Iconophages

Iconophages

A History of Ingesting Images

Jérémie Koering

Translated by Nicholas Huckle

ZONE BOOKS · NEW YORK

2024

ZONE BOOKS
633 Vanderbilt Street
Brooklyn, NY 11218

Originally published as *Les Iconophages: Une histoire de l'ingestion des images* © 2021 Actes Sud. The publisher would like to thank the French Ministry of Culture for assistance with this translation.

Printed in the United States of America
Distributed by Princeton University Press,
Princeton, New Jersey, and Woodstock, United Kingdom

Library of Congress Cataloging-in-Publication Data

Names: Koering, Jérémie, author. | Huckle, Nicholas, translator.
Title: Iconophages : a history of ingesting images / Jérémie Koering; translated by Nicholas Huckle.
Other titles: Iconophages. English
Description: New York : Zone Books, 2024. | Includes bibliographical references and index. | Summary: "In the history of human societies, images have not only been destined for contemplation. They have also been eaten or drunk. But what purposes and what structures of the imagination can explain such behavior? These are the questions that this book aims to answer" —Provided by publisher.
Identifiers: LCCN 2023043900 (print) | LCCN 2023043901 (ebook) | ISBN 9781890951276 (hardcover) | ISBN 9781890951368 (ebook)
Subjects: LCSH: Image (Philosophy) | Eating (Philosophy) | Food—Symbolic aspects. | Food—Religious aspects.
Classification: LCC N7428 .K6413 2024 (print) | LCC N7428 (ebook) | DDC 704.9—dc23/eng/20231206
LC record available at https://lccn.loc.gov/2023043900
LC ebook record available at https://lccn.loc.gov/2023043901

For my parents, with happy memories
of their welcoming kitchen

Contents

INTRODUCTION

Amuse-Bouche

'Tis still man with whom we have to do,
of whom the condition is wonderfully corporal.
—Michel de Montaigne,
"On the Art of Discussion," 1585–1588[1]

That a person might eat an image—welcoming it inside their body, and sending it, in solid or liquid form, from mouth to stomach, lodging it in the secret recesses of their guts, making themselves, in a word, an *iconophage*[2]—what a very strange idea! And yet, there was a time when icons, frescoes, sculptures, devotional engravings, stamped eucharistic hosts, waffle cookies, marzipan figures, and sculpted dishes were not simply looked at but also ingested. There was once a time when figured artifacts, from the crudest to the most highly wrought, were drunk, chewed up, and devoured. Now, who remembers this time? Who understands it? Surely, very few people do. Because, as we must admit, this singular use of images is in large part foreign to us today. Even though we continue to eat biscuits, lollipops, or other figured candies, even though we still decorate our birthday cakes with portraits and stereotypical representations, the long process of rationalization that forms our heritage—the process that has brought about a deep division between body and mind just as it has induced a growing specification of the abilities assigned to our various sense organs—has triumphed over the beliefs, commands, and dreams that justified, in times past, such physical dealings with images.[3] To physically consume a representation, especially an inedible representation like a painting, a sculpture, or an engraving is surely something that, quite literally, defies reason.

If we want to get a sense of this, we have only to look to the products of the contemporary imagination. Consider, for example, how the madness of Francis Dolarhyde, one of the main characters in the movie *Red Dragon* (2002), is depicted on screen by the director Brett Ratner in his adaptation of Thomas Harris's novel.[4] It is by eating a masterpiece of Western art history that the serial killer, played by Ralph Fiennes, reveals to the viewer the full extent of his madness (fig. I.1). In the drawing section of the Brooklyn Museum, Dolarhyde regards with disturbing fascination a William Blake watercolor, *The Great Red Dragon and the Woman Clothed in the Sun* (1805). He moves toward it, leans in, and then suddenly knocks unconscious the curator standing beside him, and finally he starts to devour the work of art he has just frantically seized.[5] What should have been held at a distance, simply contemplated, is torn up, swallowed, destroyed. This wild ingesting of an image, along with the loud gasps and contorted facial expressions accompanying the act of manducation, transforms Dolarhyde into an animal, a being devoid of *ratio intellectualis*, the faculty that in ordinary times would enable him to distinguish the edible from the inedible, to see the difference between good and bad uses of the sense organs, and whose absence here delivers him over completely to the supreme domination of an oral drive.[6]

We are very much here, of course, in the fictional register of cinematographic fable, and perhaps more exactly that of mass entertainment. This might explain the extreme character of the iconoclastic act that we are given to see. But we would be wrong, I think, to see in this only a piece of sensationalism, a screenwriter's eccentricity, something that reflects no presuppositions about our normal relations with images. In fact, popular culture is not alone in having made *iconophagy* into an exemplary transgressive

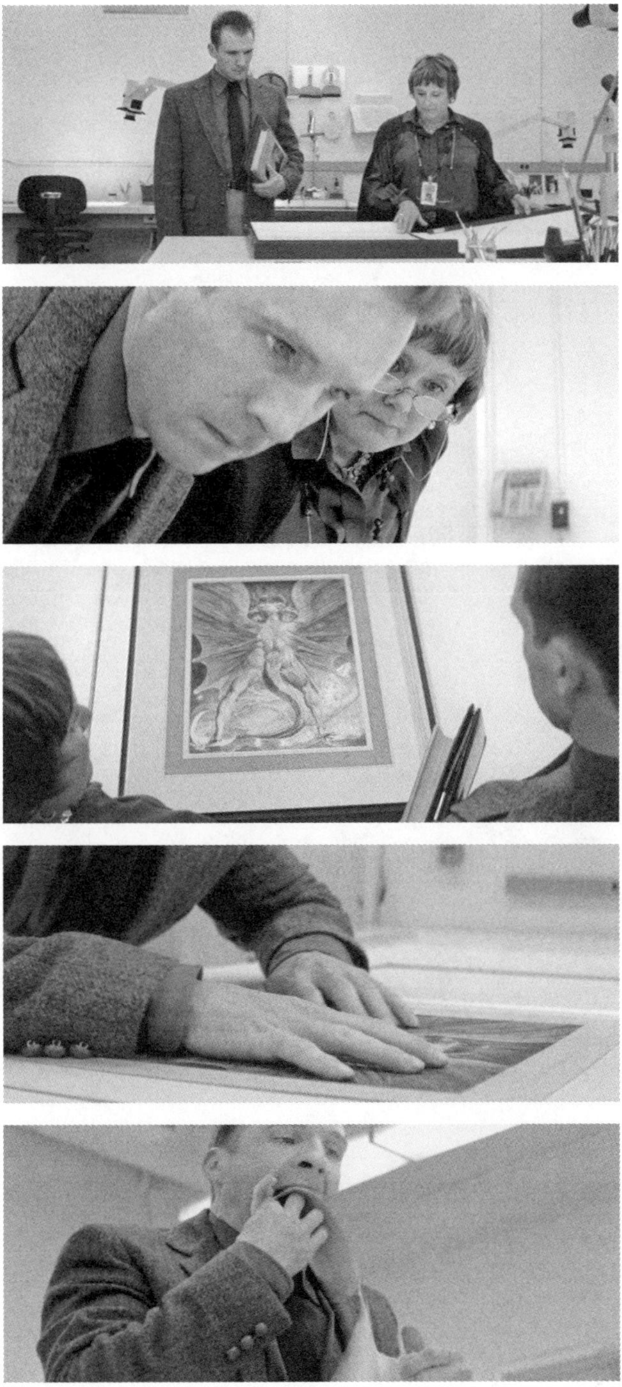

Figure I.1. Brett Ratner, *Red Dragon* (2002),
35 mm film, 5 screenshots, MGM.

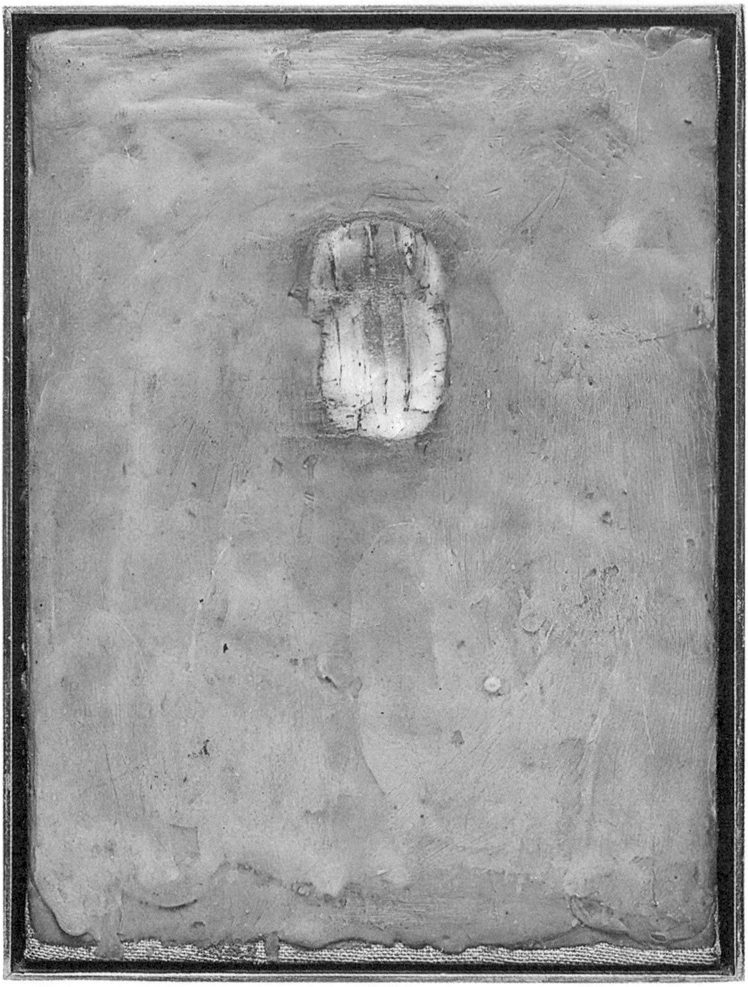

Figure I.2. Jasper Johns, *Painting Bitten by a Man*, 1961, encaustic on canvas mounted on type plate, 9.5 × 6.9 in. New York, Museum of Modern Art, Gift of Jasper Johns in memory of Kirk Varnedoe, Chief Curator of the Department of Painting and Sculpture, 1989–2001 (© 2023 Jasper Johns/Licensed by VAGA at Artists Rights Society, NY).

act. Although aimed at the entirely different public of the artistic avant-garde, Jasper Johns adopts the very same approach in order to overturn the primacy of the visual relation to art objects. In *Painting Bitten by a Man* (1961; fig. I.2), a monochrome in encaustic on canvas bearing the trace of a deep bite, Johns effectively suggests that a painting might awaken in the viewer a desire to ingest rather than a wise and considered need for contemplation.[7] While with *The Critic Sees* (1961), a piece in sculp-metal on plaster with glass that depicts a pair of glasses behind which there are not eyes but mouths with bared teeth, he stigmatizes the blindness and voracity of the critics.[8] In each of these two cases, *devouring* becomes the archetype of a disturbing and aberrant relationship with artifacts, and at the same time, it is the operator of a change in our perspective on art.[9]

Faced with the outrageousness of this approach, that is, consuming something not intended to be eaten and feeding oneself on art, it is easy to accept that ingesting such inedible images might have been banished to the rank of oddities and that no one would have bothered to explain it or write down its history. But what about images specifically made to be eaten? Have they posed fewer problems? Have people been more at ease with figured cakes, anthropomorphic gingerbreads, and sculpted dishes? Have people paid more attention to these? In truth, these items have not received much more attention. Even though certain culinary traditions are today well-identified (I am thinking of figured biscuits like the *minne de Sant'Agata* in Sicily, the marzipan Santa Claus of the Germanic world, and the gingerbread men of the English world, all of which are still eaten today), and even though modern artists and their works such as Piero Manzoni's *Uova* (1960), Dennis Oppenheim's *Gingerbread Man* (1970), Filippo Tommaso Marinetti's *The Futurist Cookbook* (1932), Claude and François-Xavier Lalanne's *Cannibal Feast* (1970), and John Cage's series *Wild Edible Drawings* (1990) have brought back within our artistic horizon this oral relationship with visual objects, the ingestion of edible images attracts the historians' antennae no more than does the ingestion of inedible images.

The reasons are easy enough to see. On the one hand, an image that can be physiologically assimilated seems destined for no great fate, at best a paltry one, and on the other, the approach involving eating a figured representation appears to modern eyes as an act that is futile and infantile, betraying a regression in the scale of our relationship with things from the spiritual to the basely material. This way of being with images, therefore, is struck with a double indignity.

Should we therefore strike a line through all these practices? Should we forget the unusual occurrences, the stakes involved, the reasons behind them? Should we give up on doing their archaeology? No, of course not. But how are we to confront this obliteration, this hole in history? How can we stitch together the narrative of what, with very few exceptions, has been taken to be the most negligeable, cursed perhaps, share of our culture?[10]

Confronting this difficulty will require, first of all, that we make a few methodological choices: we must hold in suspense the already traced lines of a triumphant art history, the one of big names and big artistic aims, and we must instead take an interest in objects that are forgotten today, focusing on types of sensory relations that are often neglected. Secondly, we must appeal to other fields of knowledge, such as historical anthropology, material history, the history of sensations, medical history, philosophy, and semiology so as to remove the epistemological bolts keeping works of art, and images more generally, within the register of the optical. And thirdly, we must return to a few simple questions: How are images configured? What are the technical procedures and the materials involved? What is the nature of the iconographic repertoire of the images in question? How does one go about ingesting an image? Who are the people who form part of the relational network established by ingestion? What social functions can we assign to this "paradoxical" experience? What place must be accorded to the senses in the perception of images and in the emergence of aesthetic relations? These are so many guiding questions that will allow us to understand these various behaviors and to refresh our knowledge of images, their status, their uses, and their relations to the human body.

Eating an image is all well and good, but what image? A few specifications are called for here. The meaning of the term "image" that I adopt in these pages connects the meaning that prevails in the fields of philosophy, theology, and semiotics — the image as representation, archetype, and sign[11] — with the meaning that attaches to it in anthropology, that is, the image as a configured object that plays the role of a social *operator*.[12] In carrying through this connection, I adopt in particular the definition proposed by the anthropologist Philippe Descola. An image is any

> material object invested in an ostensible way with a socially defined "agency" following an act of fashioning, arranging, ornamentation, and situational setting aiming to give it the potential to iconically evoke a real or imaginary prototype that it denotes in an indicial manner (through delegation of intentionality) by playing upon a direct mimetic resemblance or on any other type of motivation identifiable in a mediated or unmediated manner.[13]

My assumption throughout this study is that the *equiformity*, to take a term from Jean Wirth, of the image will not depend solely upon figurative similarity, but also on a "structural conformity" between the image and its model.[14] I speak, moreover, of images in the context of coats of arms, and I even extend the meaning of the term to attend to an abstract artifact, if the latter demonstrates self-reflexive qualities that make it, like an image to the second degree, a *representation* of its own genre. Hence Cage's *Wild Edible Drawings* (fig. I.3) are, as I see them, images of abstract art to the extent that they are not just abstract compositions or, yet, artifacts made of edible ingredients, but objects that, through the materials put to work in them, appear *like* abstract drawings.

The present study, in terms of its place in the general history of images in its ways of conceiving, perceiving, and analyzing them

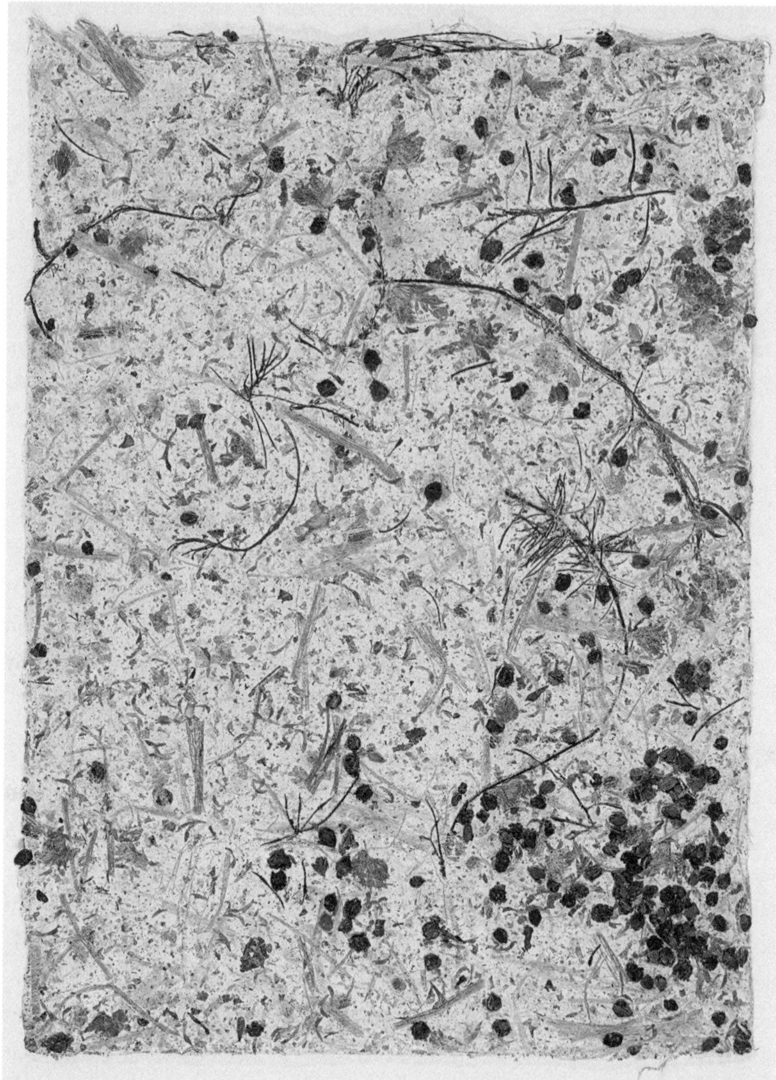

Figure I.3. John Cage, *Wild Edible Drawing #6*, 1990. Handmade paper of mulberry, burdock, hibiscus stems, barley, hijiki, and clover. 17 × 12 in. New York, Museum of Modern Art, Gift of Sarah-Ann and Werner H. Kramarsky (© 2023 John Cage Trust).

and writing their history, follows upon the debate carried on for some forty years now by Hans Belting, Gottfried Boehm, Horst Bredekamp, Hubert Damisch, Georges Didi-Huberman, James Elkins, Alfred Gell, W. J. T. Mitchell, and, once again, Wirth.[15] And I would like to express the hope that this work might bring, along with others, a few additions and perhaps a few nuances to an exclusively visual approach to images. I do not believe, in fact, that it is possible to limit the image solely to the *iconic difference*, as Gottfried Boehm does in his essay "Die Wiederkher der Bilder."[16] Although Boehm's analysis is of crucial importance for understanding some of the most basic aspects of the image, in particular its status as "visual evidence," it is not sufficient to account for the polysensory complexity of images and the experiences that can be had with them. Wirth has it right, I think, when he notes, "Images, even those that today we are compelled to put into the category of the visual, are not made *just* to be seen."[17] I would add that any analysis that makes the image's existence *qua* image depend solely upon the optical relation inevitably misses many characteristics relating to the materiality of the object or medium thanks to which the image makes itself perceptible, and consequently it misses other important stakes involved with these two aspects.[18] History, phenomenology, and anthropology teach us that other senses, such as the sense of taste or of touch, can be engaged in the perception of an image.[19] In order to give rightful place to these other sensory relations, I shall not hesitate, following Jean-Claude Bonne, Jean-Claude Schmitt, and Jérôme Baschet, to use the concept of the *image-object*. This is a notion that, by recognizing the role of the imaging substance and the image's site or location, allows for a more complex understanding of the image's reality.[20]

As we shall discover, people have eaten or imbibed images since ancient times, in widely varied forms, in numerous regions of the world, on very particular occasions, such as times of worship, ceremony, or feasting, and at more simple, everyday events. They have done this with different and sometimes radically opposing views of the world. The question arises, therefore, as to whether the objects and attitudes that this study deals with can have any sort of unity. How is it possible to encompass so many differing artifacts, behaviors, and discourses? To manage this heterogeneity, it is not enough to do what I did just previously, which was to make a blanket distinction between inedible images (e.g., icons, frescoes, sculptures, and devotional engravings) and edible ones (e.g., eucharistic hosts, waffle-cookies or *cialde*, marzipan figurines, sculpted dishes, breads decorated with images, and so forth). A simple classification such as this does not give us the tools to specify the functions assigned to these various manifestations: edible images, for example, are sometimes consumed for the same reasons as inedible ones; or an engraving and a wafer representing one and the same saint can both be swallowed to cure a sickness. In order to overcome this aporia, it will be necessary to add to this overly simple typological distinction, that is, edible or inedible, a functionalist system of classification based on criteria that are essentially more anthropological, and doing this allows us to understand this very particular experience with images by shifting the center of the analysis away from the object as such and towards the relation connecting, on the one hand, the artifact with its consumer (internal relation), and on the other, the consumer with the collective (external relation). Beyond the dichotomy of the edible/inedible, we should, in fact, distinguish between two functions at work in ingestion. The first of these, linked to the care of body and soul, has a healing or protective purpose. Essentially vertical, this function establishes a relationship between the consumer and the power or *virtus* of a prototype that is represented by the image. I shall call this first form of image ingestion *constituting ingestion*, with the dual meaning, physiological and ethical, of the term. The second function, generally regulated by ritual (although rituals can include ingestion with a constituting purpose) and ceremony or meals, is essentially horizontal and its main goal is to accept and recognize the consumer as part of a specific community.[21] I shall call this second category *instituting ingestion*, referring to the meaning that Bourdieu gives the term in his 1982 essay "Rites as Acts of Institution." Ingestion is here a way of granting the consumer a social place or position, entailing a certain "duty-to-be" and a specific relationship to others.[22]

On one side of this distinction, the image appears as a vehicle for establishing a continuity (which is magical through configuration, real through imprint, conventional through representation) with the prototype that it makes present, in such a way that the consumer can claim to capture its power and obtain its benefits by ingestion; on the other side, the image is an operator allowing the one who makes use of it to model and define his or her identity in relation to the other participants in the same ritual. Of course, these two poles are not divided by an impermeable barrier, and certain of the images that we shall study, such as the stamped eucharistic hosts, are able to fulfill both functions. To avoid there being too much rigidity in this division, we shall therefore speak of relations that are *primarily* constituting or *primarily* instituting.

In adopting this system of classification, I look at the phenomenon through a functionalist lens. However, employing this approach still only partially completes the investigation. To go even deeper into the ingestion experience, we must take account of the practical ways in which this type of use of images have been carried out.[23] In other words, we must look at the "how" and not just the "what," and perhaps more precisely, we must examine the procedures that establish or realize a relationship rather than the imperatives that might call for such procedures to be done in this or that fashion. Fortunately, we do have available to us texts, visual accounts, and, in more recent times, ethnographic material that supply us with a basis from which we can isolate certain procedures, gestures, and feelings.[24] Indeed, it is through this examination of a lived experience or a "modality of being"—and not through setting out a flat relationship between cold intellectual terms—that we are really able to understand the relational dynamics that interest us here.[25]

Because it is not simply a question of looking at how the act of ingestion changes the one who ingests, that is, person A becoming person A1 by virtue of an event marking a change in time (Arnold Van Gennep),[26] nor of simply considering what it institutes, that is, the places it assigns and the social configuration it establishes (Pierre Bourdieu); it is, rather, in addition to these things, to investigate the inner experience of the change. In other words, we must examine the ways that ingestion involves bodies that are not only constrained and regulated but also *lived*. As Tim Ingold writes, "Life will not be contained, but rather threads its way through the world along the myriad lines of its relations."[27] Consequently, we cannot ignore the ontogenies, narratives, depictions, and other configurations of the imagination that report on this other way of being with images.[28] The main task is to identify what it is in these accounts that belongs to the foundation of this way of being with images as a social practice, and what, on the other hand, falls outside of the social frame, representing a random or utterly unique event. To the structural approach favored in the study of social relations, therefore, I shall add a modal approach, allowing thus for an accounting not only of the various customs that I shall identify, but also of the various ways of ingesting images seen not so much through the lens of technique or procedure, but rather in formal terms.[29] History, art history, and anthropology therefore move forward together in a dialectical relationship.

Finally, I would like to stress one point. The two forms of ingestion, constituting and instituting, that I have so far distinguished one from another will only have meaning if we keep in mind their strict relation to the image. It is the eaten-image, always as a sequential syntagm, that is the operator through which a physical, psychological, and social transformation takes place. Consequently, this is not the history of an aberrant form of consumption. Rather, it is the history of a conjunction, a knotting of an act (ingestion) and an object (the image) that transforms the very nature of the representation. The ingested image is not just the instantiation of a real or imaginary archetype. It is an *operator*, acting and producing very specific effects that are distinct from other modes of experience such as vision, hearing, smell, and touch.

The origin of ingesting images lies, no doubt, in the unreachable regions of the far-distant past. There is nothing to indicate that this very specific use of images emerged alongside writing, when it would first have been possible to preserve it in memory.[30] I am inclined to think even that people have consumed images in one way or another since their first appearance, at a time when no written traces existed. Still, although the beginnings of this history are destined to remain obscure, we must begin somewhere—but where and when to begin?

Since my aim is to cover, as much as possible, the entirety of the phenomenon, I have not limited my investigation to a single area. It has been the sources available to me that have, so to speak, established the geographical perimeter of this narrative. The geographical areas will change, therefore, in accordance with the periods of history under consideration. Up to the modern area, I look primarily at the European and Mediterranean region, extending my study after the twentieth century to any region subject to the "naturalist" paradigm.[31]

In terms of chronology, the reader will not find a smooth and regular progression through time. I do not intend to retrace the history of ingesting images from its origins up to its most recent developments, and this is for one simple reason: there cannot possibly be an evolution of the phenomenon in the Darwinian sense of the term.[32] This history, therefore, will have no beginning and no end. It will be synchronic and polyrhythmic. If it happens that certain sequences do follow upon one another chronologically, the reader should not assign these concatenations any sort of teleological value.

CHAPTER ONE

Ingesting Images

Magicam operari non est aliud quam maritare mundum.
—Jean Pic de la Mirandole, *Conclusiones magicae*, 1486, XIII

A man pours lustral water over a statue covered in hieroglyphs, and, as he does so, he recites an incantation. Gathering up the precious liquid, now charged with the power of the gods, a power emanating from their names and figurative representations, he offers it to a sick person, who will thus, or so the man probably hopes, be cured by ingesting it. A young boy grinds up an earthen token bearing the figure of a hermit saint. He then mixes it with water to create a beverage that he believes will allow him to draw on its protective power if he can drink it with faith. A woman scrapes the surface of a fresco that bears the images of Saints Cosmas and Damian, and she then ingests the pigments so as to be delivered from ills no physician can cure. Now comes the turn of a young girl in labor: after cutting out an engraving of a Miraculous Virgin Mary, she introduces it into her body, trusting in the Mother of God to save the child that she herself is unable to bring into the world...

Such behaviors, roughly reconstructed, are fairly representative of what we find in accounts involving ingesting images. But how are we to understand these practices? In what cultural context should we place them? From what underlying concept of the image do they derive? Of what ways of thinking and experiencing the human body are they the symptoms?

To answer these questions, let us take the images out of the display cases where we normally keep them, and let us observe them now in the act, as they are put to work, in the multifarious array of their many uses, and in the various societies that saw them arise.

Eating and Drinking the Gods

The oldest sources, both written and iconographic, that have come down to us concerning these customs date from Pharaonic Egypt, during the years between the Middle Kingdom (2045–1781 BCE) and the Ptolemaic period (305–330 BCE).[1] Indeed, the magical and religious culture of the Ancient Egyptians reserved an important place for contact and ingestion as a means of appropriation of the sacred.[2] We should also note that for modern sensibilities, while magic and religion are two opposing cultural fields, here they do not constitute two distinct poles of experience.[3] Three types of figurative artifacts offer us especial evidence in this regard: the stelae known as Horus on the Crocodiles, the healing statues, and the body paintings.[4]

Horus on the Crocodiles

We turn first to the stelae of Horus on the Crocodiles. These are among the objects used for the purposes of ritual magic, and they all include, on the front side, the same iconographic nucleus: the figure of Horus the Child standing on one or several pairs of crocodiles (fig. 1.1).[5] They are found in a variety of forms: medium to large votive plaques (30–80 cm in height) used in places of worship, amulet pendants, and also small and easily transportable stelae (roughly 8–12 cm in height) that were typically kept in houses. These objects have been documented as early as the New Kingdom (1539–1069 BCE) and, in increasing numbers, up to the Ptolemaic period.[6] In terms of materials used, the larger pieces were made of hard stone (e.g., basalt, steatite, serpentine), while the smaller objects (e.g., small stelae, amulets) were often made of ceramic or even metal.[7] Beyond the primordial iconographic depiction of Horus perched upon

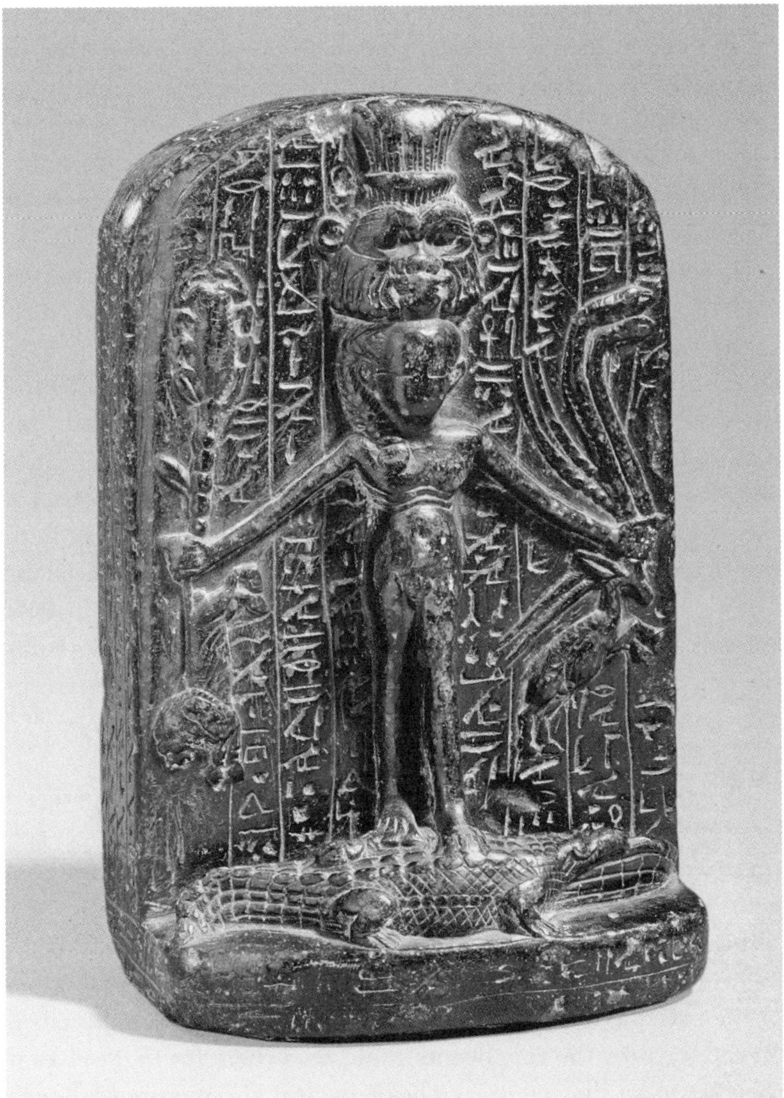

Figure 1.1. *Stela of Horus the Child on the Crocodiles.* Magic Stele: Horus overpowering vermin. Ptolemaic Period (332–330 BCE), serpentinite, 7.4 × 3.3 × 2.2 in. Paris, Louvre Museum. Photo: Christian Décamps (© RMN—Grand Palais/Art Resource, NY).

crocodiles, we find, more often than not, other accompanying figurative features such as animals, venomous scorpions, and snakes, or fearsome lions, oryxes, and hyenas,[8] and deities that figure in the story of Horus the Child, such as the adult falcon-headed Horus, Isis, and the ibis-headed Thoth, as well as with reputedly protective deities, such as the god Bes who occupies an increasingly important place towards the end of the Ptolemaic period.[9]

In each case, the sculpted image in bas-relief is closely connected with the hieroglyphic inscriptions more or less extensive according to the height of the object. These inscriptions are of two main types: on the one hand, brief *historiolae*[10] (etiological accounts) telling the story of Horus the Child who, after having been hidden away by his mother in the marshes of Chemmis as a safeguard against his uncle Set, was cured of a scorpion's sting by the magician god Thoth. On the other hand, prophylactic magic formulae intended as protection against venomous stings and bites, and that were also used for driving out venom and healing wounds and illnesses caused by wild animals. These magical texts are believed to have been employed by the deities for their own healing.[11] They date, for the most part, to the second millennium BCE, and they were handed down by tradition until the end of the Ptolemaic period.

It appears, from a reading of the medical and magical papyri and from an examination of the material remains, that these images and texts were not simply read and contemplated, but they were also *put to work* physically in a way that involved both the human voice and the human body. The supplicant, desiring protection or healing, was required, among other things, to listen to the incantation of the priest as the latter read out loud the hieroglyphs inscribed on the stela (or the supplicants could read them for themselves if their status so allowed it), and he or she was also required to touch the surface of the object. In many cases, there are evident traces of wear on the face of the figure of Horus, suggesting that this part of the stela was considered particularly powerful, and for this reason it was touched and perhaps kissed or licked.[12] At the same time, and of particular interest for us, the supplicant was required to *drink* the water that had been poured over the surface of the artifact.[13] Moreover, a number of stelae, such as one from the middle of the Ptolemaic period in the collection of the Louvre, include at their base a concave feature formed out of a pair of intercoiled crocodiles, allowing the supplicant or priest to collect the liquid that had been in contact with the image and the inscriptions.[14]

The stela's magic effect, it is generally understood, rests upon both the connection between the image and the hieroglyphics and upon the relationship of the priest or supplicant with the icono-textual ensemble. The central image, bringing together the actors and elements of the story through the figure of Horus the Child (shown at the base and center of the composition), along with attributive figures arranged around him (the wild and threatening wild beasts that he has subdued and that he now grasps in his fists, as well as the priests and deities who helped him) offers itself as a visual sign of the magician god's victory over the dangers lying in wait for humanity throughout the world.[15] As Annie Gasse notes in her study on Horus and the Crocodiles, in appearing as both "the model of suffering humanity" and "the paragon of the 'saved'," Horus "is transformed into a Savior."[16] The image is situated at the intersection of two vertices, one of which is horizontal, with Horus as the model of the healed patient, representative of all of humanity, and the other vertical, as the child god is saved by the deities. But the image here is not simply an emblematic or memorial representation, but rather it is an actual recreation of past events. The central iconic feature is, at once, the matrix, the echo, and the product of a hieroglyphic account, and it is often accompanied by a narrative figuration in the peripheral registers, as we see in the Metternich stela,[17] with the latter including as many as two hundred and fifty figures (fig. 1.2). This narrative, replayed as it is read aloud, reactivated and made present the mythical healing.[18] The represented scene (fig. 1.3), set in movement by the reading or by the running water, opens onto a moment in the story when the healing is not

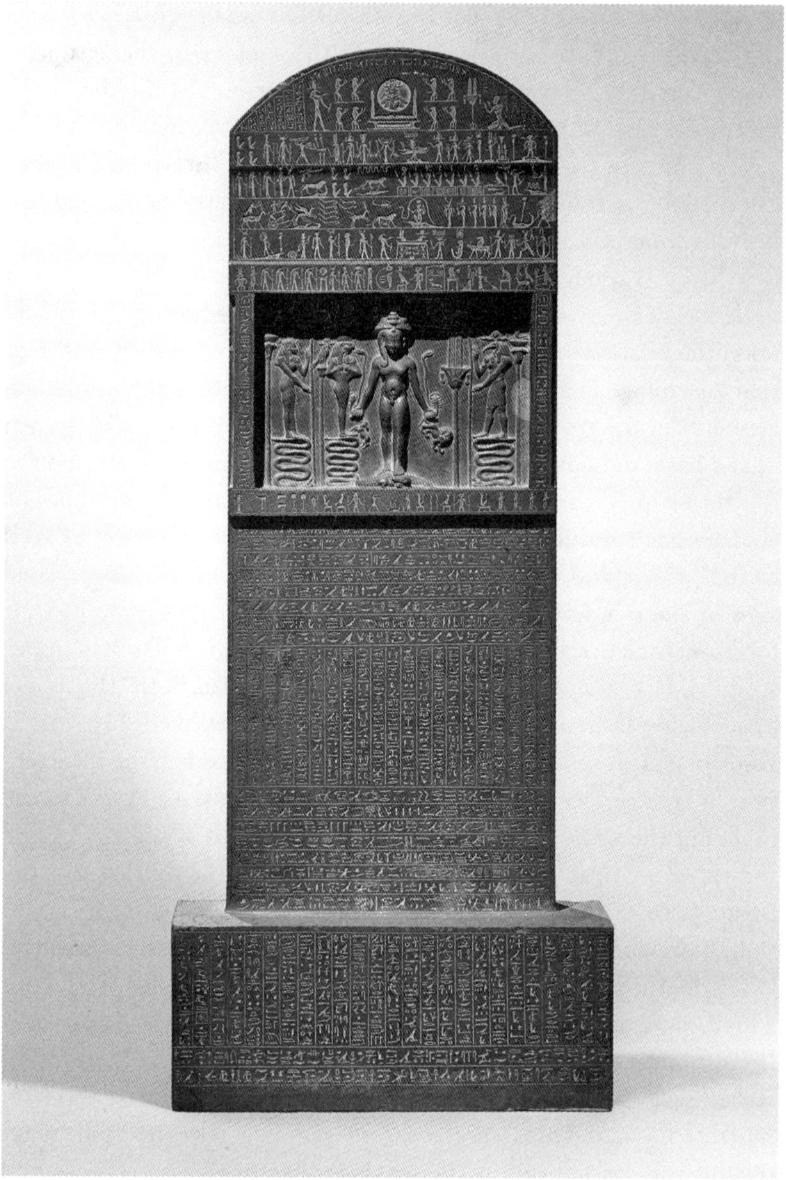

Figure 1.2. *Magical Stela (Cippus of Horus)*, Late Period (360–343 BCE), meta-graywacke, 32.9 × 13.2 in. New York, Metropolitan Museum of Art, Fletcher Fund, 1950.

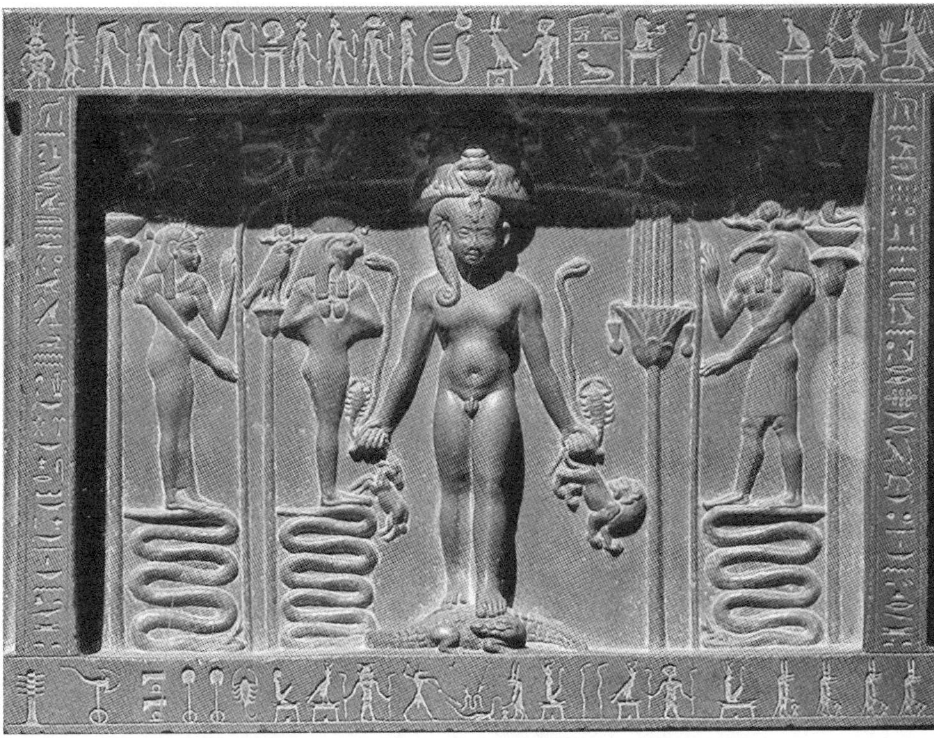

Figure 1.3. *Magical Stela (Cippus of Horus)*, Late Period (360–343 BCE), meta-graywacke, 32.8 × 13.1 in. New York, Metropolitan Museum of Art, Fletcher Fund, 1950 (detail of Figure 1.2).

hoped for, but rather is in the process of being carried out. What happened at the beginning (the healing of Horus) *is* reproduced in the *here and now* (the healing of the patient) through the dual power of the presence of the image and the invocation of names.[19]

Looking at this magical operation as a whole, Egyptologists have, naturally enough, emphasized the role played by the incantation since the uttered hieroglyphs plainly appear to function as illocutionary *acts*, performative utterances that *do* something in the saying, and indeed it is in this sense that the hieroglyphs are, properly speaking, magical, according to the Egyptian terms *nty/ntt*.[20] Through vocal repetition, the gods came to relive their great deeds, and in the retelling men were allowed to become their contemporaries. Sharing thus the same temporal space, men were able, through the priests as intermediaries, to benefit from the gods' good deeds, and to direct magical incantations to them. Consider, for example, this prayer, inscribed on the surface of the Metternich stela:

> [To Horus] Come to me quickly, quickly, today, as you did when you rowed the divine boat, repulse from me every lion of the desert, all crocodiles on the water, all mouths which sting, in their holes. Make them for me like a stone of the desert, like a potsherd in the street. Extract for me the rushing poison which is in every limb of the sufferer . . . Behold, your name is pronounced today, "I am Horus the Savior!"[21]

The noticeable use here of the active voice and direct style highlight unequivocally the role of the speech act in the magical operation. The priest, as reader-reciter, calls on the deities to ward off the dangers of bites, stings, or other wounds. Furthermore, as can be seen in another text inscribed on the Metternich stela, the priest can himself become the Savior-god incarnate, addressing the personified Evil through venom even more directly, exhorting it to depart from the sick person's body:

> Flow out, poison, approach, come forth on earth. It is Horus who exorcises you, he cuts you to pieces, he spits you out so that you cannot mount up on

> high but fall to earth. You are weak, you have no strength, you are miserable and cannot fight, you are blind and cannot see, your head is turned upside down and you cannot raise your face. You wander without being able to find your way, you grieve and cannot rejoice, you wander and cannot open your eyes—in accordance with the speech of Horus, potent of magic.[22]

If it is true that the hieroglyphic text was seen by the ancient Egyptians as the receptacle of divine power,[23] the image's role in the functioning of the artifact should not be underestimated. Alongside the invocations, the image is the very means by which the natural and supernatural worlds come to be connected and to share the same temporality. In order to see this more clearly, we must now consider the healing statues, as the latter will allow us to follow in greater detail the ritual involving the drinking of the water that was poured over the images, and the inscriptions making up the magical object.

The Healer Djedhor

Named after Pierre Lacau's 1921 article,[24] the ancient Egyptian "healing" statues are, so to speak, outgrowths of the stelae with Horus on the Crocodiles (fig. 1.4).[25] Fairly widely distributed in the temples of the Delta from the 26th Dynasty (664–526 BCE), they show a human figure in the round of about 80 cm in height, a figure denoting a member of the upper class and not an ordinary person, standing or kneeling and holding in his hands or between his legs a Horus stela. The most well-known of these artifacts is surely the statue of the Healer Djedhor in the Cairo Museum (fig. 1.5).[26] Sculpted around 320 BCE during the reign of Philip III Arrhidaeus and discovered at Athribis (present-day Tell Atrib) in the Nile Delta in Lower Egypt, it is remarkable evidence of the functions of image-objects in the religious, medical, and magical culture of Egypt during the Macedonian period. The statue includes a wide variety of magical, biographical, and dedicatory inscriptions, and we find a dual system of basins carved into its plinth. The first of these, running around the main figure, allowed for the collection of

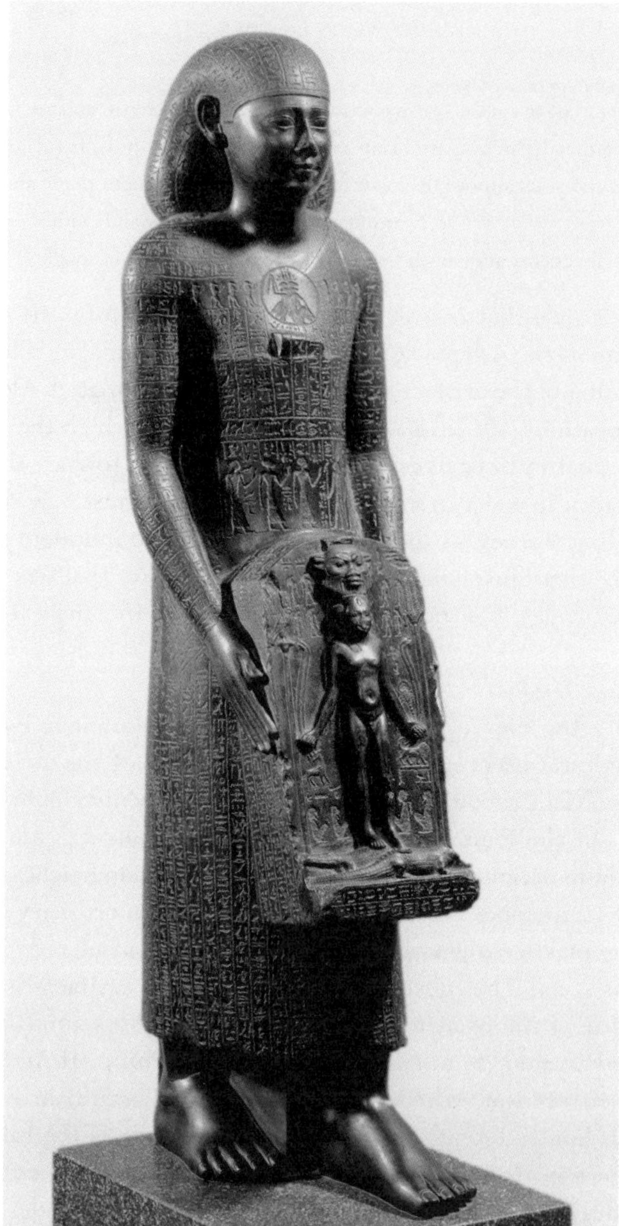

Figure 1.4. *Healing statue of a priest of Bastet* (the Tyszkiewicz statue), Late Period (380–343 BCE), meta-graywacke, 26.5 in. Paris, Louvre Museum (© RMN—Grand Palais; photo © RMN—Grand Palais/Les frères Chuzeville).

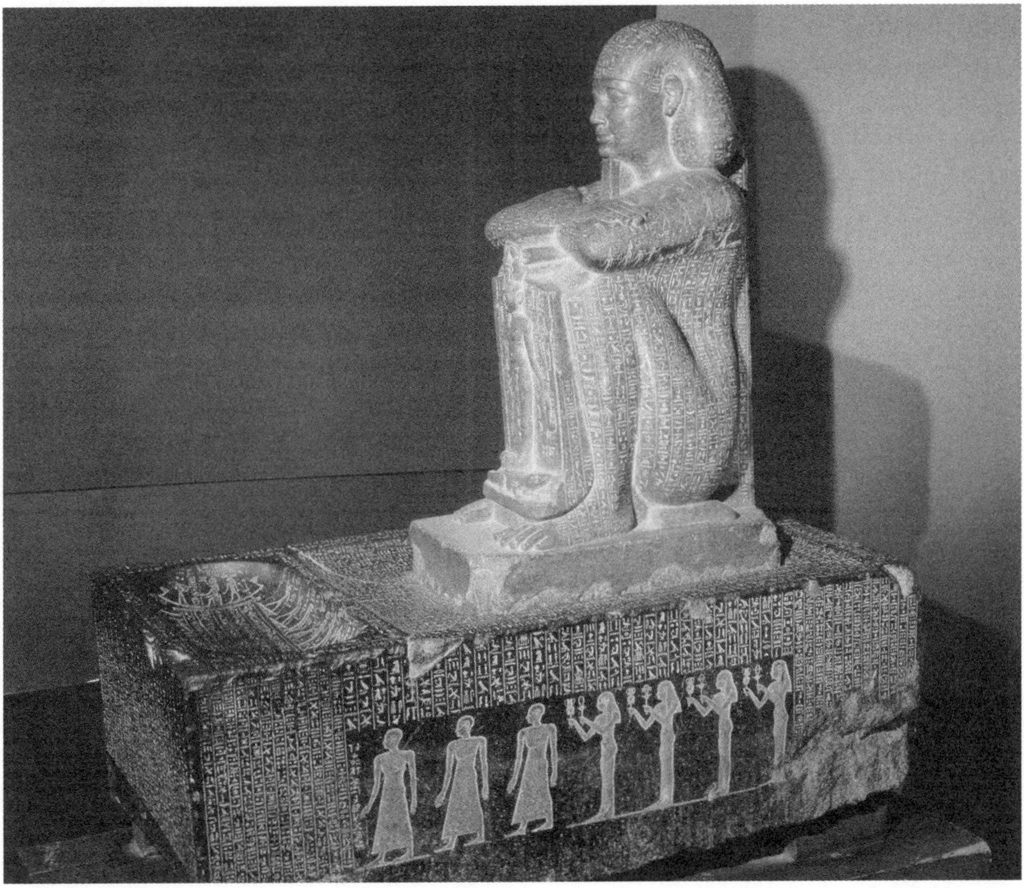

Figure 1.5. *Statue of the Healer Djedhor*, ca. 320 BCE. Cairo, Egyptian Museum (© akg-images/Werner Forman).

water poured over both it and the stela, while the second, sculpted deeper and connected to the first by a channel, formed a sort of reservoir into which a container might be dipped. The two basins were clearly intended to be the statue's magico-medical end point.

From evidence pointed out by Lacau, we can see that the object was intended primarily for a procedure of "washing"[27] rather than for reading. Firstly, the magical inscriptions that were believed to ensure healing are consistently placed on the parts of the object (i.e., the healer figure, the stela, and the basins) that would come into contact with the water as it was poured over the head of the healer figure. The "biographical" inscriptions, on the other hand, are found only in the vertical columns on the sides of the plinth and thus would have been untouched by the running water.[28] At the same time, the magical inscriptions are generally positioned so as to face the healer figure, notably so with the second basin, in such a way that they appear intended to be read not so much by the officiating priest, but rather by the statue itself.[29] Consequently, the artifact was principally activated by the running of the water that the sick person, or an intermediary, would then draw from the basin.[30] The liquid poured over the surface of the object is a substitute, therefore, for the ritual of incantation.

But how are we to understand this piece of *legerdemain*? What could authorize such a slippage? It is hard to believe that the invocation, whose importance is so well known in ancient Egyptian culture, might have been entirely sidelined, at least conceptually. The solution is most likely to be found in the analogy one could make between the act of reading and the running water. The contact and the movement of the water were possibly likened to the experience of reading: the physical action of the water, running from top to bottom and adapting itself to all the reliefs and hollows of the engraved object, must have seemed equivalent to the work of the reader's eyes, moving down the sculpture from the top to the base, activating the magical potential of the written story. This interpretation of the "washing" procedure seems to me, moreover, to offer us an important clue for understanding the arrangement here, involving as it does the depiction of a man whose profession was that of a healer, and therefore also a reader, along with a whole set of texts arrayed around him. The liquid, as it is poured over his body and over the stela of Horus, might be likened to the flow of a murmured voice. Essentially, the water would be called upon to activate an always possible, potential reading.

What can we say about the water here in terms of its relation to the image? For many of the Egyptologists who have studied these objects, it is the inscriptions that are the real vector of magical power,[31] with the image being, so to speak, of secondary importance.[32] But, here again, Lacau breaks from his peers in that he is one of the few to assign a central place to the images. As he sees it, the image is a catalyst: "The water itself, flowing over the stela, takes up all of the virtues of the representations at once—in this way, it concentrates their effectiveness."[33] In fact, the water, coupled with the image, appears to be so very useful and beneficial because it does more than simply offer itself as a substitute for the reading; indeed, it brings something extra, an addition to the incantation, and it does so for two reasons. First, the water running over the stela carries out a process that reading aloud is unable to achieve, mixing image and text in a flow that makes no distinction between these two material parts of the object. It gathers the trace of the images and writing into a material, dynamic, and continuous substance, creating thus a remedy that, still active and in motion, could then be taken and given to the sick person. Indeed, there is no reason not to suppose that the water could have been collected up and transported some distance from the temple housing the healing statue or stela of Horus on the Crocodiles.[34] And, secondly, in the ancient Egyptian demiurgical imagination, water was endowed with a special plasmatic power. For the ancient Egyptians, all forms of life arose out of Nun, the primeval waters; indeed, they arose and rose again since the dead were also regenerated in them.[35] And part of our world was believed by the ancient Egyptians to have been created out of bodily fluids—liquid substances. The god Atum, born out of the primeval chaos and who was linked, well before Ra, with the sun, gave birth to his son Shu through masturbation and ejaculation, and to his daughter Tefnut through spitting.[36] If the divine essence could be formed out of liquid, and if the image was that essence's congealed form, then the liquefaction of an image by means of water poured over its surface could make real once again the original creative power, giving life to whomever might consume it.

Licked Images

With the stelae of Horus on the Crocodiles and with the healing statues, the image is not swallowed directly; the water, rather, functions as intermediary. Other magical practices, however, did involve the direct ingestion of an image. This is the case with the paintings done on skin, and evidence of these paintings exists from the beginning of the Middle Kingdom. In certain magic rites, these paintings required licking in order for their desired benefits to be realized.[37] In chapter 81 of the Coffin Texts, there is notably mention made of the creation, "on a man's hand," of a painting, in Nubian ochre, showing the Ogdoad of Hermopolis, that is, the eight primordial spirits: the primeval waters Nun and Naunet, what-is-hidden Amun and Amaunet, the darkness Kuk and Kauket, and the infinite in its spatial and aquatic form Heh and Hauhet.[38] The magical text specifies that every day at the rising of the sun Ra, and following the recitation of the magic spell,[39] the image was to be licked. Given both the funerary context of the inscription and its relative vagueness, it is hard to determine the ultimate goal of the ingestion of the image and the exact assignment of roles; indeed the inscription says "a man's hand" but gives no further details. Did the ritual bring together a living person and a dead person, or did it involve two living people? We cannot be sure.[40]

The first possibility evidently makes us question for whom the procedure was designed. If it were the case of an image placed on the hand of a dead person, was the officiant supposed to draw something from it for himself, or did he act solely in the interest of the deceased? The significance and variety of acts specifically carried out for the dead in ancient Egyptian funerary rituals, the most well known being the Opening of the Mouth, do possibly suggest that this act could have formed part of the attention given to the dead in order to keep them alive in the afterworld. However, it is equally conceivable that the act might have been directed towards the earthly living person and, if so, that it had a prophylactic or even therapeutic purpose. Our modern ideas about medicine and pharmacy prevent us from imagining that a dead person might be of some help to the living; however, we tend to forget that most other ways of seeing the human body and its healthcare were not based upon "naturalist"[41] systems of thought. We must remember that, in ancient Egypt, and indeed up until quite recently in parts of Europe, pieces of human body in the form of *mumia/mummies* went into the composition of many medicines.[42] People sought to cure themselves with human hair, skin, or ground-up bone. It is, therefore, conceivable that one might lick a dead person's hand bearing a painting of the Ogdoad in order to draw from it some life-giving force. For Robert Kriech Ritner, who makes a particular study of the licking ritual, there can be no doubt that the magical spell, with its close similarity in terms of its component parts to the non-funerary magical writings, did involve a therapeutic element—it was, therefore, designed for the living.[43]

What can we say now about the second possibility? What meaning and what purpose can we attach to the licking of an image painted upon the hand of a living person? If we accept that the effective power of the ancient Egyptian images depended upon their being ritually brought to life, then the bodily support and the licking, alongside the incantations and the washing carried out with the stelae and the healing statues, could possibly have served as a "natural" device for the activation of the images. This is intuitively quite understandable since the heat of the body, the sensitivity of the epidermis, and the movement of a bodily member all go into the animation of the image painted on the skin. Licking an image that has been painted on the surface of a body is not the same as licking an inert figure; it is, rather, licking a living image, capable of transmitting the power of which it is the vehicle. And we can go further in saying that the liquification of the representation through the action of the tongue succeeds in changing the image, as it animates it from a visible to a comestible state. Yet, what function can we assign to this in a funerary ritual? What possible meaning could there be for the deceased if the exchange involved two living persons? The answer probably lies in the spell's origins. As with many other magical incantations appearing frequently on the sarcophagi, this one was most likely initially used among the living, in everyday life, so to speak, only to be then added to the sarcophagi as a precaution for the life beyond. Therefore, it may not have been first implemented during the funerary ceremonies. Perhaps it was later offered to the dead, as a potential help to them in their future life.

Several magic papyri show, moreover, that this practice was equally current during the Ramesside period, and in a more specifically medical context. Again, Ritner mentions the case of a spell found on the 1993 P. Turin papyrus that was linked with an image showing Atum, Isis, and two figures of Horus on the hand of a person who had been stung by a scorpion. The image, licked by the suffering person, was intended to act as a repellant and to neutralize the poison's effect:[44]

> Words to be recited over an image of Atum and of Horus-of-Praise, a figure of Isis, and an image of Horus, drawn (on) the hand of the sufferer and licked off by the man; do likewise on a strip of fine linen, placed on the sufferer at his throat. Its plant is scorpion plant. Or ground up with beer or wine, it is drunk by the man who has a scorpion sting. It is what kills the poison — truly effective, (proved) a million times.[45]

We should note here, in passing, that while the wording "truly effective, (proved) a million times" is a common and clearly rhetorical turn of phrase, it does nonetheless indicate that this remedy was itself a common one.

Licking was not the only means of introducing an image for prophylactic or curative purposes. Magical forms could also be painted upon reeds, and then these latter dissolved in a liquid, before being swallowed in a potion. Chapter 341 of the Coffin Texts includes a prescription, intended for any person wanting to protect themself against evil, requiring the consumption of an image bearing the *oudjat*, the seven eyes of Horus: "This spell is to be spoken over seven sketched Sound Eyes, dissolved in beer and natron and drunk by a man."[46] The exact nature of the evil is not specified, probably because the remedy was intended to be used for any type of illness. Indeed, the left eye of Horus, stolen and cut into six pieces by Set and then partially recovered, reconstituted, and augmented with the missing sixth part by Thoth, protected the body against any form of illness. It did this because, following the principles of analogy and metonymy—which connect things beyond their discontinuity or distance—it was able to obstruct the opening through which, in Egyptian thought, pathogens entered the body.[47]

Hygieia

The culture of ancient Egypt was not the only one in Antiquity to have produced healing statues or figurative artifacts designed to protect or cure the suffering.[48] From the sixth century BCE, in Greece we find statues of athletes or Trojan heroes that were held to contain powers that were potentially healing.[49] However, our knowledge of the individual attitudes coinciding with the rituals of devotion in the temples is far too limited for us to be able to claim that practices similar to those that we have seen in Egypt, such as the consumption of lustral water or of any other substance having come into contact with an image, might have been common in Greece. Still, as Toni Hölscher has written, insofar as "relations with the gods were carried out through an exchange of gifts,"[50] it is conceivable that the care given to statues in the form of clothing, offerings, or sacrifices[51] set up expectations that were just as substantial as those we have noted in Egypt.

For example, thanks to Herodotus (*Histories*, II, 47), we know that dishes of food were often offered to the gods as substitutes for animal offerings, and this perhaps for symbolic or economic reasons (the gift of animals was onerous, and not all worshippers could afford the expense[52]). These comestible offerings, presented first to the gods, were sometimes divided among the participants in the sacrifice. Indeed, this is what we see in the *Mimes* of Herondas (third century BCE), where in Book IV the poet describes an offering made to Asclepius, the god of medicine. Entering his temple in Cos, two women friends, Kunno and Kokkale, bring a rooster and a votive image as offerings that they lay at the feet of the statues of Asclepius and his assistants, Hygieia, Panaké, Epio, and Iaso, in thanks for a cure:

> Kokkalê, remember to cut the little leg of the bird off carefully and to give it to the attendant. Put the cake-coin offering in the serpent's box in holy silence and moisten the barley-cakes. We'll eat the rest at home; you there, don't forget to take away some of the holy bread. Hand [it] out as much as you like, for certainly at sacrifices . . . of the share.[53]

As the Herondas text indicates, in the ritual, the two women divide the rooster up between the god, the attendant, and themselves, adding to it "sacred bread," probably bearing the image of the god Asclepius and the word *hygieia* ("health"[54]). Much like the Egyptian images, and alongside incubation (i.e., the oniric path most often taken by sacred medicine[55]), the figure of the god linked with the sacred foodstuff was, therefore, the vehicle of a curative power capable of bringing health to whomsoever consumed it.[56]

The combination of the god's image and the foodstuff is meaningful when we consider the ties binding together health and the celestial world — the microcosm and the macrocosm — in ancient Greek sacred medicine. Unlike Hippocratic medicine that rested upon relations of natural causality, sacred medicine considered foodstuffs and digestion to be inescapably bound with divine manifestations.[57] We should note that as the end result of his catasterization, Asclepius formed the constellation of the serpent bearer Ophiucus and that his daughter Hygieia was often shown as feeding the serpent.[58]

Lithophagy

While we know very little about the ritual consumption of images in the Greek sanctuaries, the situation is less obscure with personal and domestic practices. The works devoted to semiprecious stones (i.e., the lapidaries or *lithika*) inform us that engraved gems could be used as amulets for prophylactic purposes, and that they were employed in the composition of *pharmakoi*[59] (medicines). This is true, in particular, of the magical, or gnostic stones, that bring together, most often, on one or both of their *characteres* (faces, images, signs), *voces magicae* or *logoi* (names), or inscriptions that are, for the most part, in Greek.[60] These magical intaglios, particularly widespread during the Imperial period (first century BCE–third century CE), notably in the Mediterranean region and to a lesser extent in the northern parts of Europe, are characterized by an iconographic repertoire deriving from the major Mediterranean and Eastern cultures. The Egyptian gods such as Horus, Thoth, and Isis, as well as the Greek deities such as Aphrodite, Helios, Ares, and Marsyas, are found side by side down the centuries with figures emerging from traditions such as the Persian Mithra, Jewish Moses, and Christian Jesus. But, equally so, we find representations of animals and of unnamed individuals engaged in various acts.[61] This syncretism is evident in the mixture of Greek, Hebrew, and Latin languages and in the hybridization of the iconographic traditions, common at the time. Hence, for example, we have the raptor-headed bird god, seemingly the product of the merging of the Zoroastrian bird god, the Egyptian serpent god Kneph, and the human-headed serpent god Agathos Daimon worshipped at Alexandria.[62]

In accordance with an analogical view of the world—for which a correspondence always exists between macrocosm and microcosm and therefore between celestial and sublunary entities—these engraved gemstones were believed to act through sympathy or antipathy. They operated first in a natural way through the intermediary of their substance and then magically, due to their preparation that is notably figurative and a result of their consecration.[63] The choice of stones took place, consequently, according to the therapeutic properties that they were supposed to have, and we have the record of this in the Greek and Latin lapidaries of the Imperial period (e.g., *the Lapidary Kerygmata*, *the Cyranides*, *Socrates and Dionysus*, *Damigeron-Evax*, and so forth), in the treatises on Theophrastus's and Pseudo-Plutarch's natural philosophy as well as in Dioscorides's and Galen's medical works.[64] Thus, hematite, also called "bloodstone" due to the red color it produces when diluted in water, was chosen for the treatment of inflammations of the eye, diseases of the blood, hemorrhages, stones, and types of hepatitis.[65] The images worked, here again, according to the principle of analogy. The entities depicted on the gemstone were chosen by the magus for their sympathetic links or their resemblances with the targeted illness. Consider, for example, the figure of Chnoubis (fig. 1.6), a hybrid being with the body of a serpent and a radiant lion's head, reputed to act upon the abdominal parts and especially on the stomach, intestines, and uterus.[66] Two characteristics make this figure especially effective for the healing or protection of these bodily parts. First, its iconographic origins link it to two deities in the Egyptian tradition: Khnum, the ram-headed creator god, and Sekhmet, the first decan of Leo; both of whom were recognized by the Egyptian magi as having a positive effect on the stomach and lower abdomen.[67] Second, and this is where we see the strictly analogical component, the very form of the figure recalls through its serpentine features the twisted and coiled intestine, the target of the treatment. To attain the source of the sickness more effectively, the magus also took pains to carefully design the images.

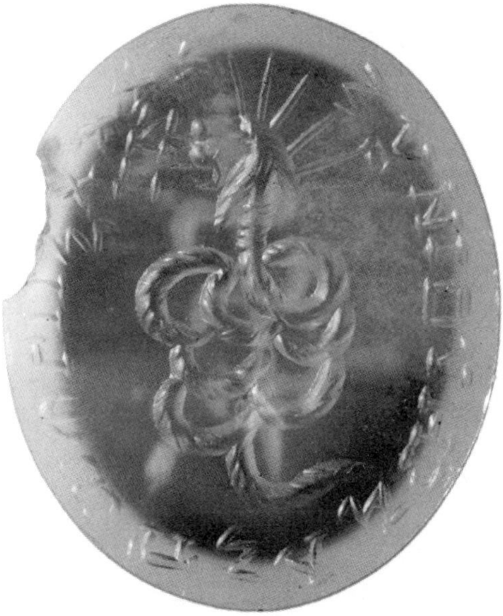

Figure 1.6. *Etched Stone with Figure of Chnoubis*, third century BCE, serpentinite, .7 × .5 in. London, British Museum (© The Trustees of the British Museum—Creative Commons).

This involved more than merely engraving the figures of Artemis, Horus, or Hercules following the classical tradition; it was also necessary to strengthen and direct the figures' power by endowing them with specific attributes, showing them many times over, or producing hybrid forms. This is what we see included in certain a formula listed on a Greek magical papyrus with the figure of the goddess Hekate:

> Take a lodestone, on which let three-faced Hecate be engraved. And let the middle face be that of a horned virgin, and the left that of a dog, and the right that of a goat. After engraving the stone, clean it with natron and water and dip it into the blood of someone who has died a violent death. Then make an offering of food to it and utter the same invocation during the rite.[68]

The inscriptions, deliberately shaped either with the doubling of letters or a geometric arrangement, worked alongside the material and figurative pieces to activate the magical object, calling up a particular *numen* (presiding spirit) through its own secret name, or producing a similar story of healing that would signal, in some way, the sick person's remission.[69] As was the case in the Egyptian tradition, these writings fulfilled a performative function. They served as both connector as well as prescription, connecting the powers thus invoked with specific individuals; indeed the inscriptions frequently mention the name of the object's owner, the one who was to benefit from the object's positive effects,[70] and they mention specific ailments, where these same inscriptions often specify the part of the body aimed at by the magic (e.g., the heart, stomach, uterus, etc.).[71] The frequent use of injunctions in the imperative mood such as "Digest, digest!" "Tantalus, you are hungry—drink blood!" or "Gout, be gone, Perseus is after you!" show, furthermore, that the object's agency was also a delegated one.[72]

Although each of the components here, the substance, image, *characteres*, and text, works its own effect, it is their conjunction, their being joined together in one object, that made these amulets powerful magical artifacts in the eyes of those who used them. The bringing together of these various material, iconographic, and textual parts, often reinforced at the time of the object's mounting as a piece of jewelry by the inclusion of astrological signs or natural elements (e.g., animal, vegetable, or mineral), was to compel in a certain fashion the invoked beings (e.g., deities, decans, or *daimones*) to act or to force the evil spirits to flee. Indeed, in both Egyptian and Greek culture, illness was often seen as the presence of an evil spirit in the body.

We know from the magic papyrus, medical treatise, and lapidary texts and from certain material traces, such as the style of the mountings and the presence of holes, that the magical and talismanic intaglios were most often placed in contact with body, sewn into clothing or worn as rings or pendants attached to chains,[73] with the idea here being, as Galen indicates in his treatise *On Simple Medicines*, to keep the engraved stone close to the sick organ:

> The testimony of some authorities attributes to certain stones a peculiar quality which is actually possessed by the green jasper. Worn as an amulet, it

> benefits the stomach and oesophagus. Some also set it in a ring, and engrave on it the radiate serpent, just as King Nechepsos prescribed in his fourteenth book. I myself have made a satisfactory test of this stone. I made a necklace of small stones of that variety and hung it from my neck at just such a length that the stones *touched the position of the cardiac orifice*. They seemed just as beneficial even though they had not the design that Nechepsos prescribed.[74]

And yet, if it is true that gems were most often worn on the person, so that, in this way, their powers might be administered, other ways of using them, including ingestion, could be foregrounded. As Erika Zwierlein-Diehl has shown, the presence of clean cuts, traces of scraping, and missing pieces on the stones (figs. 1.7a–b) demonstrates that parts of them may well have been removed and used as a base for potions.[75] Reduced to a powder, the fragments of intaglios were mixed with water or wine and then drunk. These observations only confirm what we know from the lapidaries and the magical papyri.[76] In the *Cyranides*, for example, the author offers a recipe requiring that the engraved image, alongside natural elements, be soaked in a liquid solution and then drunk with the aim of curing mania or preventing bouts of madness:

> If anyone engrave a *Phoenicopterus*, and at its Feet a Scorpion, and put under the stone the Root of the Herb, he will have a Phylactery. . . . If anyone be bitten by a mad Dog, and grow hydrophobic, he cannot drink a more precious Liquor. Take therefore the Ring, and put it in Water, and give him to drink, and he will be safe; and if you give it before Madness, he will not be mad.[77]

Given the large number of stones bearing traces of cutting or scraping that are now held in collections, there is every reason to believe that this practice was quite widespread, or, at least, much more widespread than was thought up until very recently.[78] Once again, we should consider the ingestion of images to have been a privileged or recurrent form of therapeutic treatment. And indeed, it seems very much that the figure itself fulfilled a

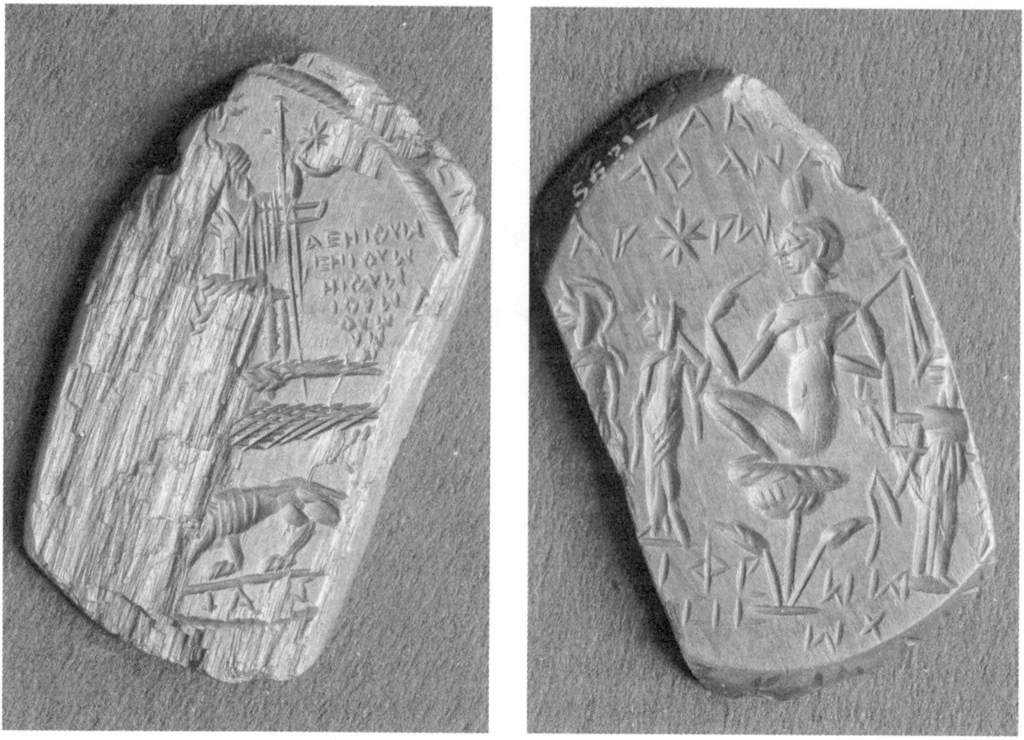

Figures 1.7a and b. *Magical Gem,* third century BCE, intaglio (front and back), jasper, 1 × .6 in. London, British Museum (© The Trustees of the British Museum).

primordial function in this magical medicine. An examination of the marks on the stones indicates that the effectiveness of the cure depended upon the proper "treatment" of the image. The physician or the patient took care that the image not disappear as the cuts are often in the middle of the images. Conceivably, this was so that the magical object would continue to function in the future. Indeed, it is very likely that the medicinal power of the emblemized gem derived, in part, from the establishment of a relation between the celestial *numen*, its representation on the stone, and its residence deep within body of the sick person, in the hidden place from where the illness was to be removed. Through this process of triangulation, the sick patient was placed at the heart of a network of correspondences in which microcosm and macrocosm reverberated, allowing thus for the rebalancing of the humors, an essential process for healing.

Ingesting Images in the Christian World

Contrary to what centuries of theological rationalism have led people to believe, the perception and understanding of images in the Christian world[79] was never a purely visual affair. From the studies carried out by Marc Bloch, Jean-Claude Schmitt, André Vauchez, and Caroline Walker Bynum,[80] it has become clear that if we wish to understand how ingesting images functioned as a form of relation with the sacred, we must first rid ourselves of the idealist and anti-materialist concept of religious experience. And to do this, it is essential that we avoid setting up, as a first principle, any sort of watertight barrier between religious and magical practices.

Let us start therefore with the magical images. Such images did not disappear after the fall of the Egyptian, Greek, and Roman civilizations. Indeed, the truth is quite otherwise.[81] Although magic was subject to repressive legislation in the Christian world during the time when Christianity was established as the imperial religion (by Theodosius in 392 CE) to replace polytheistic cults, and despite the fact that the Church Fathers often forbade it, magical practices mostly survived the Christianization of the Roman world that took place between the fourth and sixth centuries.[82]

To demonstrate, in his study on the medicinal uses of Byzantine artifacts, Gary Vikan indicates the sizable distribution in Byzantium of magical and personal objects such as rings, bracelets, necklaces, intaglios, and seals bearing the inscription *hygieia* (health).[83] This term, linked with an image, advertised the prophylactic or therapeutic purpose of the figured artifacts. Among such images, we frequently find the figure of the lion-headed serpent Chnoubis, who was already widespread during the Hellenic period, used as a cure for abdominal ills.[84] Or again, we see a holy rider, often Solomon or Saint Sisinios, riding over and trampling a female demon.[85] The configuration of this last image, with a horseman striking down a figure of evil, gives visibility to the principle of evil annihilated by a representative of God. A hematite in the collection of the British Museum (fig. 1.8) bears, on the front side, the inscription *sphragis theou* (Seal of God), and on the back, the figure of Solomon trampling over Evil (in this case, Lilith). Véronique Dasen has identified this item as a medicinal seal effective for all types of illness, the term *sphragis* echoing here the *terra sigillata* used by the physicians of the time.[86] If it is true that this object did have a healing purpose, as seems to be confirmed by other Solomon figures appearing in conjunction with inscriptions using a medical vocabulary, it is conceivable that this piece of "God's medicine" took the form of an imprint made on a malleable substance such as a gum, paste, or resin, and that this substance was then given to the patient as an ingestible medicine. Thanks to various sources, we know that magical seals were used to produce healing images intended to be ingested, and the ingestion of an imprinted token in *terra sigillata* could very well have figured among the cures prescribed by certain physicians in the Middle Ages.[87] In Book VI of his medical treatise *Inventarium sive Chirurgia Magna* (1363), Guy de Chauliac recommended for a cure for a nephritic colic, also called the sickness of the stone, the consumption of an astrological image made from a seal:

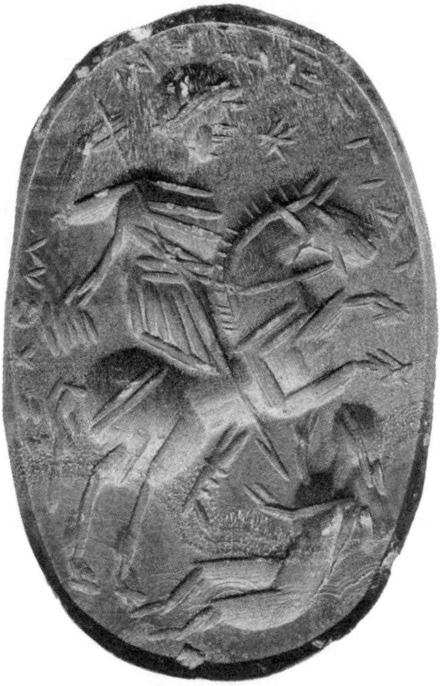

Figure 1.8. *Magical Gem with rider (Solomon) stabbing Lilith*, fourth century, intaglio, hematite, 1 × .15 × .68 in. London, British Museum (© The Trustees of the British Museum).

> And Hermes said, as Arnaud [de Villeneuve] and the Conciliator [Pietro d'Abano] bear witness, that the image of the lion, engraved in most pure gold when the sun is in Leo [and] the moon is not in Saturn and is not receding, [and] worn in a band (*bracali*) or a belt (*zona*) in leather of a lion or a seal, protects against kidney and other stones. And incense bearing this mark (*sigillatum olibanum*) or even goat's blood prepared with the same image and at the same hour, can break the stones and cause urination if pulverized and given with wine.[88]

Here, the medical prescription is coupled with an astrological computation: the image must be made at a specific time in order to establish a sympathetic connection between macrocosm and microcosm, that is, between the celestial spheres, the magical object, and the sick patient. The astrological component reflects the medical importance assigned since Antiquity to *melothesia*, the idea that each part of the body came under the influence of a particular planet and zodiacal constellation.[89] We shall need to return to this point in more detail during our later discussion of the reasons for the choice of *ingestion* as a privileged way of enabling healing. For now, one should note that the seal was not necessarily worn on the person; it could also be imprinted on incense or dried goat's blood and then mixed in wine and drunk.[90] Furthermore, the fact that various substances could serve equally well as receptacles of the image shows the overriding importance of the image itself in the working of the artifact's magical effect. The substance certainly does have its role to play; however, its role appears less crucial than that of the image in the channeling of celestial influxes, the magical procedure seeming to take precedence over the natural power, that is, the specific properties of substances and gems noted in the *Empirica*,[91] of the form-bearing substance.

This medieval seal, of course, takes us a long way both spatially and chronologically from the Byzantine examples that we looked at previously (Chnoubis or Solomon). However, we should note along with Nicolas Weill-Parot, Árpád Nagy, Zwierlein-Diehl, and Dasen, that lines of transmission allowing for the communication of magical knowledge were not lacking in the Middle Ages (e.g., through Techel, Al-Kindi, Thomas of Cantimbré, Vincent de Beauvais, and Albertus Magnus),[92] and that the practice of ingesting images for therapeutic purposes in the late classical and medieval worlds was quite conceivably much more widespread than it would appear from the textual sources alone.

As we have already noted, with the Christianization of the Roman Empire, there was no letup in the production of intaglios, seals, and other talismanic objects. However, the industry was transformed by contact with the Christian culture, and we can measure the change by looking at the iconographic evolution of the magical objects. Between the fourth and sixth centuries, the representations coming out of the syncretic Greco-Roman culture are increasingly linked with Christian figurations. Examples of this include a silver bracelet, now in The Cairo Museum, on which the magical figure of Chnoubis is inserted in an iconographic sequence

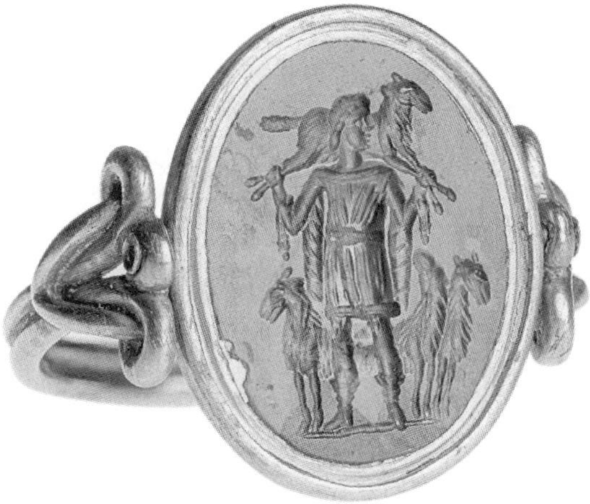

Figure 1.9. Oval gem with the Good Shepherd and Hekate on reverse, Roman, Late Imperial Period (250–400 CE), jasper with gold mounting, .625 in. Boston, Museum of Fine Arts (Bartlett Collection—Museum purchase with funds from the Francis Bartlett Donation of 1900 03.1010).

reserved in large part for episodes from the New Testament, such as the Annunciation, Nativity, Baptism, Crucifixion;[93] a gem, today in the collection of the Boston Museum of Fine Arts, bearing a Good Shepherd on the front side and on the back, a Triple Hekate (fig. 1.9);[94] and a clay pendant of Syrian origin, now in the collection of the American Numismatic Society in New York, one side on which we see an Anguipede and on the other, a Jonas figure.[95] The two figurative traditions have the same objective, namely, the protection or cure of whomsoever might have recourse to either the saints or magical artifacts.[96] Indeed, as Vikan adds, "while one's local bishop, town physician, and neighborhood sorceress were almost certainly at odds over how best to evict the demon that possessed one, the possessed did not indulge in the luxury of subtle differentiations. If need be, he called upon Christ, Solomon, and the Chnoubis in one breath . . . ."[97]

And yet, while certain "pagan" figures were to continue to appear on prophylactic and therapeutic objects (e.g., Chnoubis, the Anguipede scheme[98]), by the end of the sixth century it was the Christian repertoire that was to form the major presence on this sort of artifact.[99] Hence, a bracelet, today in the Jeffrey Spier collection bearing the inscription "*hygieia*," displays scenes from the New Testament, along with a holy rider, probably Solomon, which strongly suggests that healing power was, at this point and henceforward, attributed to Christian images.[100] Likewise, we have a reliquary pendant locket (seventh–eighth century), in the British Museum, depicting, on the front of the lid, both the Nativity and the Adoration of the Magi, and with, on the back, a magical number and the inscription, "Secure salvation and repulsion of all evil things." Along the side of the lid, there is an inscription referring to Saints Cosmas and Damian. The iconography here shows us that codes originating in the magical practices of the Imperial era had been wholly taken up by Christian culture.[101]

The main reason for the continued presence of magical objects in the Christian world was the persistence of the analogical thinking that had characterized most of the civilizations of Antiquity. The coherence of the magical system depended upon analogy, and analogical thought was not to be put into serious question until the dawn of modernity.[102] Before the Cartesian "revolution," the world functioned in much the same way for both pagans and Christians. It was a world inhabited by devils, and the natural elements, human bodies, and humors were all in correspondence with one another. This is not to say, however, that for the religious authorities, from Tertullian to Martin Luther and by way of Saint Augustine, this mixture of genres did not create problems.[103] For the Christian theologians, magic was always "other people's religion,"[104] and it was important to condemn the practice to avoid turning any use of images into a form of idolatry. Indeed, as we shall see later, the iconoclasts were to build their arguments against holy images on the identification of the "deviant" use of such images with magical practices.[105] Such practices involving the configuration, preparation, and consecration of an image in order for it to act remotely on a substance or to force an entity to manifest itself were vigorously condemned and marginalized, and any and all pagan magical procedures were treated as vain superstition. The worshipped *numina*, identified with demonic figures, were to be progressively replaced by relics and then by images conveying a divine power that was henceforth held to be uncontrollable. The strictly human magical procedure, while it was to remain a possibility in certain circles,[106] receded into the background before a presence that was now supernatural, mysterious, and infused in people by God. It was God Himself who had chosen to communicate His *virtus* through certain people, natural elements, or artifacts. Healing was thus a gift—the work of divine grace, something miraculous, and no longer, in principle, the result of human action.

The Saints' Eulogiae

In Miracle 232 of the *Vita* of Saint Symeon Stylites the Younger (521–592), a work of hagiography like dozens of others dating from the sixth century, we find the singular story of one Theodore Pikaridios, a praetorian prefect in Africa from 569 to 582. Suffering from intestinal distress, Pikaridios is cured by ingesting a token bearing the stamped iconic image of the stylite saint.[107] This text is well worth quoting because it shows, in the clearest manner possible, the sort of relationship that Christians in the East maintained with the saints:

> For reasons that are of interest for the good of all souls, the Servant of God [Saint Symeon] sent down into the imperial town Thomas, God's well-beloved priest, who was also his apocrisiary, with two other monks. Theodore, the very illustrious praetorian prefect, whose nickname was Pikridios, seeing these men speaking freely in the palace, asked where they were from. Those who knew them told him that they were from the monastery of Saint Symeon on the Wondrous Mountain, near to the great city of Antioch. The prefect had Thomas summoned, and he invited him to come and sit with him in the praetorium. Thomas did so, and, over the course of many hours, they talked of the saint, and Thomas told of the miracles that God had worked following the saint's prayers. Believing these words, the prefect said: "I am secretly afflicted with a terrible illness, and there is no remedy

that I have not tried, and yet it only gets worse. I pray, therefore, that the circumstances of my illness be made known to the saint, so that I myself might be cured by the saint's prayers, and that, accordingly, I also become, along with everyone else, a herald of his marvelous works." Thomas asked what this illness was. The prefect said to him: "Everything that I eat is turned to blood and worms, and it comes right out of me, causing me great suffering because the worms tear at me." Thomas said: "Make these details known to the saint, as you have suggested; for my part, I shall write to him myself. But we have here some of his holy hair and dust of his blessing. Take some, and dip it in pure water, then drink it while fasting and rub yourself with the water, and you will see the glory of God." The prefect took the consecrated objects and, after having done as he was told, the healing took place, the demon having immediately fled and his bowels begun to function normally. And yet, when he saw that the hemorrhage of blood and worms had stopped, the prefect, his mind deranged by fear, sent for Thomas, and, in a state of great agitation, he explained to him what had happened, saying: "I fear that the worms, prevented from coming out, are tearing at me from another side; but, because of that, I wish to send a magistrianos to inform the saint of this." Accordingly, he made the request himself, and designated the one who was to leave. Meanwhile, a reply arrived from the saint to Thomas and the prefect, relating in full their conversation, and saying how, after having taken the consecrated objects, soaking them in water, and then drinking it, the prefect had been cured. The saint also let it be known that he knew of the prefect's mistaken idea, and he accused him of a lack of faith. He strengthened the priest anew in his faith and confirmed his cure. And the man remained in good health until the end of his days, glorifying God and his Holy Servant because of the miracle that was worked on him, and because of Symeon's written prophesy about the remarks exchanged between himself and Thomas.[108]

The author of the *Vita* does not specify in his account exactly how Symeon is depicted. However, seen in the context of pilgrimages to the Miraculous Mountain, the terms *eulogia* (εὐλογία; "blessing") and *sanctified objects*[109] may well allude to circular tokens,

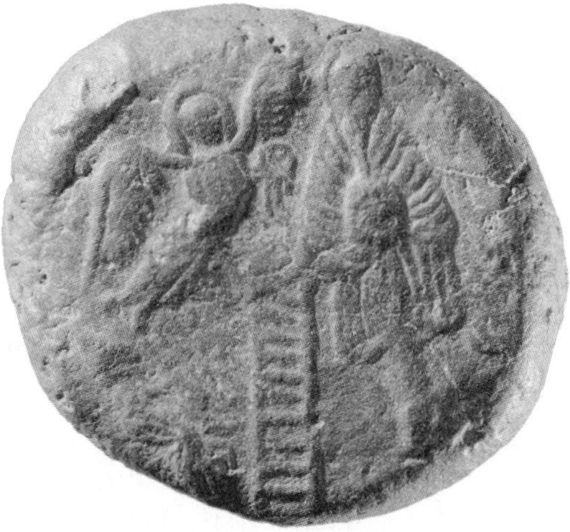

Figure 1.10. *Pilgrim token depicting Saint Symeon Stylites*, sixth–seventh century, terracotta, diameter 1.14 in. London, British Museum (© The Trustees of the British Museum).

measuring some two to five centimeters in diameter, made from sanctified earth, and that bore the figure of the saint (fig. 1.10).[110] A token in the Museum of Bobbio Abbey in Italy shows the head and shoulders of Saint Symeon placed atop his column. A ladder leans against the column, and a monk is climbing it, holding in his hand an incense censer. In the accompanying inscription, the token is clearly marked as a "eulogia": "Eulogia of St. Symeon of the Miraculous Mountain."[111]

It may seem strange that, as is made clear in the Pikridios story, the saint himself offers an emblemized object such as this.[112] But, if we are to believe the account of Miracle 231 in the *Vita*, in which the presence of an effigy on his blessing is explicitly mentioned, then this would appear to have been the custom.[113] A priest from Baliseia, whose eldest son was ill, comes to the holy man to ask for his help. After having received the grace of God and the cure of his son, he returns home, only to find that his second son has also fallen ill. He left once again for the monastery, and again seeks the saint's help. The latter extends "his right hand" over the child, and, after having marked him with the sign of the cross, says to the priest:

"Take this other one who is now returned to life and leave at once." The priest said: "Allow us, Servant of God, to stay a few days with you. Your hand will touch and bless us, and our presence at your side will guarantee a more complete cure." Symeon became angry at the priest, saying: "Why does he who leads astray by lack of faith fool you so in this? The power of God, in fact, is at work everywhere. Take, therefore, this blessing made from my dust, leave, and when you see the imprint of our image, it is us that you will see.[114]

The expression, "blessing made from my dust" and the one used in Miracle 232, "the dust of my blessing," suggest that these two objects were one and the same, and that, in Miracle 232 just as in Miracle 231, which includes a clear mention of an "image," it is in each case an emblemized token that is being offered to the pious believer.[115]

Still, although the image is clearly present here, it does not appear to be directly involved in Miracle 232. The author of the *Vita* speaks of ingesting a "pure water" into which the hairs of the saint and the earth of his blessing, had been dipped.[116] It was thus the material substances having been in contact with the saint that, in this case, establish a state of continuity with the sick person.[117]

Relics

To fully understand how this transitivity was believed to work, let us look at the role played, from the fourth century onwards, by the Christian saints.[118] According to the fourth- and fifth-century theologians Theodoret of Cyrus and Gregory of Nyssa, the saints were "intimate friends" of men, and yet also "invisible"; they were intercessors capable of passing prayers on towards God, examples to conform to (namely, both to resemble and to follow) in the hope of winning a place in the heavenly kingdom and, finally, a genuine source of life during one's time on earth.[119] The commerce with the saints was physical as much as it was spiritual. It happened not only through prayer and meditation, as the latter developed during the Middle Ages in the monastic communities, but also through a more concrete relationship with their body, living or not. Even when deceased, and perhaps above all when deceased if we judge by the many accounts of *postmortem*[120] miracles, the saints continued to act through their relics.[121] Gregory of Nyssa explains: "Those who behold them embrace, as it were, the living body in full flower: they bring eye, mouth, ear, all the senses into play, and then, shedding tears of reverence and passion, they address to the martyr their prayers of intercession as though he were present."[122] From late Antiquity until the end of the Middle Ages, in both East and West, the bodies of the saints, especially the bodies of martyred saints, were reputed to be the receptacles of divine power. Proof of this was seen in their incorruptibility, in their "odor of sanctity," and in the many miracles attributed to them.[123] It was desirable, therefore, to look on the bodies of the saints,[124] to get close to them, and even to touch them,[125] and we can see this in the numerous injunctions coming from the Church Fathers and Church Doctors.[126] Basil of Caesarea proclaimed it thus in a homily on Psalm 115: "anyone who has touched the bones of a martyr receives some share of the holiness that comes from the grace inherent in the body."[127] Given the importance of physical contact in the healing miracles in the New Testament — the fundamental Christian paradigm for the majority of its attitudes and practices with regard to the sacred — it is easy to understand the great role played by physical contact as a means of communicating grace. In the New Testament, it is by the placing of his hands upon bodies that Christ transmits his divine power and that he heals men and women of faith.[128] By this very same gesture, the majority of the saints, hermits, or monks dispensed their miraculous healing, and indeed it is also by this very same gesture that the kings of England and France were to display their thaumaturgical power.[129]

From the fourth century onwards, in conjunction with the growth of the cult of saints and their relics, an increasing number of shrines were to be erected on the sites of *martyria* (martyrdom) or in cemeteries.[130] This was, of course, a way to preserve the remains of the saints and holy martyrs, and to ensure their veneration. At the same time, we see the beginnings of the custom of consecrating altars by burying holy remains under the *mensa* (the altar table).[131] Efforts were made, furthermore, to widely distribute the relics' *praesentia* (presence) throughout all of Christendom, even inside the towns (breaking thus with the classical ban on burying the dead within the bounds of the city[132]), through the parceling out and transporting of the various body parts (head, arms, feet, hands, and hair), it being understood that "each fragment keeps . . . all of the *virtus* of the entire body."[133]

Faced with this practice of dismembering, and concerned above all to avoid the bodies being completely destroyed, the religious authorities supported the distribution, even the industry, surrounding the *eulogiae*, the blessed substances that pilgrims could take back to their communities.[134] Any substance having had direct physical contact with the body of a saint was deemed capable of carrying the *virtus* associated with it.[135] The material substance did not actually hold the power within itself; indeed, to avoid any confusion in the matter, Saint Thomas took pains to distinguish between the *virtus* peculiar to the divine, and the *potentia* attaching to the substances through which God acted.[136] However, any earth, water, oil, fabric, stone, ceramics, metal, or leather that had been placed in contact with a saint living or dead, or with his or her relics or tomb, could become a vector of divine grace.[137]

An entire array of objects allowing for the transportation of the *virtus* emerged at this time: ampullae or phials in which holy oil flowing from saints' tombs had been collected, as we see for example with Saint Demetrios in Thessaloniki or Saint Nicholas in Bari,[138] but also holy water coming from holy sources and rivers such as that of Saint Menas (Abou Mena) in Egypt (fig. 1.11).[139] These ampullae were also used to carry the precious liquids to members of the community who were unable to travel.[140] There were also the insignia that had touched the relics and, that, like the saint him- or herself, accompanied and protected the pilgrims on their way home

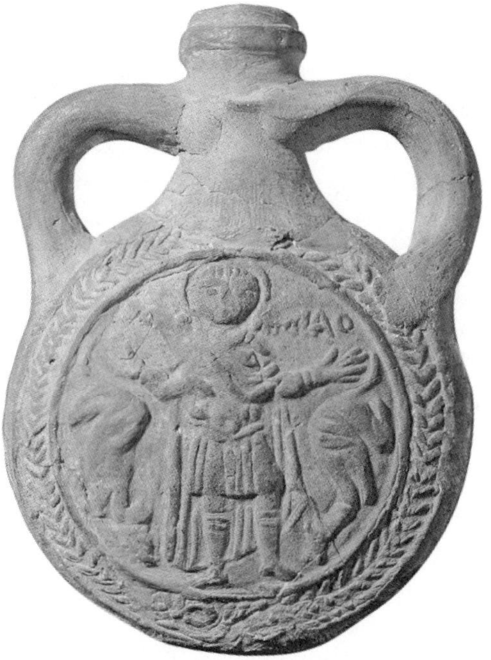

Figure 1.11. Saint Menas Ampulla, ca. 480–650 CE, terracotta, 5.9 × 4.2 in. London, British Museum (© The Trustees of the British Museum).

before being stitched into clothing, pinned into books of hours, hung on the walls of homes, buried with the dead, or thrown into rivers in order to sanctify "the land."[141] And again, halfway between these two types of objects, we have the *tortae*, "made with holy soil gathered up from around the holy site," "marked with an image," and able to spread the "holy substances" to distant places, far and wide.[142]

With the massive growth of pilgrimages in the twelfth century, the relics were to become more and more protected from the public. The pilgrims were kept increasingly distant from the holy remains, and they were thus obliged to find other ways to obtain the *virtus*. In addition to the relics by way of contact (e.g., *brandea*, *tortae*, emblems, etc.), one of the expedients that the pilgrims used was a mirror, either carried along with them or purchased in the vicinity of such holy sites as Aachen, Brussels, Nuremberg, Venice,

Saint-Nicolas-de-Port, etc.[143] As we can see from a 1487 engraving by Peter Vischer, part of the Nuremberg *Heiltumbusch* (fig. 1.12), the pilgrims directed the reflecting surface towards the "inaccessible relic," in hopes of "capturing . . . the grace contained in its reflection." The mirror, therefore, paradoxically allowed for a sort of contact at a distance.[144] Later, when the moment arose, all one had to do was bring out the object to benefit from the power contained within it. One pilgrimage account mentions the surprising (to say the least) ingestion of a piece of bread that had been put in contact with a mirror that had previously taken in the reflection of a relic.[145] The operational logic of this transmission of power cannot, of course, be understood without including the fact that, for the medieval mind, the image reflected in the mirror was the result of the material diffusion of rays.[146] The *virtus* deposited in the relic radiated out thanks to the *spiritelli* emanating from the object and broadcast into space. These "material" spirits could consequently be captured, imprisoned, and then released by mirroring.

Judging from the pilgrimage accounts from late Antiquity and the Middle Ages, the artifacts brought back from the holy sites were used not only as protective objects but also as medicines for the suffering.[147] Ingestion did not have the sole goal of a blessing or an internal unction; very often it served the purposes of physical healing.[148] Like the aforementioned tokens, one could use oil, holy water, or earth. Once mixed with other ingredients, in the form of a pomade or after having been transformed into pills or drinkable solutions, the substance was ingested to cure all sorts of diseases. Accounts involving ingesting relics or, more frequently, materials having been in contact with them are not uncommon. A pilgrim from Piacenza in Northern Italy who had made the journey to the Holy Land around the year 570, for example, mentions that as they went into the Church of the Apostles on Mount Zion in Jerusalem, the faithful would consume water that had been put in contact with the head of the holy martyr Theodota: "I saw a human head enclosed in a reliquary of gold and adorned with gems, which they

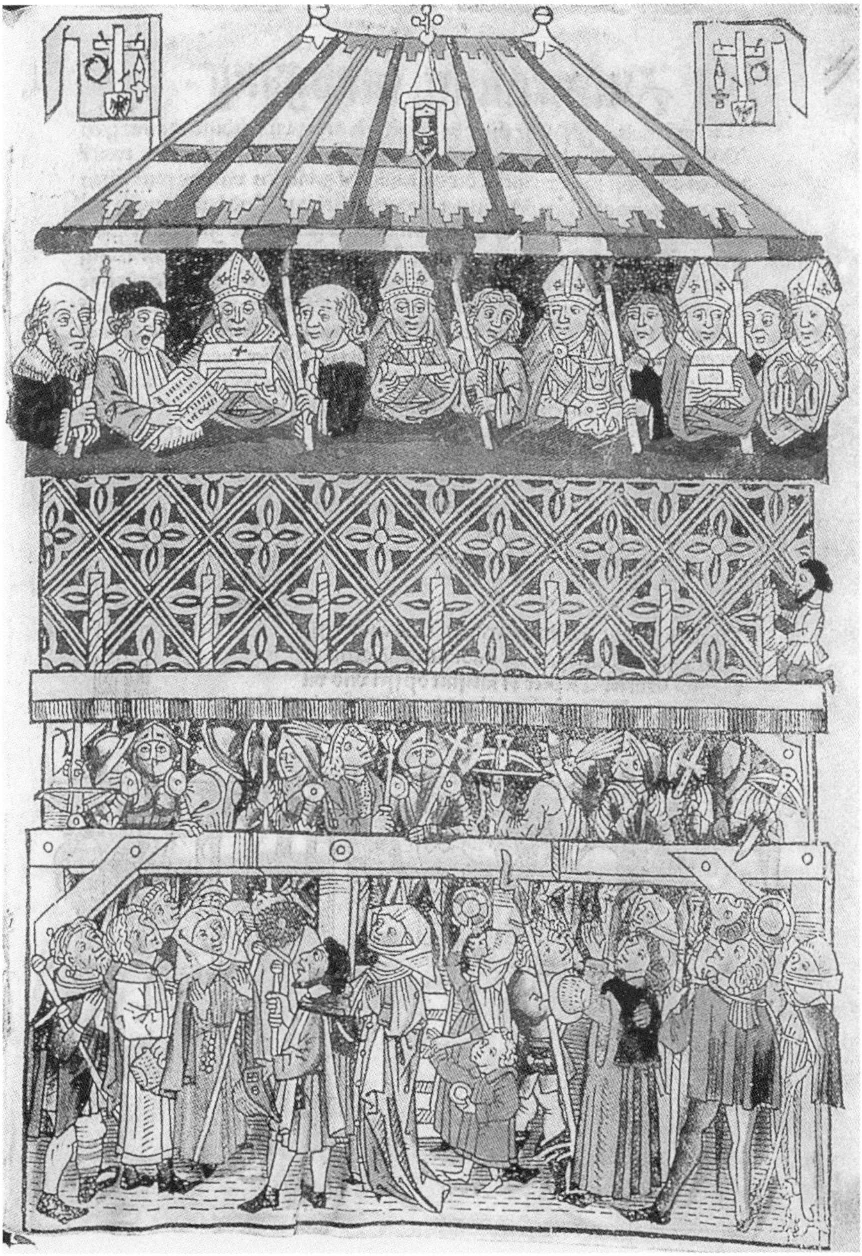

Figure 1.12. "The Annual Display of Relics," in Peter Vischer's *Nuremberg Relic-Book* (Nürnberg: Heiltumsbüchlein, 1487), woodcut, 8.2 × 5.5 in. Nuremberg, Staatsarchiv (Wikimedia Commons).

say is that of St. Theodota the Martyr. Many drink out of it to gain a blessing, and so did I."[149]

Saint John Chrysostom, for his part, recommended drinking and anointing oneself with oil of the martyrs: "Have a contrite mind; raise a blessing from the tomb . . . embrace the coffin, nail yourself to the chest. Not just the martyrs' bones, but even their tombs and chests brim with as great deal of blessing. Take holy oil and anoint your whole body—your tongue, your lips, your neck, your eyes—and you'll never fall into the shipwreck of drunkenness."[150]

In similar fashion to the consecrated water or oil, the holy earth could equally well be transformed into a remedy. Hence, in the *Vita* of Saint Symeon the Younger, we find a miracle account following the ingestion of a medicinal paste made up of holy dust and saliva.[151] Ingesting these substances was equivalent to incorporating a vestige of holiness, and that, as Gary Vikan points out, made it into a genuine "*prophylactikos*."[152]

Ingesting relics, real ones or those by way of contact, was not limited to the holy sites in Palestine and the East, nor was it limited in time to the sixth and seventh centuries.[153] Analogous scenes took place in the majority of the places of worship of the Roman Catholic Church throughout the Middle Ages. Gregory of Tours mentions the case of a child who found a way to health after having drunk water that had been in contact with the royal cloak of Guntram, the Merovingian king of Burgundy who was canonized shortly after his death, around 592–593:

> The faithful had a story which they used to tell about Guntram. There was a woman whose son was seriously ill of a quartan ague. As the boy lay tossing on his bed, his mother pushed her way through the vast crowds and came up behind the King. Without his noticing she cut a few threads from his cloak. She steeped these threads in water and then gave the infusion to her son to drink. The fever left him immediately and he became well again. I accept this as true, for I have often heard men possessed of a devil call upon Guntram's name when the evil spirit was in them, and through his miraculous powers confess their crimes.[154]

At the Benedictine Finchale Abbey in England, it was said that pilgrims visiting "the tomb of Saint Godric . . . were often cured by drinking water in which the bones of the saint had been dipped."[155] At Canterbury in 1170, shortly after the murder of Thomas Becket, the archbishop's bloodstained shirt was soaked in water and then used to cure a woman suffering from paralysis.[156] Similarly, during the canonization of Saint Peter Thomas in Famagouste, Cyprus (1366), a witness claimed to have seen certain women piously pouring water over the tomb of the patriarch, and then drinking it.[157] Finally, in the modern era, pilgrims to the Roman catacombs were able to collect a sort of "human paste," a mixture of earth and bones from the first martyrs, and this went into the manufacture of amulets (*Brevis de Marcha*) or *Agnus Dei* having a curative function.[158]

These practices were so widespread that, from the High Middle Ages, Sophronius of Jerusalem (ca. 550–639) was obliged to "remind the faithful that it was more profitable to commune with the body and blood of Christ than to drink oil from the lamps in front of the tombs of the martyrs."[159] The customs were, nonetheless, widely accepted by the religious authorities. Certain bishops even encouraged them to the extent that they were signs of *reverentia*, of social submission to the saints.[160] Gregory of Tours (538–594), for example, recommended that pilgrims make tokens out of the holy ground of Golgotha, and that they ingest them.[161] And again, in the fourteenth century, as we see from the account of a lay witness to the canonization of Peter of Luxembourg, a Dominican bishop could use "a small quantity of earth from the tomb mixed with wine" to heal the sick.[162] Patriarchs, bishops, and cardinals made no comments about this, quite simply because they themselves shared the same belief.[163] During this period, as André Vauchez notes, "a bishop dedicated himself to a saint in exactly the same way as his manservant."[164]

The Image on the Eulogiae

But let us return now to the image that was linked, in all likelihood, to the eulogia mentioned in Miracle 232 of the *Vita* of Saint Symeon the Stylite. What role and what status could possibly have been accorded it? If the earth of the holy site and the hairs of the saint were the active substances, should we conclude that ingesting the image was, in contrast, simply an accessory activity, or should we grant it an agency of a different nature?[165]

To judge from the iconography of the tokens associated with Saint Symeon the Stylite, which would have typically been a conventional picture of the bust of the saint set upon a column, and from the way in which these images were produced in imprints from engraved molds,[166] the depictions establish a relation, at once memorial and indicial, between the eulogia and the saint or with his or her shrine. And yet, although the image could certainly bear witness to a pilgrimage already undertaken, it was primarily a sign certifying the earthen token's origin. In fact, the owner of a blessing was not necessarily one who had traveled to obtain it; rather, the blessing, so to speak, may have traveled to them. In this way, the eulogiae functioned much like the seals that we find on those earthen *sphragis* or *terra sigillata* (medicinal tablets; fig. 1.13) that had been in fashion since Antiquity, and that were sold by apothecaries for their healing powers.[167] The famous clay and limestone quarries, such as those at Lemnos, Malta, and Samos, generated enormous profits, and, in an attempt to foil counterfeiters—who were, indeed, increasingly numerous with the growth of trade in the Middle Ages into the modern era—the producers placed sigillary images on the small spherical, cylindrical, cubic, or truncated blocks of earth, so as to guarantee the remedy's provenance. Such images included a figure of Philoctetes, a goat, or stars identifying it as Lemnos clay; a portrait of Saint Paul or a Maltese cross designating limestone from the cave at Ir-Rabat in Malta; or a scene from the life of Christ, usually the Crucifixion or the Resurrection (fig. 1.14), indicating the holy land of Bethlehem or the *terra Hierosolymitanae* (Holy Sepulcher).[168]

In the case of the earthen sigillary pieces like the tokens from the shrines, the image imprinted on the substance had a function

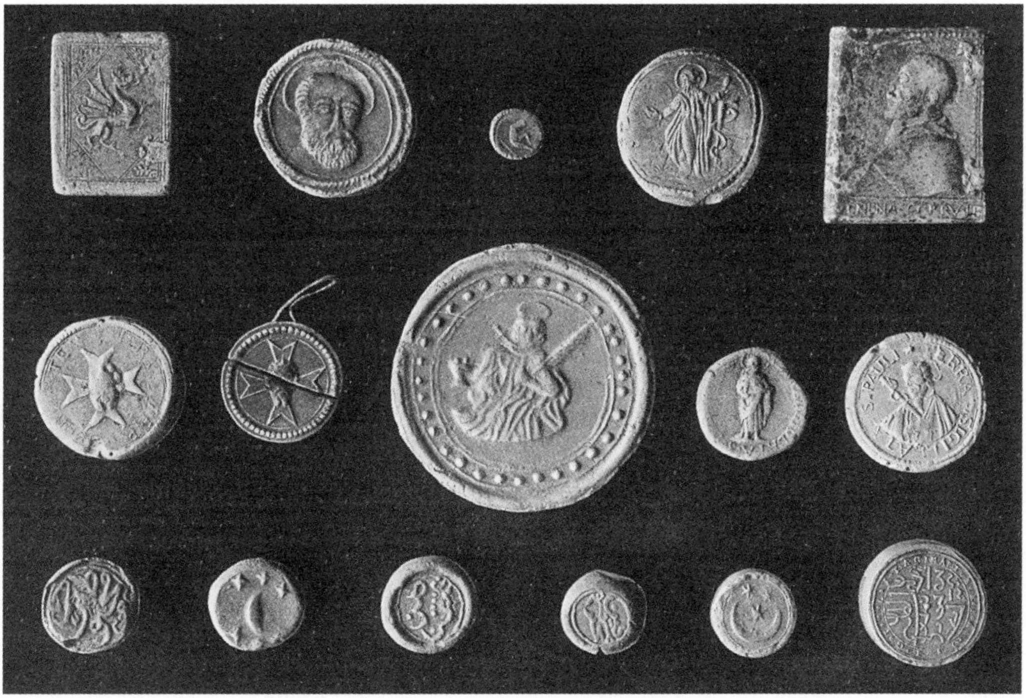

Figure 1.13. Terra sigillata tokens with varying provenance, in Josef Anton Häfliger, *Pharmazeutische Altertumskunde und die Schweizerische Sammlung für Historisches Apothekenwesen an der Universität Basel* (Zurich, Buchdruckerei zu alten Universität, 1931).

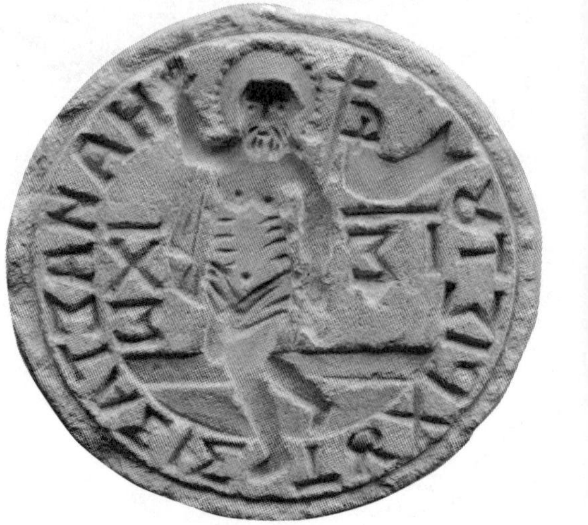

Figure 1.14. *The Resurrected Christ*, fifteenth century, terra sigillata (clay), limestone pharmacy seal, 1.3 × 2.4 in. London, Science Museum (© The Board of Trustees of the Science Museum—Science Museum Group Collection—Creative Commons).

that was basically memorial and indicial. And yet, we would be wrong to reduce these representations to simple figurative reminders or signs of provenance.[169] The image established a connection that was much more active than one produced by a mere "souvenir" or a certificate of origin since it was believed to have the real power of making the divine present. The above cited passage from Miracle 231 in the *Vita* of Saint Symeon the Younger is very clear about this: addressing the priest, the saint says, "The power of God, in fact, is at work *everywhere*. Take, therefore, this blessing made from my dust, leave, and *when you see the imprint of our image, it is us that you will see*."[170] The image could act in all places because it had the power of making the saint present and visible, even though the latter remained physically absent.

Here we touch upon a central fact about the Byzantine world's thinking with regard to the material image. Although it underwent variations through time and location,[171] this thinking rested upon one basic principle: the icon made visible the natural and invisible image of the holy being. As Venance Grumel writes, paraphrasing

Theodore the Studite (759–826), "any artificial image is the resemblance with that of which it is the image and shows, in itself, the figure of the archetype."[172] The point is well known, but we should take care to spell it out in detail. The icon is not a mere representation, rather, it is "the economy of the image."[173] It "aims at resemblance to its prototype without trying to maintain it with the relation of similitude that the prototype maintains with its own substance."[174] The icon makes the archetype present through the iconic *homoiôsis* (formal resemblance) resulting from the mimetic act generally accompanied by prayer; and yet, given all of this, it is not identical with its model. This is so because, although the icon does literally make present the "model in its image" and "participates" thus "in the divine nature of the prototype," as Olivier Boulnois defines it, its substance, for its part, is fundamentally different.[175] According to Theodore the Studite: "The nature of the material representation and the nature of Christ are indeed different ones, but the hypostasis is not different—rather, it is one, and the one of Christ and the one that is represented in the icon are the same,"[176] and again, "with the (artificial) image, it is not nature, but personhood that is expressed."[177] This means that, through the icon, the holy being is made present while, significantly, not being confused with it. The image, connected with the prototype, brings together the worlds of sensation and intelligence, and it becomes "a sacred mediation" deserving, "in itself, of veneration."[178] John of Damascus (676–749) was to sum up this idea with the remarkably simple phrase: "The image of a saint is a saint."[179] But, according to certain theologians of the image, this simplicity, and we shall return to this point later, did not go without creating confusion in the minds of the "simple."

Through this sensory making present, the image allows the pious believer, by contemplating it, to find him or herself in an analogous position to where they would be if they were, in fact, before the saint in the latter's own flesh and blood. Miracle 321 of the *Vita* puts particular emphasis on this power of making present, a power that permits the image to act as a *doorway*: after having obtained the cure of his second son, the priest discovers that his third-born son is also in "a desperate state." The child asks that he also be taken to the holy site, but the priest replies: "Saint Symeon, my son, has the power to come to visit you here, and you will be healed, and you will live." The child then sees the saint, though it is unclear whether this was a vision with material basis or a material image and says to his father: "Get up quickly, throw on incense, and pray, for the servant of God, St. Symeon, is before me."

The iconography traditionally used in the eulogiae from the Miraculous Mountain helps us to understand how the representation functioned within the mechanism of connection. As we can see from the Saint Symeon token held in Bobbio, the image, through its component parts, reflected the pilgrim's experience within the holy site: Saint Symeon appears atop a column, and the individual, dispensing incense during prayer, uses a ladder to get closer to the saint and to obtain his benediction.[180] By looking at the image, the pious believer is thus in the middle of the holy site. In this way, the material image becomes, itself by way of analogy, a *ladder* upon and through which the viewer can meet the saint, and the saint meet the believer. It is a path of access that abolishes the spatial and temporal distance separating the believer and the holy site. Like a visionary apparition, it puts right before one's eyes what is, in reality, absent, and it places everything within its purview under the saint's influence.[181] It is in this way that the icon, therefore, is a connector. It is not the saint, in the sense that it would transport to the here and now the invisible archetype, making it absent where it came from; rather, it renders the saint present both here and there through the establishment of a formal relation. As Marie-José Mondzain defines it, "Christ is not in the icon; the icon is *toward* Christ."[182]

It was due to this ability to lift spatial constraints that the images of the saints, and especially those of the stylite saints, were so widespread, going well beyond the Near East. And if, as is reported by Theodoret of Cyrus, a very great number of images of Saint Symeon the Elder were placed in the entrances of Roman shops, it was not merely to keep alive the memory of a past pilgrimage (or even a pilgrimage that may not always have been carried out), it was also, and perhaps above all, to obtain the protection of the saint in the "here and now."[183]

The Image's virtus

Cast one's eyes upon the saint and be healed! But was this visual connection all that was needed to capture the entirety of the sacred power carried by the artifact? The dust of the image in Miracle 231 seems to answer this question in the affirmative, and yet this initial visual functionality did not exclude other uses of the image. Visual contact could have been coupled with a much more physical, a more bodily relation with the representations. Miracle 231, depicting the swallowing of the *eulogia*, does not say what the priest did with the figured eulogia; however, judging from Miracle 232, the eulogia could well have been ingested. The following question, therefore, arises: if the image brought grace to the pious believer by making the saint present, could taking the image into one's own body have been a way to intensify the power carried by these contact relics? To answer this, we must look at other examples that can help us understand, in a more global way, the status of the image during late Antiquity and the Middle Ages, in the East as in the West.

A Byzantine hagiographical text from the end of the sixth or beginning of the seventh century known as the Miracle 15 in the *Vita* of Saints Cosmas and Damian relates the story of a woman of Constantinople, pious and suffering from sickness, who was supposedly healed of an internal affliction after ingesting a potion in which a painted representation of the two unmercenary saints had been dissolved.[184] Healed already many times through their intercession, the woman, as the anonymous author of the account of the miracle tells it, went constantly into their "admirable dwelling" to venerate them. Yet even this was not enough to assuage her devotional ardor, and she had the two saints painted in her own house:

> Upon her return home, the woman painted images of the saints "on all the walls of her house, being, as she was, insatiable in her desire to see them." One night, the text continues, while alone in her house, the woman came down with an acute stomachache. "Perceiving herself to be in danger, she crawled out of bed and, upon reaching the place where these most wise saints were depicted on the wall, she stood up leaning on her faith as upon a stick and scraped off some plaster with her fingernails. She put the plaster into water and, after drinking the mixture, she was immediately cured of her pains by the visitation [*epiphoitêsis*] of the Saints."[185]

Similar in its narrative to the accounts of healing that we see in the *Vita* of Saint Symeon the Younger, this story is, nonetheless, different from the two preceding miracles in one detail: grace is not obtained by the contemplation of an image, as in Miracle 231, or by ingesting a substance that had been in contact with the saint, as in Miracle 232; rather, it is acquired by ingesting a material representation. The woman was healed by eating an image.

As the author of the narrative explains, merely contemplating the image was not enough to satisfy the sick woman since she was "insatiable in her desire to see them."[186] The presence of the saints on the walls was still too external and distant to carry out the healing, hence the choice of ingestion, a genuinely physical meeting with the representation. The relation between the pious believer and the image passes no longer through the medium of sight, but through the mouth, the body, and its internal organs. Saints Cosmas and Damian act here by the intermission of their pictorial representation in the very insides of the sick body, where the eye cannot go.[187] Consequently, the image acts through its substance, and not only through the relation of conventional resemblance that it maintains with the saintly entities.

But what authorized and justified this transformation in the status of the image? Two historical processes, it seems to me, were involved in this metamorphosis: the likening of the image to a body and the singling out of ingestion as the paradigm of contact.

For the artificial image to be endowed with a *potentia* similar to that of a relic by way of contact, it was first necessary for the saints to be linked with images—an identity had to be established between the natural body and the artificial body.[188] The account of the death of Saint Daniel the Stylite shows, in a very concrete manner, how this identification was able to work in the imagination of the first Christians of the East. The events that took place at the time of the saint's funeral set up a continuity between the saint's remains and the icon:

> Our glorious father Daniel died at the third hour on the following day, a Saturday, December 11th in the second indiction (A.D. 493), and at the time of his death he worked a miracle in that the man with an unclean spirit was healed.... When they took down the railing they found the saint's knees drawn up to his chest, and his heels and legs to his thighs. And whilst his body was being forcibly straightened, his bones creaked so loudly that we thought his body would be shattered; yet when he was laid out, he was quite entire.... They clad him, as was his wont, in a leather tunic, and a plank was brought up and laid on the column and he was placed on it.... At early dawn the Archbishop Euphemius, dearly beloved of God, came and went up the column by the spiral way and kissed the precious corpse, and thus, too, did all the faithful high dignitaries and officials, for they went up to the head of the column, gave their benediction and kissed his blessed body and came down. But the people demanded that the holy man should be shown to them before his burial, and in consequence an extraordinary tumult arose. For by the Archbishop's orders *the plank was stood upright—the body had been fixed to it so that it could not fall—and thus, like an icon, the holy man was displayed to all on every side*; and for many hours the people all looked at him and also with cries and tears besought him to be an advocate with God on behalf of them all.[189]

The deceased, set upon a board and brandished before the crowd, appeared *like* an image. Now, an identification such as this suggests that the observers replaced the saint with his figuration, suspending thus the ontological distinction that normally separates a natural body from its artificial representation.[190] Setting to one side the question of the substance in favor of an immaterial continuity, this merging was not only to authorize the transfer of the relic's *potentia* to the representation, but to promote, in the following centuries in both the East and the West, the extension of the veneration of relics to that of images.[191]

Let us accept, therefore, the idea that the bodies of the saints could be likened to images. But was the reverse true? Were images holy objects or, to put it in other terms, were they the sensory and material manifestations of saintly entities? We have seen that the theologians did conceive of images as a way of rendering present something absent, and yet there was one important point of difference between the image and its archetype, namely, its substance. The image did not share in the material reality of its model.[192] This is how it differed from a relic. The bodily remains of a saint made present the very substance of the saint, while the image for its part made present only the form.

The difference between the icon and the relic had to do with the way in which the former established this presence. Again, Theodore the Studite makes clear that it is "by virtue of imitation [that is, *mimesis*], the image and the model are one."[193] With the image, "the relation to the sacred" is no longer, as Boulnois explains, "one of simple contiguity, as in the case of relics, but . . . of resemblance."[194] This conventional resemblance on which the principle of the icon depended established an artificial, and not a natural or physical, continuity between the image and the archetype. For this reason, it reiterated and maintained the gulf separating the image from the being.

But is it possible that this understanding of resemblance could still have given birth to the idea of a "material" and "physical" presence of the represented entity? Certainly, it is possible; however, for this to be the case, it would be necessary to go beyond indexing resemblance just to the artifact's external qualities. One would have to connect resemblance once again with the process that allowed it (i.e., the image mapped onto the artifact) to come into being. For it is on the basis of this process, whether it be real or in principle, that the image drew its link with the archetype. We should not forget that for the Byzantine iconodule theologians and patriarchs, the paradigmatic form of resemblance was the imprint,[195] because printed or stamped images, appearing through contact, maintained, in this way, an auratic link with the mold that issued them.[196] In fact, for Saint Augustine in the fifth century,[197] and then for Theodore the Studite at the beginning of the ninth century, it was the seal that served as a paradigm for explaining the continuity through resemblance and the difference in substance that existed between an artificial image of Christ and its archetype:

> Let us now consider a ring that is imprinted with the image of the emperor, and let the image be imprinted in wax, or in pitch, or in clay. The seal will indeed be one and the same, without any difference in all the materials. The latter, however, are different one from the other; the seal did not remain the same in virtue of the distinct materials but rather in virtue of the fact that it does not have anything in common with the materials. The seal did remain in the ring, but conceptually it is distinct from the materials in which it was imprinted. And the same applies also to the likeness of Christ, whenever the latter is imprinted in any material you can think of, as the likeness of Christ does not have anything in common with the material in which it is imprinted; rather, the likeness remains in the hypostasis of Christ, of which it is also a property (*idion*).[198]

This continuity belonging to representations produced by seals is at the heart of another miracle that was worked by ingesting an image. In the *Varia graeca sacra*, a mid-seventh-century compilation of miracles, the anonymous author relates the story of a man called Sergios of Alexandria who, suffering from a hernia, receives a visit in a dream from Saint Artemios. The latter gives him a golden coin and commands him to "drink" it to be cured. The following morning, the man awakes, and he finds between his hands not the golden coin, but a piece of wax imprinted with the saint's image. He swallows the seal mixed with water and is cured.[199]

In this case, the artifact's power clearly came from its method of manufacture — the image healed because it was in a relationship of identity with its archetype. Despite the difference in substance separating it from its template, where the seal was not of the same material as the resultant image, it was indeed in a relation of continuity with it. Whether the saint was fully present in physical reality or not was of no importance once the image had been established as his or her vestige.

This type of holy medicine, in which the archetype heals because it is instantiated in an imprint that is then ingested, cannot fail to remind us of the magical remedies that we have already seen in Byzantine society and in the medieval world of the West. In fact, the intaglios inherited from the Greco-Roman world could, themselves, be used as seals, producing healing effects.[200] As with the Christian seals, resemblance through contact assured a continuity with the heavenly powers, and this was how the remedy was able to work its effect. For certain doctors in the modern era, this process was even considered the true active principle behind certain *terra sigillata* ("stamped medicines"). For Galen, Cassius Felix, and Theodorus Priscianus, the image stamped upon therapeutic clay had no function other than to authenticate the remedy's origin; however, for other doctors and apothecaries, it was endowed with its own therapeutic power.[201] In a text from the eighteenth century, devoted to the history of pharmacology, John Hill explains, for example, that the "Ancients" attributed more virtues to the imprints than they did to the substances: "Our Forefathers thought the Earth obtained its Virtues from the Stamp of the Seal, and that if it had that it was no Matter whence it came, or what it was."[202]

As we can see from these many examples, the image's power of making the archetype present tended towards a progressive assimilation of the icon to the human body, and it was to be used to justify, in the arguments of the theologians, their being seen as equal in terms of the diffusion of grace. Saint Basil of Ancyra, aligned with the iconodule party, was to grant an equal measure of holiness to both icons and relics:

> I call on the intercession of the Virgin, the heavenly powers, and the saints. I accept the relics of the saints that I kiss and before which I prostrate myself because I have faith that by doing these things I participate in the process of sainthood. In the same way, I kiss with my lips and hold fast in my arms and prostrate myself out of respect before the icons of the carnal economy of Christ, the Virgin, the angels, apostles, prophets, martyrs, and all the saints.[203]

In making representations into the alter egos of relics, the theologians pushed the pious towards maintaining a genuinely physical relationship with images. As a sign of devotion, a believer might hold close an icon in their arms or kiss it, and all of this despite the difference in substance separating the image from its archetype. Physical evidence of this, moreover, is not at all rare. We find, notably and in both the East and the West, a great many illuminated manuscripts and icons that show signs of wear from the kisses of the faithful (fig. 1.15).[204]

As is noted by Gilbert Dagron, and later by Aurélie Barre and Olivier Leplatre, certain of the Church Fathers, champions of images, were nonetheless to take a position that was even more materialist. John of Damascus, for example, considered that, since God had made himself into man,[205] matter itself was a manifestation of the divine:

> Of old, God the incorporeal and formless was never depicted, but now that God has been seen in the flesh and has associated with human kind, I depict what I have seen of God. I do not venerate matter, I venerate the fashioner of matter, who became matter for my sake and accepted to dwell in matter and through matter worked my salvation, and I will not cease from reverencing matter, through which my salvation was worked. I do not reverence it as God.... I reverence the rest of matter and hold in respect that through which my salvation came, because it is filled with divine energy and grace.

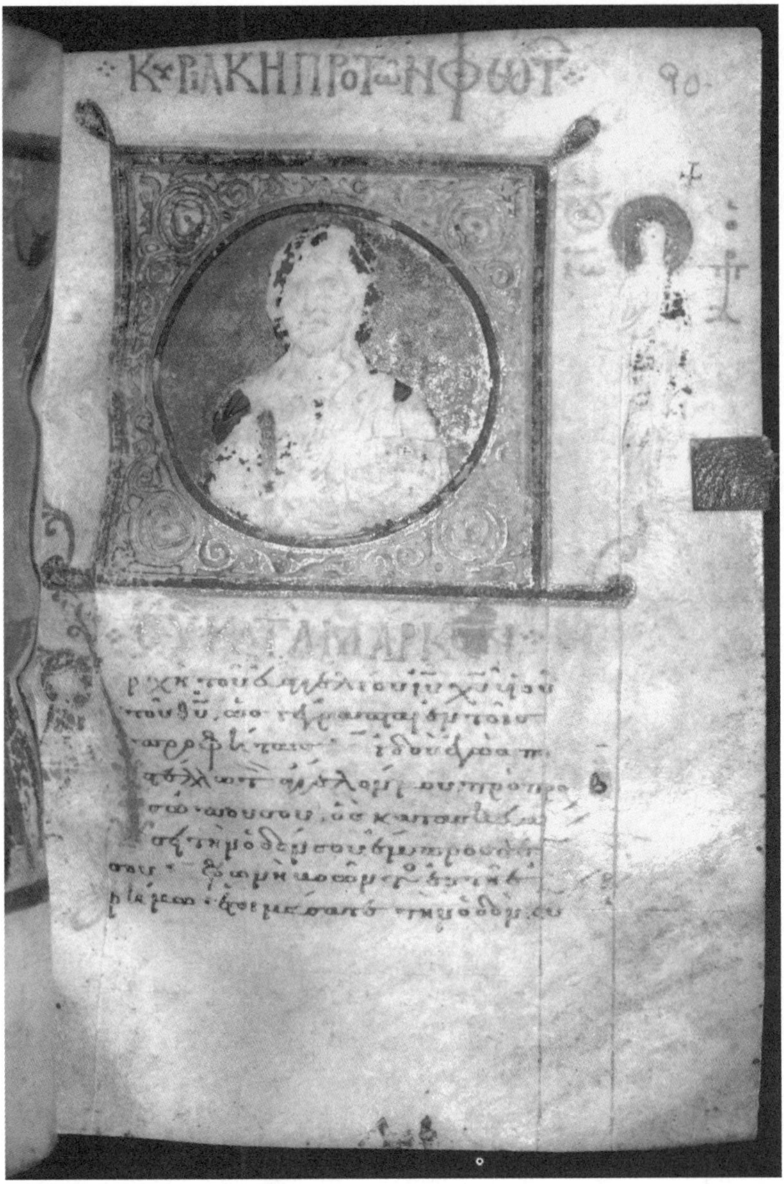

Figure 1.15. *The Gospel Book of Eusebius of Caesarea*, ca. 1080–1100 CE. Baltimore, Walters Art Museum, Ms. W 522, fol. 90r (© The Walters Art Museum).

> Is not the thrice-precious and thrice-blessed wood of the cross matter? Is not the holy and august mountain, the place of the skull, matter? Is not the life-giving and life-bearing rock, the holy tomb, the source of the resurrection, matter? Is not the ink and the all-holy book of the Gospels matter? Is not the life-bearing table, which offers to us the bread of life, matter? Is not the gold and silver matter, out of which crosses and tablets and bowls are fashioned? And, before all these things, is not the body and blood of my Lord matter? Either do away with reverence and veneration for all these or submit to the tradition of the Church and allow the veneration of images of God and friends of God, sanctified by name and therefore overshadowed by the grace of the divine Spirit. [206]

The image had no less power than did a contact relic since it gathered up and conveyed materially the divine *potentia*.[207] Not only was it in a relationship with its archetype by virtue of the principle of resemblance on which its own manufacture was based, but the substance used by the painter was itself holy. For Finbarr Barry Flood, this divine assumption of materiality must, in fact, be seen as the sign of a relative eclipsing of the distinction between image and archetype,[208] a blurring of boundaries that pushed the pious, in the East and then in the West, to employ images in a thoroughly material fashion—in other words, to perceive icons, statues in the West, and mural paintings as living *bodies*, able to walk and talk, to weep and bleed.[209]

The Ground Icon

Returning to the practice of consuming images in the context of our discussion of Miracle 15 in the *Vita* of Cosmas and Damian involving the ingested fresco, we should mention another document, coming this time from the iconoclast's camp. This is a letter from the Emperor Michael II to King Louis the Pious in 824 in which the iconodules are accused of mixing icons with the bread and wine during the Eucharistic rite:[210] "Certain priests and clerics scraped the paint of images and, mixing this with the eucharistic bread and wine, let the communicants partake of this oblation after the celebration of the mass. Others again placed the Body of the Lord in the hands of images and made the communicants receive it therefrom."[211]

The pictorial substance is here likened to the body, and the scraping equated to a sacrificial act.[212] Mixed with the bread and wine, the icon inserts the real presence of Christ into a rite that was still, at the time, essentially symbolic.[213] We shall come back to this later in our discussion of the ritual ingesting of comestible images. For now, we should note that this "confusion" between image and physical reality did not affect only lowly people, and it was not always incompatible with the rites commanded by the Church.[214] In other words, "improper" customs and officially established practices coexisted in the experience of many of the Eastern Christians.[215]

Reading the letter of Michael II, however, does tell us that the procedure by which the *potentia* (power) of relics was carried over to icons, and by which images were assimilated to a thoroughly material reality, did not happen without opposition. Indeed, it was this that lay, in large part, at the heart of the Iconoclastic Controversy since the physical power transferred to images had the effect, in the opinion of the iconoclasts, of bringing icons perilously close to idols.[216] The text by John of Damascus, and the account in Miracle 15 discussed above of the ingestion of the painted representation of Saints Cosmas and Damian, can be seen as being under the broader umbrella of the Iconoclastic Controversy, the debate between iconoclasts and iconodules that took place at the end of the eighth century. Indeed, John of Damascus thinks of his theological argument as a *defense* of images. As for Miracle 15, although the account was drawn up before the Iconoclasm, it was used by the iconodules at the time of the Second Council of Nicea (787)[217] as evidence against the arguments of the denigrators of images. The miracle justified and normalized the veneration of icons by linking the image of the unmercenary saints to the obtaining of a blessing of grace. However, to avoid any chance of conflating this practice with any form of idolatry, the author of the account, troubled by the thought that the iconoclasts as was probably often the case would associate the events and gestures in the story of the sick woman with pagan practices, felt obliged to distinguish the use of images that he was describing from those reprehensible customs stigmatized by the iconoclasts: "Let no one imagine that in this miracle there was any innovation on the part of the saints or that the sick woman was cured simply by drinking the potion."[218] The saints were *vehicles* of divine power, and their image was the *channel* through which that force could become manifest on earth. As the anonymous author explains, "Our Lord accomplishes them [miracles] by the intermission of the saints," before letting it be understood that this operational chain was not unknown to the woman who received the act of grace: "After her cure, she came into the august temple, giving thanks to our master the Christ, who has given such great charisma to his saints. She told everyone of the healing that had come to her, through the intercession of the saints, in the course of the deed that she had done."

In giving thanks to Christ, the woman establishes, as the apologist sees it, a clear distinction between potential potency and effective power, and, at the same time, between an image and an idol. The image is not itself the saintly entity, at least not so independently of the saint's manifestation. Instead, the image rather *makes present* the saintly entity. And this capacity was visibly recognized as such. Arguing against the idea of a reduction of the divine to the finite world of matter, the defenders of images among the Church Fathers generally valorized the principle of *participation*.[219] And yet, the fact remains that these displays of piety were indeed physical rather than spiritual, and this is precisely what was disturbing.

To avoid their being associated with the *hylolaters*[220] or worshippers of matter, the iconodules pointed to the principle of the *transitus* as the essential justification for the veneration of images. This principle, which asserts that "the honor paid to the image passes on to the prototype,"[221] was introduced in the fourth century by Basil of Caesarea, before being taken up again at the time of the First Iconoclasm (726) by John of Damascus in the context of the defense of icons,[222] and then elevated to a definition of *horos* ("faith") in the conclusions of the Second Council of Nicea:

> We decree with full precision and care that ... the revered and holy images ... are to be exposed .... The more frequently they are seen in representational art, the more are those who see them drawn to remember and long for those who serve as models, and to pay these images the tribute of salutation and respectful veneration [*timètikè proskunesis*]. Certainly this is not the full adoration [*latreia*] in accordance with our faith, which is properly paid only to the divine nature, but it resembles that given to the figure of the honoured and life-giving cross, and also to the holy books of the gospels and to other sacred cult objects. Further, people are drawn to honour these images with the offering of incense and lights, as was piously established by ancient custom. Indeed, the honour paid to an image traverses it, reaching the model, and he who venerates the image, venerates the person represented in that image.[223]

As Dagron explains, it was "through inert matter, that the faithful venerated the person represented."[224] Power did not reside in matter; it was not immanent in the artificial image; it only moved through it. The material dimension was thus attenuated by the transformation of the representation into a sign.[225]

This way of understanding the relationship between the image and its protoype, despite the opposition it was to meet from the Carolingians as we can see from the *Libri carolini*,[226] was to be progressively recognized by the Roman Catholic Church, and Basil of Caesarea's judgement was to be accepted, from the twelfth century onwards, by Hugh of Saint Victor,[227] Albertus Magnus, Thomas Aquinas, Bonaventure,[228] and after the Middle Ages by many of the theologians of the Counter Reformation.[229] There was, nonetheless, a difference between the Greeks and the Latins regarding their concept of the image and the *transitus*. For the former, "something of the original model passes *into* the image," and honor had to be rendered to the icon to reach the prototype, while, for the latter, the image was nothing more than a channel permitting access to the original, and no honor was due it directly.[230] However, this distinction had little impact on actual practice. For whatever the angle of interpretation, the Greek and Latin clerics were all concerned to make the claim that the image *in itself* did not hold any power; rather, it was the vehicle of divine power, and this was precisely the point that separated accepted from abusive devotional practices, the latter being censured as superstitions. Concerning the *Agnus Dei*, in his *De legibus*, William of Auvergne (1190–1249) writes:

> If, in fact, the waxen forms, that have all the appearance of lambs, receive, through the benediction of the Roman Pontiff, this virtue of diverting and stopping bolts of lightning so that they [the lightning bolts] do not hurt those that carry them [the waxen forms]; if bells, that, in any case, do not have animal form nor nature, can receive at the time of their benediction the same virtue that ensures that those within hearing of the bells at the time [of such events] do not suffer from storms and lightning bolts; if salt and water can receive through benedictions and exorcisms the virtue of chasing away demons and the power of benediction; if the candles that are blessed on the Feast of the Purification of the Blessed Virgin Mary receive from this blessing the virtue of diverting lightning bolts; then one cannot doubt that all these virtues are divine. It might appear plausible to those in error, however, that it is through their own cursed benedictions and execrations that such virtues are conferred upon images. Now, it is manifest to you that *the things we have reported to you happen only through virtue of the all-powerful Creator; hence, Christian devotion does not require of the blessed water that it chase away demons, nor of the bells, lambs, or blessed candles that they divert lightning bolts and storms, but rather of the all-powerful Creator.*[231]

It was God's *virtus*, moving through the blessed object, that was made manifest to men. And conversely, it was by way of images that men's prayers could reach God.[232]

In the Bosom of the Saints

If it is true that the theory of the *transitus* allowed most theologians (most, but not all, since the religious authorities did not always decide these issues entirely without ambiguity) to transform images into quasi signs, this conceptual metamorphosis was not enough to convince people to see images as transparent representations. Indeed, the situation was quite otherwise. In reality, the material substance of icons, mural paintings, and statues played a much greater role than is suggested in the written texts. In the Byzantine world, for example, the idea of the image as *transitus* led very quickly to the custom, among the members of the aristocracy, of having themselves depicted alongside the saints.[233] The patron, whose image was placed as close as possible to the intercessor, was thus incorporated into the representation—the very place where the saints continued to live as social actors.[234] As André Grabar writes, they sought:

> To associate themselves *ad sanctum* in the saint's image, as one might be placed, after death, near to the saint's tomb, communicating with the saint through one's own depicted form, with the added gesture of piety, condensing, in some way, the prayer recited before the icon. Clearly, this demonstrates the utmost confidence in the virtue of the image, i.e., in its capacity to formulate and prolong the words of invocation, the transport of the soul and fleeing thoughts, and to increase, therefore, the value of a movement of piety, and thus the chances of the prayer's fulfilment.[235]

This practice, especially widespread in the Byzantine society, was to flourish also in the Latin world. In the Middle Ages, from the thirteenth century and up until the beginning of the modern era, the donors depicted at the foot of saints entered, so to speak, into the very body of the image. Furthermore, this was not simply a case of the patrons, through a simple representation, showing publicly and symbolically their place of choice alongside the saintly beings; it was, rather, and perhaps above all, a way for them, through the images, to approach the depicted saints' spheres of influence. In

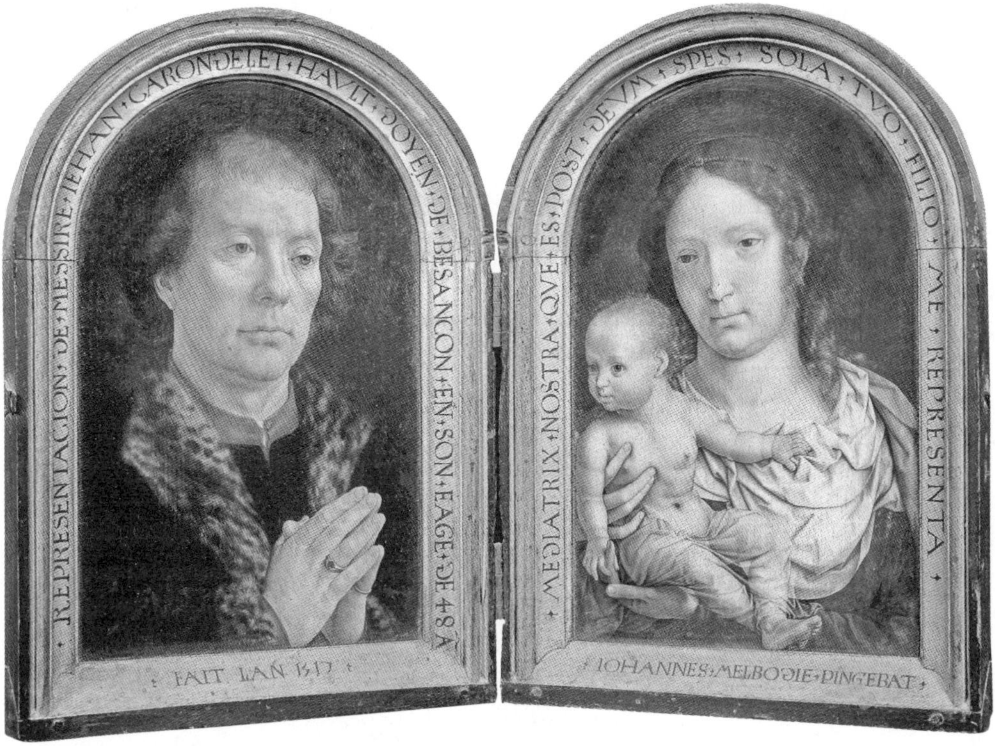

Figure 1.16. Jan Gossaert (also known as Jan Mabuse), *The Diptych of Jean Carondelet*, 1517, oil on panel, 20.8 × 14.5 in. Paris, Louvre Museum (© Josse/Bridgeman Images).

other words, it was a way to enter into the bosom of the saints.[236] Personal and private images, crafted with this same concern for proximity to the sacred entity, prove, moreover, that the intention behind the depiction of the donor cannot be reduced to a simple issue of representation. The devotional diptychs (fig. 1.16) and triptychs that flourished into the fifteenth century throughout Europe are evidence of this. When such pieces are opened, the viewer can see, in fact, a man or a woman set in a prominent and privileged place beside Christ, the Virgin, or a saint. But the object is not made solely to be seen; the artefact designed expressly for the *viewer* was an invention of the Renaissance centuries later. Once it was closed up, the object remained active, and the depicted figures, far from disappearing in their withdrawal from the viewer, continued to "live" in it. The relationship between donor and saintly entity was even reinforced: the worshipper, placed on one of the panels, removed from people's gaze, and far from the public world, comes close and touches the saintly being, murmuring, in the silence of the darkness, his or her prayer.[237]

Many other customs that existed during the Middle Ages provide evidence of this attribution of a form of existence to images, both in the East and in the West.[238] We have the especially widespread incidence of graffiti marks on the representations of the saints, as we see, for example, in the Martyrium at Baouit in Egypt, the cave churches in the Soğanlı Valley in Cappadocia, and again, among so many other instances, in the Basilica di San Zeno in Verona.[239] In these various shrines, the pious believers scratched the painted substance, inscribing their prayers, wishes, and their thanks for grace obtained and attaching to these inscriptions, most often, a name and a date. The image was thus considered as both a "doorway" through which one could make "contact" with the saintly being (as if the written word were projected in the direction of the *numen*), and also as a *body* that one could touch and in which it was possible to seek "refuge," where the inscribed name making the person present, thereby, a sort of power of invocation.[240] The placement of the inscriptions suggests that the depictions were seen as genuine persons, possessing a material substance that was potentially holy. For although the words and signs traced on the paintings were generally put around the figures, as if out of respect for the integrity of the painted body, there are cases where they appear on the figures themselves. At San Zeno, we find the case of a worshipper having taken the care to inscribe the name of someone close to them, Andrea of Mantua, who died, according to the inscription, on January 24, 1460. The name appears upon the very heart of the Virgin (fig. 1.17), in other words, in the very place that was considered, at the time, to be the seat of love and compassion, and so in the very site where the memory of the deceased had every chance of receiving mercy.[241] In the same way as with the portraits of patrons, the inscription allows the worshippers to come as close as possible to the holy figure, to find a lodging place within that figure, rather as if, by engraving their name, they would find themselves wrapped within the cloak of a Virgin of Mercy, or, even better, curled up in the open arms of a Virgin, welcoming into her bosom God the Father, Christ, and the community of Christians. In this regard, the piece of graffiti is an "ornament," much like the precious objects of necklaces, rings, broaches, and headpieces offered to the Virgin and to the representations of the saints that were intended to accompany a prayer. An example of such objects exists in the necklace of precious stones that "the noble Godiva, on the eve of her death, ordered hung around the neck of a statue of Mary in Coventry" to oblige the image of "the Virgin to remember" her "and to grant her her intercession."[242]

In the light of this propensity to ascribe a certain physicality to images, we can legitimately ask what became of the plaster and pigments that were removed from the painted representations. Dominique Rigaux and Mario Sensi, who have studied the devotional gestures addressed to images in the Italy of the Middle Ages, have suggested that this dust from the frescoes could have been ingested for prophylactic purposes.[243] The documentation is unfortunately lacking for us to be entirely sure about this; however, if we consider the custom attaching to the fresco of Saints Cosmas and Damian in the Byzantine miracle that we looked at earlier, or again if we consider the common practice at the shrine in Loreto, of collecting up the dust of the House of the Blessed Virgin Mary, and of making small sachets of the *polvere* to be served in potions to the sick, then we may well be tempted to agree with them.[244]

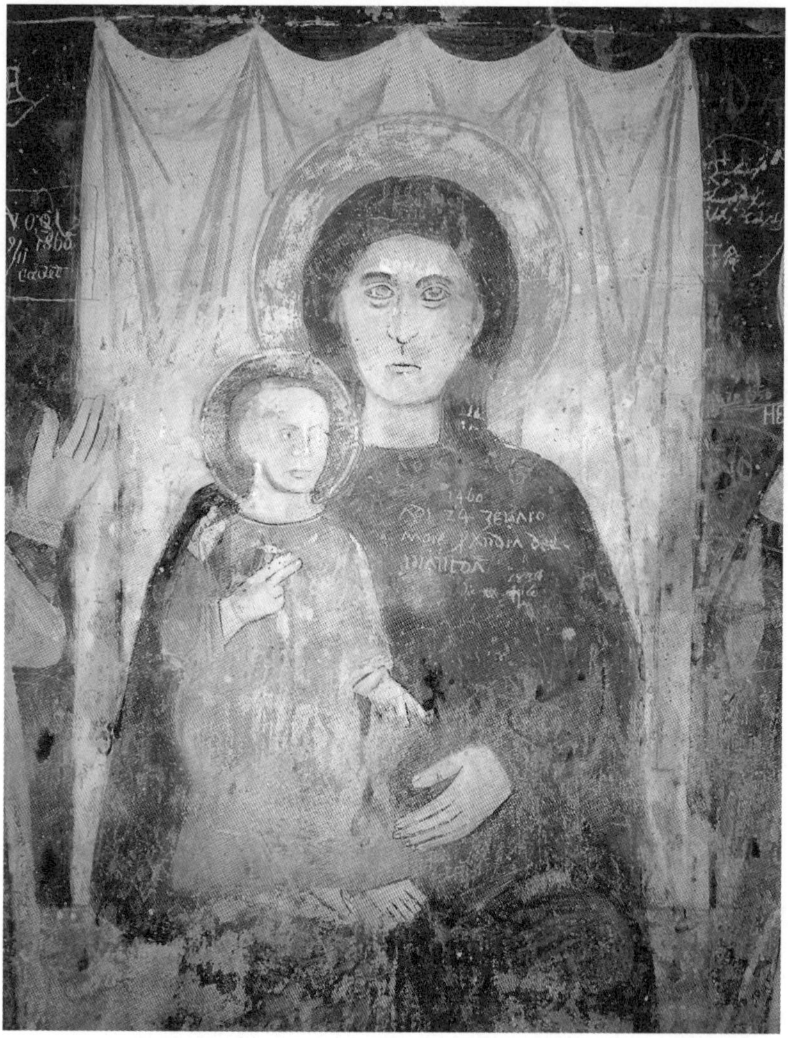

Figure 1.17. *Madonna and Child with Saint Catherine and a Holy Bishop*, fifteenth century, fresco. Verona, Basilica of San Zeno (Creative Commons).

A Taste of Miracle

Up until this point, the images that we have dealt with have been "generic" images, revealing their power to the believers *after* the act of healing. This was notably the case with the Saint Symeon token and with the Cosmas and Damian fresco in Byzantium. The images that we shall look at now, without being fundamentally different in terms of material composition, enjoyed a special status in that they already had a reputation for being miraculous before they were deliberately used for healing or sanctifying purposes.[245] Their power had already been made manifest, and it was, moreover, often recognized and guaranteed by the religious authorities. People hoped and expected, therefore, that it would become active again.[246] Thus, these miraculous images constituted a privileged means of access to the divine, and they attracted fervent believers, the sick, and, more generally, anyone wanting to protect themselves from the traps ceaselessly set by the "Devil." The hope of seeing oneself healed or made holy by the grace of an image that had, so to speak, already shown its colors, was enough to incite the pilgrims to cross mountains to see, touch, and commune with the venerable image.[247]

These miraculous objects were typically extremely plain: Romanesque statues in wood or stone, stereotypical paintings in the *maniera greca*, and icons.[248] However, to distinguish them from other images, and to highlight their special character, they were displayed, particularly from the fifteenth century, in architectural niches, in marble and golden tabernacles, and wearing richly ornamented vestments and all sorts of precious and revered accessories, such as necklaces, rings, and crowns.[249]

There was a quite straightforward reason for this contrast: it was important that the bright and showy aspects of the depicted figure be confined to the accessories, and not to the image itself since the faithful should not be led to identify the miraculous object's power with its material basis, that is, the wood, stone, and lead. Above all, it was essential that the faithful not believe that the image was inherently miraculous, and that its power was permanent. For the theologians, let us repeat, images did not possess their own power, but they had a *potential potency* that only the divine being, God the Father, could activate.[250] In the same way as the host, undergoing its miraculous metamorphosis in the celebration of Eucharist, the material substance of the icon, making visible Jesus, the Virgin, or the saints, was, for the period of time in which the miraculous manifestation took place, a divine substance and not simply plaster, wood, pigment, or stone.[251] For this reason, the image's power was fragile, relative, and mysterious. Any miraculous statue or painting that was worshipped unsuitably might run the risk of no longer being "visited" by its heavenly prototype. For this reason, the fervent believers directed their efforts as much towards maintaining the connection between the image and the divine being as they did towards actualizing its power—a power that was, by definition, uncertain and requiring of people two of the three "theologal" virtues: faith and hope.

In Contact with Images

As was the case with the relics and depictions of the saints in the churches, the miraculous images often gave rise to excessive desires on the part of the pilgrims (figs. 1.18 and 1.23). A certain number of the pilgrims would want to touch, kiss, and even take away some of an image's substance, or failing that, to procure some of the material substance of the place where the image was displayed, with the aim of protecting themselves for a period of time that exteneded beyond the time of the pilgrimage. Michel de Montaigne's journal of his travels in Italy (1581) gives a detailed account of this practice in Loreto in the sixteenth century (fig. 1.19). The essayist, in fact, includes the text of an inscription expressly warning pilgrims against any attempt to write on the walls or to take away any of the substance of the House of the Blessed Virgin:[252]

> People are forbidden to scratch anything from this wall; and if it were permitted to take anything away, there would not be enough to last three days. This place is full of innumerable miracles, for which I refer to the books; but

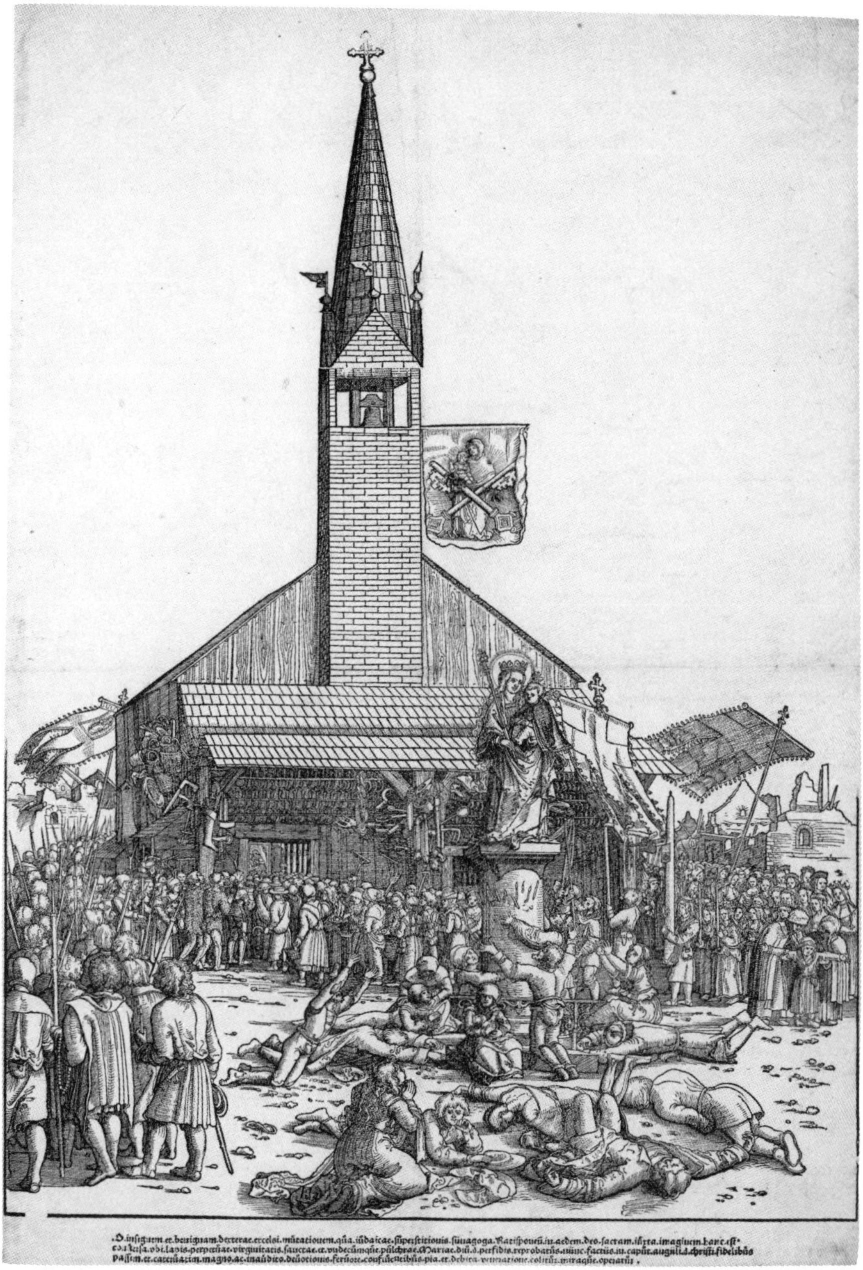

Figure 1.18. Michael Ostendorfer, *The Pilgrimage to the Beautiful Virgin at Regensburg*, 1519–1523, woodcut, 22.9 × 15.3 in. London, British Museum (© The Trustees of the British Museum).

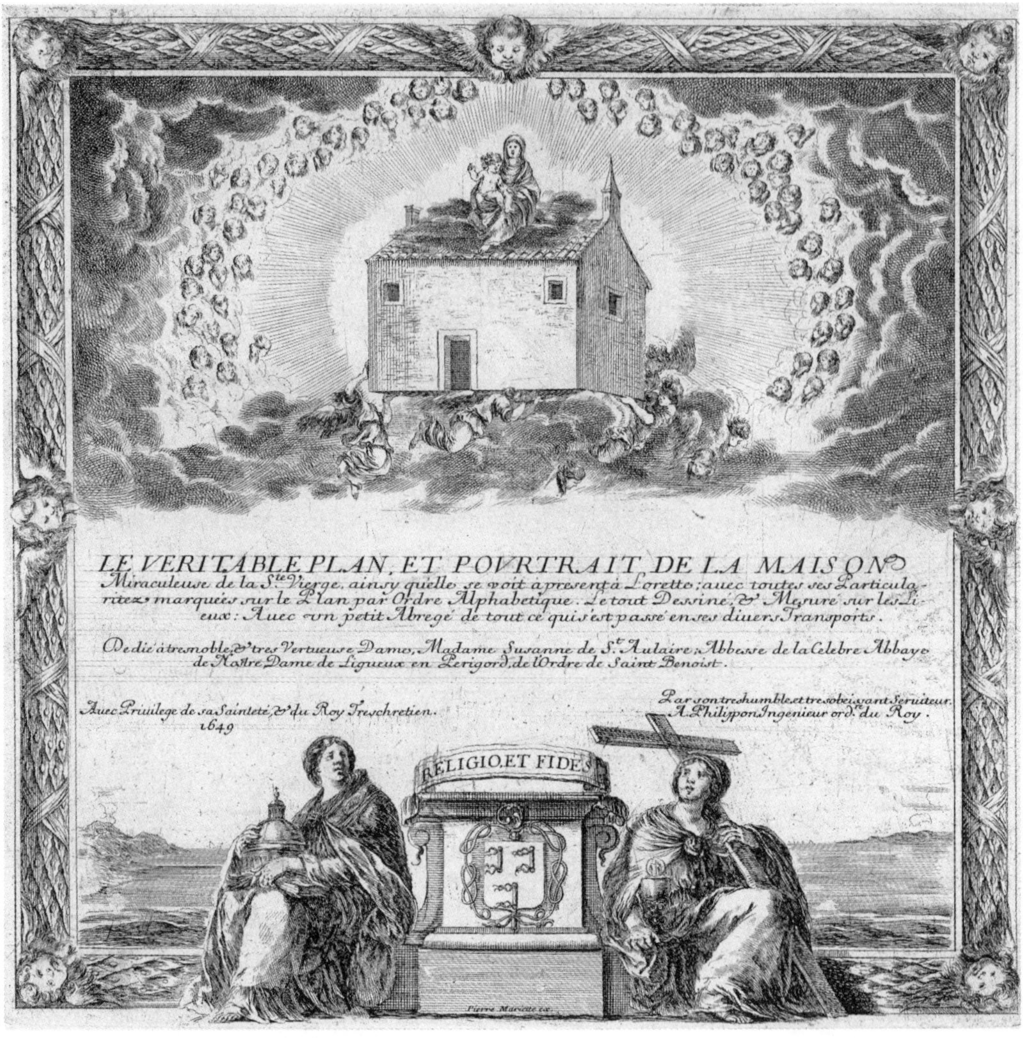

Figure 1.19. Stefano della Bella, after Adam Philippon, *Frontispice du véritable plan et portrait de la maison miraculeuse de la Sainte Vierge ainsy qu'elle se voit à present à Lorette*, 1649, etching, 9.2 × 13.5 in. Amsterdam, Rijksmuseum (© Rijksmuseum, Amsterdam).

> there are several, and very recent ones, involving mishaps that have befallen those who out of devotion have carried away something from this building, even with the Pope's permission; and a small fragment of brick which had been removed at the time of the Council of Trent has been brought back.[253]

Although this concerns an architectural structure, la Santa Casa, and not a specific image, the interior walls of the House of the Blessed Virgin were covered with frescoes (fig. 1.20), works that have since been destroyed in the lower parts either by fires or by the likely samplings.[254] The ban that Montaigne refers to here clearly suggests that this behavior was widespread enough to be of concern for the clergy in charge of the shrine. Thus, to prevent the images of majesty, and the architectural niches in which they were displayed, from being destroyed by these repeated contacts, the religious authorities adopted the policy of denying people access to them, choosing rather to distribute to the believers dust that had fallen naturally from the walls to the ground, as well as other figures (e.g., engravings, sculptures, and casts) and aniconic objects that had been put in contact with the holy images, and that were reputed, by this means, to carry the *virtus* of a venerated image.[255]

The efficacy of this procedure of substitution depended on the authority of ancient accounts, such as the story of the bleeding woman of Paneas (present-day Banias, Syria) who, in thanks for miraculous healing wrought by Jesus, had a bronze statue of him erected (fig. 1.21). We know of this mainly through a passage in the *Ecclesiastical History* of Eusebius (ca. 260–339):

> They say that the woman who had an issue of blood, mentioned by the evangelists, and who obtained deliverance from her affliction by our Saviour, was a native of this place and that her house is shown in the city and the wonderful monuments of our Saviour's benefit to her are still remaining. At the gates of her house, on an elevated stone, stands a brazen image of a woman on her bended knee, with her hands stretched out before her like one entreating. Opposite to this there is another image of a man, erect, of

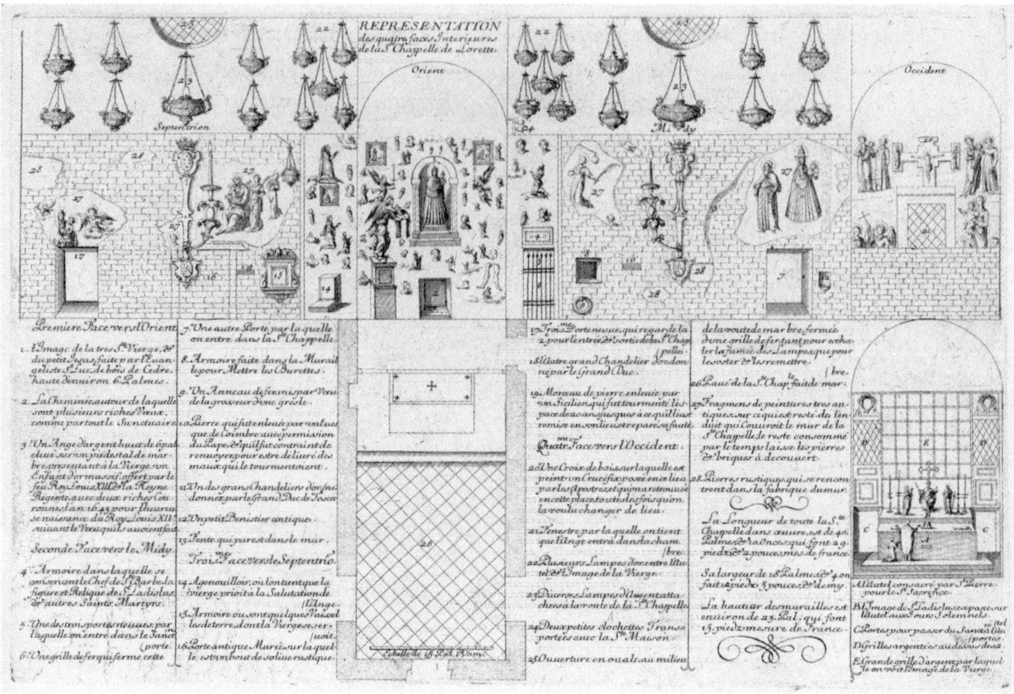

Figure 1.20. Stefano della Bella, after Adam Philippon, *Santa Casa Interior*, 1649, etching, Amsterdam, Rijksmuseum (© Rijksmuseum, Amsterdam).

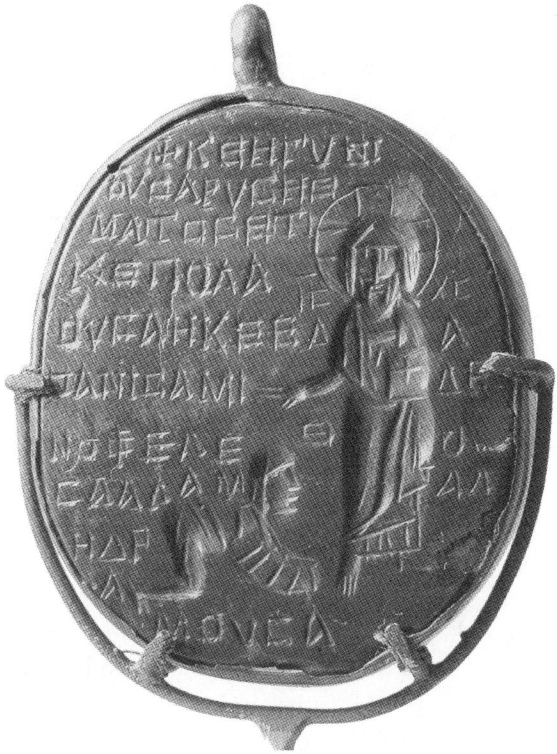

Figure 1.21. *The Bleeding Woman and the Christ of Paneas*, sixth–seventh century, amulet carved in intaglio, hematite, 1.9 × 1.4 × .4 in. New York, Metropolitan Museum of Art, Gift of J. Pierpont Morgan, 1917.

the same materials, decently clad in a mantle (*diplois*) and stretching out his hand to the woman. Before her feet and on the same pedestal, there is a certain strange plant growing, which rising as high as the hem of the brazen garment, is a kind of antidote to all kinds of diseases. This statue, they say, is a statue of Jesus Christ, and has remained even until our times; so that we ourselves saw it while tarrying in that city. It is not to be wondered at, that those of the Gentiles who were anciently benefited by our Saviour should have done these things. Since we have also seen representations of the apostles Peter and Paul, and of Christ himself, still preserved in paintings; it is probable that, according to a practice among the Gentiles, the ancients were accustomed to pay this kind of honor indiscriminately to those who were as saviours or deliverers to them.[256]

In this particularly detailed narrative, the linking of the thaumaturgical power of Jesus, Himself the incarnated *image* of God, with the potency of his represented form[257] is especially remarkable.[258] Just as with the bleeding woman in the Gospels (Matthew 9:20–22; Mark 5:25–34; Luke 8:43–48), who was healed of a continuous loss of blood by touching the hem of Jesus's garment, those who used the plant that was "rising as high as the hem of the brazen garment" received, by this device, a "a kind of antidote to all kinds of diseases."

As both a way of legitimizing the production of images resembling Christ, and of justifying those images' role in the Christian economy of Salvation, this account in Eusebius was much touted by the Church Fathers (Basil the Great or John of Damascus), historians (Sozomen), and theologians (Nikephoros Kallistos, or Ludolph of Saxony[259]) in their attempts to justify the veneration of images. Indeed, the passage was held up as a proof in the argument for the cult of images at the Second Council of Nicea.[260]

Much later, in the fifteenth century, the passage in Eusebius was to be used by Antonio degli Agli, the priest at Impruneta from 1439 to 1477, in his argument in support of the devotions rendered to the Miraculous Virgin at the shrine of Santa Maria dell'Impruneta (fig. 1.22):[261]

> [A] bronze statue of Jesus was fashioned on the outskirts of Syria, at the feet of which lay a woman who had been cured of the flow of blood by him, as if she were worshiping; a certain plant of unknown type is said (with Eusebius as witness) to have risen up from beneath the edges of the statue itself, which, although previously it was of no use, infused with a wonderful strength where it had touched the garment, became useful for various illnesses and weaknesses.[262]

The story was again brought up, for the same reasons, in the sixteenth century, notably by Alberto Pio da Carpi, who used it in his argument against Erasmus (1531),[263] and it came up again in seventeenth century, having undergone some changes, in Louis

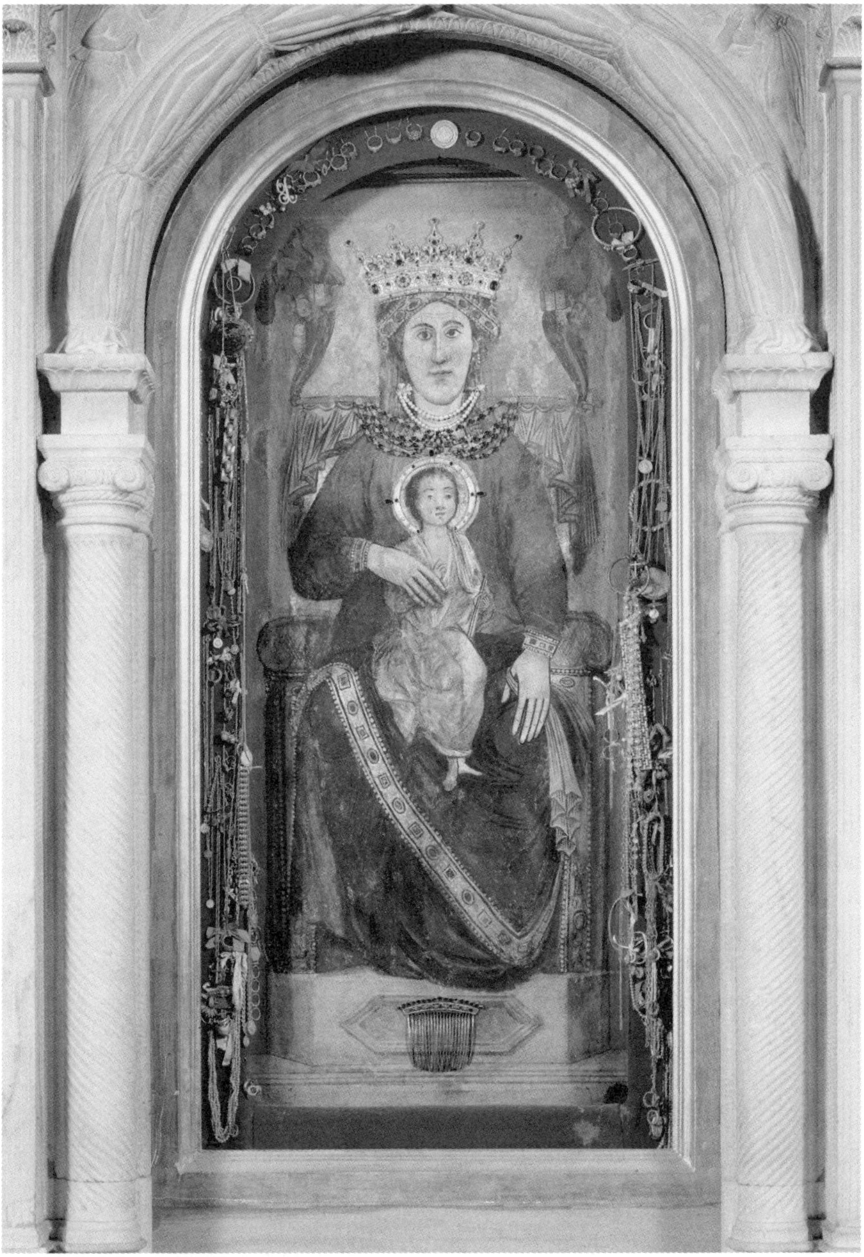

Figure 1.22. *Our Lady of Impruneta*, eleventh–fifteenth century, painting on panel. Impruneta, Church of the Santa Maria dell'Impruneta, Tempietto della Madonna (© Scala/Art Resource, NY).

Richeome's work, *L'idôlatrie huguenote* (1608): "The image of the Savior erected by the bleeding woman was worshipped by all the Christians of the East, and God honored it so that the herb growing around it, as soon as it touched the hem of the gown, was made a heavenly medicine, able to chase away all manner of sickness."[264]

In this latter account, Richeome takes some liberties with regard to the story as told by Eusebius since he mentions only the statue of Christ, the effigy of the bleeding woman having, for its part, disappeared. Could this be because Richeome was trying to avoid the suspicion that the bleeding woman might herself also have been a vector of miraculous power? The story is recorded in an anti-Protestant treatise, and so this is a distinct possibility. But apart from this, emphasis is always put on the role of contact in the transmission of the *virtus*:[265] the representation of Christ transmits its power to the bronze garment, the garment gives off its virtue to the plant that touches it, and the latter heals anyone who uses it, and the expression "celestial medicine" is placed at the end of the chain to show that the power remains intact despite its successive transfers.[266]

Despite the silence surrounding the ways in which the remedy was taken, there is reason to believe that the transmission of the *virtus* happened by infusion. It was, in fact, mainly in the form of a beverage (e.g., decoction, wine fortification, etc.) that the faithful introduced into their own bodies the substances that had been placed in contact with miraculous images.[267] The text of the *Miracula Sancti Ithamari episcopi* (Miracles of Saint Ithamar), written at Rochester around 1140, relates the case of a sick woman having requested "that they wash the feet of the saint's image attached to the side of the reliquary with water, and that she be given the water to drink."[268] Linked, therefore, with the relics contained in the coffer, it is the image that makes present the saint's earthly remains, communicating the saint's *virtus* to water poured over its surface. Here, it will have been noted, the material representation is not directly introduced into the body. But it remains the case that the image is clearly marked as the element through which the sacred power is in transit and made present to the senses. We should say here, in passing, that we are very close to the mode of operation that we saw in ancient Egypt with the stelae of Horus on the Crocodiles, so despite the repeated efforts of the churchmen to establish a clear boundary between Christianity and paganism, there are numerous similarities bringing together these two worlds. These homologies show that these practices and ways of being vis-à-vis images belonged to a single scheme of thought. Ingesting the holy power through the intermediary of a substance that had been in contact with the image made perceptible, if not to say intelligible, the paradoxical inscribing of the invisible into the sensory. All of these "strategies" of transmitting grace by way of images and substances were ways of infusing, in a miraculous way, God's spiritual power into the world.

Awesome Cure

Later accounts show that infusion was to remain for a long time something of a standard practice in "holy" or "miraculous" medicine.[269] In the region of Nantes, we find, especially throughout the seventeenth century, mention of pilgrims who, once inside the church of Trans-sur-Erdre, would take away fragments of the plinth supporting a sculpture representing Saint Maudez in order to get hold of his *virtus*. In fact, during a pastoral visit in 1686, the archdeacon Antoine Binet noted "that the corbel on which" the statue rested "had been dug into and seriously scratched in various places," and that the whole thing was in danger of collapsing. He went on to add that, based on what he had been told, this was due to "women who came to the aforesaid chapel to cure their children's stomach aches, and who, following the usual superstition, carried away with them the stone scrapings to put in their children's porridge."[270] As Bruno Restif suggests, the pilgrims probably scratched the corbel rather than the statue itself because the latter was placed too high.[271] Once again, this indicates that, for the believers, the *virtus* dwelt not only in the representation but also in everything that came into contact with it.

Recently, Ralph Dekoninck investigated the unusual case of the statue of Notre Dame de Montaigu in the Dutch Brabant (figs. 1.23 and 1.24). Placed within a cross-shaped oak tree in the sixteenth century, the statue became the object of intense worship after it was shown to have punished a young shepherd who had tried to steal it.[272] The oak tree that housed the image was cut down at the beginning of the seventeenth century, and its wood was then used to make statuettes of the miraculous Virgin, and these were then sent out to many parts of the world. Now, according to a report published by the Premonstratensian Abbot of Tongerlo, Augustin-François Wichmans, in *Brabantia Mariana tripartita* (1632), the believers regularly used the wood to make potions:

> Everyone knows, in fact (and I shall make it clear enough to those who do not in what follows), how many stupendous wonders have shone and continue to shine, in various places, through the Marian figures made from chips and fragments from the Montaigu Oak. Even better, ordinary fragments and scrapings from the afore-mentioned tree, when thrown into water and consumed, performed miraculous healings more than once.[273]

More specifically, Wichmans gives the example of a healing effected by ingesting a wood chip:

> [F]ollowing the orders of an exorcist from the Presbyterian community of Capuchins, the chip was taken, eaten and swallowed by a young girl inhabited by evil spirits. The spirit showed itself in her throat, crying out that it was burning and was tormented by the wood. Suddenly, by the power and intercession of Mary of Montaigu, the spirit, along with two evil accomplices, was forced to leave its refuge; and finally, it let out this loud cry: "Long live the Lady of Montaigu who has forced me to come out."[274]

In the author's telling of the story, it was seemingly the substance having been in contact with the miraculous image of the Virgin that transported the *virtus*. However, although the wood did not have to keep the Virgin's form to be effective, no one could doubt that it drew its force originally from the holy image, the

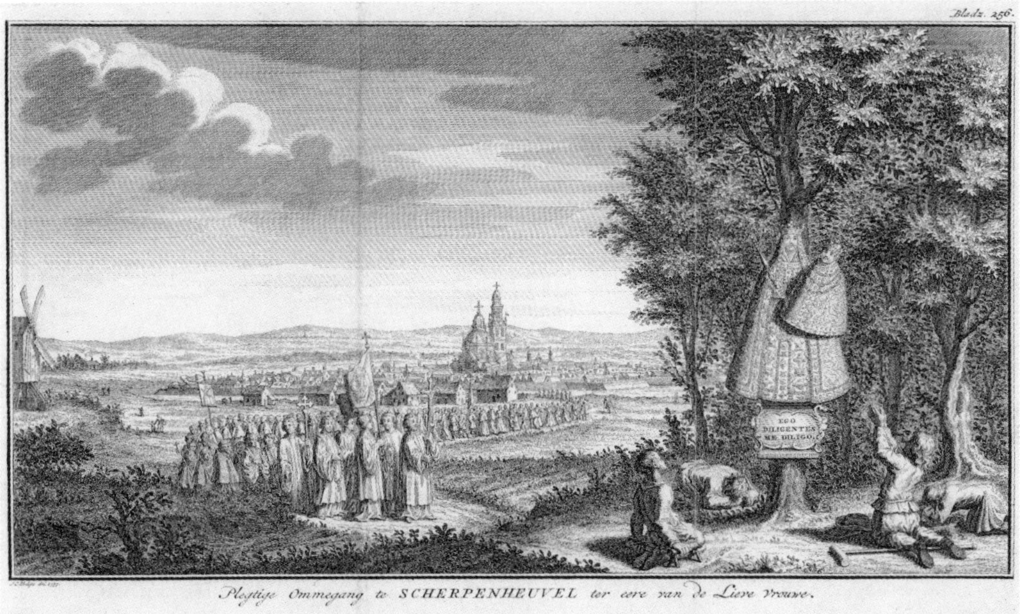

Figure 1.23. Jan Caspar Philips, *Pilgrimage on the way to Our Lady of Scherpenheuvel*, 1737, etching, 7 × 11.6 in. Amsterdam, Rijksmuseum (© Rijksmuseum, Amsterdam).

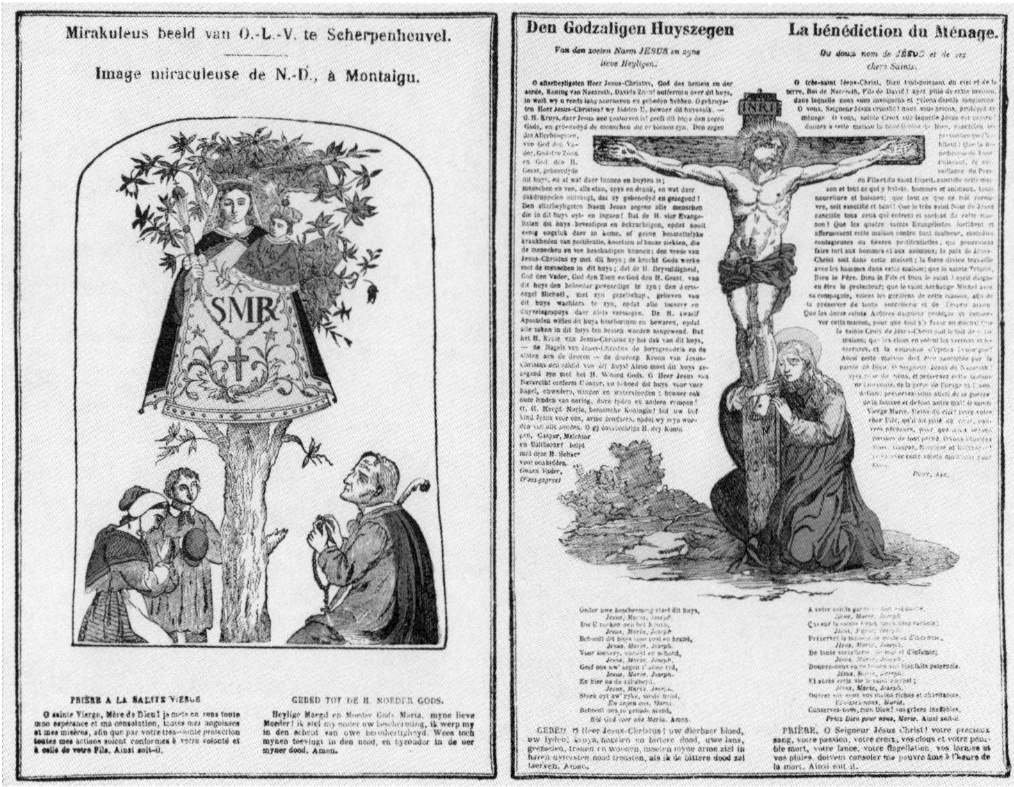

Figure 1.24. *Miraculous Image of Our Lady of Scherpenheuvel: The Blessing of a New Home.* 1827–1894, etching published by M. Hemeleers-van Houter, 12.87 × 16.6 in. Amsterdam, Rijksmuseum (© Rijksmuseum, Amsterdam).

latter functioning as a means of making present the heavenly archetype. As Wilhelm Gumppenberg (1659) writes concerning another miraculous image, Notre-Dame-de-Foy (fig. 1.25), "such a power comes . . . from the holy image."[275] It was because the wood had been in contact with the image that it was able to take on the holy power of its prototype. The image is the primary earthly agency of the heavenly entity, and it was by ingesting it, even in a dissimilar form, that the believer obtained divine grace.

Despite its not being absolutely necessary to the transportation of the *virtus*, the secondary image did nonetheless reinforce the miraculous potential of the substance. The case of the wood of Our Lady of Montaigu is evidence of this. The wood was sent in the form of little statuettes to religious communities that were on the other side of the Atlantic in the New World.[276] For the faithful believer, distant by hundreds if not thousands of miles from the miraculous statue, the image reproducing the appearance of the Virgin as worshipped in the original shrine, reactivated the presence of the *numen* as it showed itself in the statue of the Virgin, making thus visible the invisible link that the substance, prior to its being shaped into the second image, maintained with its model.

Schabmadonnen

As we can see from the statuettes in the likeness of Notre-Dame-de-Foy or Notre-Dame de Montaigu, copies of miraculous images were relatively common. They certainly were so in Brabant, but also in other regions of Europe such as Lower Austria (Sonntagberg), South Bavaria (Altötting), and the German-speaking part of Switzerland (Einsiedeln), areas where, between the seventeenth and nineteenth centuries, little terracotta statuettes in the form of *Gnadenbild* (an image of majesty) were produced in series for prophylactic or curative purposes.[277] These figures, called *Schabfiguren* or *Schabmadonnen* (literally, madonnas for scratching and scraping), were mechanically reproduced from a template in the shape of the miraculous image, and, like the Brabant statuettes, they were made

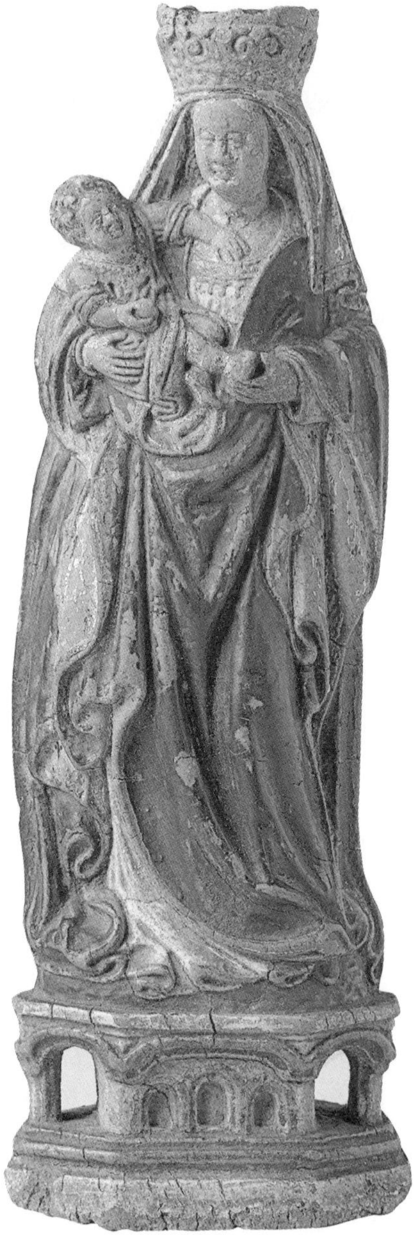

Figure 1.25. *Statuette of Our Lady of Foy.* After 1609 (based on an Utrecht model from the second quarter of the fifteenth century), polychrome earthenware and other organic material, 7 in. Amsterdam, Rijksmuseum (© Rijksmuseum, Amsterdam).

from a sanctified substance, such as clay having been in contact with the statue or earth containing relics from the shrine.

Claude Jacquet, the canon of the church at Besançon, and the author of a history of the Einsiedeln shrine that was published in 1699, points out that the little figurines of Notre-Dame-des-Ermites were produced from a small amount of "loam [with] which one [mixed] several precious relics" (fig. 1.26).[278] The Benedictines gave the statuettes to pilgrims after they had worshipped at the shrine, and the faithful could then, upon their return home, scrape the surface of the statuette with a knife and collect the powder, mixing it with water or wine to make a healing beverage for all sorts of ailments.[279] Further evidence of these practices appears in a later edition of Jacquet's work (1750), that includes the miracle of a woman who safely survived a desperate childbirth by ingesting an image of the Einsiedeln Virgin:

> The Reverend Récolet Father Antoine di Monzana at Belinzone assures us, by a letter written in his own hand in 1724, that Madame his Mother, after a labor that was as difficult as it was extraordinary, would have perished along with himself during the childbirth if she had not swallowed a little of the powder of an image of Notre-Dame-des-Ermites, the powder having the effect of bringing her to give birth immediately and very happily.[280]

The increase in the number of miracles attributed to the Black Madonna in the seventeenth and eighteenth centuries, the huge influx of pilgrims to the shrine, and the fact that the "images" were designated as "ordinary medicine/remedy and almost always reliable [against] fevers,"[281] led naturally to such an increase in demand that "charlatans" seem to have taken advantage of all this enthusiasm by selling fake statuettes in the vicinity of the shrine. In the revised edition of the *Histoire de la Sainte-Chapelle de Notre-Dame-des-Ermites* at Einsiedeln (1750), the anonymous author explains that the "earthen images," given "gratis at the Abbey doors," were sometimes shamelessly "counterfeited" and "sold" by "shiftless people, always on the lookout for a sordid profit." And the author goes on to specify that

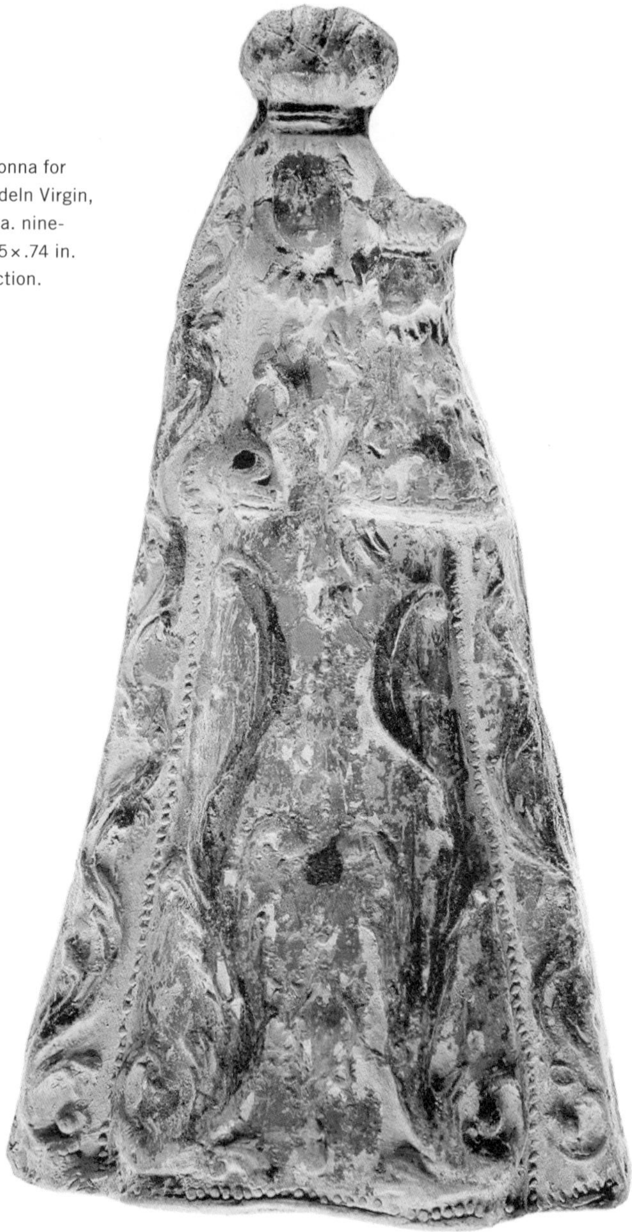

Figure 1.26. Schabmadonna (Madonna for scraping) in the form of the Einsiedeln Virgin, called Notre-Dame-des-Ermites, ca. nineteenth century, terracotta, 5.3 × 2.5 × .74 in. (Creative Commons). Private collection.

"despite the assurances of the sellers," these "little earthen images of the Holy Virgin" were "not those from which one might expect to obtain [miraculous] effects." Indeed, the author adds, the "true" images were "made of Relics, earth, the walls, and the oil from the Chapel of Grace that had all received a special blessing, had touched the miraculous Image, and were marked on the back with the Abbey arms, surmounted by a miter, crosier, and sword."[282]

Judging from these remarks, the resemblance between the statuette and the miraculous image was not enough to ensure the object's effectiveness. The replica's power resided more precisely in the material substance of the artifact (e.g., relics from the chapel or earth from the shrine), in its having been in contact with the miraculous image, and in the sacerdotal gesture that had transformed it into a sacrament.[283]

Blessed Images

Thus far, we have examined the importance of contact and material substance in the attribution of power to images, and we turn now to the blessings conferred on them. The benediction of images was not, in fact, widely accepted in Christian Europe. Unlike what we see in the Eastern Church since late Antiquity, where the blessing of figured artifacts was standard practice, the blessing of material images of statues and paintings was not particularly common in the West before the end of the Middle Ages.[284] Evidence does exist for the practice of this sort of ritual, especially in Canterbury around 1100, where the words of the blessing of the images of the Virgin and of Saint John show that it was thanks to the "episcopal benediction and unction" that "the image was endowed with *virtus*,"[285] but the practice remained for a long time more the exception than the rule.[286] It was only with the serial production of images, first the *Agnus Dei* and then the prints and molded earthenware statuettes, that the blessing of images was to become more generally adopted by the Church of Rome.

Three main causes for this change come to mind. In the first place, the mass-reproduced image underwent a loss of holiness through its very reproducibility—what Walter Benjamin called the loss of its aura.[287] In this situation, the blessing could appear as a means of bringing an added charge of holiness to the artifact. Secondly, the serial production of images ran the risk of separating the believers from the Church. If the images were all that one needed to practice one's devotions, and if all the faithful were in possession of them, then the link with the Church would be attenuated; on the other hand, if it were only the images that had been blessed that could transmit grace, then the blessing forced the sacerdotal act into the proceedings. Finally, faced with the mechanical reproduction of images, and their possible counterfeiting, the blessing allowed for the strategic control of a part of the devotional print market by rendering unblessed objects null and void, and therefore ineffective. Henceforth, therefore, there would be two kinds of images: the true and the fake.

Agnus Dei

The practice of benediction undoubtedly played an essential role in the growth and "success" of certain sacramental objects. The *Agnus Dei*, for example, were small wax figurines in the form of lambs (fig. 1.27) that appear as early as the eleventh century and whose production was under the control of the papacy (fig. 1.28). Made from wax that was poured into a mold in the shape of the Lamb recumbent upon the Book of the Apocalypse and holding with one of its forelegs the Standard of the Resurrection, these *Agnus Dei* were produced in the hundreds of thousands. Blessed and consecrated by the Pope at Easter celebrations, they were then sent out all over the world.[288] From their first appearance in the Middle Ages, these figures enjoyed a special privilege since, despite being produced in series, they were considered miraculous images. As William of Auvergne writes, in his previously cited *De legibus*, "the waxen forms, that bear a strong resemblance to lambs, receive *through the benediction* of the Roman Pontiff the virtue, for those who carry them, of warding off and stopping lightning strikes."[289]

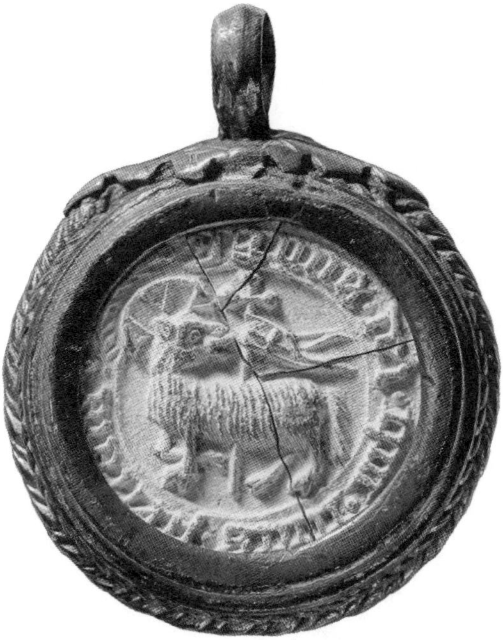

Figure 1.27. Agnus Dei medallion, second half of the fifteenth century, shell, copper, gold, niello, silver, .63 in. London, British Museum (© The Trustees of the British Museum).

The *benediction* made the wax figure into an object destined for the miraculous, and it was therefore seen as such even before it had demonstrated its effectiveness. In his 1539 pamphlet on the *Agnus Dei*, Luther strongly criticized the principle according to which God was transformed into little wax *gods* that were just like pagan deities,[290] but, despite the Reformers' repeated attacks against these images, this belief in the power of sacramental objects did not disappear in the modern age. A broadsheet, published by the Apostolic Chamber in 1662, and that Bernard Picart was to reproduce in 1723 in his *Cérémonies et coutumes religieuses de tous les peuples du monde* (fig. 1.29), underlines the importance of the benediction in the transformation of the *Agnus Dei* (just one waxen image among so many others) into a remedy that was effective against storms, hail, snow, furious winds, evil spirits, tricks of the Devil, and difficult childbirths.[291]

Because of this miraculous potential, the *Agnus Dei*, normally worn on the body, often set in brooches or attached to a chain,

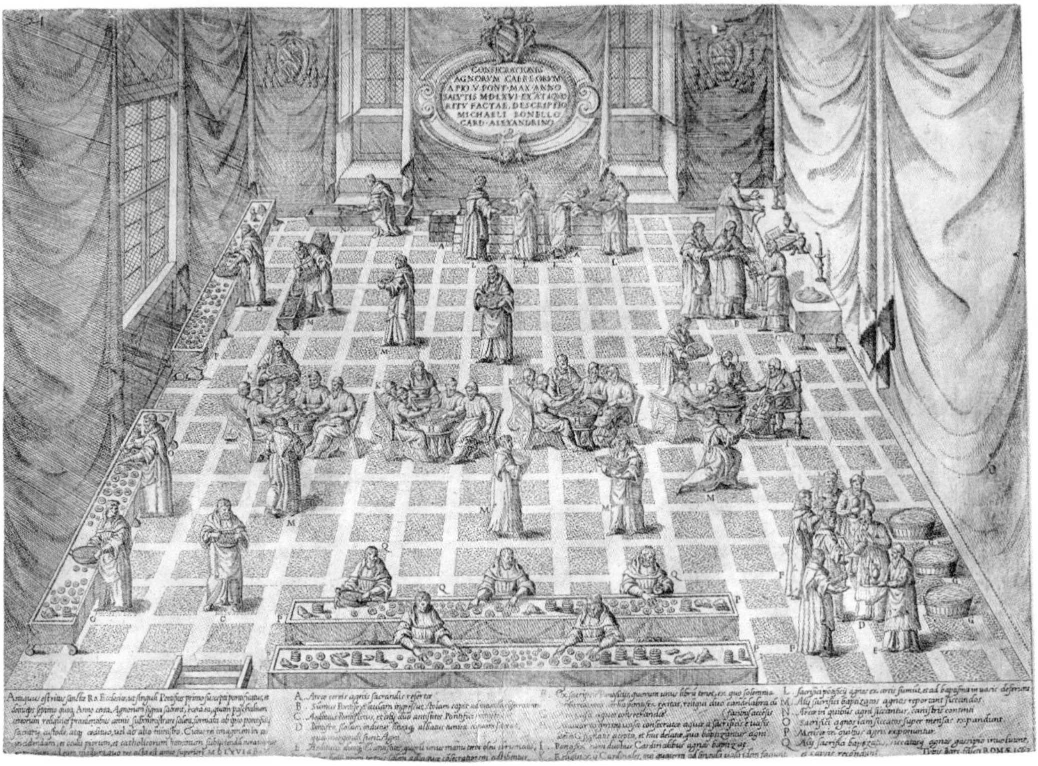

Figure 1.28. Bartolomeo Faleti, *Pope Pious V Consecrating the 'Wax Lamb'*, 1567, etching on paper, 15.7 × 21.2 in. London, British Museum (© The Trustees of the British Museum).

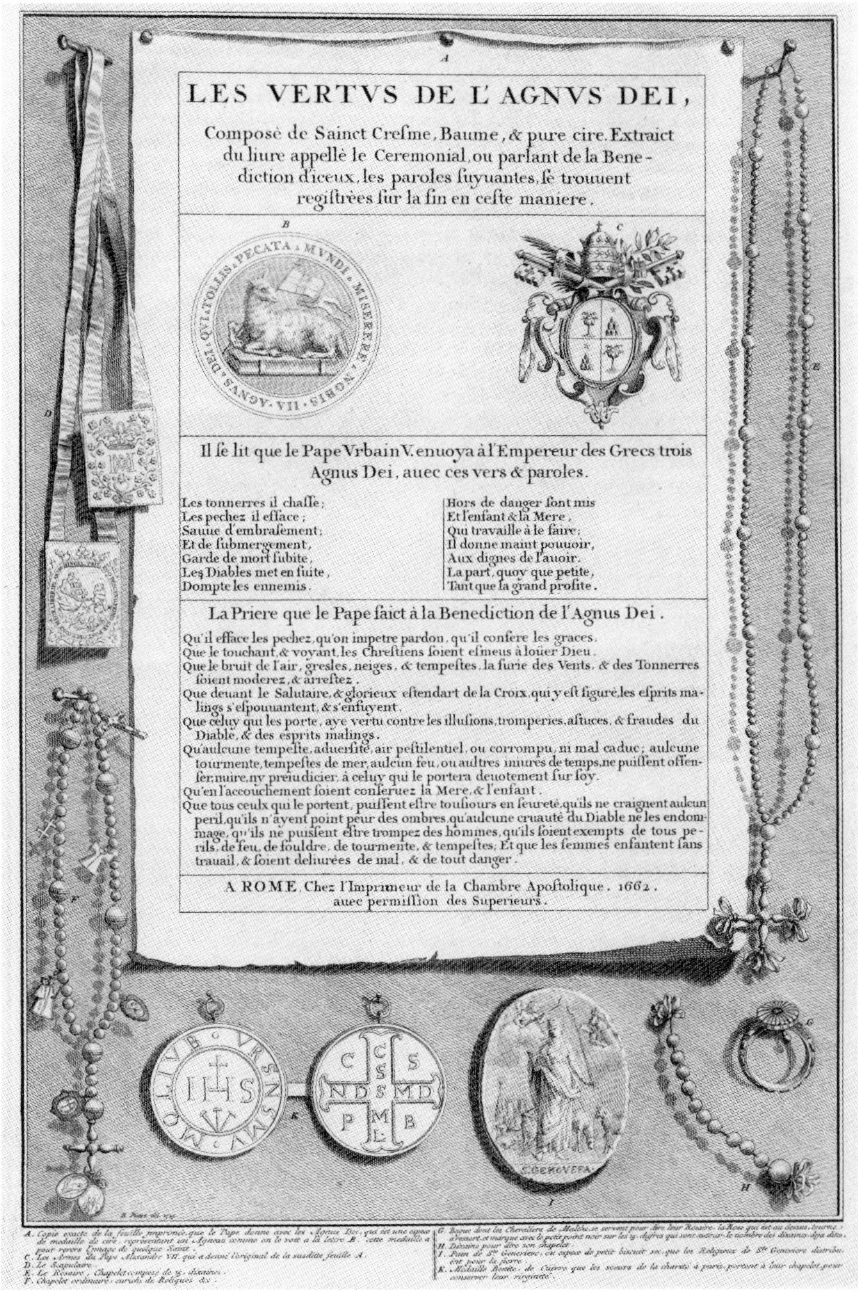

Figure 1.29. Bernard Picart, *The Virtues of the Agnus Dei*, in Jean Frederic Bernard and Bernard Picart, *Cérémonies et coutumes religieuses de tous les peuples du monde, (*Amsterdam: J. F. Bernard, 1723) (© Bibliothèque nationale de France).

or placed inside a monstrance, could equally well have been ingested. In an opuscule of some twenty pages titled *Miracoli operati dall'Onnipotenza divina per mezzo degli Agnus Papali Benedetti dalla Santa Memoria d'Innocentio XI*, published in Venice in 1691 but reporting events that had taken place in 1690, the doctor and historian Girolamo Bertondelli relates the case of Sister Maria Giuseppa, a novice of the Order of the Poor Clares at the monastery of Sant'Anna in Borgo Valsugana in Feltre, Italy, who was healed of a malignant fever by ingesting a tiny piece of *Agnus Dei*.[292] Since the doctors and physicians were unable to cure the young woman, Mother Cecilia, the mother superior of the novices, "resolved . . . to give her, as part of her fasting, and at the height of her fever, a little of the papal Agnus, but not without having first exhorted her to take it with the greatest faith and devotion, so that the Holy Pontiff Innocent might obtain for her perfect health."[293] And, as Bertondelli relates it, "Three days after having received the aforementioned papal Agnus" the nun was completely cured.

In the same booklet, Bertondelli reports a second miracle, this time in connection with Mother Eleonora Serafina Teresia who, suffering from terrible toothache, turned towards Mother Superior Cecilia, and asked for "a little of the aforesaid papal Agnus with which she had seen the novice freed from her infirmity." A piece of the wax lamb was put in her "mouth, and a little afterwards she was freed from her pain."[294]

Let us note that, in each of these two cases, the doctor avoids using the term *Dei*, since he designates the wax figurine with the expression "*papal Agnus*."[295] Now, the ellipsis here, as we can see from the title, is not just the result of a desire to simplify the language; rather, it is a sign of the stranglehold of the Church, and above all of the pontiff, over the production and use of these sacramental objects. The object stands out, in fact, as the material configuration of a continuity existing between God and His intermediaries: Christ, the pope, and the Church. The grace that is obtained through the intermediary of the *Agnus* (material instance) is actually granted through the intercession of the pope, and then by members of the clergy acting under his authority; indeed, in these accounts, it is the mother superior who gives a piece of the *Agnus*. The Lamb of the Resurrection announces a promise of healing, where it is through Christ's sacrifice that sin, the archetypal form of evil, is confronted and overcome, as is recalled in the inscription on the *Agnus Dei*: "*Ecce Agnus Dei qui tollit peccata mundi*." This promise of healing is one that the pope, as certified by the pontiff's arms and name and the date imprinted on the artifact, makes real through his benediction and that the Church, with its material image imprinted in the wax, has the power to distribute and administer.[296] The *Agnus Dei* is at once the symbol of God's power, the icon of pontifical authority, and the sign of the power of the *Ecclesia*. To eat an ounce of *Agnus Dei* with the intention of being healed was, therefore, to call to one's bedside God, the pope, and the Church, making a remedy out of their intermingled images.

A Woodcut in the Mouth

In addition to the three-dimensional reproductions of miraculous images, there were many two-dimensional representations of these same images in circulation. It was, in fact, customary to make woodcuts of the images venerated in the shrines to further promote their worship, and to ensure the transporting and diffusion of their *sacredness*.[297] Here again, these artifacts, considered sacramental objects, allowed the believer to experience contact with the image of majesty without having to touch it directly.

The book of the miracles of the Madonna delle Carceri de Prato, written in 1505 by the jurist Giuliano di Francesco Guizzelmi, is a particularly instructive piece of evidence concerning the link established between the miraculous image and its engraved replicas. The book provides us with details about the ways in which the woodcuts were used by believers and particularly for healing purposes.[298]

Before going into these details, we should recall the origin of the miraculous image itself (fig. 1.30).[299] According to Guizzelmi's

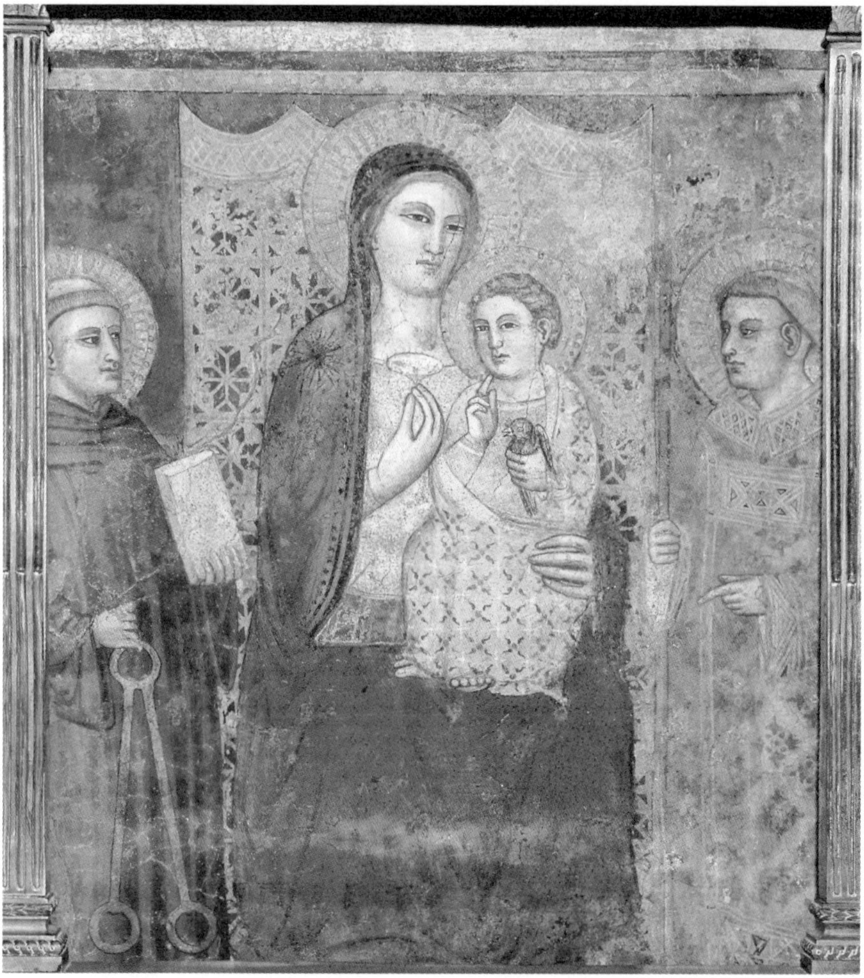

Figure 1.30. *Madonna and Child with Saints Stephen and Leonard*, fourteenth century, fresco. Prato, Basilica of Santa Maria delle Carceri (© photo Bibliotheca Hertziana—Max-Planck-Institut für Kunstgeschichte, Rome).

account, a fresco showing a Madonna and Child with, on either side of them, Saints Stephen and Leonard, and painted on the external wall of a ruined prison in the area surrounding Prato, miraculously sprang to life on July 6, 1484, to the amazement of a young boy who saw it happen. According to this boy, the painted Virgin came forth from the wall, took the Child from her knees, placed Him on the ground, and proceeded to clean the place up. This task accomplished, she took the Child again into her arms and became once again fixed in position. As one might expect, news of this event spread rapidly, and the representation became the object of intense devotion. New miracles then followed, confirming its miraculous nature: the Madonna changed color, bled, healed several of the faithful, and all this prompted the authorities to invest in the construction of a church to serve as casket.[300]

Among the ninety-four miracles presented in the work, we should especially note the cure of Mona Lisabetta, a twenty-six-year-old woman from Pisa. Guizzelmi tells the story of how, in the month of July 1485, a certain Ser Davino came to see him and "asked . . . for a Virgin Mary which had touched the Madonna of the Carceri of Prato to put on a woman who had been in a faint and as if dead for three days and who he judged would be dead in a matter of hours if she were not given miraculous help by the Lord God."[301] Guizzelmi accordingly gave the man "a figure of the Most Glorious Virgin Mary of the Carceri [*una figura della Vergine Maria del Carcere*] which had touched her most glorious figure [*Sua Gloriosissima figura*]," and this "paper figure [*figura di charta*]," was carried to the sick woman, and "put . . . to Mona Lisabetta's mouth." Immediately, "the said Mona Lisabetta who had first been as if dead, came round."[302] Shortly afterwards, the woman was once again able to speak, and "she told how she had seen that the Most Glorious Virgin Mary placed at her mouth, and how she had commended herself to her with a good heart and how she had received grace from Her Majesty."[303]

As Guizzelmi makes clear, the woodcut is not the sole determining factor in the miracle. It is just one link in a causal chain involving the Virgin (the prototype), the miraculous image (the figurative archetype kept in the shrine), and the engraved replica (its *figura di charta*), all of these being held together by two operative conditions: the production of a represented likeness (e.g., Guizzelmi speaks of "*una figura della Vergine Maria del Carcere* [a figure of the Virgin Mary of the Prison]" and not a generic representation of the Virgin[304]) and the establishment of contact between the miraculous image and the woodcut. We should stress once again here the importance given to contact in the miraculous functioning of the woodcut: the *virtus* of the miraculous image is *communicated* to its "double" by the physical, material meeting of the two images.[305] Yet we should note also that the reproduction itself, through its own figurative characteristics, its resemblance, is no less a determining factor in the operation.[306] In the eyes of the believers, the reproduced likeness crystalized all the powers involved in the process, and this is made explicit in Guizzelmi's account. Shortly after having related the ordeal of Mona Lisabetta, the jurist points out that he had heard about the miracle from the husband of the miraculously healed woman, Santi dell'Orechiata, and that the latter had been particularly insistent about the role played by the image in the wondrous event, saying that it was "through the mediation of the image of the Most Glorious Madonna of the Prison" that Mona Lisabetta had been healed by the Virgin.

But what sort of figure was it exactly that Guizzelmi offered to the sick woman? Reading his text, it is hard to be sure which type of image was involved. However, as Robert Maniura has suggested, it is very likely it was a woodcut identical to the one pasted into the jurist's manuscript of his miracle book, a document that is today in the collection of the Roncioniana Library in Prato (fig. 1.31).[307] Guizzelmi appears to have had in his possession several examples of this woodcut, dating from the end of the fifteenth century, showing a Madonna and Child framed by Saints Stephen and Leonard. In 1490, Guizzelmi noted in his *Memoriale*: "I recall how, on the 18th of May, I bought in Florence a number of Madonnas of the Prison. I spent 16

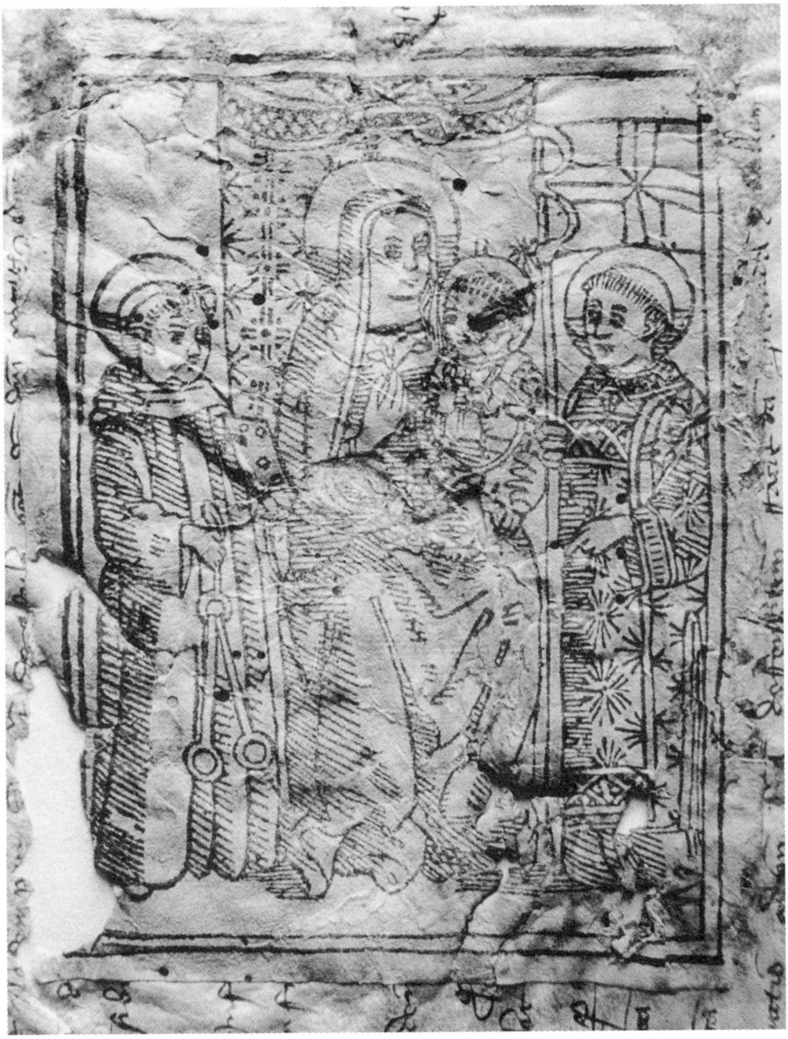

Figure 1.31. *Madonna delle Carceri*, ca. 1480, woodcut, 4 × 5.4 in., pasted in Giuliano di Francesco Guizzelmi, *Historia della apparition et altri miracoli di Madonna Sancta del Carcere di Prato* (Prato: Biblioteca Roncioniana, 1505), codex 87 (© Robert Maniura).

soldi. Now I have more Virgin Marys on paper."[308] The fact that the woodcuts are called specifically "Madonnas of the Prison" removes any doubt about their direct link with the miraculous image, and this last remark of Guizzelmi's proves that this was not his first purchase.

At this juncture, let us look at how the image was actually used. According to Guizzelmi's text, the woodcut was taken to the sick woman, and then put in her mouth. Now, if the woodcut used here was, in fact, just like the one pasted into the jurist's book, it would have been necessary for the helpers to fold it or cut it into pieces before placing it in the sick woman's mouth. Its relatively large dimensions (10.2 x 13.8 cm) would have precluded any more "direct" insertion. In the absence of absolute certainty about the exact nature of the image used, this must remain on the level of conjecture. But the point is ultimately of no great importance for us. What is of overriding importance here is the method by which the healing was carried out and the experience that it generated: the healing was obtained through the placing of a material object in the mouth, through touch, and consequently through the establishment of a physical relationship with it. It would appear, therefore, that the figurative representation (i.e., the part that one might expect to be designed solely for viewing) carried with it a material portion that was as necessary to its status as an image as was its iconicity.[309] The choice of the term *figura* to designate the woodcut (*figura di charta*) and the fresco (*la gloriosissima figura*) is, moreover, very likely linked to the desire to stress the material aspect of the representation. As Eric Auerbach has shown, the term *figure* was used by Saint Augustine, Saint Isidore, and Dante Alighieri to refer to the waxen image resulting from the stamping process[310]—without, however, it being fused with its heavenly prototype.[311]

Yet we should note that, as it is presented in the book of miracles, the experience of the image was not exclusively material. Although, in the world of facts, it was still an image stamped on paper that was put into her mouth, what the possessed woman received was of another nature. In fact, in contrast to the expression Guizzelmi uses to refer to what was put in her mouth by those close to her ("*Quella* figura di charta, *puosono alla bocca* [this paper figure, put to her mouth"]), the phrasing used by Mona Lisabetta ("*porsi alla bocca quella Gloriosissima Vergine Maria* [the Most Glorious Virgin Mary placed at her mouth"]) does not include words pertaining to the material aspect of the image. In fact, the terms *figura di charta* have disappeared. It is possible that the signified substitutes here for the signifier purely for reasons of narrative economy. However, I think it more likely that, through this omission, the author was wanting to make room for an indeterminacy that would allow for a certain play on the effects of substitution and equivalence between the figure and the object.[312] The absence of the term *figura* invites the reader to identify the *Gloriosissima Vergine Maria* with the Virgin herself and, this comes down to the essence of the miracle, that the graven image is the *thing* through which the Virgin herself was able to return to earth, just as the fresco painted on the prison wall in Prato was the *device* that made possible her appearance before the young boy.

Given all of this, questions remain: how was it that Guizzelmi, as a lay person and a doctor of canon and civil law, could become the apologist of the miraculous image, the purveyor of its graven replicas, and the memorialist of the miracles worked by the stamps? Did he have a more official position within the administration of the shrine? Although the biographical information gathered by Maniura is not sufficient to enable us to fully answer these questions,[313] we can still safely conclude, from the role played by the jurist, that the administering of the venerated and miraculous images did not always happen within strict official boundaries. It certainly seems to be the case that, during this period, there existed a degree of flexibility within these customs and practices. It is for this reason, perhaps, that we see these seemingly heterodox uses of visual artifacts.

Schluckbildchen, Esszettel, *and Photographs*

Among the early modern devotional prints, a special category emerged after the sixteenth century in response to the desire for contact and incorporation. These were the *Schluckbildchen* ("tiny images for swallowing") or *santini eduli* ("little edible saints").[314] Particularly widespread in Catholic Germany such as in Bavaria, Tyrol, and Styria, where there were a great number of Marian shrines (e.g., Altenberg, Altötting, Landshut, Mariahilf at Innsbruck, Mariazell, etc.),[315] these images specifically intended to be ingested were to proliferate also over much of Europe up to the middle of the twentieth century (figs. 1.32 and 1.33).[316] Easy enough to identify from their dimensions that rarely exceed 4–5 cm in length or width, they are also recognizable from their iconography since they mostly depict miraculous images, relics, or saints.[317] Without being exactly reproductions of *Gnadenbild*, they belong, for the most part, to the same category. They were, therefore, images of images, showing a painting, sculpture, or mosaic that was venerated in a specific place.

Printed in sheets that could include as many as one hundred thirty individual figures, though most having from twelve to thirty images, the *Schluckbildchen* were offered to the faithful in response to demonstrations of piety, or they were sold in the vicinity of the shrines.[318] The evidence that we have indicates that they could be blessed, before or after their acquisition, and then, like the *Schabmadonnen* or the larger woodcuts such as the ones of the Madonna delle Carceri, they were placed in contact with the miraculous image, either by the believer (probably a less common occurrence) or by the shrine's religious authorities.[319] The prints could then be put on spice breads or biscuits as an ornament,[320] and indeed more usually, they could be scratched, cut, or grated before being mixed with an edible substance or dissolved in a drinkable liquid and thus eaten or drunk as a remedy.[321]

It was the miraculous image itself that determined the ailments against which the images for swallowing were supposed to act, with each thaumaturgical figure, therefore, having its own special field of action. The Virgin of Mariazell, for example, was reputed to come to the aid of barren or gestating women.[322] At the same

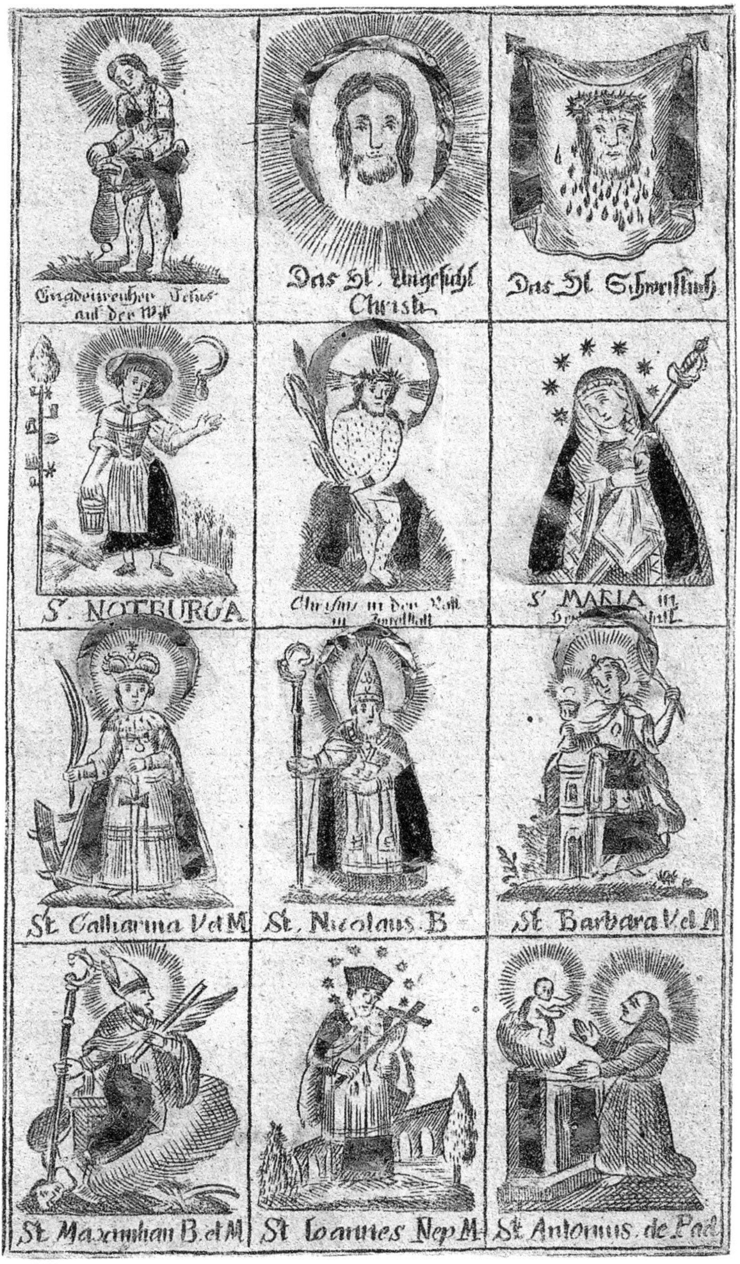

Figure 1.32. Edible devotional images, ca. 1780, woodcut. Private collection.

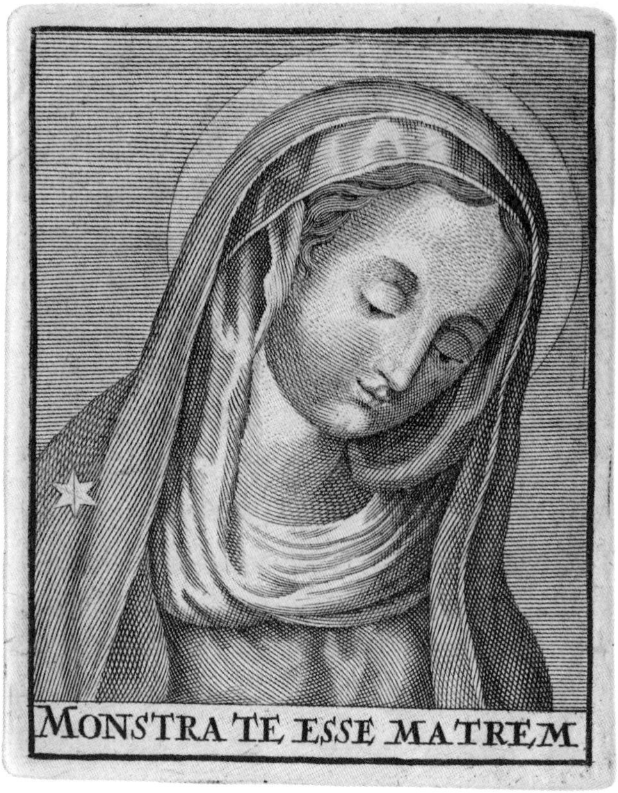

Figure 1.33. *Little Picture to Eat* (Schluckbildchen) *after the Miraculous Virgin of the Ursulines Convent at Landshut* (Die Mutter mit dem geneigten Haupt), ca. 1780, etching, 3.5 × 2.3 in. Collection of Jérémie Koering.

time, a certain number of images were believed to be effective against an almost unlimited number of sicknesses and dangers. The Brown Madonna of Santa Maria del Carmine Maggiore in Naples, it was said, cured leprosy, hemorrhages, blindness, Saint Anthony's fire, and guarded against drownings, shipwrecks, and wild animals.[323]

Similar in many ways to the *Schluckbildchen* were the *Esszettel* ("tickets for eating") that could also be ingested for therapeutic or prophylactic purposes.[324] The majority of these artifacts included only a written prayer, but a few of them, like the tickets of the Three Magi, Saint Anthony of Padua, Saint Francis, Saint Walpurga, or Saint Agatha, might come with an illustration.[325] The power ascribed to them was, as before, based upon the principle of analogy. The *Dreikönigszettel* ("Three Kings tickets"), for example, were thought, among other positive benefits, to protect travelers, while the *Agathenzettel* ("Saint Agatha tickets"), sold mainly on February 5th, the saint's holiday, were deemed effective against burns, barrenness, and difficult childbirths. For the virtue of these pieces of paper to work, they had to be carried on the body, or, once again, mixed with water and swallowed.[326]

With the development of new techniques of reproduction in the nineteenth century, and, above all, with arrival of the widespread access to photography in the twentieth century, certain believers were to replace the prints for eating with photographs of the saints. This practice of substitution has been recorded as late as the end of the twentieth century, particularly in Egypt[327] and Uganda.[328] Heike Behrend, who has studied devotional practices in eastern Africa, reports on a number of cases involving the ingestion of photographic images of Father Bill, a charismatic priest of Indian origin who had lived in Kampala, and who was reputed to be a miracle worker. After his sermons, certain believers would gather up the earth on which he had walked, apply it to a photograph of him, mix the resulting object with water, and then drink the sanctified liquid to obtain its benefits.[329]

Power of the Multiple

Unlike the Marian statues of Montaigu or Einsiedeln, the images printed on paper, such as woodcuts and photographs, did not share the same sacral substance as the prototype. Their virtue derived either from contact with a miraculous image, or from benediction, or again from the resemblance between the two images.[330] The following question then arises: Could an image that had not had any contact with a miraculous image, and that also had not been blessed, be considered effective?[331] There is some reason to believe so. A few sheets, presenting not a single repeated figure but rather a whole selection of miraculous images, would suggest that the visual aspect was not a mere accessory for the believer and that it might even have been enough to ensure a connection with the figured archetype. A sheet published by Johann Friedrich Carl, probably around 1780, bring together representations of twelve miraculous images of the Virgin (including those of Altötting, Loreto, Gennazano, Landshut, Innsbruck, and Mariazell). Another sheet, engraved by Johann Michael Söckler in Munich, also around 1780, depicts a group of miraculous images that included not only the Virgin (of Altötting, Landshut, Innsbruck, etc.) but also Jesus (e.g., Jesus von der Ruhe, Jesus Kindlein zu Altenhochenau, etc.). These examples show that these woodcuts were transported and sold at great distances from the shrines, enabling the faithful believers to benefit from several miraculous images at the same time and without their necessarily having to undertake all the pilgrimages.[332] Now, in these specific cases, it is hard to imagine that the prints were systematically placed in contact with the miraculous paintings or statues. Their effectiveness must have resided, above all, in their power of making present, a power that allowed, despite the absence of contact, for the transmission of "a piece of that infinitely shareable sacral power, held to be inexhaustible . . . as long as the original image existed."[333]

The fact that the image used was both general (i.e., one example among a multitude of other identical ones) and specific (e.g., one representing a particular saint or miraculous image) probably did have some importance on a theoretical or theological level, irrespective of whether the individual believers were aware of that. On the one hand, its status as a reproduction prevented the faithful from confusing the representation of the saint with the saint's actual incarnation, that is, from conflating, as I have said, the signified and signifier. On the other hand, this same status allowed for the establishment of a sensory link between the model and its multiples. It is by virtue of the resemblance between the multiple and the material figure of the prototype (the *Gnadenbild*, or miraculous image) that the effectiveness of the duplicated image can be understood.

The replicas of miraculous images were different from the images of saints that we looked at earlier, such as the tokens, seals, and frescoes, because the latter were in principle not images of images, but rather conventional representations of saints. With the reproductions of miraculous images, the artifact was a substitute for an image of majesty and not for a prototype. Even if the replica was still a channel for making present a heavenly entity, this making present happened, so to speak, at a second remove.

Ingestion in Network

One last aspect of the believer's relationship with the miraculous image must be addressed: the insertion of the practice of ingestion in a global pattern of distribution and manifestation of the faith. As we can see from Wichmans's report on the miraculous image at Montaigu,[334] these practices involving incorporation were spread by way of a network created by the members of the religious community, and the same emerges from a reading of the texts pertaining to the Einsiedeln image. Because of this fact, ingesting an image was neither an isolated act, a response to a single individual's "superstition," nor was it a gesture that was condemned by the entire community of clerics. Quite the contrary, this approach to images appears to have become a normal way of living one's faith. Evidence discovered by Ralph Dekoninck in connection with the miraculous statue of Notre-Dame-de-Foy (present-day Dinant, Belgium) seems to confirm this interpretation.[335] In a 1670 letter addressed to Father Chaumonot, Father Claude-Alix de Véroncourt, who was a Jesuit missionary charged with converting the Huron Amerindians in New France (Québec), explained that the wood of the tree in which the Virgin of Notre-Dame-de-Foy had been discovered possessed a genuine healing power, especially when it was ingested:

> I am communicating to you now the secret of how we obtain the favors of Our Glorious Dame de Foy. After we learned that it was not only the miraculous image of Notre-Dame de Foy that healed all who recommended themselves to it in good faith, but that pieces of wood and sawdust from the oak in which she had been found, and with which other images had been made, that the earth of the place where the said oak grew, and that certain stones from the same piece of land, worked miracles for those who wore them and used them with devotion. . . . We send to the sick [one of these stones, or] a piece of oak, or a rosary bead made from the same wood, so they can dip it in their drink, and several of them recover their health in this way.[336]

By prescribing to his correspondents this practice involving substances having been in contact with the miraculous image, the Jesuit father is literally raising ingestion to the level of a devotional act that should be shared within the community.[337] Therefore, far from it being systematically seen as suspect and punished, ingesting substances that were the vehicles of the power of images was understood, against all expectation perhaps, as one of the practices on the basis of which a Christian community could ultimately be established and consolidated.

The recommendations provided by the author of the history of the shrine at Einsiedeln shed a different light on the importance of the links between miraculous images, molded or engraved replicas, and the religious community of believers. As the reader will recall, the signs allowing one to distinguish the genuine statuettes of the Black Madonna from the fake ones sold outside the shrine included "the Abbey arms, surmounted by a crosier, miter, and sword."[338] This mark was not just a way of authenticating the origin of the effigy, as the seal identified the provenance of a capsule of *terra sigillata*, but also a sign connecting the power of the artifact with a particular community, in this case the Benedictines of Einsiedeln. As we know, a shrine's reputation, its fame, was essential to the social, economic, political, and spiritual standing of any religious institution, and it depended as much upon the accounts of miracles as it did on the distribution of those sacramental objects that made those miracles possible. I would argue that proof of this can be seen in the scrupulous addition of the names of the sites associated with the miracles accomplished by way of the miraculous image in the *Histoire de la Sainte-Chapelle de Notre-Dame-des-Ermites* (Einsiedeln). The geographical origin of the people who received the benefits of these miracles is close to being consistently indicated. Mentioned as healed by the ingestion of "a little powder of an image of Our Lady," we have Ursule Topf at Brand in Austria (p. 523), Abbot Saint-Pierre of Salzburg (p. 525), Jean Kober from Munich (p. 525), the Hermit Brother François Kopfer at Bercken in Alsace (p. 526), Joseph Beitelrock at Konstanz (*ibid.*), the Reverend Father Christophe in Venice (*ibid.*), and so on. This listing of names and places allowed the reader to map out the miraculous image's range of effectiveness on a European scale, to appreciate the role played by the statuettes in the spread of its influence,[339] to become aware of the existence of a network of believers faithful to the Einsiedeln Virgin, and to see his or her own adherence to the practices described in the work as a way of participating in a community norm. Under these conditions, consuming a little terracotta, wood, or paper, bearing the heavenly image of Christ, the Virgin, or the saints, to heal or to protect oneself was, after all, merely one way, among others, of living one's life as part of the Christian community.

CHAPTER TWO

Imagining Ingestion

For thinking is digesting.
—Letter of Ludwig Wittgenstein to Norman Malcolm, June 26, 1945

The fish is brought all gleaming onto the painter's board, and,
thanks to his swiftness, it is served at table in the evening.
They eat their models!
—Letter of Eugène Boudin to Ferdinand Martin, December 15, 1864

The stomach is also an example: conversion, assimilation, rejection,
one hand on mood, the other on dreams.[1]
—David Bosc, *Mourir et puis sauter sur son cheval*, 2016

Irrespective of whether they ate, drank, or licked the images, people consumed them for apotropaic, prophylactic, or therapeutic purposes, and as we shall see in our next chapter, they used them to establish, consolidate, or participate in the life of social groups. But why was it that, in some circumstances, one would resort to ingestion rather than relying upon vision, that is, the path of sensation most readily associated with images? How was it that in some situations, it was consumption that was favored over other experiences as a remedy, a form of protection, a means of access to knowledge, or as a way of forging links within communities when other experiences, although certainly more distanced, were less invasive as far as the images were concerned? We have already seen, here and there, bits and pieces of an answer to this question. But now we must approach it more systematically by examining the worlds of medicine and psycho-physiology, theology and religion, art and literature, and politics and philosophy. We must approach it by investigating the connections, both positive and negative, they have had with ingestion in the cultures and societies under our consideration.

The Body Connected

A possible first answer to the question, *Why ingestion?*, can be found in the role in health care allotted since Antiquity to the consumption of nutritional or medicinal substances. Ancient or premodern medicine resorted overwhelmingly to the ingestion of solids or liquids as means of treating illness and fortifying the body.[2]

In ancient Egypt, the healing statues, reactivated by water poured over them, required, so to speak, drinking.[3] For the priests and doctors, evil resided specifically *in* the body, and it was necessary to introduce into the body an antagonistic agent that would dislodge the pathogen, annihilate it, or dissolve it. This accounts for why, in most of the magical *historiolae*, ingestion was the path *par excellence* of healing. One of the texts inscribed on the statue of Djedhor the Healer calls unequivocally for the *incorporation* of the god for the healing to take place:

> I have pronounced your name, I have recited your spells, I have pronounced your magic charms, I have conjured with the conjurings that you created. It is your magic art (coming out of) your own mouth that your father Geb bequeathed to you and that your mother Nout gave to you that taught you, beside the Majesty of the one who presides in Leotopolis, to ensure your protection, to renew your safeguard, to seal the mouth of all the reptiles in the sky, earth, and water, to make people live again, appease the gods, to glorify Rê by your incantations. *Come inside me*! Hurry, hurry, on this day, since you have sailed in the divine boat. May you repulse for me every lion in its desert, every crocodile in its river, and every mouth (of venomous animal) that stings in its hole.[4]

Seth, the deity that is apparently being called upon here, must penetrate inside the body of the supplicant in order to effect the cure. And it is through his liquified image that he will answer the supplication.

In parallel fashion, in the Greco-Roman world, absorption was considered an effective channel for maintaining health and for curing a large number of medical conditions. In fact, the Hippocratic and Galenic medicine that predominated throughout almost the entirety of the arc of the Mediterranean and in Europe from Antiquity up until the French Classical age saw health as "the balanced mixture of all the constitutive elements of man"[5] and as the result of a proper balance among the elementary qualities, the correct proportions of hot, cold, dry, and wet. The regulatory seat of these qualities was to be found in those internal organs, such as the liver or stomach, that carried out nutritional functions—hence the importance given to dietetics.[6] Any imbalance that was due to poor diet, the weather, or evil spirits could be counterbalanced by the introduction of something from the outside. The remedy consisted in introducing into the body liquid or solid substances whose qualities could induce the liquification and rebalancing of the humors, black bile, yellow bile, phlegm, and blood.[7] By virtue of the laws of sympathy inherent in the analogical functioning of the world, the closer an active element was to the source of disease, the more its effectiveness was ensured.

The role that the image ultimately played in this medicinal practice is more difficult to discern. Was the form supposed to be an active agent in the working of the remedy? In the case of engraved gems, Galen dismissed any idea that the image was active, judging that only the stone, ingested in a potion, could have a real effect.[8] However, other doctors and magi took an opposing view because, for them, the images did have a role to play in the therapeutic protocol to the extent that its configuration allowed for the capture of positive and curative celestial influxes.[9]

As Nicolas Weill-Parot shows, although it was not until the second half of the thirteenth century that the magical "functioning" of images was to be "based on an explanatory theoretical system," that is to say, natural magic,[10] the presence of images in magical artifacts had in fact been almost systematic since Antiquity, which certainly moves towards proving their importance in ideas about what made the remedies effective. The analogical system underlying the natural philosophy of Antiquity was enough to justify their sympathetic effects.[11] Attraction and repulsion corresponded to the Galenic system of balance among the primary qualities of hot, cold, moist, and dry, and the substances to be ingested were determined as a function of their *dynameis*, their capacity to set in motion the fluids and humors, to reverse imbalances, and to prevent congestion.[12] For example, depending upon the temperamental constitution of the subject, an excess of cold and moistness could be counterbalanced by the introduction of just the right ratio of hot and dry substances. As a result of moral pressure coming from the Church that, in Marc Augé's phrasing, saw magic as "other people's religion" and the religion of the "pagans," it began to appear necessary to justify the integration of magical practices into the Christian edifice through a logical demonstration.[13] Consequently, without abandoning the analogical system of scholastic medicine and the magic of the Middle Ages and the Early Modern period that were generally Galenic, the Christian physicians began to describe and explain the mechanisms of magic, and in particular the role played by "the imagination and the properties of the specific form."[14] This happened with mixed success. Still, before the fifteenth century, which saw an increasing number of cases in which judicial astrology was condemned (the essential problem being astral determinism), the practice of magic in its natural or empirical form and that of natural astrology (associated with melothesia) was effectively unhindered since it primarily involved revealing and setting into mutual reaction the similarities and qualities that God himself had introduced into his work, Nature.[15] The simples and minerals were held to be the expression of divine grace, and this was thought enough to render them effective.[16] To combine them or to add to them images capable of strengthening their primary quality or their specific form through allowing them to capture the virtues of the heavenly bodies was nothing other than a natural operation. In this way, Arnaud de Villeneuve (ca. 1240–1311) was to justify the preparation of magical artifacts such as image-bearing seals:

> At every hour . . . the parts of the heavenly sphere introduce one or another of the virtues into the engenderables, according to what is required by the figure of the heavenly sphere determined by the horoscope or ascendent at the hour related to the engenderable or the engendered whatever it might be. But yet the virtue that the bodies above introduce is only received by the bodies that have been prepared [or disposed] either solely by the natural agents, or with the aid of art . . . . Everything that is produced under the heavenly sphere by art or nature receives a property for undergoing [the action] of another thing or for acting on another thing, even if this property is unknown to us . . . . Consequently, whoever would know the virtues of the heavenly sphere and would recognize the substances, with the dispositions that prepare them to receive the impression of these virtues, would make amazing and, so to speak, great modifications in things below.[17]

The seal was thus "the product of the encounter of a substance prepared [in such a way as] to receive a certain virtuous influence," and the magical operation consisted in nothing more nor less than marrying art and nature.[18] At the beginning of the fifteenth century, Giorgio Anselmi was again to stress this encounter as a way of legitimizing his art: "The image is a natural resemblance induced by an artificial choice in order to reinforce natural things and marvelous operations."[19] Thus, as Weill-Parot stresses in his reading of Anselmi, "the action (always 'natural') of the *psyche* of the artisan works along with the action of the celestial influences."[20]

In like manner to the physicians who "logically" treated illnesses by way of mouth (fig. 2.1) through electuaries, decoctions, pills, and oils, the magi privileged this same method for magically healing the sick. One might drink potions containing the powder of a gem bearing, for example, the image of Chnoubis.[21] Now, the reason why the physicians could recommend such a beverage was because by drinking the graven image of a seal, the patient lodged within their body the active principle capable of attracting the celestial influxes necessary for healing.

The Arab physician and philosopher Avicenna (980–1037), whose writings were among those most commented on during the Middle Ages, provides an explanation of the mechanisms by which a remedy functioned within the body. Weill-Parot explains here the three distinct ways in which, according to Avicenna, the healing process worked:

> First of all . . . there is the thing that acts by its own quality (*sola sui qualitate*): such a thing heats the body by its own heat or cools it through its own coldness; in this way, it is not "assimilated" into the body. Then there is the thing that is ingested and that acts through its own substance. In this case, there a process of assimilation of the thing into the body: it receives, in fact, the form of one of the parts of the body; thus as lettuce is digested it is transformed into blood. Finally, there are the substances that operate by virtue of their "specific form."[22]

Following Avicenna, Arnald of Villanova was to further specify that these external agents acted upon the *spiritus*, the vital spirit linking men to the stars, either by their specific form or by their artificial configuration when the remedy included the production of a seal.[23] In the latter case, the graven or stamped image attracted the heavenly virtues to the very inside of the body in order to reestablish the balance between the four humors.

Taking into account the various commentaries that we find at this intersection of medical and magico-astrological thought, it appears entirely understandable that images could be invested with a "natural" power, even though they were the product of artificial configurations, and that, consequently, people could imagine them capable of communicating that power, on an equal level with the substances associated with them, inside the body and at the conclusion of the digestive process.

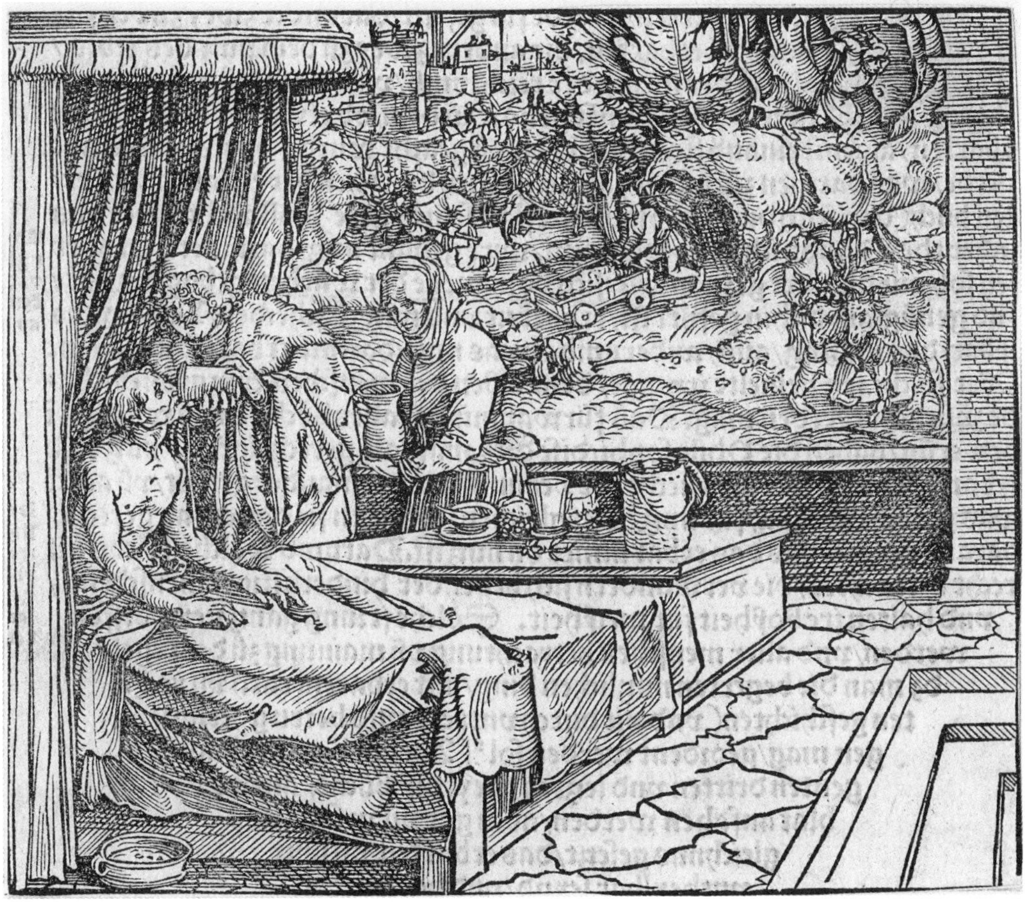

Figure 2.1. Hans Weiditz, *Physician Ministering to a Patient*, 1531, woodcut, 11.6×8 in. In Marcus Tullius Cicero, *Officia M.T.C von den tugentsamen ämptern* (Augsburg: Heinrich Steyner, 1531). London, British Museum (© The Trustees of the British Museum).

Mystical Incorporations

Corpus mysticum

Alongside the physical rationale that looms large in the medical thinking, the ingestion of images can also be explained by the importance given to the metaphor of incorporation as a way of depicting the relationship between people and the supernatural world. In Christian theology, notably, we see the all-encompassing principle of the *corpus mysticum* through which the idea of community was understood. After Saint Paul, Christians were to be seen as parts of the mystical body of the Church: "For just as in a single human body there are many limbs and organs, all with different functions, so all of us, united with Christ, form one body, serving individually as limbs and organs to one another (Romans 12:4–5)."

The Church Fathers were thus to liken the faithful to the "members" of a "mystical body" with Christ as its head.[24] In the ninth century, Rabanus Maurus declares, for his part, that the Catholic Church was a mystical body, "*Ecclesia Catholica, quae mystice corpus est* (The Catholic Church that is mystically a body)."[25]

In describing the community of believers as a body whose head is Christ, the theologians used synecdoche to designate the relationship of inclusion that lay, as they saw it, at the foundation of the Christian Church. It is quite possible to understand, after this, how a continuity might have been established between the Holy Communion and the image of the Church as a *corpus mysticum*. For Henri de Lubac, the notion of the *corpus mysticum* was close to being inextricable from the sacrament of the Eucharist, the latter being at one and the same time the body of Christ and the figure of the Church.[26] It was not until the twelfth century that the expression *corpus mysticum* was to be almost exclusively reserved for the Church, and *corpus Christi* for the Eucharist.[27]

This inclusive relationship was often translated into images, as we see with the *Vierges ouvrantes* (Opening Virgins) where the mounting of the piece materializes the identification of the Mother of God with the *Eklesia* ("assembly"[28]). Particularly widespread in western Europe between the thirteenth and fifteenth centuries, these objects, both sculpted and painted, took the form of a Virgin and Child with, on their inside, a representation of the Holy Trinity or of Christ alone, accompanied by scenes from the life of the Virgin, or again by an assembly of men and women protected by the cloak of the Virgin of Mercy.[29] One example in the collection of the Cluny Museum, originating conceivably in a priory of the Teutonic order (fig. 2.2), shows, on the inside of the body of the Virgin, God the Father, Christ on the Cross. (A sculpture dating from the eighteenth century has likely replaced a previous figure of Christ that was lost or destroyed.) On either side of these two main figures God the Father and Christ, stand a company of male and female saints, kings and queens, bishops, clerics, and lay people. However, the Church did not establish or universally recognize this type of anthropomorphized representation of the mystical body of the Church. Indeed, certain theologians strongly criticized these pieces for erring devotion. For example, the chancellor of the University of Paris, Jean Gerson (1363–1429), in a sermon delivered on December 25, 1402, proscribed their use on the grounds that "there is neither beauty nor devotion in such works, and they may well be the cause of error and indevotion."[30] And yet, by their very existence, these image-objects, despite a few condemnations, reveal that many Christians felt the need to depict the Christian community visually and literally as a human body.[31]

Drinking Christ's Blood and the Virgin's Milk

Throughout the Middle Ages and into the modern era, other figurative solutions appeared to depict this continuity between Christ and the community of believers. I am thinking in particular of the depictions of this spiritual communion involving the consumption of a flowing liquid substance, either blood or milk.[32]

The Chiarito Tabernacle (fig. 2.3) is an exemplary case of this type of depiction.[33] Painted and decorated by Pacino di Bonaguida around 1340, it brings together scenes of Christ's Passion, a mystical

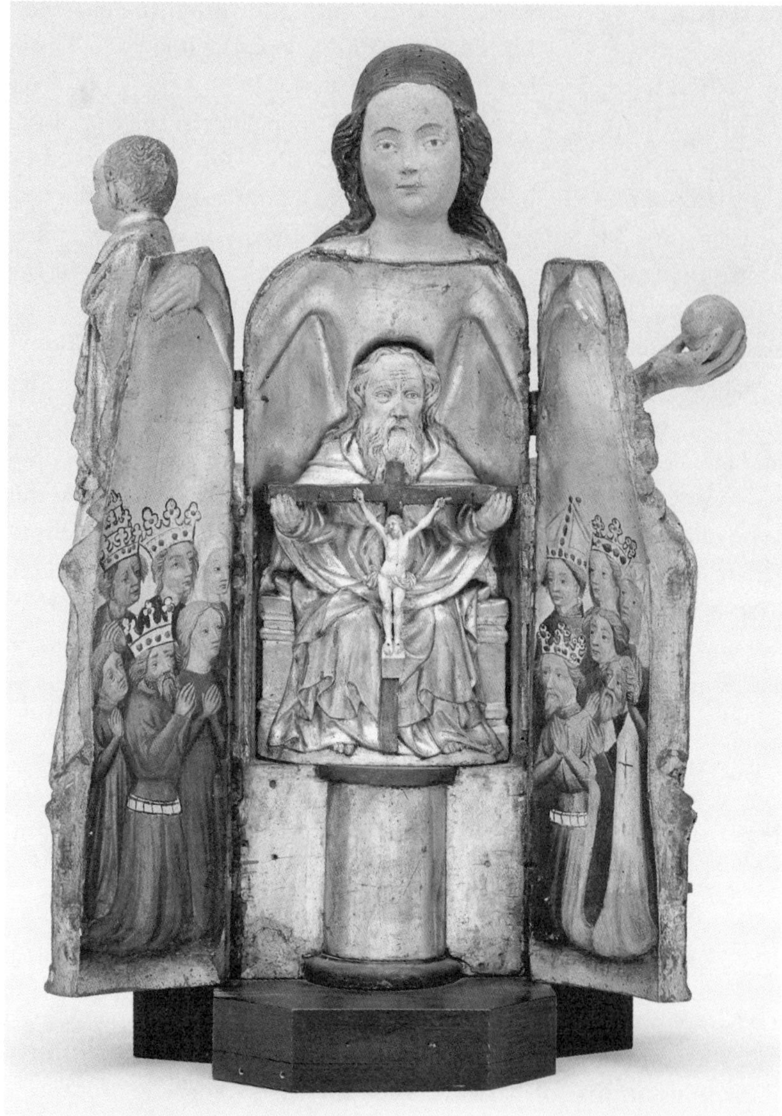

Figure 2.2. Pomeranian Studio, *Opening Virgin with the Holy Trinity*, ca. 1375–1425, polychrome wood, 3 in. Paris, Musée de Cluny—Musée National du Moyen Âge (Cl. 12060) (© RMN—Grand Palais/Art Resource, NY/Michel Urtado).

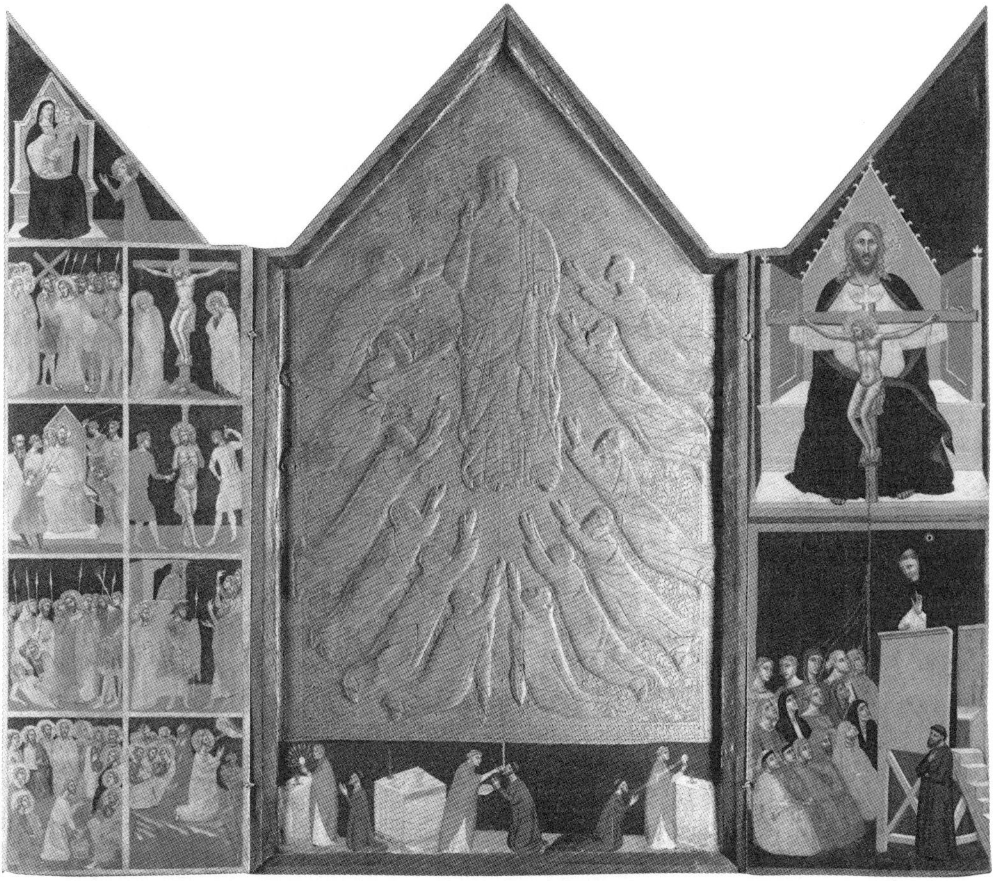

Figure 2.3. Pacino di Bonaguida, *The Chiarito Tabernacle*, ca. 1340, gilded gesso and tempera on panel, 39.7 × 44.4 in. Los Angeles, J. Paul Getty Museum (© J. Paul Getty Museum).

communion, and various episodes in the blessed life of Chiarito, a wealthy layperson who lived in Florence in the first half of the fourteenth century and who was miraculously cured of a chronic throat affliction by the intercession of Saint Zenobius, the first bishop of Florence. It was said that the saint appeared to Chiarito as the latter was in meditation before the saint's tomb, delivering him from his afflication by giving him a blessing with the sign of the cross. After this episode, Chiarito made a vow of chastity, and he helped several communities of women around the city of Fiesole in Italy. As legend has it, his good works were repaid with several other visions.

Ingestion, as a way of appropriating the sacred, is most evident in the central panel of this devotional object (fig. 2.4). In the upper section, the artist has depicted a mystical communion in gilded *pastiglia*, and this is placed above three painted scenes showing the sacrament of the Eucharist: on the left, the miraculous germination of a host, out of which several ears of wheat shoot out; on the right, the vision of a homunculus emanating from a host; and, in the center, Chiarito receiving Holy Communion. Each of these three episodes emphasizes the real presence of Christ's body in the host, reinforcing the dogma of transubstantiation that had been established at the Lateran Council of 1215, and according to which, at the moment of consecration, the species of bread and wine become the Body and Blood of Christ while retaining their original physical characteristics and appearances. However, it is only the central scene that specifically highlights ingestion. Here, in fact, the artist has chosen to materially present the transmission of divine grace in the form of thirteen golden lines of flowing liquid running out from Christ's navel, reaching not only the mouth of each of the twelve apostles, but also, in the lower part, the mouth of Chiarito del Voglia himself. It is here that spiritual communion takes a visible and most definitively material form. Christ flows down, so to speak, as if liquified, towards the lower register where He meets the host and subsequently the mouth of Chiarito del Voglia. Thus, it is through the depiction of the divine spirit as an ingested flowing

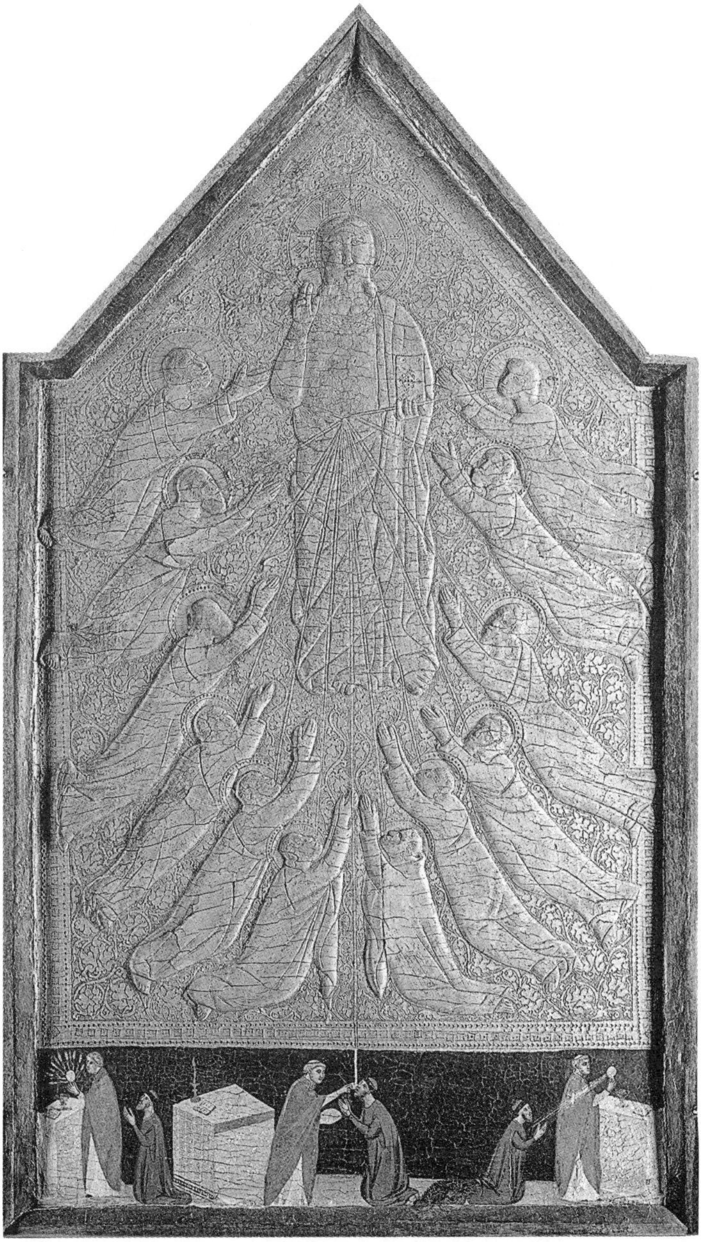

Figure 2.4. Pacino di Bonaguida, *The Chiarito Tabernacle*, ca. 1340, gilded gesso and tempera on panel, 39.7 × 44.4 in. Los Angeles, J. Paul Getty Museum (detail of fig. 2.3) (© J. Paul Getty Museum).

liquid that participation in the Christian community here acquired its full shape.

For Richard Öffner, the rays of gold reaching the mouths of communicants are a reference to the metallic tubes (known as *fistulae*) used during the mass to consume the Eucharistic wine.[34] However, this "realist" explanation should not prevent us from seeing here, just as well, an imaginative variation on depictions of, on the one hand, the flowing of Christ's blood down onto the skull of Adam, and where the skull drinks the blood as we see in the Crucifixion scene painted around 1300 by Deodato Orlandi, today in Naples's Museo di Santa Chiara; on the other hand, the consumption of Christ's blood by the male and female mystic saints. One thinks, in fact, of the considerable importance given to the flow of blood from the costal wound in the imaginations of Mechthild of Magdeburg, Catherine of Siena, Angela of Foligno, Alda (Aldobrandesca) of Siena, or Lutgardis of Tongres.[35] All these visionaries put great emphasis on their desire to drink the blood of Christ, to incorporate the suffering of God made man, and to satisfy their hunger with the holy food that was His redeeming blood.

The most complex of these mystical experiences was surely that of Catherine of Siena (1347–1380) who constantly praised the virtues of Christ's blood, exhorting those close to her to become transported by the precious liquid.[36] Raymond of Capua, her confessor and the first complier of her sayings, reports notably the saint's desire to attach her lips to the Savior's wound, with Christ acting as a nursing mother:

> Father, do you know what the Lord did to my soul that day? He behaved like a mother with her favorite child. She will show it the breast, but hold it away from it until it cries; as soon as it begins to cry, she will laugh for a while and clasp it to her and, covering it with kisses, delightedly give it her full breast. So the Lord behaved with me. That day, He showed me His most sacred side from afar and I cried from the intensity of my longing to put my lips to the sacred wound. After He had laughed for a little while at my tears—at

> least that is what He seemed to do—He came up to me, clasped my soul in His arms, and put my mouth to where His most sacred wound was, that is to say, the wound in His side. Then with its great longing my soul entered right into that wound, and found such sweetness and such knowledge of the Divinity there that if you could ever appreciate it you would marvel that my heart did not break, and wonder how ever I managed to go on living in the body in such an excess of ardour and love.[37]

Moving from a visual to a tactile relationship, this text translates the saint's irrepressible need for absorption.[38] To fully encounter God, to become one with him, it was not enough to see him. One touch, kiss, and drink him. A number of artists, including a manuscript illuminator from the Upper Rhineland in the fifteenth century (fig. 2.5),[39] or again around 1600, Santi di Tito and Francesco Vanni (fig. 2.6), have depicted this inextinguishable thirst by showing the precise moment at which Catherine, putting her lips to Christ's side, consumes the redeeming liquid as it pours forth from the wound.

If the consumption of the blood appears to be the vehicle of the mystical union, this is perhaps because this is an act that conjoins, in an exemplary fashion, the literal and the figurative. On the one hand, there is the physiological process, nutrition, indispensable to life, and that, as we shall see later, has often served as a metaphor for describing the phenomenon of spiritual absorption, and on the other hand we have a substance, blood, charged with a particularly rich symbolic meaning[40] and perceived as the vital fluid *par excellence.* As the physician Levinus Lemnius writes in 1564, "Blood is the best of sauces, the food and pasture of life."[41] Consuming liquid blood announces, in fact, a process of digestion, a breaking down and stewing in the stomach, with the function of transforming the nutriment into nourishment, and then into blood.[42] Now, in choosing the blood of the Redemption as food, the saint takes into her own body a substance that is both *absorbable* in its essence—according to Galenic medicine, blood transforms into blood—and also *irreducible* in its accident—Christ's blood, untainted by original sin,

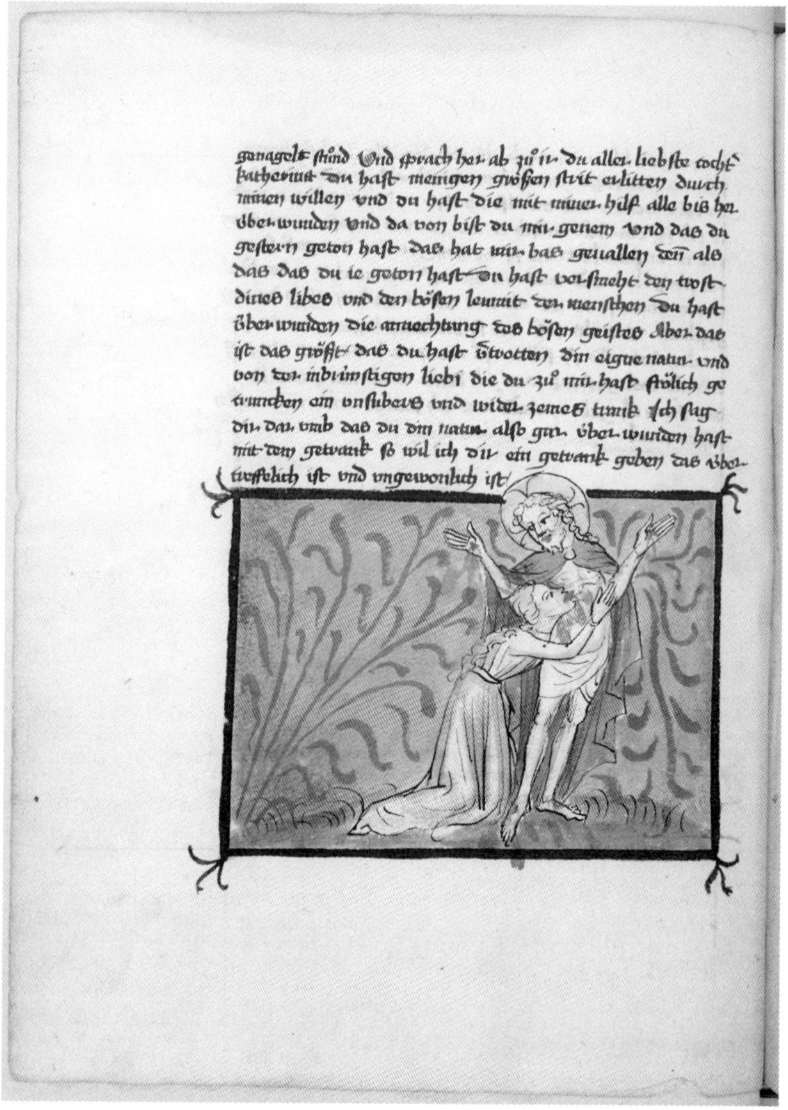

Figure 2.5. Rhineland illuminator, *Saint Catherine Drinking the Blood from Christ's Wound*, fifteenth century, in Raymond of Capua, *La Vie de Sainte Catherine de Sienne*, Paris, Bibliothèque National de France, Ms. All. 34, fol. 43v. (© Bibliothèque nationale de France).

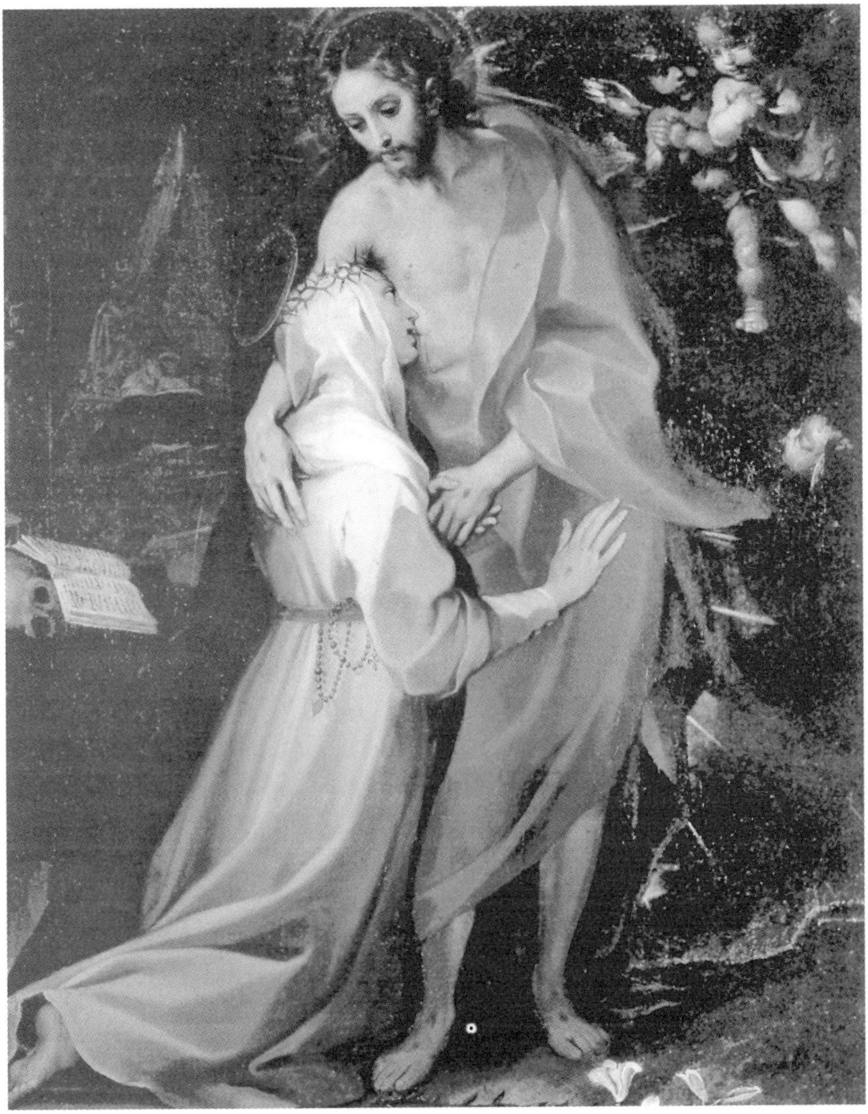

Figure 2.6. Francesco Vanni, *Saint Catherine Drinking the Blood from Christ's Wound*, 1594, oil on canvas. Siena, Duomo di Siena.

is a pure blood, unlike the blood running through the veins of the descendants of Adam.[43] To better understand this, let us recall the words of Galen: "it is impossible for anything to be assimilated by, and to change into anything else unless they already possess a certain *community and affinity* in their qualities" (*De naturalis facultatibus*, I, 10).[44] This idea prevailed through all of the Middle Ages and was still commonly accepted at the beginning of the seventeenth century. For Jean Fabre (1588–1658), the physician and alchemist from Montpellier, for example, "If the food is in its beginning different from what it feeds, it must divest itself of this difference, and by divers alterations must make itself to be similar to what it feeds, before it can be its last food."[45] Consequently, the blood absorbed by Saint Catherine can be, paradoxically, neither excreted nor completely assimilated. Ultimately, the only possible assimilation works in reverse since it consists in converting the blood of the nourished into the blood of the nourisher. Christ, through His conforming power, and by his power of subjection, replaces, so to speak, the saint's vital fluid with His own blood.

And yet this was not all. In the Christian imagination, blood could equally well be designated as the substance through which God communicated the Spirit, the *spiritus* or *pneuma*, to people.[46] Therefore, to absorb it was possibly to establish an equivalence between the way in which God distinguished humans from among the animals and the means by which He infused the truth of the Redemption. Through the absorption of the blood of the Sacrifice, the tainted spirit, sullied by the Fall, could find a way to be reformed and purified.[47] Here, we remember that for Christians, before original sin, Adam was the only one among all creatures who was endowed with a perfect equilibrium of the four humors in his blood, and this was due the associative relationship between him and his Creator: *ad imaginem Dei*.[48]

In *Holy Feast and Holy Fast*, Caroline Walker Bynum demonstrates that these mystical experiences were a response, in the Middle Ages, to the saints' desire to drink in the Christ in order to espouse his model of humility and charity, that is, to adopt by this device a model for living.[49] For Saint Catherine of Siena, drinking the blood from Christ's wound was a way of identifying with the latter and of offering her own self in sacrifice. In the tales of her life, her constant dreams of consuming Christ's blood proceed with self-debasing absorption that is nothing less than sacrificial. According to Raymond of Capua, as Saint Catherine bestows her care upon a woman named Andrea who suffers from cancer, alongside traditional washing and bandaging the saint adopts extreme personal humility and consumes the pus flowing from the wound of the suffering woman in order to obtain, in recompense, Christ's intercession and the cure of the woman:

> "Long live the Highest, the sweet Bridegroom of my soul! This which you find so abhorrent, let it enter into your bowels!" And she collected up into a bowl the fetid stuff that had that had been used to wash the sore, along with all the pus, and, going away a little, gulped it all down.[50]

Now, as the hagiographer points out, it was this self-denial that made her worthy of the divine recompense of drinking Christ's blood a second time:

> These victories, then, having been graciously granted to his bride by the Heavenly Bridegroom, on the night following the last of them, while she was praying about them, the Lord and Saviour Jesus Christ appeared to her . . . and said to her: "Beloved, many battles you have fought for the love of me . . . annihilating your bodily nature with the ardour of my charity, you cheerfully drank that abhorrent drink. I therefore say to you that since with that act you transcended your own nature I will give you a drink that transcends every human nature and expectation." And putting his right hand on her virginal neck and drawing her towards the wound in His own side, He whispered to her, "Drink, daughter, the liquid from my side, and it will fill your soul with such sweetness that its wonderful effects will be felt even by the body which for my sake you despised.[51]

It is precisely this relation of causality, with the sacrifice giving rise to a reward, that we see in Francesco Vanni's depiction of this episode in the illustrated life of Saint Catherine, *Vita, mors, gesta et miracula . . . B. Catharinae Senensis*, as engraved by Pieter de Jode in 1597 (fig. 2.7).[52] The artist intentionally places the two beatitudes one above the other, and after having mastered her disgust and having put her mouth to the wound of the woman suffering from cancer (lower part), the saint receives the supreme privilege of being able to place her lips on the "cup" of Christ, drawing the saving nectar directly from the costal stigmata (upper part).

Ideally, this experience aimed at a literal incorporation of Jesus's suffering, leading eventually to a total identification with him. In gathering the Redeemer into the innermost part of one's being by physically taking him into her body, Saint Catherine was giving fleshly form to her obsessional desire for mystical fusion.[53] Ingestion, therefore, appears as the physical operator of an experience that was nonetheless a spiritual one.

These images of the flow and consumption of the purifying blood are certainly very striking, but we would be wrong to see them as isolated cases, as if they were merely a few islands of strangeness in the course of art history. In truth, they belong alongside many other depictions of Christ's blood as a medium for the transmission of Grace. To see this, we need only turn to the iconograph of the mystic wine press, where Christ, pressed like newly harvested grapes, offers His blood to mankind to make of it the Eucharistic wine.[54] Consider also the depiction of Christ as the *fons vitae* in this woodcut (fig. 2.8), published by Georgette de Montenay in *Emblemes, ou devises chrestiennes* (1571). Here, the blood flowing from Christ's wounds feeds a fountain out of which people of all ages, those in good health as well as the sick, come to draw some of the purifying liquid. In this latter scene, Christ occupies the place taken by the statues that typically stand above the basins of Renaissance fountains (e.g., the personifications of the virtues in Nuremberg's *Tugendbrunnen*[55]), and in such a way that it is hard to tell if we are looking at a sculpture of Christ, and thus an *image*, or

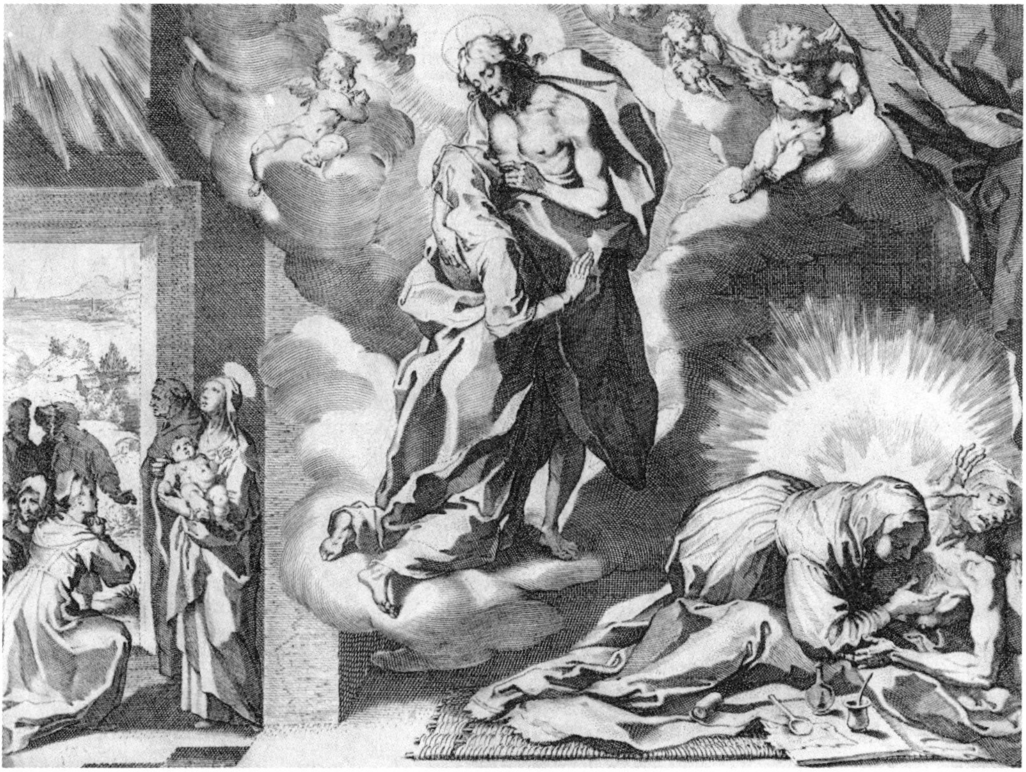

Figure 2.7. Pieter de Jode I after Francesco Vanni, *Vita, mors, gesta et miracula quaedam selecta B. Catherinae Senensis*, 1597, engraving on paper, 9.9 × 11.2 in. London, British Museum (© The Trustees of the British Museum).

EMBLE'ME CHRESTIEN 3

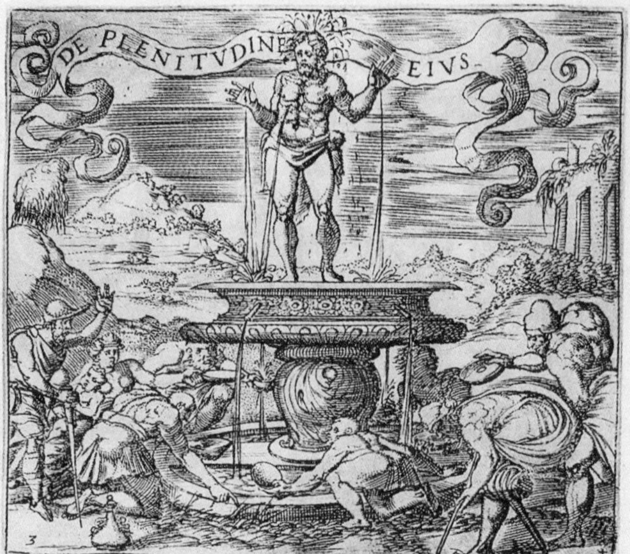

Pource que tant eſlongnés de Dieu ſommes,
Qu'impoßible eſt à nous de l'aprocher,
Naiſtre il a fait ſon fils ſemblable aux hommes,
Fors qu'il eſt net, & exempt de pecher.
Qui ſe veut donc de peché depeſcher,
Et de Satan fuir la ſeruitude,
S'en vienne à Chriſt pour ſa ſoif eſtancher:
Car nous puiſons tous de ſa plenitude.

Le

Figure 2.8. Pierre Woeiriot de Bouzey, *De Plenitudine Eius*, engraving in Georgette de Montenay, *Emblemes, ou devises chrestiennes* (Lyon: Jean Marcorelle, 1571), 3r. (Creative Commons).

if it is actually Christ himself miraculously appearing before people. The slight turn along the vertical axis in the figure of Christ in relation to the pedestal, and the forward positioning of the right foot indicating the beginning of a movement, might suggest that this is a statue of Christ in the process of becoming animate. This ambivalence, that may be only fortuitous, invites us, in a timely fashion, to repeat the question that we asked at the beginning of this investigation: Can an image be drunk, consumed, or ingested? To answer this question, let us move on to other imaginings.

The Image as Nursing Mother

In the mystical experiences that we have just considered, the saving substance does not flow directly out from an image; however certain hagiographical accounts do place images at the origin of miraculous manifestations, singling them out as vectors of the transmission of grace.[56] The Dominican Gregorio Lombardelli writes, for example, that Saint Alda of Siena (1245–1309), overcome with the desire to taste the blood of Christ's wound, saw one day several drops of blood running from the Crucifix before which she was praying.[57] She rushed, therefore, to put her lips to it, consuming the liquid dripping from the piece of sculpture, entirely forgetting that this was an image. In memory of this work of grace, she had painted a *Pietà* in which the Virgin, in a sort of inversion of the typical iconography of the *Virgo lactans*, is depicted as drinking from Christ's wound.[58] In similar fashion, in his *Vita piae Liutgardis* (1248), Thomas of Cantimpré refers to a miracle that happened to the Benedictine nun Lutgardis of Tongres (1182–1246). In prayer before a sculpted figure of Christ, Lutgardis saw blood running from the wound. She stepped towards the object, and, as in the previous case, she drank the few drops falling from the depicted wound.[59] In both of these miracle accounts, the man-made, artificial image is the vehicle of a supernatural manifestation, and, in each account, the encounter with the divine takes place through the ingestion of an image that has come to life.

From the fifteenth century, ingesting the sacred through the medium of an image (i.e., painted or sculpted altarpieces, icons, statues, etc.) was to become an increasingly common practice. The "spiritual" incorporation of a saintly entity, appearing in the form of a heavenly figure floating in air or on a cloud, was to recede somewhat before a more material absorption of substances emanating from painted or sculpted figures, which inspired the faithful to understand ingestion as a route towards a relation with the divine. Certain representations, for example, specifically highlight the flow of blood from images of Christ. An example of this is the bas-relief, *The Mass of Saint Gregory*, in the church of San Gregorio Magno al Celio in Rome and sculpted by Luigi Capponi at the end of the fifteenth century (fig. 2.9). To see this fully, let us recall that according to legend, the miracle of the Mass of Saint Gregory (540–604) followed the disbelief of certain officants concerning the real presence of Christ's body in the Eucharistic bread and wine. One day, as the pope was celebrating mass in the Basilica of the Holy Cross in Jerusalem in Rome, Christ presented Himself on the altar table, making his blood flow into the chalice and placing his foot on the corporal cloth.[60] Indeed, this is exactly what we see represented in the bas-relief in San Gregorio al Celio. To indicate the miracle of transubstantiation, the sculptor has shown an image of Christ issuing forth from the plane of the altar painting, where He pours His blood directly into the chalice placed upon the altar's *mensa*.[61] The material image is thus the tangible means through which Christ made Himself present.

Even clearer than the Mass of Saint Gregory, it was the miraculous lactation of Saint Bernard that supplies the clearest example of the transmission of divine wisdom through the absorption of a liquid issuing from an image.[62] According to the tradition, Bernard of Clairvaux was rewarded for his devotion to the Virgin by a miracle: as shown in a representation of the Madonna and Child in the Church of Saint-Vorles de Châtillon-sur-Seine, as he was praying at the foot of the Virgin, she springs to life, projecting three drops of

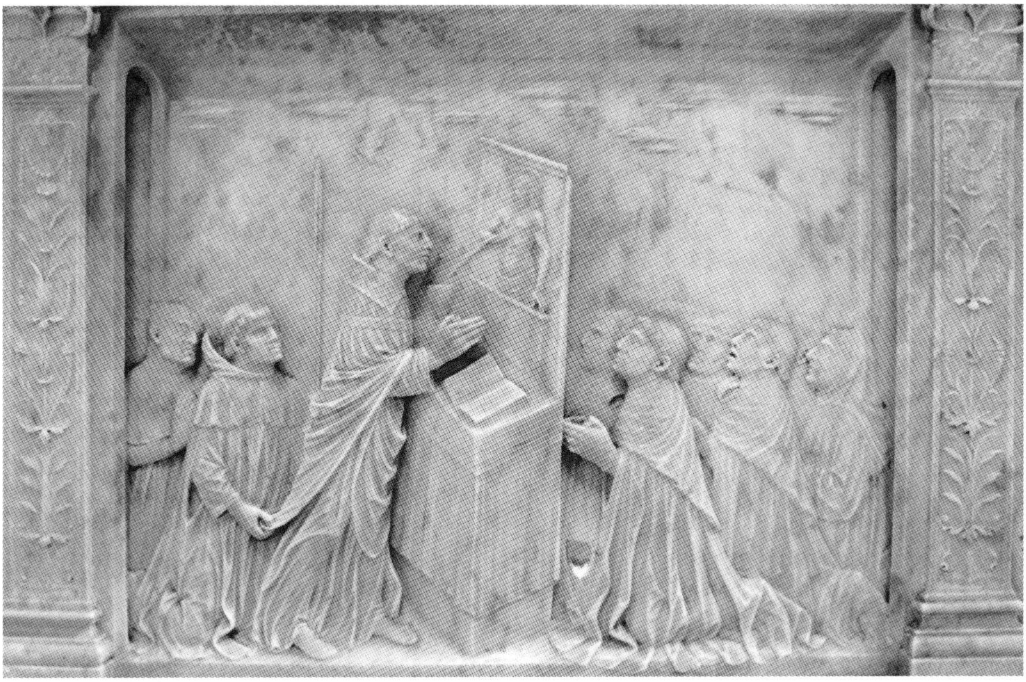

Figure 2.9. Luigi Capponi, *Saint Gregory's Mass*, ca. 1500, stone bas-relief. Rome, San Gregorio al Celio (Creative Commons).

milk into his mouth.[63] As Victor I. Stoichita shows, in his fine work on the visionary experience in the painting of Spain's Golden Age, this episode was to become one of the most popular features in the thirteenth- to the eithteenth-century representations of Saint Bernard's life. However, the miracle is, quite unexpectedly, absent from the canonical works on his life, and it was quite possibly a medieval iconographic invention, deriving from his ninth sermon on the *Song of Songs*:[64]

> Men with an urge to frequent prayer will have experience of what I say. Often enough when we approach the altar to pray our hearts are dry and lukewarm. But if we persevere, there comes an unexpected infusion of grace, our breast expands as it were, and our interior is filled with an overflowing love; and if somebody should press upon it then, this milk of sweet fecundity would gush forth in streaming richness. Let us hear the Bridegroom: "You have received my love, what you asked for, and here is a sign to show you, your breasts are better than wine; henceforth you will know that have received the kiss because you will be conscious of having conceived. That explains the expansion of your breasts, filled with a milky richness far surpassing the the wine of the worldly knowledge that can intoxicate indeed but with curiosity, not charity; it fills but does not nourish; puffs up but does not build up; pampers but does not strengthen.[65]

In fact, two centuries were to pass after the saint's death before an account of the lactation was actually consigned to writing. The first written reference is an episcopal letter of indulgence dated October 4, 1340, in which the author of the report preceding the notorized act clearly emphasizes the role of the image in the transmission of the divine *virtus*:

> In the Church of Saint-Vorles du château de Châtillon-sur-Seine, in the diocese of Langres, there stands, since time immemorial, an image made in reverence and honor of the Blessed Virgin Mary, who, as it is reported more fully in the life of Saint Bernard, miraculously offered her Son to him in this church, saying: "Bernard, receive my Son, the Redeemer of the World," and, among other things, instructed him in the Catholic faith, miraculously

> speaking to him, making him see divinely the entire Passion of Christ, and then, going beyond all human power, as if this were the natural mother of Christ, *the image took its hand to its breast and brought forth from it instantly and miraculously three drops of milk, flowing from the breast of the said image into the open mouth of its faithful saint, Bernard.* Having received these drops from the very breast of the said image, and having become the orator of Mary, Mother of god, the professor of Christ, His Son, the faithful confessor of God's Army, and the chaste lover of Mary, he composed several works of praise to the King of Heaven.[66]

In the earliest depictions of this episode, the apparition of the Virgin is generally too insufficiently defined for us to be sure how exactly she shows herself miraculously. Therfore, it is difficult to tell if it is by heavenly agency or simply through the image. In the very first known depiction, the San Bernardo altarpiece in Palma de Mallorca (ca. 1285–1290), there is, iconographically, no indication that the Virgin is a statue. She suckles Bernard from a distance, standing on a level ground with him. It is only, perhaps, the two candles held by the angels framing Mary and Jesus that potentially suggest the furnishings of an altar, which might allow us to see the Virgin here as an image. In similar fashion, in many of the Flemish illuminated manuscripts and paintings (fig. 2.10), the Virgin appears as a fully alive *Virgo lactans*, nursing Saint Bernard from her throne, and there is no indication whatsoever that this "Mother of God" is a statue or a painting. We must wait until the second half of the fifteenth century and, significantly, the sixteenth and seventeenth centuries to see artists connect this divine manifestation with an artifact. This approach is notably present in an altarpiece painted by the Master from Canapost (ca. 1450–1500) in the Girona Art Museum in which the Virgin is clearly shown upon an altar, appearing as a three-dimensional sculpture framed by two columns;[67] and in an illustration by Jacob Neeffs from the middle of the seventeenth century (fig. 2.11), where Mary appears as a statue on a pedestal; and again in an engraving from 1620 by the Flemish artist Raphael

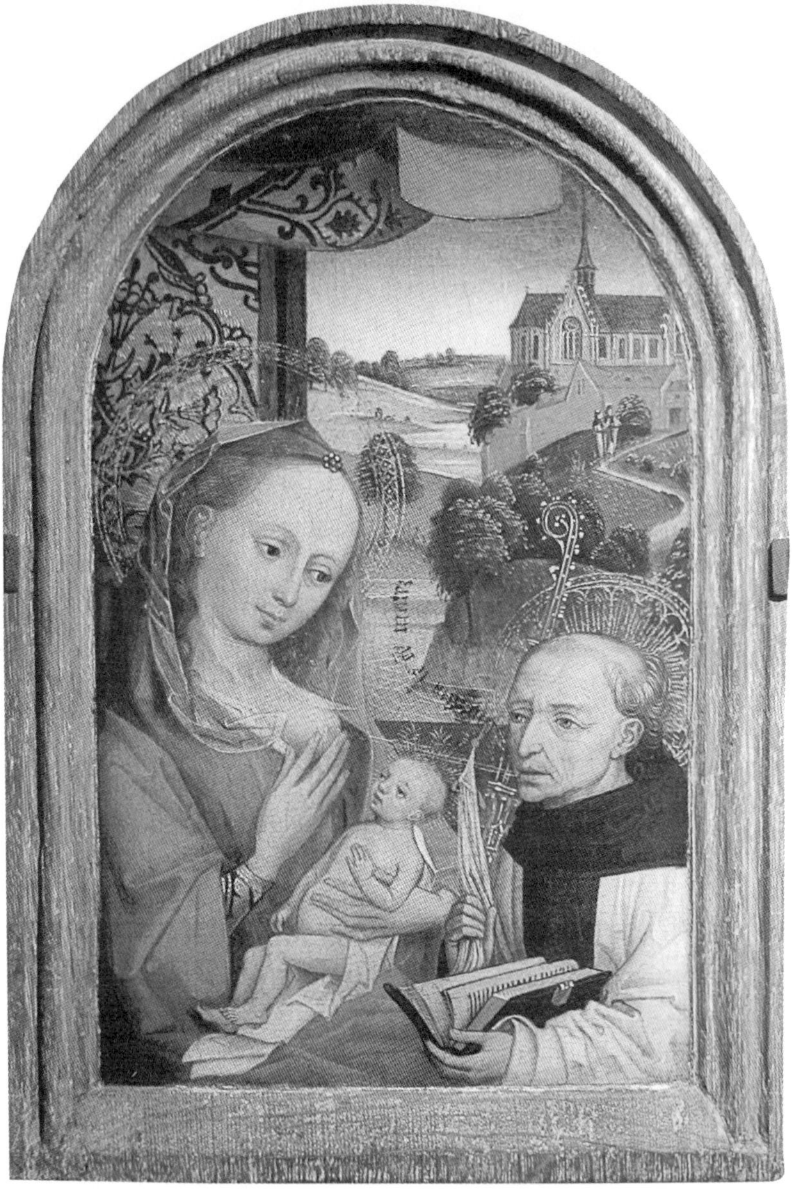

Figure 2.10. Flemish School, *The Lactation of Saint Bernard*, ca. 1480, oil on panel, 15.3 × 10.2 in. Liège, Curtius Museum (Creative Commons).

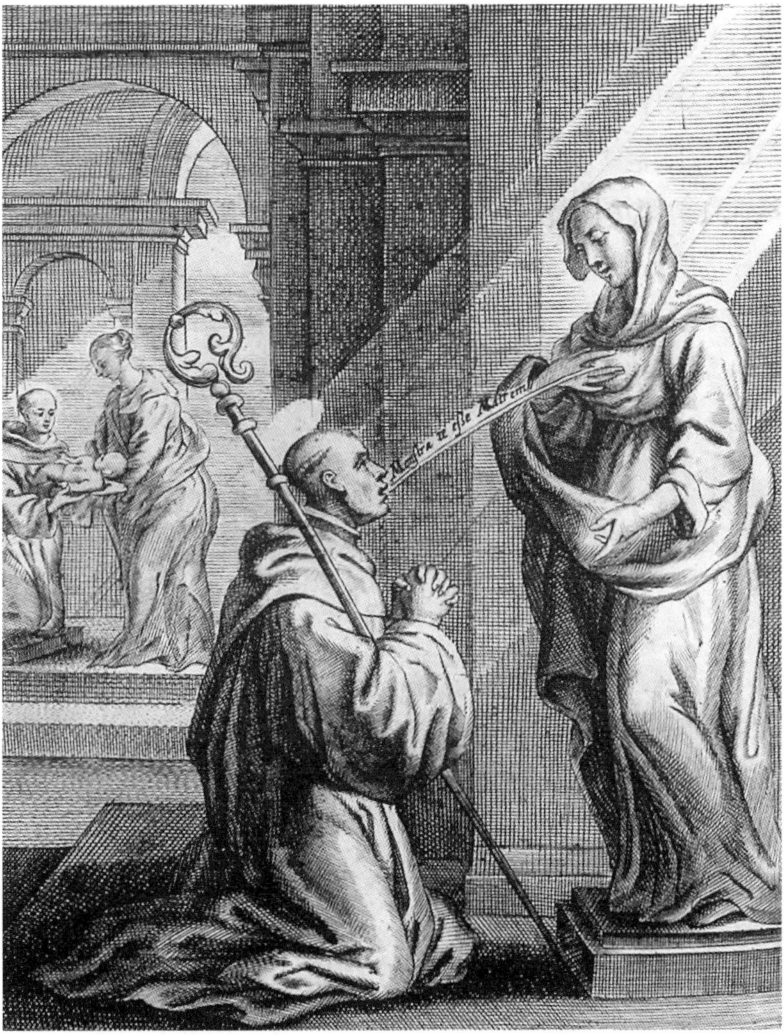

Figure 2.11. Jacob Neefs, *The Lactation of Saint Bernard*, engraving in *Sancti Bernardi Melliflui Doctoris Ecclesiæ, Pulcherrima & Exemplaris Vitæ Medulla*... (Antwerp: Apud Guilielmum Lestcenium & Engelbertum Gymnicum, 1653), p. 193, The Monks of Baudeloo (Boudelo) Abbey (Creative Commons).

Sadeler (fig. 2.12) showing, this time, a mural painting placed above an altar that comes to life and suckles Saint Bernard. It is, however, in the work of another artist, Alonso Cano in 1650, that we see the most obvious and powerful depiction of the absorption of a liquid emanating from an artificial image of the Virgin (fig. 2.13). The Spanish painter has, in fact, traced in detail the ingestion-mediated continuity between the heavenly and earthly worlds. Within the painting, the statue of Mary placed above the altar comes to life and feeds the saint's mouth with its milk. To mark this miraculous transformation of the sculpture into a living figure, suckling at a distance, the artist is careful to underline the traces of the artificiality of the figure through which the divine prototype shows itself: The reduction in size indicates the break with reality in terms of scale; the presence of a sculpted plinth come replete with the heads of cherubims; the figure is placed with its back to the chapel wall; and there is also the presence of a veil similar to those used to cover up the sculptures at certain times in the liturgical year. All these visual maneuvers designate the Virgin as a *representation* placed above the altar, a liturgical *object*. By stressing this materiality, the painter amplifies the miraculous dimension of the manifestation, and it is against a backdrop of immobility that the Virgin takes on life and projects her milk towards the saint. What Bernard drinks and absorbs, therefore, is certainly a miraculous image.

We should note in passing that, particularly popular among Catholics at the time of the Counter-Reformation, this iconography prefigures certain sculpted depictions of the Madonna and Child during the Baroque period. These representations were sometimes supplied with a hydraulic device allowing for the pouring of milk or water and intended to simulate, likely for purposes of religious instruction, a miraculous lactation promised to the pious.[68] Such systems were specifically designed to sate the thirst of the faithful, as we can see from this Madonna and Child from Saint Margarethen near Grieskirchen in Upper Austria (fig. 2.14). Here, the tube is set within the breast, and, rather than being pointed towards the

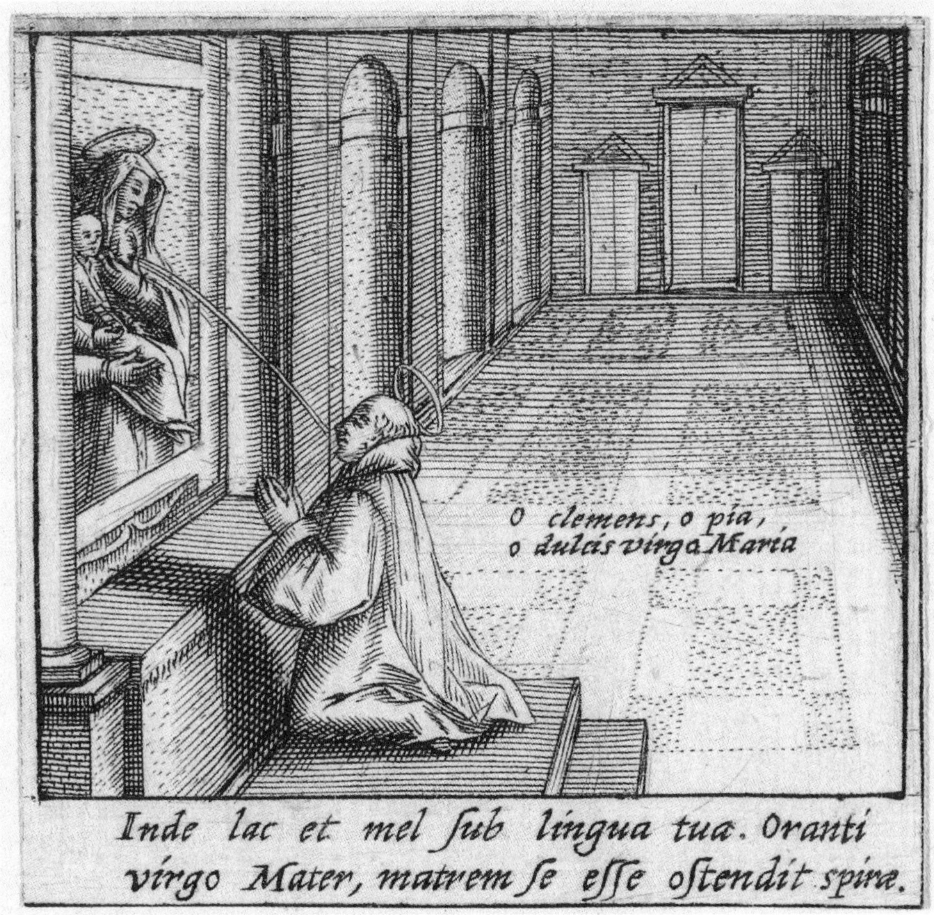

Figure 2.12. Raphael Sadeler, *The Lactation of Saint Bernard*, 1605–1628, engraving, 2 × 2 in. Amsterdam, Rijksmuseum (© Rijksmuseum, Amsterdam).

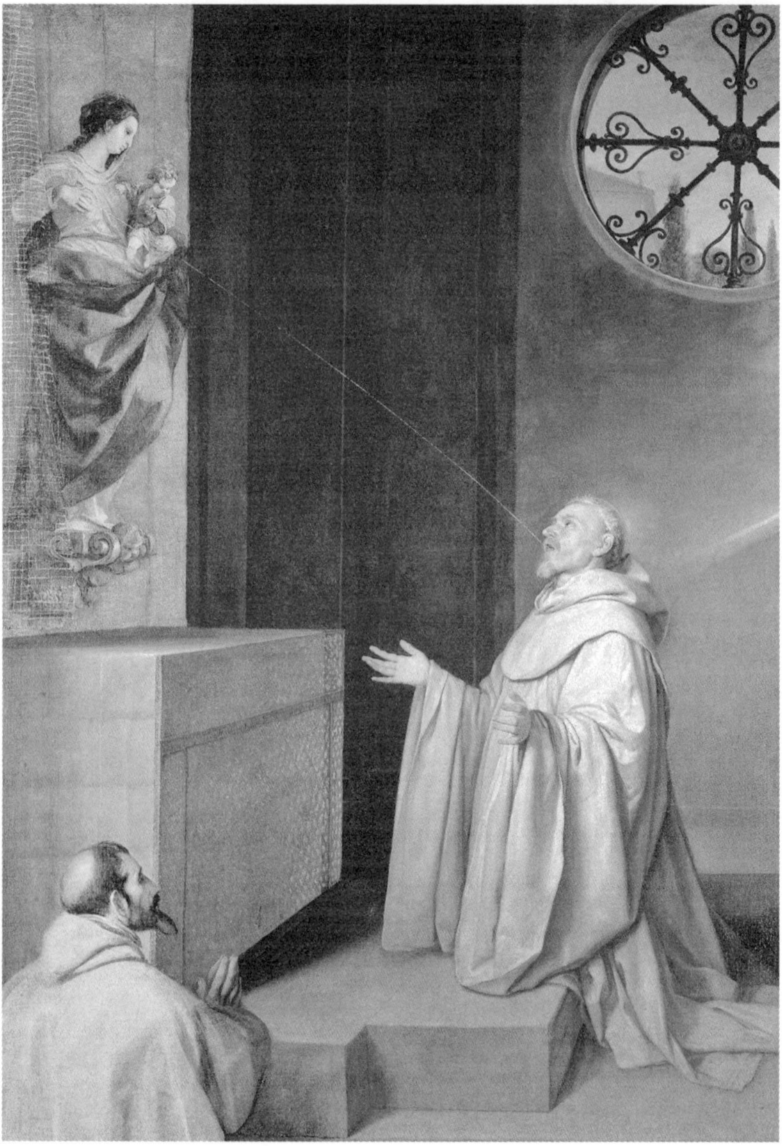

Figure 2.13. Alonso Cano, *The Lactation of Saint Bernard*, 1650, oil on canvas, 105 × 72.8 in. (Inv. P003134). Madrid, Museo Nacional del Prado (© Photographic Archive Museo Nacional del Prado).

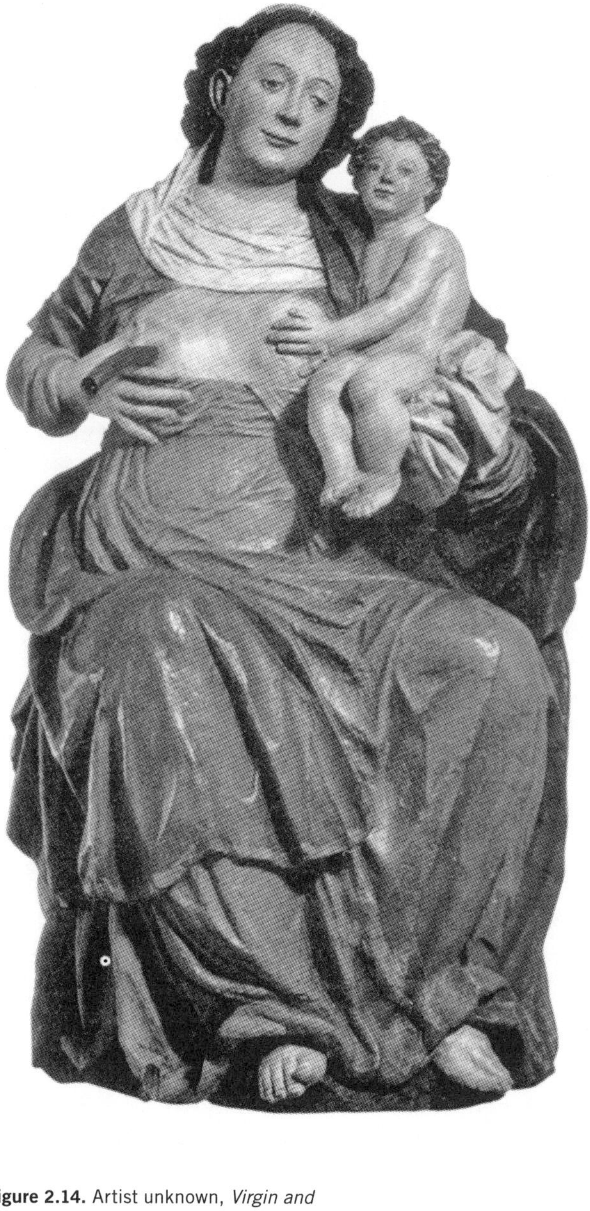

Figure 2.14. Artist unknown, *Virgin and Child with tube protruding from the Virgin's breast*, eighteenth century, polychrome wood. Grieskirchen, Margarethen.

infant Christ, it points in the opposite direction towards a potential drinker.[69] Few artifacts embody, as literally as this one, the idea that images are endowed with nutritive power.

Returning to the work by Cano, we should remind ourselves that, beyond the striking character of its figurative creation, there was, behind this iconographic choice, not only the desire to defend the role of images in the instruction of the faithful at a time when Protestants were refusing to grant them any mediating function,[70] but also the desire to show in visual form the analogy between nutrition and innutrition, between physical nourishment and the transmission of knowledge.[71] By virtue of their common etymology, the Latin and Latinate verbs *sapere/savoir/saber* and *assaparare/savourer/saborear* were in fact often deliberately conflated by the theologians, the Latin *sapere* meaning at once "to sense, have a taste of" and "to know or understand."[72] Thus, to *savor* the milk coming from the image of the Virgin in order to nourish oneself and to savor this same milk penetrated by divine wisdom were one and the same operation. By taking the divine nutriment into his mouth, Bernard ingests God's knowledge or mysterious *Sapienza*, the very same knowledge that was to allow the saint to bring, with wisdom and eloquence, the divine Word into his writings.[73]

Ruminatio

Eating the Book

The idea that knowledge could be carried by a substance and ingested was not a uniquely Christian invention. Representations of the practice are part of a very old tradition going back to Antiquity. Taking into the body a material substance that emanated from an image in order to attain knowledge was something that derived, in fact, from the shared imagination of most of the written cultures of the Mediterranean for whom the ingestion of *text* was understood as one of the ways in which divine wisdom could be communicated to men.

From ancient Egypt, in the first tale of Setne Khamwas at the Cairo Museum (CGC 30646), we have an account involving the absorption of magical knowledge by ingesting papyrus. This text, which has been known since the third century BCE, tells how the magician Naneferkaptah, after having stolen the book of knowledge from the god Thoth, demonstrates to his sister that to capture its power, she has only to write down each word present on Thoth's papyrus, to dissolve them in beer, and then to drink the solution thus obtained.[74] More generally, in ancient Egypt, ingestion represented the appropriation of knowledge and the assumption of power, and we can see this in the use of the verb *to swallow* in certain of the Egyptian myths. The Cannibal Hymn from the Pyramid Texts (504) declares that for the king to enter into contact with the gods and to take advantage of their vital power, he must "swallow their spirit" and "eat their magic." This understanding of ingestion as a form of acquiring knowledge led the priests, for example, to use the ingestion of images of the gods as a means of initiating men into their mysteries.[75]

In like manner, in all the religions of the Book (Judaism, Christianity, and Islam), ingesting text translated this possible transmission of knowledge from the heavenly to the earthly world.[76] To take into oneself, to ingest and digest writing, was essentially to encounter and to know the divine. In the *Nevi'im* (Books of the Prophets), the story of the eating of a scroll that appears in Ezekiel 2:8–10 and 3:1–3 offers us the standard model:[77]

> But you, man, must listen to what I say and not be rebellious like them. Open your mouth and eat what I give you. Then I saw a hand stretched out to me, holding a scroll, He unrolled it before me, and it was written all over on both sides with dirges and laments and words of woe. Then he said to me, "Man, eat what is in front of you, eat this scroll; then go and speak to the Israelites." So I opened my mouth and he gave me the scroll to eat. Then he said, "Man, swallow this scroll I give you, and fill yourself full." So I ate it, and it tasted as sweet as honey. "Man," he said to me, "go and tell the Israelites what I have to say to them."

This biblical passage was often accompanied by illustrations, notably in the ornamental letters or versals that mark the beginnings of the sections in the illuminated manuscripts of the Christian Middle Ages. Two bibles from the second half of the twelfth century, one in the Bibliothèque nationale de France (Ms. Lat. 16744; fig. 2.15) and the other in Lambeth Palace (Ms. 3; fig. 2.16), offer interesting versions of this scene in their versals.[78] In each of them, the prophet Ezekiel is shown opening wide his mouth in order to consume the scroll held out to him by God. The BnF version shows a book and an unfurled phylactery scroll, and we can read this inscription on the scroll: "*Comede volume istud, et vadens loquere [ad filios Israël].*" The text here corresponds to the words "eat this scroll" and "go and tell the Israëlites" in the biblical passage. This logophagy, signifying the incorporation of the divine spirit through the consumption of the word,[79] is doubled in the Lambeth Palace illumination (fig. 2.16) by a second scene in the story. In the right-hand section of the letter E versal, we see Ezekiel again, and this time, he is holding in his left hand a pot of ink, and in his right hand, a reed pen.[80] Now, all this might well give the impression that the minituarist has deliberately placed the pot on a level with Ezekiel's stomach in order to indicate that the ingested divine word, incorporated through the mouth and lodged in his belly, might henceforth reemerge from his entrails in this other liquid form so as to be communicated to men through writing. Indeed, on the page of the codex, writing is precisely what we see facing the instrument held by Ezekiel: "*(E)t factum est in trigesimo* (In the thirtieth year)" (Ezekiel 1:1).

As André Neher writes, the choice of oral transmission for the Law was probably the result of a desire to emphasize the objectivitiy of the given word. In contrast to the *ruah* (the spirit or the wind), "the *davar* . . . gives itself without ambiguity, without bivalence. It is the objective *spoken word*, that has encapsulated the revelation without letting anything escape it. The objectivity of the *spoken word* becomes manifest in its opposition to vision . . . . [V]ision is part of the domain of the *ruah*; it is obscure; it must be deciphered . . . . For *absolute authenticity* to be added to *knowledge*, the *ruah* must be

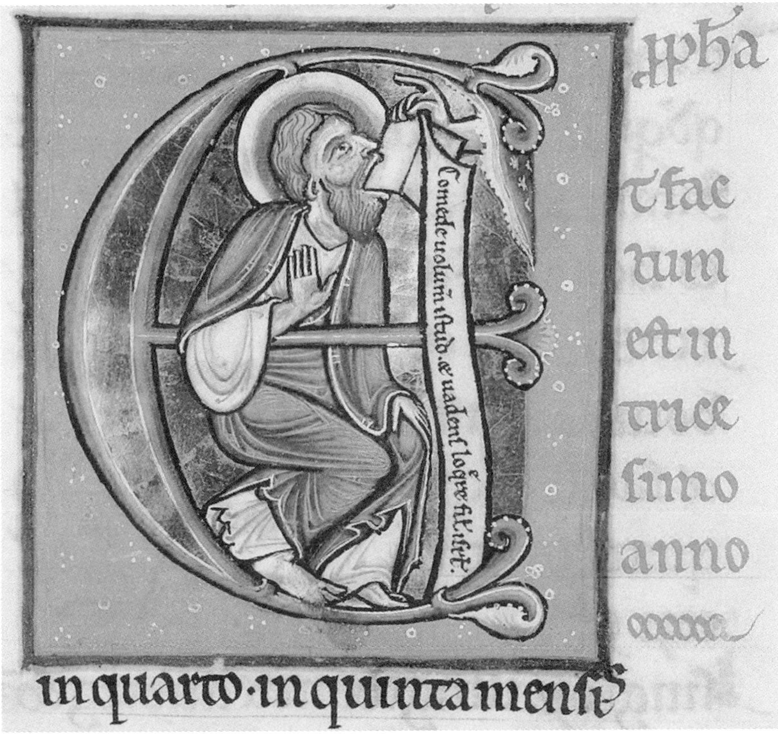

Figure 2.15. Latin Bible, illuminated initial with Ezekiel eating the Book, 1150–1200, Manuscript Ms. Lat. 16744, fol. 81r. Paris, Bibliothèque nationale de France (© Bibliothèque nationale de France).

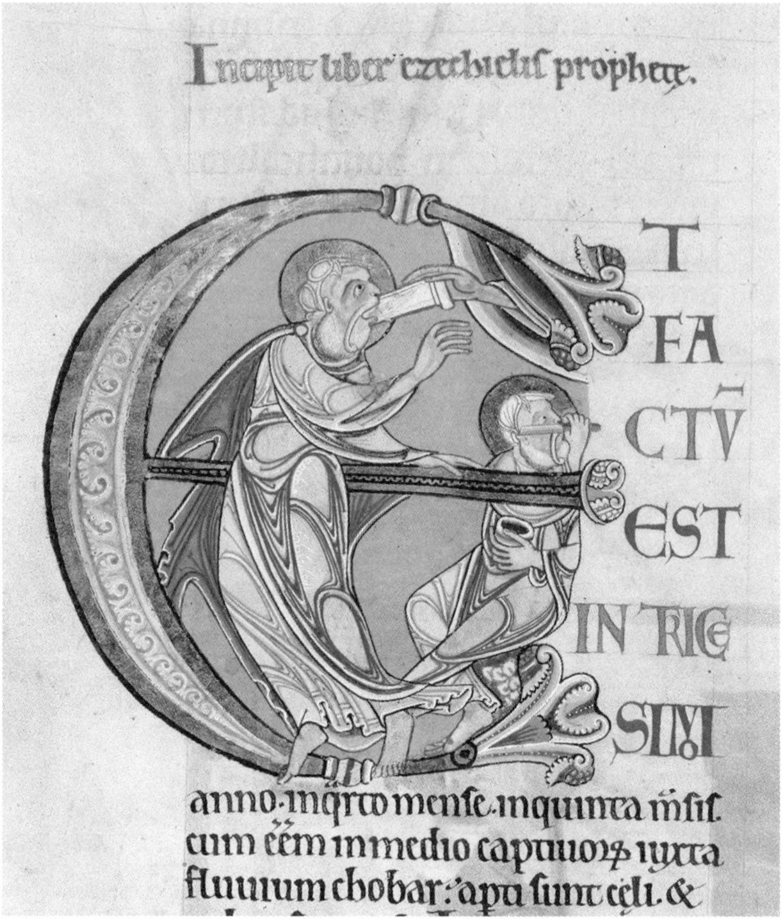

Figure 2.16. Illuminated initial E illustrating the Book of Ezekiel in the *Lambeth Bible*, ca. 1146, Ms. 3, fol. 258v. London, Lambeth Palace Library (© Lambeth Palace Library, London/Bridgeman Images).

crystalized into the *davar*."[81] These hermeneutical subtleties allow us to grasp the meaning and destiny of the eaten book, beyond its visual power as an image. Ingesting a book, more than a visual epiphany of God, inscribes the revelation into the natural world of men, thus making the body subject to the Word. Truth is not always distant and mysterious; it is transmitted in a much more concrete fashion, and through that, it becomes indisputable. It was in this way that this biblical passage was to be seized upon by a certain Christian reformist tradition. The Protestant reformer, John Calvin, for example, was to interpret Ezekiel 3:1–3 in such a way as to make the expression "eat what is in front of you" the sign of the faithful believer's submission to God:

> When the Prophet is ordered to eat all that he receives, this ought not to be extended to everything which he meets with, but, whatever may be the taste of the book, he is forbidden to refuse it: for its bitterness might possibly cause him to reject the threats of God. Lastly, the quality of the book is noted, because it contained nothing but the material for sorrow. He adds, *that he opened his mouth*, for the sake of obedience; by which he signifies that he was not curious or dainty in seeking to taste it, but that he took what was divinely offered to him, without the slightest hesitation.[82]

God is ineffable, impenetrable, but the transmission of his revealed Word is not open to discussion.

As is well known, the narrative sequence in the book of Ezekiel appeared later, in almost identical form, in the Apocalypse of Saint John (Rev. 10), and through this, it was to influence Christian culture yet more deeply.[83] There are only a few differences between the passage in the New Testament and the earlier, Old Testament model. The later version introduces an angel as God's intermediary, and it expands on the effect produced by the ingestion:

> Then the voice that I had heard from heaven spoke to me once more: "Go, take the scroll that lies open in the hand of the angel who is standing on the sea and on the land." So I went to the angel and asked him to give me

> the little scroll. He said to me, "Take it and eat it. It will turn your stomach sour, but 'in your mouth it will be as sweet as honey.'" I took the little scroll from the angel's hand and ate it. It tasted as sweet as honey in my mouth, but when I had eaten it, my stomach turned sour.

The scroll, which had been only honey-tasting in Ezekiel, is here at once sweet in John's mouth and bitter in his stomach. As Tania van Hemelryck has suggested, the addition of bitterness here certainly "refers to the ambivalent nature, both exalting and constricting, of the actions implied by the divine verbal injunction."[84] But, reading Calvin's interpretation of this biblical motif, we might also add that this transformation in the taste is yet another way of saying that people must submit to the divine plan, however harsh or bitter the revelation might be.

As with the vision of Ezekiel, the scene from the Book of Revelation gave rise to numerous artistic depictions, and we should note among these a striking engraving by Albrecht Dürer (fig. 2.17), where we see John taking fierce hold of the book that the angel hands to him, then opening wide his mouth to bite it.[85] The latter figurative feature shows us that Dürer was perfectly aware of the biblical text and the theological stakes at play in it. In a study devoted to the metaphor of the chewed book, Massimo Leone points to the semantic richness of the accounts in Ezekiel and Saint John, noting that the terms used to designate the ingestion of the book, *'akal* (□□□) in Hebrew in the Torah and *katephagon* (κατέφαγον) in Greek in the New Testament, are in fact closer to the French *dévorer* ("to devour") than they are to *manger* ("to eat"). They both carry within them the idea of an active ingestion, fully involving teeth and mastication.[86] John does not want only to taste the Word of God with the tip of his tongue; he wants to chew it with fervor. The decision to depict Saint John as a man experiencing great hunger, as a devourer of God's words, is in no way accidental. It places the viewer squarely within a metaphorical interpretation of the gesture that many medieval and modern texts attempted to lay out.

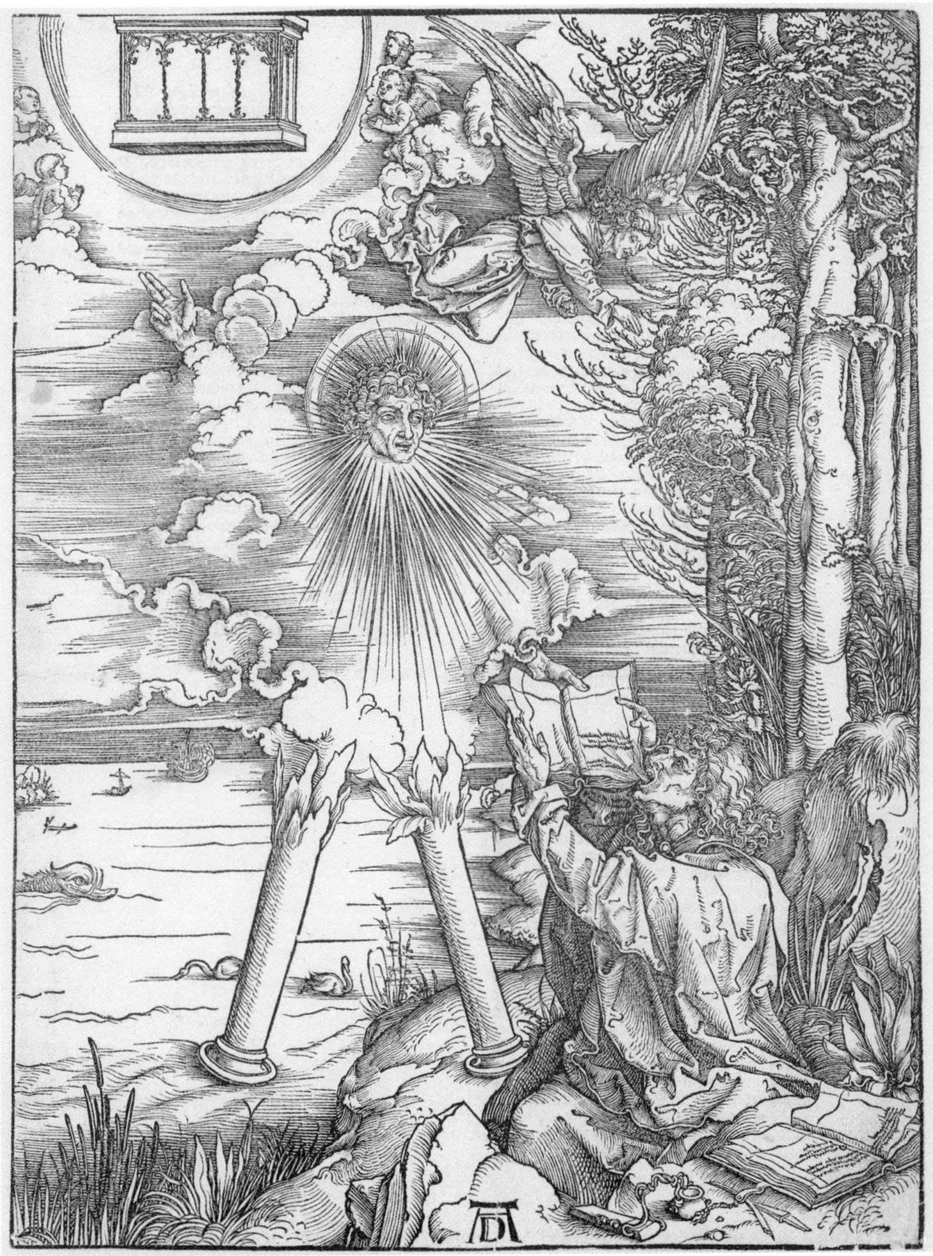

Figure 2.17. Albrecht Dürer, *Saint John Devouring the Book*, 1497–1498, woodcut, 15.3 × 11 in. London, British Museum (© The Trustees of the British Museum).

The *Opus imperfectum in Matthaeum*, a commentary of the Gospel of Saint Matthew that was for a long time attributed to the early Church Father, John Chrysostom, and that was often drawn upon by the theologians of Middle Ages, includes a particularly detailed explanation for this logophagic urge:

> For speech has many properties in common with food. For just as he who puts a piece of bread or whatever kind of food into his mouth first softens it with his teeth and sends it down to his stomach, so also when we hear every word, we must meditate in the mouth of thought and soften it by handling it as by teeth and see what it is that it is saying or why he says it or for what sake he says it. For just as we do not perceive a food's flavor, whatever the food may be, unless we chew it with the teeth, so also we cannot understand the power of that word.... And just as after we chew the food, we send it down to the stomach, so also after we have mulled over the Word well, we entrust it to our memory as if to our stomach. For just as food cannot benefit us unless it is chewed and goes down to the stomach, so the Word cannot benefit us for salvation unless it has been handed over to the intellect and memory. Just as food does us no good if we eat it and then spew it from the stomach, so the word that we hear and forget immediately does not help us. The food that stays in the stomach comforts it and the speech that remains in memory saves.[87]

To chew the divine Word, in the form of text or oral discourse, so as to receive it within oneself thus constituted an effective metaphor for illustrating the necessarily progressive assimiliation of the meaning of Scripture. For it was never believed to be sufficient to read or hear only once the words of God. In order to make the words fully one's own, one had to savor them, bite them, grind them repeatedly. In 1297, in his *Lectura super Apocalypsim*, the Franciscan theologian Pierre de Jean Olieu took hold of this idea, condensing its elements into this remarkably succinct statement:

> Consider the fact that God does not say "read" but *devour*, and He does not say "look" but *take*. He does so because He wants the spiritual and intellectual to be chewed, savored, and transmitted within us through a taste and attachment that is both very fervent and sapid.[88]

Through ingestion and the progressive transformation of solids into liquids, therefore, the truth of Scripture was believed to find its way to total absorption.[89]

Moreover, it was essentially on this basis that the practice of monastic reading was instituted. As Hugh of Saint Victor points out, following the twelfth-century theologians Bernard of Clairvaux, Alan of Lille, and Peter Cellensis, to gain access to the quintessence of the text, one had to absorb it, chew it, and ruminate on it so that it might penetrate into the innermost depths of one's being:[90]

> Just as we receive food though our mouth, it is through the power of intelligence that we receive the food of holy reading. And . . . just as we chew food with our teeth, it is through the practice of meditation that we are able to taste the subtleties of the life-giving bread of reading. [91]

Ingesting the book brings about a metamorphosis, the transformation of what is commonly understood into what is intensely personal. It involves, therefore, a passage from externality to interiority, and this is precisely what is at issue in the act of knowledge. As Charles Taylor writes in *Sources of the Self*: "In contrast to the domain of objects, which is public and common, the activity of knowing is particularized; each of us is engaged in ours. To look towards this activity is to look to the self, to take up a reflexive stance."[92]

A Word in Your Mouth

It is certainly worth emphasizing that the idea of followers being able to encounter knowledge by ingesting the written word, and thus through a "mechanics of taste," was not something unique to the history of religions.[93] The notion was also omnipresent in the early modern period in the minds of physicians, alchemists, and other philosophers of nature. Incorporation was, in fact, the paradigm par excellence for thinking about the acquisition of knowledge about the natural world.[94] In the thirteenth century, the surgeon Henri de Mondeville used the model of the ingestion of food to conceptualize the transmission and incorporation of knowledge:

> It is as if we are wet-nurses giving babies our milk and teaching them to accept and to swallow solid food. We first chew it for them and then offer some of it for them to swallow. So it is that we men of our Art (i.e., surgeons) and physicians must not only chew the science for illiterate students, but we must process it like cud, twice or more times to render it swallowable.[95]

This continuity between "scientific" learning and the way in which theology imagined the ground-up and eaten word did not depend solely on the figural felicity of the trope. It rested just as much upon foundations that were thoroughly concrete. In fact, we can connect it with the emergence, since Antiquity, of pedagogical practices that prescribed recourse to edible letters for the purposes of teaching students to read. We find in the Talmudic tradition, for example, evidence of the initiation to reading by means of ingesting writing. Gérard Haddad gives this example:

> His elders get this child to eat the first egg laid by a hen, an egg on which the teacher writes a formula mentioning the Name. . . . In certain communities, the first reading lesson is on a tablet containing certain letters written down and then covered in honey. For the first lesson, the young pupil needn't decipher the inscriptions but simply lick the honey until the writing's erased—which is to say, swallowed, incorporated.[96]

Evidence for this very material mode of instruction exists also in Classical Latin culture. In the first book of his *Satires*, Horace explains that "coaxing teachers sometimes give children little cakes, to give them the incentive to learn the basic rudiments."[97] Erasmus, in the sixteenth century, extolled similar recipes for making children find some enjoyment in learning: "Teachers of antiquity . . . would bake cookies of the sort that children like into the shape of letters, so that their pupils might, so to speak, hungrily eat their letters; for any student who could correctly identify a letter would be rewarded with it."[98] Children were thus able to memorize words by incorporating them *in figura*.

The same procedures were sometimes used with matters other

than words, such as, for example, with antiquarian culture in general. In 1792, the German archaeologist and teacher Karl August Böttiger reported on the fashion in Rome of giving children from wealthy families sugar cameos showing scenes from mythology or depicting historical figures so that they might absorb, by eating them, those treasures of classical history:

> It is doubtless a characteristic of our most current fine-living that we refine and spiritualize our sensual pleasures by bringing to them a touch of the love of art and science . . . . Proof of this can be seen in those *Classical Candy Boxes*, much in fashion today among those of good taste, and that take pride of place, at dessert, on the dinner tables of Roman high society. One sets out very carefully . . . paper carton boxes . . . filled with sugar pastilles . . . all of them sculpted from glass paste templates after the most beautiful intaglios . . . , and they offer, in such a way, all sorts of multi-colored, edible classical gems. One has before one, therefore, a complete little sugar gem box, in which one might find, for example, the Olympian Jupiter, a beautiful Strozzi Medusa, an Andromache in tears, a Ulysses, a Caesar, . . . a Homer, . . . or a Leda, offered to you to put on your plate before letting it melt on your tongue. It is, in fact, an amusing confection, very subtle and in fine taste, that lends itself to endless games of wit and good humor at dessert. What a joy for the soul! [Johann Bernhard] Basedow, who allowed children to make letters of the alphabet out of gingerbread dough that he then allowed them to eat, would not have been displeased with this invention for studying at dessert the art and mythology of the ancients.[99]

The use of these edible alphabets and these "sugar gem boxes" was, more often than not, treated with indulgence, but we should note that it was also sometimes the subject of mockery.[100] In the eighteenth century, in a hilarious passage in *Gulliver's Travels* (1726), Jonathan Swift described the bizarre school in Lagado where knowledge of mathematics was transmitted by the intermediary of wafers on which formulae were inscribed by means of a "cephalic tincture":

> I was at the mathematical school, where the master taught his pupils after a method scarce imaginable to us in Europe. The proposition and demonstration

> were fairly written on a thin wafer, with ink composed of a cephalic tincture. This the student was to swallow upon a fasting stomach, and for three days following eat nothing but bread and water. As the wafer digested, the tincture mounted to his brain, bearing the proposition along with it.[101]

Whether celebrated or derided, these material methods for dispensing a teaching were fine fodder for dinner table conversation. In fact, during the modern era, we find edible letters in contexts that are no longer educational but primarly festive. Certain recipe books from the seventeenth century recommend the confection of sugar alphabets for the adornment of the tables of the great homes, such as, for example, those "*cinnamon letters made by art*," mentioned by John Murrell in his *Delightfull Daily Exercise for Ladies and Gentlewomen* (1621).[102] According to Wendy Wall, who has studied the intersection of high culture and culinary practice in Early Modern England, there is strong evidence for this special place accorded edible letters at banquets. The confections were offered to the guests so that they might construct, in a spirit of play, monograms, anagrams, or acrostics that would then be deciphered and eaten.[103] Not only did these textual combinations give a concrete value to the puns punctuating the festivities (since Antiquity, sharing a table has always been bound up with the exchange of words[104]), but swallowing the signifier allowed one to envisage a yet more material outcome for the signified, a real incorporation of meaning, giving an unexpected twist to the theories of physicians and philosophers on the absorption of knowledge, servings and sayings flying off to live happily ever after, attaching the mind to the life of the body.

Traces of these alphabetical recreations exist also in the visual culture of the French Ancien Régime. Cookies in the form of letters appear in several still lifes from the seventeenth century, as in those by Clara Peeters (1611; fig. 2.18) and Peter Binoit (1615; fig. 2.19).[105] The inclusion of these edible initials within painted compositions, however, goes beyond the simple referential and documentarian function. Through their presence, the painting offers itself

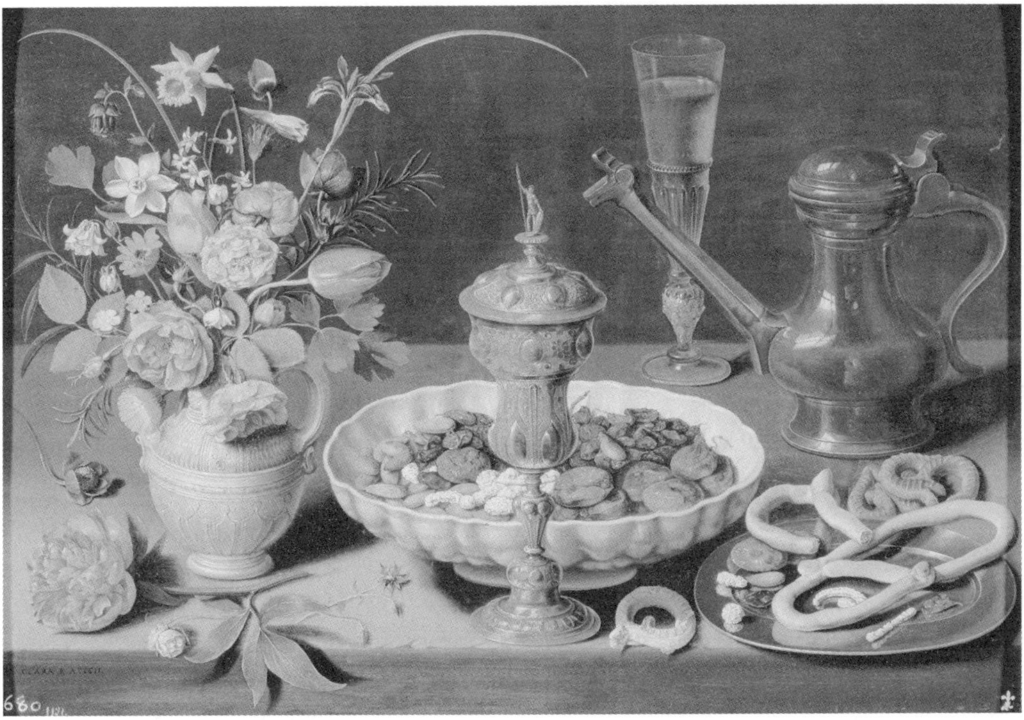

Figure 2.18. Clara Peeters, *Still Life*, 1611, oil on panel, 20.4 × 28.7in. (Inv. P001620). Madrid, Museo Nacional del Prado (© Photographic Archive Museo Nacional del Prado).

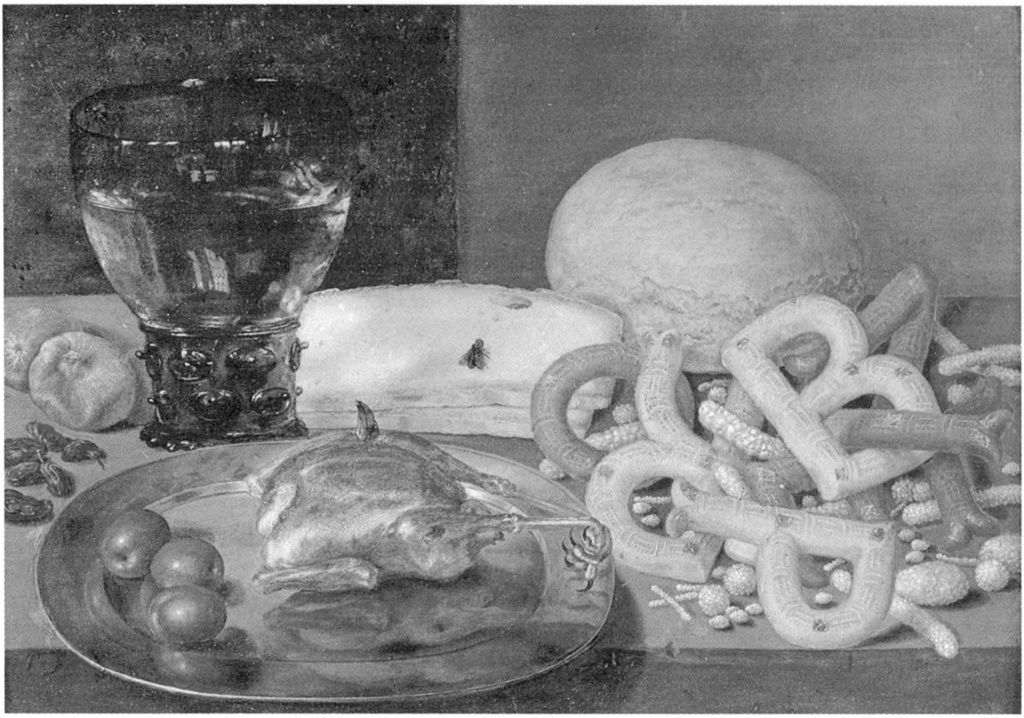

Figure 2.19. Peter Binoit, *Still life with Letter Pastry*, ca. 1615, oil on panel, 10.4 × 14.3 in. Groningen, Groninger Museum (Creative Commons).

as a meditation on the circulation of meaning, from the material towards the immaterial and back again.[106] Taste, smell, sight, and touch come together in these table-paintings, turning perception into the *athanor*, the alchemical furnace of all intellectualizing. The figurative cookie becomes thus emblematic of the fusion of the senses, of seeing and tasting, lending legitimacy to a literal, one might say letter-perfect incorporation of knowledge.

Art's Flesh

The process of thought, therefore, would supposedly come down to a synchrony of seeing and having: carving, cutting, cooking, tasting, and digesting the visible as much as the readable.[107] We should not be surprised to see, after this, ingestion established as a model not just by monks, philosophers, and pedagogues, but also by poets and artists as a way of giving form to the mystery of artistic transmission. In fact, since Antiquity, in the writings of poets, orators, artists, and theoreticians of art we find the idea that to imitate is nothing other than to feed oneself and digest.[108] Proof of this exists in metaphors that attempt to overcome "the logical 'perplexity'" posed by the idea of spiritually incorporating tropes and physical images[109] by likening artistic inspiration or the appropriation of the art of the old masters to an act of absorption; for example, one drinks at the source of the old masters and one butters one's toast with them.

In Letter 84 of Seneca's *Epistles to Lucilius*, we read:

> This is what we see nature doing in our own bodies without any labour on our part; the food we have eaten, as long as it retains its original quality and floats in our stomachs as an undiluted mass, is a burden; but it passes into tissue and blood only when it has been changed from its original form. So it is with the food which nourishes our higher nature — we should see to it that whatever we have absorbed should not be allowed to remain unchanged, or it will be no part of us. We must digest it; otherwise it will merely enter the memory and not into our own being. Let us loyally welcome such foods

> and make them our own, so that something that is one may be formed out of many elements.[110]

This missive was to inspire the Petrarch to communicate his own theory of *innutrition* to Giovanni Boccaccio in a letter dated October 1359:

> I have read Virgil, Flaccus, Severinus, Tullius not once but countless times, nor was my reading rushed but leisurely, pondering them as I went with all the powers of my intellect; I ate in the morning what I would digest in the evening, I swallowed as a boy what I would ruminate upon as an older man.[111]

In the same way, in *La Défense et illustration de la langue française* (1561), Joachim Du Bellay was to speak of the Latin writers of Antiquity who achieved their own genius by

> imitating the best Greek authors, transforming themselves into them, devouring them, and, after having thoroughly digested them, converting them into blood and nourishment, selecting, each according to his own nature and the topic he wished to choose, the best author, all of whose rarest and most exquisite strengths they diligently observed and, like shoots, grafted them, as I said earlier, and adapted them to their own language.[112]

These metaphors typically involve solids; however, François Rabelais, for his part, used liquid images to describe the absorption of poetic material. In the Prologue of the *Cinquiesme livre* (1564), the poetical work is no longer just swallowed, but rather drunk down:

> Topers, I give you timely notice, lay in a good provision of them [R's books] as soon as you find them in bookstores, and you have not only to shell them but also to devour them like an opiate for the heart and incorporate them into yourselves; it is then that you will discover the good they reserve for all nice bean-shellers.[113]

The recourse to ingesting as a way of imagining the process of imitation was not limited to the sphere of literature. It was just as much a feature in the understanding of the visual arts. We can see this in Chapter 27 of Cennino Cennini's *Libro dell'arte* (ca. 1400) in which studying the old masters is likened to a enjoying a nourishing meal:

> Having practiced drawing a sufficient time on tablets as I have before directed, always take pains in drawing the best subjects which you can find, done by the hand of great masters; turn them into delicacies for you... if you continually follow the method of one master, your intellect must be very dull indeed if it gets no food.[114]

It is equally present in Giorgio Vasari who, in his *Lives* (1568), compared the work of the sculptor Brunelleschi to food, and the artistic gaze to an act of digestion:

> Donato... saw the Crucifix of Filippo, placed in a good light; and stopping short to study it, he found it so perfectly finished, that, being overcome and full of amazement, like one distraught, he spread out his hands, which were holding up his apron; whereupon the eggs, the cheese, and all the other things fell to the ground, and everything was broken to pieces. But he was still marvelling and standing like one possessed, when Filippo came up and said with a laugh, "What is thy intention, Donato, and what are we to have for dinner, now that thou hast upset everything?" "For my part," answered Donato, "I have had my share for this morning."[115]

Another metaphor in the liquid register comes from the pen of Federico Zuccaro. In his *L'idea de'pittori, scultori ed architetti* (1607), the painter and theoretician personifies painting and drawing as parents mutually feeding themselves with their milk. The *Disegno*, "true milk, nutriment and unique substance of these professions," nourishes Painting, before the latter, itself having become mother, gives to Drawing "the milk of its breasts."[116] A few years after this, it was the turn of the historian André Félibien to use the image of milk. In 1637, writing about Poussin in his *Entretiens*, he writes, "His instruction was in the school of Raphael, of which... one might say that *he sucked the milk and received the food*, and the spirit of its art as he progressively saw its works."[117]

Despite the fact that, in all logic, the practice of painting relates primarily to the eye, Félibien describes the learning process in artistic production through the metaphor of suckling, the only metaphor capable of really getting across to the reader the way in which Raphael's artistic sensibility was progressively infused into that of Poussin. Here, we must recall that, since the time of Hippocrates, milk had been thought to be a derivative of blood, a substance through which the spirit could therefore pass.[118]

Finally, let us consider a famous passage in Karel Van Mander's *Schilder-Boeck* in which, in an attempt to break away from the Italian model he found a little too "idealist" for his taste, the Flemish historiographer describes the process of imitation in Pieter Breughel the Elder as a devouring and sees the production of his painted landscapes as a sort of vomiting onto the canvas of previously ingurgitated features:[119]

> On his travels he drew many views from life so that it is said that when he was in the Alps he swallowed all those mountains and rocks which, upon returning home, he spat out again onto canvases and panels, so faithfully was he able, in this respect and others, to follow Nature.[120]

These variations on the principle of *innutrition* show the extent to which imitation, and more generally the artistic process as a whole, was assimilated to an act of ingestion. For the artists and theoreticians of the early modern era, the practice of painting came down to eating at the table of the old masters and drinking at Nature's breast.

We should not really be surprised to learn that artistic production was seen in the early modern era as a form of dietetics. One notable reason for this view of the matter was the fact that artists and cooks were understood, at this time, as practicing the same kind of occupation. Painters, sculptors, musicians, and goldsmiths ranked alongside pastry cooks and sellers of roast meats because they were all, following the medico-astrological view of the professions, linked to the planet Mercury. This shared destiny can be seen very clearly in the depiction of the *Children of Mercury* by the Master of the Housebook (1475–1485; fig. 2.20). In the right hand part of this scene, a young woman seated at table offers a glass to a sculptor who stands beside her, establishing by this gesture a connection between the world of the table and that of art. As the engraver sees it, the artist cannot sculpt without taking refreshment. The porosity between artistic production and taking sustenance emerges in a strikingly concrete way in the journal of Jacopo da Pontormo (1554–1556) in which dietetic instructions, lists of dishes, self-auscultation, drinks and artistic illustrations are mixed seamlessly together.[121]

Now, although this attention paid to diet might appear to be merely anecdotal, it had, in reality, a genuinely determining influence. For the artists of this period, falling into acedia or melancholy was a constant danger for anyone in the intellectual professions who did not take proper care of their own body. As Paolo Pino was to say, in his *Dialogo di Pittura* (1548):

> And because painting does not call for physical effort, but keeps man still and melancholy, with his natural virtues fixed on the idea, it will be of help towards the preservation of this individual to exert himself riding, playing ball, wrestling, fencing, or at least walking some distance while conversing with a friend about joyous things, for such practices limber up the person, settle the digestion and destroy melancholy, and moreover purify man's virtue. ... And above all, the painter must abhor all vices, such as avarice (in man a vile and reprehensible thing); scoundrelly and pernicious gambling; gluttony, mother of ignorance and idleness; nor should he live to feed himself, but nourish himself soberly for the sake of self-preservation.[122]

And for his part, artist Romano Alberti (1585) explains that the peril of melancholia results from the fact that painters,

> wishing to imitate ..., must retain the phantasms fixed in the intellect, so that afterward they can express them in the way they first saw them when present; and, being their work, this occurs not only once, but continually. They keep their minds so much abstracted and separated from nature that consequently melancholy derives from it.[123]

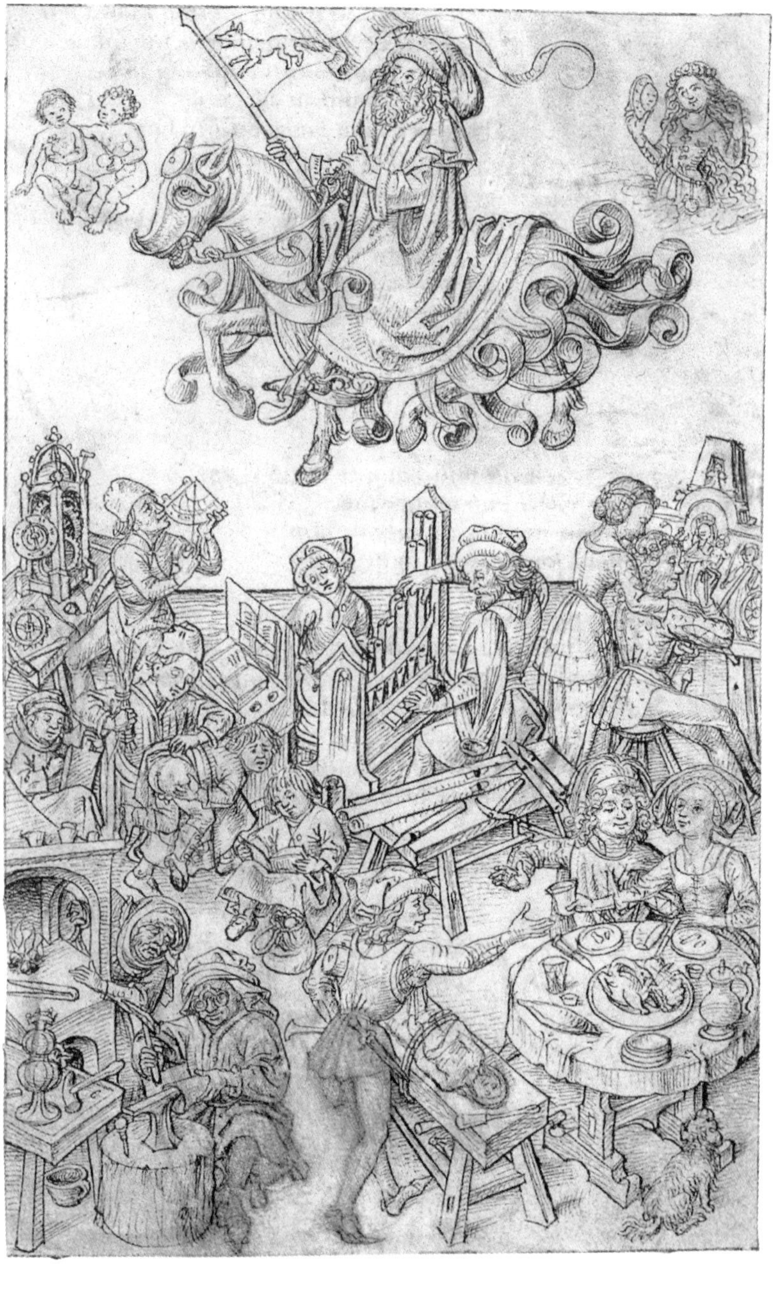

Figure 2.20. Master of the Housebook, *The Children of Mercury*, ca. 1475–1485, woodcut, 9.2 × 5.6 in. Schloss Wolfegg (Creative Commons).

In the more or less parodic and satirical depictions of the healing of melancholics produced in the "Autumn" of the Renaissance, we can see not only a profusion of images weighing down and shackling the mind, but also the important role played by the ingestion of a liquid substance as a means of medication. In engravings such as Johann Theodor de Bry's *Arte mea cerebrum nisi sit sapientiatotum* (1596; fig. 2.21)[124] and Martin Droeshout's *To This Grave Doctor Millions Do Resort* (1620; fig. 2.22), the melancholic, subjected to a superabundance of phantasmata that take the form of genuinely material images lodged both in the head and the stomach, is cured by, among other remedies, ingesting a filter.[125] The expelling of the images is helped by the circulation of a beverage setting in movement the bodily fluids. The liquid thus taken in absorbs the images and allows the excess to be eliminated through evaporation, micturition, or defecation. The stress on excretion as a remedy here indicates still more the importance of digestion, in other words, the process of sorting out of the beneficial and waste products in the "managing" of images and ideas.[126]

Devouring

In the preceding survey of the medical, religious, and artistic imaginations, I have highlighted the positive value attached to innutrition as a way of conceptualizing the functioning of the human body, the human relation to the divine, the acquisition of knowledge, and artistic production. However, ingestion, and more specifically ingesting visual artifacts, was not always seen in a positive light. Indeed, this was very far from being the case. Ingestion was frequently seen as an "other" and aberrant way of interacting with images, and it was severely criticized for reasons that were theological and philosophical as much as they were political.

To take the measure of this, let us consider an engraving by satirist William Hogarth. This work crystallizes, in an exemplary manner, many of the outward signs that brought condemnation down upon the practice of ingesting images.[127] The engraving, titled

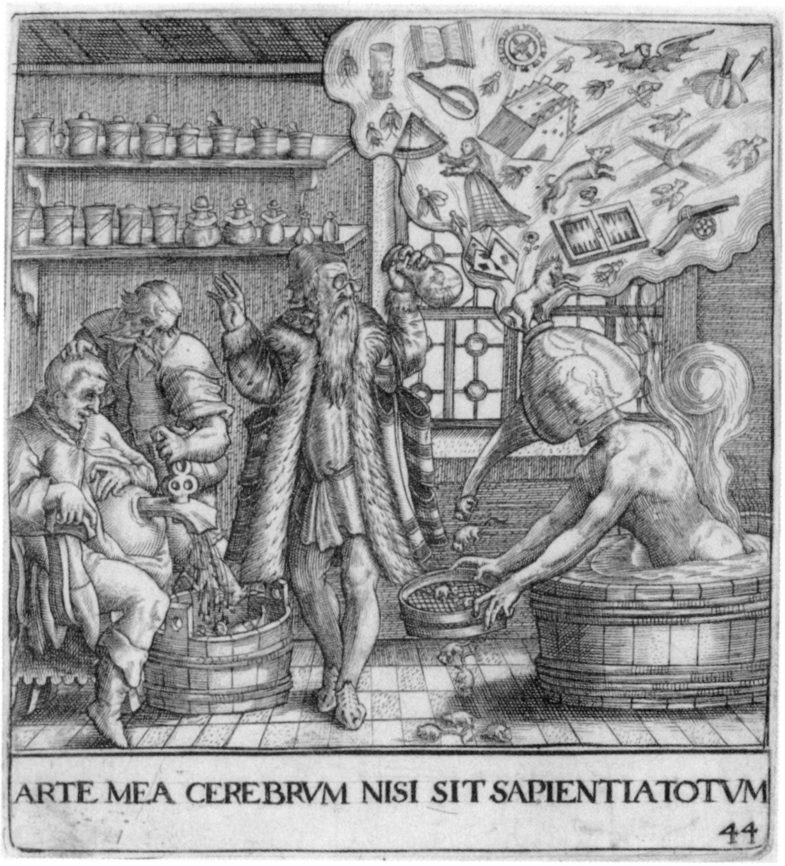

Figure 2.21. Johann Theodor de Bry, *Arte mea cerebrum nisi sit sapientatotum*, engraving, 4 × 3.8 in., in *Emblemata saecularia mira et iucunda varietate saeculi huius mores ita exprimentia*, 1596. Strasbourg, Cabinet des estampes et des dessins (© Creative Commons).

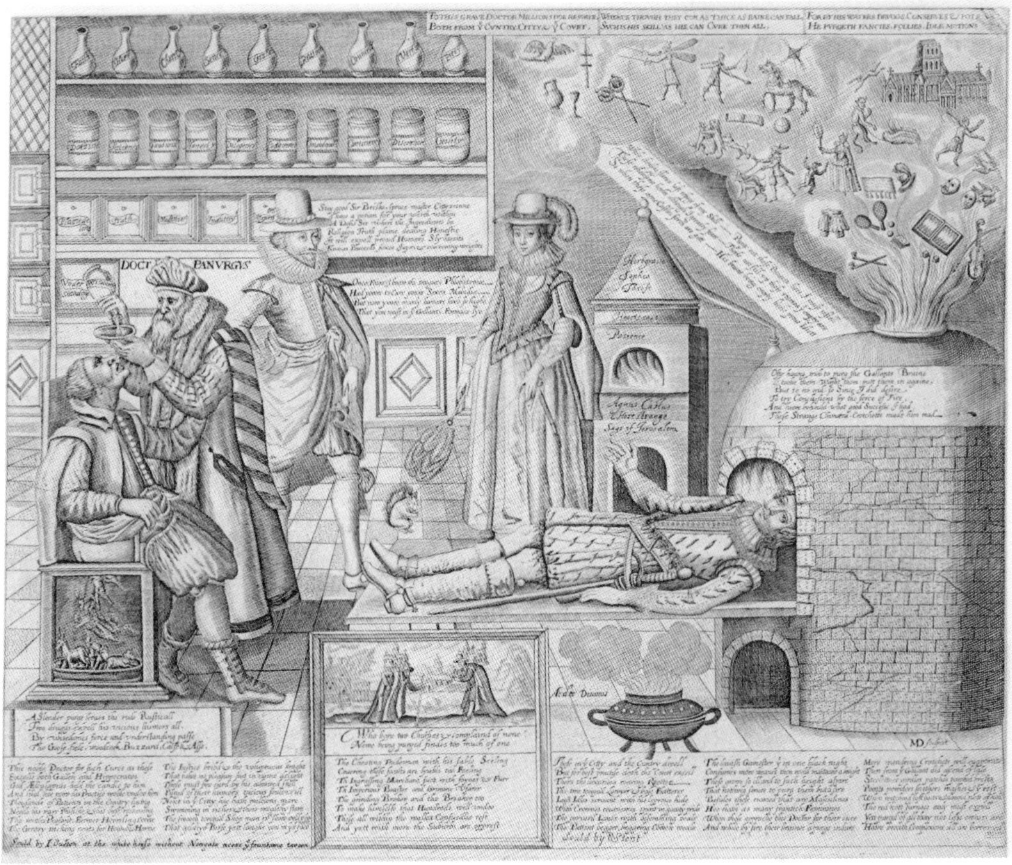

Figure 2.22. Martin Droeshout, *To This Grave Doctor Millions Do Resort*, 1620–1630, etching, 13.7 × 16 in. London, British Museum (© The Trustees of the British Museum).

Enthusiam Delineated (1760–1762; fig. 2.23), has often been seen as a broad response by Hogarth to critic Joseph Warton and painter Joshua Reynolds's panning of his work.[128] And yet, in parallel to this artistic backlash, the work takes aim, in the most cutting fashion, at Christian supersititions, and most particularly at the use made of images in the religious context. Hogarth's scene shows a group of men and women at a Methodist service. We can see that this is a Methodist service from several details: the name "Whitfield" [sic] written on the collar of the dog sitting below the preacher as well as on the sheet attached to the lectern and also the inscription "Methodist's brain" at the bottom of the "thermometer" of the emotions. Now, as a free thinker, Hogarth is here sarcastically depicting Methodism, the schismatic current in the Anglican Church that was born in the middle of the eighteenth century from the preachings of John Wesley (1703–1791) and George Whitefield (1714–1770). He does this by showing the faithful believers adopting, for the most part, irrational behaviors. Some of them are eating effigies in the image of Christ (fig. 2.24), and we see others kissing and embracing the very same statuettes, while another takes advantage of the innocence of a young person by slipping a hand inside her bodice.[129] The generalized delirium here is connected to the enthusiasm that characterized the sermons of Wesley and Whitefield. Both of these preachers favored extreme collective expressions of devotion, such as songs, tears, and shouting, turning these assemblies into genuinely charismatic experiences.[130] But if the link with Methodism is quite clear here, the presence of material images, whether statuettes of Christ or the puppets that the preacher holds forth from his raised pulpit, relates more specifically to the use of images within the Church of Rome.[131] The explanatory note that goes along with the scene makes it quite clear that the mockery extends to the Church and to religion in general: "The intention of this Print is to give a lineal representation, of the strange Effects of litteral and low conceptions of Sacred Beings as also of the Idolatrous Tendency of Pictures in Churches and Prints in religious books, etc."[132]

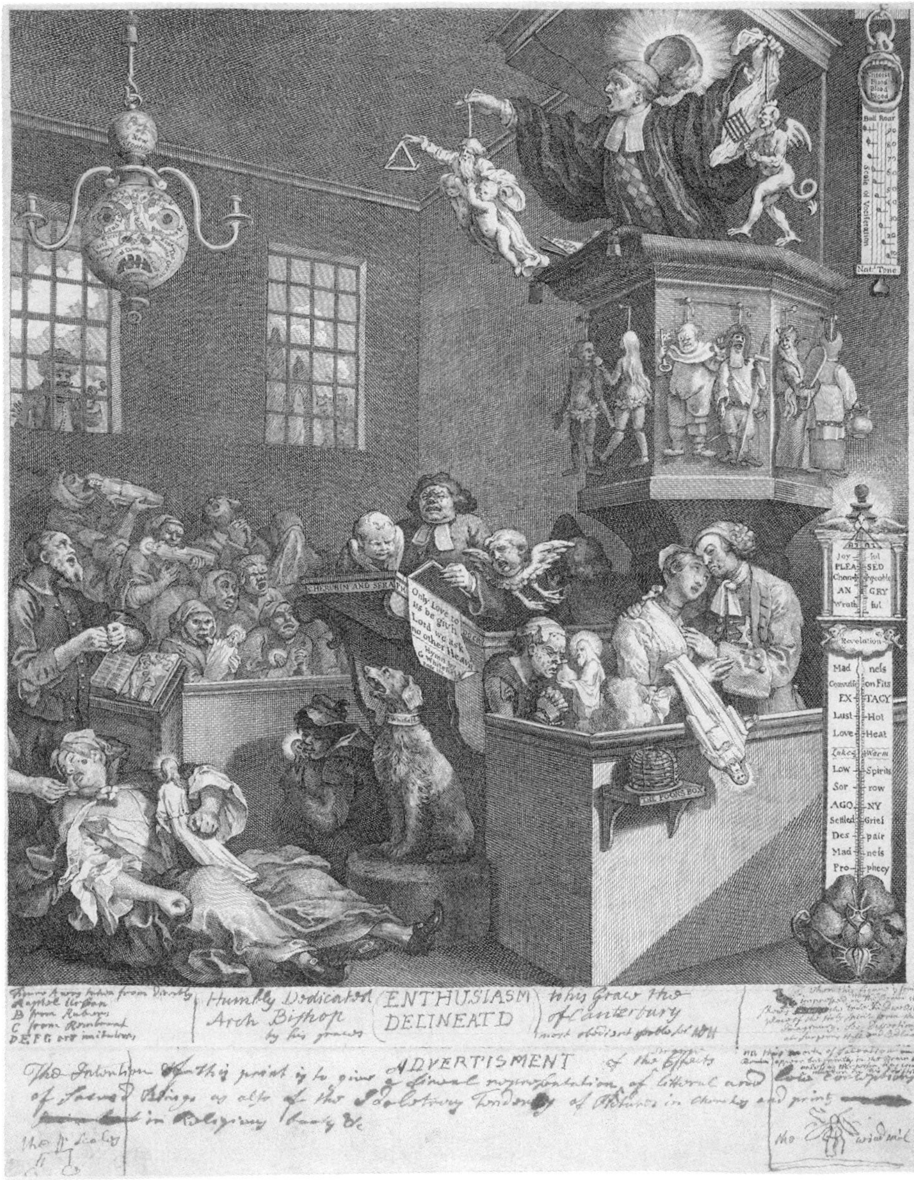

Figure 2.23. William Hogarth, *Enthusiasm Delineated*, 1760–1762, etching, 16.4 × 12.5 in. London, British Museum (© The Trustees of the British Museum).

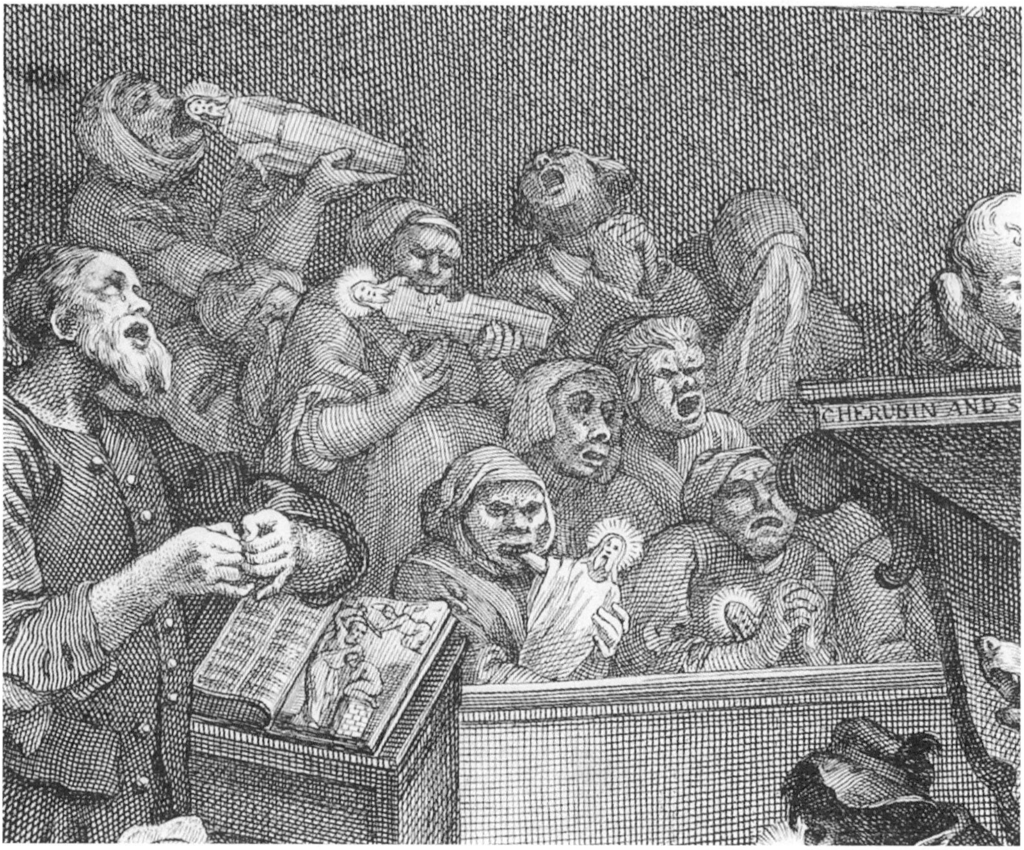

Figure 2.24. William Hogarth, *Enthusiasm Delineated*, 1760–1762, etching, 16.4 × 12.5 in. London, British Museum (detail of fig. 2.23) (© The Trustees of the British Museum).

Within this teeming orchestration, our interest is drawn principally to those extraordinary, bestial-looking "image eaters." How, in fact, are we to understand the meaning of their behavior? What lies behind this grotesque, simian characterization of the eaters of images? How does this show of iconophagy relate to the other little scenes in the engraving?

To answer this question, we must view the print within a larger history than that of the immediate context of its creation. And to do that we must make a few detours, and we shall have to backtrack a little.

Superstition

As I have already had occasion to point out, behaviors involving the eating of representations of divine figures as a means to incorporate their grace were very often not looked on favorably by the public and by religious authorities. For the iconoclast emperor Michael II the Amorian at the time of the Second Iconoclastic Controversy (813–843), ingesting icons was quite clearly a form of idolatry.[133] At the dawn of the modern era, a great many theologians in the West, such as Jean Gerson, Baptista da Mantova, Nicholas of Cusa, and Bernardino Busti, were to take up the terms of Michael's condemnation, albeit without going along with his iconoclastic conclusions, describing these practices as "vain superstitions" betraying an "aberrant" relation to images.[134] In their eyes, eating an image in order to obtain its *virtus* was something to be expected only of simple folk who were unable to see the difference between the simulacrum and its heavenly prototype and who were therefore mistaking the signifier for the signified.[135]

This condemnation of *stolidi* or *stulti* ("stupid folk"), who maintained a lowly and material relationship with images,[136] rarely had any real consequences; however, it could take on dramatic importance in cases where ingestion was seen as evidence of devilish practices. In fact, the preparation and absorption of a drinkable solution containing fragments of images was at times seen as an essentially magical procedure, carried out with evil intentions. For example, in Innsbruck in 1507, the repeated scraping and ingestion of a statue of Saint Christopher occasioned a trial for witchcraft with the charges brought against a certain Peter Wenbrenner.[137] Similarly, in 1685, in the region of Val Gardena in the Italian South Tyrol, a number of pregnant women were accused of scratching away at a figure of the devil in the Church of Saint Jacob and of ingesting the dust in order to get rid of the children they were carrying in their wombs.[138]

Whether superstitious, simpleminded, or engaged in witchcraft, the eater of images was always, for Catholics, a potential idolator, partaking with the "savages" in devilish practices.[139] The jurist François Lemée, in *The Treatise on Statues* (1688), saw the ingestion of images as a common denominator uniting heretics, pagans, and barbarians who mistook the figurative representation "for the thing itself, and not the image of the thing."[140] Comparing the sacrifices carried out by the Cataphryigians, a second-century Christian sect, with Aztec rituals, Lemée draws a direct connection between ingesting images and the horrors of such bloody sacrifices:

> In the month of May, the Mexicans would celebrate the Feast of Vitziputli, and during this feast the high priests of Mexico would make an idol out of a paste made up of human blood and all sorts of flours, giving it the size and shape of the wooden God that they had in their temple. Did this superstition bear relation to the heresy of the Cataphyrigians who used to pierce a one-year-old child on all sides, and then dip into his blood the bread that they called Eucharist?[141]

If we put this passage in its historical context, it must surely refer to the feast of Panquetzaliztli, such as described by the Franciscan Brother Bernardino de Sahagún in his *Historia General de las Cosas de Nueva España* (1577). According to de Sahagún, in the fifteenth month of *Panquetzaliztli* (the Aztec calendar), the officiants would make a cake out of *tzoalli* (amaranth flour) in the form of the god Huitzilopochtli, and they would carry it to the top of the temple where right after the close of the ceremony the edible image was shared out before being eaten.[142] However, far from just following de Sahagún's relatively neutral description, Lemée proceeds to denounce the idolatry of the Aztecs by introducing a detail from an account by Brother Juan de Torquemada, according to which human blood was mixed in with the edible images of the god.[143] In Lemée's eyes, therefore, the pagan sacrifice was accompanied by a devotional gesture that was truly abominable, and in which teeth were substituted for eyes, devouring took the place of contemplating, and cannibalism replaced communion. As part of his building up of this demonic picture of the Aztec rites, Lemée appropriates the picture of the god Huitzilopochtli that was current at the time. In *La description de l'univers*, published in 1683 by Allain Manesson-Mallet (fig. 2.25), for example, the statue of the god is nothing more nor less than a figure of the devil, a hybrid being seemingly right out of the imagination of Hieronymous Bosch with his goat hooves, bat wings, and his belly the face of a monster.[144]

Theophagy

Although the Catholic Church itself did often issue pronouncements against these "strange" practices, it was, we must stress, more fundamentally the Reformers who were to make ingesting images into the major sign of a deviant relationship with God. In the sixteenth century, the "image eater" or "crucifix eater" was before all else a "papist." A pamphleteer from Zürich wrote that if anyone were to travel through the lands of Germany (where they do not teach God's Laws), "he would find everywhere people gnawing away at images as if they wished to devour their feet."[145] The defamatory picture of the statue nibbler was to become a commonplace weapon with which to strike the sanctimonious adherents of the Church of Rome, marking them with the seal of infamy. Thus, in the midst of the Wars of Religion (1562–1598), the Calvinist poet and philologist Florent Chrestien was to use this idea in an epigram directed at François d'Amboise, accusing the latter of treachery in the service of the League:

Figure 2.25. Alain Manesson-Mallet, *Vitzlipuztli*, in *La Description de l'univers* (Paris: Denys Thierry, 1683), vol. 5, p. 311.

Ha! I know the reason and I shall say it softly:
There is among us a traitor and false brother
He belongs to the Leaguers and I am against them,
He is an image eater and I am not.[146]

The metaphor here is not simply a stylistic figure. Its force is twofold. It is both a condemnation of the Catholic veneration of images, or, idolatry, and a direct critique of the sacrament of the Eucharist since the Protestants denounced both the mass and the host as belonging to the wider practice of literally ingesting images. Indeed, the target was even clearer when the Eucharistic wafers were themselves endowed with figurative images.[147] As Frank Lestringant and Aden Kumler show, the Calvinists generally adopted two attitudes in their attempts to discredit the "holy sacrament": horror and derision.[148] If the consecrated host really did make present the body of Christ, as was claimed by Catholics adhering to the dogma of transubstantiation, then ingesting it was an abominable act of theophagy; on the other hand, if the Holy Communion were only a symbolic sacrifice, as was believed by the partisans of consubstantiation, then it was nothing more than a sham designed to satisfy the bigotry of the "saint eaters."[149]

This last, essentially satirical interpretation of the Eucharist was widely adopted by the Reformers because it was easily understood and effective. Notably, it lay behind the legend of *Jean le Blanc* (1574), an anti-Catholic poem in which the transubstantiated Christ, the perishable product of a cheap pastry confection, is presented as a "pastry god" to be nibbled on by children.[150] An engraving titled *The Genealogy of Jean Le Blanc* (ca. 1575–1600; fig. 2.26), is a gloss on this derisory economy that turned Christ into the equivalent of a bushel of wheat that had been harvested, beaten, milled, cooked, fashioned, and consumed amid the vapors of a filthy kitchen with hens and chickens scratching and pecking around.[151]

We can see better now, after having been "fed" by the preceding examples, that it is really this dual tradition that Hogarth is

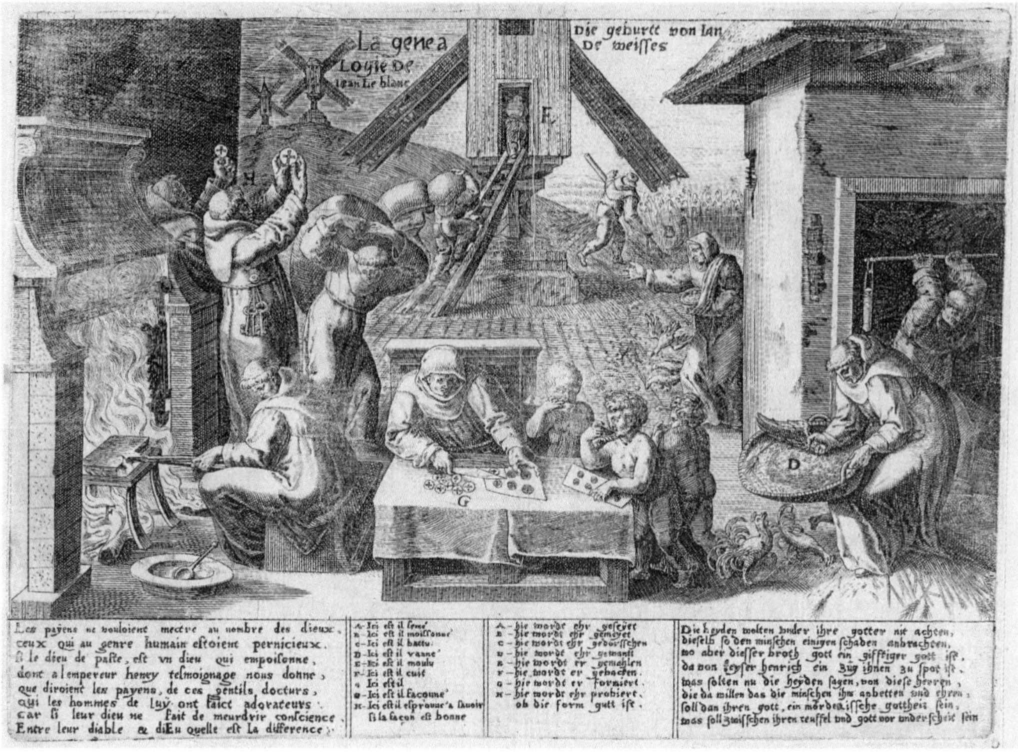

Figure 2.26. *La Genealogie de Jean Le Blanc*, ca. 1575–1600, etching, 7.6 × 10.3 in. London, British Museum (© The Trustees of the British Museum).

carrying forward in his engraving. The statuettes of Christ in the hands of the devourers and the sanctimonious bigots in the foreground are so many varied metaphorical depictions of the Eucharistic wafers swallowed by Catholics.[152] This interpretation is supported, moreover, by the drawing that Hogarth places in the lower right of the print (or on the left in the initial engraved plate). This is a sketch of a windmill, and it refers directly to one of Hogarth's paintings titled *Transubstantiation Satirized*, which has disappeared but is known through an engraving of it made shortly after its creation, in which the Virgin Mary holds up her son by the feet above a mill or mincer producing Eucharistic wafers that are sent straight to the mouths of the kneeling communicants (fig. 2.27). The reference to this painting, a twist on the medieval "mystic mill,"[153] places the theophagical act at the threshold of Hogarth's illustrated assembly.

Blasphemy

In addition to condemning this "devotional cannibalism," certain Protestant writers also sought to denounce as obscene what they saw as the "carnal" relationship that Catholics maintained with images. In doing so, they brought up once again, as support for their argument, the ingestion of figurative representations. The cult of Saint Guerlichon in the town of Bourg-Dieu, France, thus served as an example for the Humanist Reformer Henri Estienne as he criticized with calculated derision the blaspheming behavior of the Catholics. In his *L'Introduction au traité de la conformité des merveilles anciennes avec les modernes ou Traité préparatif à l'Apologie pour Hérodote* (1566), he relates that the statue of

> *S. Guerlichon* (in the Abbey of the city *Bourg de Dieu*, near to *Rommorantin*, and in sundry places elsewhere) braggeth that he can get as many women with child as come, be they never so many; if whilst they are going with child, they fail not to stretch themselves devoutly upon the holy Idol which lieth all flat upon his back, and standeth not upright as the rest do; besides, that *they drink every day a certain potion mingled with the scrapings of the said*

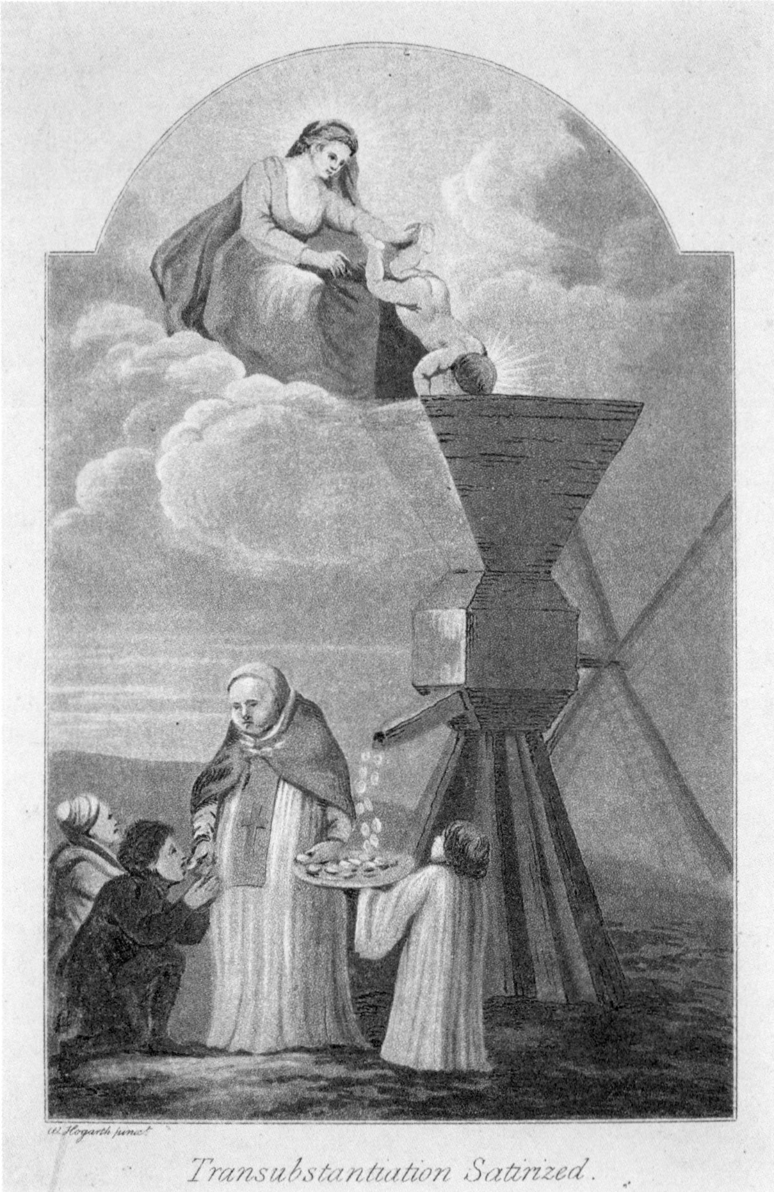

Figure 2.27. Samuel Ireland, after William Hogarth, ca. 1794, *Transubstantiation Satirized*, etching and aquatint, 9.3 × 6.6 in., in *Graphic Illustrations of Hogarth*, London, British Museum (© The Trustees of the British Museum).

> *image, and by name with the scraping of that part which I cannot name with modestie.* Now whether this do get women with child or not, I leave to be decided by those that have forged it or approve of such devilish devotion: *which would have been holden a wonderment to the world, if it had been recorded by any barbarous or heathen people*; what shall we say then to see it in use even amongst those who profess themselves Christians. Yet I am not very certain whether this Saint be in as good credit at this present, as he was in times past: sith they that have seen him (to whom I am beholden for this report) affirm it to be about tewelve years ago, since he had that part almost worn away by continual scraping.[154]

The unseemliness of the physical, not to say sexual, relations between the faithful and the statue, along with the consumption of the fragments of what passed for an idol, certainly recalls the lack of dignity of Christian pilgrims who, as Erasmus facetiously puts it, were willing to do anything for a few drops of the Virgin's milk.[155] But this attack goes further. Stretching oneself out over statue of Saint Guerlichon and then scraping his genitals and consuming the powder was, for Henri Estienne, a "devilish devotion" that brought Catholics close to pagans. Ingestion, insofar as it established a basely material relationship with images, erased the barrier that "normally" separated Christians from "barbarous peoples."

Turning again to Hogarth's engraving, we can now see that it is likewise a receptacle for this critical tradition. The image eaters figure here alongside other sanctimonious believers, each more ridiculous than the next, some of whom are giving themselves over to acts of blasphemy. This is quite particularly the case with the young woman at the bottom left of the print who has fainted. She is holding the statue of Christ as if she wants to physically join herself with it. Bernd Krysmanski has suggested a similarity here with the position of the Virgin in Antonio da Corregio's *The Lamentation of Christ* in Parma at Galleria Nazionale.[156] The connection is all the more convincing in that, beyond the artistic reference that allowed Hogarth to take a stab at Reynold's "sublime style,"[157] it underscores, on a purely moral level, the irreverence of the young woman's behavior. Indeed, as Krysmanksi has argued, Corregio's representation of an incestuous Christ "making love" to his mother is, in some ways, a visual and satirical translation of one of Whitefield's sermons that took as its subject *mutual union*, and that was titled "Christ the Best Husband" (1740).[158] But there is more to add to *Enthusiasm Delineated*: Hogarth likens the Virgin here to a woman of loose virtue; her left hand pressing the Christ down between her legs can leave no doubt as to her sexual intentions, and the outrageous beauty spot that she displays marks her as belonging squarely on the side of artifice, makeup, and fakery. Moreover, John Ireland, the first to comment on Hogarth's engravings, saw in this young woman a reference to Jenny Douglas, a famous madam of the 1750s.[159] For Hogarth, therefore, religious enthusiasm went hand in hand with plain lust.

Hypocrisy and Manipulation

Although, as we have just seen, the expression *image* or *crucifix eater* was to spring from the pens of Protestants as a means of denouncing the "deviant" habitus of the Catholics, it became over time more universally used to stigmatize the lies and dissimulations of the *faux dévots* (false believers). Thus, Brantôme was to condemn the "women eaters of images" who "beneath this hypocrisy . . . hide and brood on their fires, so that by such feints and false seemings, no one can see it, and everyone considers them very prudent, even half-saints";[160] and again, describing positively the genuine faith of Filippo Strozzi, he takes up the expression to mark a negative contrast, Strozzi "was certainly not a zealot, a hypocrite, an eater of images, nor a great attendee at Masses and sermons, but he believed very well, moreover, what should be believed."[161]

This sense of the "eater of images" as a hypocrite and false believer was to pass quickly into everyday language. Indeed, the following entry appeared in the first complete edition of the *Dictionnaire de l'Académie française* (1694): "One says of a sanctimonious person, a false believer, that he is a Crucifix-eater, an eater of images."[162] This figurative sense of the term "eater," used sometimes for comic and sometimes for critical effect, was to show up in most dictionaries in the eighteenth and nineteenth centuries, from Pierre Bayle's (1702) to Jules Trousset's (1885–1891) and including along the way Philibert-Joseph Le Roux's (1750), Louis-Nicolas Bescherelle's (1856), and Émile Littré's (1873–1874). Ingesting images becomes thus the exemplary figure for depicting the artfulness of the ruses deployed by hypocrites to hide their intentions and take advantage of the weakness of poor souls.[163]

On this fertile ground, the critique of idolatry, impiety, blasphemy, and sanctimoniousness was to be joined, in the seventeenth century, by attacks aimed at the clergy for taking advantage of credulous idiots devoid of common sense. As the poet Sieur de la Vergne put it, describing how a young girl is deprived of her inheritance, they made fools eat images so as to delude them and to quietly whisk away their possessions:

> They give her as antidote
> The feelings of a dévote;
> And by such convincing,
> Occupying her with holy duty,
> So that only one will eat the property,
> They set her to image eating.[164]

Beyond this metaphor, however, the most powerful tool for making the Church the subject of derision was bringing to mind those edible images that the institution really did produce. In an anticlerical pamphlet titled *Le moine sécularisé* (1678), Jean Chastain draws, in the form of a dialogue, a comical account of the sacraments fabricated by the Church for controlling credulous souls. Alongside the worship of "Relicks," such as the holy Thorn, Saint Margaret's bones, Charles Borromeo's Hose, there appears the consuming of St. Nicholas Bread, a baker's specialty, widely seen in France, Italy, and Spain during the modern era, that bore the saint's image:[165]

> Patrick: We have, says he, the holy Thorn, one of St. Margarets' Bones, one of Charles Borromeo's Hose. These are curious Relicks, replies the sick Woman; but what virtues hath St. Nicholas Bread? So many, says the Monk, that sometimes several thousands of poor people have been cured by it of the Ague in one City or Country. It quells the rage of evil spirits, it quencheth fire, and preserves houses from an irreparable conflagration, calms the wind and the waves of the Sea, diverts hail and tempests from fields, and helps to defend from thunder, nay, it makes a person Musquet-proof.... It makes barren women fruitful, and preserves the fruit of the womb after conception, and eases their pains in Child-birth. It maintains in health whosoever eats it, it keeps from ill luck those who carry it about them; it brings away from the tender throats of young Children the bones of fish, bits of glass, needles, nails and the like, which they may have swallowed unawares. It cures all Fevers, nay evil and pestilent, also Epidemical ones, and the most incurable diseases; preserves from all poysons, delivers whole Cities, nay Provinces from the Plague. In short, it operates many other Miracles of the like nature.[166]

While the author is here picking out for particular vilification the Saint Nicholas Bread insofar as it was used as a means to literally nourish the credulity of the pious believers, his account ultimately takes aim at all objects said to be miraculous. This text recalls, moreover, the sheet given with the Agnus Dei in 1662 reproduced by Bernard Picart in *Cérémonies et coutumes religieuses de tous les peuples du monde* (1723; see fig. 1.29). In this engraving, there is also a Saint Geneviève Bread that we can see placed around the shown paper sheet, scapulars, rosaries, and other blessed medals. The caption at the bottom tells us that it was made by the nuns of the Saint Geneviève Abbey to cure fevers. Eating the saint's image ensured a cure that was nothing short of miraculous. Now, it is exactly this sort of bread that the young woman asks for in *Le Moine sécularisé*: "Father (says the good Woman) how much shall I be obliged to you, if you will be so kind as to bring me a little of that blessed bread, and of those holy Relicks?" And through expedients such as these the priest falsely obtains the confidence of the poor fool:

> To which he agreed, and in the morning comes and brings I know not what sowed up in a fine bit of Taffity, tyed with a Ribbon at the end; and after a small Preamble made in commendation of those Relicks, beg'd leave of the Lady to tye them about her neck; then presenting them to her to kiss, he pull'd the pin from her smock, and puts this mystical remedy between her two brests [sic].
>
> Florimond: O the Knave! She was a weak Woman.

Once again, reading this passage, we are reminded of Hogarth's print. In the right-hand section, what do we see but a woman smiling a smile of beatitude as she is seduced by a man whose grimacing look makes clear his sly intentions. The gentleman, who is of course not a gentleman, is taking advantage of the young woman's religious transport to slip his hand inside her bodice. As she gives herself to him, she lets drop the statuette of Christ, just as others devour its like in the background.

Madness and Animality

This dual denunciation of sanctimonious sensuality and of the manipulative abuse that exploits it, opens an essential perspective on our topic. Ingestion was seen as the archetypal abuse of images because, as a practice, it brought the tactile and gustatory experience of the image down to a level that was purely sensual and material. The monstrous deformation of the image eaters in Hogarth's engraving must be understood in the light of this. The artist gives them simian features because, as a good inheritor of Idealist and Cartesian thought, he saw ingesting images as the equivalent of reason being levelled by the senses.[167] As we know, since Aristotle, the classification of *scala naturae* (the chain of beings) had been determined on the basis of the superiority of the intellect to the senses. Furthermore, the latter had their own hierarchy, with gustatory taste being placed at the very bottom of the scale.[168] What differentiated men from all other animals was their capacity to think and to reason; take away that faculty, and men were no more than beasts. For Hogarth, as would have been the case for any other educated person in the eighteenth century, anyone who was a captive of the materiality of things was, quite simply, an animal. The scowling, holier-than-thou congregants, gnawing at the statuettes like monkeys or rats were thus living examples of a humanity subjected to its passions, and as a result, perfect prey for the voracity of a hypocritical and scheming clergy.

Another figure in Hogarth's engraving deserves comment as part of this depreciatory analysis. This is the man wearing a turban, who looks down at the scene before him from up behind the window's gridwork as he puffs on his pipe.[169] This onlooker, who is nothing less than our alter ego in the picture, was evidently, according to the terminology of the time, to be seen as a Turk or so-called Mahommedan; in other words, for Christians he was the typical heretic, the worshipper of a false god.[170] Now, to have given this onlooker this specific identity and this distinct position with respect to the rest of the assembly suggests that Hogarth was seeking to upend the usual teachings of the religious authorities and to bring about a change of philosophical perspective: the one whom Christians ordinarily condemn for his error now observes the errors of the image worshippers, the Christian idolators who behave like madfolk.[171]

Madness—the word is not excessive. These image eaters really do look like people who have lost their reason. And if we are justified in speaking of madness here, it is not only because the various depicted actions were seen at the time as being, strictly speaking, beyond the bounds of reason,[172] perpetrated by a lack of *ratio intellectualis*. (As Foucault has defined it, the French Classical age is the age of the *ratio*, and madness "is precisely a condition of impossibility for thought."[173]) However, it is also because Hogarth's satirical scene takes place in what looks very much to be a place of confinement. The bars through which the Turk contemplates the superstitious congregation encourage us to identify the place as a "house of correction," the sort of place where, up until the beginning of the nineteenth century, "madfolk," "prostitutes," "vagabonds," and "prisoners" were kept.[174] Indeed, Hogarth is careful to slip into his engraving a number of inscriptions that designate the assembly quite clearly as a community of madfolk. In fact, the heading of the sermon placed on the pulpit's lectern reads "I Speak as a Fool," and "Madness" figures at the top of the list of the rules of the emotions.

Based on these observations, we summarize Hogarth's position: image eating is unreason is madness. This simple equation was to apply, moreover, beyond the eighteenth century. Consider, for example, the attitude of Francis Dolarhyde, the protagonist of the film *Red Dragon*, already referred to in the introduction. He is a man who emits wild, animal cries, far from the rational logos, and who throws himself like a savage beast on a William Blake watercolor in order to eat it. This can only be a madman. To take another contemporary example, we have the perspective of the writers of a television series devoted to the female prison environment, *Orange is the New Black*. In season 3's episode 13 titled "Trust No Bitch," the inmate Angie Rice ingests the "miraculous" piece of toast bearing the image of Norma, another incarcerated woman who was seen by the community as a sort of saint.[175] Leanne Taylor, one of the protagonists, says in fact that her friend Angie "ate toast Norma," which shares a miraculous "resemblance" with Norma through the contrast between white and dark sections—and is thus acheiropoetic[176]—because "she thought it would give her powers or some stupid shit!" In the same episode, a flashback to an earlier moment in the life of another inmate, Lorna Morelli, invites us to witness the first communion celebration in which young children receive the "redeeming" host from the hands of a priest. In this scene, Lorna is so delighted to show off her new white dress that she forgets to swallow the host. Her parents, utterly devastated, castigate her, yelling out, "she didn't eat the Eucharist!" and reminding her that what counts is not the communion dress but what Lorna's mother calls the *cracker*: "The cracker is the whole point!" Now, the term "cracker" is precisely the one that Angie uses to describe "toast Norma" when she discovers the image printed on it. "It's so over-toasted, you could pretend it was a cracker." The assimilation of toast and host, these two "pieces of bread," seems deliberate. Ingesting the toast is a way for the screenwriters to bring together two worlds that are normally kept apart, conferring on the scene all its critical and satirical density. The scene targets all at once the trappings of the Catholic Church, the delirium of charismatic communities, the uncontrollable addictions of drug abusers, and the credulity of members of New Age cults. Religion—opium of the people?

Childish Ways

In parallel with the religious and devotional sphere, there was yet another area of human experience that became negatively characterized through the figure of image eating. This was the world of childhood. Certainly, the so-called senseless individual had for long been thought of as being only one step away from the child, and most people were quick to make the connection.[177] Before the advent of modern psychiatry, the observers of madness often likened the incoherence of the insane to the *debility*, in the etymological sense of the term, of the *infans*. Likewise, but in reverse direction, the observers ascribed the child's thoughtlessness to an absence of reason.[178] The "unreasonable" nature of the child was, in fact, frequently stigmatized. Children were understood to maintain basely material relations with things, and more specifically, they were said to have an insatiable desire to devour, the appetite being the sign and symptom of this psychic incompleteness.[179] As Bernard de Gordon wrote in the fourteenth century,

> children are very attached to pleasure, to food and drink, . . . it is quite clear, therefore, that reason is not or scarcely useful to them since they have not reached the years of discernment, and it is for this reason that Galen and other learned men say of an adult man presenting the least signs of madness that he has the stupidity of a child.[180]

Children were believed to be incapable of reflective thought, and they were thus considered unable to resist their own inclinations. Always moved by their emotions, they would give in to all their desires, and so, quite naturally, they would succumb to gluttony—the vice that generally subsumed all others.

Given this, it is easy to see that, as a victim of his or her emotions, the child might have put on the costume of the "eater of images," not to say of "illusions." An example that comes easily to mind is Jacob and Wilhelm Grimm's tale, "Hansel and Gretel," in which an old witch manages to lure the two children into her clutches by offering them nothing less than a house to eat.[181] In Ludwig Richter's illustration (1860; fig. 2.28), the "little gingerbread house" has the form of a tiny structure partly covered with little people and animals, all made of gingerbread and pretzel bread. To underscore how effective the offer was, Richter shows us Gretel holding in her hand, hidden behind her back, a partially eaten piece of the roof.

The Brothers Grimm did not invent the idea of an edible house. It derived, in reality, quite directly from the houses that we see in certain depictions of the mythical land of Cockaigne. A similar building appears, in fact, in an illustration by Erhard Schön for the poet and humanist Hans Sachs's poem "Das Schlaraffenland" (ca. 1530; fig. 2.29). The artist shows us a *Lebkuchenhaus* with doors and shutters made of gingerbread figures, including a saint, some members of the nobility, and an imperial eagle.[182] In his poem, Sachs describes the land of Cockaigne, a land where everything is easily available and where even the houses can be eaten. But, as he warns the reader, in this world the vices prosper! And the real reason why the elders created this land was to punish the young gluttons who lead an indolent life and who make no effort in life.[183] The edible image is a trap for all those who, like children, march to the sound of their own stomach.

Tyrants

Continuing on from this critique, caricaturists looking to denounce the despotism of princes and politicians happily adopted the motif

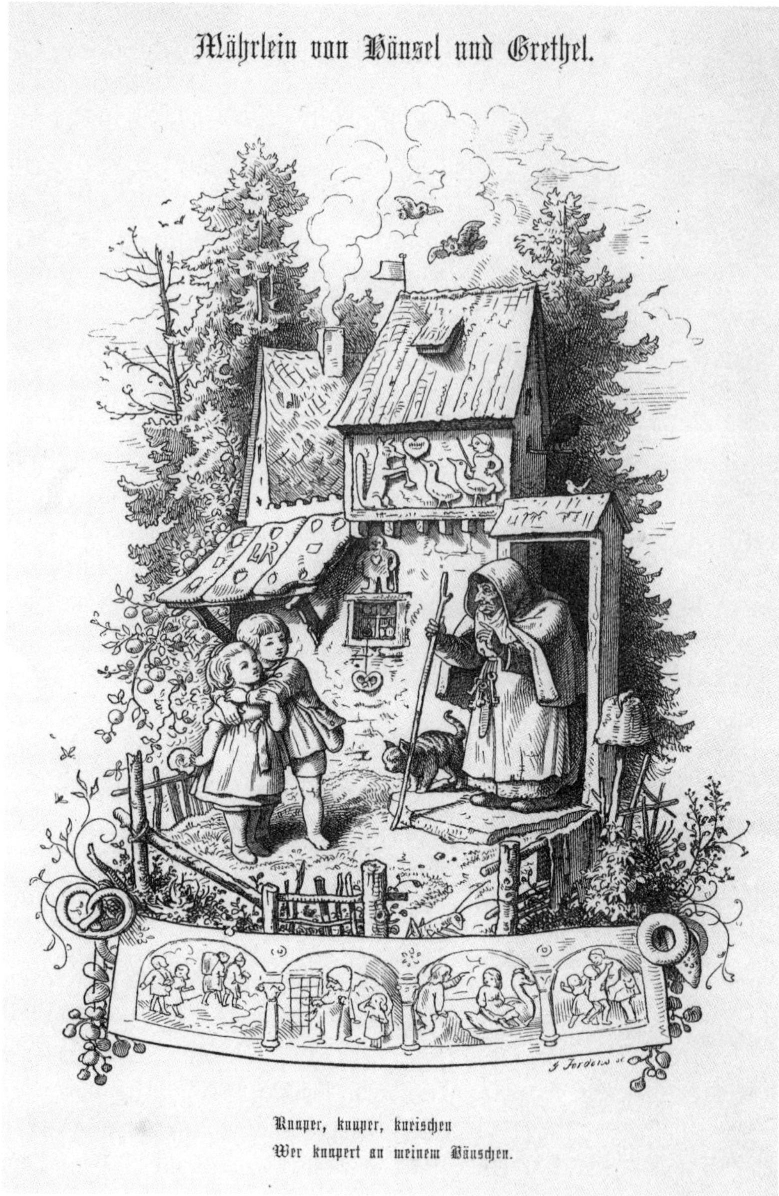

Figure 2.28. Adrian Ludwig Richter, *Wer knuspert an meinem Häuschen*? 1860, woodcut, 11.8×9.4 in., in Jacob Ludwig Carl Grimm and Wilhelm Grimm, *Hänsel und Gretel*, Bad Oeynhausen, Deutsches Märchen- und Wesersagenmuseum (© Deutsches Märchen- und Wesersagenmuseum).

Das Schlauraffenlandt.

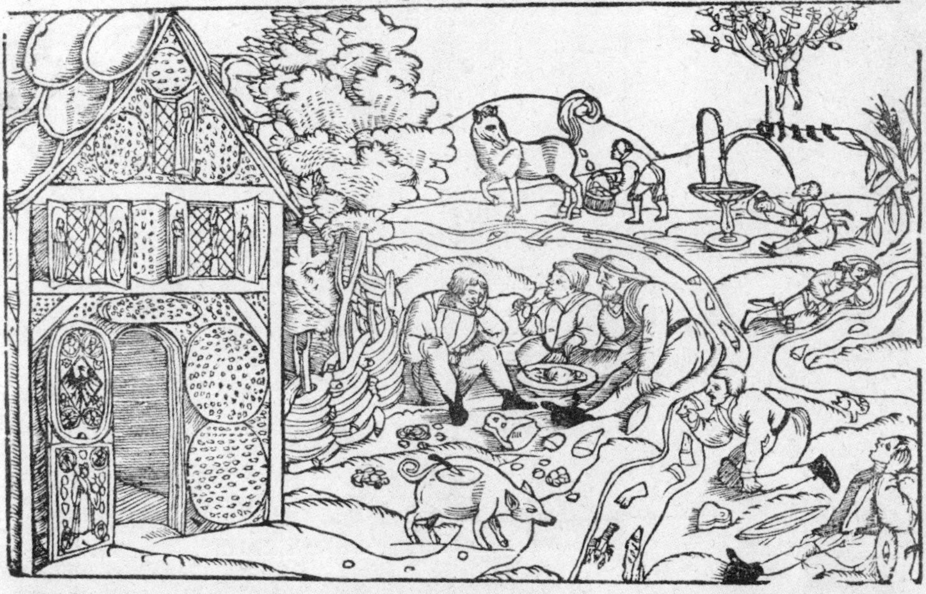

EIN gegend heyst Schlauraffenlandt
Den faulen Leuten wol bekandt
Do sindt die Heuser gedeckt mit Fladen
Leckkuchen die Haußthür vnd Laden
Von Speckkuchen Thielen vnd wend
Die Tröm von Schweynen braten sendt
Vmb yedes Hauß so ist ein Zaun
Geflochten von Bratwürsten braun
Von Malmasier so sind die Brunnen
Kommen eim selbst ins Maul gerunnen
Auff Weyden koppen die Semmel stehn
Darunter Bech mit Milch gehn
Die fallen dann in Bach herab
Das jederman zu essen hab
Auch gehn die Visch in den Lachen
Gesotten/bratten/gsultzt vnd bachen
Vnd gehn bey dem Gestadt so nahen
Lassen sich mit den Henden fahen
Auch fliegen vmb/mügt ihr glauben
Gebraten Hüner/Genß vnd Tauben
Wer sie nicht facht vnd ist so faul
Dem fliegen sie selbst in das maul
Die Sew all Jar wol geraten
Lauffen im Landt vmb sind gebraten
Yede ein Messer hat im Ruck
Damit ein jeder schneidt ein stuck
Vnnd steckt das Messer wider drein
Creutz Käß wachsen wie die Stein
So wachssen Bawren auff den bawmen
Gleich wie in vnserm Land die Pflaumen
Wenns zeytig sind so fallens ab
Yeder in ein par Stiffel rab
Wer Pferd hat wird ein reicher Meyer
Dann sie legen gantz Körb vol Ayer
Am weg vil Gelds man finden ist
Ein Junck Brun ist im Land alle frist
Darinn veriungen sich die alten
Viel kurtzweyl man im Landt thut halten
So zu dem ziel schiessen die Gest
Der weitest vom blat gewind das best
Auch ist im Landt gut Gelt gewinnen
Wer sehr faul ist vnd schlefft darinnen
Dem gibt man von der stund zwen pfenig
Er schlaff jhr gleich viel oder wenig
Ein furtz gilt ein Binger heller
Drey gröltzer einen Jochims Thaler
Vnd welcher sein Geld auch verspielt
Zwifach man jhm das wider gibt
Vnnd welcher auch nicht gern zalt
Wenn die schuld wird eins Jares alt
Muß jhm jhener zu geben ohn klag
Vnnd welcher wol trincken mag
Dem gibt man von dem trunck ein batzen
Vnd welcher wol die Leut kan fatzen
Dem gibt man ein Plappart zu lohn
Für ein grosse Lüg ein Kron
Doch muß sich da hüten ein man
Aller vernunfft frey müssig stan
Wer Sinn vnd Witz brauchen wolt
Dem würd kein Mensch im Lande holdt
Vnd wer gern arbeyt mit der handt
Dem verbeut mans Schlauraffen Landt
Wer zucht vnd erbarkeyt het lieb
Den selben man des Landts vertrieb
Wer vnnutz ist will nichts nit lehren
Der kumbt im Land zu grossen ehren
Dann wer der feulest wirdt erkandt
Derselbig ist König in dem Land
Wer wüst vnd wild vnsinnig ist
Grob vnuerstanden zu aller frist
Auß dem macht man im land ein Fürsten
Wer gern ficht mit leber würsten
Auß dem ein Ritter wirdt gemacht
Der schlüchtisch ist vnd nichts nit acht
Denn essen trincken vnd vil schlaffen
Auß dem macht man im Land ein Graffe
Wer tölpisch ist vnd nichts nit kan
Der ist im Land ein Edelman
Wer also lebt wie obgenandt
Der ist gut ins Schlauraffen Landt
Das von den alten ist erdicht
Zu straff der jugendt zu gericht
Die gewönlich ist faul vnd gefressig
Vngeschickt heyloß vnd nachlessig
Das man sie weiß in Schlauraffen
Damit jhr schlüchtig weyß zu straffen
Das sie haben auff Arbeyt acht
Weyl faule weyß nichts gutes bracht.

Zu Nürnberg/bey Wolff Strauch.

Figure 2.29. Erhard Schön (after the poem by Hans Sachs), *Das Schlauraffenlandt*, ca. 1530, engraving. Vienna, Albertina Museum (© The Albertina Museum, Vienna).

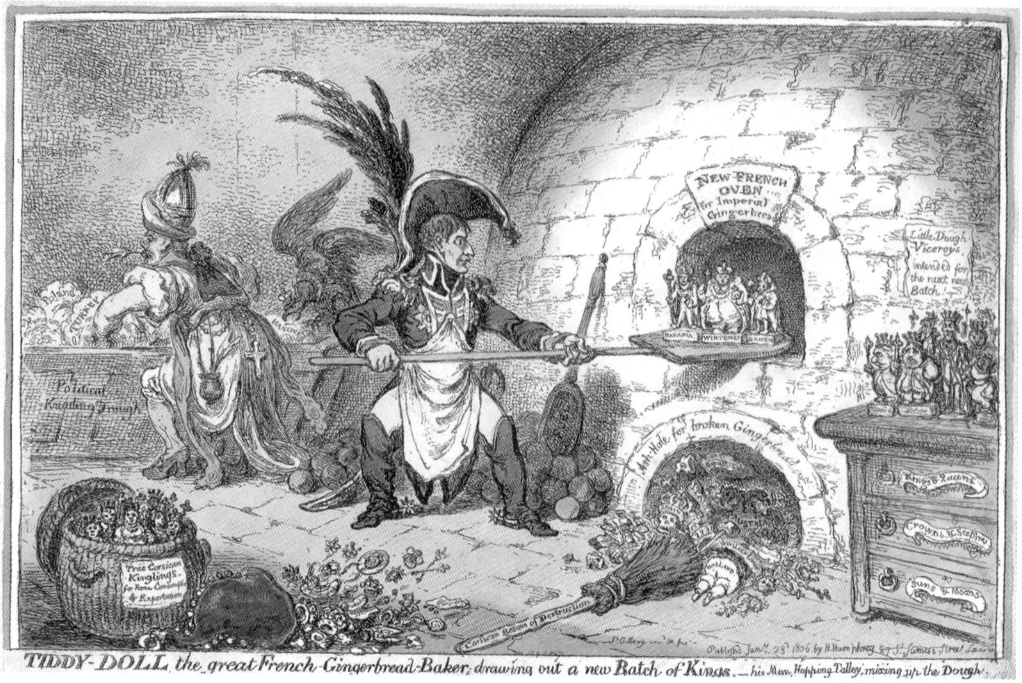

Figure 2.30. James Gillray, *Tiddy Doll: The Great French-Gingerbread-Baker*, 1806, hand-colored etching, 10.2 × 15 in. London, British Museum (© The Trustees of the British Museum).

of baking and eating gingerbread figures, a practice generally associated with children and the idle young in the modern age.[184] An engraving by James Gillray (1823–1825; fig. 2.30) depicts Napoleon, after his victories in 1805 and 1806, dressed as a baker and putting in the oven gingerbread cookies in the shape of the kings of the Germanic Bavaria, Württemburg, and Baden.[185] In the English caricaturist's rendering, Napoleon, nicknamed Tiddy Doll, is a maker of kings who is "unable to rely on the privilege of heredity" and who thus tries to solidify his authority over continental Europe by creating new kingdoms on the basis of a "gingerbread aristocracy."[186] But all these kings are ephemeral *gingerbread men*, simply edible images destined for a gastric dissolution.

A few years after this, in 1814, the caricaturist George Cruikshank (fig. 2.31) was to bring this reversal of fate to its logical conclusion by offering a follow-up to Gillray's print. Now exiled on the Island of Elba, Napoleon appears in rags carrying a plate bearing bits of broken gingerbread. As we gather from the bubble coming out of his mouth, nobody wants his already broken and half-eaten gingerbread kings: "*Buy my image! Here's my nice little gingerbread: Emperor & kings. Retail & for exportation!*"

The insolent force of the comparison between rulers and edible little men relied, in part, on the fact that these confections were commonplace, if not low-class, commodities. Typically, "gingerbread men" were little cookies costing only a few pennies, and street sellers would yell out their prices in all the cities and towns of Europe.[187] Furthermore, as we can see from the street stand in *Le marchand de pain d'épice* by Carle Vernet, engraved in 1823 by François-Séraphin Delpech (fig. 2.32), the little men offered up to children's taste buds often took the form of the characters from the *commedia dell'arte*, such as Polichinelle, Scapin, and Pierrot. In other words, these were servants and jesters, swindlers and clowns, occupying a place at the antipodes of prudent and serious rulers.

Intended for consumption, these anthropomorphic culinary specialties also echoed, in the political imagination, the figure

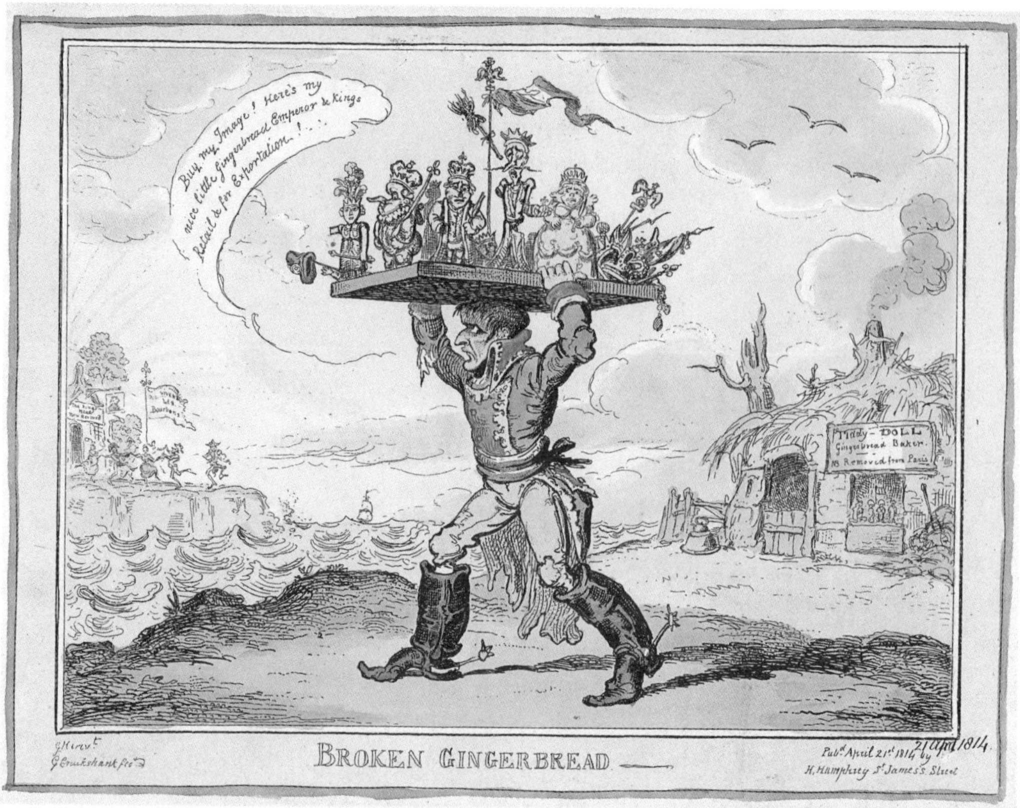

Figure 2.31. George Cruikshank, *Broken Gingerbread*, 1814, hand-colored etching, 8.4 × 10.8 in. London, British Museum (© The Trustees of the British Museum).

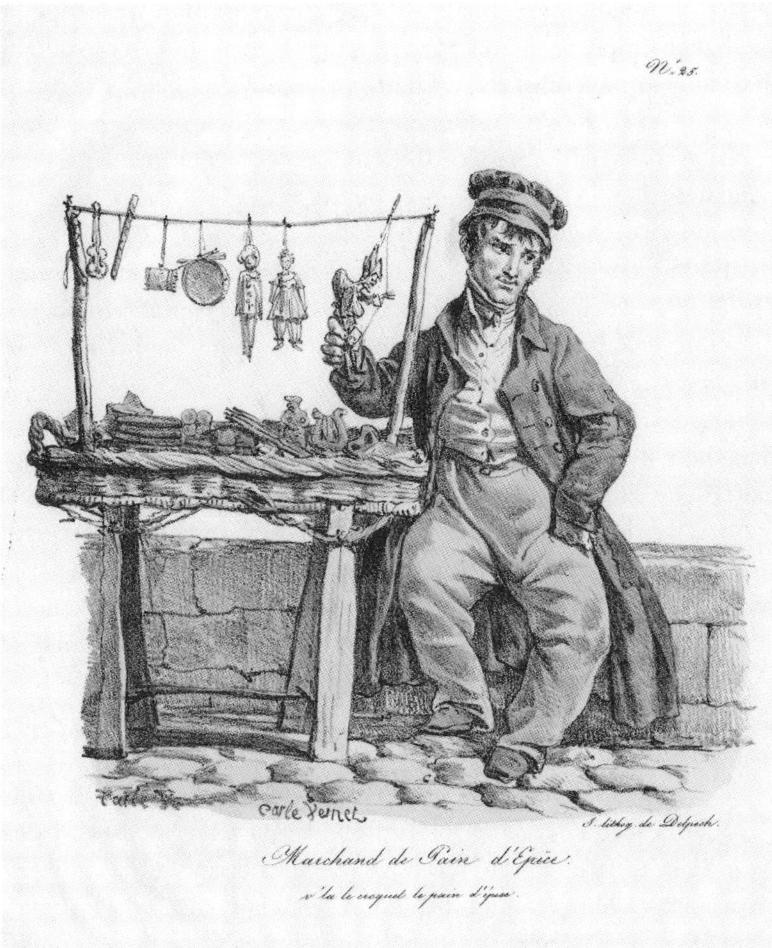

Figure 2.32. Carle Vernet, *The Gingerbread Seller*, 1823–1825, lithograph, 12.5 × 10.6 in. Paris, Musée Carnavalet (Creative Commons).

of the cannibal king.[188] Behind the relatively inoffensive image of the baker-emperor lay the idea of a monarch who was capable of devouring his enemies and even his own entire people. Caricatures of Napoleon as an ogre swallowing the globe whole, or as an anthropophage roasting the nations like chickens on a spit occurred with regularity during the last years of the reign of the "Little Corsican." Examples worth citing here include *An Attempt to Swallow the World*, an etching dated April 6, 1803, and published by William Holland; *The Plum-Pudding in Danger, or State Epicures Taking un Petit Souper*, drawn in 1806 by Gillray; or again an anonymous engraving from 1814–1815, *L'ogre dévorateur du genre humain*.

The caricature of Napoleon as a baker, however, is unlike those that show him as a cannibal despot because, in its attempt at stigmatizing political violence, it connects imaginatively with childhood. The child holds up the mirror, in fact, to the all-powerful ruler gobbling up everything he wants. Hence it is not just the abomination represented by the eater of men that is criticized here, but more generally the unmindfulness of the political world in general. The governing classes certainly do behave like cannibals, but those that they devour on the political chessboard are nothing other than puppets or cheap biscuits.

A later occurrence of the gingerbread eater lends support to this view. This is an engraving by André Gill (fig. 2.33) published in *La Petite Lune* in April 1879 in which we see Jules Ferry eating a gingerbread priest. This scathing depiction relates to the French parliamentary bill of March 15, 1879 that Ferry brought to the Assemblée nationale with the aim of forbidding all forms of religious instruction in schools. The parliamentarian Ferry chews into his adversary like a devouring tyrant, but at the same time, the religious authority that he makes his delight appears as no more significant than a simple confection.[189] The caricature thus targets both eater and eaten.

As we have seen, just as the tyrant could be likened to a confectionar or a devourer of gingerbread, the anthropomorphic cookie could itself become the object of ridicule. In the same spirit as

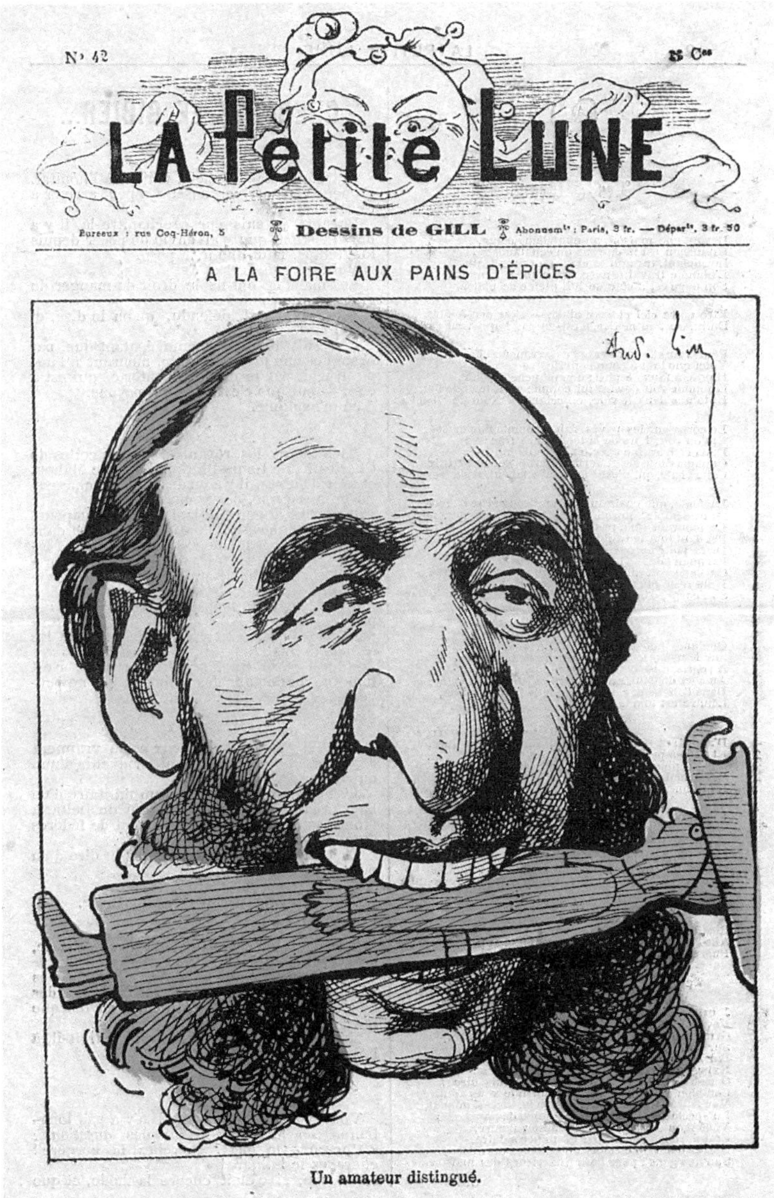

Figure 2.33. André Gill, *The Gingerbread Fair, A Distinguished Amateur* (satirical portrait of Jules Ferry), in *La Petite Lune*, April 1879, lithograph, 10.7 × 7.3 in. Paris, Musée Carnavalet (Creative Commons).

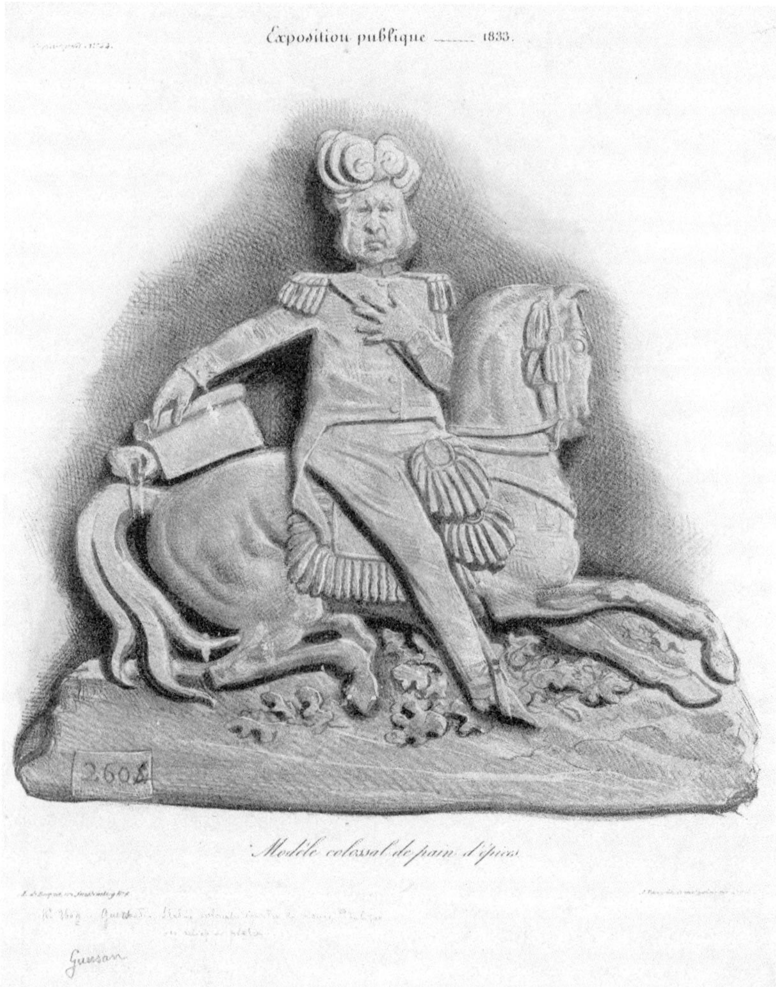

Figure 2.34. Honoré Daumier, *Colossal Model of a Gingerbread*, 1833, lithograph, 12.9 × 9.9 in. Paris, Musée Carnavalet (Creative Commons).

the satires of Gillray and Cruikshank, the gingerbread man was to become, during the nineteenth century, the archetypal image of the puppet king, liable to be wolfed down and to disappear at any moment. Similarly, in 1833, in an engraving by Honoré Daumier (fig. 2.34), the king Louis-Philippe appears thus as a gingerbread cavalier, his horse giving way under his enormous weight.[190] As the artist has stressed with his title, *Modèle colossal de pain d'épice*, this is a model not made of bronze but of flour mixed with honey, and through this substitution of ingredients it is the essential insignificance of Louis-Philippe, "Mr. Chose," that is offered up to the palate.[191] A few years later, in 1851, the same Daumier was again to use gingerbread to make fun of Léon Faucher, the member of parliament for the Marne and the last Minister of the Interior of the Second Republic (fig. 2.35).[192] Putting under his illustration the caption, "*Bas-relief en pain d'épice destiné à faire passer à la posterité la plus reculée le souvenir de l'entrée triomphale du général Léon Faucher dans la ville de Rheims* (Bas-relief in gingerbread destined to send to the most posterior posterity the memory of General Léon Faucher's triumphal entry into the city of Reims)," Daumier audaciously predicts the rapidly approaching oblivion that was in store for the politician. The edible aspect of the image, evoking the whole alimentary cycle from mastication to defecation, is the basis of the satire through the association of an edible item ("gingerbreads" were a speciality of Reims) and a pun (i.e., "postérité," which shares its etymology with "postérieur"). Daumier points up how the fame of this man who, as interior minister and under the guise of a military "general," had pursued between 1849 and 1851 decidedly anti-socialist and authoritarian policies would eventually turn into pure excrement.[193]

The rage for using gingerbread in caricatures can also be explained by the huge increase in popularity of the Paris Gingerbread Fair over the course of the nineteenth century (fig. 2.36). The fair took place traditionally on the Monday after Easter, and it was the usual practice for people to munch on these little gingerbread

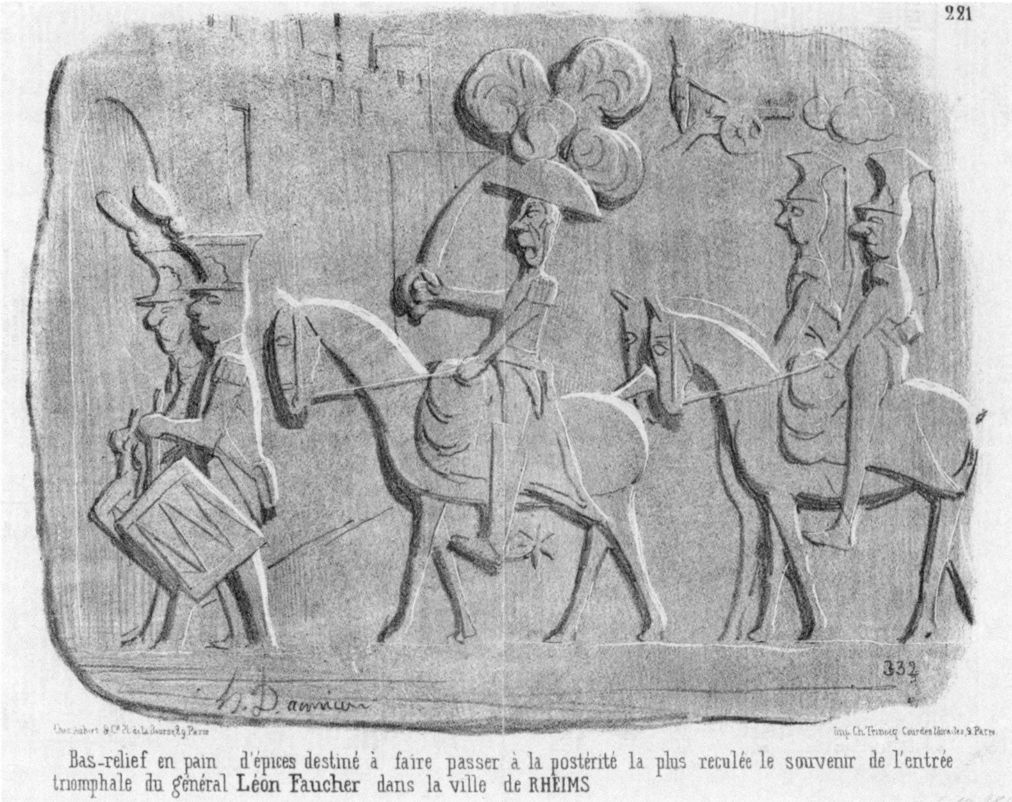

Figure 2.35. Honoré Daumier, *Bas-relief in Gingerbread Destined to Send to the Endmost Posterity the Memory of General Léon Faucher's Triumphal Entry into the City of Reims*, 1851, lithograph, 10.2 × 14 in. Paris, Musée Carnavalet (Creative Commons).

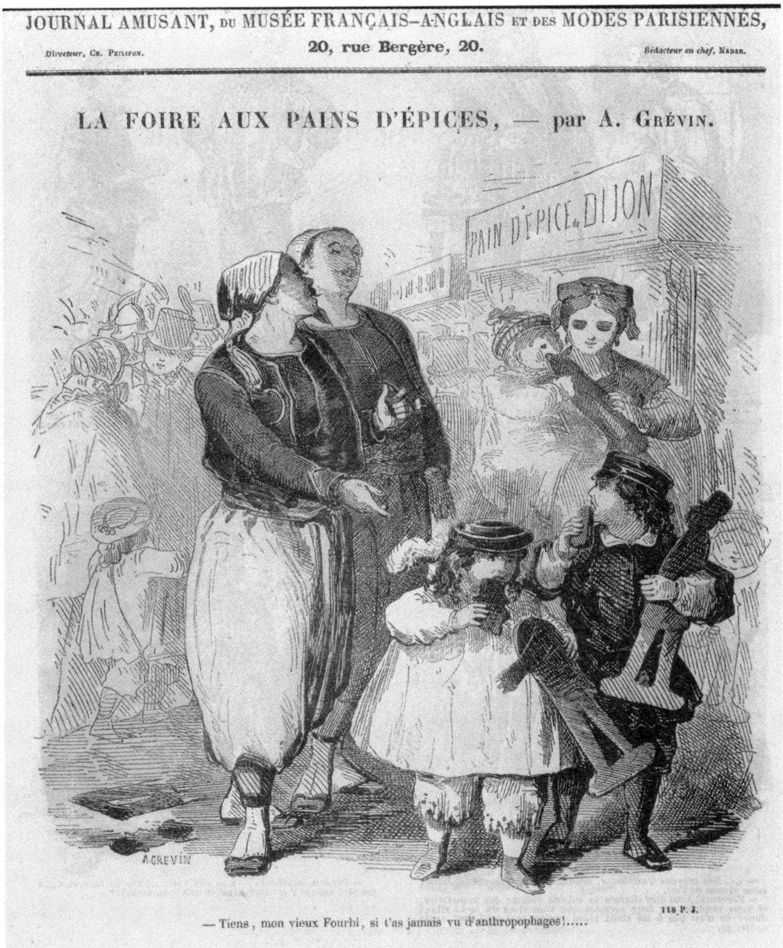

Figure 2.36. Alfred Grévin, *The Gingerbread Fair*, ca. 1860–1870, lithograph, in Charles Philipon, ed., *Le petit journal pour rire*. Private collection.

effigies of public figures.[194] The humorous account of a certain Argus, published in *La semaine des familles* (1872) shortly after the demise and exile of the Emperor Napoleon III, provides us with a good picture of this tradition:

> The gingerbread is typically made in the form of a *bonhomme* [a little man], and, the usual practice of the manufacturers of the Place du Trône has been to delicately flatter (so they thought) the Emperor Napoleon III by making the little men more or less in his image. This year, as one would expect, they have refrained from making their figures in the shape of the fallen sovereign, but they have not thought to replace him with the image of M. Thiers. Another symptom! Such is, for some, the prestige of the power of the throne! . . . A President of the Republic can give dinners at the Elysée Palace, have his own aides-de-camp, bestow on himself military honors like a king or emperor; but he cannot immediately attain the apotheosis of supreme power that is represented by his own effigy in gingerbread.[195]

Although, as Argus indicates, in the spring of 1872 the "manufacturers" of the fair in Place du Trône did not appear to have sold from their stands little gingerbread men with the image of President Adolphe Thiers, a few years later, on May 7, 1876, the illustrator Gill was to have fun with these satirical effigies and the possible substitution by personifying the French Republic as a gingerbread man with a little goatee and moustache, a walking cane, tailcoat, top hat, and monocle (fig. 2.37)—the French Republic taking *la place* du Trône. Now this pastry "Republic," that, for the readers of the satirical weekly *L'éclipse* probably recalled the appearance on the scene of the Republicans recently victorious in the legislative elections of March 1876, finds itself seized and devoured by a very young girl.[196] As the Republicans were unwilling to accept a monarchist president, Patrice de Mac Mahon, and France seemed "ungovernable," here once again, the ephemeral gingerbread effigy appears as both the sign of political instability and as the derisory plaything of a child who could, with no more ado, consume the image of power.[197]

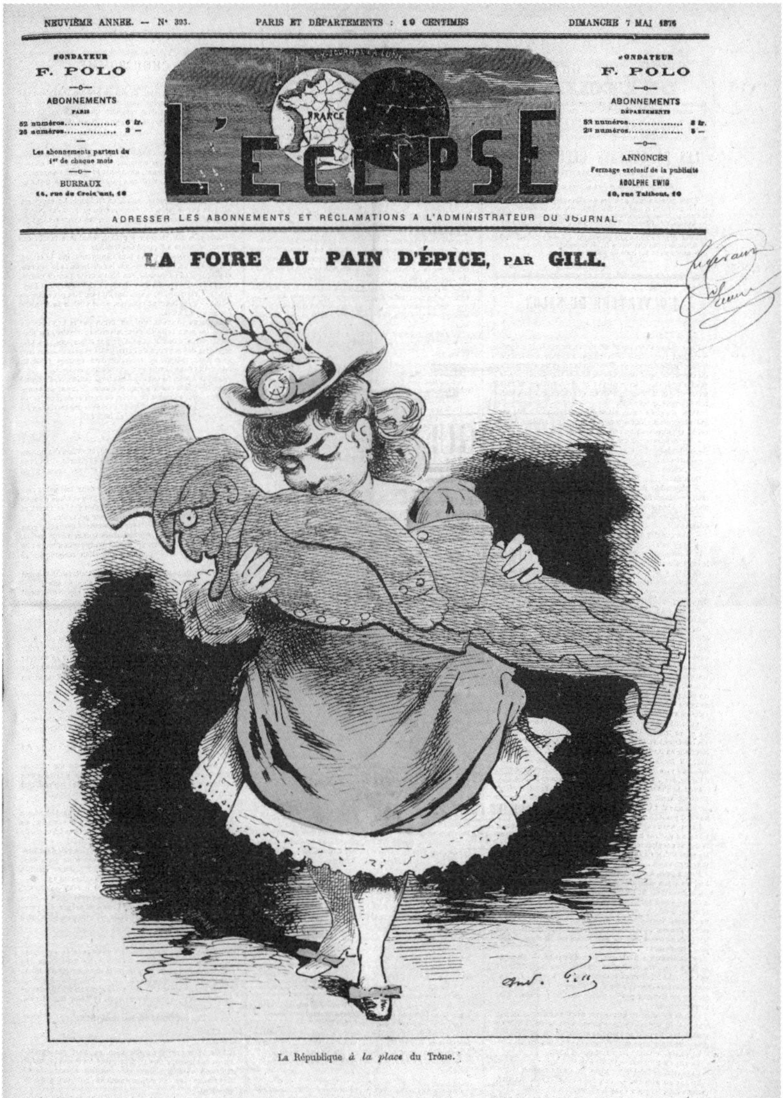

Figure 2.37. André Gill, *The Gingerbread Fair, the Republic Replaces the Throne*, in F. Polo, ed., *L'Éclipse*, May 7, 1876. Paris, Musée Carnavalet. Private collection (Creative Commons).

Zeuxis's Fruits of Reason

In the same way that ingesting and dissolving a gingerbread man departs from the inclusive and coextensive ideal of the *corpus mysticum*—because a child might eat the image, moved only by her own desire and without consideration for its potential significance—the real devouring of a painting, or of any other work of art for that matter, constitutes the polar opposite of the alimentary metaphor running through the discourse of artists and poets as it pertains to the mimetic procedure. A painting cannot be really offered up to the mouth or teeth of the viewer. It must be contemplated from a distance through the wise and educated eye of a connoisseur. The story of the Grapes of Zeuxis (fig. 2.38), one of Pliny the Elder's myths that has been the most frequently called upon in writings on art since Antiquity, shows this clearly: eating a work of art is the height of error and *unreason* in one's approach to art. In his *Natural History*, Pliny, in fact, presents the rivalry between Zeuxis and Parrhasius. Zeuxis's

> contemporaries and rivals were Timanthes, Androcydes, Eupompus and Parrhasius. This last, it is recorded, entered into a competition with Zeuxis, who produced a picture of grapes so successfully represented that birds flew up to the stage-buildings; whereupon Parrhasius himself produced such a realistic picture of a curtain that Zeuxis, proud of the verdict of the birds, requested that the curtain should now be drawn and the picture displayed; and when he realized his mistake, with a modesty that did him honor he yielded up the prize, saying that whereas he had deceived birds Parrhasius had deceived him, an artist.[198]

With this anecdote, Pliny seems to be adhering to the Aristotelian distinction between the judgement of the senses and that of the intellect.[199] The senses allow us to identify the things of this world by introducing distinctions between the parts that make it up, but the senses are only the first stage on the way to knowledge. We must go beyond appearances, beyond the aspects of things, in order to reach a genuine and fully intellectual understanding of phenomena.[200] For Pliny, anyone who limited themselves to the

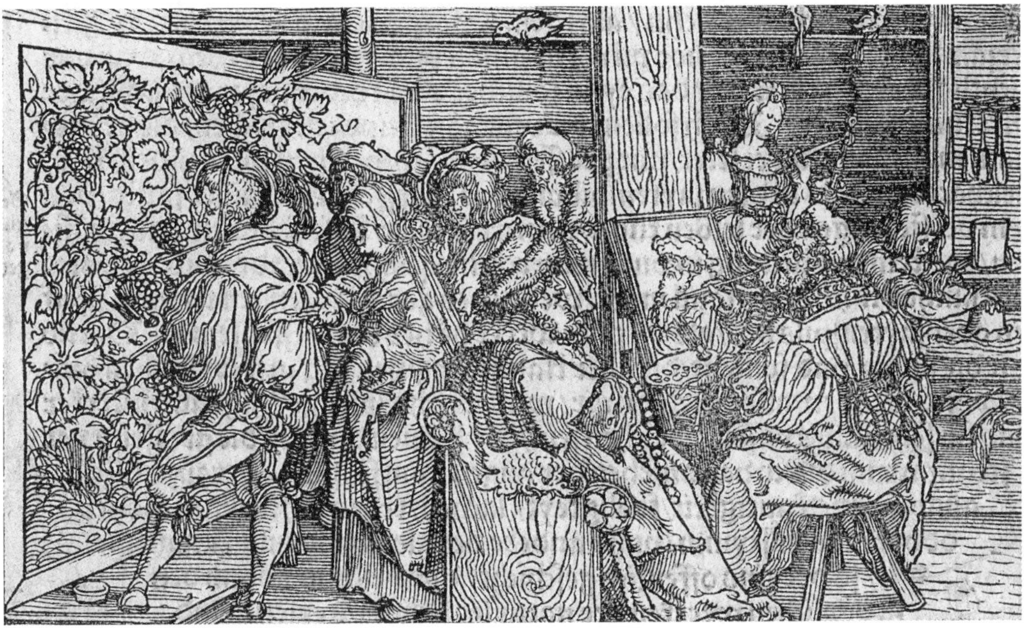

Figure 2.38. Hans Weiditz, *Painter's Studio*, engraving, 3.7 × 6 in., in Petrarch, *Von der Artzney bayder Glück* (Augsburg: Heinrich Steiner, 1522). London, British Museum (© The Trustees of the British Museum).

judgement of the senses alone was running the risk of being fooled, like an animal before a painting; while anyone who called upon his or her intelligence, and upon the faculty of reason, would break free from illusion. But there is more in Pliny's story, where the author indicates furthermore that a painting cannot be "consumed" other than by the eye. To touch a painting, and *a fortiori* to taste it, was an improper way to experience it, and the viewer who allowed himself or herself to descend to such relations with a painting would cede control to the animal within.[201]

This setting of the image at a distance, along with its relative dematerialization, was to find its point of culmination in the French Classical age with René Descartes's treatise *La dioptrique.* For Descartes, it was the soul and not the body that received the sensations,[202] and although in the eighteenth century the proponents of sensualism and empiricism — most notably John Locke, David Hume, and Étienne Bonnot de Condillac — were to restore epistemological importance to the senses, the aesthetic object was still to be entirely reserved for the sense of sight, excluding therefore the senses of taste or touch.[203] The argument about which was more important, drawing or color, partly involved the distinction between optical and haptic perception.[204] But even those defenders of color who believed that a painting could satisfy our senses of taste and touch by endowing the eye with a tactile and gustatory sensitivity did not go so far as to think that a painting could really be eaten. Consider, for example, Denis Diderot's superb analysis:

> When I look at other artists' paintings, I feel I need to make myself a new pair of eyes; to see Chardin's I only need to keep those which nature gave me and use them well. . . . For the porcelain vase is truly of porcelain: those olives are really separated from the eye by the water in which they float; you have only to take those biscuits and eat them, to cut and squeeze that orange, to drink that glass of wine, peel those fruits and put the knife to the pie.[205]

Yet, as Jean-Claude Lebensztejn points out, Diderot "might well be able to eat Chardin's biscuits," but he still "has to stand back a bit":[206]

> This magic is beyond comprehension. There are thick layers of paint, laid one on top of the other, which interpenetrate from the bottom to the top layer. In other places, it is as if a vapor had been breathed on the canvas; in others still, as if a light foam had been thrown on it. Rubens, Berghem, Greuze, Loutherbourg could explain this technique better than I, for all of them could make your eyes feel its effect. Come close, and everything becomes confused, flattens out and vanishes; move back, and everything takes shape once again and recomposes itself.[207]

There can be no genuinely gustatory appreciation of painting. Everything must pass through the eye to the mind.[208] Jacqueline Lichtenstein reminds us that "the pleasure of seeing requires that this desire be contained"; rather, it "requires one to keep one's distance."[209]

Certain eighteenth-century critics, glossing on the potential confusion between "natural taste" and "acquired taste"[210]—the result, according to Roger de Piles, of transferring the taste of "the tongue" to that of "the mind"[211]—were to seize on the vocabulary of cooking to denigrate those painters they saw as daubers seeking to flatter the senses rather than the intelligence through an excessive foregrounding of the substance of the paint.[212] Such painting was thus seen as a cheap cuisine that offered up its dishes to the appetites of viewers so unsophisticated as to be unable to distinguish between "natural and artistic beauty"; in other words, between still life and life's own stillness.[213] Indeed, the comparison between painting and cooking was to become the subject of satires. In 1755, the Genevan minituarist painter and art critic Jean André Rouquet ridiculed Diderot's 1755 essay, *L'histoire et le secret de la peinture en cire* in his pamphlet titled *L'art nouveau de la peinture en fromage, ou en ramequin, inventée pour suivre le louable projet de trouver graduellement des façons de peindre inférieures à celles qui existent.* This was a project that Rouquet's friend Hogarth would have probably applauded. In his text, Rouquet describes a fictive technique of "painting in cheese" that he considers perfect when applied to bread:[214]

> This way of painting is not applicable on wood, and neither is it applicable on muslin, taffeta, nor even on ordinary canvas, for which painting in soap is so marvelously adapted. Cheese rejects all these substances in favor of its natural association with bread. In order to prepare the surface on which you wish to paint, take wheat flour and make a dough with some whey (pure milk will make it too crumbly because of the butter it contains). The dough will take any form you wish, and you will even see that it spreads out under the rolling pin.[215]

The facetious author makes it clear that a recipe such as this runs the risk of being a little too appetizing. So, to prevent the work from disappearing, he suggests spoiling the binder:

> It will be good to mix into your dough a small quantity of extract of bitter apples so that the bitterness will stop the worms, mice, and children from eating your paintings. This is what happened to the first painting I did, through my having omitted to take this precaution. If the painting in ramekin does not appear sufficiently debased, you can debase it some more by eliminating the bitter apples and exposing it thus to the inconvenience of being eaten.[216]

Echoing a previous point, animals and children are both designated in these lines as the viewers most likely to fall into the trap of illusion and to try to eat the picture. Rouquet then takes this absurdity to its logical conclusion. He suggests that the technique could, in fact, provide nourishment for the "poor painters in ramekin," who would thus be able to "immediately eat their paintings for dinner, & more easily than Painters of other genres."[217]

This type of culinary satire, still relatively rare in the Age of Enlightenment, was to become widespread during the nineteenth century. It was used to denigrate in a single stroke works by artists of the day that were either too academic or too modern. Jacqueline Lichtenstein and Frédérique Desbuissons each show how, in the reviews of the *Salon*, paintings were frequently likened to "a sickly mush of overripe fruit," "a crust," "a stew of colors," "meat and cabbage soup," "a turnip," "a slice of bread and butter," or "a buttery mess."[218] Quite naturally, going along with this line of criticism denigrating works of art is the suggestion that ingesting a painting was the most commonplace sign of error in matters pertaining to art, a sign not only of a wrong approach on the part of the viewer in using their sensual faculties as a means to enter into relations with the products of the fine arts but also, and perhaps even more so, a sign of poor taste on the part of the artist insofar as the latter was seeking to appeal to the sense of touch and not to that of sight, aiming thus to seduce the senses rather than the intellect.[219] Eating paintings was the result of the perfect ignorance of certain viewers, falling into traps set for them by a whole brigade of sauce-chef, baker, and baker's-boy painters deliberately confusing art and cooking. In turn, Émile Zola uses precisely this culinary vocabulary to stigmatize the visitors who "gorge themselves" on the academic paintings that win success at the *Salon*:

> You know the effect that M. Manet's paintings have at the Salon. Quite simply, they crack open the walls. All around them are arranged the sweet offerings of the fashionable artistic confectioners: sugar-candy trees, houses in pâté crust, gingerbread gentlemen, and vanilla cream ladies. The candy store is becoming more and more sweet and rosy, and our artist's canvases seem to take on a certain bitterness in the midst of this milky river. You only have to see the ugly looks on the faces of the grown-up children walking about in the room. You couldn't get them to pay tuppence to swallow a piece of real flesh endowed with the reality of life. But, like unhappy souls, they gorge themselves on all the disgusting sweets offered them.[220]

Zola's disparaging of the gluttonous gaze as it enjoys a painting in almond paste is an amplification of Pliny's myth of the difference in judgement between both a humanity endowed with reason and the lower animals, and human children, that are guided by their sensations alone. But it is also at work in a certain view of painting as something detached from any referent, opposed to all forms of illusionism, and entirely devoted to the conquest of the work's own surface layer—a view that was to triumph in the 1950s in the writings of the American art critic Clement Greenberg. Indeed, it is very much starting from and, in a particular way, going against this distancing of the sense of touch in aesthetic matters that the violence erupts for us in the two works by Jasper Johns that we considered briefly at the outset, *The Critic Sees* and *Painting Bitten by a Man* (see fig. I.2). The latter painting's title speaks loudly the complete aberrance in the modern era of seeing a work with one's teeth, or consuming it with one's mouth.

CHAPTER THREE

Sharing Images

They did assemble there indeed, like the early Christians,
not to partake merely of a material nourishment,
which was incidentally exquisite, but in a sort of social Eucharist.
—Marcel Proust, *The Guermantes Way*, 1920

Eating images to heal oneself, to protect oneself, and to have dealings with a supernatural entity; dreaming that statues or paintings come to life and offer their flowing milk or blood for one to drink in order to fill oneself with wisdom; imagining that tyrants grind up with their sharp teeth an edible humanity; and that children unthinkingly gobble down the pictures surrounding them. These are so many ways in which individuals might practice and imagine for themselves the ingestion of images. Yet, these are only a few scenarios among a multitude of others that have punctuated the course of our history, either openly or in secret. Aside from these mouthfuls (wise or wild, literal or metaphorical), there were indeed many other forms of ingesting that we must keep in mind. These were *agapae* (image love feasts) that took place at meals, ceremonies, and festivals, either ritualized, merely routine, or extraordinary or everyday, and that which involved the sharing of signs and stories to establish, extend, and perhaps even transform the lives of communities.[1] In the Roman world, for example, sacrificial cakes were eaten to consolidate membership in a social class. In the Christian sphere, eucharistic wafers bearing stamped images were eaten to reduce the distance separating men from God. In the medieval towns and cities, people ate molded gingerbreads to establish a community on the inclusive model of the *corpus mysticum*. During the Renaissance, they ate wafers bearing heraldic symbols to celebrate a genealogical line and to ratify marriages between noble and patrician families. The social order of the state was confirmed or attacked through an alimentary architecture just as people used sculpted dishes to celebrate the unique identities of artists' corporations. As we shall see, all these forms of iconophagy had one thing in common: they made edible images the operators of *social* relations.[2]

The Sacrificed Image

To begin, let us start the service with Hubert Damisch:

> Curiously, V. [Valerio Adami] chooses the moment when I have just finished reading Madeleine Biardeau and Charles Malamoud's book on *Le Sacrifice dans l'Inde ancienne* (Sacrifice in Ancient India) to let me know, rather out of the blue, that he has always understood art as a form of atonement for and redemption from cannibalism.
>
> Intended, as it was, to ensure the cohesion of beings and things, to make them hold together, the Vedic sacrifice forbade any recourse to images. Now, it seems likely that *the latter were first introduced into the ritual in the form of effigies intended to replace certain victims* (primarily human?). It was a prelude, therefore, to the replacement of blood sacrifices by temple worship, and to the eventual iconic proliferation that characterizes India. This led, accordingly, to the establishment of another economy of consumption (of sacrifice), and another way of *expenditure*.
>
> The atonement for cannibal orality takes place in and through language—the organ of taste becomes that of the spoken word. If there is, and if there must be, devouring, and firstly predation, it will henceforth happen either by way of the ear or the eye.[3]

According to Damisch's philosophical *rêverie*, images would thus have intervened in religious rituals in India to replace blood sacrificial rites. In other words, representations would have been introduced in place of meat, bringing about a move from a real sacrifice to a symbolic sacrifice as the real sacrificial victim was progressively replaced with its representation. As a result of this radical change, the worshipper would allegedly have passed from a tactile relationship with the supernatural to an oral, auditory, and visual relationship with the transcendent world.

A good number of historians and anthropologists have likewise seen this double sequencing—from the real to the symbolic and from the palate to the eye—in the Mediterranean civilizations, and even more so in the religions of the Book. From his reading of ancient Greek and Roman texts, Jean-Louis Schefer has recently written:

> According to the accounts of Firmicus Maternus, Justin, and Plutarch (*Isis, On the Obsolescence of Oracles, The Roman Questions*), primitive omophagy (the eating of raw flesh) was replaced by a meal during which bread was shared.... Christianity emerged, as did the eastern religions, at the end of a process of ritual simplification through which the offerings become symbolic, the eating of raw flesh and the consumption of blood being replaced everywhere by bread and a beverage, a mixture of wine and water.[4]

But can we be so sure about this chain of events? And can we really conclude from these ancient readings of Firmicus Maternus, Justin, or Plutarch that Christianity opted for a bloodless sacrifice for exactly the same reasons as did the Eastern religions?[5] Marcel Detienne and Jean-Paul Vernant show, in the works assembled in their book, *The Cuisine of Sacrifice Among the Greeks*, that this universal and teleological substitution has, in reality, very little historical foundation.[6] A study of the ancient Greek, Egyptian, and Roman textual corpus explodes the idea that symbolic sacrifices put an end to blood sacrifices in the area of the Mediterranean.[7] There was no more a progressive essentializing of sacrifice than there was a substitution of one form for another. Images coexisted with animal-blood sacrificial practices. Animal sacrifice in Hellenistic Egypt, Greece, or Rome was often accompanied by effigies in the form of the sacrificed animals, and yet, for all that, the images did not substitute for the real animals, save for economic reasons. Furthermore, as Jean-Claude Lacam explains, describing the *vestiça* (an Italic sacrificial cake):

> This offering does not fit . . . within the context of the rejection of bloody sacrifice; it does not represent, as has been said of inanimate offerings, an evolved form of sacrifice since it does not substitute for the putting to death of the animal, and it underscores, on the contrary, the refinement of the process by which the victim is transformed into edible meat . . . . The cakes join the animal offering when the latter, to use the terms of Lévi-Strauss' famous "culinary triangle," leaves the sphere of the "raw" for that of the "cooked," or at least to approach it since, as Lévi-Strauss has shown, the "roasted" is an intermediate category situated between the two poles. The cakes are positioned thus, just as much as the cooked meats, and even more so because with cakes there is no half-cooking, on the side of civilization and culture.[8]

Given this, what can we say now about Damisch's idea of the substitution of the eye for the mouth? Even if we were to prove the existence of such a development for India, could it be generalized to all societies? The production and use of *edible* images for use in rituals suggests not. Such artifacts, consciously made to be seen and consumed, dissuade us from a too rapid disassociation of the eye from the mouth, holding us back, therefore, from abandoning one sense organ for another.[9]

The Sacrificial Cakes of Antiquity

Bearing in mind these two points, and before looking more closely at Christianity, let us consider in more detail the edible images associated with the ancient rituals. In fact, across the entire area of the Mediterranean in this period, we do find cakes decorated with recognizable figures that were used in a sacrificial context, either as complementary offerings[10] or as substitutes, especially when the sacrificial animal was rare or too expensive.[11] The archaeologist Margarete Bieber has interpreted a 13 cm in diameter cake mold in

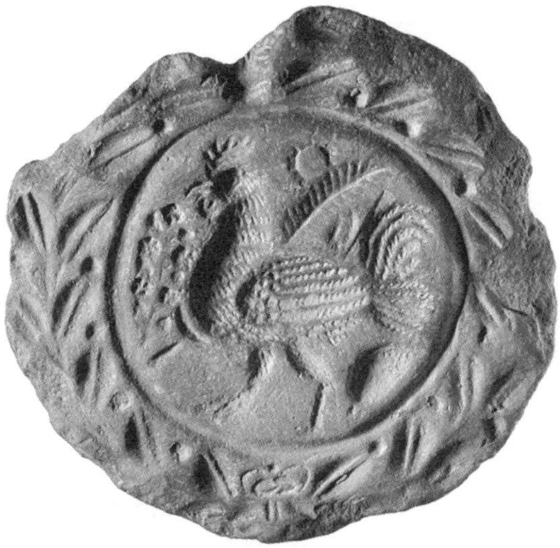

Figure 3.1. Bread-stamp with standing cock, Ptolemaic Period, terracotta, 4.3 in. London, British Museum (© The Trustees of the British Museum).

the Berlin Humboldt-Universität showing a temple, poppy flowers, dogs, torches, and in the center the *omphalos* circle as having conceivably been used to make edible images for the cult of Artemis Hekate or for the Eleusinian Festival at Athens.[12] Similarly, a terracotta mold that once belonged to Heinrich Schliemann (Staatliche Museen in Berlin, inv. 9579) showing busts of Isis and Serapis would have been used, according to Bieber, as fashion cakes for the festival of a divinity worshipped in a Trojan sanctuary.[13] These ritual foods were prepared most often with molds, but stamps could also be used to mark the dough with an image prior to cooking. Indeed, The British Museum has several objects from the Ptolemaic period bearing images of sacrificial animals, which were probably used in this way (fig. 3.1).

These archaeological traces, relatively rare before the Roman period, do nonetheless find echoes in a certain number of ancient written accounts. Plutarch, for example, in his *Isis and Osiris* (50), mentions the baking of cakes bearing the image of a hippopotamus for the festival of Typhon:

> At Hermopolis they point out a statue of Typhon in the form of an hippopotamus, on whose back is poised a hawk fighting with a serpent. By the hippopotamus they mean to indicate Typhon, and by the hawk a power and rule, which Typhon strives to win by force, oftentimes without success, being confused by his wickedness and creating confusion. For this reason, when they offer sacrifice on the seventh day of the month Tybi, which they call the "Coming of Isis from Phoenicia," they imprint on their sacred cakes the image of an hippopotamus tied fast.[14]

In Rome, among the vast array of cakes made for the religious ceremonies, we know that the *liba* ("offering") often bore images.[15] In his *De lingua Latina* (VII, 44), Varro points out that these pastries were made by *fictores* ("image makers"), placed under the authority of *pontifices* ("pontiffs"), and whose role, such as we assume it from the name attaching to their profession, was to produce elaborately shaped cakes.[16] Servius, for his part, mentions in his commentary on Virgil's *Aeneid* a zoomorphic cake often used by the officiating priests as a substitute when it was impossible for them to obtain a real sacrificial animal:[17] "And one should know that in the rites the pretend is often taken for the true. When it is necessary to sacrifice animals but difficult to procure them, the sacrifice is carried out with [figured] breads or waxen figures, and these are accepted in place of the true."[18]

These pastries were generally offered to the divinities during public or private sacrifices. Typically placed at the foot of the statues of the gods, the offerings were then burned—destruction by fire making disappear the part owed to the gods, miming thus the consumption of the offering by the divinity.[19] It did, however, sometimes happen that in the course of certain rituals, a portion of the offerings was taken and distributed among the people according to their rank and function.[20] The return of the offering, materializing the pact binding men with the gods, lent substance to the principle of "sharing" that, as John Scheid shows, was "characteristic of [Roman] sacrifice."[21] As Scheid writes, "sacrifice was a way of establishing, by way of a feast to which the gods were invited, and through the sharing of food or a victim, the relations setting everyone in his or her place: men in relation to gods, citizens in their relations one with another."[22] The shared and consumed image would thus be, in fact, one of the religious operators allowing for the renewal, at regular intervals, the structure of the community. In other words, it allowed, like any other sacrificial food, for sharing to take place between men and gods, the living and the dead, and between the various classes that made up society.[23]

Cakes decorated with figures were also used as part of a more specific form of ritualized ingestion of images in Antiquity, the initiatory ingestion that we find notably in the Egyptian religion.[24] According to a Greek papyrus (PGM XIII) dating from the fourth century BCE and concerning Egyptian rituals, the initiation into the mysteries of the deacons took place through the making of "three figures from fine flour," "one bull-faced, one goat-faced, one ram-faced, each standing atop a celestial sphere, having an Egyptian flail." Everything was to be "censed" and "eaten" during the reciting of a magical formula addressed to "the gods of the hours."[25] The purpose of the operation was to initiate the successful candidate into the decons' mysteries by giving him the means to incorporate, literally and symbolically, the magical knowledge shared by the priests. The act of eating, furthermore, allowed the candidate to be "inhabited" by the divinities, and to become, by this means, one of their servants. Ingesting the image, therefore, had a dual effect: not only did it assign the initiated a new place in society, but it also carried out a transformation of his very nature, endowing the initiated individual with the new knowledge that authorized his taking up of this new place in society. The change in social position was thereupon essentially a change of state.

The Christian Sacramental Bread

Unlike the Egyptian, Greek, and Roman religions, Christianity limited the type of offerings by making bread the principal, but not the only,[26] consecrated substance around which the liturgy was organized.[27] In the early days of the Church, before the emperor Justinian's establishment of the pentarchy in the sixth century, the bread used for the mass was offered up by the faithful as an oblation. The dough was usually a leavened dough, less commonly unleavened (unraised bread was adopted later by the Armenian Church and was to become predominant in the Latin Churches after the Council of Toledo in 693), and it was stamped with the aid of a bread stamp[28] or marked with a cross either by knife or with the finger (e.g., in the fourth century, the disciples of Marcion marked it with a red cross using the eucharistic wine[29]). With stamps, the symbols used could be relatively complex. Indeed, in Coptic Egypt, seals and molds have been found that show a dove, a lamb, and a fish. The early Christians adopted the latter figure as a sign of recognition and eucharistic symbol since the Greek term *ichtys* (ἰχθύς; "fish") is the acrostic of the expression "Jesus Christ, Son of God, Savior."

In the Orthodox Church, a seal bearing symbols and an inscription was gradually to become the predominant tool for marking leavened bread.[30] Typically made in two superposed parts representing Christ's dual nature, human and divine, this bread called *prosphera* was blessed by the priest and was the subject of a complex liturgy, traditionally attributed to Saint John Chrysostom.[31] In the Slavic rite, these *prospherae* were small in size, and they are typically contrasted with the large ones used in the Greek rite.[32] In both cases, however, the *prosphera* bore the mark of a quadripartite and cruciform seal with the letters *IC XC NI KA* (Jesus Christ Victorious), the idea being to signify, by the inscription and the geometrical shape, Christ's sacrifice and its redeeming power.[33] This part of the prosphera, known as the *Amnos* ("Lamb"), was identified with the body of Christ at the moment of the *epiclesis* (invocation of the Holy Spirit). During the *proscomidia* (the preparation of the bread and wine for the Eucharist), preceding the *anaphora* (the thanksgiving prayer of the Eucharistic liturgy), it was detached from the lower part of the bread by means of a "lance," as the celebrant recited the prophesy of Isaiah (53:7–8), whereupon, placed with its upper side facing the paten, it was incised with a cross. The *Amnos* was once again turned around, upper side uppermost, and then pierced by the lance in memory of the wounds in Christ's side inflicted by Longinus. Next there came the second phase of the ceremony, called *panaghia* in the Slavic rite, during which the celebrant extracted from a second oblation triangular pieces representing the Virgin Mary and referring symbolically to the Holy Trinity.[34] Finally, a third phase involved the extraction of nine sections of bread from another oblation in memory of the saints, before the ceremony concluded with the cutting up of the parts commemorating the living and the dead. All the selected bread pieces were then gathered and placed upon the paten according to an order established by the Divine Liturgy of Saint John Chrysostom, and they were then brought to the altar for the consecration. Only a small portion of the bread from the part designated as the "Body of Christ" was distributed to the believer for the communion. Dipped first in the chalice, containing wine mixed with a little water,[35] the eucharistic bread was then placed in the mouth of the communicant who saw him or herself thus transformed, in the words of John Chrysostom, into the dwelling place of the Spirit.[36] Christ's sacrifice was thus replayed symbolically through the association of gestures, letters, geometrical shapes, and prayers.[37]

Corpus christi

In the West, a quite different "image" was to serve as the essential vector in the eucharistic celebration: the stamped host.[38] Ephemeral by its very nature, we nonetheless know this image-object—through all the variations of its material inscriptions from the iron host presses (fig. 3.2) and, to a lesser extent, the engraved stones—was used by religious communities for making the sacrificial bread, at least as early as the ninth century.[39] The most ancient examples of these date from the twelfth century, but their use prior to this is attested by an account of a vision had by Saint Ildephonsus

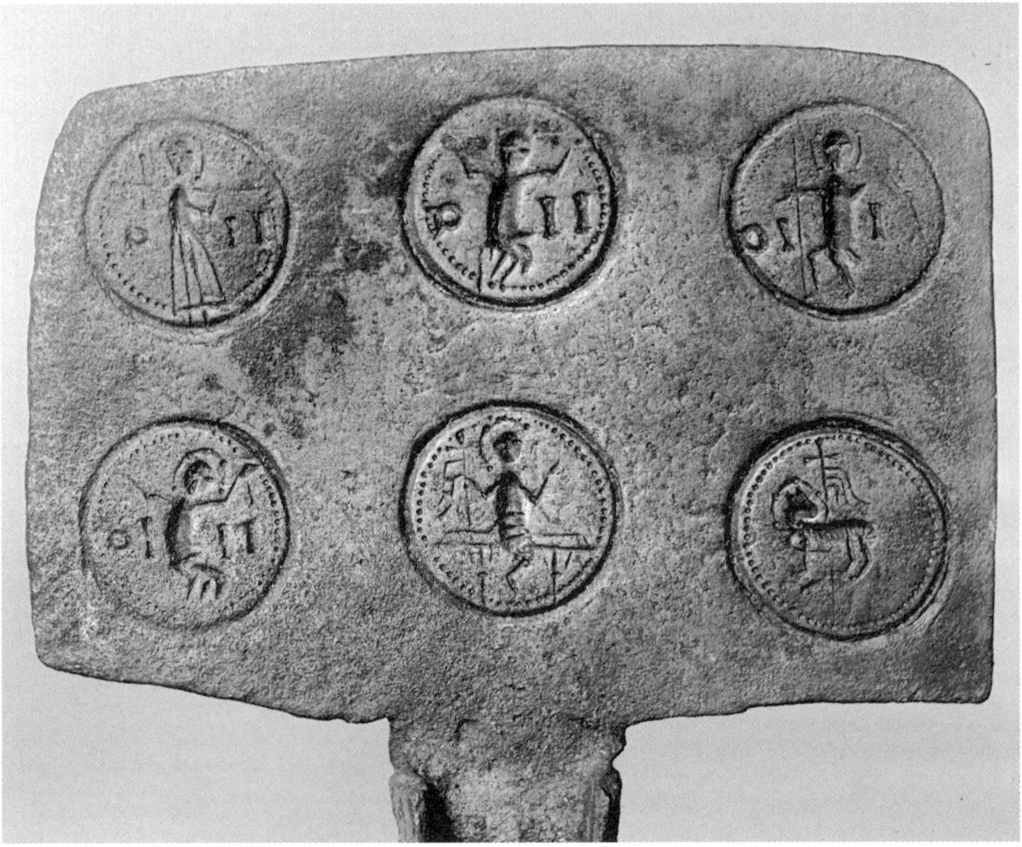

Figure 3.2. Wafering iron, thirteenth–fourteenth century, iron. Stockholm, Statens Historiska Museum (Creative Commons).

on a Sunday in November 845. The saint was said to have seen a double figure of the host in the form of "two wheels engraved by two irons."[40] Such presses, made of two plates riveted together, usually included several molds *in forma* ("in the form of") *rotulae* ("wheels") or *nummi* ("coins").[41] The iron molds were typically filled with unleavened dough, unlike what was customary in the Orthodox Church,[42] made from a mixture of white wheaten flour and water, and then were placed in the oven for cooking.[43]

Communion rituals and practices varied slightly over the course of time and from region to region, and this led to variations in the preparation of the host. During the Early Middle Ages, it was customary for the faithful to receive the *corpus Christi* in their hand; however, from the end of the ninth century, the host was more often received by the mouth in order to avoid the purity of the consecrated bread being sullied by any hand other than that of the celebrant. A distinction was made also between the larger host wafers that were broken by the priest in order to reiterate the sacrifice before being offered symbolically to the community, and the smaller unbroken wafers that were given to the communicants.[44] The frequency of taking communion also changed over time. According to the recommendations of the Fourth Lateran Council (1215), the faithful were to take communion at least once a year at Easter,[45] but certain theologians such as Nicholas of Cusa, Bernardino of Siena, and Meister Eckhart were to defend a greater frequency of communion-taking. Finally, we should note that social and geographical factors came into play: people took communion more often when they belonged to the upper classes and when they lived in urban areas, and communion-taking was less frequent among those who cultivated the land and lived farther from churches.

As far as concerns the iconographic repertoire, the host presses itself, and numerous written accounts that have come down to us provide a reasonably precise idea of the development of the molds. In the absence of any strict legislation pertaining to the host's appearance, the images in the presses were relatively diversified.[46]

According to Jean Mabillon, the first signs engraved on the inside of the circles were in the form of a cross.[47] But more complex representations of the Passion or of Christ Himself were progressively substituted for this simple geometric design. In 1136, Honorarius of Autun recommended, for example, that in the bread made in the form of a coin there be stamped an image of God made man:[48]

> Which bread, moreover, is formed in the manner of a coin [*denarii*] because Christ, the living bread, was sold for the price of coins, and he himself is the true coin, which according to the Decalogue of the law shall be given as a reward to those laboring in the vineyard.[49]

Around 1220, Pope Honorius III, for his part, promoted the use of a host depicting Christ on the Cross.[50] After this insertion of the "historical" and anthropomorphic figure of Christ, the depicted scenes were to become more diverse. Nonetheless, certain representations were to occur more frequently than others (figs. 3.3 and 3.4), and these included the Agnus Dei, the Suffering Christ, Christ Crucified, the Crucifixion with Saint John, the Virgin Mary and Mary Magdalene, the Entombment of Christ, the Last Supper, or the Resurrection — so many subjects relating to the Eucharist, the Passion, and Christ's sacrifice. The sacrificial dimension was also present in the use, after the thirteenth century, of the term itself, *hostia* ("victim").[51] In addition to this iconographic repertoire, inscriptions might accompany or even substitute for the images. These inscriptions ranged from the monogram "IHS" to extracts from the New Testament, and they included more didactic statements such as, for example, in the inscription on a host iron today in the Episcopal Museum in Vic: "*Qui mi mangara la benedicio de Deu aura* (Whoever eats me will have God's blessing)."[52]

Unlike the letters and symbols that figured on the Byzantine prosphorae, all of which corresponded to moments in the Divine Liturgy, the images stamped on the bread used in the Latin mass had no such function within the eucharistic ritual. From a purely liturgical point of view, the images were mere accessories.

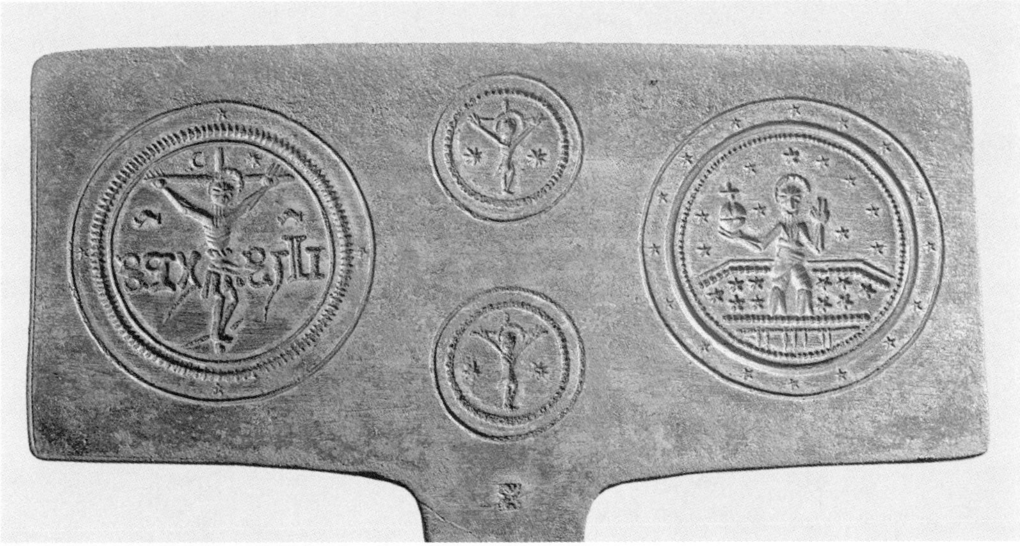

Figure 3.3. Wafering iron, fifteenth century, iron. Church of Saint-Céols (Cher). Photograph by Henri Heuzé (© Ministère de la Culture/Médiathèque du Patrimoine, Dist.RMN—Grand Palais/Art Resource, NY/Henri Heuze).

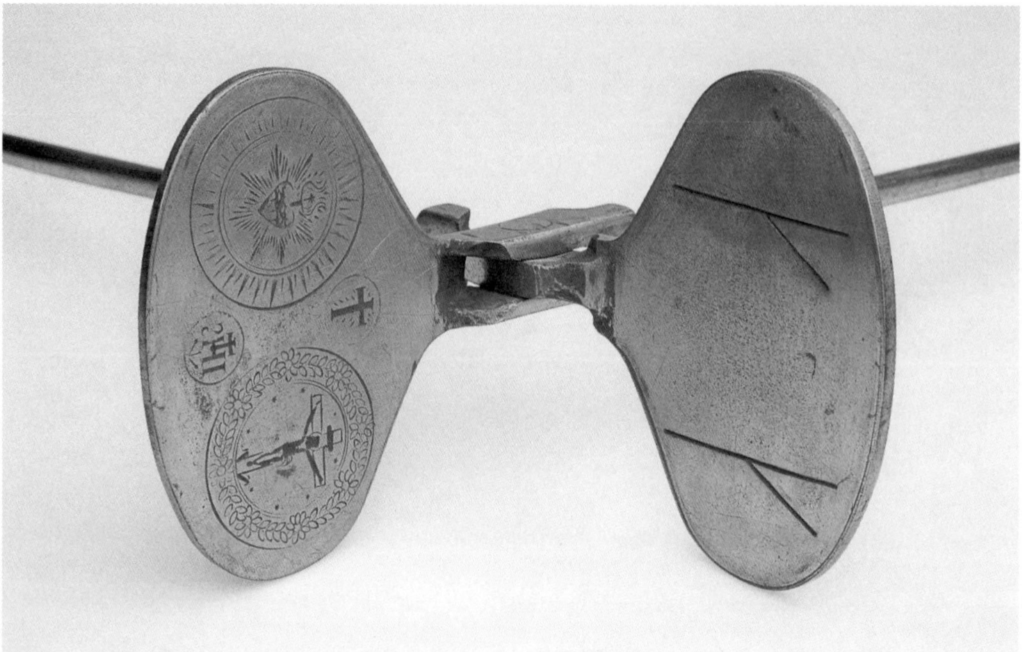

Figure 3.4. Wafering irons from Köbölkut (Hungary), ca. 1880, iron, 7 × 3 × 31 in. Victoria, Museums Victoria Collections (Creative Commons).

Consequently, we might wonder about their real status and the reasons for why their use became so widespread and well established. A possible answer, I think, might be found in the growing importance of the image of Christ in the ecclesial space from the end of the early Middle Ages, along with the progressive affirmation of the dogma of transubstantiation following the Fourth Lateran Council in 1215.[53] It is possible that the images adorning the host wafers had the function of making manifest in a concrete way the mystery of the *imago*, that is, the Incarnation of the Son of God "in the image of the Father," mentioned repeatedly in the eucharistic sacrament, and which was intended as imaginative support in the minds of the priest and the faithful during the mass. Their purpose was to be a sort of visual relay encouraging the perception of the real presence of Christ's body under the guise of the consecrated bread — the image thus suggesting in some way the process of transubstantiation to come and to be realized once the priest uttered the words: "*Hoc est enim corpus meum* (For this is my body)."[54] This hypothesis is supported by the fact that the religious authorities wanted very much to link the host with the image of Christ. Evidence for this can be seen in the following: the adoration of the *corpus Christi* on the universal feast of the same name established by Pope Urban IV in 1264 and reaffirmed by Clement V's bull *Si Dominum* in 1314;[55] the creation and use, from the end of the fourteenth century, of eucharistic monstrances allowing the faithful to contemplate and experience *per manducatio in visum* (communion with the consecrated host from a distance);[56] the increasingly systematic presence of the image of Christ at the altar in sculptures and paintings;[57] the cults associated with a miraculous host such as the one at Dijon where the stigmata of the imprinted Christ bled, making thus manifest the miracle of transubstantiation;[58] and finally the growth, in the fifteenth century, of depictions of the *Mass of Saint Gregory* during which the principle of real presence was reaffirmed by the miraculous intervention of the Christ on the altar (figs. 3.5 and 3.6). The raising of the figured host, introduced around 1195 by the bishop of

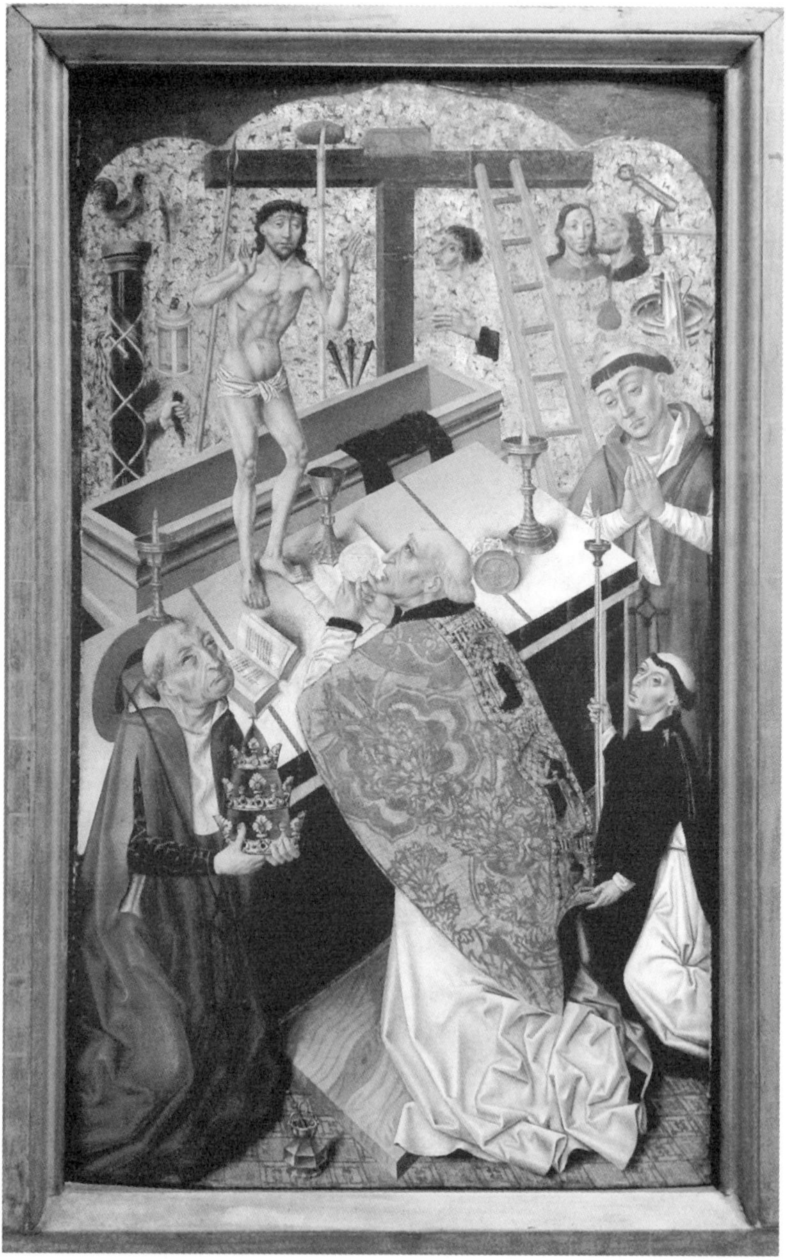

Figure 3.5. Diego de la Cruz, *The Mass of Saint Gregory*, ca. 1490, oil and gold leaf on wood, 45.9×27.5 in. Purchased with the W. P. Wilstach Fund, the George W. Elkins Fund, and with the bequest of Miss Anne Thompson (by exchange), 1993. Philadelphia Museum of Art, Philadelphia (Creative Commons).

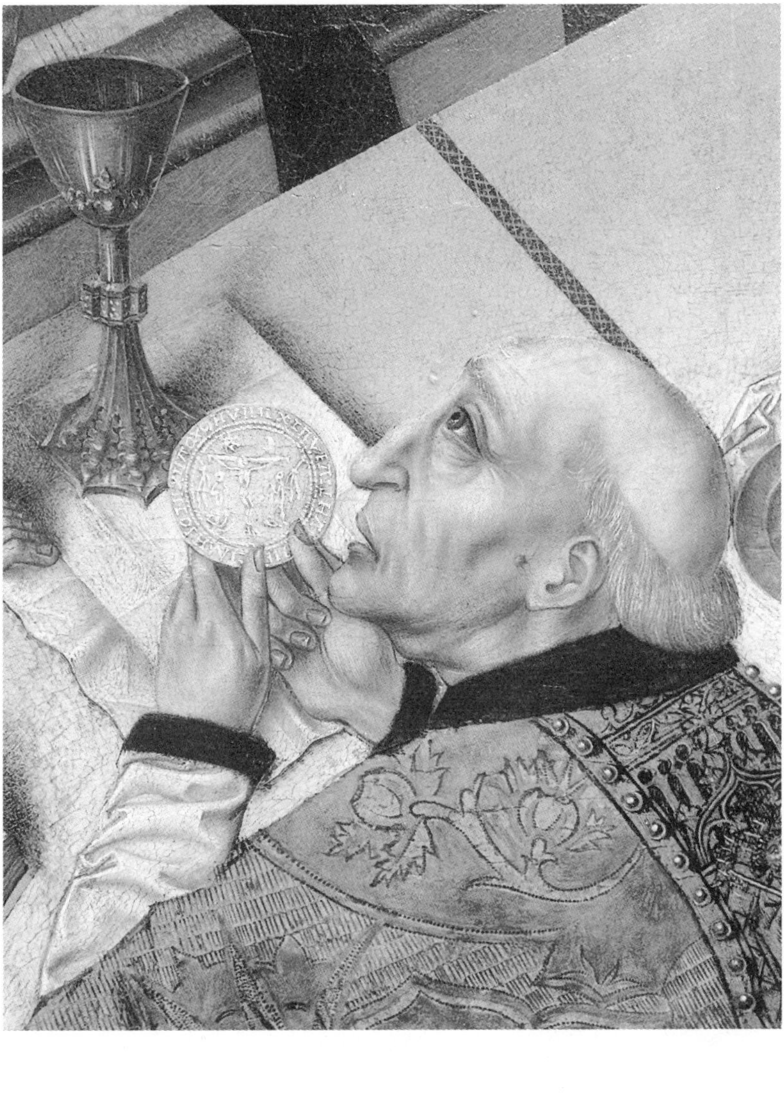

Figure 3.6. Diego de la Cruz, *The Mass of Saint Gregory*, ca. 1490, oil and gold leaf on wood, 45.9 × 27.5 in. Purchased with the W. P. Wilstach Fund, the George W. Elkins Fund, and with the bequest of Miss Anne Thompson (by exchange), 1993. Philadelphia Museum of Art, Philadelphia (detail of fig. 3.5) (Creative Commons).

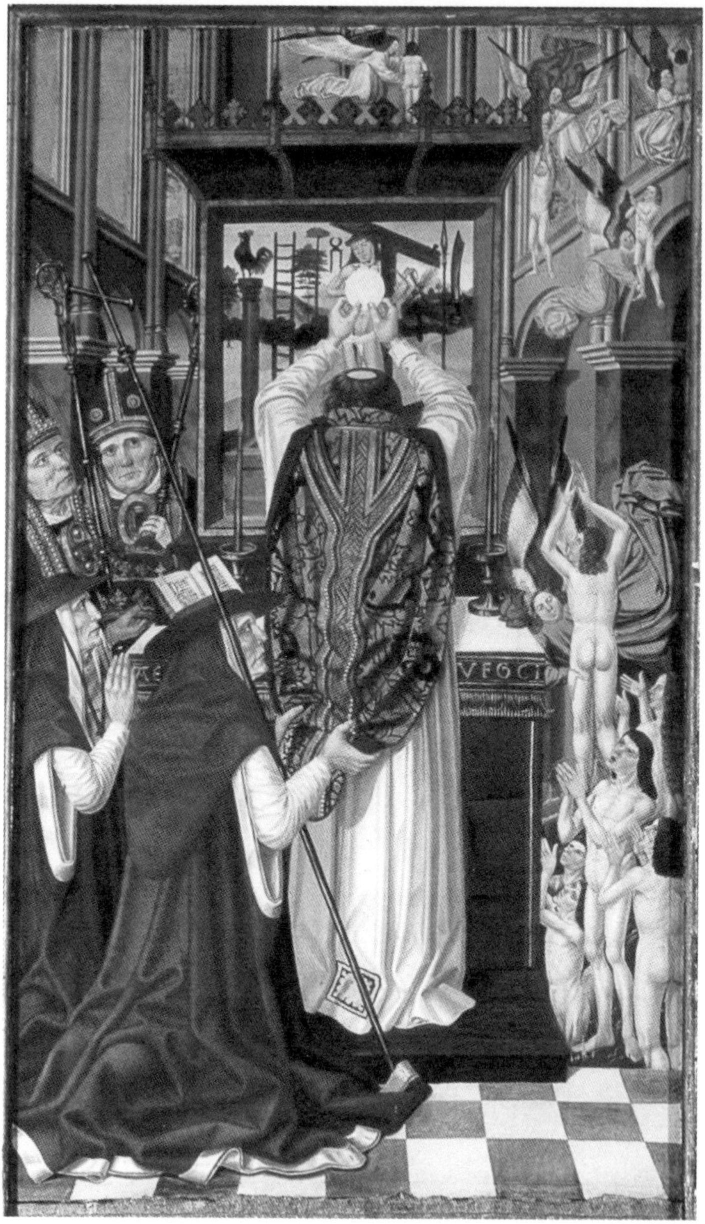

Figure 3.7. Wilm Dedeke, *Saint Gregory's Mass*, 1496, paint on panel, 39.3 × 20.4 in. Detail of the Altar of the Corpus Christi Fraternity of Lübeck (formerly in the Burgkirche). Lubeck, St. Annen-Museum (© St. Annen—Museum der Hansestadt Lübeck).

Paris, Eudes de Sully (1196–1208), and generalized in church services from the fourteenth century through its mixing of the image with the bread and wine, was also a response to the desire on the part of the faithful to see the body of Christ.[59] In Wilm Dedeke's *Mass of Saint Gregory* (fig. 3.7), the priest raises the host in such a way that it is inscribed into the figure of Christ's body in the altarpiece — the sacramental bread and the image seeming to fuse together.[60]

All these explanations for the widespread use of figured eucharistic wafers have merit. But beyond the desire to see Christ within the space of worship, another yet more fundamental reason seems to me to be possible: the stamped host, by virtue of the means of production of which it is the trace, materializes the principle governing all at once the Christian economy of the image (condensed in the Genesis formula, *ad imaginem dei*), the dogma of the Holy Trinity, the idea of the Mystical Body of Christ, and the eucharistic rite — the principle, in other words, of the many in the One.[61]

To understand this fully, we must go back to the process of stamping and sealing (fig. 3.8). As Georges Didi-Huberman points out in *La ressemblance par contact*, the stamp's power rests upon a paradox: the copresence of the unique and the multiple:

> On the one hand, the contact (or the striking) guarantees in itself the power of the *unique*; on the other hand, the production (or the putting into circulation) guarantees in itself that this power is capable of being reproduced indefinitely — at least, as long as the mold exists — and, above all, that it will not be lost or dissipated in the dissemination that it authorizes.[62]

Didi-Huberman adds, "the element of contact remains a guarantee of uniqueness, authenticity, and power ... beyond [the] very reproduction" of the images.[63] Thus, the seal certifies and authenticates, even as it is reproduced *ad infinitum*.

Research carried out by Brigitte Miriam Bedos-Rezak shows the extent to which, on the basis of this form of production, the sigillary imprint became a material paradigm in the Middle Ages for conceptualizing truth and identity.[64] She writes:

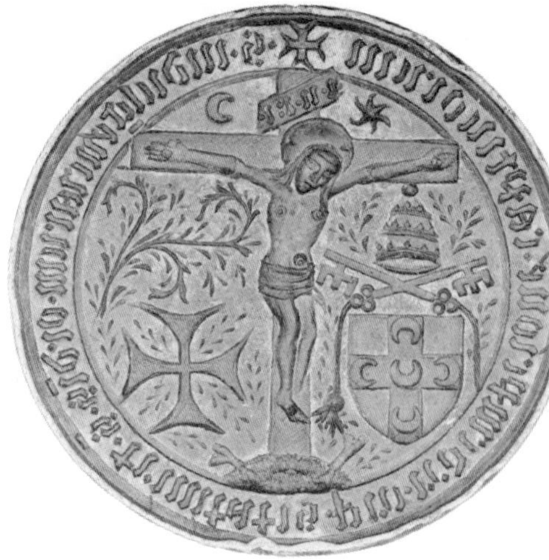

Figure 3.8. Seal template for indulgences of the Order of the Holy Trinity for the Ransom of Captives, 1458–1464, bronze. Paris, Musée de Cluny—Musée national du Moyen Âge (Cl. 23918) (© RMN—Grand Palais/Art Resource, NY/Michel Urtado).

> In twelfth century culture . . . the impressed image, *imago impressa*, signaled that the true portrait of the sealer on his seal resided not so much in the image as form but in the image as marked matter. Imprinting rendered tangible an action by an agent, whereby the agent left something of itself within the matter.[65]

Therefore, on the semiotic level, "immanence rather than transcendence governed the rapport between signifier and signified."[66] This transformation in the approach to the sign allowed for the affirmation of the process of production and materiality in the creation of the sigillary image. "Carnal child . . . of its parental form," as Didi-Huberman elegantly puts it, the seal maintained a genealogical link with the image-mold from which it came.[67]

From a technical point of view, the host press functioned exactly like the seal: it produced an image, the vestige of a contact, that certified the uniqueness of the multiple. In this way, despite the mass production of the eucharistic wafers, it was always the same Christ that was sacrificed and offered up at communion.[68] Not only did "the pressed image form part of . . . a fundamental economy . . . , an economy of transubstantiation and 'real presence,'"[69] but the

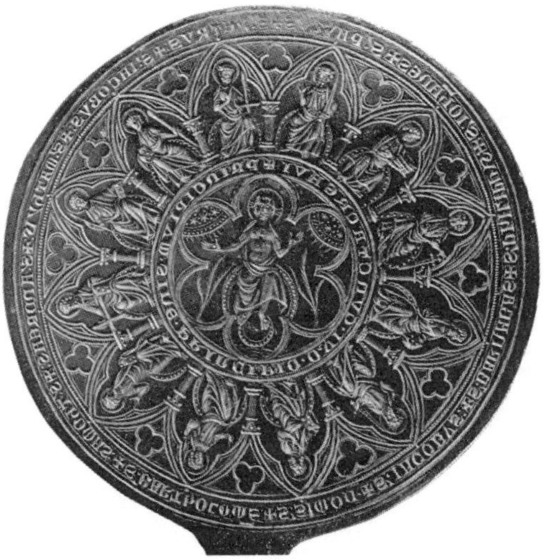

Figure 3.9. Host iron template bearing a representation of Christ surrounded by the Apostles, second half of the thirteenth century, iron, 2.16 in. Paris, Musée de Cluny—Musée national du Moyen Âge (Cl. 2067) (© RMN—Grand Palais/Art Resource, NY).

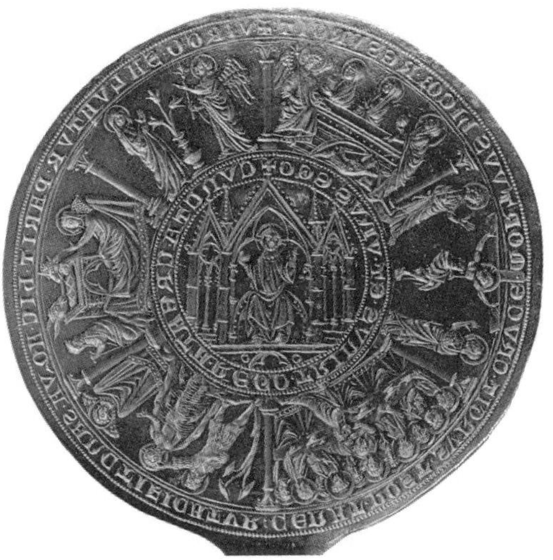

Figure 3.10. Host iron template with scenes from the Life of Christ, second half of the thirteenth century, iron, 10.15 in. Paris, Musée de Cluny—Musée national du Moyen Âge (Cl. 2067) (© RMN—Grand Palais/Art Resource, NY).

ingestion of this same image by all the faithful allowed each one of them to be symbolically connected with all of the other members of the Christian community who, like him or her, incorporated the image coming from the mold.

In accordance with this idea, certain host presses bore representations depicting this principle very explicitly and in ways that show evidence of much thought. A particularly remarkable example can be seen in a Parisian double-template press dating from the second half of the thirteenth century, today in the collection of the Cluny Museum (figs. 3.9 and 3.10).[70] The circular templates show, on one of them (fig. 3.9), Christ showing his stigmata and around him in a radiating circle are the twelve apostles (though in contrast to the disciples of Christ, Judas Iscariot and Thaddeus are replaced by Paul and Barnabas), and, with the other one (fig. 3.10), Christ appears enthroned within an aedicula, surrounded by six scenes from the New Testament, the Annunciation, Nativity, Baptism, Last Supper, Crucifixion, and Resurrection. The whole is enriched by various inscriptions: accompanying the scene showing Christ and his apostles, we read in the center "*Principium sine principio qui cuncta creavit* (The principle that created all things from all eternity)," and around the edge, we see the names of the apostles. Moreover, in the scenes showing the life of Christ (fig. 3.10), we read in the exterior circle the *tituli* of the various episodes from the New Testament. Lastly, around Christ the King we see "*Cuncta Creata Rego Trinus et Unus Ego* (I rule over the created things, I am one and three)."[71]

In addition to the superior figurative quality of this double press, measuring no less than 25 cm in diameter, it is essentially the visual configuration of the side showing Christ surrounded by the apostles that deserves our attention here. By virtue of its concentric and radiating arrangement, the image makes visible the force of attraction exerted by the action of grace: through the taking of communion, in other words, by receiving the host, all the members of the Christian community can unite, like the apostles, around Christ, and they can thus maintain with him the same relationship of identity.[72] The theological reasoning behind this relational dynamic was not new. Its roots lay in the Gospel of Saint John, according to which anyone who incorporated Christ also and at the same time incorporated him or herself in Him: "Whoever eats my flesh and drinks my blood remains in me, and I in them" (John 6:56).[73] This principle of mutual incorporation was often to be glossed during the Middle Ages and at the dawn of the modern era. Let us consider here a few instances. Saint Augustine, for example, brings up in his *Confessions* (VII, X, 16) his own paradoxical knowledge of God, emphasizing the turning around of incorporation:

> I knew myself to be far away from you in a region of unlikeness, and I seemed to hear your voice from on high: "I am the food of the mature; grow

> then and thou will eat me. You will not change me into yourself like bodily food: you will be changed into me."[74]

This idea reappears, in slightly altered form, in one of Bernard of Clairvaux's Sermons on the Song of Songs 71:6–7. In a number of inspired pages, the Cistercian theologian weaves through his discourse the metaphor of mutual devouring as a way of making clear the unity of the Father and the Son, man and God:

> Yet I . . . am not afraid to say that I am one spirit with God, if ever I shall have been convinced by sure experience that I cleave to God, after the manner of those who abide in charity, and therefore abide in God and God in them [John 4:16], feeding somehow upon God, and being fed by God. For I think that it was about such a union that it was said, "he who cleaves to God is one spirit with him [1 Corinthians 6:17]." So what? The Son says, "I am in the Father and the Father in me [John 10:38], and we are one [John 10:30]." Man says, "I am in God, and God is in me, and we are one spirit."
>
> But do the Father and the Son not feed upon each other, that they may be in each other, just as God and Man, by feeding mutually upon each other, abide as one spirit even though they are not one? Not so; for they do not indwell the one the other in the same way, nor is their unity the same.[75]

At the end of the thirteenth century, William Durand of Mende was to take up and carry further this reversed absorption. In his *Rationale Divinorum Officiorum* (1286–1296), one of the most widely read texts of the Middle Ages, the Bishop of Mende argued, in fact, that the Christian was "in ymaginem Dei reformamur (reformed in the image of God)" through the ingestion of the image of Christ.[76] As Aden Kumler has noted, Durand borrows here from Honorarius of Autun: "through this bread the image of God is restored in us and our name is written down into the book of life [*et per hunc panem imago Dei in nobis reparatur, et nomen nostrum in libro vitae notatur*]."[77] But, unlike his predecessor, who speaks of *reparatur* ("restoration") without specifying how this return action was to operate, Durand uses the term *reformamur* ("reformed"), introducing thus the idea of movement, conversion, and the subjection even of the communing person to God's form.

This idea of communion as, so to speak, a dynamic process was to persist through the centuries: At the threshold of the seventeenth century, in his *Brevi et divotissime meditationi del Santissimo Sacramento* (1600), the Jesuit, Luca Pinelli, wrote: "Consider . . . that our Saviour in the institution of this divine Sacrament showed his desire to make us one thing with himself, for that is such a kind of meat, that it *converts* into itself all those who worthily eat the same."[78]

This movement of inverted conversion, where the communicant, as host of the sacrament, is brought to espouse the form of the one that he or she receives, fits aptly with Saint Paul's idea of *symmorphon* (process of taking on likeness), which, as Giovanni Careri shows, was the foundation on which the greater part of Christian anthropology has been built.[79] On the Last Day, according to Saint Paul, Christ "will transform our lowly bodies so that they will be like his glorious body" (Philippians 3:21).[80] This then is the essential eucharistic project: to strip oneself of one's difference, one's sinful condition, in hopes of recovering a lost resemblance through *symmorphon* (the process of taking on likeness).[81] Now, this project is carried forth, not to say revealed, by the image stamped on the consecrated host. Far from being a mere accessory, the image makes visible the power inherent in the Eucharist of reducing the many to the One.[82] Consequently, the figured host presents us with an image-vestige whose essential function is to produce an identity link that is both horizontal and vertical. The full realization of this function is possible thanks to the image engraved on the host press. As a result of its having properties that are genetic (it arises from a stamp), visual (its design rests upon a principle of natural or conventional resemblance), and syntactic (the representation is an encoding), the image is an amalgam of three signs in a *representamen*—at once *index*, *icon* and *symbol*.[83] Yet these three signs, far from being mutually exclusive as they are in the Peircean tripartition, are here superposed. In the first place, insofar as it is a stamp or index, the host *certifies* the presence of the One in the many, allowing for all the communicants to recover a lost unity. Secondly, as an icon, the image makes the prototype present and *signals* the real presence of the one who is sacrificed.[84] Finally, insofar as it is a symbol, the image *reveals* the theological meaning of the Eucharist, turning the host into the "bread of life." Unlike a painted image that can only be looked at, the host, insofar as it is swallowed, allows for the image's triple power to act very directly within the body. In other words, it establishes a physical and material continuity between the communicants and Christ. The edible image becomes thus the *operator* through which the individual Christian *re-forms* themself and through which the Christian community itself is instituted.[85]

Trials by Ordeal

The importance of ingesting the eucharistic image—and more generally of any shared image in a ritual or in the context of worship—as a means of establishing community can be measured if we compare it with its opposing principle: ingestion that effectively disestablishes. Going back as far as antiquity, there are traces of this latter type of ingestion in the rites of trial by ordeal. To see this more clearly, let us open the Bible to the Book of Exodus (32:19–28). When Moses comes down from Mount Sinaï and discovers the children of Israel worshipping before the Golden Calf, in his fury he decides to submit them to the judgement of God by making them drink the ashes of the melted idol mixed with water:[86]

> When Moses approached the camp and saw the calf and the dancing, his anger burned and he threw the tablets out of his hands, breaking them to pieces at the foot of the mountain. And he took the calf the people had made and burned it in the fire; then he ground it to powder, scattered it on the water and made the Israelites drink it.

Convinced that his people were guilty of "such great sin," Moses then called upon the Levites to put to the sword those among the children of Israel who were "prone . . . to evil"; "the Levites did as Moses commanded, and that day about three thousand of the people died." The text does not specify how the people's guilt was revealed; however, the immediate consequence, namely death, suggests that ingesting the image—the height of idolatry—was here the operative factor in this exclusion from the community.[87]

The trial of the *sotah* (woman suspected of adultery) by bitter water, described in the Book of Numbers (5:11–31), seems to confirm this interpretation since it echoes directly that original trial by ordeal underwent by the people of Israel. As the Lord dictates to him, Moses is to tell the priests to expose the adulterous woman by making her ingest water in which biblical scriptures and some dust from the tabernacle floor have been dissolved. This ritual, that according to tradition had to be carried out in the Temple of Jerusalem, condemned "to become a curse among [her] people" any woman who, upon drinking the potion, experienced pain and swelling in the abdomen.[88]

In Imperial Rome, *iudicium offae* (trial by mouthful) was practiced. According to the Pseudo-Acron, slaves suspected of theft were led before the religious authorities and made to ingest a small quantity of bread in which magical words had been placed. If they hesitated to do so, they were declared guilty, and were banished.[89] In India among Hindus, an image was used in the trial known as *Cósha* to confute any man suspected of theft:

> Trial by the Cósha is as follows: the accused is made to drink three draughts of the water, in which the images of the Sun, of Dévì, and other deities, have been washed for that purpose; and if, within fourteen days, he has any sickness or indisposition, his crime is considered as proved.[90]

The Christian world was no stranger to these practices. Between the ninth and fourteenth centuries, trials involving recourse to the Eucharist and the *iudicium panis et casei* (ordeal by bread and cheese) were applied to men suspected of either theft, fornication, or murder.[91] As stipulated in the Ordines Romani, the suspect was set before the altar and forced to swallow either a piece of consecrated bread and cheese that had been marked with a cross, or a host bearing the stamped image of Christ.[92] If the accused were to choke or start to tremble and faint, then he would be held to be guilty "by the body and blood of Christ."[93]

This latter practice was so widespread in the Middle Ages that Boccaccio made fun of it in the *Decameron* (VIII, 6), describing a scene in which partners in crime Buffalmacco and Bruno, after having secretly stolen a pig from Calandrino, propose that they resort to the *iudicium panis et casei* to expose the thief whom they pretend is to be found among Calandrino's neighbors:

> "Why," replied Buffalmacco, "'tis certain that no one has come from India to steal thy pig: it must have been one of thy neighbors, and if thou couldst bring them together, I warrant thee, I know how to make the assay with bread and cheese, and we will find out in a trice who has had the pig."[94]

While the host ingested during the mass guarantees the faithful believer a place within the community, the ritual of the *iudicium panis* punishes and excludes any person found guilty of breaking the pact of peaceful order that allows the community to prosper. The process of conformation worked by eucharistic communion, allowing the believer to come closer to the image of God by divesting themself of their sins, is here reversed. In the ritual of the *iudicium panis*, ingestion intensifies the dissimilarity separating the sinful person from their creator — the damned is consigned to hell.

Sweet Holy Days

A Multitude of Breads

The trial of ingesting bread stamped with the symbol or natural image of Christ could, therefore, lead to exclusion from the community. But this was a rare occurrence. The Church and conventual establishments were much more inclined to single out this food item and other analogous specialties for their capacity to *unite* the community of believers around them, and this happened throughout the year.[95]

In the Eastern and Byzantine traditions from the fifth century, various types of stamped breads were in fact distributed in parallel with the sacraments: the *antidoron*, for example, was given out immediately following the Divine Liturgy to those who had not taken communion, and the *eulogiae* were distributed on the eve of certain liturgical feast days, such as at Epiphany or on the feast of the particular saint to which a given church was dedicated.[96]

The presses and molds that have come down to us generally have very simple designs. What we see, for the most part, are either images symbolically depicting Christ (e.g., the fish, cross, or lamb) or simple figures of saints accompanied by inscriptions that contain the word *eulogia* ("blessing"). However, the wooden molds from the Monastery of Saint Catherine at Mount Sinai show that these images could also be much more elaborate: around the saint, who is shown standing and wearing a crown, a cross, and a palm branch, are her traditional attributes, which are the open book, referring to her wisdom, and the toothed wheel, the instrument of her martyrdom, and both features are linked with the representation of the Monastery of Mount Sinai.[97]

Similar practices were to take root also in the West through the Middle Ages and into the modern period. On precise dates in the calendar, and essentially during the period starting with All Saints' Day to Easter, depending on the circumstances the conventual communities would offer or sell to the lay society molded cakes such as gingerbreads or stamped breads and pastries (waffle, *waffel*, *cialde*, or *oublies*[98]) bearing images or symbols of Christ, the Virgin, or the saints. Here again, these items, made of fine flour mixed with water were typically very plain; however, they could be endowed with much more complex forms. An especially fine example of the latter can be seen in two graphite molds, today in the collection of the Cluny Museum in Paris. These culinary tools have been associated with the studio of the goldsmith and engraver Hans von Reutlingen, who was active in Aix-la-Chapelle between 1500 and 1547.[99] One of them shows a Virgin accompanied by the angel Gabriel (fig. 3.11), and the other depicts a *Virgo lactans* (fig. 3.12). Their respective iconographies suggest that they were mainly used for two specific feasts: the Annunciation, for the Virgin and Angel Gabriel, and the Nativity, for the Virgin nursing the Child.[100] In the absence of any information pertaining to the history of these two objects, it is hard to say exactly how the cakes were used. We do not know if they were sold, given out, or otherwise shared by the members of the religious community. But the fine quality of the design in its treatment of the figures and in the abundance of its ornamentation surely implies that these were instruments of prestige intended for select consumers who were able to appreciate the image's quality before making it disappear. We know that it was a custom among the nuns to give out gingerbreads as a way of thanking a convent's benefactors, their confessors, and passing clerics,[101] so it is very likely that the cakes made from the Cluny molds were used for a similar purpose. With this in mind, the *Virgo lactans* mold suggests perhaps, in the form of a *mise en abyme*, the convent's act of charity in giving out these items: just as the Virgin feeds Christ with her milk, the nuns feed the recipients of the gingerbreads with their love and gentleness.

Although the religious communities produced these cakes primarily for the holy days dedicated to Jesus or the Virgin, they also made and sold pastries for village festivals and local saint's days.[102] Thus, in Paris, the nuns of the Abbey of Saint Genevieve, as we have seen, made the Saint Genevieve biscuits (fig. 3.13). Collin de Plancy describes the cake as "a small dry biscuit, oval in shape, on which there figures the saint keeping her sheep, with a shepherd's crook, a prayer book, and with a few angels above her." Once blessed, these "little breads" were sold "as guaranteed cures against fevers."[103] In the small towns of Sarule and Orani in Sardinia, they made the *pani' a vintichimbe* for the Feast of the Annunciation on March 25th, marking the dough with a stamp in the image of the Virgin and Child before putting it in the oven. And in the town of Catania, in Sicily, they made, and still make today, the *minne* or *minnuzze di*

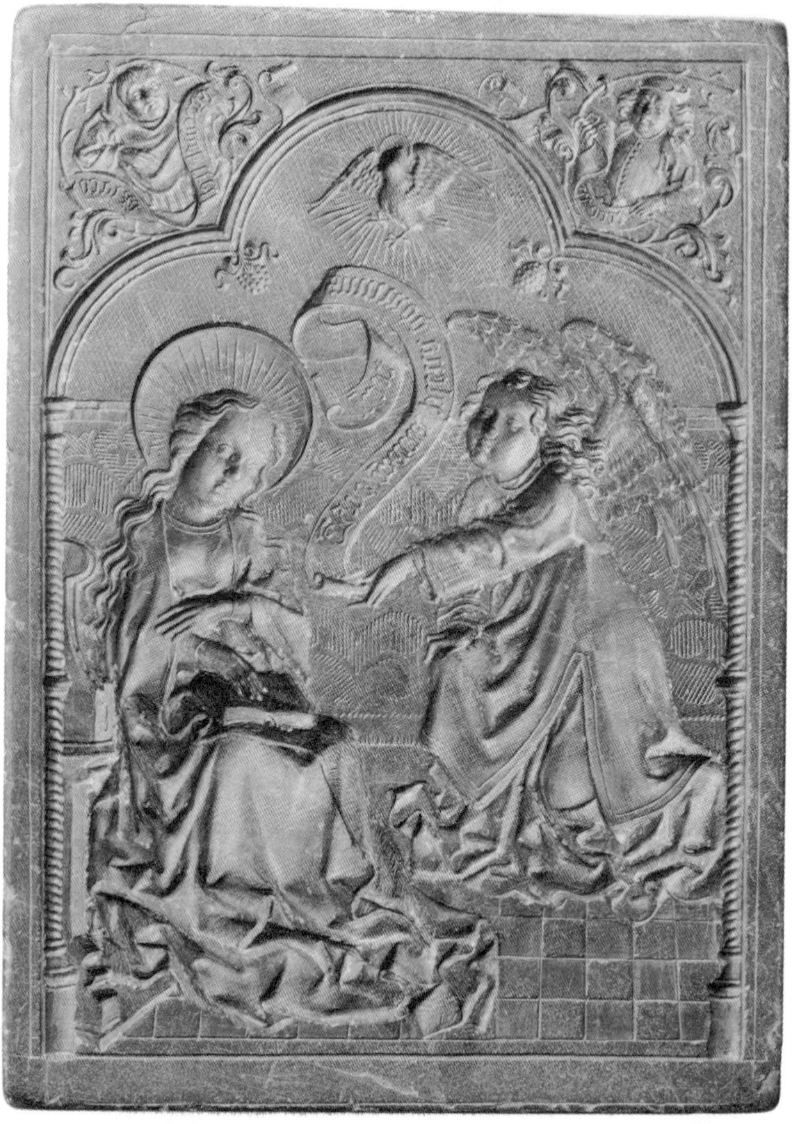

Figure 3.11. Studio of Hans von Reutlingen (?), *Gingerbread mold from the region of Aachen with a depiction of the Annunciation*, ca. 1475–1500, graphite, 7.6 × 5.3 in. Paris, Musée de Cluny—Musée national du Moyen Âge (Cl. 14096) (© RMN—Grand Palais/Art Resource, NY/Jean-Gilles Berizzi).

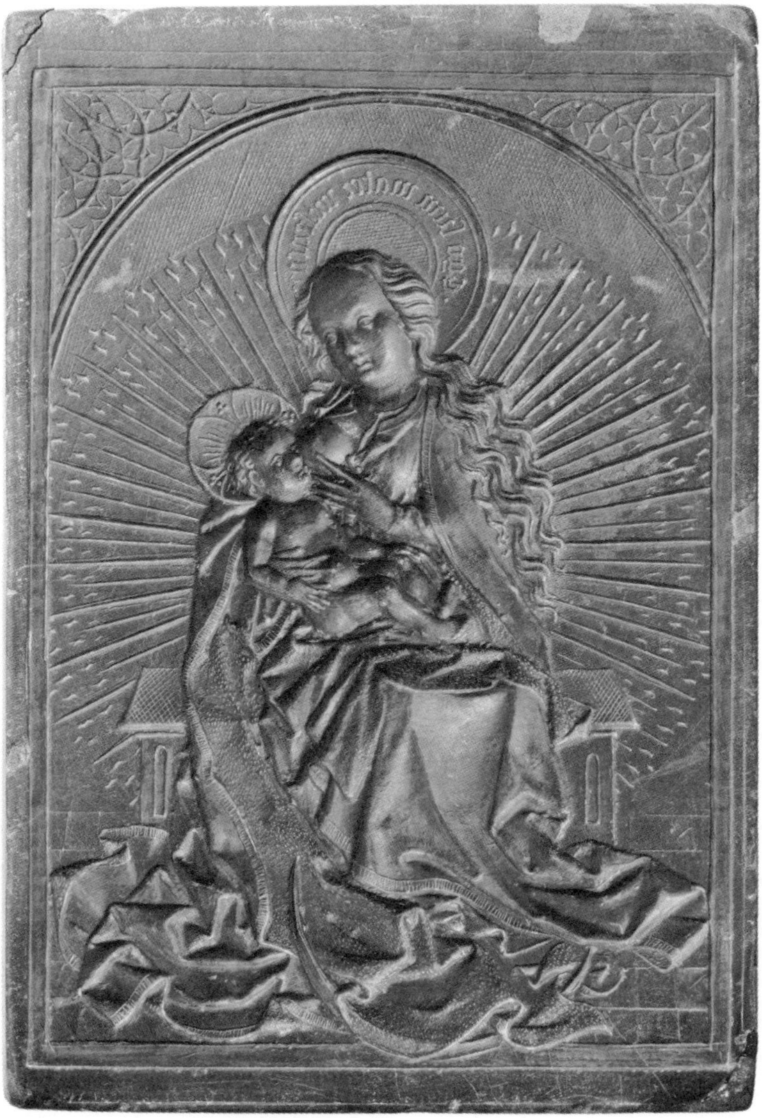

Figure 3.12. Studio of Hans von Reutlingen (?), *Gingerbread mold from the region of Aachen with a depiction of the Virgo lactans*, ca. 1475–1500, graphite, 7.2 × 5 in. Paris, Musée de Cluny—Musée national du Moyen Âge (Cl. 14097) (© RMN—Grand Palais/ Art Resource, NY/Jean-Gilles Berizzi).

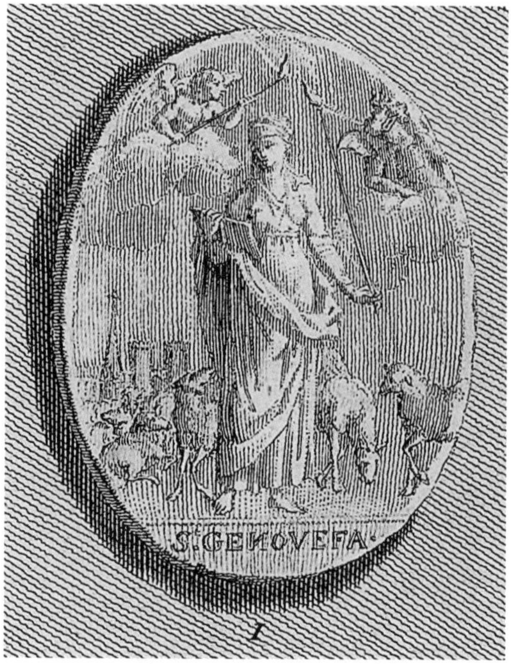

Figure 3.13. Bernard Picart, *Saint Geneviève Biscuit*, 1723 (detail of fig. 1.29). Paris, Bibliothèque nationale de France (Creative Commons).

sant'Agata from the third to the fifth of February in celebration of their patron saint. Fashioned first by the nuns of San Andrea delle Vergini in Palermo, before migrating to Catania and the Benedictines of San Nicolò l'Arena, this latter dessert, prepared from a mixture of flour, eggs, ricotta, and maraschino cherry, was formed in the shape of a woman's breast, a reference to the martyrdom of Saint Agatha whose breasts were torn off.[104] Due to the metonymical properties of the image, lactating virtues were attributed to the pastry.[105] Everyone would eat them during the festival, but it was the mothers of newborn children who were, for this reason, most interested in them.

Beyond the therapeutic or benedictive benefits that we might ascribe to these delicacies, their gastronomic qualities added to the reputation of a convent and, by extension, to the prestige of a town.

Consequently, this shared renown was a vector of social cohesion.[106] The preparation, distribution, and consumption of the cakes and pastries established links between various social strata, solidifying their interrelation at regular intervals. The lay people came to form a single body surrounding the nuns, and the Christian community came thus to see itself as linked, so to speak, *by mouth* to the convent.[107]

Blessed Wafers

In addition to figured gingerbreads and biscuits, the religious communities also made *cialde* or *oublies* (waffle-cookies or wafers), and they did so with engraved iron presses like the ones used for the manufacture of the eucharistic wafers. In certain cities, as for example in Paris, these sweet desserts were almost always sold in front of the doors of churches by tradespeople, the pastrycooks, and *oublieurs*,[108] but a few convents, especially in Italy and Germany, also took this on as a specialty. The wafers sold by the sisters differed from those of the street hawkers in terms of their stamping. Whereas the professional pastrycooks made their wafers in iron presses with square indentations, and that were sometimes adorned with simple religious symbols, the sisters of the convents used irons with more complex designs, bringing together inscriptions, coats of arms, and religious images. Indeed, the images and inscriptions we find on the iron presses used by the nuns indicate that their wafers had a genuine spiritual and social function, and this was not so much the case with the "secular" *oublies*. Looking at a pair of wafering irons forged in 1547 for the convent of the Poor Clare nuns at Monteluce in Perugia, we can get an idea of this (fig. 3.14). One of the templates has, in the middle, the monogram "IHS," and, around the edge, we see the inscription: "*Sic[u]t nomen d[omi] ni benedicto c[um/con] questi ferri si sonno di monte luce furo[no] factte MD47* (Just as the lord's name is blessed, so too are [the waffles made with] these irons of Monte Luce, made in 1547)." Just as the lord's name is blessed, so too are [the waffles made with] these

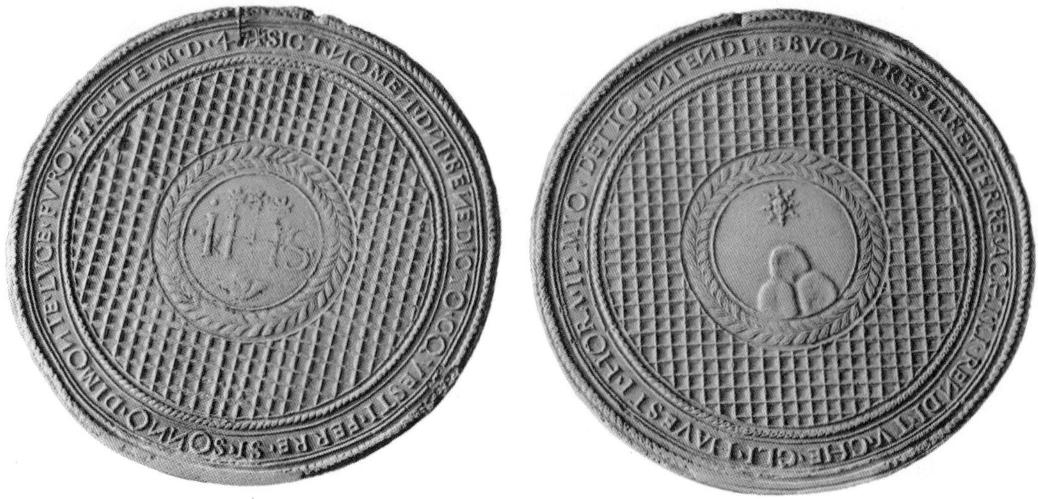

Figure 3.14. Plaster casts bearing the stamps of the wafering irons of the Convent of Monteluce, 1547, plaster, 7 in. Perugia, Galleria Nazionale dell'Umbria (© Kunsthistorisches Institut in Florenz—Max Planck Institut).

irons of Monte Luce, made in 1547 The wafers produced from this template, consequently, bore an image (the monogram of the name of Jesus) that appeared as a blessing offered by the religious institution to the community of the believers.[109] The grouping of text and image transformed the stamped wafer into an operator of the Poor Clares' power to spiritually and physically nourish the community, and it transformed the consumption of this food item into a channel of blessing: the term *sicut* ("in the same way" or "as") is fundamentally important here since it puts the wafer on the same level as the name of Jesus.[110] The inscription on the other plate complicates matters further by opening yet another perspective on the use of the *cialde*: "*È buon prestare i ferre a chi li rendi tu che gli havesti hora il mio detto intendi* (It is good to lend out these irons to one who will return them; you who now hold them, hear what I say)." The wafers made from this pair of irons bore the emblem of the Poor Clare Sisters of Monteluce (three mountains under the sun) in the center, and, around the edge, we have this imperative statement, showing that, on the one hand, the irons were lent out by the sisters, and, on the other hand, that the wafers produced by the irons would always bear a stamp indicating their provenance. In other words, even in cases where the *cialde* were not produced directly by the nuns, the wafers would still appear as an indirect offering of the convent. The concatenation of property ("*sonno di Monteluce*"), loan ("*è buon prestare*"), and restitution ("*chi li rendi*") gives a very concrete picture of the interdependent relationship linking the convents with their communities of believers. For their part, the nuns are doing a work of charity, the primary mission of their order, by lending out their irons, and, for their part, the lay people are required to remember the nuns' role in their everyday lives, and, consequently, the need to make some sort of donation to them in return. Now, it is remarkable that this entire economy of sharing and exchange finds itself in condensed form in the consumption of these figured desserts.

We must note, before coming back to this point later, that the notion of lending, introduced by the verb *prestare* in the inscription on the irons from Monteluce, was in no way unusual; indeed, it was quite common in Italy.[111] The majority of the irons that have come down to us contain analogous formulae. These pieces were relatively expensive to have forged and engraved, and not all families could afford to own them. Hence, they were often lent out. Furthermore, this circulation of cooking equipment in the pastry economy of the Middle Ages and the modern era is clear evidence of a porosity existing at that time between the temporal and religious spheres.

Lebkuchen *and* imitatio christi

Although the molded desserts such as the gingerbreads and waffles were at first produced mainly in the convents, they were gradually to infiltrate the princely, patrician, and bourgeois homes over the course of the Renaissance. Indeed, the figured gingerbreads and waffles were often prepared by the laity, and as was the case with the religious communities, these edible images played a not insignificant role in the lives of secular groups.

The gingerbreads or *lebkuchen* (fig. 3.15) that were made, from the fifteenth century, in the German-speaking areas such as Germany, Switzerland, and Austria, in the Low Countries, and in Hungary give us a sense of how this worked. The Christmas or Easter cakes, evidence of which we have from stone, wood, or tin molds conserved today in many European ethnohistorical museums, often carried images drawn from the Bible, and they were endowed with a social and spiritual function akin to that attributed to the host. We can see this clearly and without ambiguity in a sermon given in 1507 by the preacher Johannes Geiler of Kaysersberg on the precise topic of this culinary specialty. The Strasbourgian preacher explained, in fact, that the *lebkuchen* were neither more nor less than secular substitutes for the "bread of the angels," or the host:[112]

> I shall now have you partake of the delicious honey cake, commonly called *lebkuchen*, with which we shall nourish you spiritually throughout Lent, bringing health to your soul once every day. This cake is the most delicious property of Christ, for Jesus, our Lord, was God and man hidden under the white veil of the bread of the angels.[113]

Point by point, Geiler established a parallel between the baking of the cake and the life of Christ, describing the cake's manufacture and consumption in twenty-one steps, in which cooking instructions and Christ's Passion are intermingled. He specifies first that the dough for the *lebkuchen* is to be made from three types of flour symbolizing the Trinity: a *bonen mehl* (bean flour) representing the Holy Spirit, a *alten mehl* (wheat flour) depicting the body, and a *rocken mehl* (rye flour) for the soul: "And our lebkuchen of Jesus Christ are made with bean flour for divinity, wheat flour for the moistness of the flesh, and new rye flour for the soul. These three are in Christ: divinity, body, and soul."[114] To these three ingredients

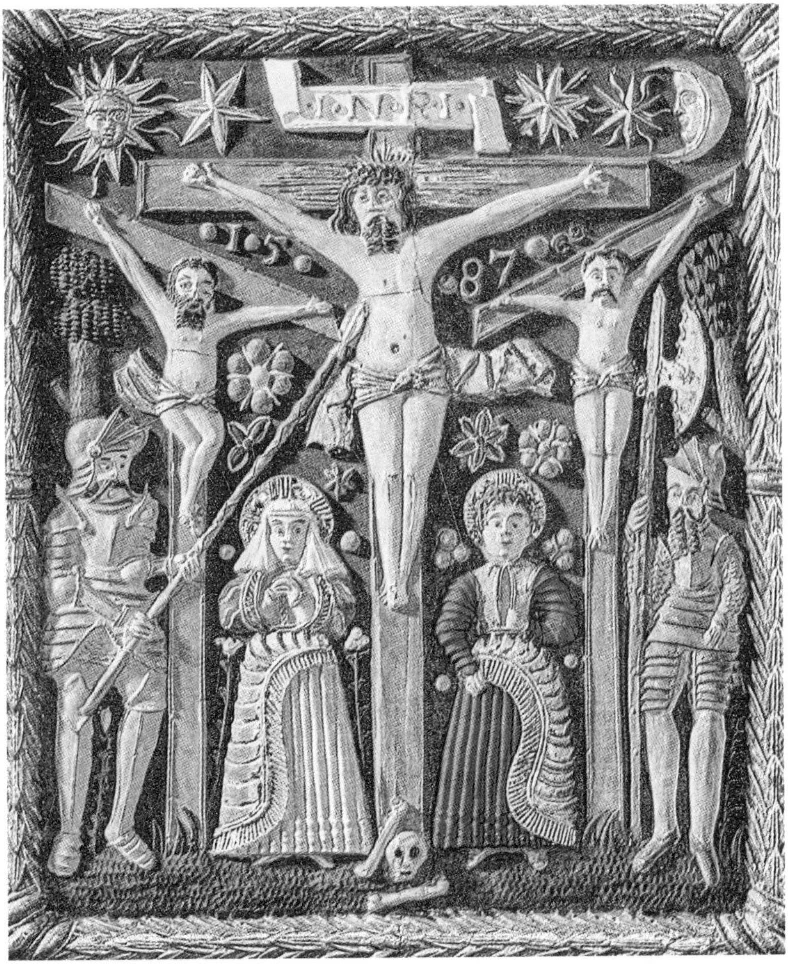

Figure 3.15. *Crucifixion*, 1587, plaster cast after a model in wood. Munich, Bayerisches Nationalmuseum (Creative Commons).

are added the honey and spices.[115] As Geiler characterizes it, the preparation is then worked on and transformed in a way that is a little like Joseph working with wood.[116] Once the dough has been kneaded, raised, and rested, it is given shape in imitation of Christ's incarnation:

> Just as gingerbread is made in many shapes, Christ, our Lord, was conceived and formed by the Father and the mother.... First of all, the Father: the Father engendered and formed [the Son] in his own likeness, and therefore, even if that is not written, the son is born of the father completely the same, and the father is neither better, nor more powerful, nor greater, nor wiser than the son, and the Father is totally and entirely imprinted, represented, and engendered in the son.... In the sixth chapter of the Gospel of John, Christ himself speaks of this taking on of form [*formierung*] by which he was made by the Father. According to this idea, God the father also made and formed the Lord Jesus.... This is why, just like [the son in relation to] the father, our gingerbread was formed and made with its own mold. Then, our gingerbread was also figured and formed by the mother with her own shape. And, if he had no father in the flesh, we must remember that he had the form and aspect of his mother.... He was therefore born of the flesh of his mother alone, but thanks to the aid of the Holy Spirit.... This is why, in our interest, this gingerbread that is Jesus Christ has been designed and shaped.[117]

For Geiler, the identity relation linking the stamped item to the mold was analogous, therefore, to the relation that existed between Christ and the Father.[118] And just as Jesus was himself the incarnated image of God, given birth by the Virgin Mary, the individual *lebkuchen* was the counter-form, the progeniture even, of the mold used in its own manufacture.[119]

The analogy continues with a setting in parallel of the cooking of the cake and Christ's ordeal. Just as Christ was wounded by the crown of thorns, the gingerbread is pricked before baking (steps 8 and 9),[120] carried to the oven, cooked and, so to speak, sacrificed (steps 10, 11, and 12).[121] "Taken from the Cross," the cake is then placed in "white linen cloth" and set upon "a stone to cool" (step 13).[122] After three days of rest, it is divided up like "the bread of the twelve" (steps 14, 15, and 16),[123] and finally offered to the guests "by the father of the family for the meal."[124] Thanks to this *liba* or offering,[125] each person could be fortified, protected against disease,[126] and they would be able to remember the sacrifice (steps 17 and 18):

> Thus we break the *lebkuchen* . . . and it is shared among all the men as a snack, so that by this means they might find strength . . . . But also so that every Christian, during the time of fasting, might each day take on a tiny part of the suffering and Passion of our Lord; and that he might contemplate in his soul and mystical flesh something that will allow him to draw strength and virtue. This is why, I myself, at this time of fasting and as a father, I have stamped [or beaten],[127] shared and arranged for you the gingerbread of our lord martyr, according to the ancient custom.[128]

Each guest, as they took their share of the living cake, received a fragment of Christ's image. But in each of the fragments it was always the one and the same Christ who dwelt in it.[129] For, as Geiler specifies, "each piece is marked and decorated . . . after the aspect of the figure that was stamped on the cake from the original mold."[130] The stamped image is the double of the image from which it comes. As a matter of pure fact, it strictly resembles its model. And, thanks to this adherence, the shared image, exactly like the eucharistic wafer, is an operator of unity. Through the sharing and ingesting of the *one* image, the table guests participate in the establishment of a community in which each member divests him or herself of their difference in order to enter into the unity of Christ.

An engraving accompanies the written text, introducing Geiler's sermon and lending support to his words. The print shows very precisely the dynamic of gathering into one through the sharing of the edible image (fig. 3.16): six men and a woman of varying social rank (e.g., a cleric, a patrician, a magistrate, and others of the bourgeoisie) are seated at table around the *hausvater* ("house father") who, knife in hand, cuts up the parts of a *lebkuchen* bearing the

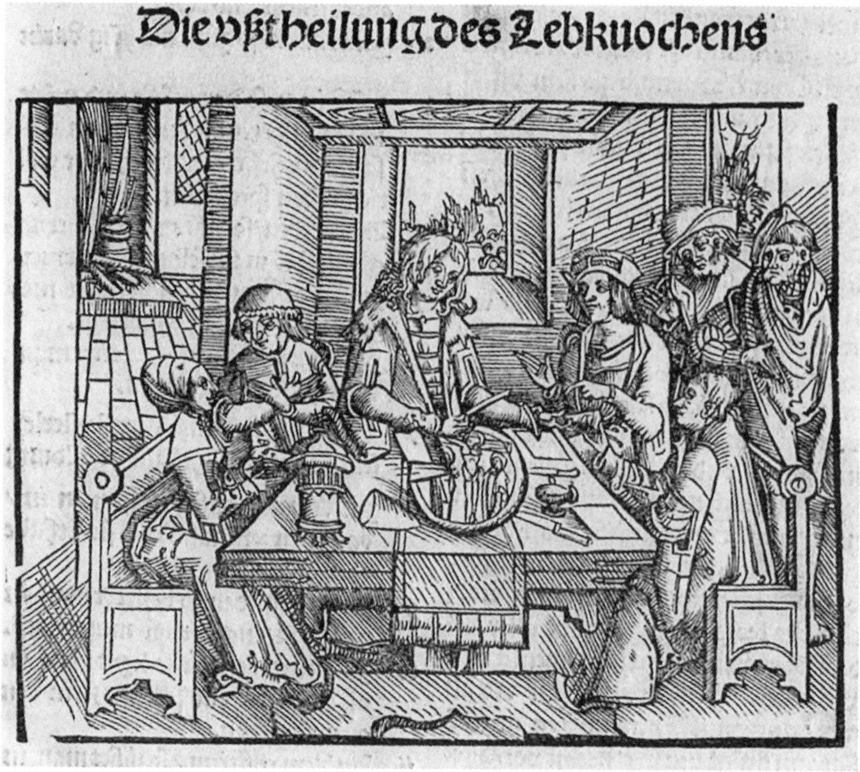

Figure 3.16. Johannes Geiler von Kaysersberg, *Doctor Keiserspergs Passion Des Here(n) Jesu, Fürgeben und geprediget gar betrachtiglich (particuliert) und geteilt in Stückes weiß eins süßen Lebkuochen vßzuogeben (per quadragesima[m]) als durch die gantze fasten allen tag wol ein Predig daruß zuonem ist* (Strasbourg; Johannes Geller von Kayersberg, 1514), p. 7, 11.4 in. (Creative Commons).

image of the Crucifixion, becoming in this way the sacrificer who must right his wrong, and sharing thus with the representatives of Strasbourgian society the living model of humility and sacrifice depicted by the *Christ on the Cross.*[131]

We should note that the function assigned here to the *lebkuchen* did not come out of nowhere. It fit in perfectly with the way in which Geiler envisaged the organization of the social fabric of the city of Strasbourg as having to mirror as strictly as possible the Christian *oikonomia*. The city was, in his words, *leib* ("body"); the citizens its *glieder* ("members");[132] the *weltlich menschen* ("lay people") were the arms, trunk, and legs; *gaistlich menschen* ("clergy")[133] the head. And just as with any body, it was the head that must lead. In Geiler's ideal vision, the city thus reflects the Heavenly Jerusalem: the city would live under the *lex divina*, finding its perfect form of governance and functioning in the model of the monastery.[134] We recall, once again, that this model consolidated the image of the *corpus mysticum*, and the adherence and participation of an entire society in a single eucharistic model is, for Geiler, a necessary condition for the social reform that he had been seeking to establish since his accession to the chair of Strasbourg Cathedral.[135]

The figured *lebkuchen*, as the preacher sees it, brings to the fore, in the establishment of a given social group, all the symbolic force of a "horizontal" sharing. However, another aspect is worth noting in this "spatial" leavening of the organization of society, and this is the role of time in the making and ingesting of the image. The sharing of the image is not solely an operation that allows for the *distribution* of places within society, thus implying thus a relation of contiguity between all its members, it relates also to a certain use of time.

As I have noted earlier, the figured cakes made by the religious communities were consumed on specific dates determined by the liturgical calendar. It was no different for the gingerbread that, although belonging to the lay sphere, was itself a device for inscribing the lives of men into the time of the Church, and more fundamentally into the eschatological time of Salvation. This was a point, it seems to me, on which Geiler was particularly insistent. Throughout his sermon, the preacher returns, in fact, to the regular distribution of pieces of the cake during the forty days of Lent. Each day, the father of the family was to offer a piece of cake. This regular rhythm to which the lay community subjected itself through the consumption of the gingerbread seems to have been, for Geiler, a very concrete way to combat what appeared to him to be the source of worldly failing: the increasing autonomy and temporal power of the laypeople.[136] In his eyes, the entire city was to be molded within the time of the Church. Now, on a symbolic level, what better way to achieve this goal than to offer an edible image of Christ that, being ingested, not to say sacrificed, regularly every day, allowed each member of the community to demonstrate penance and repentance, submitting themselves to the moral injunctions of the clergy.

Eating the Family

Pastries and Rites of Passage

As universally applicable as it might appear, Geiler's way of understanding the economy of the *lebkuchen* was far from reflecting all the uses to which these dessert items were put. We must consequently beware of generalizing too quickly. Most of the figured breads and pastries played a more limited role, remaining within the confines of the family.[137] Although several Christian feasts, such as Epiphany, the Circumcision, and the Visitation, did extend themselves into the domestic space (marking thus the interdependence of Church time and family time), other events, such as births, marriages, and deaths, were linked more with the rhythms of biological and social life.[138] While still tied in some way to the sacraments, these latter events did not form part of the liturgical calendar. Now, for all these family "rites of passage," people also made figured desserts.[139]

Fortunately, certain iconographic details can help us to differentiate the cakes made for family events from those that were intended solely for religious festivals. For example, a *Baptism of*

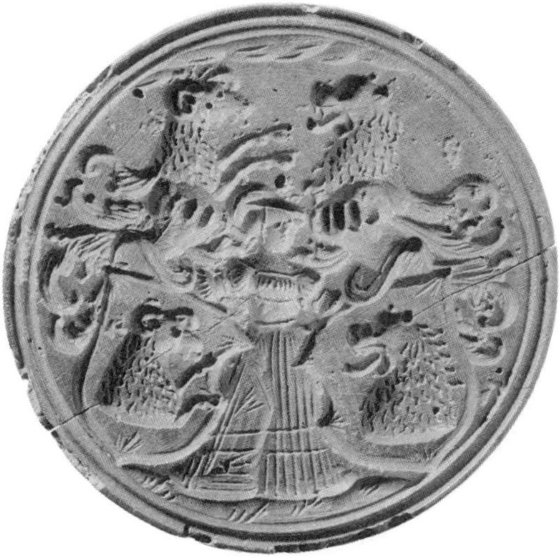

Figure 3.17. *Marzipantorte mold with the conjoined arms of the Thurn and Schultheiss families*, 1541. Zürich, Schweizerisches Nationalmuseum (inv. LM-51573) (© Landesmuseum Zürich).

Jesus, such as the one we find mentioned in 1521 in an inventory of cake molds, was very likely used for banquets following births. The inventory was drawn up by Claus Stalburg (1469–1524), an extremely wealthy Frankfurt patrician who, before becoming burgomaster of the town, had made his fortune in the silk and precious stones trade.[140] In the same way, we can be almost certain that a *gebäckmodel* ("pastry mold") dating from 1541 and bearing the adjoining *Allianzwappen* ("coats of arms") of the families Thurn and Schultheiss (fig. 3.17), was fashioned for the wedding of Beat Wilhelm Im Thurn and Dorothea Schultheiss.[141] We can also be quite sure that a mold for making *marzipantorte* ("marzipan tart") from the sixteenth century, depicting the biblical event Wedding Feast at Cana (fig. 3.18) and though directly connected with Christian culture, was a home emblem for a newly married couple. In this latter example, Jesus's miraculous intervention, filling the empty jars by turning water into wine, is brought into the present day through the modernization of the clothing of the people figuring around the married couple. By placing this pre-eucharistic miracle at the heart of the family economy (i.e., the sharing of a meal, the attention

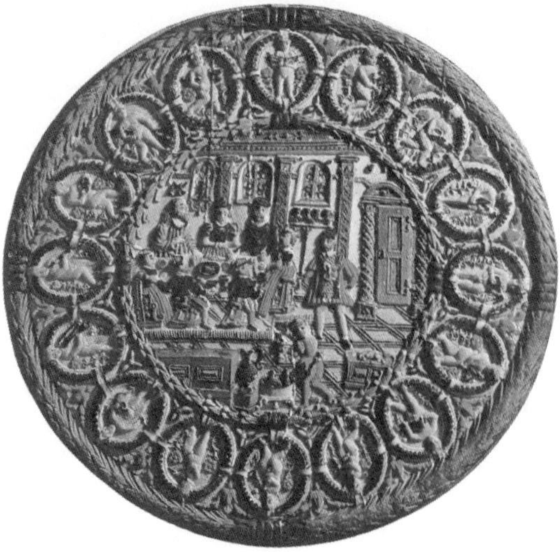

Figure 3.18. *The Wedding Feast at Cana*, second half of the sixteenth century, colored plaster cast from a *marzipantorte* mold, Nuremberg, Germanisches Nationalmuseum (photograph taken from Hanse, 1968) (Creative Commons).

given to the table guests, the commissary), the couple instantiate Jesus's redeeming promise in their own life in the present. However, just as they identify their life with the Christian model, the two spouses resort also to a profane register, placing their marriage under the ruling influence of fecundity, where the ornamental edge running around the circumference includes sixteen nude *putti* that, by force of their number, musical and dancing activities, and variety of poses, appear to guarantee the young couple fertility, harmony, and abundance.

To take an even more unusual example, a mold signed by the Swiss engraver Conrad Rosenbaum from Schaffhausen depicts the Judgement of Paris (fig. 3.19), a representation which quite certainly served as food for thought for a married couple (perhaps mainly the husband) confronted with the dangers of a life entirely devoted to carnal love and earthly pleasures. Paris embodies, in fact, the perfect example of the poor judge, blinded by his passions, having chosen the beauty of Aphrodite, goddess of sensuality and symbol of vanity, over the wisdom of Athena or the authority of Hera. The presence, on the back side, of another mold representing the

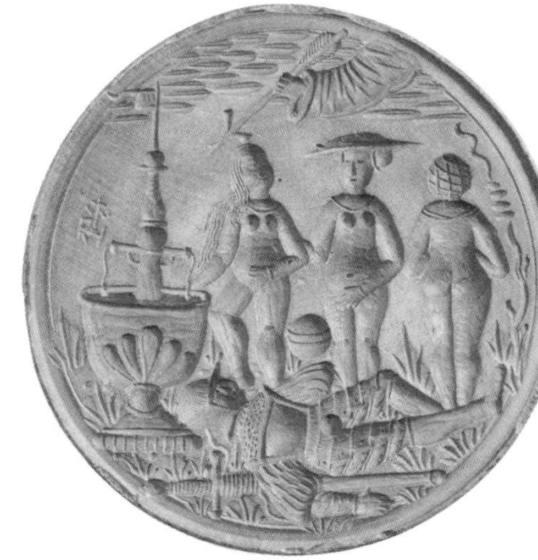

Figure 3.19. Conrad Rosenbaum, *The Judgement of Paris*, before 1520, wooden *marzipantorte* mold (front), 7.6 in. Zurich, Schweizerisches Nationalmuseum (inv. LM-52821) (© Landesmuseum Zürich).

biblical story of Samson and the Lion (fig. 3.20) would seem moreover to indicate that the Greek myth on the front side, while it displays naked figures likely to please the eyes of the owner and his table company, could also be read as a moral tale. Over against the young Trojan's laziness and lust, one was required, in all probability, to set the model of assertiveness, faith, and courage represented by Samson. Yet there is something surprising about this figurative coupling. Both the story of Paris and that of Samson involve a dreaded, even impossible, union with an enemy party: a Trojan (Paris) abducts a Greek (Helen); Samson, a member of the Israelites, goes "to the uncircumcised Philistines to get a wife" (Judges 14:3). In the first case, the transgression provokes war; in the second, it leads a people towards their freedom. Is it possible that this dual iconography was a direct reflection of the couple's situation? Might not the husband have married a wife from an opposing clan, and might he not see a model of "redemption" in the biblical story? Nothing prevents us from seeing it this way.

The aforementioned inventory compiled by the burgomaster Claus Stalburg contains another piece of information concerning

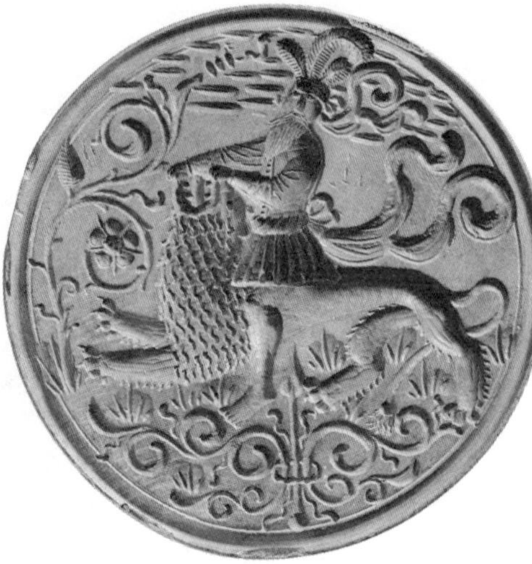

Figure 3.20. Conrad Rosenbaum, *Samson Slaying the Lion*, before 1520, wooden *marzipantorte* mold (back), 7.6 in. Zurich, Schweizerisches Nationalmuseum (inv. LM-52821) (© Landesmuseum Zürich).

the importance of these culinary utensils. The list shows, in fact, that the iconographic subjects chosen for these cakes were not only varied, but also regularly renewed over time. Between 1510 and 1519, no fewer than thirty or so molds were noted, and some of these were created by Hartmann Kistener, a goldsmith who was active in Frankfurt from 1512 to 1529.[142] The abundance and the fine decoration of these *kuchelsteine* ("cake stones") give the strong impression that edible images such as these played an indispensable role in the social representation of patrician families in this Germanic area.[143] For every situation in life, the images offered an *exemplum* that, being shared and consumed, demonstrated their owners' adherence to certain common moral and cultural values.

Cialde *as Operators of Family Lineage*

As with the gingerbreads, the *cialde* very soon infiltrated aristocratic and bourgeois households.[144] From the fourteenth to the ninteenth centuries,[145] they spread over almost all of Europe, and they bore witness, as did the gingerbreads, to the shifting of the stakes of social identity from the sacred to the profane world.[146]

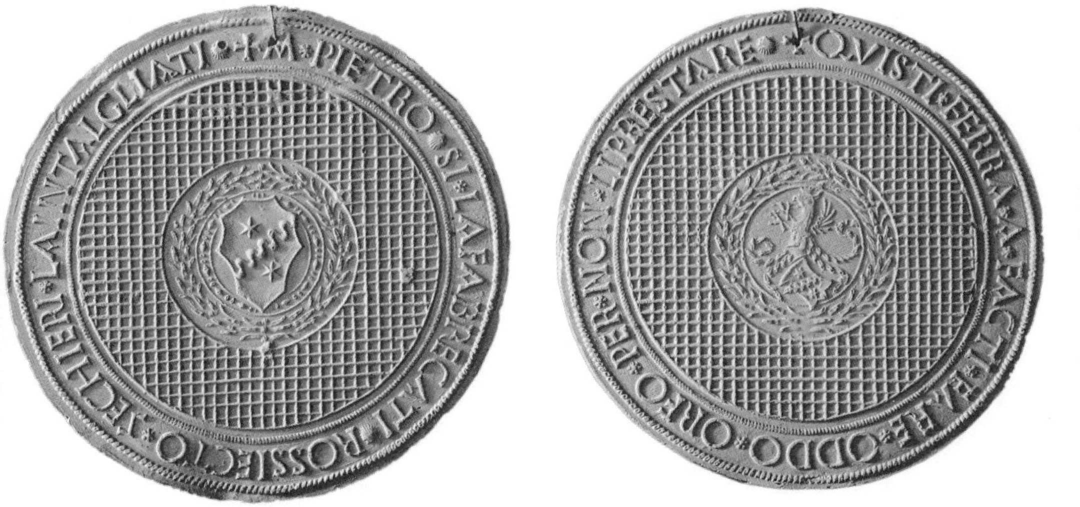

Figure 3.21. Federico di Francesco Rossetti, ca. 1490–1500, plaster casts from wafering irons bearing the arms of Oddo Orfo, 7 in. Perugia, Galleria Nazionale dell'Umbria (© Kunsthistorisches Institut in Florenz—Max Planck Institut).

The wafering irons, like the ones used for baking *oublies*, derived from those employed in the making of the host wafers. As with the host presses, the wafering irons consisted of two plates that could be pressed together, and each of the plates bore an engraved image (figs. 3.21, 3.22, and 3.23). Engraved inscriptions were often put along the border, and these typically mentioned the owner's name, a date, a motto, a commemorative phrase or a moral proverb. In terms of ornamentation and figuration, the irons traditionally showed an escutcheon or crest bearing the coat of arms of the sponsoring family. Depending upon the historical period and the quality of the craftsmanship, the irons might also display an emblematic image, such as a *memento mori* (fig. 3.23), a portrait (much less common;

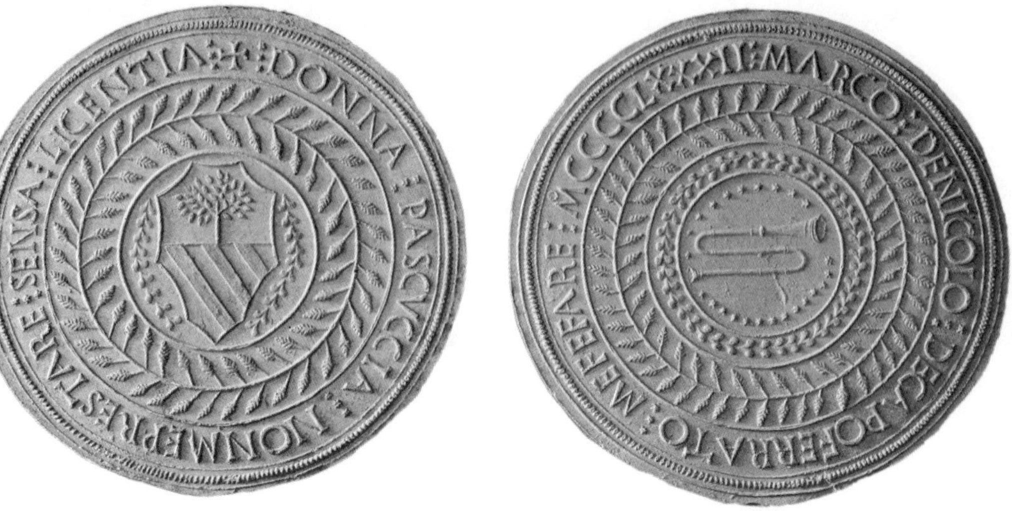

Figure 3.22. Plaster casts from wafering irons bearing the arms of Nicolo Capoferrato, 1482, 6.6 in. Perugia, Galleria Nazionale dell'Umbria (© Kunsthistorisches Institut in Florenz—Max Planck Institut).

fig. 3.24), or yet decorative features (garlands, foliate scrolls, bows, résille patterns, etc.).[147] The variety and abundance of the ornamentation was designed to visually indicate the family's material wealth and comfort in public settings where its honor might be at stake, notably on the occasion of weddings, baptisms, funerals, and other festivals and holy days throughout the year.[148] In this, these dessert items were anything but bit players in the banquet economy since they could on occasion be produced in great numbers. For example, in June 1466, Giovanni Rucellai ordered 4,000 *cialde* for the marriage of his son Bernardo with Nannina de' Medici, the daughter of Piero de' Medici,[149] and the cook and master of ceremonies Cristoforo da Messisbugo informs us, in his *Banchetti, compositioni di vivande e apparacchio generale* (1549), that on June 24, 1529 Hercule d'Este, who was

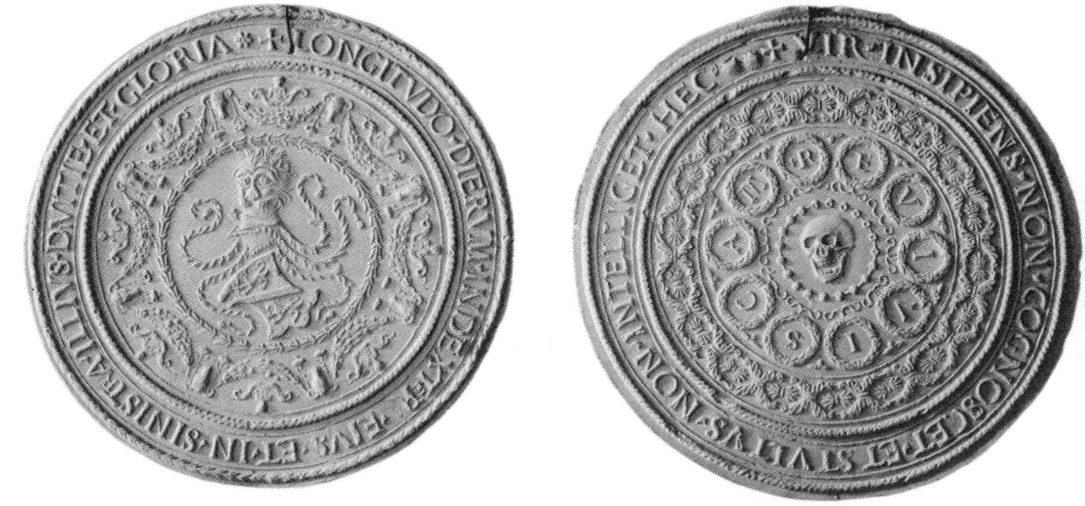

Figure 3.23. Plaster casts from wafering irons, ca. 1501–1515, 7 in. Perugia, Galleria Nazionale dell'Umbria (© Kunsthistorisches Institut in Florenz—Max Planck Institut).

at that time Duke of Chartres, served at dinner no fewer than 1,500 *cialde* to his fifty-four invited guests, among whom were assembled the Duke of Ferrara, Alphonse d'Este, the Archbishop of Milan, Hippolyte d'Este, the Marquess of Mantua, Isabelle d'Este, as well as the ambassadors of Venice and the King of France, François I.[150] The great need for ornamental ostentation at these banquets explains why certain templates were particularly elaborate and why the families, especially the princely ones, called upon famous goldsmiths, such as Francesco di Valeriano (Il Roscetto), to do the engraving.[151]

The obvious connection, in terms of use and design, between the *cialde* irons and the host presses (fig. 3.25) allows us, by extrapolation, to uncover the essential social purpose served by the production and consumption of the *cialde* in the context of family

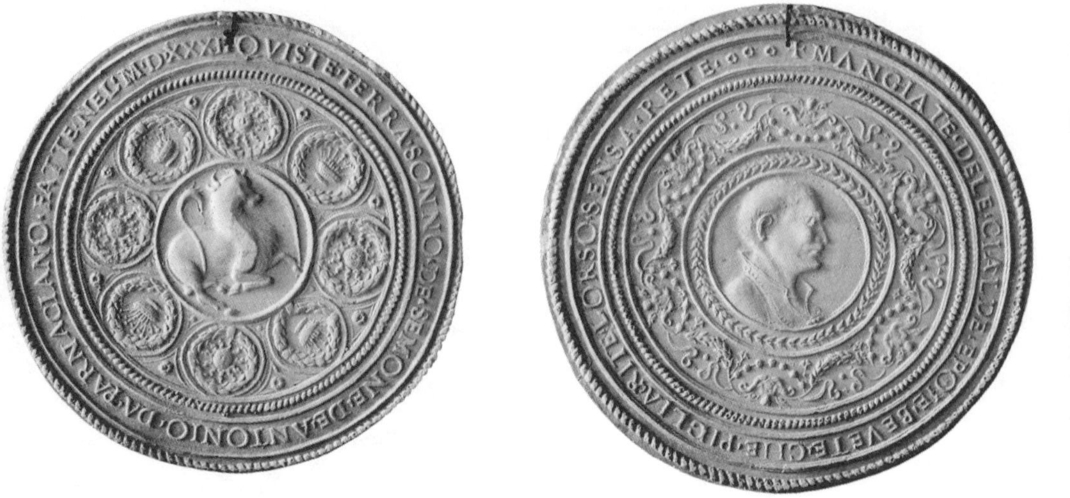

Figure 3.24. Plaster casts from wafering irons bearing the arms of Simone de Antonio da Parnaciano, 1532, 7 in. Perugia, Galleria Nazionale dell'Umbria (© Kunsthistorisches Institut in Florenz—Max Planck Institut).

banquets. Just like the host wafers, each individual figured wafer, although one of many, was identical to all the others. Accordingly, by ingesting it the family members were granted a chance to reaffirm their place in the community.

Seen from this perspective at least, the coat of arms, the iconographic feature most often found on the irons, takes on its fullest meaning. In offering his family the *cialde*, the *paterfamilias* was tacitly inviting all those partaking to share in what, in an essentially patrilineal society, defined their identity, their line of descent.[152] In fact, as Hans Belting notes, the "heraldic abstraction" identifies "not an individual but the bearer of a familial or territorial genealogy; that is to say, it defined the body of a social estate."[153] With this definition in mind, we can highlight the fact that the individual *cialda*

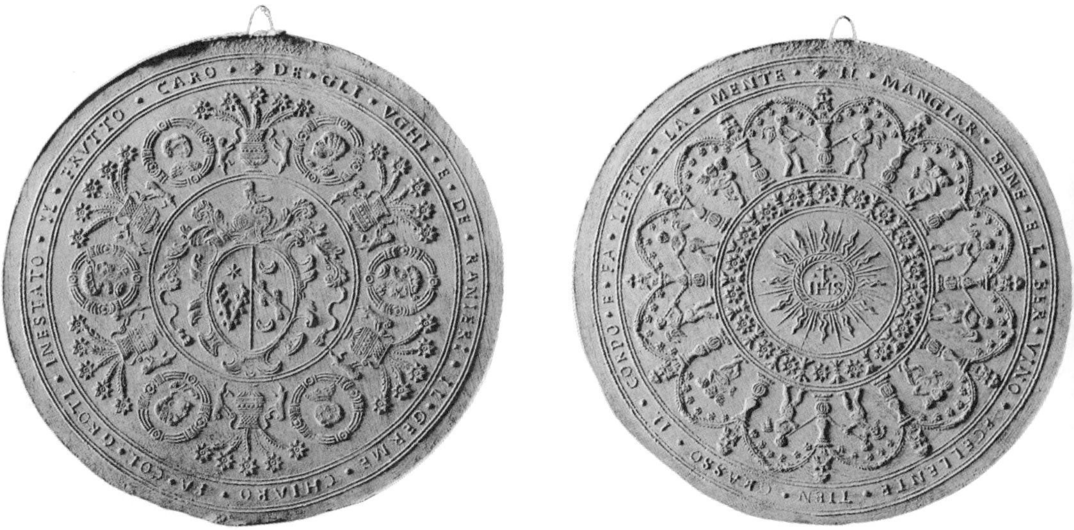

Figure 3.25. Plaster casts from wafering irons bearing arms and the monogram IHS, 1576–1600, 7.8 in. Perugia, Galleria Nazionale dell'Umbria (© Kunsthistorisches Institut in Florenz—Max Planck Institut).

functioned, as did the host wafer, like a seal. During the Middle Ages and into the Renaissance, seals traditionally bore the heraldic emblems of their sigillants, and it is for this reason that the arms engraved on the plates were generally designated by their owners as "*imaginis nostre*."[154] The almost complete absence of portraits on the *cialde*, at a moment in history when that form of representation was undergoing spectacular growth, adds support to this idea. If history here appears *out of joint*, so to speak, this certainly suggests that what was really being celebrated with these *cialde* were family lines of descent and not the individual family members.[155]

By eating one of the pressed wafers, the partaker was ingesting the coat of arms of the father of the family, assimilating that which constituted the eater's own identity, his own genealogical heritage. Indeed, incorporating the iconic cipher of a line of descent also meant taking into one's own body a symbolic image of the hereditary blood, and we should not forget that during the Renaissance, in remembrance of Rome, a line of descent was understood as essentially a transmission of blood.[156] The wafer-eater was thus transforming into blood what had before been only an image,[157] and so it was the continuity between food and blood that lay behind the choice of *ingestion* of the heraldic image as the preferred way of binding together the members of a single family.[158]

We should note, extending the range of our argument here, that at this time in history the idea of the family was not limited to the nuclear grouping of father, mother, and children. The family included, rather, anyone possessing a wider kin relationship, and it even encompassed those employed in the service of the *paterfamilias*.[159] Under these conditions, the centrifugal link forged by ingesting the *cialda* was even more powerful if the partaker did not share a direct blood relationship with the family, not to mention that the extension of the perimeter of the family went even further when the wafering irons were lent out. The frequent use of the pairing *lend/return* in the inscriptions on the irons[160] suggests, in fact, that *cialde* bearing a family's coat of arms could well have been consumed beyond the immediate family circle, for example, by such "clients" as friends and neighbors, who thus came to form an "artificial lineage."[161] On such occasions, the eaters, although set at a distance, might see themselves as situated within the sphere of influence of the *patron*, the owner of the irons.

Given the family's variable limits, the relation of dependence and inclusion established by the consumption of the *cialde* quite naturally found its fullest application at marriage celebrations.[162] Like certain marzipan molds, the irons engraved for weddings often showed the coats of arms of the two families, one on each of the two plates—the two sides of the *cialda* materializing the meeting of the two groups. One example of this, in the collection of the Victoria and Albert Museum (fig. 3.26), includes an inscription

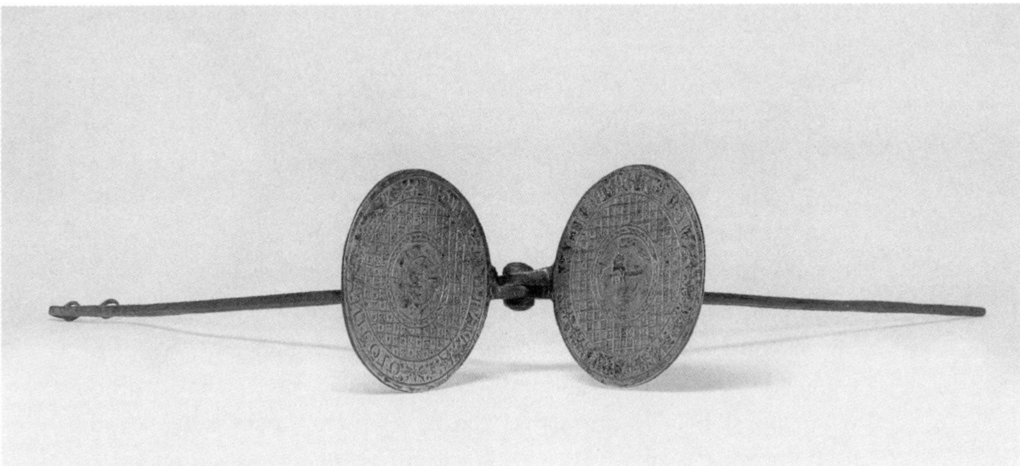

Figure 3.26. Wafering irons for the wedding of Nicolo and Paulina Lugli, ca. 1500, iron, 6.4 in. London, The Victoria and Albert Museum (inv. M.454-1924) (Creative Commons).

linking husband and wife, "Nicolo e Paulina Lugli."[163] This adjoining of names is also materialized by each of the irons' facing templates: on one of them, around the emblem of the gloved hand holding a baton, the initials "NL" for Nicolo Lugli; and on the other, inscribed within a shield containing a stylized heart, the initials "NPL" for Nicolo *Paulina* Lugli. On the latter template, the framing of the P inside the N and L, within a form traditionally associated with genealogy (i.e., the shield), seems to depict the newly wed husband's incorporation of his bride. Consequently, by virtue of its shape and use, the stamped wafer became both a symbol of their alliance and a vector for encompassing one group, the bride's people, within another, the husband's family.[164]

This active role played by the figured representations in the establishment of a community was, we must note, often made explicit in the inscriptions accompanying the engraved images. These inscriptions typically "speak" in the first person (see fig. 3.22): "*Marco de Nicolo de Capoferrato* me *fe fare MCCCLXXXII* (Marco de Nicolo de Capoferrato had me made in 1482)." Indeed, the text might even address the eater in the imperative: "*Donna Pascuccia non* me *prestare sensa licentia* (Donna Pascuccia[,] do not lend me without permission)."[165] Through this direct form of address, the inscription points to the edible image not only as a "speaker" activating a symbolic link between producer and consumer, but also as an *operator* capable of "impacting upon the feelings, thoughts and motivation of engaged observers."[166] Understood in this way, the *cialda* occupies what Horst Bredekamp calls "the zone of the image act," which he defines as "a sphere in which the difference between observation and action, between the living and the anorganic, is ever more sharply marked."[167]

We can be certain, therefore, bringing together all these disparate pieces, that ingesting *cialde* fulfilled the following functions: it established a *tie* of dependence with the holder of the template, it *depicted* the principle of symbolic feeding (I am fed by the *patrone*, the master of the house),[168] and finally, it *transformed* the eater internally, making him or her into a member of the family—feeding his or her blood with the image of a *blood tie*.[169]

Eating the Dead

Yet, there is more. A pair of wafering irons dating from the beginning of the sixteenth century (see fig. 3.23) and today in the Galleria Nazionale dell'Umbria in Perugia encourage us to add a more "vertical" line representing family memory to the "horizontal" line of social relations. These irons were probably used for making *cialde* intended for private masses, and the two templates contain both images and text.[170] The first plate bears a heraldic crest with the proverb, "*Longitudo dierum indextera eius et in sinistra illius divitie et gloria* (Long life is in her right hand; in her left are riches and honor," Proverbs 3:16), while the second plate has a skull in its center entirely surrounded by letters forming the inscription "*Reviviscam* (I shall come back to life)," and along the border, the verse "*Vir insipiens non cognoscet et stultus non intelliget h[a]ec* (The senseless man shall not know: nor will the fool understand these things," Psalms 91:7)." The presence of the lines from Proverbs and Psalms in connection with the two emblems certainly gives a Christian coloring to the *cialda*. So much so, in fact, that we might see the term *reviviscam* as translating a belief in eternal life, set in opposition to the *memento mori* represented by the skull. The *cialda* would thus be a sort of *ersatz* host. But this is perhaps not the main point. Since the template gives equal weight to the heraldic helmet, we can assume that the *rebirth* offered to the eater was not to be based entirely on the latter's adopting the Christian denial of worldly possessions; it would result, rather, from the regeneration offered by the consumption of the wafer bearing the image of the family lineage. Symbolically ingesting the coat of arms was not only a way of nourishing and nurturing the family for its living members, but it was also a way of keeping alive the family's ancestors by preserving their memory. The family, as represented by its living members, and itself now a source of life, would thus be destined for perpetual rebirth through its near and distant descendants.

This preserving of memory through ingestion fits, moreover, with certain stories from antiquity in which eating one's ancestors features as a way of keeping alive family members and other loved ones. We might recall, for example, the story of Artemisia and Mausolus (fig. 3.27), as told in Aulus Gellius's *Attic Nights* (x:18):

> Artemisia is said to have loved her husband Mausolus with a love surpassing all the tales of passion and beyond one's conception of human affection. Now Mausolus, as Marcus Tullius tells us, was king of the land of Caria; according to some Greek historians he was governor of a province, the official whom the Greeks term a satrap. When this Mausolus had met his end amid the lamentations and in the arms of his wife, and had been buried with a magnificent funeral, Artemisia, inflamed with grief and with longing for

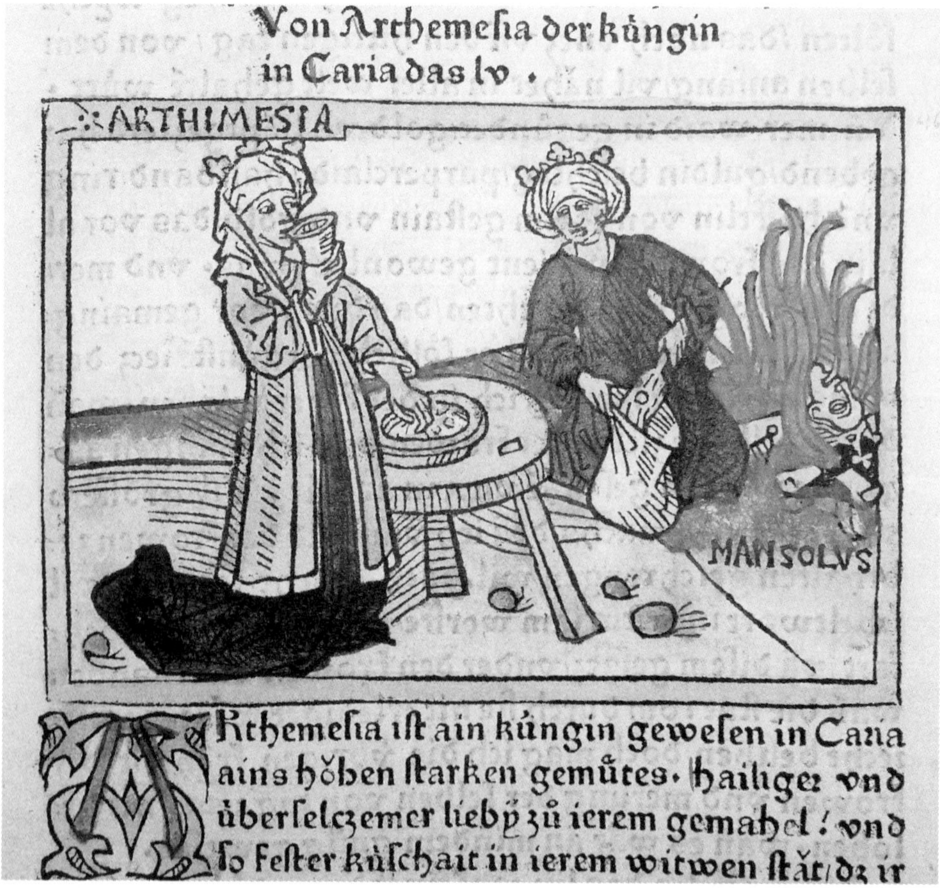

Figure 3.27. *Artemisia, Queen of Caria, Drinking Mausolus's Ashes*, woodcut, in Giovanni Boccacio, *De claris mulieribus* (Ulm: Johannes Zainer, 1474) (Creative Commons).

> her spouse, mingled his bones and ashes with spices, ground them into the form of a powder, put them in water, and drank them.[171]

As Girolamo Tartarotti was to put it in the eighteenth century, the desperate Queen of Caria "devises a way to resuscitate" her husband "by identifying him" through ingestion "with herself."[172] She turns her own body into Mausolus's sepulcher, "making eternal the being that she so loved, by changing him into her own substance."[173] The *other*, now made into the *self*, is thus kept alive in a way that goes beyond any naturalistic explanation.[174]

As strange as it may appear, the story is consistent with some well-known ancient funereal practices, such as a son's eating the corpse of his father, a custom that existed, according to Herodotus (*Histories*, III, 38), among a tribe in India called the Calliatae. In the sixteenth century, in his essay *The Apology of Raymond Sebond*, Michel de Montaigne was to give a remarkable analysis of the funereal ritual involving eating a deceased's ashes:

> The nations which had this custom in ancient times, however, regarded it as testimony of piety and good affection, trying thereby to give their progenitors the most worthy and honorable sepulture, lodging in themselves and as it were in their marrow the bodies of their fathers and their remains, bringing them to life in a way and regenerating them by transmutation into their living flesh by means of digestion and nourishment.[175]

Digestion here produces a transmutation of the substances, making possible a father's reincarnation in his son.[176] The father's ashes are changed into blood; the blood becomes bone marrow; and the father finally surges back, in unrecognizable form, in the son's semen (since Antiquity, semen had been thought of as originating in bone marrow).[177]

Along with the *cialde*, the bones of the dead (fig. 3.28) offer another example of the mixing of food with the symbolic incorporation of one's ancestors. This particular food specialty is to be found most notably in Sicily, and it is inextricably linked with the

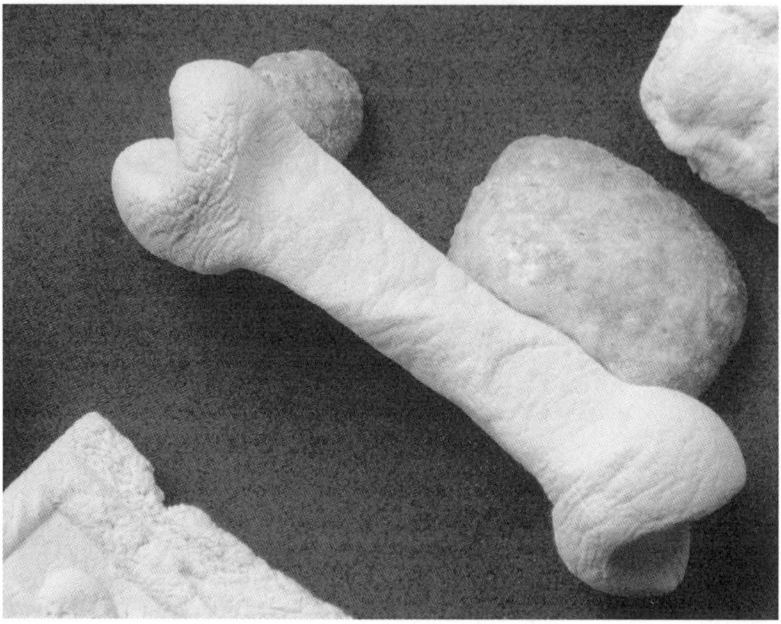

Figure 3.28. Bones of the Dead (*ossa dei morti*), flour and sugar (Creative Commons).

Sicilians' relationship with their forebears.[178] The cakes are made specifically for the Feast of the Dead, the day on which children receive gifts called *i cosi di morti*.[179] As the anthropologist Salvatore D'Onofrio writes in his compelling study on bodily fluids in southern Italy, "the parents [at the time] have the children believe that it is their recently deceased relatives who . . . brought [gifts], during the night of November 1 to November 2, while they [the children] had been processing to the mass given for them [the ancestors]."[180] In addition to these gifts, the parents also give to their children cakes made of "hard pastry" called *ossa dei morti* ("bones of the dead"). These cakes are distinguished by a particular combination of hard and soft textures, and by their white and red coloration. There are two distinct parts to the cake: an inner layer made of caramelized sugar that is given a red coloring, and an outer layer made of flour, white in color and extremely hard after cooking. The whole piece is often, but not always, placed in a mold in the form of a bone, skull, or skeleton in such a way that it "matches" the hardness of bone on the outside and the softness of marrow on the inside. Through their appearance and texture, therefore, these cakes become the bones of the ancestors, and ingesting them becomes an act of "symbolic patriphagy."[181] D'Onofrio further explains that, for children before the age of puberty, this act of incorporation symbolically enacts the transmission to them of the *virtus* ("seminal power") of the dead.[182] By eating the marrow-like inner part of the cake, the child is taking in the very substance that is responsible for the transmission of the family's line of descent.[183] In this way, eating the bones of the dead ensures continuity through the various generations of a single family, establishing "a symbolic channel of communication . . . allowing, through an exchange of food . . . items, for the cultural regulation of the return of the dead to earth . . . and the cultivation of their loving memory."[184]

This same relationship between the living and the dead is also at the heart of the *calaveras de azúcar* tradition in Mexico (fig. 3.29). On the Day of the Dead (November 2), it is customary to offer children sugar skulls, representing one of their relatives, where the name printed on the skull determines the candy's identity.[185] This custom, shot through with vestiges of pre-Columbian and Christian practices (Sergei Eisenstein revealed their analogical sparks in *Que Viva Mexico!*), can be explained in several different ways.[186] Firstly, it reflects the unique status of death in Mexican culture. For a large part of Mexican society, death does not stand in opposition to life. As the ethnologist Kristin Congdon explains it: "For Mexicans . . . , death is simply a *part* of life. It is not separate from life, as an entity from somewhere else."[187] Hence, we see in Mexican culture numerous points of contact between the world of the living and that of the dead. Most Mexicans set up altars in their homes to celebrate

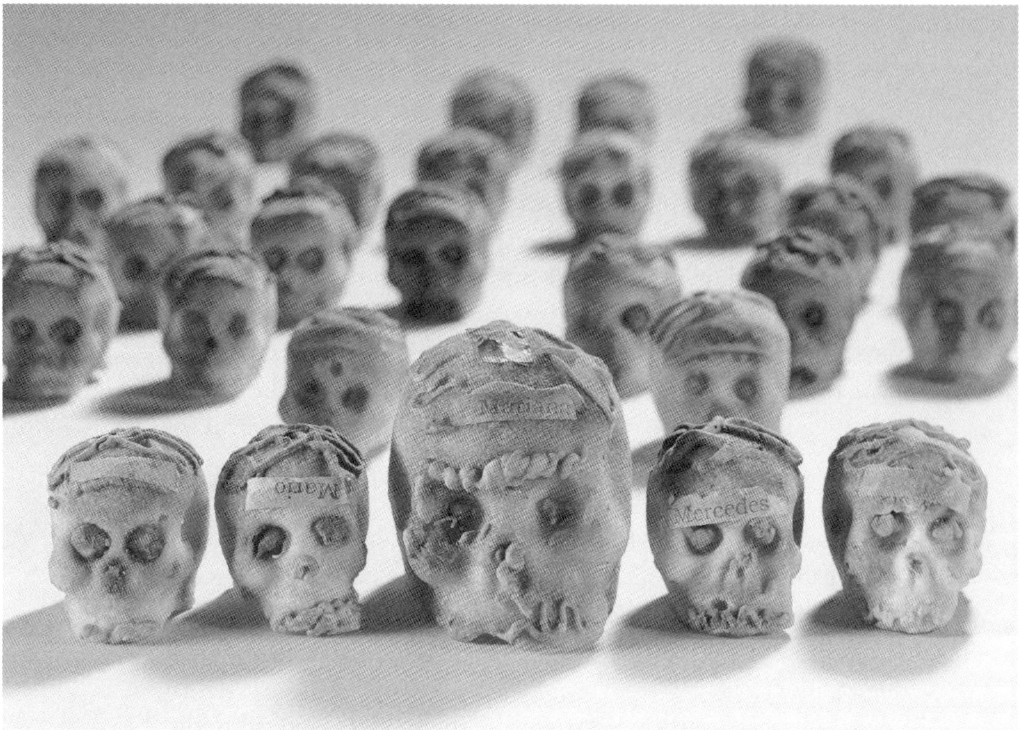

Figure 3.29. Miniature sugar skulls (*calaveritas de azúcar*), twentieth century, sugar, ink, and paper, between 1.5 and 3 in. Paris, Musée du Quai Branly—Jacques Chirac (© Musée du quai Branly—Jacques Chirac, Dist. RMN—Grand Palais/Art Resource, NY/Claude Germain).

their ancestors, and they eat "with them" in the cemeteries. With this in mind, we can see the eating of skulls as a way of living with death, becoming aware of death's presence, and even laughing at it. But there is still more to it. As Congdon explains further, "we all carry death within us,"[188] and the skull in particular, a *memento mori*, when it bears this conventional "likeness," brings to our consciousness this essential part of our being. To consume one's *own* death, and not death in general, is way to overcome our fear of it: "By consuming a sweet skull the eater is inoculated against fear of death because she or he has taken in the peace of death or the dead."[189]

There is, however, another way of understanding the sugar skulls, and this is prompted by the fact that eating the skulls frequently happens in family settings. The *calaveras*, insofar as they constitute in each case a specific tribute or homage, allow a family to preserve a connection with the dead, demonstrating the family's care and attention for their ancestors. Eating an ancestor materializes the continuity of exchange between the living and the dead. In a sense, therefore, the sugar skulls are counterparts to the *ofrendas* ("offerings") made to the dead in the form of prepared foods, arranged on altars in homes and on tombs.[190] Moreover, the specific name attached to a skull encourages us to think that the human sense of identity is bound up with this relationship to the ancestors. Indeed, we might ask, could there even be such a thing as a name, often handed down from generation to generation, without this tie of memory, that is, if not for this handing down?

A work by the artist Stephanie Jones, titled *The Shadow of Love* or *Butade's Biscuits* (fig. 3.30) offers an interesting coda to these customs. In 2009, Jones depicted her friends and relatives in the form of Royal Icing silhouettes set on Arnott's biscuits,[191] creating thus a poetic variation on the story of the discovery of drawing as told in Book XXXV of Pliny the Elder's *Natural History* (fig. 3.31):

> Modelling portraits from clay was first invented by Butades, a potter of Sicyon, at Corinth. He did this owing to his daughter, who was in love with

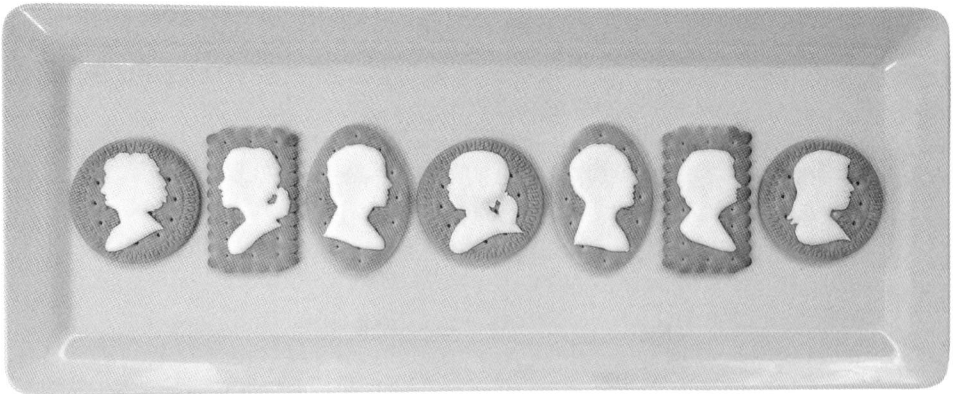

Figure 3.30. Stephanie Jones, *The Shadow of Love (Butade's Biscuits)*, 2009, icing sugar on Arnott's biscuits, plastic dish, 7.8 × 18.8 in. (© Hilary Cuerden-Clifford). Private collection.

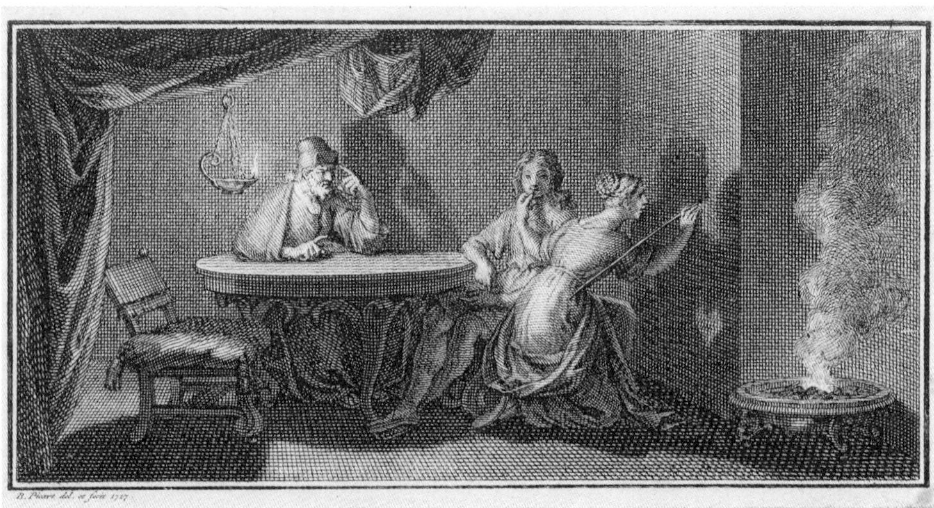

Figure 3.31. Bernard Picart, *Butades's Daughter Tracing Her Lover's Silhouette*, engraving in Bernard de Fontenelle, *Oeuvres diverses qui contient l'histoire des oracles* (The Hague: Gosse & Neaulme, 1728–1729), vol. 2, p. 245. Amsterdam, Rijksmuseum (© Rijksmuseum, Amsterdam).

> a young man; and she, when he was going abroad, drew in outline on the wall the shadow of his face thrown by a lamp.[192]

Like the young woman of Corinth, Jones resorts to line to preserve the contours of a life. However, over against the emptiness contained within the line drawn around the shadow, she sets the completeness of the solidified fondant, filling from within to the edge of the design. Offered up first to our gaze, the image here promises to lodge the memory of the loved one within the innermost part of us. Instead of the deceased's absence in the hollowness bound within a line, the sugar silhouette offers something like the edible body of their fugitive presence. This is a physics of memory, inviting the eye and then the mouth to feast on the portrait, transforming the viewer's body into a tomb as much as it makes of it a mausoleum of appearances.[193]

Political In(di)gestion

At work in spiritual communities and in families, eating images was also an effective way of establishing, consolidating, celebrating, and even contesting political power in the city. We can identify at least three types of edible images used in civic situations and for political festivals: cakes or breads made and distributed as an act of *evergetism* or private liberality for public benefit, figured dishes celebrating and demonstrating the magnificence of princes and city councilors, and edible architectural structures symbolizing the relations between governing classes and their communities.

Panem et circenses

Thanks to an archeological discovery made at the beginning of the twentieth century, we can better document the role of the figured molds and templates in the making of cakes and breads for civic occasions. In the former Roman Ostia Antica, in the years 1904–1905, almost 400 terracotta pieces were found in the *Caseggiato dei Dolii* (a storehouse for large containers) connected to a *pistrinum* (bakery).[194] Now, the context in which the objects were found suggests that they belonged to a baker.[195] Of particular interest for our present purpose is the fact that a good number of the scenes depicted concern public games, such as scenes from the circus and amphitheater, hunting scenes, depictions of tragic and comic theater, and scenes with animals. For Angiolo Pasqui, the first to report on the find in 1906, these breads, given their iconography, were probably served at the feast of Epulum Iovi and the Ludi Plebeii, or the Plebian Games.[196]

The establishment of public largesse in the Greece of the Hellenistic period, a practice subsequently copied by the dignitaries of the Roman towns, created a favorable context for the production and distribution of edible gifts designed to satisfy what Juvenal referred to as the "idle" Roman populace: "For the People who once upon a time handed out military command, high civil office, legions—everything, now restrains itself and anxiously hopes for just two things: bread and circuses."[197] In the Roman world during the Imperial Period, any wealthy person granted public office or honor made an act of *euergesia* (*ob honorem*), that is, a large-scale private generosity. This gift to the community was not offered primarily in exchange for the power and new privileges bestowed on the individual. It was much more a matter of bringing honor to the latter's own dignity, bolstering his superior authority.[198] In the gift economy of ancient Roman society, the figured breads, through the image stamped on their crusts, allowed for a symbolic link to be made between the care and upkeep of the people, where the city councilors were responsible for making wheat always available in order to maintain public order,[199] and the pleasures of the games, paid for and presided over by the magistrates. The iconography of the breads was a way of reminding the people that this largesse, repeated every year at specific times to honor this or that divinity, was a contribution to the maintenance of the temporal order on which the stability of Roman society depended—the stamped breads were a guarantee of good government.[200]

Princely Dishes

Alongside the public circulation of figured breads ensuring the permanence of social institutions and the stable stratification of society, we also find in the ancient world evidence of figured dishes whose ingenious designs were part of a strategy of prestige, allowing the wealthy patricians to show their economic and cultural power within the world of interpersonal relations.[201] Hence Petronius, in his *Satyricon*, reported on the extravagance of Trimalchio, saying that the latter went so far as to offer "a huge boar . . . surrounded by rather small piglets made of hard cake," out of whose gashed side "thrushes flew out," and that he dumbfounded his guests by making "a fish out of a sow's belly, a pigeon out of bacon, a turtledove out of ham, a chicken out of a pork knuckle."[202] In these wild and lavish banquets, Trimalchio was looking to surprise and astonish his guests by "changing the true nature of the dishes by turning them into forms unlike their usual appearance."[203] The dishes offered here to the palate belonged to an aesthetics of astonishment that relied for its effect on transforming foodstuffs into images of what they were not, or no longer were. For, as Aristotle explains it, "Our wonder is excited, firstly, by phenomena which occur in accordance with nature but of which we do not know the cause, and secondly by those which are produced by art despite nature for the benefit of mankind."[204] Creating surprise requires dissimulation, masking, and keeping your technique secret.[205]

Over the course of the Middle Ages and into the modern era, these practices were naturally to find a place on the tables of princes and city dignitaries when it was a matter of celebrating emperors and kings, subjugating diplomatic delegations, and astonishing the guests at princely wedding banquets.[206] On May 29, 1475, for example, for the wedding of Costanzo Sforza, the lord of Pesaro, with Camilla Marzano of Aragona, the guests were served around thirty sugar and pastry creations among which there figured the following: Towers, castles, trees, animals, a triumphal chariot bearing Justice personified, an ox-drawn gallows bearing a figure of Chastity, coins

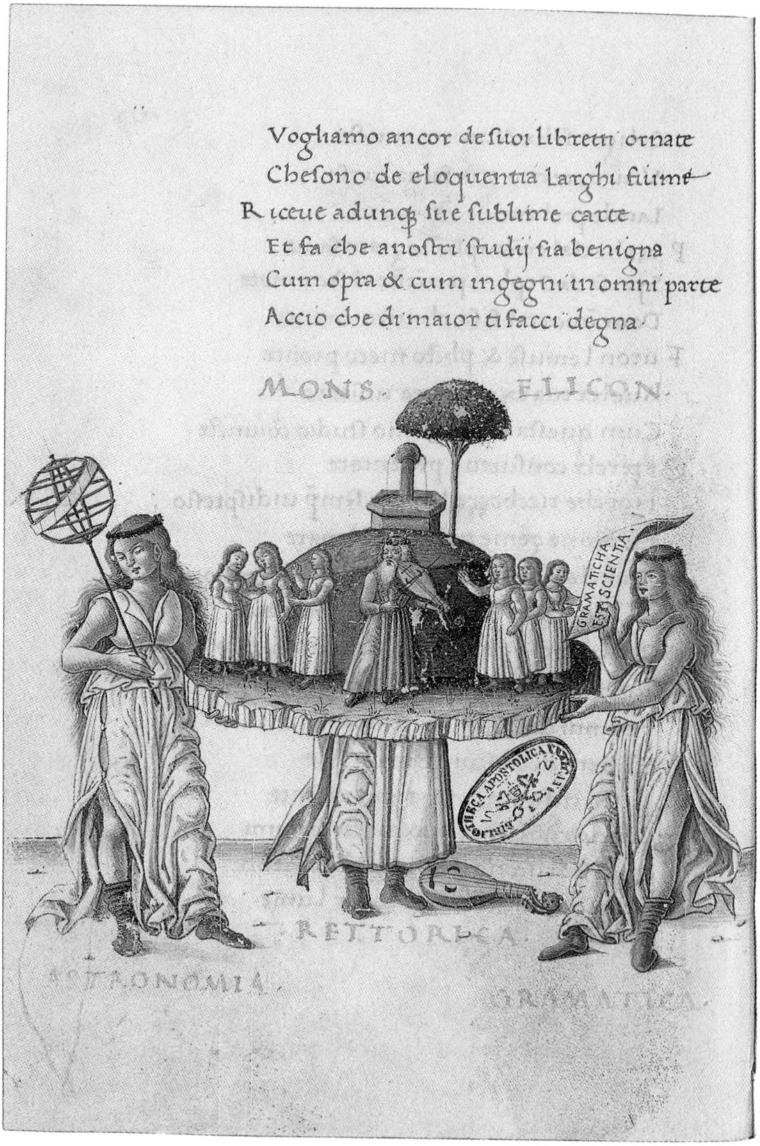

Figure 3.32. *Astronomy, Grammar, and Rhetoric carrying Mount Helicon with Apollo and the Muses*, 1475, illustration in the dishes offered at the wedding feast of Costanzo Sforza and Camilla of Aragona. The Vatican, the Vatican Library Urb. Lat. 899, fol. 110 (© The Vatican Library).

stamped with the images of the young couple, and a Mount Helicon with the Muses and Apollo playing the *lira de braccio* (fig. 3.32), all of these being creations "good to eat."[207] Likewise, on May 22, 1529, Ippolito II d'Este, Archbishop of Milan, had similar creations made for the festivities he organized at the Palazzo Belfiore in Ferrara in honor of his brother Ercole II d'Este and his bride Renée de France. The first course included "fifteen sugar figures," partly decked out in "gold and paint" and representing "Venus, Cupid, and Bacchus," and then, for the ninth course, "fifteen naked Moors" (i.e., eight men and seven women) made of "sosamelli dough," "vegetables," and "flowers."[208] On all these occasions, the honor rendered the guests was the direct result of the creativity of the cooks and artists. The greatest court sculptors, therefore, were quite naturally made to contribute, as we see, for example, with Giambologna in Florence who, for the marriage of Marie de' Medici and Henry IV of France in June 1600, supplied no fewer than forty models for making sugar statues, among which figured a Hercules and the Centaur, a Dwarf Morgante, a Pluto Raping Proserpina, and equestrian statues of Ferdinand I and Cosimo II.[209]

The tributes made on these occasions took their force essentially from the gustatory and ornamental qualities of the dishes and confections; however, a similar purpose could be achieved in a more referential way, particularly through allegory and the language of heraldry, moving things, therefore for such occasions, from the pictorial surface to the palate. For the banquet given to celebrate the coronation of Henry VI of England on November 6, 1429, there appeared among the figured dishes offered to the guests a pie bearing a golden lion, the symbol of the English monarchy, grasping in its claws a fleur-de-lys, the symbol of France. As the Hundred Years' War was playing itself out, heraldic codes were taking the route of cooking to express, in a way that was as simple as it was effective, the Yorkist claim to the throne of France.[210]

In similar fashion, the culinary arts did not fail to contribute to the symbolic rhetoric accompanying Prince Ernest of Bavaria on his entrance into the town of Liège in 1581. In his account of the event, Jean Polit describes a banquet with several courses that included a huge number of emblemized dishes that were there both to celebrate the prince's line of descent, and to flatter his taste for hunting:[211]

> The guests being already well amused by the dinner that had gone off pleasantly, a long train of servants brought the sweet course to the table. One of the first serving trays had on it his highnesses' coat of arms, adorned with a green miter, and held up at the sides by two angels.[212]

After this:

> There came a dual hunting scene, for boar and stag, one divided into thirteen, and the other into twenty sections. Next came two tournaments depicted as in life. One could see real knights in armor, with their lances down, as if moved by the sound of the eight trumpeters standing near them, and ready to charge. An equal number of other jousters faced them, distinguished by their colored cloaks, but equally ready for the imminent confrontation. Standing close by was the field steward of the joust, escorted by three knights with their pages on foot. His highness was shown as a spectator at the contest.[213]

We might add to this example the feast given on June 16, 1585, in Düsseldorf for the wedding of John William, Duke of Jülich-Cleves-Berg, Count of La Marck and Ravensberg (1562–1609) and Jakobea of Baden (1558–1597). At this event, the riot of dishes on offer was designed to mix sensation and political judgement. The engraving by Frans Hogenberg accompanying the description of the meal (fig. 3.33) gives an idea of the variety and complexity of the edible creations on offer at the table: we find a large number of real animals (e.g., dogs, a camel, an elephant, bears, fish, and a horse) and fantastical ones (e.g., unicorn), as well as trees, human figures (e.g., an ostler, men at arms), a castle, and all of this set up around the coats of arms of the two families and the emblem of the Holy Roman Empire, the two-headed eagle, perched upon

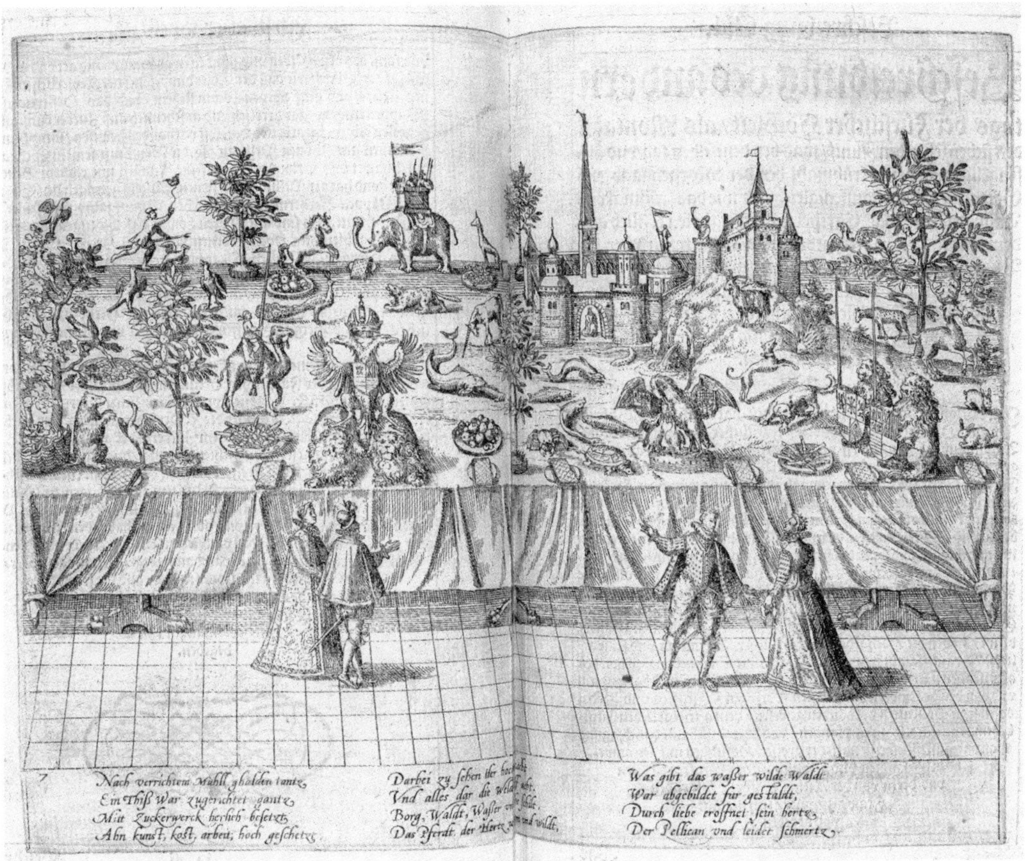

Figure 3.33. Frans Hogenberg, *Table Setting of Sugar Paste Sculptures for the Wedding of Johann Wilhelm, Duke of Jülich*, 1587, engraving in Theodor Graminaeus, *Beschreibung derer fürstlicher güligscher etc. Hochzeit* (Cologne, 1587), pl. 7 (© The Getty Research Institute).

two lions.[214] As with the banquet in Liège, the political dimension comes through in the association of heraldic images with symbolic figures, and these were readily understandable.[215] To take just one obvious example, the presence of the *Pelican feeding its young with its blood*, a traditional symbol of Christ the Savior, seems to take on here an overtly political meaning since the bird bears on its wings the heraldic shields of the two princely families.[216] Seen in this light, the bird is quite conceivably praising the reciprocal love of the couple, as well as their love of charity, a sign of their future good government. Indeed, all these images made to be eaten and arranged around this allegorical figure invited the guests to consume, and through this prompting they transformed what might have been a simple *petitio principii* (sharing, love, and charity) into a real demonstration of the newlywed couple's liberality *in action*.

Food City

Feeding one's guests with allegorical images to celebrate a fertile union or to predict the coming state of plenty ushered in by new rulers can take on an entirely new meaning when the banquet is held in the city streets and when the guest list is no longer limited specifically to those members of high society that one needs to impress with a show of expense and novelty but includes rather the ordinary people over whom a prince wields authority. An engraving included in Francesco Orilia's political treatise, *Il Zodiaco, over, idea di perfettione di prencipi* (1630),[217] shows a triumphal arch (fig. 3.34) whose facing is made up of various foods, such as hams, piglets, and vegetables. The illustration memorializes an ephemeral decoration that was set up in Naples on June 23, 1629, for the entrance into the city of its viceroy, Antonio Álvarez de Toledo y Beaumont, Duke of Alba.[218] Erected in front of the Porta del Caputo (also called the Porta San Giovanni), the structure was one of a great many staged sets produced to celebrate, in symbolic fashion, the prince's virtues as he marked his seventh year in government (the Duke of Alba had

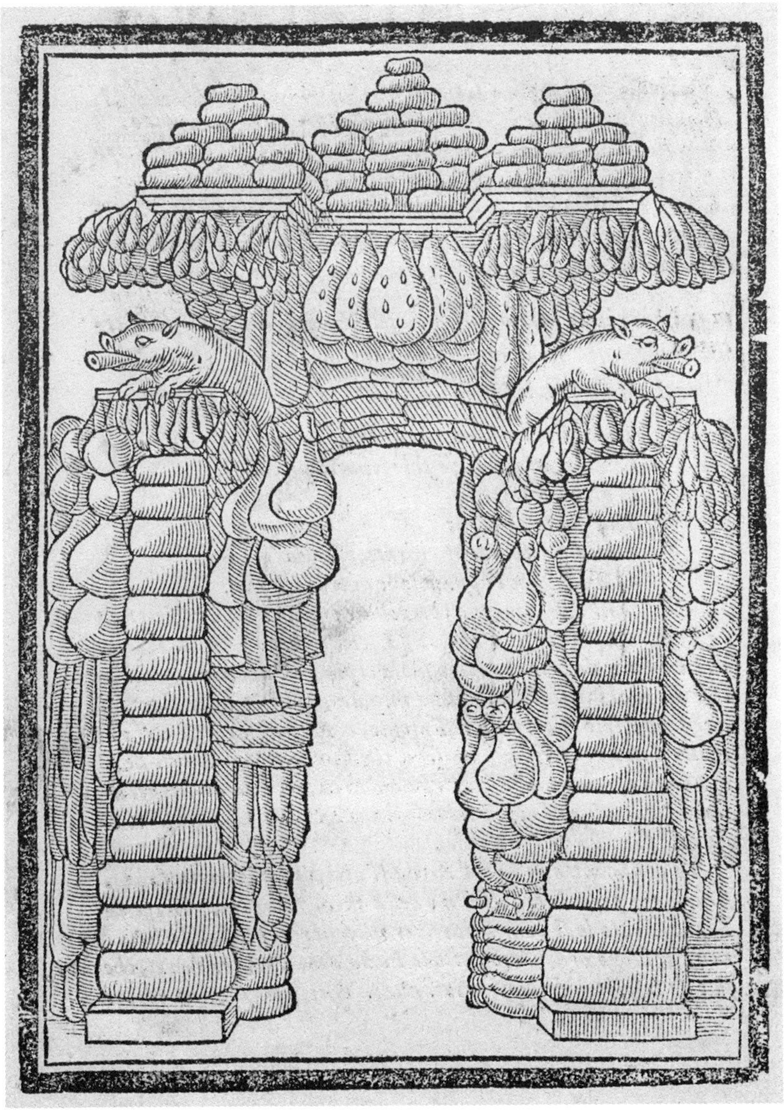

Figure 3.34. *Triumphal Arch in honor of Antonio Alvarez of Toledo*, in Francesco Orilia, *Il Zodiaco, over, idea di perfettione di prencipi . . .* (Naples: Apresso Ottauio Beltrana, 1630), p. 457r, Getty Research Institute, Los Angeles (94-B11818) (© The Getty Research Institute).

been made viceroy of Naples on September 14, 1622, by Philip IV of Spain). Now, according to Orilia, at the close of the festivities, the arch of vittles, representing the virtue of Vigilance and illustrating the material support given by the prince to his people, was taken down and its edible parts offered to the people who then ate them. The arch is transformed thus from a symbol of the viceroy's ability to offer sustenance to his people into an actual operator of the prince's largesse.[219] The political impact of such a device is easy to see. By sharing the very sign of his princely power, the prince unites the people under his own image, forming thus around him a community that is bound, by mouth and stomach, to his own good government.[220]

Much more recently, on June 13, 1971, the Haus-Rucker-Co group harnessed the same performative power of the edible image to stage a citizens' action event in Minneapolis. The project, conceived by the artists and architects Günter Zamp Kelp, Klaus Pinter, Manfred and Laurids Ortner, was titled *Food City I* (fig. 35). The goal of the Minneapolis project, however, was quite different from that of the artists and political advisors working for the Duke of Alba since the edible architectures, made essentially out of sliced bread, butter, ham, eggs, tomatoes, and cucumbers, were designed to make the town councillors and residents aware of the decrepit state of many of the city's neighborhoods and of the need for them to be transformed.[221] The group's purpose was thus to symbolically forecast the neighborhoods' disappearance by bringing those who lived there to be the very agents of the alteration of their own living space. As the architects explained in an interview: "The city is killing itself with urban problems, *Food City* [allows participants] the opportunity to destroy obsolescence by gobbling the city up."[222] Ingestion here is no longer the germinating leaven of a social pact linking a people's future with the good government of their prince; rather, it is rather a *modus operandi* by which the people could bring about a *redistribution of the sensible*, participating thus in the radical utopia offered by a total transformation of the city.[223]

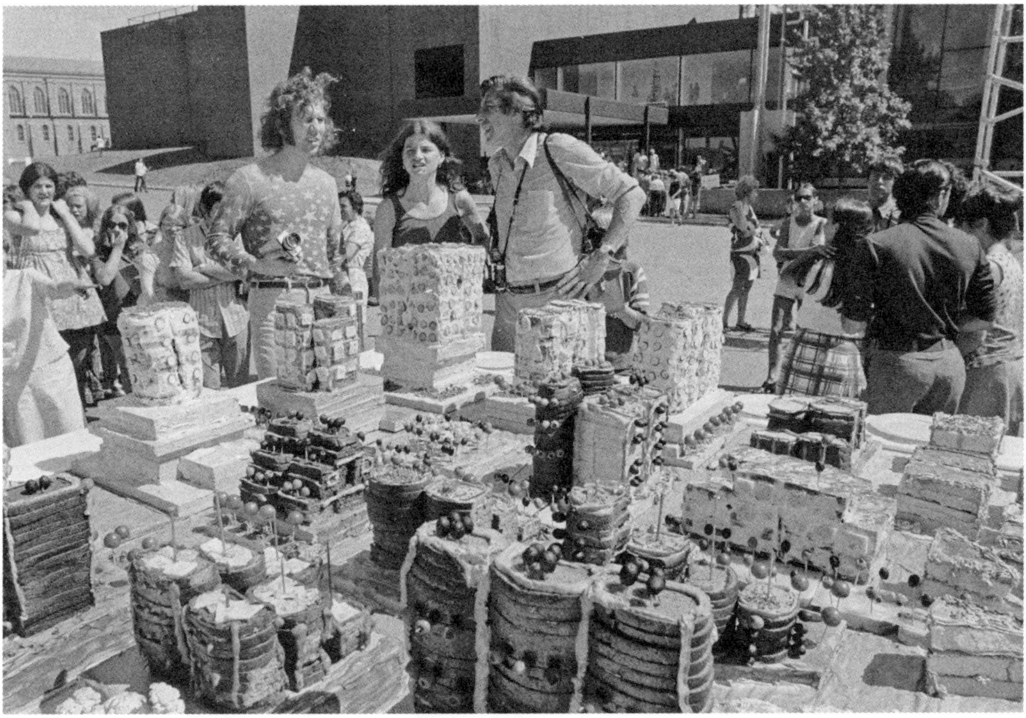

Figure 3.35. Haus-Rucker-Co, *Food City I*, June 13, 1971. The Armory Gardens (now the site of the Minneapolis Sculpture Garden). Photograph by Powel Krueger. Minneapolis, Walker Art Center (Creative Commons).

A Consummate Art for Consumption

With all these stratagems, we should not forget that the individual sculpted food items, like the edible architecture just discussed, were not made entirely for political causes and interests. Behind the orgy of intentions, there was an orgy of inventions. The art of producing, building, and arranging images using malleable, brittle, sticky, soft, and irremediably perishable substances has its driving force in the overriding (and doubtless febrile) desire to launch into existence so many ingenious, beautiful, and capricious forms in the full knowledge that they will not survive longer than a single day. Each piece of edible sculpture is a clever snub to the empire of Chronos—an impertinent reversal of the order of things.

Praising of the Unique

We have only to read the pages that Giorgio Vasari devotes to the *Compagnia del Paiuolo* (the Company of the Paiuolo) in his account of the life of the sculptor Giovan Francesco Rustici to appreciate how much purely artistic motivations have been at play since the Renaissance in the history of these ephemeral images:[224]

> There used to assemble in his rooms at the Sapienza a company of good fellows who called themselves the Company of the Paiuolo, and these, whose numbers were limited to twelve, were our Giovan Francesco, Andrea del Sarto, the painter Spillo, Domenico Puligo, the goldsmith Robetta, Aristotile da San Gallo, Francesco di Pellegrino, Niccolò Buoni, Domenico Baccelli, who played and sang divinely, the sculptor Solosmeo, Lorenzo called Guazzetto, and the painter Ruberto di Filippo Lippi, who was their proveditor. Each of these twelve could bring to certain suppers and entertainments of theirs four friends and no more. The manner of the suppers, which I am very willing to describe because these companies have fallen almost entirely out of fashion, was that each man should bring some dish for supper, prepared with some beautiful invention, which, on arriving at the proper place, he presented to the master of the feast, who was always one of their number, and who then gave it to whomsoever he pleased, each man thus exchanging his dish for that of another. When they were at table, they all offered each

other something from their dishes, and every man partook of everything; and whoever had hit on the same invention for his dish as another, and had produced the same thing, was condemned to pay a penalty. One evening, then, when Giovan Francesco gave a supper to that Company of the Paiuolo, he arranged that there should serve as a table an immense cauldron, in the centre of which came the viands arranged in a circle; and the handle of the cauldron, which curved like a crescent above them, gave out a most beautiful light from the centre, so that, looking round, they all saw each other face to face. Now, when they were all seated at table in the cauldron, which was most beautifully contrived, there issued from the centre a tree with many branches, which set before them the supper, that is, the first course of viands, two to each plate. This done, it descended once more below, where there were persons who played music, and in a short time came up again and presented the second course, and then the third, and so on in due order, while all around were servants who poured out the choicest wines. The invention of the cauldron, which was beautifully adorned with hangings and pictures, was much extolled by the men of that company. For that evening the contribution of Rustici was a cauldron in the form of a pie, in which was Ulysses dipping his father in order to make him young again; which two figures were boiled capons that had the form of men, so well were the limbs arranged, and all with various things good to eat [*cose tutte buone a mangiare*]. Andrea del Sarto presented an octagonal temple, similar to that of S. Giovanni, but raised upon columns. The pavement was a vast plate of jelly, with a pattern of mosaic in various colours; the columns, which had the appearance of porphyry, were sausages, long and thick; the socles and capitals were of Parmesan cheese; the cornices of sugar, and the tribune was made of sections of marchpane. In the centre was a choir desk made of cold veal, with a book of lasagne that had the letters and notes of the music made of pepper-corns; and the singers at the desk were cooked thrushes standing with their beaks open, and with certain little shirts after the manner of surplices, made of fine cauls of pigs, and behind them, for the basses, were two fat young pigeons, with six ortolans that sang the soprano. Spillo presented as his dish a smith, which he had made from a great goose or some such bird, with all the instruments wherewith to mend the cauldron in case

> of need. Domenico Puglio represented by means of a cooked sucking-pig a serving girl with a distaff at her side, who was watching a brood of chickens, and was there to scour the cauldron. Robetta made out of a calf's head, with appurtenances formed of other fat meats, an anvil for the maintenance of the cauldron, which was very fine and very beautiful, as were also all the other contributions; not to enumerate one by one all the dishes of that supper and of many others that they gave.[225]

This remarkably vivid and precise description provides a huge number of details on the makeup and regulations of the company, the nature of the images produced, and on how the edible creations were sculpted, shaped, arranged, and finally eaten. Yet, to make the stakes involved in creating and consuming these representations fully clear to us, we must highlight a few important points.

Created, in all probability, around 1512 in the studios of the Sapienza, in the neighborhood of the Santissima Annunziata, the Company of the Cauldron, as Vasari tells us, was a group of twelve artists, including famous painters and sculptors, such as Domenico Puligo, Aristotile da Sangallo, Solosmeo, and Andrea del Sarto. The number twelve is obviously not accidental since it establishes a parallel between the group of artists and the company of Christ, where the number twelve doubtless corresponds to Christ and the eleven disciples who did not betray him.[226] The company's distinguishing characteristic was that they organized banquets or *tornate* ("sessions") during which its members would concoct, out of vegetables, fruits, cheeses, meats and pâtés, architectural settings, landscapes with animals, heroic figures (Ulysses, Anchises, et. al.), various tools and instruments, and so on. The company rule was that each member was to bring along a dish decorated with recognizable figures, and the dish had to be clearly different from all the others, so much so that any resemblance to another dish entailed a forfeit.[227] Now, unlike the cakes that were prepared for sacred rituals or domestic celebrations (*lebkuchen, cialde*, etc.), the edible creations of the Company of the Cauldron never involved the use of molds or templates. Each of the dishes made for the company banquets was totally unique, bearing witness thus to the manual skill of its maker. Once the dishes were collected together, the edible artifacts were given over to the member designated to be the banquet's organizer, the *signore* (the master of the feast), and it was the latter's responsibility to give out a portion of each image to every one of the guests.[228] Once the decorated dishes had been shared out in this way, each was judged according to its degree of creativity.

As Vasari describes it, this custom resonates perfectly with the rituals and ceremonies we have looked at previously. Here, as before, it is a question of instituting a community and recognizing its members through the making, sharing, and eating of edible images.[229] However, unlike the stamped breads and molded cakes (e.g., the host, *cialda*, or *lebkuchen*), which involved the sharing and eating of a single image common to the whole community, the sculpted dishes made for the Company of the Cauldron were all different—twelve entirely unique creations were offered to the guests. The image's function here is thus no longer that of bringing together a multitude of distinct individuals in the unity of Christ or the family. The aim here is, in fact, quite the opposite: each member of the group differentiates himself from the others, defining himself by what is uniquely his, namely, his *ingenium* ("artistic ingenuity"). In other words, the cement that binds together the fraternity is, paradoxically, each member's personal idiosyncrasy—their own individual uniqueness. Despite the possible link with the Christlike model of a company of twelve, the ideal sought here is no longer one of *conforming*—the taking on of a form that would lead to resemblance with the divine—but rather of *individuating*, as it is an artist's originality that assures him a place in history.[230] The reversal of the Christian paradigm could not be more complete.

All these edible sculptures with which the Florentine artists competed among themselves, as they vied with each other to be the most creative and ingenious, were no doubt counterparts of the dishes created for the princely and political banquets of the same period in time. Now, this is not without significance: the artistic one-upmanship that emerged from these artist's productions was to have its effect on the evolving forms and uses of similar dishes served at princely courts during the early modern period. The increasingly evident artificiality of those dishes, such as, for example, with the sugar sculptures produced by the sculptors Giuseppe Mazza, Sebastiano Sarti, and Giovanni Battista Zaccarini, for the table of the senator Francesco Ratta in 1693 as part of the celebration of the end of his period of office as Gonfalonier of Bologna (fig. 3.36),[231] were to lead to such an "artification" of food as to transform it into an inedible "object." The silver and gilt highlighting tended to turn the sugar figures into purely visual objects (fig. 3.37) that could not be physically tasted. Indeed, once the festivities were over, these trophies were put away in closets where they became food only for mice.[232] Henceforth, art was to call for contemplation, keeping the aesthetic object at a distance, in such a way that the eye was to thoroughly eclipse the mouth.[233]

Nouvelle Cuisine

Culinary games and banquets laced with images were not the prerogative of ancient times. Indeed, in the works of twentieth-century artists, the *agapae* of the Renaissance and Baroque periods were to extend well beyond the modern era as their forms were modified, often upturned and deliberately transgressed. From the Futurists, Filippo Tommaso Marinetti and Luigi Colombo to the actors of Eat Art, Daniel Spoerri, Claude and François-Xavier Lalanne, and including Surrealists such as Wilhelm Freddie, Jørgen Roos, and Meret Oppenheim, or the conceptual artist Piero Manzoni, iconophagy was to continue to haunt contemporary artists.

In 1960, Manzoni created an edible sculpture titled *Uova* (fig. 3.38), placing it at the center of a work of performance art called *The Consumption of Dynamic Art by the Public, Devouring Art.*[234] Performed on two occasions (the first on June 10th in the Koepke Gallery in Copenhagen and the second on July 21st in the Azimut

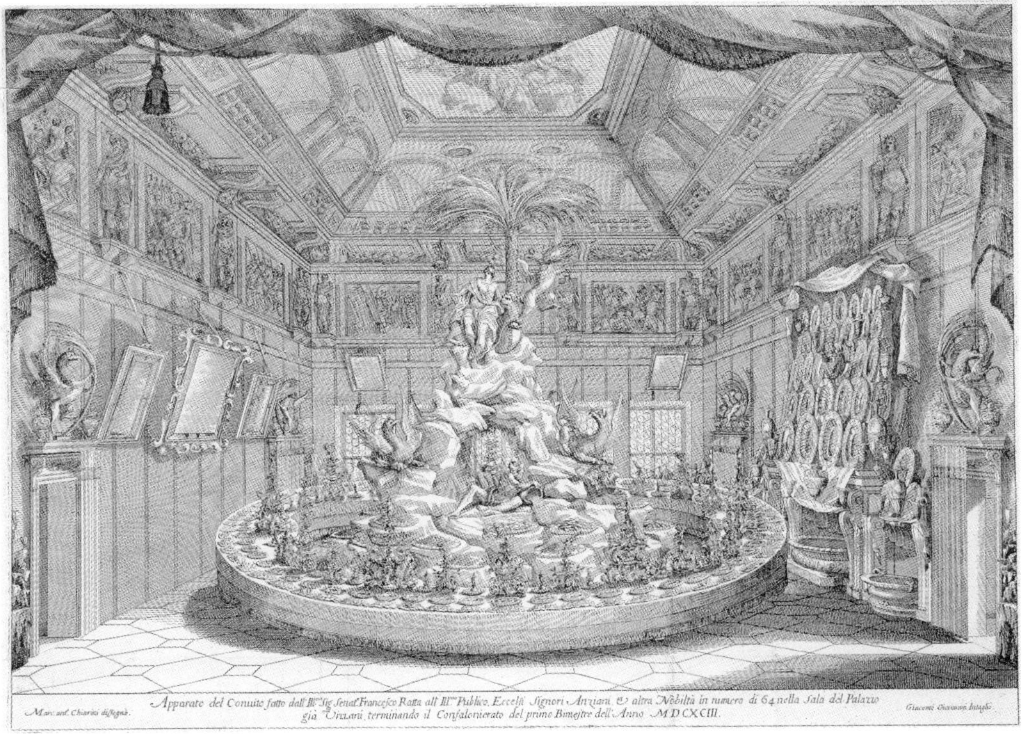

Figure 3.36. Print made by Giacomo Giovanini after Marcantonio Chiarini, *Sugar Sculptures made by Giovanni Battista Zaccarini and Giuseppe Mazza for the Banquet in Honor of Senator Francesco Ratta Held on February 28, 1693, at the Palazzo Vizzani*. Etching on paper, 20.7 × 26.4 in. Frontispiece in *Disegni del convito fatto dall'illustrissimo signor senator Francesco Ratta all'illustrissimo publico, eccelsi signori anziani & altra nobiltà terminando il suo confalonierato* (Bologna: Per li peri, 1693) (© The Getty Research Institute).

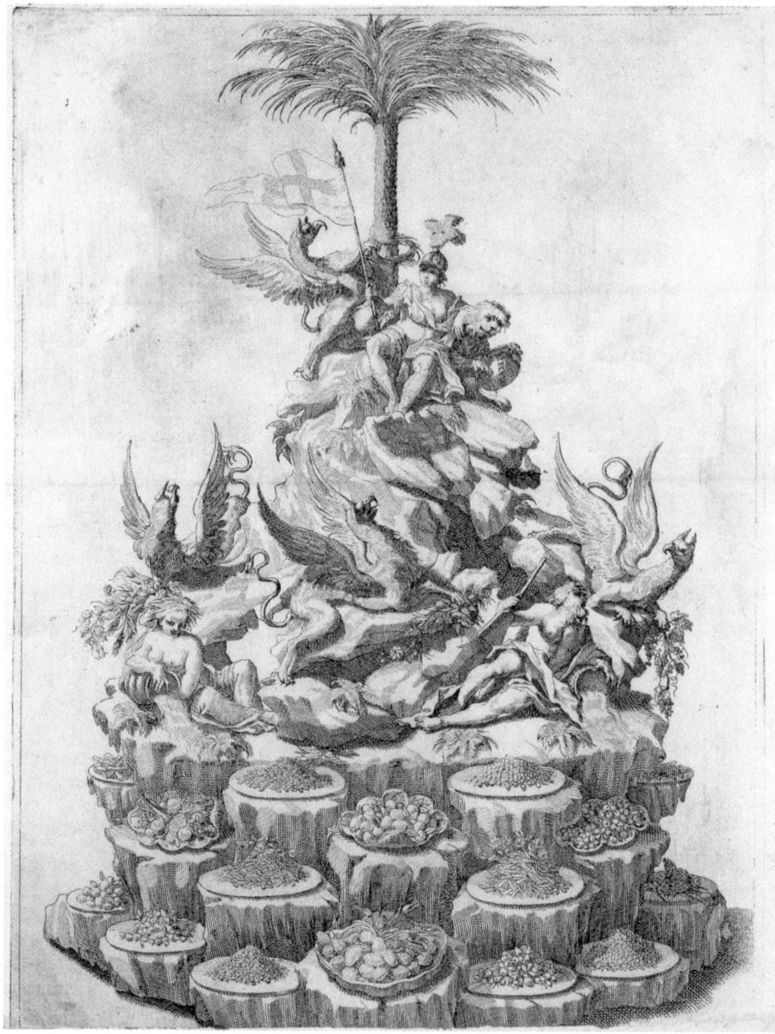

Figure 3.37. Print made by Giacomo Giovanini after Marcantonio Chiarini, *Sugar trophy, known as "La Felsina," made by Giovanni Battista Zaccarini and Giuseppe Mazza for the Banquet in Honor of Senator Francesco Ratta Held on February 28, 1693, at the Palazzo Vizzani.* In *Disegni del convito fatto dall'illustrissimo signor senator Francesco Ratta all'illustrissimo publico, eccelsi signori anziani & altra nobiltà terminando il suo confalonierato* (Bologna: Per li Peri, 1693) (© The Getty Research Institute).

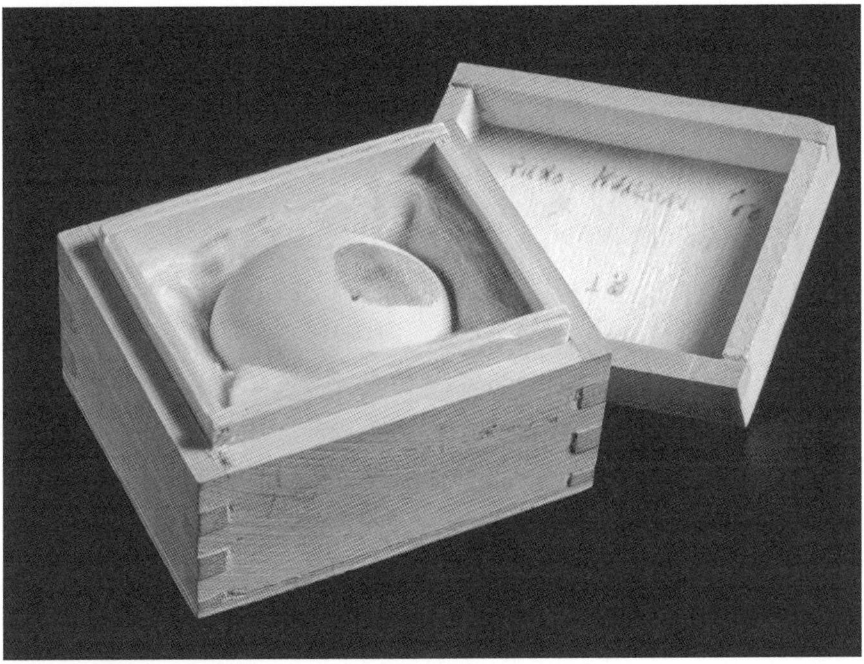

Figure 3.38. Piero Manzoni, *The Consumption of Dynamic Art by the Art-Devouring Public, ex. No 34*, 1960, boiled eggs, wood, 2.2 × 3.2 × 2.6 in. Milan, Museo del Novecento (© Luisa Ricciarini / Bridgeman Images / 2023 Artists Rights Society (ARS), New York / SIAE, Rome).

Gallery in Milan), Manzoni's performance condensed and cross-fertilized the stakes at play in certain of the edible images, such as the stamped hosts and the *cialde* that we have already considered. As with the eucharistic hosts, it is the principle of the digital print, placed here upon an egg, that determines the relationship established between the prototype and the ingested object. Moreover, the artist himself stressed the connection between the "happening" and the eucharistic rite. In interviews he gave at the time, Manzoni speaks of eggs being "consecrated" by "the artist's personality" and "communion."[235] At the same time, Manzoni makes no mention of the possible connection between his imprint on the egg and the production process involved with the eucharistic hosts. It does seem, however, that the artist's thumbprint relates quite directly to the imprint on the host—the sign of the real presence of Christ. By substituting his own natural imprint for the one produced by the stamping irons—a substitution where we also see an image disappearing into a purely indicial sign—Manzoni inserts his performance into a history of cultural practices that, in line with Christian thinking, raise art to the level of a universal rite. Yet, unlike the stamped host that calls upon the communicants to divest themselves of their differences in order to clothe themselves in the "glorious body" of Christ, Manzoni, for his part, beckons the public to commune directly with the artist.[236] His performance immediately transforms the nature of the society it institutes since in the place formerly occupied by the Christian community, Manzoni founds a collective whose spiritual project is no longer salvation and life in the heavenly hereafter, but the transformation of this world into a work of art. He redefines, therefore, the outer limits of artistic practice: the concept of art is no longer to be attached solely to the production of an object, either a painting or sculpture, but can now be extended to artists' gestures shared with their public.[237]

Eating the artist, even in the condensed form of a thumbprint placed on an egg, borders on anthrophagy, and it recalls the "cannibal art" so dreamed of by the Futurists and Surrealists. In *The Futurist Cookbook* (1930), for example, Marinetti recounts a dinner shared with Giulio Onesti during which, to cure Onesti of his depression caused by sadness over losing the woman he loved and to dissuade him from carrying out his declared intention to commit suicide, Marinetti offers his friend an edible reproduction of her.[238] Marinetti and his fellow artists, the "aeropainters" and "aerosculptors" Luigi Colombo (known as Fillìa) and Enrico Prampolini, prepare a dinner made up of twenty-two dishes in which chestnut flour, wheat flour, ground almonds, rye flour, cornmeal, cocoa powder, red pepper, sugar, eggs, oil, honey, and milk form an "aerocomplex" that Onesti and his sidekicks will savor with great delight:[239] "With the mouths of friendly cannibals Giulio Onesti, Marinetti, Prampolini and Fillia restored themselves with a tasty morsel of statue every now and again." And then came the night, and Onesti decides to feast alone on the anthropomorphic figure:

> All at once Giulio, with the wary back of a thief, turned his head a fraction to right and left, making sure that the sculptors and sculptress of life were fast asleep. Springing lightly to his feet, without making a sound, he ran his eyes around his great armoury and then resolutely made for the towering sculpture of The Curves of the World and Their Secrets. Kneeling before it he began like a lover to adore it with his lips, tongue and teeth. Searching and overturning the pretty little sugar palm tree like a ravenous tiger, he bit off and ate a sweet little foot skating on a cloud. At three that morning, with a terrible writhing of his loins, he bit into the dense heart-of-hearts of pleasure.... At dawn he devoured the mammellary spheres of all mothers' milk.[240]

By placing "the fleeting eternal feminine in ... [his] stomach," Onesti imprisons the woman he adores in his own body, like Artemisia with the ashes of her husband. He takes pleasure in this "edible art" and is at peace, "unencumbered, liberated, empty and bursting.... Possessor and possessed. Unique and complete,"[241] his sadness fading away to the rhythm of the disappearing image.[242]

Marinetti's cannibal meal, as he imagined it in 1930, was yet only a piece of fiction, but it presaged the *Edible Plastics* that Fillía, Prampolini, Bruno Munari, and the chef Mario Tapparelli were to exhibit at the Galleria Pesaro in Milan on June 16, 1933, as well as the edible creations made from casts of body parts that the artists Claude and François-Xavier Lalanne were to offer their guests at the Restaurant Spoerri in Düsseldorf during the famous *Dîner Cannibale*.[243]

Echoing these anthropophagic obsessions, the Surrealists were to play on the collusion between the anthropomorphic image and cannibalism, more often than not replacing the *image* of a woman with a real woman. In *Eaten Horizons* (1950), a seven-minute short film directed by Wilhelm Freddie and Jørgen Roos, the anthropophagic act becomes the highlight of an oneiric banquet.[244] Here again, the eucharistic dimension makes its return, but this time in the form of a nightmare: a woman's open back reveals a simmering pot of blood sausage meat, and the bread is dipped into it. The scene repels the viewer, the better to keep the eucharistic dimension at a distance.[245] Close in spirit to this sequence, Meret Oppenheim's installation, *Das Frühlingsfest* or *Cannibal Feast*, produced twice in 1969, one time with friends in Bern, and then in Paris with the support of members of the Surrealist group EROS (Exposition inteRnatiOale du Surréalisme, Cordier Gallery), shifted the critique of sacrificial rites towards modern sacrifices, denouncing women's submission to male desire and men's destructive appetites.[246] For the first performance, the artist used a mannequin around which she arranged fruits and vegetables along with table settings, inviting the public to devour the composition. For the second performance, however, she placed a live, flesh-and-blood woman in the middle of the table, setting her artist friends around the table.[247] The feast takes an uncanny turn: the body offered up to the table guests is transformed into a living image, and as it is devoured by the gaze of surrounding observers who watch from behind bars, the image withers and disappears.

The Digested Image

The disappearing image, as has often been said, was the ultimate goal of a large number of twentieth-century artistic experiments. As many critics and commentators have noted, the "death" of the image was the ultimate goal of a large number of twentieth-century artistic experiments. From the avant-gardes at the beginning of the century to the conceptual art of the 1960s and 1970s—including American postwar abstraction—the idea of art as a representative or referential agency has had several burials. These interments have often been quiet and discrete, but they have sometimes taken on spectacular forms. Iconophagy, raised to the rank of art, figures among the latter.[248]

In 1971, the conceptual artist Dennis Oppenheim enacted the dissolution of the image by filming himself eating three gingerbread men cookies (fig. 3.39).[249] The performance carried out, not without humor and sarcasm, the dethroning of the anthropomorphic figure as model (the representation here being a rudimentary human form, as if produced by a child), by staging the destruction of the edible image, reduced to formlessness by the action of the teeth, digested, and finally transformed into excrement. We might imagine that the artist sees parallels with Manzoni's *Merda d'artista* (1961) when Oppenheim documents this final phase of the procedure by producing a series of photographic enlargements of various samples of his fecal matter seen under a microscope—"the residue becomes the finished work."[250] As Oppenheim made in clear in the statement accompanying the installation, the destruction of the image is not an end in itself; it is, rather, the leavening yeast of a transformation in which life and *technè* are linked. Through the digestive process, the body itself is the agent of "making (changes)."[251]

Engaging the body and its vital processes in artistic action was also to be at the heart of John Cage's practice. Towards the end of his life, the composer and conceptual artist conceived a series of twelve edible abstract drawings (*Edible Drawings* and *Wild Edible Drawings*, 1989–1990; fig. I.3) based on the macrobiotic diet he was following. The abstract composition is the result of the color variations of

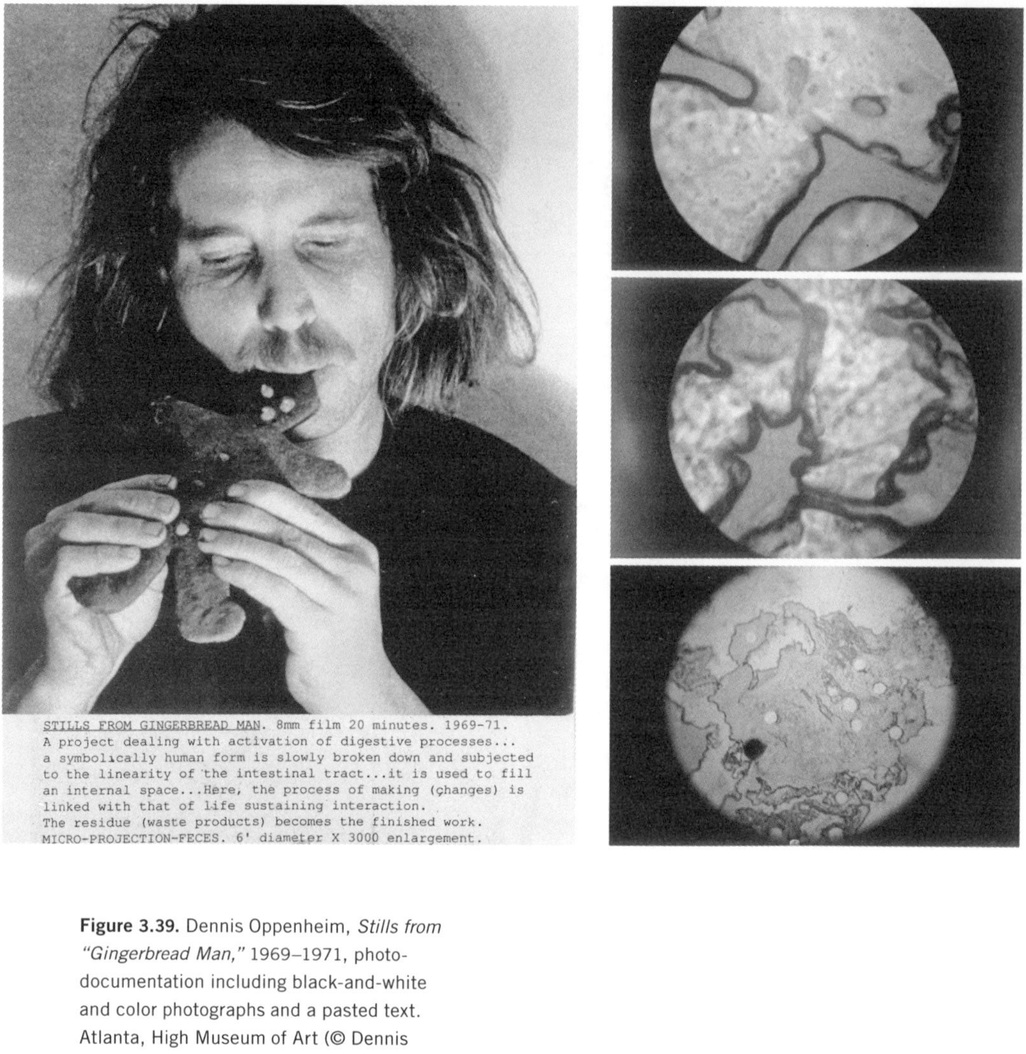

Figure 3.39. Dennis Oppenheim, *Stills from "Gingerbread Man,"* 1969–1971, photo-documentation including black-and-white and color photographs and a pasted text. Atlanta, High Museum of Art (© Dennis Oppenheim Estate).

the pressed grains, berries, and wild mushrooms that make up the fibers of the paper sheet.[252] The dissolution of the image had already taken place, abstraction having for a long time already supplanted figurative representation in Cage's artistic imagination. However, maintaining a mimetic relation with Jackson Pollock's "dripping compositions" and Mark Tobey's "calligraphic" abstractions, Cage's sheets offer themselves, so to speak, as *images* of abstract paintings just as much as they constitute *images* "of the abstraction offered by the natural world."[253] In working this transmediation of the artistic field into the culinary, Cage makes the edible drawing into a *representation*. Now, the image-substance here, as it has become an object, is not offered up by the artist to the gaze alone. It is intended also to be ingested.[254] The promise is therefore dual: on the one hand, the macrobiotic component of the drawing makes the object an *artifact* that is beneficial to one's health, and here we find, in a New Age version, the physically *constituting* function of ingesting images; and on the other hand, in parallel, the paper sheet, insofar as it is a representation of an abstract composition, enables the sharing of a certain idea of art that allows for the establishment of a new community and therefore shows the *instituting* function at work. In the place of the symbolic sacrifice of the image, Cage puts up art itself. For him, it is no longer a question of entering into a community of believers, nor is it about communing with an artist such as Manzoni; it is, rather, about living off art—making art the substratum of life itself.

CONCLUSION

A Short Sweet

To Eat or be Eaten — That is the Question.
— August Strindberg, *The Father*, 1887

As we have seen, ingesting an image, converting it into one's own flesh and being, and finding oneself, in turn, transformed by it, is a simple gesture that has served as a cure, an operator, even a disjunctor in the relations that we forge with the world and with the time that beats its rhythm. A type of behavior that seemed at the outset so unheard of, bizarre, and perhaps aberrant, has now emerged as a pragmatic practice — something that fulfills a function. And it is justifiably so since we found, as we looked closer within this hard-to-understand custom a very concrete form of the dealings that people have maintained, and continue to maintain in more or less discrete ways, with images both material and immaterial. Necessary as it is for us to concur with the Aristotelian aphorism, "the soul never thinks without a mental image,"[1] we shall be quick to add that the soul has no sensory life without an incorporated image, real or imagined. Let us welcome, therefore, this hunger for images!

And yet, if we eat too many of them, over-indulging our taste buds, do we not run the risk of being swallowed up by them in our turn? The film director David Cronenberg suggested as much with his horror movie Videodrome (1983) in which, displayed on a television screen, an erotic mouth, the lips and teeth of the protagonist's lover, attracts, and eats the protagonist who gazes at it.[2] Surely the endless stream of images to which we surrender ourselves today (beyond all reason, as some would like to believe) is glaring proof of it. But, in the face of this fear of being unable to stop the flow, and of being unable to grasp and make sense of the images, do we not just have to take the risk of being swallowed up? Do we not just have to expose ourselves to this danger in order to feel, think, and simply live?

In a notebook entry during the 1950s, Jasper Johns neatly sums up the ambivalence of things observed, saying that always, when observed by us, things look at us and eat us up in return: "'Looking' is and is not 'eating' and 'being eaten.'"[3] And when August Strindberg's character, Captain Adolph, proclaims "To eat or to be eaten—that is the question," there is no indication that either one of the two options is preferable to the other. The difficulty is not in the choosing, but rather, as with Hamlet, it is in the question of the sudden awareness of the pendulum movement of being—to be or not to be, to look at or to be looked at, to eat or to be eaten—and we might put it this way: to be and not to be, to look at and to be looked at, to eat and to be eaten.

When I was a child, at the dinner table, my mother would often take a spoon and draw on my plate, forming a tree, a flower, or an animal. This was so long ago now that I am no longer quite sure why she did it. Was it to encourage me to eat my vegetables, their fearsome taste disappearing as they became images? But I like to think also that this metamorphosis provided something else: the pleasure of contemplating both the birth of a figure (some recognizable form emerging from the muddle of my Moulinexed vegetables) and its disappearance under the repeated attacks from my fork.

I am fond of thinking of image-eating in general as something a bit like a children's game, swirling together creation and destruction, and summoning up being's vertigo. The pancake held up by the young boy in Godfried Schalcken's painting, *Boy with a Pancake Mask* (1670–1680; fig. C.1), bitten on and playfully turned into a face

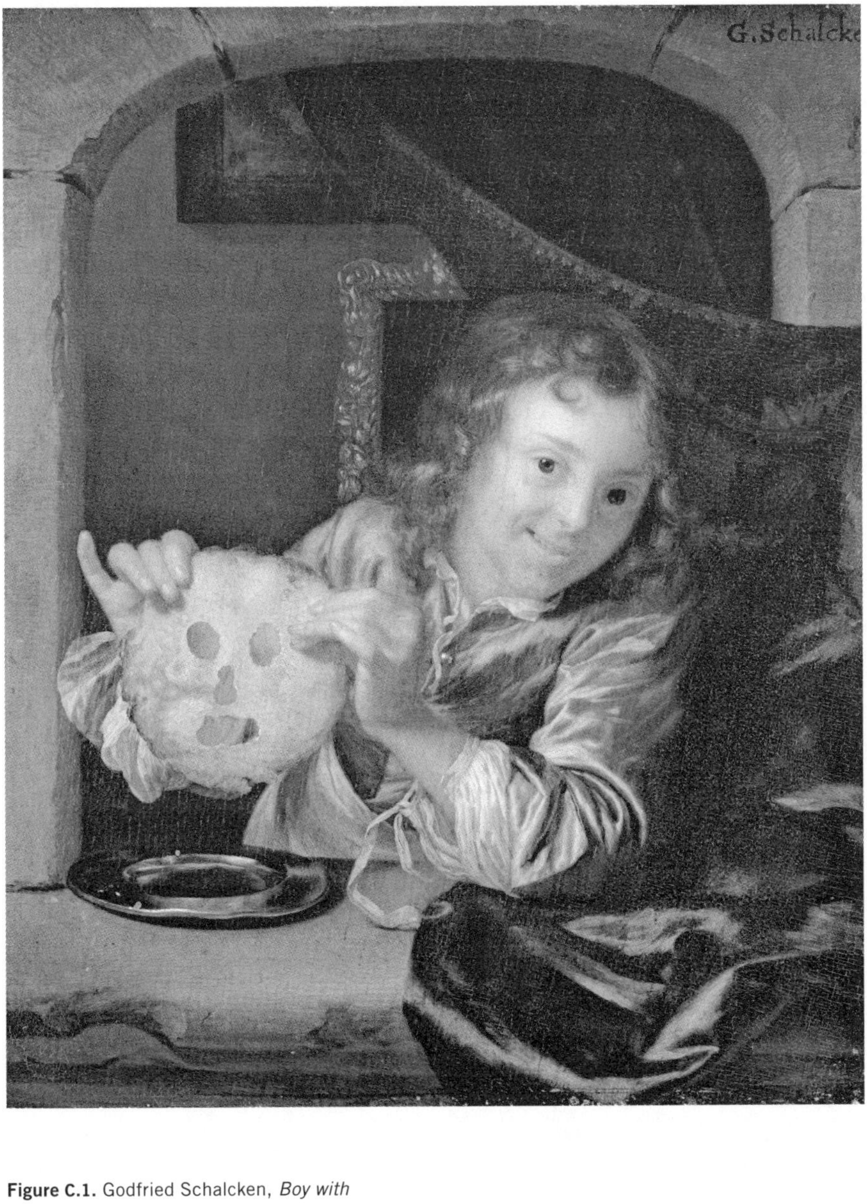

Figure C.1. Godfried Schalcken, *Boy with a Pancake Mask,* 1670–1680, oil on panel, 7.7 × 6 in. Hamburg, Kunsthalle (© Hamburger Kunsthalle, Hamburg/Bridgeman Images).

before its certain devouring and, at the same time, clear proof of the painter's artistic mastery,[4] speaks to the figured representation's constant oscillation between being and nothingness, presence and absence, joy and sadness.[5] As Maurice Blanchot writes:

> The image, we feel, is joy, for it is a limit beside the indefinite, the possibility of suspension at the heart of a shifting movement: through it, we believe ourselves to be the masters of an absence become form, and the dense night itself seems to open itself to the resplendence of an absolute clarity. Yes, the image is joy — but close to it lies nothingness; nothingness appears at the limit of this image, and all the power of the image, drawn from the abyss in which it is founded, cannot be expressed except by calling to nothingness.[6]

Ingesting an image would thus be a way of bringing into harmony the two poles of the world, a means of holding together presence and absence. Eating an image might come down to turning around the sense and direction of the sign, transforming the trace of a lack into an experience of presence. Perhaps here, at the root of it all, lies the paradoxical desire inciting us to produce images before this urge turns us into iconophages: the wish to make being eternal by rendering it absent, so that we might experience it as present, here, in the dark night of our own bodies.

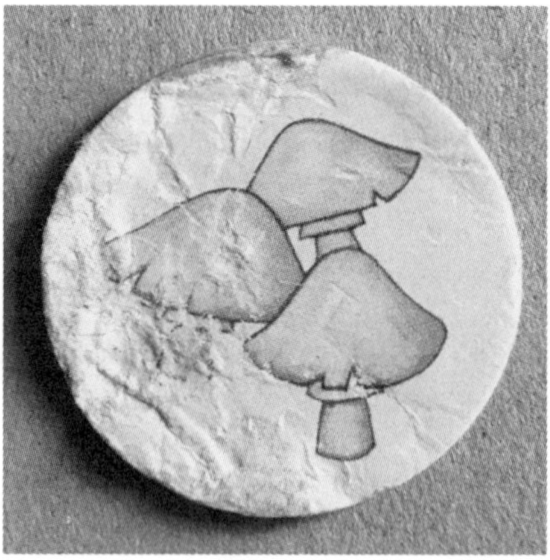

Figure C.2. Théophile, *Mushrooms are good!*, 2014 (© J. Koering).

Acknowledgments

This book was many years in the making. Although I conducted my research mostly alone, I was fortunate to be able to regularly share its progress at a number of seminars and conferences. For their generosity and insights, I am deeply grateful to my hosts at the Academia Belgica in Rome (2015), the Collectif d'Histoire de l'Art de la Renaissance (2015), the Centre André Chastel (2016 et 2017), the Bibliotheca Hertziana (2018), the Institut National d'Histoire de l'Art (2018), the Harvard University Center for Italian Renaissance Studies at the Villa I Tatti (2019), and the Université catholique de Louvain (2020).

Adopting the Rabelaisian principle that one gains knowledge "whilst eating and drinking," the text was composed in part at the dinner table, in the delightful and nourishing company of the following: Francesca Alberti, Jean-Marc Alexandre, Grégoire Aslanoff, Michele Bacci, Andreas Beyer, Dominic-Alain Boariu, Yve-Alain Bois, Hervé Brunon, Stephen J. Campbell, Giovanni Careri, Guillaume Cassegrain, Giordana Charuty, Claudia Cieri Via, Emanuele Coccia, Pierre Curie, Véronique Dasen, Ralph Dekoninck, Vincent Delieuvin, Philippe Descola, Georges Didi-Huberman, Pierre-Olivier Dittmar, Thierry Dufrêne, Sybille Ebert-Schifferer, Isabelle Ewig, Pierre-Antoine Fabre, Patricia Falguières, Finbarr Barry Flood, Dominique de Font-Réaulx, Frédéric Keck, Caroline

Gaillard, Dario Gamboni, Carlo Ginzburg, Fabien Gourdon, Allen J. Grieco, Aude Gros, Carl Havelange, Sefy Hendler, Viktoria von Hoffmann, Étienne Jollet, Stephanie Jones, Rémi Labrusse, Anne Lafont, Johanne Lamoureux, Guillaume Le Gall, Olivier Leplatre, Anne Lepoittevin, Robert Maniura, Isabelle Marchesin, Philippe-Alain Michaud, Philippe Morel, Alina Payne, Arnauld Pierre, Ulrich Pfisterer, Monica Preti, François Quiviger, Marcia Reed, Kathryn Rudy, Jean-Claude Schmitt, Mathieu Somon, Gennaro Toscano, Tanguy Viel, Pierre Von-Ow, Lise Wajeman, Tristan Weddigen, Teri Wehn Damisch, David Zagoury, and Henri Zerner. From amongst all my dinner companions, I would like to single out Jean-Pierre Criqui, Antonella Fenech, and Jean-Claude Lebensztejn for having added their own special seasoning to the meal.

For the present edition, my warmest thanks go to Jonathan Crary, Meighan Gale, Nicholas Huckle, and Lily Brewer.

Isolde Pludermacher, once again, lent me her eyes, her ears, and her voice to give meaning to what, without her, would have been an absolute rat's stew. My thanks go also to my children, Eliot, Oreste, and Théophile. They have waited patiently for so long at the table that I must now promise them some less-complicated fare.

A final note of thanks to the late Cyril Gerbron. I wish so much that he could have read these pages, and that we could have continued our discussions, too soon cut short.

Notes

INTRODUCTION: AMUSE-BOUCHE

1. Michel de Montaigne, "The Art of Discussion," in *The Complete Essays of Montaigne*, trans. Donald M. Frame (Stanford: Stanford University Press, 1998), book 3, chap. 8.

2. To make matters easier, I have chosen to group together under the one heading of *iconophagy* a number of practices involving ingesting images. The practices referred to as such in this study will include not only eating images, but incorporating them by drinking, nibbling, and swallowing them whole, by mouth, either directly or indirectly.

3. On this "tropism," see Bruno Latour, *We Have Never Been Modern,* trans. Catharine Porter (Cambridge, MA: Harvard University Press, 1993); Bruno Latour, *Sur le culte moderne des dieux faitiches,* suivi de *Iconoclash* (Paris: La Découverte, 2009); and Philippe Descola, *Beyond Nature and Culture*, trans. Janet Lloyd (Chicago: University of Chicago Press, 2013).

4. The scene comes directly from Thomas Harris's novel *Red Dragon* (New York: Putnam, 1981).

5. On his back, as a way of showing that he identifies with the creature, Francis Dolarhyde has a tattoo of William Blake's *The Great Red Dragon and the Woman Clothed in Sun* (1805).

6. Both Harris's novel and Ratner's film adaptation of it stress the psychoanalytic view of incorporation. As the reader may recall, since Sigmund Freud and Karl Abraham, this view has been that the assimilation of the power of the father happens through incorporation. Now, with Dolarhyde, everything connects to an original problem: he suffered from childhood abuse, and this prevents him from going beyond the oral stage

of incorporation. The serial killer believes that he can extricate himself from the power of the dragon by making its force his own, that is, by swallowing its image.

7. Richard Shiff, "Johns Metanoid, Metanoid Johns," in James Rondeau and Douglas Druick, eds., *Jasper Johns: Gray* (Chicago: Art Institute of Chicago, 2007), exhibition catalog, p. 133: "investigative touching (with the mouth) displaced investigative looking." See also Alexander Nagel, *Medieval Modern: Art out of Time* (London: Thames & Hudson, 2012), p. 186.

8. The origin of *The Critic Sees* lies in a dialogue between Johns and an art critic over a work in which Johns had used casting as a technique, the critic having refused, on account of this, to call it a "sculpture." Cf. Lilian Thone, cited in Kirk Varnedoe, "Introduction: A Sense of Life," in Kirk Varnedoe, ed., *Jasper Johns: A Retrospective* (New York: MoMA Publications, 1996), p. 192.

9. Shiff, "Johns Metanoid, Metanoid Johns," p. 133.

10. In carrying out this study, I have been fortunate in having available to me a certain number of works that include mention of ingesting iconic artifacts or that focus on one or another of the edible images that are to be found in the history books. Nothing of what follows could have been formulated and organized without the works of Hans Jürgen Hansen and George Galavaris on stamped breads and dishes decorated with figures, Robert Ritner on magic in ancient Egypt, Véronique Dasen and Árpád Nagy on intaglios in the Greco-Roman world of late Antiquity, Gary Vikan on the medical uses of images in Byzantium, Finbarr Barry Flood on devotional practices in the Islamic world, Dominique Rigaux on the apotropaic uses of medieval Italian frescoes, Jean-Louis Schefer and Aden Kumler on the eucharistic host, Maria Attilia Fabbri Dall'Oglio, Marcia Reed, and Gregory Ems on sculpted dishes in the modern era, Salvatore D'Onofrio on the "bones of the dead," Giordana Charuty on votive breads, and finally, Olivier Leplatre on the phenomenology of the iconophagic imaginary. I refer the reader to the general bibliography for the works cited.

11. For a detailed account of the meaning of the term "image" within these three fields, see Jean Wirth, *Qu'est-ce qu'une image?* (Geneva: Droz, 2013).

12. Alfred Gell uses the term "social agent"; however, I prefer *operator* since this term implies a necessary exchange as part of its functioning. Alfred Gell, *Art and Agency: An Anthropological Theory* (Oxford: Clarendon Press, 1998), p. 22.

13. See especially the courses at the Collège de France that Philippe Descola taught from 2003 to 2011 on "The Ontology of Images" and "The Anthropology of Figuration

or Image-Making." Summaries of these courses are available online. For example see, "Ontologie des images (suite) (1)," Collège de France, March 10, 2010, https://www.college-de-france.fr/fr/agenda/cours/ontologie-des-images-suite/ontologie-des-images-suite-1-0.

14. Wirth, *Qu'est-ce qu'une image?,* pp. 25–26.

15. References to the works of these authors can be found in the bibliography. In addition to these works, see also the texts collected by Emmanuel Alloa, ed., *Penser l'image* (Dijon: Les Presses du réel, 2010).

16. Gottfried Boehm, "Die Wiederkehr der Bilder," in *Was ist ein Bild?* (Munich: Wilhelm Fink, 1994), pp. 11-38. Jean Wirth has called this idea into question, recalling that for Saint Augustine, Peirce, and Wittgenstein "the visual characteristics . . . is not constitutive of the notion of the image." Wirth, *Qu'est-ce qu'une image?,* p. 14.

17. Ibid., p. 24. My emphasis.

18. Wirth, Belting, and Didi-Hubermann all differ from Boehm on this point. See also Thierry Davila, "Esthétique et clinique: Brève introduction à l'art médecin," *Les Cahiers du MNAM* 67 (1999), p. 101.

19. It is important here to note the significant contribution of medievalists, such as Jérôme Baschet, Brigitte Bedos-Rezak, Caroline Walker Bynum, Jean-Claude Schmitt, and Wirth, to our appreciation of this material dimension. I should add also here the work of historians of modern and contemporary art, such as Hubert Damisch, "La peinture est un vrai trois," in Hubert Damisch, *Fenêtre jaune cadmium, ou Les dessous de la peinture* (Paris: Seuil, 1984), pp. 275–305. Among the American theorists, I should mention W. J. T. Mitchells's use of the term picture as a *fusion* of image and object. See W. J. T. Mitchell, *What Do Pictures Want?: The Lives and Loves of Images* (Chicago: University of Chicago Press, 2005), pp. 28–56. In the field of phenomenology, I am thinking mainly of the works of Maurice Merleau-Ponty and Roland Barthes.

20. Jean-Claude Bonne, "Représentation médiévale et lieu sacré," in Sofia Boesch-Gajano and Lucetta Scaraffia, eds., *Luoghi sacri e spazi della santità* (Turin: Rosenberg & Sellier, 1990), p. 566; Jérôme Baschet and Jean-Claude Schmitt, eds., *L'image: Fonctions et usages des images dans l'Occident médiéval* (Paris: Le Léopard d'or, 1996), p. 20; Jérôme Baschet, *L'iconographie médiévale* (Paris: Gallimard, 2008), pp. 33–39; and Jean-Claude Schmitt, "Introduction," in Jérôme Baschet and Pierre-Olivier Dittmar, eds., *Les Images dans l'Occident médiéval* (Turnhout: Brepols, 2015), p. 11.

21. On the meal as a "social fact," see Milad Doueihi, *A Perverse History of the Human*

Heart (Cambridge, MA: Harvard University Press, 1997), p. 15, and Jean-Jacques Boutaud, *Le sens gourmand: De la commensalité, du goût, des aliments* (Paris: Jean-Paul Rocher, 2005), p. 19.

22. *Instituo, ere* means originally to "give a place." Cf. Pierre Bourdieu, "Les rites comme actes d'institution," *Actes de la recherche en sciences sociales* 43 (June 1982), pp. 59–63. I add to this approach Descola's interpretation, *Beyond Nature and Culture*, pp. 112–25, 248, 278–80.

23. In connecting ingestion with ritual, I concur with Michael Houseman and Carlo Severi in *Naven, or, The Other Self: A Relational Approach to Ritual Action* (Leiden: Brill, 1998) who write: "We . . . look to stress the specificity of ritual as a particular modality of action, insisting upon the generative quality of ritualization." Houseman and Severi, *Naven, or, The Other Self*, p. 201.

24. I refer here to Tim Ingold's nonrelationist model in anthropology, set out in his works *Being Alive: Essays on Movement, Knowledge, and Description* (London: Routledge, 2011); *Marcher avec les dragons* (Le Kremlin-Bicêtre: Zones sensibles, 2013), especially chaps. 2–4; and *Faire: Anthropologie, archéologie, art et architecture* (Paris: Éd. Dehors, 2017). On this alternative to relationism, see the debate between Ingold and Descola in *Être au monde: Quelle expérience commune?* (Lyon: Presses universitaires de Lyon, 2014), a debate presented by Michel Lussault, especially p. 37; see also Albert Piette, *Contre le relationnisme: Lettre aux anthropologues* (Lormont: Le Bord de l'eau, 2014) for a more polemical statement of the position.

25. Cf. Piette, *Contre le relationnisme*, p. 32, quoting Gilbert Simondon, *De l'individuation psychique et collective* (Paris: Aubier, 2007), p. 24. This attention given to ontogenies helps also to overcome an overly strong impermeability between ontologies. Within each of us, in fact, there coexist many ways of being in the world: naturalist, animist, analogist, and so forth. Descola concedes this, moreover, when he says that he is an animist when he talks to his cat.

26. Arnold Van Gennep, *The Rites of Passage*, trans. Monika B. Vizedom and Gabrielle L. Caffee (Chicago: University of Chicago Press, [1909] 1960).

27. Tim Ingold, *Lines: A Brief History* (London: Routledge, 2007), p. 103.

28. Ingold in Descola and Ingold, *Être au monde*, p. 37.

29. I take the expression "modal approach" from the Marielle Macé's illuminating commentary on Marcel Mauss's article "Techniques of the Body" in *Techniques, Technology and Civilization* (New York: Durkheim Press/Berghahn Book, 2006), *Journal de Psychologie* XXXII 3–4 (1936), pp. 271–93. See Marielle Macé, *Styles: Critiques de nos formes de vie* (Paris: Gallimard, 2016), pp. 70–81.

30. The oldest molds for putting geometrical form to a pastry dough date from 3000–2500 BCE and have been found in Mesopotamia and in the Indus Valley. See Hans Jürgen Hansen, ed., *Kunstgeschichte des Backwerks: Geschichte und Entwicklung der Gebäckarten und ihrer Formen* (Oldenbourg: Gerhard Stalling, 1968), p. 43.

31. Descola, *Beyond Nature and Culture*, pp. 172–200.

32. Many phenomena, admittedly and with some regret perhaps, will be left to one side, or only treated in passing.

CHAPTER ONE: INGESTING IMAGES

1. The chronology used here is the one established by Pierre Tallet, Frédéric Payraudeau, Chloé Ragazzoli, and Claire Somaglino, *L'Égypte pharaonique: Histoire, société et culture* (Paris: Armand Colin, 2019).

2. In chapter 3 of his work, Robert Kriech Ritner describes three magical acts involving the mouth, and notably includes ingestion: spitting, licking, and swallowing. More generally, concerning contact as a way of magical transmission, see the well-known pages in, for example, Frazer, "Things that have once been in contact with each other continue to act on each other at a distance after the physical contact has been severed." See James George Frazer, *The Golden Bough: A Study in Magic and Religion*, 2 vols. (New York: Macmillan, 1922), vol. 1, p. 11.

3. This point was already noted by Gaston Maspéro, *Études de mythologie et d'archéologie égyptiennes* (Paris: Ernest Leroux, 1893), vol. 1, p. 106. For further study, see Robert Kriech Ritner, *The Mechanics of Ancient Egyptian Magical Practice* (Chicago: Oriental Institute of the University of Chicago, 2008); Marc Étienne, *Héka: Magie et envoûtement dans l'Egypte ancienne* (Paris: RMN, 2000), p. 35; and Yvan Koenig, *La Magie en Égypte: À la recherche d'une définition* (Paris: La Documentation française/Musée du Louvre, 2002), pp. 9–13, 399–413.

4. See Pierre Lacau, "Les statues 'guérisseuses' dans l'ancienne Égypte," *Monuments et mémoires de la Fondation Eugène Piot* 25.1–2 (1921), pp. 189–210; Ritner, *The Mechanics of Ancient Egyptian Magical Practice*; Annie Gasse, *Les stèles d'Horus sur les crocodiles* (Paris: RMN, 2004); Étienne, *Héka*, pp. 65–67; and Koenig, *La Magie en Égypte*.

5. The iconography of Horus the Child often overlaps with that of the Greek Harpokrates.

6. Gasse indicates however that the great majority of the stelae that have been discovered are from the Ptolemaic period and come from Lower Egypt. Gasse, *Les stèles d'Horus sur les crocodiles*, p. 14.

7. See the catalogue in ibid.

8. As is noted by Gasse, among the fearsome animals, the oryx is consubstantial with Set. Ibid., p. 20.

9. Ibid., pp. 17–18.

10. For more on this idea, see David Frankfurter, "Narrating Power: The Theory and Practice of the Magical *Historiola* in Ritual Spells," in Marvin Meyer and Paul Mirecki, eds., *Ancient Magic and Ritual Power* (Leiden: Brill, 1995), pp. 457–76, and David Frankfurter, "The Laments of Horus in Coptic: Myth, Folklore, and Syncretism in Late Antique Egypt," in Ueli Dill and Christine Walde, eds., *Antike Mythen: Medien, Transformationen und Konstruktionen, Fritz Graf zum 65. Geburtstag* (Berlin: De Gruyter, 2009), pp. 229–47.

11. Lacau, "Les statues 'guérisseuses' dans l'ancienne Égypte," p. 206; Frankfurter, "The Laments of Horus in Coptic."

12. Gasse, *Les stèles d'Horus sur les crocodiles*, p. 22. The licking of images, as we shall see, was possibly one way of taking hold of a power. See Ritner, *The Mechanics of Ancient Egyptian Magical Practice*, p. 92 et seq.

13. According to Lacau, through contact, the water takes on the virtues of the images and the magic formulae. Lacau, "Les statues 'guérisseuses' dans l'ancienne Égypte," p. 191. In similar fashion, small objects could be submerged directly in the water. Cf. Gasse, *Les stèles d'Horus sur les crocodiles*, p. 22. On the persistence of these practices in the Islamic world, see Finbarr Barry Flood, *Technologies de dévotion dans les arts de l'Islam: Pèlerins, reliques et copies* (Paris: Musée du Louvre/Hazan, 2019), pp. 120–23.

14. Gasse, *Les stèles d'Horus sur les crocodiles*, p. 101.

15. The various parts of the image, symbolizing Evil (i.e., crocodile, snake, lion, scorpion, etc.) and Good (i.e., Thoth and Bes) are in conformity with the analogical functioning of images that is based upon the principle of a bringing together at the same time of both the terms of the problem and the solutions that might be applied to it. See the exhibition catalog, Descola, dir., *La fabrique des images: Visions du monde et formes de la representation* (Paris: Somogy/Musée du quai Branly, 2010).

16. Gasse, *Les stèles d'Horus sur les crocodiles*, p. 13.

17. New York, Metropolitan Museum of Art, 83.5 cm in height, dating from the reign of Nectanebo III (360–343 BCE). The stela was set up by the priest Esatum, probably in a temple at Heliopolis. See Heike Sternberg-el Hotabi, *Untersuchungen zur Überlieferungsgeschichte der Horusstelen: Ein Beitrag zur Religionsgeschichte Ägyptens im 1. Jahrtausend v. Chr.* (Wiesbaden: Harrassowitz, 1999), vol. 1, pp. 106, 110; and Gasse, *Les stèles d'Horus sur les crocodiles*, p. 23.

18. The earthly healings were the direct result of healings that took place "in the divine world." Étienne, *Héka*, p. 66. And "in all cases, the mythological tale concludes with the healing of the sick divinity; the earthly sick person is cured as a consequence." Ibid., p. 67. See also Yvan Koenig, ed., "Conclusion," in *La magie en Égypte: À la recherche d'une définition* (Paris: La Documentation française/Musée du Louvre, 2002), p. 408.

19. The story of the secret name of Ra is one of the etiological explanations that account for the power of invocation: for "the Egyptians, the name was at the heart of the divine essence, and . . . to possess it was to take hold of the very power of the god." Christiane Zivie-Coche, "Noms divins et pratiques magiques en Égypte ancienne," in Olivier Boulnois and Brigitte Tambrun, eds., *Les noms divins* (Paris: Cerf, 2016), pp. 69–84.

20. Philippe Derchain, "À propos de performativité: Pensers anciens et articles récents," *Göttinger Miszellen: Beiträge zur ägyptologischen Diskussion* 110 (1989), pp. 13–18; Alessandro Roccati, "Qu'est-ce que le texte magique?," in Yvan Koenig, ed., *La magie en Égypte: À la recherche d'une définition* (Paris: La Documentation française/Musée du Louvre, 2002), esp. pp. 72–73. This idea that certain hieroglyphic texts were "performative" owes much, of course, to John L. Austin. See John L. Austin, *How to do Things with Words*, eds. J. O. Urmson and Marina Sbisà (Oxford: Clarendon Press, 1975).

21. Gasse, *Les stèles d'Horus sur les crocodiles*, p. 23. English translation in Nora E. Scott, "The Metternich Stela," *Metropolitan Museum of Art Bulletin* 9.8 (April 1951), p. 212.

22. Nora E. Scott, "The Metternich Stela," p. 205.

23. For Marc Étienne, for example, "the curative virtues [of the] stelae are a result of the texts that they bear." Étienne, *Héka*, p. 65.

24. Lacau, "Les statues 'guérisseuses' dans l'ancienne Égypte."

25. Lacau refers to a statue from the Ptolemaic period (fourth–third century BCE) showing a priest of Bastet named Padimahes.

26. Lacau, "Les statues 'guérisseuses' dans l'ancienne Égypte"; Eva Jelinkova-Reymond, *Les Inscriptions de la statue guérisseuse de Djed-Her-le-Sauveur* (Cairo: Institut français d'archéologie orientale, 1956); E. J. Sherman, "Djedhor the Saviour: Statue Base OI 10589," *Journal of Egyptian Archaeology* 67 (1981), pp. 82–102; Ritner, *The Mechanics of Ancient Egyptian Magical Practice*, pp. 107–108; Campbell Price, "On the Function of 'Healing' Statues," in Campbell Price, Roger Forshaw, Andrew Chamberlain and Paul T. Nicholson, eds., *Mummies, Magic and Medicine in Ancient Egypt: Multidisciplinary Essays for Rosalie David* (Manchester: Manchester University Press, 2016), pp. 169–82, esp. pp. 175–78 for the

intended public for these statues. Price considers that they were reserved for an elite, but the use of water seems to me to weaken this perspective.

27. Lacau, "Les statues 'guérisseuses' dans l'ancienne Égypte," pp. 193, 203.

28. Ibid., p. 192.

29. Ibid., p. 193.

30. Ibid., p. 201, and later Ritner in *The Mechanics of Ancient Egyptian Magical Practice*, p. 107, have moreover stressed the fact that many of these objects were produced or reemployed during the Ptolemaic period, and, therefore, at a time when very few people had the skills to read the hieroglyphs of the Old Kingdom. Furthermore, certain artifacts, such as stela no. 9402 in the Cairo Museum, include a dedication by a Phoenician citizen who probably could not actually read the hieroglyphs. On this last point, see Lacau, "Les statues 'guérisseuses' dans l'ancienne Égypte," pp. 195, 200.

31. See Ritner, *The Mechanics of Ancient Egyptian Magical Practice*, p. 107; Price, "On the Function of 'Healing' Statues," pp. 170–71.

32. Étienne, *Héka*, pp. 47–48, for example, writes: "One had to drink the water that one had run over the statue, and that was impregnated with the curative powers generously dispensed by the magical texts engraved upon it." See also ibid., pp. 65–67.

33. Lacau, "Les statues'guérisseuses' dans l'ancienne Égypte," pp. 196 (for the quotation) and 199.

34. Price uses a bas-relief from the tomb of Amenemopet to illustrate the use of the healing statues, and, in particular, how the lustral water was used. It was poured over the statue, collected in an earthenware jar, and then drunk. See Price, "On the Function of 'Healing' Statues," pp. 173–74. Ritner also refers, in the same way, to the Tyszkiewicz healing statue in the Louvre Museum. This statue includes an inscription stating explicitly that the water was intended for the "sick person." See Ritner, *The Mechanics of Ancient Egyptian Magical Practice*, p. 107.

35. Erik Hornung, *Conceptions of God in Ancient Egypt: The One and the Many*, trans. John Baines (Ithaca, NY: Cornell University Press, 1982), p. 161.

36. Ritner, *The Mechanics of Ancient Egyptian Magical Practice*, chap. 3.

37. There exist many variants of this practice where we see an inscription take the place of the image. Cf. Ibid., pp. 96–102, and Carina Kühne-Wespi, "Papyrus trinken und Hieroglyphen essen: Praktiken der Schriftverinnerlichung im pharaonischen Ägypten," in Carina Kühne-Wespi, Klaus Oschema, and Joachim F. Quack, eds., *Zerstörung von Geschriebenem Historische und transkulturelle Perspektiven* (Berlin: De Gruyter, 2019),

pp. 341–58. A magic spell inscribed on a healing statue in the Turin Museum recommends drawing an ibis right above the sick person's heart. Accompanied by an incantation, the painted image on the skin was supposed to heal the sick person immediately. Cf. Maria Elena Gorrini, "Healing Statues in the Greek and Roman World," in Ildikò Csepregi and Charles Burnett, eds., *Ritual Healing: Magic, Ritual and Medical Therapy from Antiquity until the Early Modern Period* (Florence: Sismel, 2012), p. 126.

38. Ritner, *The Mechanics of Ancient Egyptian Magical Practice*, p. 94; Harco Willems, *The Coffin of Heqata (Cairo JdE 36418): A Case Study of Egyptian Funerary Culture of the Early Middle Kingdom* (Louvain: Peeters, 1996), p. 276. Ochre was thought by the ancient Greeks, specifically the physician Pedanius Dioscorides, to be an anti-inflammatory. See Pedanius Dioscorides of Anazarbus, *De materia medica*, trans. Lily Y. Beck (Hildesheim: G. Olms-Weidmann, 2005), vol. 5, chap. 93, p. 374.

39. Willems offers a variant: "*Saying words over eight Heh-gods drawn in yellow and in white on a man's hand and licked off daily very early in the morning.*" Willems, *The Coffin of Heqata*, p. 276.

40. In his study of the Heqata sarcophagus, Willems stresses this same difficulty.

41. Cf. Philippe Descola, *Beyond Nature and Culture,* trans. Janet Lloyd (Chicago: University of Chicago Press, 2013).

42. Kamal Sabri Kolta and Doris Schwarzmann-Schafhauser, *Die Heilkunde im Alten Ägypten: Magie und Ratio in der Krankheitsvorstellung und therapeutischen Praxis* (Stuttgart: Franz Steiner, 2000); Paula Alexandra da Silva Veiga, *Health and Medicine in Ancient Egypt: Magic and Science* (Oxford: BAR International Series [1967] 2009), pp. 44–45. There is an equally rich literature for the more recent periods, see Piero Camporesi, *The Incorruptible Flesh: Bodily Mutation and Mortification in Religion and Folklore*, trans. Tania Croft-Murray and Helen Elsom (Cambridge, UK: Cambridge University Press, 1988), esp. pp. 11–14; Piero Camporesi, *Les baumes de l'amour* (Paris: Hachette, 1997), p. 24 et seq.; Louis Noble, *Medicinal Cannibalism in Early Modern English Literature and Culture* (New York: Palgrave Macmillan, 2011), esp. chap. 1; Richard Sugg, *Mummies, Cannibals and Vampires: The History of Corpse Medicine from the Renaissance to the Victorians* (London: Routledge, 2011); and Angelica A. Montanari, *Il fiero pasto: Antropofagie medievali* (Bologna: Il Mulino, 2015), chap. 5.

43. Ritner, *The Mechanics of Ancient Egyptian Magical Practice*, p. 94.

44. Ibid., p. 95.

45. Ibid., and James B. Pritchard, *Ancient Near Eastern Texts Relating to the Old Testament* (Princeton, NJ: Princeton University Press, 1969), p. 14.

46. Ritner, *The Mechanics of Ancient Egyptian Magical Practice*, p. 104; and Willems, *The Coffin of Heqata*, p. 276.

47. Étienne, *Héka*, p. 57. Étienne notes, "one of the explanations supplied by these medical texts on the causes of illnesses is based upon the propagation of a pathogenic or miasmic breath called *deheret*, 'what is bitter.' Transmitted by ambient air, dispersed by the winds, this nefarious breath could be easily contracted, and it had a determining effect upon the illnesses that it brought about." Étienne, *Héka*, p. 56.

48. On the living statues, see Françoise Frontisi-Ducroux, *Dédale: Mythologie de l'artisan en Grèce ancienne* (Paris: La Découverte, 2000), pp. 95–120; Christopher A. Faraone, *Talismans and Trojan Horses: Guardian Statues in Ancient Greek Myth and Ritual* (Oxford: Oxford University Press, 1992), p. 4; Françoise Dunand, *Corps vivants des Dieux: Les statues animées dans le monde méditerranéan antique* (Paris: Picard, 2018); Tonio Hölscher, *La vie des images grecques: Sociétés de statues, Rôles des artistes et notions esthétiques dans l'art grec ancien* (Paris: Hazan, 2015), p. 98 et seq. The latter recalls that the statues were, at one and the same time, material objects and living beings.

49. Gorrini, "Healing Statues in the Greek and Roman World."

50. Hölscher, *La vie des images grecques*, p. 74.

51. For example, once each year, the Athenian Palladium was carried in procession all the way to Phalerum where it was bathed in the Mediterranean Sea. Cf. Frontisi-Ducroux, *Dédale*, p. 104.

52. Cf. George Galavaris, *Bread and the Liturgy: The Symbolism of Early Christian and Byzantine Bread Stamps* (Madison, WI: University of Wisconsin Press, 1970), pp. 23–25. We shall see, in the third part of this book, that the same was true in Rome. Cf. John Scheid, *Quand faire, c'est croire: Les rites sacrificiels des Romains* (Paris: Aubier, 2011).

53. English translation quoted from Herodas, *Mimiambs*, edited with an introduction, translation and commentary by Graham Zanker (Oxford, Oxbow Books, 2009), p. 103.

54. Galavaris, *Bread and the Liturgy*, p. 20. See also Hugo Blümner, *Technologie und Terminologie der Gewerbe und Künste bei Griechen und Römern* (Leipzig: B. G. Teubner, 1875), vol. 1, p. 85; Waldemar Deonna, "Notes d'archéologie suisse, V: ΥΓΙΕΙΑ," *Anzeiger für schweizerische Altertumskunde* 21 (1919), pp. 87–95; and Franz Joseph Dölger, "Heidnische und christliche Brotstempel mit religiösen Zeichen," in *Antike und Christentum: Kultur- und-Religionsgeschichtliche Studien* (Munster: Aschendorff, 1929), vol. 1, pp. 1–46.

55. Cécile Nissen, *Entre Asclépios et Hippocrate: Étude des cultes guérisseurs et des médecins en Carie* (Liège: Presses universitaires de Liège, 2009), pp. 227–59.

56. For more on the medical role of Asclepius and his assistant Hygieia, see Michael T. Compton, "The Association of Hygieia with Asklepios in Graeco-Roman Asklepieion Medicine," *Journal of the History of Medicine and Allied Sciences* 57.3 (2002), pp. 312–29, esp. p. 325.

57. Cf. Jackie Pigeaud, *La maladie de l'âme: Étude sur la relation de l'âme et du corps dans la tradition médico-philosophique antique* (Paris: Les Belles Lettres, 1981), pp. 62–65; Jacques Jouanna, *Hippocrates*, trans. M. B. DeBevoise (Baltimore, MD: Johns Hopkins University Press, 1999), pp. 181–209. On the transformation of the idea of sacred medicine into that of miraculous healing, see notably Gabriela Signori, *Wunder: Eine historische Einführung* (Frankfurt: Campus, 2007), pp. 94–136.

58. Cf. Compton, "The Association of Hygieia with Asklepios," pp. 314–15, 327.

59. These stones were also used to ward off enemies, to charm people, etc.

60. Armand Delatte, "Étude sur la magie grecque: V. Akephalos Theos," *Bulletin de correspondance hellénique* 38 (1914), pp. 189–249; Campbell Bonner, *Studies in Magical Amulets Chiefly Graeco-Egyptian* (Ann Arbor: University of Michigan Press, 1950); Jacques Schamp and Robert Halleux, eds., *Les lapidaires grecs: Lapidaire orphique, kérygmes lapidaires d'Orphée, Socrate et Denys, lapidaire nautique, Damigéron-Evax* (Paris: Les Belles Lettres, 1986); Michaël Martin, *Magie et magiciens dans le monde gréco-romain* (Arles: Errance, 2005), pp. 198–202; Véronique Dasen and Árpád M. Nagy, "Le serpent léontocéphale Chnoubis et la magie de l'époque romaine impériale," *Anthropozoologica* 47.1 (2012), pp. 291–314; Erika Zwierlein-Diehl, "Magical Gems in the Medieval and Early-Modern Periods: Tradition, Transformation, Innovation," in Véronique Dasen and Michel Spieser, eds., *Les Savoirs magiques et leur transmission de l'Antiquité à la Renaissance* (Florence: Sismel, 2014), pp. 87–130; Árpád M. Nagy, "*Daktylios Pharmakites*: Magical Healing Gems and Rings in the Graeco-Roman World," in Ildikò Csepregi and Charles Burnett, eds., *Ritual Healing: Magic, Ritual and Medical Therapy from Antiquity until the Early Modern Period* (Florence: Sismel, 2012), pp. 71–106; Christopher A. Faraone, "Text, Image and Medium: The Evolution of Graeco-Roman Magical Gemstones," in Chris Entwistle and Noël Adams, eds., *"Gems of Heaven": Recent Research on Engraved Gemstones in Late Antiquity, c. AD 200–600* (London: British Museum, 2011), pp. 50–61; Attilio Mastrocinque, *Les intailles magiques du département des Monnaies, Médailles et Antiques* (Paris: Éditions BnF, 2014); Véronique Dasen and Árpád M. Nagy, "Gems," in David Frankfurter, ed., *Guide to the Study of Ancient Magic* (Leiden: Brill, 2019), pp. 416–55; and Véronique Dasen, "Le pouvoir des pierres: De la *sphragis* au médicament estampillé dans le monde

gréco-romain," in Thomas Galoppin and Cécile Guillaume-Pey, eds., *Ce que peuvent les pierres: Vie et puissance des matériaux lithiques entre rites et savoirs* (Liège: Presses universitaires de Liège, 2021), pp. 135–62. Faraone notes that the oldest gems were not necessarily inscribed. See Faraone, "Text, Image and Medium," p. 50.

61. On the variety of this repertoire, see Bonner, *Studies in Magical Amulets Chiefly Graeco-Egyptian*; Dasen and Nagy, "Le serpent léontocéphale Chnoubis," p. 295; Nagy, "*Daktylios Pharmakites*," pp. 85–86; Mastrocinque, *Les intailles magiques*; Dasen and Nagy, "Gems." The figures of men, animals, and vegetables are often mentioned in the *lithika*.

62. Mastrocinque, *Les intailles magiques*, pp. 106–109.

63. For a discussion of the notions of sympathy and antipathy, see the well-known pages in Michel Foucault, *The Order of Things: An Archaeology of the Human Sciences*, trans. Alan Sheridan (New York: Vintage Books, 1994), pp. 23–24. Naturally, I align myself with Foucault's nonnormative position on magic, seeing it as operational. Among the lapidaries, the most detailed, in terms of the preparation, are *Socrates and Dionysus* and *Damigeron-Evax*. The latter is particularly interesting for the part it accords to astrology. On this doctrine in Greek culture, see Patricia Gaillard-Seux, "Sympathie et antipathie dans l'*Histoire Naturelle* de Pline l'Ancien," in Nicoletta Palmieri, ed., *Rationnel et irrationnel dans la médecine antique et médiévale: Aspects historiques, scientifiques et culturels* (Saint-Étienne: Publications de l'université de Saint-Etienne, 2003), pp. 113–28, and for the later period, see Mireille Ausécache, "Le minéral au secours du corps dans la pharmacopée médiévale occidentale (XIIe–XVe siècle)," in Danielle Jacquart and Nicolas Weill-Parot, eds., *Substances minérales et corps animés / Mineral Substances and Animates Bodies (1100–1500)* (Montreuil: Omniscience, 2012), pp. 147–77.

64. Fernand de Mély, *Les Lapidaires de l'Antiquité et du Moyen Âge, tome 3: Les lapidaires grecs (French translation)* (Paris: Ernest Leroux, 1902).

65. Dioscorides, *The Greek Herbal of Dioscorides*, ed. Robert T. Gunther (Royal Oak: Hafner Publishing, 1968), V, 126, p. 392. See also Dasen and Nagy, "Gems."

66. For more on Chnoubis, see Bonner, *Studies in Magical Amulets Chiefly Graeco-Egyptian*, pp. 54–60; Simone Michel, Peter Zazoff, and Hilde Zazoff, eds., *Die magischen Gemmen im Britischen Museum* (London: British Museum Press, 2001), pp. 194–95; Véronique Dasen, "Métamorphoses de l'utérus, d'Hippocrate à Ambroise Paré," *Gesnerus: Revue trimestrielle d'histoire de la médecine et des sciences naturelles* 59 (2002), pp. 167–86; Faraone, "Text, Image and Medium," pp. 50–52; Dasen and Nagy, "Le serpent léontocéphale Chnoubis"; Mastrocinque, *Les intailles magiques*, pp. 93–104; Véronique Dasen, "Magical

Milk Stones?," in Juan Francisco Martos Montiel, Cristobal Macias Villalobos, and R. Caballero Sanchez, eds., *Plutarco, entre dioses y astros: Homenaje al profesor Aurelio Pérez Jiménez de sus discípulos, colegas y amigos*, (Zaragoza: Libros Pórtico, 2019), vol. 2, pp. 1037–1039; and *Socrate et Denys*, 35, in Schamp and Halleux, eds., *Les Lapidaires grecs*, p. 170.

67. Dasen and Nagy, "Le serpent léontocéphale Chnoubis," pp. 299 and 309.

68. PGM IV, 2880–90. Cited in *An Anthology of Classical Myth: Primary Sources in Translation*, eds. Stephen Trzaskoma, R. Scott Smith, Stephen Brunet, Thomas G. Palaima (Indianapolis: Hackett, 2004), p. 433.

69. Attilio Mastrocinque, "Le pouvoir de l'écriture dans la magie," *Cahiers "Mondes anciens": Histoire et anthropologie des mondes anciens* 1 (2010).

70. See the list of inscriptions in Dasen and Nagy, "Le serpent léontocéphale Chnoubis," appendix 8, p. 310.

71. For more on these invocations, see Mastrocinque, "Le pouvoir de l'écriture"; Dasen and Nagy, "Le serpent léontocéphale Chnoubis," p. 302; Nagy, "*Daktylios Pharmakites*," p. 80; and Faraone, "Text, Image and Medium."

72. The inscription "Digest, digest!" (in Greek) is engraved upon a chalcedony now at Ann Arbor's Kelsey Museum of Archaeology at the University of Michigan; see Dasen and Nagy, "Le serpent léontocéphale Chnoubis," p. 310. "Tantalus, you are thirsty: drink blood!" (in Greek) is inscribed upon a hematite, today in the collection of the Département des Monnaies, Medailles et Antiques of the Bibliothèque nationale de France. See Mastrocinque, *Les intailles magiques*, no. 353, no. 354, pp. 133–35. And finally, we find "Gout, be gone, Perseus is after you!" (in Greek) on the Perseus gem found in the Hermitage Museum in Saint Petersburg. See Árpád M. Nagy's study, "Engineering Ancient Amulets: Magical Gems of the Roman Imperial Period," in Dietrich Boschung and Jan N. Bremmer, eds., *The Materiality of Magic* (Paderborn: Wilhelm Fink, 2015), pp. 205–40, esp. pp. 220–32, and Mastrocinque, "Le pouvoir de l'écriture," pp. 17–18.

73. See, for example, Hermes Trismegistus, *Les Cyranides*, I, K, 20–28, in Fernand de Mély, ed. and trans., *Les lapidaires de l'antiquité et du Moyen Âge*, vol. 3: *Les lapidaires grecs* (Paris: Ernest Leroux, 1902), pp. 51–52. Cf. Martin, *Magie et magiciens dans le monde gréco-romain*, p. 199; Véronique Dasen, "*Probaskania*: Amulets and Magic in Antiquity," in Dietrich Boschung and Jan N. Bremmer, eds., *The Materiality of Magic* (Paderborn: Wilhelm Fink, 2015), pp. 177–203.

74. Galen, *De simpl.* 10, 19. See Galen, *Claudii Galeni opera omnia*, 20 vols., ed. and Latin trans. C. G. Kühn (Leipzig, 1821–33, reprinted Hildesheim, 1964–65), vol. 12, p. 207.

Cited and translated in Bonner, *Studies in Magical Amulets Chiefly Graeco-Egyptian*, p. 54 (my emphasis).

75. Erika Zwierlein-Diehl, *Magische Amulette und andere Gemmen des Instituts für Altertumskunde der Universität zu Köln* (Opladen: Westdeutscher Verlag, 1992) p. 50; Dasen, "Métamorphoses de l'utérus, d'Hippocrate à Ambroise Paré," p. 170; Véronique Dasen, "Magic and Medicine: Gems and the Power of Seals," in Chris Entwistle and Noël Adams, eds., *"Gems of Heaven": Recent Research on Engraved Gemstones in Late Antiquity, c. AD 200–600* (London: British Museum, 2011), pp. 71–72; Nagy, "*Daktylios Pharmakites*," p. 81; and Dasen, "Le pouvoir des pierres," p. 138.

76. Zwierlein-Diehl, *Magische Amulette*, and Nagy, "*Daktylios Pharmakites*." In addition to magical stones, the Greco-Roman physicians also prescribed other image-bearing remedies. Asclepiades the Younger, cited by Galen, mentions, for example, a remedy of Antigone's "called little lion because the image of a lion was imprinted upon it." See, Dasen, "Magic and Medicine," p. 71.

77. Trismegistus, *Les Cyranides*, I, Ω, 32–34, p. 69. This English version (slightly modernized) is from an anonymous 1685 English translation of an 1158 Latin translation from the Greek original: *Magick of Kirani, King of Persia, and of Harpocration containing the Magical and Medicinal Vertues of Stones, Herbs, Fishes, Beasts and Birds*. . . . Early English Books Online, London, 1685, pp. 20 and 63. See also the *Orphei lithica kerygmata* (pp. 8, 16, 20, 20) and Socrates-Dionysus (*Orphei lithika kerygmata*, pp. 39, 3, 5), in Schamp and Halleux, eds., *Les lapidaires grecs*, p. 172. For the stones cut in two, see the *Orphei lithika kerygmata*, 20, 23, in Schamp and Halleux, eds., *Les Lapidaires grecs*, p. 162. Nagy also points out in the *Cyranides* (I, 22, 23–31) a "*Golden oriole . . . standing on a dorade on a* chrysites *gem: against problems of stomach, kidney and womb; it is to be worn, but soaked in wine it can also be used as a medicinal drink*." See, Nagy, "*Daktylios Pharmakites*," p. 85.

78. See Dasen, "Le pouvoir des pierres," p. 146 et seq.

79. I am using this expression to mean the temporal rule of Christianity, and not to postulate any unity of Christian practice within the Western world.

80. I refer the reader to the general bibliography for the works of these various authors. Particularly interesting, however, is the position taken by Caroline Walker Bynum, "Why All the Fuss about the Body?: A Medievalist's Perspective," *Critical Inquiry* 22.1 (1995), pp. 1–33.

81. See especially the examples given by Mastrocinque, *Les intailles magiques*, pp. 187–96.

82. Michel Spieser, "Christianisme et magie du IIIe au VIIe siècle," in Véronique Dasen and Michel Spieser, eds., *Les savoirs magiques et leur transmission de l'Antiquité à la Renaissance* (Florence: Sismel, 2014), pp. 333–34.

83. Gary Vikan, "Art, Medicine, and Magic in Early Byzantium," *Dumbarton Oaks Papers* 38 (1984), p. 69.

84. Vikan, "Art, Medicine, and Magic," p. 69. See especially Vikan's account of a silver ring, dating from the seventh or eighth century, and now in the Menil Collection in Houston.

85. Ibid., p. 79. See also Jeffrey Spier, "An Antique Magical Book Used for Making Sixth-Century Byzantine Amulets?," in Véronique Dasen and Michel Spieser, eds., *Les savoirs magiques et leur transmission de l'Antiquité à la Renaissance* (Florence: Sismel, 2014), pp. 43–66.

86. Dasen, "Magic and Medicine," p. 72; see also Dasen, "Le pouvoir des pierres," p. 146.

87. Nicolas Weill-Parot, *Les "Images astrologiques" au Moyen Âge et à la Renaissance: Spéculations intellectuelles et pratiques magiques (XIIe–XVe siècle)* (Paris: Champion, 2002), p. 454: "Certain seals were intended to be dissolved or simply dipped in drinks, and then ingested." Weill-Parot also gives the example of a seal placed inside a drinking vessel so that it would confer its *virtus* on any drinks consumed from it. See Weill-Parot, *"Images astrologiques" au Moyen Âge et à la Renaissance*, pp. 538–39.

88. *Inventarium sive Chirurgica Magna*, tract. VI, Doct. 2, cap. 7. Cited in Weill-Parot, *"Images astrologiques» au Moyen Âge et à la Renaissance*, p. 532.

89. See especially Wolfgang Hübner, "La mélothésie zodiacale à la Renaissance," in Véronique Dasen and Michel Spieser, eds., *Les savoirs magiques et leur transmission de l'Antiquité à la Renaissance* (Florence: Sismel, 2014), pp. 301–30.

90. There is a similar recipe, this time with the image of a scorpion, in the *Centiloquium Ptolemei*. See Weill-Parot, *"Images astrologiques" au Moyen Âge et à la Renaissance*, p. 479.

91. According to Pietro d'Abano, there are two species of poison: one that "works its effect through its own quality or complexion," and one that "does the same thing through a virtue deriving from its entire species, what the physicians call specific form." And he defines specific form as "precisely nothing other than what is obtained and won from the influences of the fixed stars by each composite according to the greater or lesser proportions of these same elements in the composite." Cited in Weill-Parot, *"Images astrologiques" au Moyen Âge et à la Renaissance*, p. 526.

92. See Weill-Parot, *"Images astrologiques" au Moyen Âge et à la Renaissance*; Erika Zwierlein-Diehl, "Antike Gemmen im Mittelalter: Wiederverwendung, Umdeutung, Nachahmung," in Dietrich Boschung and Susanne Wittekind, eds., *Persistenz und Rezeption: Weiterverwendung, Wiederverwendung und Neuinterpretation antiker Werke im Mittelalter* (Wiesbaden: Reichert, 2008), pp. 237–84; Zwierlein-Diehl, "Magical Gems"; Dasen and Spieser, eds., *Les savoirs magiques*; Árpád M. Nagy, "Étude sur la transmission du savoir magique: L'histoire post-antique du schéma anguipède (Ve–XVIIe siècles)," in Véronique Dasen and Michel Spieser, eds., *Les savoirs magiques et leur transmission de l'Antiquité à la Renaissance* (Florence: Sismel, 2014), pp. 131–55.

93. Vikan, "Art, Medicine, and Magic," pp. 75–78.

94. Spieser, "Christianisme et magie," pp. 341–42.

95. Jeffrey Spier, *Late Antique and Christian Gems* (Wiesbaden: L. Reichert, 2007), p. 113. Numerous other examples are cited in Nagy, "Étude sur la transmission du savoir magique," p. 136 et seq., and see Spieser, "Christianisme et magie."

96. For Brigitte Pitarakis, "the Byzantines, in their everyday life, were haunted by the fear of demons, and they warded these off through constant recourse through magical practices, subtly integrated with individual piety." Brigitte Pitarakis, "Magie, santé, piété privée: Les vertus du motif du lion sur les amulettes paléobyzantines," in Véronique Dasen and Michel Spieser, eds., *Les savoirs magiques et leur transmission de l'Antiquité à la Renaissance* (Florence: Sismel, 2014), p. 371.

97. Vikan, "Art, Medicine, and Magic," p. 86.

98. Nagy, "Étude sur la transmission du savoir magique."

99. Henry Maguire, "Magic and the Christian Image," in Henry Maguire, ed., *Byzantine Magic* (Washington, DC: Dumbarton Oaks Research Library and Collection, 1995), pp. 51–71.

100. Vikan, "Art, Medicine, and Magic," pp. 79–80.

101. Ibid., p. 84. Another hematite, in the New York Metropolitan Museum, bears an engraving of Christ and the woman with a hemorrhage (sixth–seventh centuries). For more on this object and its magical function, see J. Tuerk, "An Early Byzantine Inscribed Amulet and its Narratives," *Byzantine and Modern Greek Studies*, 23 (1999), pp. 25–42, esp. pp. 30–31 on the ingestion of the hematite.

102. Spieser, "Christianisme et magie"; Foucault, *The Order of Things*; Descola, *Beyond Nature and Culture*.

103. Spieser, "Christianisme et magie," pp. 333–34, 344. Brown, Grabar, Schmitt,

Vauchez, among others, recall that the early days of Christianity were marked by the (at least partial) religious rejection of images in the context of worship, with images often understood as being inseparable from idolatry.

104. Marc Augé, *Génie du paganisme* (Paris: Gallimard, 2008), p. 141.

105. Maguire, "Magic and the Christian Image," pp. 52 and 66, et seq.; Weill-Parot, *"Images astrologiques" au Moyen Âge et à la Renaissance* (for William of Auvergne); André Grabar, *L'iconoclasme byzantin: Le dossier archéologique* (Paris: Flammarion, 1984), p. 105.

106. On this continuity into the medieval and modern eras, see especially the volume edited by Dasen and Spieser, *Les savoirs magiques*.

107. The author of the *Vita*, who remains anonymous, was probably one of the saint's disciples, living in the latter's vicinity during the years 545 and 592. Cf. Paul Van den Ven, *La vie ancienne de S. Syméon Stylite le Jeune (521–592),* 2 vols. (Brussels: Société des Bollandistes, 1962–1970), vol. 1, p. 105.

108. Van den Ven, *La vie ancienne*, vol. 2, pp. 233–35. Vikan also cites this passage, likening the eulogia to a token bearing the image of the saint. See Gary Vikan, "Ruminations on Edible Icons: Originals and Copies in the Art of Byzantium," in *Studies in the History of Art* 20: Symposium Papers VII: Retaining the Original: Multiple Originals, Copies, and Reproductions (Washington, DC: National Gallery of Art, 1989), pp. 55–56.

109. As Vikan points out, throughout the 259 chapters that make up the *Lives of Saint Symeon the Younger*, the word *eulogia* appears about a dozen times as a term for a substance that has been blessed. Such substances might be water coming from a place near near the column, bread that had been blessed, or locks of hair. See Vikan, "Art, Medicine, and Magic" and "Ruminations on Edible Icons."

110. Numerous pilgrim tokens bearing the image of Saint Symeon are held today in the collections of the Menil Foundation in Houston and the Walters Art Museum in Baltimore. It is, however, hard to say whether these are connected with the Church of Saint Symeon the Elder, at Qal' at Sem'an outside of Aleppo, or with the Monastery of Saint Symeon the Younger, in the area outside of Antioch. Cf. Vikan, "Art, Medicine, and Magic," p. 73, and Vikan, "Ruminations on Edible Icons," pp. 55–56. Tokens such as these were also produced during the mid-Byzantine period, between 843 and 1204, but their iconography and function are different. See Vikan, "Art, Medicine, and Magic," p. 74. See also Finbarr Barry Flood, "Mimesis, Mediation and the Ingestion of the Sacred in Christianity and Islam," in Sally M. Promey, ed., *Sensational Religion: Sensory Cultures in Material Practice* (New Haven, CT: Yale University Press, 2014), pp. 463–64; Flood,

Technologies de dévotion dans les arts de l'Islam, p. 82 et seq.; and Jean-Pierre Sodini, "La terre des semelles: Images pieuses ramenées par les pèlerins des Lieux saints (Terre sainte, Martyria d'Orient)" *Journal des savants* (2011), pp. 77–140.

111. See Vikan, "Art, Medicine, and Magic," pp. 67–68.

112. After the death of Saint Symeon, these tokens continued to be made and sold to pilgrims journeying to the holy site in order to seek communion with themselves there. Cf. Martine Gerard et alii, "Argiles et eulogies en forme de jetons: Qal'at Sem'an en est-il une source possible?," in Henry Maguire, ed., *Materials Analysis of Byzantine Pottery* (Washington DC: Dumbarton Oaks Research Library and Collection, 1998), pp. 10–11.

113. Van den Ven, *La vie ancienne*, vol. 2, p. 231, cited by Sodini, "La terre des semelles," pp. 101–102.

114. Van den Ven, *La vie ancienne*, vol. 2, pp. 230–31.

115. Vikan mentions the discovery, in the 1970s, of a hoard, probably of Syrian origin, containing more than ninety clay tokens, and with the following depictions: The Adoration of the Magi, Solomon, Baptism, Bust of Christ, Nativity, Women at the Tomb, Annunciation, Transfiguration, etc. Added to this list is a St. Symeon clay token. For Vikan, it is very likely that these objects, made with the earth coming from a holy place, were used as medicines and were ingested like the blessings or *eulogiae* of St. Symeon. See Vikan, "Art, Medicine, and Magic," pp. 81–82. The hoard was not found in an archaeological context, and Vikan makes a few hypotheses about how it came to be formed, suggesting the tokens were discovered among the remains of a storeroom or workshop at a holy site, or in a box belonging to a physician or a churchman. See Vikan, "Art, Medicine, and Magic," p. 82n115.

116. As Paul Van den Ven explains, "the instruments of healing were many and various" and "chapter 41 of the *Vita* gathers together the principal ones among them: the sole contemplation of the saint (in flesh and blood or in spirit), his words, the placing of his hands, touching his palm stick or the hem of his clothing, contact with earth blessed or given by him, or a simple request made to him in faith. Individual stories of healing add yet other means: the consumption of water into which one had put some of the saint's hair or dust of the earth blessed by him, a clod of earth soaked with water blessed by the saint . . . , anointing with saliva." This was not unique to St. Symeon the Younger: "Symeon the Elder also used dust of the earth gathered from around the foot of his column, and the sick were supposed to rub themselves with it, if they did not actually drink water in which it had been mixed." See Van den Ven, *La vie ancienne*, vol. 2, pp. 187–88.

117. The substances that had been in contact with the saint were reputedly of such potency that, after the transferal of the bodily remains of St. Symeon Stylites the Elder to Antioch, the pilgrimage site at Qal'at Sem'an was to remain equally important, the column and earth having retained the saint's power. Cf. Michel Kaplan, "De la dépouille à la relique: Formation du culte des saints à Byzance du Ve au XIIe siècle," in Édina Bozóky and Anne-Marie Helvétius, eds., *Les Reliques: Objets, cultes, symboles* (Turnhout: Brepols, 1999), p. 23.

118. Cf. See the classic study by Peter Brown, *The Cult of the Saints: Its Rise and Function in Latin Christianity*, 2nd ed. (Chicago: University of Chicago Press, 2015); Robert Markus, *Au risque du christianisme: L'émergence du modèle chrétien (IVe–VIe siècle)* (Lyon: PUL, 2012), p. 210 et seq.

119. Brown, *The Cult of the Saints*, pp. 50, 60–63, 75–78.

120. André Vauchez, *Sainthood in the Later Middle Ages*, trans. Jean Birrell (Cambridge, UK: Cambridge University Press, 1997), pp. 430–31. Vauchez does, however, point out that, while remaining essential to the Middle Ages, the material and sensory dimension of the relation to the saints is increasingly paralleled by a spiritual dimension "with the passage of time." Vauchez, *Sainthood in the Later Middle Ages*, p. 439.

121. "The saints, in return for their merit and for the suffering they endured, are granted by God a force (virtus) that remains present and continues to act within their remains after their death." Ibid., p. 497. Peers speaks of them as living or animated things. See Glenn Peers, "Object Relations: Theorizing the Late Antique Viewer," in Scott Fitzgerald Johnson, ed., *The Oxford Handbook of Late Antiquity* (Oxford: Oxford University Press, 2012), p. 980. See also Brown, *The Cult of the Saints*, pp. 75–76; Markus, *Au risque du christianisme*, p. 199 et seq.; James Robinson and Lloyd De Beer, eds., *Matter of Faith: An Interdisciplinary Study of Relics and Relic Veneration in the Medieval Period* (London: British Museum, 2014); and for the modern period, see Stéphane Baciocchi and Christophe Duhamelle, eds., *Reliques romaines: Invention et circulation des corps saints des catacombes à l'époque moderne* (Rome: EFR, 2016).

122. Cited in Brown, *The Cult of the Saints*, p. 11. See also Michele Bacci, *Il pennello dell'Evangelista: Storia delle immagini sacre attribuite a San Luca* (Pisa: GISEM, 1998), pp. 42–44.

123. Vauchez, *Sainthood in the Later Middle Ages*, p. 428.

124. On the role of the gaze in the pilgrim's experience, see Georgia Frank, "The Pilgrim's Gaze in the Age before Icons," in Robert S. Nelson, ed., *Visuality before and beyond the Renaissance: Seeing as Others Saw* (Cambridge, UK: Cambridge University Press, 2000), pp. 98–114.

125. See Brown, *The Cult of the Saints*, p. 75, for more on the necessity of maintaining close physical proximity to the relics. See also Grabar, *L'iconoclasme byzantin*, pp. 104–105; Vikan, "Art, Medicine, and Magic," p. 66.

126. In both the East and the West, the fathers and doctors of the Greek and Latin churches generally favored the cult of relics. This was true in late ages. The cult of relics was reaffirmed in 1563 during the final session of the Council of Trent (Session XXV, Decree 2). Cf. Pierre-Antoine Fabre, *Décréter l'image?: La XXVe Session du Concile de Trente* (Paris: Les Belles Lettres, 2013), pp. 4–7. Relics, however, were sometimes the subject of controversy. Julian the Apostate, as is well known, was opposed to the cult, as was the prefect Vigilance. See Brown, *The Cult of the Saints*, pp. 7 and 35.

127. *Saint Basil the Great: On Christian Doctrine and Practice,* trans. Mark Del Cogliano (Yonkers, NY: St. Vladimir's Seminary Press, 2012), p. 224. Gregory of Nazianzus spoke thus of the martyrs: "*whose very bodies possess equal power with their holy souls.*" *Julian the Emperor*, trans. C. W. King (London: George Bell & Sons, 1888), p. 39.

128. As Vauchez has shown these miracles occur after a clear demonstration of faith and piety. See André Vauchez, *Saints, prophètes et visionnaires: Le pouvoir surnaturel au Moyen Âge* (Paris: Albin Michel, 1999), pp. 40–41.

129. Marc Bloch, *Les rois thaumaturges: Étude sur le caractère surnaturel attribué à la puissance royale particulièrement en France et en Angleterre* (Paris: Gallimard, [1924] 1983).

130. See Brown, *The Cult of the Saints*, p. 40, on the cemetery at Tebessa that was made into a pilgrimage site, and, again on the tomb of Saint Felix, developed into holy site by Saint Paulinus of Nola. See also Markus, *Au risque du christianisme*, p. 207 et seq.

131. Cf. Markus, *Au risque du christianisme*, pp. 206–207. Markus cites Letter XXII of Saint Ambrose concerning this new practice that he established in Milan: "Let the triumphant victims take their place where Christ is the victim. Let Him be above the altar who suffered for all; let them be beneath the altar who were redeemed by his suffering. This is the spot that I had destined for myself, because it is fitting that a bishop rest where he was wont to offer the Holy Sacrifice. But I yield the right-hand portion to the sacred victims, that place is owed the martyrs." Saint Ambrose, Letter 61 "to the lady his sister." See Saint Ambrose, *The Fathers of the Church: Saint Ambrose, Letters 1–91*, trans. Sister Mary Melchior Beyenka (Washington, DC: Catholic University of America Press, 1954), pp. 380–81.

132. Brown, *The Cult of the Saints*, pp. 4–5, and Markus, *Au risque du christianisme*, pp. 207–10.

133. Jean-Claude Schmitt, *Le corps des images: Essais sur la culture visuelle au Moyen Âge* (Paris: Gallimard, 2002), p. 280; See also Brown, *The Cult of the Saints*, chap. 5; Patrick J. Geary, *Le vol des reliques au Moyen Âge* (Paris: Aubier, 1993). On the things done with the physical remains, see Kaplan, "De la dépouille à la relique," pp. 19–21, 24.

134. These precautions are analogous to those taken to prevent the destruction of holy sites such as the Holy Sepulcher and the Golden Gate. Many pilgrims, in fact, tried to get hold of pieces of the Christian monuments that they visited. The Franciscans in charge of the administration of such places in the Holy Land, moreover, threatened with excommunication anyone who tried to take away such relics. Cf. Brian Spencer, *Pilgrim Souvenirs and Secular Badges* (London: Boydell & Brewer, 2010), pp. 1–3. The boxes containing holy earth or the flasks full of water from the Jordan could serve as substitute "relics." In typical fashion, the Sancta Sanctorum in Rome possesses a reliquary containing earth from several of the holy sites in Palestine. Cf. Herbert Kessler and Johanna Zacharias, *Rome 1300: on the Path of the Pilgrim* (New Haven, CT: Yale University Press, 2000), pp. 51–52; and Guido Cordini, "*Non est in Toto Sanctior Orbe Locus*: Collecting Relics in Early Medieval Rome," in Martina Bagnoli, Holger A. Klein, and C. Griffith Mann, eds., *Treasures of Heaven: Saints, Relics, and Devotion in Medieval Europe* (New Haven, CT: Yale University Press, 2010), pp. 69–78.

135. On *virtus*, see Vauchez, *Sainthood in the Later Middle Ages*, pp. 425–39, 444–77. Relics of the Passion, and acheiropoietic images of Christ such as the Mandylion, the Veil of Saint Veronica, or the Holy Shroud, allowed for the belief in the idea of transmission of *potentia* through contact. On the images not made by human hand, see Ernst Kitzinger, "The Cult of Images in the Age before Iconoclasm," *Dumbarton Oaks Papers* 8 (1954), pp. 112–15; Grabar, *L'iconoclasme byzantin*, p. 105; Vikan, "Ruminations on Edible Icons," pp. 52–53; Hans Belting, *Likeness and Presence: History of the Image before the Era of Art*, trans. Edmund Jephcott (Chicago: University of Chicago Press, 1996), pp. 49–57; Bacci, *Il pennello dell'Evangelista*; and Marie-José Mondzain, *Image, Icon, Economy: The Byzantine Origins of the Contemporary Imaginary* (Stanford, CA: Stanford University Press, 2005), p. 84.

136. Vauchez, *Sainthood in the Later Middle Ages*, pp. 433–34.

137. Brown, *The Cult of the Saints*, pp. 88–89, and Vauchez, *Sainthood in the Later Middle Ages*, pp. 429–30. Concerning the popularity of emblems as relics by way of contact, see Spencer, *Pilgrim Souvenirs and Secular Badges*, pp. 16–17.

138. On Saint Demetrios, see André Grabar, "Quelques reliquaries de saint Démétrios et le martyrium du saint à Salonique," *Dumbarton Oaks Papers* 5 (1950), pp. 1–28;

André Grabar, "Un nouveau reliquaire de saint Démétrius," *Dumbarton Oaks Papers* 8 (1954), pp. 305–14; Grabar, *L'iconoclasme byzantin*, p. 104. Concerning the sanctuary of Saint Nicholas, the pilgrim Georges Lenguerant described in 1485 a scene that unfolded around the tomb: "We saw from below something like a lamp showing great light, and it was full of oil, and there underneath is the dead body of Saint Nicholas, from which is rendered the said Oil, that is called manna, and they give some of it to each pilgrim in an ampulla." Cited in Denis Bruna, *Enseignes de plomb et autres menues chosettes du Moyen Âge* (Paris: Le Léopard d'or, 2006), p. 35. Gentile da Fabiano imagined a similar scene in one of the predella panels (Washington, DC: National Gallery, 1425) of his altarpiece for the Quaratesi Palace. For more on the world of images surrounding the dead bodies of male and female saints, see Camporesi, *The Incorruptible Flesh*, pp. 3–24.

139. Vikan, "Art, Medicine, and Magic," p. 81.

140. Bruna, *Enseignes de plomb*, p. 37. See also Catherine Metzger, *Les Ampoules à eulogie du musée du Louvre* (Paris: RMN, 1981).

141. Bruna, *Enseignes de plomb*, p. 43 et seq., and p. 173: "The emblem *is* the saint"; and, on the presence of emblems in water, see ibid., pp. 187–90.

142. Bruna, *Enseignes de plomb*, p. 45, and Spencer, *Pilgrim Souvenir and Secular Badges*, p. 18.

143. Kurt Köster, "Mittelalterliche Pilgerzeichen," in Lenz Kriss-Rettenbeck and Gerda Möhler, eds., *Wallfahrt kennt keine Grenzen: Themen zu einer Ausstellung des Bayerischen Nationalmuseums und des Adalbert Stifter Vereins, München* (Regensburg: Verlag Schnell & Steiner, 1984), p. 218; Spencer, *Pilgrim Souvenirs and Secular Badges*, pp. 17–18; Bruna, *Enseignes de plomb*, p. 178.

144. Spencer, *Pilgrim Souvenirs and Secular Badges*. See also Schmitt, *Le corps des images*, p. 285.

145. "One way of releasing the benefits was to aim the mirrors at portions of bread, which could then be eaten by those in need of a cure." Spencer, *Pilgrim Souvenirs and Secular Badges*, p. 18, and Köster, "Mittelalterliche Pilgerzeichen," p. 218.

146. Schmitt, *Le corps des images*, p. 285. This theory is notably expounded by Galen, *De placitis Hippocr. Et Plat.*, VII, 615, taken up by Saint Augustine and Vincent de Beauvais. Cf. Robert Klein's pioneering study "*Spirito peregrino*," in *Form and Meaning: Writings on the Renaissance and Modern Art,* trans. Madeline Jay and Leon Wieseltier (New York: Viking Press, 1979), pp. 68–71 on "Magic," and pp. 71–73 on "Medicine and Psycho-physiology." See also Carl Havelange, *De l'oeil et du monde: Une histoire du regard au seuil de la modernité* (Paris: Fayard, 1998), pp. 147–83.

147. In Miracle 41 of the *Vita* of Saint Symeon, the author enumerates the various medicinal powers of the eulogiae. The ways of healing are diverse: "contemplation of the saint, in flesh and blood or by the spirit, his words, the placing of his hands, touching his palm stick or the hem of his clothing, contact with dust blessed or given by him, and a simple request made in faith." These are some of many ways in which miracles happened. Cf. Van den Ven, *La vie ancienne*, vol. 1, pp. 186–87. For more on the distribution of these practices in the West, see also Köster, "Mittelalterliche Pilgerzeichen," pp. 208–10, and Spencer, *Pilgrim Souvenirs*, p. 18.

148. Pilgrimages themselves were made, above all, for purposes of healing. Cf. Hippolyte Delehaye, "Les recueils antiques de miracles des saints," *Analecta Bollandiana* 43 (1925), pp. 11, 24, 64. On miraculous healing as an alternative to traditional medicine, see Brown, *The Cult of the Saints*, pp. 114–15 et seq. Vauchez indicates that 90 percent of the attested miracles in canonizations from the thirteenth and fourteenth centuries were therapeutic. Vauchez, *Sainthood in the Later Middle Ages*, p. 468.

149. Gary Vikan, *Byzantine Pilgrimage Art* (Washington, DC: Dumbarton Oaks Trustees, 1982), p. 11.

150. *John Chrysostom,* trans. Wendy Mayer and Pauline Allen (London: Routledge, 2000), p. 96. See also Hippolyte Delehaye, *Les Origines du culte des martyrs* (Bruxelles: Bureaux de la Société des Bollandistes, 1912), p. 141. This practice is also mentioned in the *Vita* of Saint Athanasia of Aegina. Cf. Kaplan, "De la dépouille à la relique," pp. 34–35.

151. Chapter 214 of the *Vita* of Saint Symeon mentions the ingestion by the sick person of a paste obtained from mixing sanctified earth and water (or saliva). Van den Ven, *La vie ancienne*, and Vikan, "Art, Medicine, and Magic," p. 69.

152. Vikan, "Art, Medicine, and Magic," p. 68, and Theodoret of Cyrus, *Historia religiosa*, c. 21; PG82, cols. 1431ff.

153. This practice was not unique to Christianity. Similar cases of ingestion can be found in the Islamic and Indian cultures. On this point, see the fine article by Flood, "Mimesis, Mediation and the Ingestion of the Sacred."

154. Gregory of Tours, *The History of the Franks,* trans. Lewis Thorpe (London: Penguin, 1974), p. 510. See also Bloch, *Les rois thaumaturges*, pp. 33–34.

155. Bruna, *Enseignes de plomb*, pp. 35–36. A variant involved using a holy book, as Dominique Rigaux notes in "Réflexions sur les usages apotropaïques de l'image peinte: Autour de quelques peintures murales novaraises du Quattrocento," in Jérôme Baschet and Jean-Claude Schmitt, eds., *L'image: Fonctions et usages des images dans l'Occident*

médiéval (Paris: Le Léopard d'or, 1996), pp. 155–77: "The Venerable Bede claims to have seen how the Irish protected themselves from snake bites by consuming the scrapings from manuscripts mixed with water" (p. 160).

156. Cf. Bruna, *Enseignes de plomb*, p. 36 et seq. for the other miracles involving the consumption of "Saint Thomas's water." Jacobus de Voragine relates this miracle by ingestion: "Many a sick man has been healed by touching the water which was used to wash the clothes stained with the blood of Saint Thomas." Jacobus de Voragine, *The Golden Legend of Jacobus de Voragine,* trans. and adapt. Granger Ryan and Helmut Ripperger (New York: Arno Press, 1969), pp. 70–71.

157. Vauchez, *Sainthood in the Later Middle Ages*, p. 430n12: "*Aliquis mulieres patients, ut sibi videbatur, quae cum devotione fundebant aquam super tumulum dicti domini patriarchae, quam ipsae bibebant*."

158. The expression "human paste" is from the man of letters Edmond Lafond. Cf. Baciocchi and Duhamelle, *Reliques romaines*, p. 17. On the reuse of this paste, see ibid., p. 18. See also Peter Karl Jaksch, *Gesetzlexikon im geistlichen: Religions- und Toleranzfache, wie auch in Güter- Stiftungs- Studien- und Zensurssachen für das Königreich Böhmen von 1601 bis Ende 1800* (Prague, 1828), p. 42. On the persistence of these practices, see also Lenz Kriss-Rettenbeck, *Bilder und Zeichen religiösen Volksglaubens* (Munich: Georg D. W. Callwey, 1963), pp. 44–45. The practice of ingesting images has continued into the modern era. Cf. Dominique Julia, "L'Église post-tridentine et les reliques: Tradition, controverse et critique (XVIe–XVIIIe siècle)," in Pierre Boutry, Pierre Antoine Fabre, and Dominique Julia, eds., *Reliques modernes: Cultes et usages chrétiens des corps saints des Réformes aux revolutions*, 2 vols. (Paris: EHESS, 2009), vol. 1, p. 81. Julia refers us to a work by the Jesuit Jean Ferrand, *Disquisitio reliquiaria sive de suscipienda, et suspecta earundem numero Reliquiarum, quae in diversis Ecclesiis servantur, multitudine* (Lyon: Lavrentii Anisson, 1647), pp. 468–74, esp. p. 468 for the "saint vinage."

159. Christoph Schönborn, *L'icône du Christ: Fondements théologiques* (Paris: Cerf, 1986), p. 154n3 referring to PG 87, c. 3552 D-3557 C. See also Aurélie Barre and Olivier Leplatre, "L'iconophagie byzantine: Aspects du rituel eucharistique dans le christianisme oriental," *Food and History* 6.2 (2008), p. 79; Olivier Leplatre, *"Un goût à la voir nonpareil": Manger les images, essais d'iconophagie* (Paris: Kimé, 2018), pp. 176–93.

160. Brown, *The Cult of the Saints*, pp. 118–19.

161. Peers, "Object Relations," p. 980; Gregory, et al., *In gloria martyrum*, in *Gregorii Turonensis Opera* (Hannover: Impensis Bibliopolii, [1885] 1969), pp. 42.21–26. The practice

of ingesting earth on which a saint had trod did not die out with the end of the Middle Ages. We still find today examples of ingesting holy earth. Heike Behrend relates the case of Father Bill, a charismatic preacher of Indian origin, who lived in Uganda during the 1990s, and who was believed to perform miracles. After his sermons, the faithful were in the habit of collecting, and then ingesting, the earth on which he had stood. Heike Behrend, "Photo Magic: Photographs in Practices of Healing and Harming in East Africa," *Journal of Religion in Africa* 33.2 (2003), p. 139.

162. Vauchez, *Sainthood in the Later Middle Ages*, p. 430n12; Rigaux, "Réflexions sur les usages apotropaïques de l'image peinte," pp. 158–59.

163. Cf. Brown, *The Cult of the Saints*, pp. 20–22, 29–30, and Vauchez, *Sainthood in the Later Middle Ages*, pp. 436, 476.

164. Vauchez, *Sainthood in the Later Middle Ages*, p. 476.

165. Vikan asks the same question in "Art, Medicine, and Magic," pp. 72, 82–83.

166. We have marble molds from the holy site of the Miraculous Mountain, such as one, two-sided, discovered at El-Fauz near Jisr al-Shughur, on which the representations (on one side, the saint placed atop a rock, on the other, a bust-length portrait of the saint) are hollowed out so as to produce an imprint on the raw earth, before its firing and drying. An inscription accompanies the two images: "Eulogia of our Father Saint Symeon the Thaumaturge." Cf. Sodini, "La terre des semelles," p. 102 and fig. 19; and Martine Gerard et al., "Argiles et eulogies en forme de jetons: Qal'at Sem'an en est-il une source possible?," in Henry McGuire, ed., *Materials Analysis of Byzantine Pottery* (Washington, DC: Dumbarton Oaks Research and Collection p. 10. See also Jean Lassus, "Une image de saint Syméon le Jeune sur un fragment de reliquaire syrien du musée du Louvre," *Monuments et mémoires de la Fondation Eugène Piot* 51 (1960), pp. 149–50.

167. Cf. Pliny the Elder, *Natural History, XXXV*, 14, trans. H. Rackham, ed. Jeffrey Henderson, Loeb Classical Library, 394 (Cambridge, MA: Harvard University Press, 1952), pp. 285–87. On the history of the *terra sigillata* with a therapeutic function, see Marie-Hélène Marganne, "Les médicaments estampillés dans le corpus galénique," in Armelle Debru, ed., *Galen on Pharmacology: Philosophy, History, and Medicine* (Leiden: Brill, 1997), pp. 153–74; Dasen, "Magic and Medicine," pp. 70–71; Arthur MacGregor, "Medicinal *Terra Sigillata*: A Historical, Geographical and Typological Review," in Christopher J. Duffin, Richard T. J. Moody, and Christopher Gardner-Thorpe, eds., *A History of Geology and Medicine* (London: Geological Society of London, 2013), pp. 113–36.

168. Respectively in MacGregor, "Medicinal *Terra Sigillata*," pp. 115, 118–21, 121–23, 123. See

also Dasen ("Le pouvoir des pierres," p. 148), who cites the text of Dioscorides (*De materia medica*, V, chap. 97, pp. 375–76) in which there is mention of a seal with the image of a goat. These seals did not in any way impede the counterfeiters (MacGregor, "Medicinal *Terra Sigillata*," pp. 113–14). Certain quarries, such as the one in Malta (MacGregor, "Medicinal *Terra Sigillata*," p. 122) were authenticated by around twenty different seals, making the enterprise confusing and ineffective. On the uses of *terra sigillata* and seals for curative purposes in the Islamic world, see Flood, *Technologies de dévotion dans les arts de l'Islam*, pp. 89–101.

169. See Vikan, *Byzantine Pilgrimage Art*, pp. 30–32.

170. Van den Ven, *La vie ancienne*, vol. 2, p. 231. My emphasis.

171. Gilbert Dagron, *Décrire et peindre: Essai sur le portrait iconique* (Paris: Gallimard, 2007), p. 34.

172. Venance Grumel, "L'iconologie de saint Théodore Studite," *Échos d'Orient*, XX, 123, (1921), p. 259. See also Vikan, "Ruminations on Edible Icons," p. 50.

173. Mondzain, *Image, Icon, Economy*, pp. 82, 84: "the question then becomes one of justifying the resemblance of the figure to an absent original, rather than being about submission to a real model."

174. Mondzain, who refers notably to Nikephoros, *Antirrhetics*, I, 227 A: "an icon is a likeness of the archetype, and on it is stamped, by means of its resemblance, the whole of the visible form of what it is a likeness of, and it is distinct from its model only in terms of a different essence because of its material." Ibid., pp. 83, 86.

175. Cf. Olivier Boulnois, *Au-delà de l'image: Une archéologie du visuel au Moyen Âge, Ve–XVIe siècle* (Paris: Seuil, 2008), p. 192.

176. *Theodore the Studite: Writings on Iconoclasm*, trans. Thomas Cattoi (New York: Newman Press, 2015), p. 138. Cited also in Grumel, "L'iconologie de saint Théodore Studite," pp. 257–58.

177. Theodore the Studite, paraphrase by Grumel, "L'iconologie de saint Théodore Studite," p. 258.

178. Boulnois, *Au-delà de l'image*, p. 192.

179. Saint John of Damascus, *Three Treatises on the Divine Images,* trans. Andrew Louth (New York: St. Vladimir's Seminary Press, 2003), p. 42. For more on John of Damascus, see Schönborn, "L'icône," p. 191 et seq.

180. As Vikan writes, "*The scene on the token is to be understood as reflecting the experienced reality at the shrine . . . , the censing suppliant is not at the shrine at all, but . . . he is offering up*

his incense prayer from another location." Vikan, "Art, Medicine, and Magic," p. 71. Vikan also points out that the incense used by the pious believers helped with this "traveling."

181. Ibid., p. 73.

182. Mondzain, *Image*, p. 88. My emphasis.

183. "*Of [pilgrimages from] Italy it is unnecessary to speak, since they say that this man [Symeon the Elder] has become so famous in Rome, the greatest city, that they have set up small images of him in the vestibules of all the workshops for the warding off of danger and as a means of protection.*" *Historia religiosa*, 26.11, passage cited by Vikan, *Byzantine Pilgrimage Art*, p. 32, after H. Leitzmann, ed., *Das Leben des heiligen Symeon Stylites*, Texte und Untersuchungen zur Geschichte der altchristlichen Literatur (Leipzig, 1908), vol 4., ser. 32, p. 1. See also Kitzinger, "The Cult of Images," p. 94.

184. Miracle 15 in the *Vita* of Cosmas and Damian, that we know from Sophronius of Jerusalem (550–634 CE), has as *terminus ad quem* the year 634. We find this same miracle in Greek in *Kosmas und Damian*, ed., Ludwig Deubner (Leipzig: B. G. Teubner, 1907), pp. 137–38; in Latin in Jean-Dominique Mansi, *Sacrorum conciliorum nova et amplissima collectio* (Florence, 1759), XIII, col. 67; PL, 129, 0272; and in French in *Collections grecques de miracles: Saint Thècle, Saints Côme et Damien, Saint Cyr et Jean (extraits), Saint Georges*, ed., André-Jean Festugière (Paris: Picard, 1971), pp. 130–31. See also Delehaye, "Les recueils antiques de miracles des saints," pp. 16–17. The miracle is often mentioned in the studies devoted to the Byzantine images and, more generally, in those devoted to devotional practices involving images. See among others Kitzinger, "The Cult of Images," pp. 107n89 and 147–48; Dagron, *Décrire et peindre*, pp. 46, 248n29; Rigaux, "Réflexions sur les usages apotropaïques de l'image peinte," pp. 159–60; Barre and Leplatre, "L'iconophagie byzantine," pp. 79–80; Maguire, "Magic and the Christian Image," p. 66; François Lecercle, "L'infigurable" in Jean Céard, Marie-Madeleine Fontaine and Jean-Claude Margolin, eds., *Le Corps à la Renaissance: Actes du XXXe Colloque de Tours, 2–11 juillet 1987* (Paris: Aux amateurs de livres, 1990), pp. 173–86.

185. Patricia Cox Miller, *The Corporeal Imagination* (Philadelphia: University of Pennsylvania Press, 2009), p. 132. Peers considers that the terms *visitation* and the expression *dream visit* do not correctly translate the experience designated by the Greek term *epiphoitêsis* used in the miracle account, suggesting rather "*manifestation, intervention*, or even *haunting*." Peers, "Object Relations," p. 983.

186. The Greek term ἀκόρεστος is ambivalent. It means that the sick woman wanted constantly to see the saints, but that, for all that, she was never satisfied.

187. Cf. Vikan, "Art, Medicine, and Magic," p. 74; Peers, "Object Relations," pp. 970–87, esp. pp. 970, 983–84 for the example of the Cosmas and Damian fresco; Vasileios Marinis, "Piety, Barbarism, and the Senses in Byzantium," in Sally M. Promey, ed., *Sensational Religion: Sensory Cultures in Material Practice* (New Haven, CT: Yale University Press, 2014), pp. 321–40; Flood, "Mimesis, Mediation and the Ingestion of the Sacred," pp. 463–65. The latter writes (p. 465): "*In this sense, [images] acted as flesh . . . , color and enfleshment often being coincident in the painted body—fragments of the saints imbued with the sacrality of body fragments that otherwise served as relics.*"

188. This process was evidently made possible by what lies at the basis of Christian anthropology, namely, the idea that man is made in the image and likeness of God ("*ad imaginem et similitudinem nostrum*," Genesis 1:27). On this point, see the remarks made by Jean-Claude Schmitt, "La culture de *l'imago*," *Annales: Histoire, sciences sociales* 51.1 (1996), pp. 3–36. The evolution of the notion of the image in Neoplatonism also contributed to the establishment of a possible link between the spiritual and material worlds. There was, however, resistance to this in Origen, Augustine, et al. Cf. Jean Wirth, *L'image à l'époque romane* (Paris: Cerf, 1999), pp. 35–40.

189. *Three Byzantine Saints*, trans. Elizabeth Dawes and Norman H. Baynes (New York: St. Vladimir's Seminary Press, 1996), pp. 68–69 (my emphasis). See also Belting, *Likeness and Presence*, p. 60; Kaplan, "De la dépouille à la relique," pp. 19–38; and James A. Francis, "Living Icons: Tracing a Motif in Verbal and Visual Representation from the Second to the Fourth Centuries C.E." *American Journal of Philology* 124.4 (2003), p. 591.

190. Vauchez speaks of the "identification of the saint's image with his or her body." Vauchez, *Saints, prophètes et visionnaires*, p. 82.

191. Most medievalists and specialists in Byzantinology, from Grabar to Peters, including on the way Brown, Dupront, Vauchez, Schmitt, Francis, Boulnois, Sansterre, and Baschet, have thought that images were added to and progressively substituted for relics in the devotional economy. André Grabar, *Martyrium: Recherches sur le culte des reliques et l'art chrétien antique* (Paris: Collège de France, 1946); Alphonse Dupront, "Pélerinages et lieux sacrés," in *Mélanges en l'honneur de Fernand Braudel: Méthodologie de l'histoire et des sciences humaines*, 2 vols. (Toulouse: Privat, 1973), vol. 2, pp. 189–206; Peers, "Object Relations," p. 971; Vauchez, *Saints, prophètes et visionnaires*, pp. 12, 79–91; Vauchez, *Sainthood in the Later Middle Ages*, pp. 448–53; Schmitt, *Le corps des images*, pp. 291–92; Jean-Marie Sansterre, "Sacralité et pouvoir thaumaturgique des statues mariales (Xe siècle–première moitié du XIIIe siècle)," *Revue Mabillon* 22 (2011), pp. 53–77, esp. p. 54;

Boulnois, *Au-delà de l'image*, pp. 192–93; Jérôme Baschet, *La civilisation féodale de l'an mil à la colonisation de l'Amérique* (Paris: Flammarion, 2006), p. 711.

192. Saint Augustine was also to maintain this idea in his own definition of the image. Cf. Wirth, *L'image à l'époque romane*, p. 32 et seq.

193. Cited in Vikan, "Ruminations on Edible Icons," p. 50.

194. Boulnois, *Au-delà de l'image*, p. 204.

195. As Boulnois notes (*Au-delà de l'image*, p. 205), this "theory" had, however, a "price," namely, the sidelining of the role of the artisan. The paradigmatic perfect icon is an image not made by the hand of man.

196. Georges Didi-Huberman, *La Ressemblance par contact: Archéologie, anachronisme et modernité de l'empreinte* (Paris: Éd. de Minuit, 2008), pp. 71–91.

197. Saint Augustine, Sermon 9, in *The Works of Saint Augustine: Sermons,* trans. Edmund Hill, OP (New York: New City Press, 1990), p. 32.

198. *Theodore the Studite*, p. 138. Cited also in Louis Marin, *Les pouvoirs de l'image, Gloses* (Paris: Seuil, 1993), p. 209n29. See also Vikan, "Ruminations," p. 51.

199. Cf. *Varia graeca sacra*, ed., Athanasios Papdopoulos-Kerameus (Petropoli, 1900), Miracle 16; *The Miracles of Saint Artemios: A Collection of Miracle Stories by an Anonymous Author of Seventh-Century Byzantium*, eds. Virgil S. Crisafulli and John W. Nesbitt, trans. Virgil S. Crisafulli (Leiden: Brill, 1997), pp. 107–109. On the collection and the miracle 16, see Delehaye, "Les recueils antiques de miracles des saints," pp. 32–38; Kitzinger, "The Cult of Images," p. 107; Vikan, "Art, Medicine, and Magic," p. 73n45; Dagron, *Décrire et peindre*, p. 248n29: "another practice consisted in grinding up a wax tablet bearing the saint's effigy, and then using it as a bandage or eating it." In the same note, Dagron points out that "these customs assimilated the image with those relics that were bathed or boiled in water, concoctions that were then given to the faithful."

200. Cf. Dasen, "Magic and Medicine," p. 71.

201. MacGregor, "Medicinal *Terra Sigillata*," pp. 130–31.

202. John Hill, *A History of the Materia Medica* (London: T. Longman, C. Hitch & L. Hawes, 1751), p. 186. Cited in MacGregor, "Medicinal *Terra Sigillata*," p. 130.

203. Mansi, *Sacrorum conciliorum nova et amplissima collectio*, XII, 1010–11, cited in Barre and Leplatre, "L'iconophagie byzantine," p. 81.

204. Cf. Grabar, *L'iconoclasme byzantin*, pp. 104–105; Rigaux, "Réflexions sur les usages apotropaïques de l'image peinte," p. 160n23; Belting, *Likeness and Presence*, pp. 59–63;

W. J. T. Mitchell, *What do Pictures Want? The Lives and Loves of Images* (Chicago: University of Chicago Press, 2005), p. 39; Barre and Leplatre, "L'iconophagie byzantine," p. 80; Caroline Walker Bynum, *Christian Materiality: An Essay on Religion in Late Medieval Europe* (New York: Zone Books, 2015), pp. 22–23, 64–65.

205. Dagron, *Décrire et peindre*, p. 35, and Barre and Leplatre, "L'iconophagie byzantine," p. 89.

206. Saint John of Damascus, *Three Treatises*, pp. 29–30, Cf. Schönborn, *L'icône*, p. 194, and Barre and Leplatre, "L'iconophagie."

207. Cf. Belting, *Likeness and Presence*, pp. 59–63.

208. Flood, "Mimesis, Mediation and the Ingestion of the Sacred," p. 465.

209. On the Eastern Christians, see Kitzinger, "The Cult of Images," pp. 98–100; Grabar, *L'Iconoclasme byzantin*, p. 105; Robert S. Nelson, "To Say and to See: Ekphrasis and Vision in Byzantium," in Robert S. Nelson, ed., *Visuality before and beyond the Renaissance: Seeing as Others Saw* (Cambridge, UK: Cambridge University Press, 2000), pp. 143–68; Francis, "Living Icons"; Catherine Mayeur-Jaouen, "La fonction sacrale de l'image dans l'Égypte contemporaine: De l'imagerie traditionnelle à la révolution photographique," in Bernard Heyberger and Silvia Naef eds., *La Multiplication des images en pays d'Islam: de l'estampe à la télévision (17e–21e siècle)* (Wurzbourg: Ergon, 2003), pp. 59, 67; Dagron, *Décrire et peindre*, pp. 46–48; Boulnois, *Au-delà de l'image*, p. 194; and Marinis, "Piety," pp. 322–27. For the Christians of the West, see Belting, *Likeness and Presence*; David Freedberg, *The Power of Images: Studies in the History and Theory of Response* (Chicago: University of Chicago Press, 1989), pp. 283–316; Vauchez, *Saints, prophètes et visonnaires*, p. 79; Schmitt, "La culture de *l'imago*," pp. 14–25; Jean-Claude Schmitt, "Introduction," in Jérôme Baschet and Pierre-Olivier Dittmar, eds., *Les images dans l'Occident médiéval* (Turnhout: Brepols, 2015), p. 12; Rigaux, "Réflexions sur les usages apotropaïques de l'image peinte"; Jean-Claude Bonne, "Entre l'image et la matière: la choséité du sacré en Occident," in Jean-Marie Sansterre and Jean-Claude Schmitt, eds., *Les Images dans les sociétés médiévales: Pour une histoire comparée*, special issue of the *Bulletin de l'Institut historique belge de Rome* 69 (1999), pp. 77–111; and Sansterre, "Sacralité," p. 72 (for the tears and movements of the Virgin of Déols).

210. This letter is often quoted (Dagron, *Décrire et peindre*, p. 46), but the most penetrating analysis of it can be found in Barre and Leplatre, "L'iconophagie."

211. Cited in Cyril Mango, *The Art of the Byzantine Empire: Sources and Documents* (Englewood Cliffs, NJ: Prentice-Hall, 1972), p. 158. See also Schönborn, *L'icône*, p. 155;

Rigaux, "Réflexions sur les usages apotropaïques de l'image peinte," p. 159; and Dagron, *Décrire*, p. 46.

212. For Barre and Leplatre, "added to the host in the chalice, the scraped paint is . . . directly a metaphor of the suffering body of Christ." Barre and Leplatre, "L'iconophagie," p. 83. However, I do not think that we can follow them when they write, "The divine presence resides, therefore, in this substance and not in an image depicting Christ." Ibid., p. 76. As I see it, the substance would be nothing if it were not the receptacle of the image, that is, the place where the prototype is made present. The divine presence resides in the image-object.

213. Marie-Hélène Congourdeau writes, "the perception of the symbolic nature of the Eucharist in Byzantium wove a course between two perilous reefs: a hyper-symbolism that reduced the Eucharist to being only a . . . 'symbol' in the reductive sense of the term (the bread is a symbol of the body, the wine is a symbol of the blood, in the same way that the light of the candles is a symbol of the light of Christ that illuminates all men), and a hyper-realism in which the mystery was likely, at any moment, to slip into the ambiguous shades of ancient human sacrifices." Things were to progressively change, particularly in the Roman Church during the Middle Ages, and to culminate in the dogma of real presence and transubstantiation. Marie-Hélène Congourdeau, "L'enfant immolé: Hyper-réalisme et symbolique sacrificielle à Byzance," in Nicole Bériou, Béatrice Caseau, and Dominique Rigaux, eds., *Pratiques de l'Eucharistie dans les Églises d'Orient et d'Occident (Antiquité et Moyen Âge),* vol. 1: *Institution* (Turnhout: Brepols, 2009), p. 291.

214. This point is equally true of the Western medieval world. Rigaux, "Réflexions sur les usages apotropaïques de l'image peinte," p. 156: "The need to use images for apotropaic ends did not arise from any supposed 'popular mentality' that we might ascribe to a certain category of the population. It was shared by all levels of society, civil and religious, beginning with the Pope himself."

215. This expression comes from Dagron, *Décrire et peindre*, p. 72; See also Flood, "Mimesis, Mediation and the Ingestion of the Sacred," p. 465; Ann Freeman, "Carolingian Orthodoxy and the Fate of the Libri Carolini," *Viator* 16 (1985), p. 100; Charles Barber, "From Transformation to Desire: Art and Worship after Byzantine Iconoclasm," *Art Bulletin* 75.1 (1993), p. 8.

216. Grabar, *L'iconoclasme byzantine*. Boulnois notes, furthermore, that for Charlemagne and his theologians, those who claimed (as did Basil) that prayer passed through the image were unable to prove it. Boulnois, *Au-delà de l'image*, pp. 210–26. Cf. *Opus caroli*

regis contra synodum (Libri carolini), ed. Ann Freeman (Hanover: Hahn, 1998), III, 16, p. 407.

217. For the iconoclasts, the "supernatural power" attributed to the images of the saints did not really differentiate the icons from idols. It was necessary, therefore, to prove the images' status as intermediaries. Grabar, *L'iconoclasme byzantin*, p. 105.

218. *Collections grecques de miracles*, p. 131. See also in *Collections grecques de miracles*, n63: "It is through their power, and not by virtue of a remedy, that the saints healed."

219. Jean Wirth, "Structure et fonctions de l'image chez saint Thomas d'Aquin," in Jérôme Baschet and Jean-Claude Schmitt, eds., *L'image*, p. 52.

220. Dagron, *Décrire et peindre*, p. 71.

221. *Saint Basil Letters and Select Works*, vol. 8, ed. Philip Schaff (Grand Rapids, MI: Christian Classics Ethereal Library), p. 200 [Originally published: Buffalo: Christian Literature, 1886]. See also Wirth, "Structure et fonctions," p. 51; Wirth, *L'image à l'époque romane*, p. 41; Jean Wirth, *Qu'est-ce qu'une image?* (Geneva: Droz, 2013), p. 89 where "prototype" is replaced by "model." See also Barre and Leplatre, "L'iconophagie," p. 88, and Boulnois, *Au-delà de l'image*, p. 204. Athanasius of Alexandria, for his part, writes: "Therefore whoever adores the image also adores the emperor in it, for the image is his form (*morphē*) and character (*eidos*)." Cited in Francis, "Living Icons," pp. 586–88.

222. "The image of Christ is the Christ, and the image of a saint is a saint. And the power is not divided nor the glory shared, but the glory of the image becomes that of the one depicted in the image." Saint John of Damascus, *Three Treatises*, p. 42. Cited also in François Boespflug and Nicolas Lossky, eds., *Nicée II, 787–1987: Douze siècles d'images religieuses: Actes du colloque international "Nicée II"* (Paris: Cerf, 1987), p. 132. See Wirth, *L'image à l'époque romane*, p. 35. For Boulnois, John of Damascus invents an "*intentionality of veneration*: the icon is not a simple *object of knowledge*, coupled with the veneration of its intelligible signifier that would be limited to a reminder for us of the association in memory . . . neither is it a reality venerated in its *sole materiality*: the honor is given first to the materiality, but, since the contemplation of an image passes first through the bodily form, aiming at the original, in the same way, the veneration of the icon, passing through its materiality, aims at the reality of Christ or the saint that is represented." Boulnois, *Au-delà de l'image*, pp. 204–205. As Grumel explains, according to Theodore the Studite, "whoever venerates the image has venerated the one the image represents: he has not venerated the substance of the image, but the one who is painted in it." Grumel, "L'iconologie de saint Théodore Studite," p. 259. For more on proskynesis and the honor

rendered to the prototype in Theodore the Studite, see Grumel, "L'iconologie de saint Théodore Studite," p. 259 et seq.

223. *Decrees of the Ecumenical Councils,* ed. Norman P. Tanner, 2 vols. (Washington, DC: Georgetown University Press, 1990), vol. 1, pp. 135–36.

224. Dagron, *Décrire et peindre*, p. 70.

225. According to Dagron in *Décrire*, the name of the protoype associated with the image is enough to confer on it the value of a sign.

226. Cf. Wirth, "Structure et fonctions," pp. 32–40; Boulnois, *Au-delà de l'image*, pp. 206–81; Jean-Marie Sansterre, "Les justifications du culte des reliques dans le haut Moyen Âge," in Edina Bozóky and Anne-Marie Helvétius, eds., *Les Reliques: Objets, cultes, symboles* (Turnhout: Brepols, 1999), pp. 81–93.

227. For Hugh of Saint Victor, the "*transitus*" is the process by which "through the resemblance of visible things, we are elevated to the contemplation of invisible things." Cited in Baschet, *La civilisation* féodale, p. 695.

228. See Wirth, "Structure et fonctions," p. 51n36; Wirth, *L'image à l'époque romane*, p. 41; Jean-Claude Schmitt, "L'Occident, Nicée II et les images du VIIIe au XIIIe siècle" in François Boespflug and Nicolas Lossky, eds., *Nicée II, 787–1987: Douze siècles d'images religieuses: Actes du colloque international "Nicée II"* (Paris: Cerf, 1987), pp. 291–92. Saint Thomas (*Sum. Th.* 3rd pars, q. 25, a. 3) was to base the cult of images "on a totally rational basis by relying on, not the Fathers of the Church, but Aristotle. His well-known argument starts from the assertion that we can consider the image, insofar as it is a thing of stone or wood, independently from what it represents. But insofar as it is an image, it relates to the thing represented, and the movement of the soul towards it is, at the same time, a movement towards that thing." Wirth, "Structure et fonctions," p. 54. See also Wirth, *Qu'est-ce qu'une image?,* p. 89; Jean Wirth, *L'image à l'époque gothique (1140–1280)* (Paris: Cerf, 2008), p. 49 et seq. Vauchez also underlines the growing importance of images as *transitus*. Vauchez, *Sainthood in the Later Middle Ages*, pp. 444–48, 460.

229. This thinking was reactivated at the time of the debates about images in the sixteenth century. Cf. Fredrika H. Jacobs, *Votive Panels and Popular Piety in Early Modern Italy* (Cambridge, UK: Cambridge University Press, 2013), p. 165; Ralph Dekoninck, "Les Silènes de Gumppenberg: L'*Atlas Marianus* et la matière des images miraculeuses de la Vierge au regard du culte marial dans les anciens Pays-Bas," in Olivier Christin, Fabrice Flückiger, and Naïma Ghermani, eds., *Marie mondialisée: "L'Atlas Marianus" de Wilhelm Gumppenberg et les topographies sacrées de l'époque moderne* (Neuchâtel: Éditions Alphil-Presses universitaires

suisses, 2014), p. 213, citing the conference of Saint-Germain-en-Laye (1562) where the materiality of the image was entirely set aside, the image retaining only its power of transit.

230. Wirth, *L'image à l'époque romane*, p. 42 (my emphasis). Still, Gregory the Great writes: "We do not prostrate ourselves before the image as before the divinity, but we adore the one whom we remember through the image: newborn child, crucified, or seated upon a throne." Ibid., p. 46.

231. William of Auvergne, *De legibus*, *Opera*, I, Paris, 1674. Cited in Weill-Parot, *"Images astrologiques" au Moyen Âge et à la Renaissance*, p. 199 et seq. (my emphasis).

232. As Vauchez takes care to make clear, God acts *for* his saints and *through* his saints. Vauchez, *Sainthood in the Later Middle Ages*, pp. 461–62. For more on the image as an object putting into relation the earthly and celestial worlds, see also Baschet and Schmitt, *L'image*, p. 23.

233. This also recalls the cases of godparenting referred to by Dagron: "the baptized child being represented at the side of the saint who makes him his godchild." Dagron, *Décrire et peindre*, p. 72.

234. On the notion of the image as social agent, see Alfred Gell, *Art and Agency: An Anthropological Theory* (Oxford: Clarendon Press, 1998), chap. 7.

235. Grabar, *L'iconoclasme byzantin*, p. 104. In his analysis, Grabar makes use of the prayers written on the frescoes of Santa Maria Antica in Rome. These function as *ex-voto* offerings. Ibid., p. 99 et seq.: "they are like appeals (by way of paintings) to the saints that one had the artists depict, and that often, through the choice and close positioning of the figures, allow us to perceive the nature of the procedure that culminated in the making of the images."

236. For Vauchez, the meaning of the term *devotio* is precisely this: to put oneself in a position of dependence with regard to a saint, and to thus be under his or her protection. Vauchez, *Saints, prophètes et visionnaires*, p. 48.

237. We could say the same for the polyptychs that include the figures of donors in their panels, including those polyptychs designed to adorn altars.

238. For the East, see Bissera V. Pentcheva, *The Sensual Icon: Space, Ritual, and the Senses in Byzantium* (University Park, PA: Pennsylvania State University Press, 2010), and for the West, see Bynum, "Why all the Fuss about the Body?"

239. See especially Grabar, *Martyrium*, vol. 2, p. 208; Francesco Sabatini, Sergio Raffaelli, and Paolo D'Achille, *Il volgare nelle chiese di Roma: Messaggi graffiti, dipinti e incisi dal IX al XVI secolo* (Rome: Bonacci, 1987); Véronique Plesch, "Using or Abusing? On

the Significance of Graffiti on Religious Mural Paintings," in Luis Urbano Afonso and Vitor Serrao, eds., *Out of the Stream: Studies in Medieval and Renaissance Mural Painting* (Newcastle: Cambridge Scholars, 2007), pp. 42–68; Véronique Plesch, "Destruction or Preservation? The Meaning of Graffiti on Paintings in Religious Sites," in Virginia Chieffo Raguin, ed., *Art, Piety and Destruction in the Christian West, 1500–1700* (Farnham, UK: Ashgate, 2010), pp. 137–72; Gil Bartholeyns, Pierre-Olivier Dittmar, and Vincent Jolivet, *Image et transgression au Moyen Âge* (Paris: Presses universitaires de France, 2008), pp. 99–108; Jérémie Koering and Isolde Pludermacher, "Les graffitis d'artistes: Signes de dévotion artistique, Rome, Latium, XVe–XIXe siècles," *Revue de l'art* 184 (2014), pp. 25–34; and Marinis, "Piety," pp. 321–24.

240. On the image as body, see especially Schmitt, *Le Corps des images*; Georges Didi-Huberman, *L'image ouverte: Motifs de l'incarnation dans les arts visuel* (Paris: Gallimard, 2007), pp. 25–62; Gell, *Art and Agency*, p. 98: "Idols . . . are not depictions, not portraits, but (artefactual) *bodies*."

241. The representation of the Virgin with Child is on the right lateral wall of the nave at San Zeno, and the inscription is the following: "*1460 adì 24 zenaro morì Andre[e]a del Mantoa*." See Koering and Pludermacher, "Les graffitis d'artistes," p. 31. The inscription fits with the practice of testamentary vows.

242. Sansterre, "Sacralité," p. 56.

243. Dominique Rigaux, "Usages apotropaïques de la fresque dans l'Italie du Nord au XVe siècle," in François Boespflug and Nicolas Lossky, eds., *Nicée II, 787–1987: Douze siècles d'images religieuses: Actes du colloque international "Nicée II"* (Paris: Cerf, 1987), pp. 317–31; Rigaux, "Réflexions sur les usages apotropaïques de l'image peinte," pp. 158–60; Mario Sensi, "Santuari culti e riti 'ad repellendam pestem' tra medioevo ed età moderna," in Sofia Boesch Gajano and Lucetta Scaraffia, eds., *Luoghi sacri e spazi della santità* (Turin: Rosenberg e Sellier, 1990), pp. 141–42. This is also the hypothesis formulated by Bartholeyns, Dittmar, and Jolivet, *Image et transgression*, p. 131: "For purposes of preparations, in wine or to be used in amulets, they scratched certain images, collecting up the virtuous substance . . . . The gathered dust was held to protect its possessor from the plague, and it was, perhaps, often ingurgitated." See also Baschet, *La civilisation féodale*, p. 712.

244. The dust, mixed with water, was offered to the sick in a bowl bearing the image of the Virgin of Loreto (Cambridge, UK: Fitzwilliam Museum, inv. c. 2244–1928). Cf. Erin Giffin, "Détruire, reconstruire, redéfinir: la fragmentation volontaire de la Santa Casa de Loreto et ses altérations répliquées," *Perspective* 2 (2018), p. 211.

245. On the miraculous images, see Bissera V. Pentcheva, "The Performative Icon," *Art Bulletin* 88.4 (2006), p. 634; Freedberg, *The Power of Images*, pp. 99–135; Erik Thunø and Gerhard Wolf, eds., *The Miraculous Image in the Late Middle Ages and Renaissance* (Rome: "L'Erma" di Bretschneider, 2004); Megan Holmes, *The Miraculous Image in Renaissance Florence* (New Haven, CT: Yale University Press, 2013); and Dekoninck, "Les Silènes," p. 213.

246. Holmes, *The Miraculous Image*, pp. 168–77. As Holmes explains, the power becomes manifest most notably by animation: "moving, speaking, exuding bodily fluids like blood, tears and sweat, and demonstrating emotive states," or by changes in the image's appearance (change of color or facial expression). See also Jean-Marie Sansterre, "Vivantes ou comme vivantes: L'animation miraculeuse d'images de la Vierge entre Moyen Âge et époque moderne," *Revue de l'histoire des religions* 232.2 (2015), p. 162 et seq. for an overview of the origins of the living image in Christian culture.

247. For more on pilgrimages and miraculous images, see, among others, Freedberg, *The Power of Images*, pp. 99–128.

248. As Gilbert Simondon explains in *Imagination et invention (1965–1966)* (Paris: Presses universitaires de France, 2014), p. 183: "The movement from technicity to sacrality, without any modification of the object, is made possible by the rejecting the object's origin into the past, not into an historical past, but into the absolute past of the ancestral and mythical original sources."

249. On this dressed up simplicity, see Valeria E. Genovese, *Statue vestite e snodate: Un percorso* (Pisa: Edizioni della Normale, 2011); Dekoninck, "Les Silènes"; and Holmes, *The Miraculous Image*, pp. 163–68. For an historiographical approach to the phenomenon, see Marlène Albert Llorca, "Les statues habillées dans le catholicisme: Entre histoire de l'art, histoire religieuse et anthropologie," *Archives de sciences sociales des religions* 164 (2013), pp. 11–23.

250. Sansterre, "Vivantes ou comme vivantes," 168.

251. Bynum, *Christian Materiality*, notably p. 282. See also Holmes, *The Miraculous Image*, pp. 166, 182: "*The transcendent sacred being, the Virgin, is thus immanently and actively linked with her physical image, as she obtains the quality of visibility to human corporeal vision. Her material effigy frescoed [la Madonna delle Carceri] on the wall is conceived as a superficial skin that, through transfiguration, becomes 'unstuck' or 'detached' [dispicchar] from the plaster supporting structure and moves about freely the old prison grounds.*"

252. Montaigne was at Loreto from April 23 to 26, 1581. He made a votive offering,

presenting a silver relief depicting himself in prayer before the Virgin Mary, accompanied by his wife and daughter.

253. Michel de Montaigne, *Montaigne's Travel Journal*, trans. Donald M. Frame (San Francisco: North Point Press, 1983), p. 108.

254. One of the first historians of la Santa Casa, Silvio Serragli, attributes the disappearance of a substantial part of the frescoes to an excess of devotion: "Trè sono le Pareti, dove appariscono le figure, cominciando da alto, sino alla, mezca [sic], incirca, altezza di muro; mancando il resto, per l'antichità del tempo dice il Torsellino. Io più crederei dalla indiscrita divotione del Popolo, che sempre toccando, e stropocciando, con tanto ardore, I Santi Muri; appunto è maraviglia, che non si logorino l'istessi pietre." Silvio Serragli, *La Santa Casa, Abbellita* (Loreto: Paolo and Giovanni Battista Serafini Fratelli, 1634), p. 60. Cited in Giffin, "Détruire," pp. 211, 216n9.

255. On the principle of substitution, see Christopher Wood, *Forgery, Replica, Fiction: Temporalities of German Renaissance Art* (Chicago: Chicago University Press, 2008), pp. 36–42; Alexander Nagel and Christopher Wood, *Anachronic Renaissance* (New York: Zone Books, 2010), esp. chaps. 2 and 3.

256. *Eusebius' Ecclesiastical History,* trans. C. F. Cruse (Peabody, MA: Hendrickson, 1998), pp. 253–54.

257. Raoul Rochette had speculated that the sculpted group might represent not Christ and the bleeding woman, but rather the figure of a personified Province prostrated before the emperor. Raoul Rochette, cited by André Pératé, "Note sur le groupe de Panéas," *Mélanges d'archéologie et d'histoire* 5 (1885), p. 305. Von Dobschütz for his part, thought it was a representation of Asklepios. For my purposes, who it was that the group represented is less important than the tradition that was to be built up around Eusebius's account. Ernst von Dobschütz, *Christusbilder: Untersuchungen zur christlichen Legende* (Leipzig: J. C. Hinrichs, 1899), p. 198.

258. Holmes emphasizes the importance of physical contact in the economy of miraculous images. Holmes, *The Miraculous Image*, pp. 200–202. See also Bynum, *Christian Materiality*, p. 65 et seq.

259. Ludolph of Saxony, *Vita Christi* (1338). In his commentary, he stresses the transformation undergone by any material substance that had been contact with the Christ: "a plant that was at first ineffective grew under the image of Jesus Christ, and, once it became tall enough to touch the image's garment, it had such virtue as to heal all maladies." Cited in Pierre-Antoine Fabre, "L'image possible: La femme qui perdait son sang

à Panéas, et que Jésus miraculeusement guérit, dans le discours de l'image chrétienne," in Barbara Baert, ed., *The Woman with the Blood Flow (Mark 5:24–34): Narrative, Iconic, and Anthropological Spaces* (Louvain: Peeters, 2014), p. 324.

260. Notably in the *Letter of Germanos to Thomas of Claudiopolis* or in the *Letter of Gregory II to Germanos.* Mention of it is found also in Saint John of Damascus, *Three Treatises*, pp. 123–24. See Pératé, "Note," p. 306; *La vie d'Étienne le Jeune par Étienne le Diacre*, ed. Marie-France Auzépy (London: Routledge, 1997), pp. 191–92; Fabre, "L'image possible," p. 317.

261. Holmes, *The Miraculous Image*, pp. 20–21, 119–41.

262. Antonio degli Agli, *De rationibus fidei*, ca. 1460, fol. 50 v., ms. in the collection of the Biblioteca nazionale, Florence, Conventi Soppressi, B.9.1268, cited in Holmes, *The Miraculous Image*, p. 21. According to Holmes, and also Nagel and Wood (*Anachronic Renaissance*, pp. 40–50), certain Renaissance artists aimed to produce recreations of the *Christ* of Paneas. This was allegedly the case with Carpaccio in his *Saint Augustine in His Study* (Venise, Scuola di San Giorgio degli Schiavoni) and the bronze of Christ Blessing from the beginning of the 1490s (Milan, Galleria Poldi-Pezzoli).

263. Da Carpi, *Praeter*, fol. 142v. Cf. Giuseppe Scavizzi, *The Controversy on Images from Calvin to Baronius* (New York: Peter Lang, 1992), p. 170; Nagel and Wood, *Anachronic Renaissance*, p. 376n23; Alexander Nagel, *The Controversy of Renaissance Art* (Chicago: University of Chicago Press, 2011), pp. 135–36.

264. Louis Richeome, *L'idolâtrie huguenote figurée au patron de la vieille payenne* (Lyon : Chez Pierre Rigaud, 1608), cited in Fabre, "L'image possible," pp. 311–34 *passim.* Fabre mentions several other occurrences of the story of Paneas, including those that appear in Louis Richeome, *Les Trois Discours pour la religion catholique, des miracles, des saints, et des images* (Bordeaux: S. Millange, 1597), chaps. 15 and 35, and in Pierre Coton, *Institution catholique* (Paris: Claude Chappelet, 1610), chap. 21.

265. Fabre also stresses this point. Fabre, "L'image possible," p. 323.

266. This story is also reported by François Lemée, and with a subtle allusion to the psychological determinants of the belief (placebo effect?): the plants were "perfectly good for all sorts of sicknesses [but] perhaps these plants only had this virtue *because of the fact that people were persuaded of it.*" François Lemée, *Traité des statues*, eds. Diane H. Bodart and Hendrik Ziegler, 2 vols (Weimar: VDG, [1688] 2012), vol. 1, chap. 14, p. 375.

267. Kriss-Rettenbeck, *Bilder*, p. 45; Bartholeyns, Dittmar, and Jolivet, *Image et transgression*, p. 131.

268. Sansterre, "Sacralité," p. 74.

269. For more on this idea and its context, see Signori, *Wunder*, pp. 94–136.

270. The departmental archives of Loire-Atlantique, G 53. I am grateful to Bruno Restif for having made me aware of this source.

271. Cf. Bruno Restif, "Les statues touchées et malmenées dans le cadre de rites religieux en Bretagne (XVIIe–XXe siècle): Attestations, silences, enjeux internes au catholicisme," conference presentation *La Statuaire entre hommages et outrages: Corps rossés, blâmés ou adorés de la sculpture moderne en Europe et Nouvelle Espagne (XVIe–XVIIIe siècle)*, Toulouse, November 14–16, 2012.

272. Ralph Dekoninck, "Une idolâtrie iconoclaste? Usures et brisures pieuses des images saintes," in Agnès Lafont, Christian Belin, and Nicholas Myers, eds., *L'Image brisée aux XVIe et XVIIe siècles / Breaking the Image in the Renaissance* (Paris: Classiques Garnier, 2019), pp. 162–63.

273. Augustin-François Wichmans, *Brabantia Mariana tripartita* (Anvers: Joannem Cnobbaert, 1632), pp. 216–17.

274. Wichmans, *Brabantia Mariana tripartita.*

275. Gumppenberg, 1659, vol. 3, p. 67, cited in Dekoninck, "Les Silènes," p. 220. The Jesuit Pierre Bouille reported on the miracles following upon the ingestion of a mixture containing wood of Notre-Dame de Foy that had been made into replicas of the miraculous image. Pierre Bouille, *Dame de la Foy: Histoire de la découverte et merveilles de l'image Nostre Dame de Foy trouvée en un chesne près la ville de Dinan pays de Liège l'an MDCIX* (Liège: Jean Ouwerx, 1620), p. 220. On the statuette and its model (probably a statuette created in a studio in Utrecht at the beginning of the fifteenth century), see Ingmar Reesing and Michael Hoyle, "Notre-Dame de Foy: The Reuse and Dissemination of a Late Medieval Figurine of the Virgin in the Low Countries," *Simiolus. Netherlands Quarterly for the History of Art* 33.3 (2007/2008), pp. 145–65.

276. This practice has also been attested in connection with other miraculous images, such as Notre-Dame-des-Ermites at Einsiedeln, and also Mariahilf at Innsbruck. For a discussion of the latter, see Larry Silver, "Full of Grace: 'Mariolatry' in Post-Reformation Germany," in Michael W. Cole and Rebecca Zorach, eds., *The Idol in the Age of Art: Objects, Devotions and the Early Modern World* (London: Routledge, 2016), pp. 289–316.

277. On the Gnadenbilder, see Peter Dinzelbacher, "Religiöses Erleben von bildender Kunst in autobiographischen und biographischen Zeugnissen des Hoch- und

Spätmittelalters," in Klaus Schreiner, ed., *Frömmigkeit im Mittelalter: Politisch-soziale Kontexte, visuelle Praxis, körperliche Ausdrucksformen* (Munich: Wilhelm Fink, 2002), pp. 299–330. For more on the statuettes (*Schabmadonnen*), see Mathilde Tobler, "'Wahre Abbildung': Marianische Gnadenbildkopien in der schweizerischen Quart des Bistums Konstanz," *Der Geschichtsfreund: Mitteilungen des Historischen Vereins Zentralschweiz* 144 (1991), pp. 174–83; Franz-Josef Sladeczek, "Les copies de la statue miraculeuse d'Einsiedeln," in Cécile Dupeux, Pieter Jezler, and Jean Wirth, eds., *Iconoclasme: Vie et mort de l'image médiévale* (Paris: Somogy, 2001), exhibition catalog, cat. 102, pp. 250–51; Christoph Kürzeder, *Als die Dinge heilig waren: Gelebte Frömmigkeit im Zeitalter des Barock* (Regensburg [Ratisbonne]: Schnell & Steiner, 2005), p. 129; Rüdiger Rothkegel, "Mittelalterliche und neuzeitliche Tonstatuetten aus dem Kanton Zug," *Zeitschrift für Schweizerische Archäologie und Kunstgeschichte* 63.1 (2006), pp. 155–59; Josef Imbach, *Marienverehrung zwischen Glaube und Aberglaube* (Düsseldorf: Patmos, 2008), pp. 185–87. Similar statuettes were also made in Spain. See, especially concerning the Virgin of Granada, Felipe Pereda, *Images of Discord: Poetics and Politics of the Sacred Image in Fifteenth-Century Spain*, trans. Consuelo Lopez-Morillas (London/Turnhout: Harvey Miller, 2018), part 3, p. 147.

278. Claude Jacquet, *Histoire de l'origine, du progrès, et de l'état présent de la sainte chapelle située dans l'illustre Abaie des Ermites, ou D'Einsiedeln de l'Ordre de S. Benoit, en Suisse* (Einsiedeln: J. E. Kälin 1699), p. 489. The passage in question does not appear in the first edition of 1686.

279. Rothkegel, "Mittelalterliche und neuzeitliche Tonstatuetten," p. 155.

280. Claude Jacquet and Abbé Nicolas, *Histoire de la S. chapelle de Notre-Dame-des-Ermites . . . revue, corrigée, & augmentée de deux cens soixante miracles* (Einsiedeln: Jean-Everhard Kälin, 1750), p. 524. Several other miracles by way of ingestion are mentioned. See ibid., pp. 523–25.

281. Ibid., p. 528.

282. Ibid., p. 520.

283. On the status of sacraments in the premodern era, see Kürzeder, *Als die Dinge*, pp. 57–108.

284. Schmitt, *Le Corps, les rites*, p. 49; Wirth, *L'Image à l'époque romane*.

285. Sansterre, "Sacralité," p. 57.

286. For Freedberg (*The Power of Images*, p. 89), the blessing of altarpieces was an essential part of Christian ritual, but the act did not acquire the same value as in other cultures.

287. "Even the most perfect reproduction of a work of art is lacking in one element: its presence in time and space, its unique existence at the place where it happens to be . . . that which withers in the age of mechanical reproduction is the aura of the work of art . . . by making many reproductions it substitutes a plurality of copies for a unique existence." Walter Benjamin, "The Work of Art in the Age of Mechanical Reproduction," in Walter Benjamin, *Illuminations: Essays and Reflections*, trans. Harry Zohn (New York: Schocken Books, 1969), pp. 220–21. Recently, the artist Dieter Frölich has investigated this question, creating a work made up of hundreds of *Schabmadonnen* arranged one next to another. The idea that these figures might be vehicles of some sort of holiness is hard to maintain in the face of their obvious industrial production. See the exhibition catalog Katja Lembke, ed., *Madonna. Frau, Mutter, Kultfigur* (Dresden: Sandstein, 2015).

288. For more on these molds and on the general history of the Agnus Dei, I refer the reader to Eugène Mangenot, "*Agnus Dei*," in E. Amman, E. Mangenot, and A. Vacant, eds., *Dictionnaire de théologie catholique* (Paris: Letouzey et Ané, 1923), pp. 605–14; Aislinn Muller, "The *agnus dei,* Catholic Devotion, and Confessional Politics in Early Modern England," *British Catholic History* 34.1 (2018), pp. 1–28; Anne Lepoittevin, "*Picciolini, picolini* et *piccioli*: La fabrique romaine des *Agnus Dei* (1563–1700)," *Archives de sciences sociales des religions* 183 (2018), pp. 87–117. I am grateful to the latter for allowing me to see her article before publication.

289. Cited in Weill-Parot, *"Images astrologiques" au Moyen Âge et à la Renaissance*, p. 199 et seq. (my emphasis).

290. Martin Luther, *Von dem geweichten wasser, und des Bapsts Agnus Dei* (Augsbourg, 1539), cited in Lepoittevin, "*Picciolini*," p. 88. As a result of this change from singular to plural, the *Agnus Dei* were no longer sacred representations of the Lamb of God, but idols like the pagan simulacra.

291. The reproduction of this sheet in Bernard Picart's work did not have the same apologetic function as did the original. As Caroline Van Eck has noted, the inclusion of Christian engravings within an ensemble composed of illustrations coming from "idolatrous" religions could not help but produce a critical effect with regard to Catholicism. Judging from all these engravings, what difference could there be between Christian and pagan practices? Caroline Van Eck, *François Lemée et la statue de Louis XIV sur la place des Victoires: Les origines des théories ethnologiques du fétichisme* (Paris: Éd. De la Maison des sciences de l'homme, 2013), p. 41.

292. Girolamo Bertondelli, *Miracoli operati dall'Onnipotenza divina per mezo li Agnus Papali Benedetti dalla Santa Memoria d'Innocentio XI* (Venice: Dominico Louisa, 1691).

After having been put on the Papal index in 1691, the work was to be slightly revised and to go through several reeditions.

293. "*Si risolse la madre Cecilia Maestra di Nouitie, dargli à digiuno nel tempo de parosismi febrili un poco del Agnus Papale, esortata prima à prenderlo con ogni divotione, e fede, che il Santo Pontefice Innocentio l'impetrerebbe la sua perfetta salute, così successe, doppò per trè mattine ricevuto detto Agnus Papale restò perfetamente risanata.*" Bertondelli, *Miracoli operati dall'Onnipotenza divina*, p. 5.

294. "*Ricorse dalla sudetta Madre Maestra Cecilia, acciò gli dasse un poco de sudetto Agnus Papale col qual haveva veduto la liberatione dell'Infermità della sudetta Novitia, ricevuto in bocca, poco dopo dal dolor de Denti liberata si ritrovò.*" Ibid. The text mentions several other miracles by ingestion. See ibid., pp. 9, 15, 16, 19.

295. We note in passing that the author's function stands as "proof" of the superior power of God and his ministers over men, since this is a man from the art who recognizes the limits of medicine.

296. It was not the case that all the *Agnus Dei* consistently bore the arms, name, and date. Still, the inclusion of any one of the three was enough to signal the Pope's presence in the object.

297. We should note here the case of three prints of the Madonna of Einsiedeln, engraved in 1466 by the master craftsman E. S. for the celebration of the 500th anniversary of the monastery's founding. Several tens of thousands of these engravings were sold over the course of the festivities. Cf. Peter Schmidt, "Die Kupferstiche des Meisters E. S. zur Wallfahrt nach Einsiedeln: Einige Überlegungen zum Publikum, Programm und Kontext," in *Artibus: Kulturwissenschaft und deutsche Philologie (Festschrift für Dieter Wuttke)* (Wiesbaden: Stephan Füssel, 1994), pp. 293–318; and Suzanne Karr Schmidt and Kimberly Nichols, *Altered and Adorned: Using Renaissance Prints in Daily Life* (New Haven, CT: Yale University Press, 2011), pp. 65–67.

298. Giuliano di Francesco Guizzelmi, *Historia della apparition et altri miracoli di Madonna Sancta del Carcere di Prato* (Prato: Biblioteca Roncioniana, 1505), codex 87. Another manuscript, attributed to Andrea del Germanino, dating from the end of the 1480s, also relates many miracles worked by way of the image. Cf. Robert Maniura, "The Images and Miracles of Santa Maria delle Carceri," in Erik Thunø and Gerhard Wolf, eds., *The Miraculous Image in the Late Middle Ages and Renaissance* (Rome: "L'Erma" di Bretschneider, 2004), pp. 86–95, and Robert Maniura, *Art and Miracle in Renaissance Tuscany* (Cambridge, UK: Cambridge University Press, 2018).

299. Cf. Maniura, *Art and Miracle*, chap. 4.

300. The work of construction, starting in 1485, was directed by Giuliano da Sangallo.

301. "*[U]na Vergine Maria, che havesse toccato la Madonna del Carcere di Prato, per porla adosso, a una donna che era stata tramortita, & chome morta, presso a tre dì.*" Guizzelmi, *Historia della apparition*, fols. 42v.–44r., cited in Maniura, "The Images," pp. 86–87n9; *Art and Miracle*, pp. 124, 224–225n28.

302. "*[I]o gli donai: una figura della Vergine Maria del Carcere: la quale haveva toccato la Sua Gloriosissima figura . . . Quella figura di charta, puosono alla bocca di decta Mona Lisabetta: & poi gliela puosono in se: & incontinenti decta Mona Lisabetta, la quale prima era chome morta: tornò in se.*" Maniura, "The Images," pp. 86–87n9; *Art and Miracle*, pp. 124, 224–25n28.

303. "*& dixe chome haveva veduto porsi alla bocca quella Gloriosissima Vergine Maria: & chome a lei si racomandò, di buono cuore: & chome haveva ricevuto gratia: dalla sua Maiestà.*" Maniura, "The Images," pp. 86–87n9; *Art and Miracle*, pp. 124, 224–25n28.

304. With other miracles, he takes care to specify "*facta alla similitudine.*" Cf. Maniura, "The Images," p. 92n20.

305. Maniura points out that nine of the sixteen miracles involving an image include physical contact between the object and the miraculous image. Ibid., pp. 90–91.

306. Ibid., p. 93.

307. Guizzelmi, *Historia della apparitione*. Cf. Maniura, "The Images," p. 82; Maniura, *Art and Miracle*, p. 125.

308. "*Ricordo chome a dì 18 di magio io comperai in firence tante Vergini Marie delle Carcere. Spesi soldi sedici. Cioè Vergini Marie di charta di più fatte.*" Guizzelmi, *Memoriale A*, Biblioteca Roncioniana, Prato, Codex 759, fol. 21v. Cited in Maniura, "The Images," p. 87n10; Maniura, *Art and Miracle*, p. 135.

309. For more on the materiality of prints in the early modern period, see David S. Areford, "Print Trouble: Notes on a Medium In Between," in Colum Hourihane, ed., *From Minor to Major: The Minor Arts in Medieval Art History* (Princeton, NJ: Princeton University Press, 2012), pp. 229–54.

310. See Erich Auerbach, "Figura," in Erich Auerbach, *Scenes from the Drama of European Literature* (Minneapolis: University of Minnesota Press, 1984), pp. 13, 15, 22.

311. Auerbach explains that the term "figura" is almost always used by the Church Fathers to designate a real, material, and historical instance of an entity that is to come, for example, Joshua as a prefiguration of Christ ("*the notion of a figura under which something other, future, true, lies concealed*"). Auerbach, "Figura," p. 29 et seq., p. 45 for the quotation.

312. For Wood, "*substitution works only when the process of transmission is obscure or forgotten,*" and this, he argues, is generally impossible with an engraving. Wood, *Forgery*, pp. 224–25. Areford has shown that this was not the case. Areford, "Print Trouble," pp. 249, 252–54. The print could, despite certain signs of its production, become a real substitute for the archetype. See also David S. Areford, "Multiplying the Sacred: the Fifteenth-Century Woodcut as Reproduction, Surrogate, Simulation," in Peter Parshall, ed., *The Woodcut in Fifteenth-Century Europe* (Washington, DC: National Gallery of Art, 2009), pp. 118–53.

313. Maniura, "The Images," pp. 81–86; Maniura, *Art and Miracle*, chap. 1.

314. For more on the *Schluckbildchen*, see Kriss-Rittenbeck, *Bilder*, pp. 33–48, esp. pp. 42–45, and p. 141n79 for the references to the prior literature; Erwin Richter, "Esszettel," in *Reallexikon zur Deutschen Kunstgeschichte*, vol. 6, 1973, Munich, col. 42–48; C. Schneegasse, "Schluckbildchen: Ein Beispiel der 'Populärgraphik' zur aktiven Aneignung," *Volkskunst: Zeitschrift für volkstümliche Sachkultur* 6 (1983), pp. 27–32; Rigaux, "Réflexions sur les usages apotropaïques de l'image peinte," pp. 158–60; Bartholeyns, Dittmar, and Jolivet, *Image et transgression*, p. 131; Kürzeder, *Als die Dinge*, pp. 129–30; Michael Rintelen, "Schluckbilder und Esszettel: Fragmente zum Thema Schauen und Essen," in Daniel Hees et Gundolf Winter, eds., *Kreativität und Werkerfahrung: Festschrift für Ilse Krahl zum 65. Geburtstag* (Duisburg: Gilles und Francke, 1988), pp. 112–16; Karr Schmidt and Nichols, eds., *Altered*, pp. 68–69; Flood, "Mimesis, Mediation and the Ingestion of the Sacred," p. 484; Roland Halbritter, "Südtiroler Breverln: Amulette zwischen Magie und Glaube?" *Der Schlern* 72.1 (1998), pp. 39–64; Dominik Wunderlin, "Guérir par ingestion: La consommation d'images de dévotion bénites est censée apporter la guérison," in Cécile Dupeux, Pieter Jezler, and Jean Wirth, eds., *Iconoclasme: Vie et mort de l'image médiévale* (Paris: Somogy, 2001), exhibition catalog, pp. 256–57; Dekoninck, "Une idolâtrie iconoclaste?," pp. 160–61.

315. Cf. Dinzelbacher, "Religiöses Erleben von bildender Kunst, pp. 299–330.

316. At the beginning of the twentieth century, the editor of *L'Ami du clergé paroissial*, advised that "the swallowing of paper images for the purpose of regaining health is allowed, provided that it does not involve any merely idle observance." *L'Ami du clergé paroissial: Supplément à l'Ami du clergé* (Langres, 1899–1905), p. 561. At the same time, the practice was bitterly criticized by the anticlerical camp: *L'Éclaireur de l'Ain*, July 6, 1902, p. 2; *La petite guerre*, March 25, 1903.

317. Richter, "Esszettel," col. 43.

318. Ibid., and Rigaux, "Réflexions sur les usages apotropaïques de l'image peinte," p. 159.

319. For more on the benediction, see Wunderlin, "Guérir," p. 257. On the contact with the holy image, see Maniura, "The Images," p. 94, and Holmes, *The Miraculous Image*, pp. 177, 200.

320. Richter, "Esszettel," col. 42–48.

321. We should recall here the words of Thierry Davila in "Esthétique et clinique: Brève introduction à l'art médecin" *Les Cahiers du MNAM* 67 (1999), p. 101. Although Davila is not referring specifically to this practice, his point fits it perfectly: "Incorporation of the image, of the work, having become entirely and unto itself a physical substance that changes the body of the one who venerates it, i.e., of the one who ingurgitates it."

322. See the plate featuring twelve figures of Mary (ca. 1780) reproduced in Manfred Brauneck, *Religiöse Volkskunst: Votivgaben, Andachtsbilder, Hinterglas, Rosenkranz, Amulette* (Cologne: DuMont, 1978), p. 298.

323. Cf. Filocalo Caputo, *Il Monte Carmelo in cui si tratta della miracolosa imagine di N.S. del Carmine del Regio Convento di Napoli* (Naples: Lazaro Scoriggio, 1636).

324. According to Richter ("Esszettel"), if no *Schuckbildchen* or *Esszettel* were available, people would take other devotional images to cut up and dissolve.

325. Kriss-Rettenbeck, *Bilder*, pp. 42–45.

326. Ibid.

327. Mayeur-Jaouen, "La fonction," p. 67.

328. Behrend, "Photo Magic."

329. Ibid., p. 139.

330. For more on the transfer of sacral charge, see Olivier Christin and Fabrice Flückiger, "Introduction: *L'Atlas Marianus* de Wilhelm Gumppenberg: Une topographie sacrée à l'âge de la science Classique," in Olivier Christin, Fabrice Flückiger and Naïma Ghermani, eds., *Marie mondialisée: "L'Atlas Marianus" de Wilhelm Gumppenberg et les topographies sacrées de l'époque modern* (Neuchâtel: Éd. Alphil-Presses universitaires suisses, 2014), pp. 9–23; Dekoninck, "Les Silènes," p. 211 et seq.; and also this passage in Frédéric Cousinié, *Trajectoire des images: Culte marial et intermédialité dans la France du XVIIe siècle* (Paris: Éd. 1:1), 2017, pp. 62–63: "This operation necessarily involves the maintenance, more or less economical (regarding its symbolic effectiveness), of at least one piece of identifying data (a semiotic characteristic belonging to the ontological definition) of the original "piction" [W. J. T. Mitchell] that, itself, was held to be one of the specific incarnations of the virtual "image" of the heavenly Virgin. This piece of data could be its

title . . . ; its *form* . . . ; its *iconography* . . . ; its *substance* . . . ; the representational *medium* . . . ; the *place* of its exhibition . . . , but not the identity of its author."

331. On copies and the notion of the multiple in the medieval and modern periods, see Cupperi, "Introduction: Never Identical," in Walter Cupperi, ed., *Multiples in Pre-Modern Art* (Zurich: Diaphanes, 2014), pp. 7–28; Michele Tomasi, ed., *L'Art multiplié: Production de masse, en série, pour le marché dans les arts entre Moyen Âge et Renaissance* (Rome: Viella, 2011), pp. 7–23.

332. Another example is the plate made by J. M. Söckler, published around 1780–1790, where we see miraculous images of the Virgin (Altötting, Zell, etc.) along with images of Jesus.

333. Christin and Flückiger, "Introduction," p. 18.

334. Wichmans, *Brabantia.*

335. On the miraculous image and the devotions addressed to it, see Pierre Bouille, *Brève histoire de l'invention et miracles de l'image de Nostre Dame de Foy, trouvée en un chesne à Foy les Dinant, l'an 1609* (Liège: Jean Ouwerx, 1620); Christian Pacco, "La statuette miraculeuse de Foy Notre-Dame, état de la question," *Annales de la Société archéologique de Namur* 83 (2009), pp. 131–52; Ralph Dekoninck, Annick Delfosse, and Christian Pacco, eds., *Foy-Notre-Dame: Art, politique et religion,* special issue of the *Annales de la Société archéologique de Namur* 83 (2009); Ralph Dekoninck, "*Propagatio Imaginum*: The Translated Images of Our Lady of Foy," in Christine Göttler and Mia Mochizuki, eds., *The Nomadic Object: The Challenge of World for Early Modern Religious Art* (Leiden: Brill, 2018), p. 252 et seq.; Dekoninck, "Une idolâtrie iconoclaste?," pp. 161–62.

336. Félix Fries, *Histoire de Notre-Dame de Foy* (Namur: A. Godenne, 1909), p. 105, cited in Dekoninck, "Les Silènes," p. 219. See also André Haquin, "La dévotion à Notre-Dame de Foy au Québec (XVIIe siècle) et à New York (XXe siècle)," *Annales de la Société archéologique de Namur* 83 (2009), pp. 193–204; Dekoninck, "*Propagatio Imaginum.*" See Muriel Clair, "Notre-Dame de Foy en Nouvelle-France (1669–1675): Histoire des statuettes de Foy et des *wampum* des Hurons chrétiens," *Annales de la Société archéologique de Namur* 83 (2009), p. 180, for the extract from the letter.

337. Ingestion such as this was already noted by Bouille, *Brève histoire*, p. 29.

338. Jacquet and Nicolas, *Histoire de la S. chapelle,* p. 520.

339. This fits in with the cartographical approach taken in Gumppenberg's work. Cf. Christin and Flückiger, "Introduction." See also, for the French Marian network in the seventeenth century, Cousinié, *Trajectoire*, p. 51 et seq.

CHAPTER TWO: IMAGINING INGESTION

1. "L'estomac aussi est exemplaire: conversion, assimilation, rejet, une main sur l'humeur, une autre sur les rêves."

2. See especially Danielle Jacquart, *La médecine médiévale dans le cadre parisien (XIV*[e]*–XV*[e] *siècle)* (Paris: Fayard, 1998), pp. 477–500; Jean-Pierre Bénézet, *Pharmacie et médicament en méditerranée occidentale (XIIIe–XVe siècles)* (Paris: Honoré Champion, 1999), pp. 439–598; Nicolas Weill-Parot, *Les "Images astrologiques" au Moyen Âge et à la Renaissance: Spéculations intellectuelles et pratiques magiques (XIIe–XVe siècle)* (Paris: Champion, 2002), pp. 450–55; and Jacques Jouanna, *Hippocrates,* trans. M. B. DeBevoise (Baltimore, MD: Johns Hopkins University Press, 1999). It was only with the work of Marie François Xavier Bichat that the "anatomico-clinical method" was to supplant the Hippocratic system.

3. Paula Alexandra da Silva Veiga, *Health and Medicine in Ancient Egypt: Magic and Science* (Oxford: BAR International Series, [1967] 2009).

4. Annie Gasse, *Les stèles d'Horus sur les crocodiles* (Paris: RMN, 2004), p. 25. My emphasis.

5. Jouanna, *Hippocrates*, pp. 326–28.

6. Helen King, *Greek and Roman Medicine* (London: Bristol Classical Press, 2001); Jouanna, *Hippocrates*, esp. pp. 323–65. Jouanna stresses, however, that the stomach was not precisely defined at the time. The word *gaster* was generally used to refer to the stomach, but it could also refer to the abdomen. Jouanna, *Hipppocrates*, p. 314. On dietetics, see Innocenzo Mazzini, "Diet and Medicine in the Ancient World," in Jean-Louis Flandrin and Massimo Montanari, eds., *Food: A Culinary History from Antiquity to the Present*, trans. Clarissa Botsford, et al. (New York: Columbia University Press, 1999), pp. 141–52; Danielle Jacquart, "La nourriture et le corps au Moyen Âge," *Cahiers de recherches médiévales et humanistes* 13 (2006), pp. 259-66; Marilyn Nicoud, "Savoirs et pratiques diététiques au Moyen Âge," *Cahiers de recherches médiévales et humanistes* 13 (2006), pp. 243–44.

7. King, *Greek and Roman Medicine*, p. 42: "Although the fluids are the most important features of this body, the solid organs also have 'faculties' or powers. They can attract or repel, retain or expel. An organ can be too weak to attract the nutritive blood from the liver, but also the channels can be narrowed by obstruction, or the fluids they carry can be too thick and move too slowly, perhaps because the patient is eating the wrong foods. Illness can therefore be due to a fault in an organ, a channel or a fluid." See also Jouanna, *Hippocrates*, pp. 314–17.

8. Véronique Dasen, "Le pouvoir des pierres: De la *sphragis* au médicament estampillé

dans le monde gréco-romain," in Thomas Galoppin and Cécile Guillaume-Pey, eds., *Ce que peuvent les pierres: Vie et puissance des matériaux lithiques entre rites et savoirs* (Liège: Presses universitaires de Liège, 2021), p. 139.

9. Dasen, "Le pouvoir des pierres."

10. Weill-Parot, "*Images astrologiques*," p. 441.

11. Ibid., pp. 455–56.

12. This was Galen's point of view, but it was also the opinion of Avicenna, who was also to be considered an authority on the subject in the Middle Ages. "In his *Canon* Avicenna defines a *complexio* as that which arises out of the reciprocal action and passion of the primary qualities," Par-Gunnar Ottosson, *Scholastic Medicine and Philosophy: A Study of Commentaries on Galen's* Tegni *(ca. 1300–1450)* (Naples: Bibliopolis, 1984), pp. 134–35. See also Jacquart, *La médecine médiévale*.

13. Marc Augé, *Génie du paganisme* (Paris: Gallimard, 2008), p. 141.

14. As Weill-Parot writes, before the fifteenth century, it was essentially natural magic that was practiced. Weill-Parot, "*Images astrologiques*," p. 449.

15. Ibid., p. 455: "God conferred on things wondrous virtues." Jacques Le Goff, "The Marvelous in the Medieval West," in *The Medieval Imagination*, trans. Arthur Goldhammer (Chicago: University of Chicago Press, 1988), pp. 27–44.

16. Bénézet, *Pharmacie et médicament*, p. 440; Weill-Parot, "*Images astrologiques*," p. 538.

17. Arnald of Villanova, *De parte operativa*, fol. 127ra, cited in Weill-Parot, "*Images astrologiques*," pp. 465–67.

18. Weill-Parot, "*Images astrologiques*," p. 470.

19. Giorgio Anselmi, *Tractatus*, IV, pars 1, cap, 1, fol. 118r., cited in Weill-Parot, "*Images astrologiques*," p. 626.

20. Ibid., p. 628.

21. See the previous chapter.

22. Weill-Parot, "*Images astrologiques*," p. 451. See Avicenna, *The Canon of Medicine*, Volume 1, trans. O. Cameron Gruner and Mazar H. Shah (Chicago: Kazi Publications, Inc., 1999), p. 219.

23. Weill-Parot, "*Images astrologiques*," pp. 459–74.

24. Henri de Lubac, *Corpus Mysticum: The Eucharist and the Church in the Middle Ages*, trans. Gemma Simmonds, CJ, with Richard Price and Christopher Stephens (Notre Dame, IN: University of Notre Dame Press, 2007), pp. 13–17.

25. *De Universo*, 1. 5, c. 10, Patr. Lat., III, 131. Cf. Lubac, *Corpus Mysticum*, p. 101.

26. Ibid., pp. 13–36.

27. Cf. Jérôme Baschet, *La civilisation féodale: De l'an mil à la colonisation de l'Amérique* (Paris: Flammarion, 2006), p. 600.

28. Baschet, *La civilisation féodale*, pp. 223–26, 600–603.

29. Certain statues could serve a reserve for the consecrated host. Caroline Walker Bynum, *Holy Feast and Holy Fast: The Religious Significance of Food to Medieval Women* (Berkeley: University of California Press, 1988), p. 268, and Miri Rubin, *Corpus Christi: The Eucharist in Late Medieval Culture* (Cambridge, UK: Cambridge University Press, 1991), p. 145.

30. Jean-Claude Schmitt, *Le corps des images: Essais sur la culture visuelle au Moyen Âge* (Paris: Gallimard, 2002), p. 161. Cf. Michael Camille, *The Gothic Idol: Ideology and Image-Making in Medieval Art* (Cambridge, UK: Cambridge University Press, 1989), p. 232.

31. This idea is also present, of course, in political thought. In the twelfth century, we find the image of the commonwealth as a human body in John of Salisbury's *Policraticus* (1159), and later, above all, in Hobbes's *Leviathan* in the seventeenth century, where we can see it in the famous engraving in the frontispiece. For more on the latter, see Horst Bredekamp, *Stratégies visuelles de Thomas Hobbes: Le Léviathan, archétype de l'État moderne, Illustrations des* œuvres *et portraits*, 3 vols. (Paris: Éditions de la Maison des Sciences de l'Homme, 2003). On the figure of the king as the sum of his subjects and the body politic of the kingdom, see Louis Marin, *Portrait of the King*, trans. Martha M. Houle (Minneapolis: University of Minnesota Press, 1988), p. 209.

32. Bood and milk have abundantly irrigated the Christian imagination in the Middle Ages and the modern era. See especially, Georges Didi-Huberman, *L'image ouverte: Motifs de l'incarnation dans les arts visuels* (Paris: Gallimard, 2007), pp. 155–93; Jure Mikuž, *Le sang et le lait dans l'imaginaire médiéval* (Ljubljana: Zalozba ZRC, 2013); Frédéric Cousinié, *Esthétique des fluides: Sang, sperme, merde dans la peinture française du XVIIe siècle* (Paris: Éditions du Félin, 2011); Beate Fricke, "A Liquid History: Blood and Animation in Late Medieval Art," *RES—Anthropology and Aesthetics* 63–64 (2013), pp. 53–69; and Jutta Sperling, "Squeezing, Squirting, Spilling Milk: The Lactation of Saint Bernard and the Flemish *Madonna Lactans* (ca. 1430–1530)," *Renaissance Quarterly* 71 (2018), pp. 868–918.

33. On this triptych, see Richard Öffner, *A Critical and Historical Corpus of Florentine Painting*, section 3, *The Fourteenth Century* (New York: Institute of Fine Arts, New York University, 1956), vol. 5, pp. 141–48; Barbara Baert, "Nourished by Inwardness: The Beato Chiarito Tabernable (c. 1340)," *Annali dell'Università di Ferrara, Sezione Storia* 4 (2007),

pp. 28–50; Christophe Lakey, "The Curious Case of the *Chiarito Tabernacle*: A New Interpretation," *Getty Research Journal* 4 (2012), pp. 13–30; Fricke, "A Liquid History," pp. 57–59; and Guillaume Cassegrain, *La Coulure: Histoires de la peinture en mouvement (XIe–XXIe siècles)* (Paris: Hazan, 2015), p. 163.

34. Öffner, *A Critical and Historical Corpus*, p. 141n10.

35. We might add here the case of Saint Bernard of Clairvaux to whom an experience of the absorption of the blood of Christ is also attributed. Cf. Cousinié, *Esthétique des fluides*, pp. 28–29, and Mikuž, *Le sang et le lait*, pp. 46–47. For more on these saints, see especially Caroline Walker Bynum, *Jesus as a Mother: Studies in the Spirituality of the High Middle Ages* (Berkeley: University of California Press, 1982) and see also Bynum, *Holy Feast and Holy Fast.*

36. Cf. Saint Catherine of Siena, Letter 102 to Raymond of Capua, in *Letters of Saint Catherine of Siena*, trans. Suzanne Noffke (Tempe, AZ: Arizona Center for Medieval and Renaissance Studies, 2008), vol. 4, pp. 364–70.

37. Raymond of Capua, *The Life of St.Catherine of Siena*, trans. George Lamb (London: Harvill Press, 1960), p. 173.

38. Guillaume Cassegrain, *Représenter la vision: Figuration des apparitions miaculeuses dans la peinture italienne de la Renaissance* (Arles: Actes Sud, 2017), p. 180n173.

39. *La Vie de Sainte Catherine de Sienne*, Bnf, Ms. All. 34, fol. 43v. Cf. Jeffrey Hamburger, *The Visual and the Visionary: Art and Female Spirituality in Late Medieval Germany* (New York: Zone Books, 1998), pp. 460–61.

40. On the role of blood in the imagination, see among others Piero Camporesi, *The Incorruptible Flesh: Bodily Mutation and Mortification in Religion and Folklore,* trans. Tania Croft-Murray and Helen Elsom (Cambridge, UK: Cambridge University Press, 1988), p. 16 et seq.; Marie-Christine Pouchelle, "Le sang et ses pouvoirs au Moyen Age," in Arlette Farge, ed., *Affaires de sang* (Paris: Imago, 1988), pp. 17–41; Cousinié, *Esthétique des fluides*, pp. 76–94; Fricke, "A Liquid History"; and Mikuž, *Le sang et le lait*, p. 49 et seq.

41. Levino Lennio, *Della complessione del corpo humano libri due, sommamente necessarij a tutti colori, che studiano alla sanita . . . .* (Venezia: Appresso Dominico Nicolino, 1564), cited and trans. in Camporesi, *The Incorruptible Flesh*, p. 16. On the debates in the Middle Ages surrounding the nutritional role of blood, see Jacquart, *La médecine médiévale,* pp. 333–47.

42. See Marie-Christine Pouchelle, "Une parole médicale prise dans l'imaginaire: Alimentation et digestion chez un maître chirurgien du XIVe siècle," in Jean-Claude Margolin and Robert Sauzet, eds., *Pratiques et discours alimentaires à la Renaissance: Actes*

du colloque de Tours de mars 1979 (Paris: Maisonneuve et Larose, 1982), pp. 184–85; Cousinié, *Esthétique des fluides*, pp. 41–43; and Jean-Louis Flandrin, "From Dietetics to Gastronomy: The Liberation of the Gourmet," in Jean-Louis Flandrin and Massimo Montanari, eds., *Food: A Culinary History from Antiquity to the Present*, trans. Clarissa Botsford, et al. (New York: Columbia University Press, 1999), pp. 427–28. On digestion in the human imagination, see Gaston Bachelard, *The Formation of the Scientific Mind*, trans. Mary McAllester Jones (Manchester: Clinamen Press, 2002), pp. 172–84.

43. I refer here especially to the passage in the Gospel of Peter concerning Christ's shedding of blood for mankind: It is "the precious blood of Christ, a lamb without blemish or defect." 1 Peter 1:18–19.

44. Galen, *On the Natural Faculties*, trans. A.J. Brock. Loeb Classical Library, 71 (Cambridge, MA: Harvard University Press, 1916), p. 33. See Massimo Leone, "Le Dieu mâché: Idéologies du sens religieux et mastication," *Lexia: Rivista di semiotica*, special issue of *Cibo e identità culturale* 19–20 (2015), pp. 255–56. On feeding as the assimilation of the similar, see also Pouchelle, "Une parole médicale prise dans l'imaginaire," pp. 183–84.

45. Pierre-Jean Fabre, *L'abrégé des secrets chymiques, ou L'on void la nature des animaux vegetaux & mineraux entierement découverte* (Paris: Antoine de Sommaville, 1636), p. 15. Translation by Mary McAllester Jones in Bachelard, *The Formation of the Scientific Mind*, p. 174.

46. Laurence Moulinier, "Le sang au Moyen Âge, entre savoir et questionnements, science et imaginaire," in *1453, Rencontres européennes* (Bordeaux: Éditions confluences, 2004), pp. 53–73; Baschet, *La civilisation* féodale, p. 583; and Mikuž, *Le sang et le lait*, p. 49.

47. See Fricke, "A Liquid History," p. 64.

48. Cf. Moulinier, "Le sang au Moyen Âge"; Aurélien Robert, "Le corps d'après: La Chute entre théologie et médecine (XIIe–XIVe siècle)," in Gianluca Briguglia and Irène Rosier-Catach, eds., *Adam, la nature humaine avant et après: Épistémologie de la Chute* (Paris: Publications de la Sorbonne, 2016), p. 197.

49. Bynum, *Holy Feast and Holy Fast.*

50. Raymond of Capua, *The Life of St. Catherine of Siena*, p. 147.

51. Ibid., pp. 147–48.

52. For more on this engraving, see Michael Bury, *The Print in Italy, 1550–1620* (London: British Museum, 2001), exhibition catalog, cat. 42.

53. On the delusionary desire for fusion through the absorption of a liquid, see Frédéric Cousinié, *Images et méditation au XVIIe siècle* (Rennes: PUR, 2007), pp. 203–204, and Cousinié, *Esthétique des fluides*, p. 26.

54. Danièle Alexandre-Bidon, ed., *Le pressoir mystique: Actes du colloque de Recloses* (Paris: Cerf, 1990).

55. Bynum, *Holy Feast and Holy Fast*, p. 270.

56. We also find a certain number of miraculous images that, without necessarily giving rise to an act of absorption, show their power through running fluids: tears, blood, milk, oil, and so forth. Cf. Jean-Marie Sansterre, "Vivantes ou comme vivantes: L'animation miraculeuse d'images de la Vierge entre Moyen Âge et époque moderne," *Revue de l'histoire des religions* 232.2 (2015), p. 169, concerning the icon of the Virgin at Saidnaya (twelfth-century monastery, Syria) from whose breasts there flowed oil.

57. *Acta Sanctorum*, 1675, Aprilis Tomus Tertius, p. 470, Vigesima sexta Aprilis, caput 2, 21.

58. Chiara Frugoni, "Le mistiche, le visioni e l'iconografia: Rapporti ed influssi," in *La mistica femminile del Trecento* (Todi: Accademia Tudertina, 1982), pp. 5–45; Bynum, *Holy Feast and Holy Fast*, p. 142; Caroline Walker Bynum, *Fragmentation and Redemption: Essays on Gender and the Human Body in Medieval Religion* (New York: Zone Books, 1992), p. 162; Jean-Claude Schmitt, "La culture de *l'imago*," *Annales: Histoire, sciences sociales* 51.1 (1996), p. 35; and Sperling, "Squeezing, Squirting, Spilling Milk," pp. 874–75.

59. See Walker Bynum, *Fragmentation and Redemption*, p. 162; Baschet, *La civilisation féodale*, p. 713, and Olivier Leplatre, *"Un goût à la voir nonpareil": Manger les images, essais d'iconophagie* (Paris: Kimé, 2018), p. 153.

60. On Pope Gregory's vision, see Caroline Walker Bynum, "Seeing and Seeing Beyond: The Mass of St. Gregory in the Fifteenth Century," in Anne-Marie Bouché and Jeffrey Hamburger, eds., *The Mind's Eye: Art and Theology in the Middle Ages* (Princeton, NJ: Princeton University Press, 2005), pp. 208–40, and Dominique Rigaux, "Autour de la messe de saint Grégoire: Visée pastorale et réalisme rural," in Nicole Bériou, Béatrice Caseau, Dominique Rigaux, eds., *Pratiques de l'eucharistie dans les* Églises *d'Orient et d'Occident (Antiquité et Moyen Âge)*, vol. 2, *Les réceptions* (Paris: Institut d'Études Augustiniennes, 2009), pp. 954–57.

61. Alexander Nagel, *The Controversy of Renaissance Art* (Chicago: University of Chicago Press, 2011), pp. 84 and 237n5. This likening of Christ's wound to a chalice took a more literal turn in Spain with Gaspar Becerra's sculpted Christ for the monastery of Las Descalzas Reales in Madrid since the wooden sculpture has a wound-monstrance for the consecrated host. Cf. Didi-Huberman, *L'image ouverte*, p. 52.

62. On this miracle in the life of Saint Bernard, see Christoph Schönborn, *L'icône du Christ: Fondements théologiques* (Paris: Cerf, 1986), p. 154; Cécile Dupeux, "La lactation

de saint Bernard de Clairvaux: Genèse et évolution d'une image," in Françoise Dunand, Jean-Marie Spieser, and Jean Wirth, eds., *L'image et la production du sacré* (Paris: Méridiens Klincksieck, 1991), pp. 165–93; Patrick Arabeyre, "La lactation de saint Bernard à Châtillon-sur-Seine: Données et problèmes," in Patrick Arabeyre, Jacques Berlioz, and Philippe Poirrier, eds., *Vies et légendes de saint Bernard de Clairvaux: Création, diffusion, réception (XIIe–XXe siècles)* (Cîteaux: Commentarii Cistercienses, 1993), pp. 173–97; James France, *Medieval Images of Saint Bernard of Clairvaux* (Kalamazoo: Cistercian Publications, 2007); Cousinié, *Esthétique des fluides*, pp. 18–34; Victor I. Stoichita, *Visionary Experience in the Golden Age of Spanish Art* (London: Reaktion Books, 1995), pp. 132–61; Leplatre, *"Un goût à la voir nonpareil,"* pp. 20–23, 286–88; Sperling, "Squeezing, Squirting, Spilling Milk," pp. 894–909.

63. Cf. Arabeyre, "La lactation de saint Bernard," p. 176.

64. Stoichita, *Visionary Experience*, p. 133; Cousinié, *Esthétique des fluides*, p. 21.

65. Bernard of Clairvaux, *The Works of Saint Bernard of Clairvaux*, trans. Killian Walsh (Kildale: Irish University Press, 1971), vol. 2, pp. 58–59.

66. Cited in Arabeyre, "La lactation de saint Bernard," p. 176. My emphasis.

67. Cf. Stoichita, *Visionary Experience*, p. 139.

68. Dominique Rigaux, "Réflexions sur les usages apotropaïques de l'image peinte: Autour de quelques peintures murales novaraises du Quattrocento," in Jérôme Baschet and Jean-Claude Schmitt, eds., *L'Image: Fonctions et usages des images dans l'Occident medieval* (Paris: Le Léopard d'or, 1996), p. 166: "it is not surprising that this milk, a venerated relic in the Middle Ages, was very early on considered to be miraculous, to the point of giving rise to various subterfuges such as that of the so-called miracles attaching to icons of the Virgin where a thin line of milk flows from the breast. In reality, the 'miraculous' milk was supplied from behind the icon through a tube." For more on these devices, see Françoise Dunand, *Corps vivants des Dieux: Les statues animées dans le monde méditerranéen antique* (Paris: Picard, 2018), p. 45.

69. Cf. Lenz Kriss-Rettenbeck, *Bilder und Zeichen religiösen Volksglaubens* (Munich: Georg D. W. Callwey, 1963), p. 91 and fig. 299.

70. Cousinié, *Esthétique des fluides*, pp. 22–23.

71. Ibid., p. 22; Leone, "Le Dieu mâché," pp. 247–64.

72. Stoichita, *Visionary Experience*, p. 135.

73. Arabeyre, "La lactation de saint Bernard," p. 183, and Stoichita, *Visionary Experience*, pp. 135–36. On lactation as a metaphor for the gift of divine wisdom, see Bynum,

Jesus as a Mother, chaps. 4 and 5, and Rigaux, "Réflexions sur les usages apotropaïques," p. 165.

74. Damien Agut-Mabordère and Michel Chauveau, eds., *Héros, magiciens et sages oubliés de l'Égypte ancienne: Une anthologie de la littérature en égyptien démotique* (Paris: Les Belles Lettres, 2011), pp. 24–27, and Robert Kriech Ritner, *The Mechanics of Ancient Egyptian Magical Practice* (Chicago: Oriental Institute of the University of Chicago, 2008), p. 108.

75. See part three below for the initiation ritual described in papyrus PGM XIII.

76. See André Neher, *Prophètes et prophéties: L'essence du prophétisme* (Paris: Payot & Rivages, 2004), pp. 101–29; Leone, "Le Dieu mâché"; and Finbarr Barry Flood, *Technologies de dévotion dans les arts de l'Islam: Pèlerins, reliques et copies* (Paris: Musée du Louvre and Hazan, 2019), pp. 112–13.

77. This episode echoes the digestion of the Word of God in Jeremiah 15:16: "When your words came, I ate them; they were my joy and my heart's delight." Neher, *Prophètes et prophéties*, pp. 123–29.

78. For more on the Lambeth Bible, see Dorothy Shepard, *Introducing the Lambeth Bible: A Study of Texts and Imagery* (Turnhout: Brepols, 2007).

79. Neher, *Prophètes et prophéties*, pp. 102, 124.

80. See Leone, "Le Dieu mâché," pp. 251–52; Gérard Haddad, *Eating the Book: Dietary Rites and Paternal Function*, trans. David Jacobson (New York: Agincourt Press, 2013), pp. 94–95.

81. Neher, *Prophètes et prophéties*, p. 125.

82. John Calvin, *Commentaries, on the First Twenty Chapters of the Book of the Prophet Ezekiel,* trans. Thomas Myers (Grand Rapids: W. M. B. Eerdmans, 1948), p. 129.

83. On the differences between these two texts, see especially Haddad, *Eating the Book*, pp. 103–105. Albert Vanhoye points out that the words "I ate it and it tasted as sweet as honey in my mouth" is a direct quotation from Ezekiel 3:3. Albert Vanhoye, "L'utilisation du livre d'Ézéchiel dans l'Apocalypse," *Biblica* 43.3 (1962), p. 437.

84. Tania van Hemelryck, "Mascher l'escripture: Livre, lecture et nourriture aux XIVe et XVe siècles," in Nelly Labère, ed., *Être à table au Moyen Âge* (Madrid: Casa de Velazquez, 2010), p. 238.

85. One thinks here also of the same scene as depicted in the Apocalypse Tapestry of Angers (1373–1382) or of the Apocalypse series of engravings by Jean Duvet (1546–1556). In the latter, unlike what we see with Dürer, the teeth are not visible.

86. Leone, "Le Dieu mâché," pp. 251–52.

87. *Incomplete Commentary on Matthew (Opus imperfectum)*, ed. Thomas C. Oden, trans. James A. Kellerman (Downers Grove, IL: Intervarsity Press, 2010), vol. 2, p. 324. Cited also in Leone, "Le Dieu mâché," p. 253. We find also in Calvin the same type of justification of the ingestion of the divine word: "Those who truly consecrate themselves to God, not only learn what they speak of, but as food is eaten, so also they receive within them the word of God in the inmost recesses of their heart, so that they may bring it forth from thence as food properly dressed." Calvin, *Commentaries*, p. 127.

88. *Lectura super Apocalypsim*, cited in Leone, "Le Dieu mâché," p. 253.

89. Leone points out that the pseudo-Chrysostom certainly drew the idea of mastication from Aristotle, the latter having explained that the solid foodstuff had no taste in itself. It was necessary to chew it, and that its fragments be moistened by saliva to make it release its flavor. Ibid., p. 255.

90. Cf. Michael Camille, "Mouth and Meanings: Towards an Anti-iconography of Medieval Art," in *Iconography at the Crossroads: Papers from the Colloquium Sponsored by the Index of Christian Art* (Princeton, NJ: Princeton University Press, 1993), p. 49; Maggie Kilgour, *From Communion to Cannibalism: An Anatomy of Metaphors of Incorporation* (Princeton, NJ: Princeton University Press, 1990); Olivier Boulnois, *Au-delà de l'image: Une archéologie du visuel au Moyen Âge, Ve–XVIe siècle* (Paris: Seuil, 2008), p. 98 et seq.

91. Hugh of Saint Victor, *Sermon*, XXI (PL177, 937 AC), cited in Boulnois, *Au-delà de l'image*, p. 99.

92. Charles Taylor, *Sources of the Self: The Making of Modern Identity* (Cambridge, MA: Harvard University Press, 1989), p. 130. Taylor is here referring to the notion of interiority found in the writings of Saint Augustine.

93. Leone, "Le Dieu mâché," p. 255.

94. Kilgour, *From Communion to Cannibalism*, and Rémi Brague, *The Legend of the Middle Ages*, trans. Lydia G. Cochrane (Chicago: University of Chicago Press, 2009), pp. 145–59.

95. *The Surgery of Master Henry de Mondeville: Written from 1306 to 1320*, trans. Leonard D. Rosenman (Philadelphia: Xlibris, 2003), vol. 1, p. 300. Cited also in Pouchelle, "Une parole médicale prise dans l'imaginaire," pp. 182–83.

96. Haddad, *Eating the Book*, p. 91.

97. Horace, *Satires I*, trans. P. Michael Brown (Warminster, UK: Aris & Phillips, 1993), p. 19.

98. Erasmus, "A Declamation on the Subject of Early Liberal Education for Children," in *Collected Works of Erasmus*, ed. J. K. Sowards, trans. and annot. Beert C. Verstraete (Toronto: University of Toronto Press, 1985), vol. 26, p. 339.

99. Karl August Böttiger, "Die Römische Bonbonnière," *Journal des Luxus und der Moden* 7 (1792), p. 54 et seq., cited in Andrea Linnebach, "Das Publikum der Antiken: Kunsthaus und Museum Fridericianum in Kassel als Ziel von Bildungs- und Forschungsreisen der europaïschen Aufklärung," in Alexis Joachimides, Charlotte Schreiter, and Rüdiger Splitter, eds., *Auf dem Weg zum Museum: Sammlung und Präsentation antiker Kunst an deutschen Fürstenhöfen des 18. Jahrhunderts* (Kassel: Kassel University Press, 2016), p. 191.

100. Cf. Christine Armengaud, *Le diable sucré: Gâteaux, cannibalisme, mort et fécondité* (Paris: La Martinière, 2000), p. 106, and Linnebach, "Das Publikum der Antiken," p. 191.

101. Jonathan Swift, *Gulliver's Travels* (London: Oxford University Press, 1919), pp. 220–21.

102. John Murrell, *A Delightfull Daily Exercise for Ladies and Gentlewomen: Whereby is Set Foorth the Secrete Misteries of the Purest Preseruings in Glasses and Other Confrictionaries* (London, 1621), G2v. On Murrell's work and the making of edible letters, see Wendy Wall, *Recipes for Thought: Knowledge and Taste in the Early Modern English Kitchen* (Philadelphia: University of Pennsylvania Press, 2016), pp. 146–51.

103. Ibid., p. 150.

104. On the mixing of food and words, see Mikhail Bakhtin, *Rabelais and His World*, trans. Hélène Iswolsky (Bloomington, IN: Indiana University Press, 1984), pp. 280–84; Louis Marin, *Food for Thought*, trans. Mette Hjort (Baltimore, MD: Johns Hopkins University Press, 1989); Michel Jeanneret, *A Feast of Words: Banquets and Table Talk in the Renaissance* (Chicago: University of Chicago Press, 1991); and Massimo Vetta, "The Culture of the Symposium," in Jean-Louis Flandrin and Massimo Montanari, eds., *Food: A Culinary History from Antiquity to the Present*, trans. Clarissa Botsford, et al. (New York: Columbia University Press, 1999), pp. 96–105.

105. See Wall, *Recipes for Thought*, pp. 149–50; Gillian Riley, "'Eat Your Words!': Seventeenth-Century Edible Letterforms," *Gastronomica* 1.1 (2001), pp. 45–59.

106. Leplatre, *"Un goût à la voir nonpareil,"* pp. 85 et seq. and 239 et seq.

107. Carolyn Korsmeyer, *Making Sense of Taste: Food and Philosophy* (Ithaca, NY: Cornell University Press, 2002).

108. See Jeanneret, *A Feast of Words*, pp. 131–39. On artistic innutrition and the metaphorical range of this image, see Jérémie Koering, "Titien l'iconophage," *Venezia Cinquecento* 21.41 (2011), pp. 5–37; Jérémie Koering, "Un artiste affamé: Privation, mélan-

colie et innutrition dans la *Vie* de Taddeo Zuccaro," in René Démoris, Florence Ferran, and Corinne Lucas-Fiorato, eds., *Art et violence: Vies d'artistes entre XVIe et XVIIIe siècles, Italie, France, Angleterre* (Paris: Desjonquères, 2012), pp. 146–59; and Jérémie Koering, "To Drink Pictures: Fluids, Imagination and Image-Making in the Renaissance," in Ulrich Pfisterer and Christine Tauber, eds., *Einfluss, Strömung, Quelle: Aquatische Metaphern der Kunstgeschichte* (Bielefeld: Transcript Verlag, 2018), pp. 23–47.

109. Hans Blumenberg, *Paradigms for a Metaphorology*, trans. Robert Savage (Ithaca, NY: Cornell University Press, 2010), p. 3.

110. Seneca, *The Epistles, 66–92*, 2 vols., trans. Richard M. Gummere, Loeb Classical Library, 76 (Cambridge, MA: Harvard University Press, 1920), vol. 2, pp. 279 and 281.

111. Francesco Petrarch, *Letters on Familiar Matters: Rerum familiarum libri IX–XVI*, trans. Aldo S. Bernardo (Baltimore, MD: Johns Hopkins University Press, 1985), p. 212.

112. Joachim Du Bellay, *The Regrets with The Antiquities of Rome, Three Latin Elegies, and The Defense and Enrichment of the French Language*, ed. and trans. Richard Helgerson (Philadelphia: University of Pennsylvania Press, 2006), p. 336.

113. François Rabelais, *The Complete Works of François Rabelais*, trans. Donald M. Frame (Berkeley: University of California Press, 1991), p. 613.

114. Cennino Cennini, *The Book of the Art of Cennino Cennini*, trans. Christina J. Herringham (London: George Allen, 1899), p. 22. Translation slightly modified.

115. Giorgio Vasari, *Lives of the Painters, Sculptors and Architects*, trans. Gaston du C. de Vere (New York: Alfred A. Knopf, 1996), vol. 1, p. 365, and Giorgio Vasari, *Le Vite de' più eccellenti pittori, scultori ed architettori*, in *Le Opere di Giorgio Vasari*, ed. Gaetano Milanesi, 9 vols. (Florence: Sansoni, 1906), vol. 2, p. 399. Cf. Lise Wajeman, "Manger la peinture," in François Lecercle, Emmanuelle Hénin, and Lise Wajeman, eds., *La Théorie subreptice: Anecdotes picturales de la Renaissance aux Lumières* (Turnhout: Brepols, 2012), p. 121.

116. "Drawing, formed again by the latter as if it were her daughter, fed and mothered by painting, and finding itself placed in these three states of visible form, impalpable body, and clothed in accident [or artifice], reaches thus perfection. And this comes about when painting dresses it, ornaments it, and perfects it in chiaroscuro. And in this way, we can say that painting gives birth to drawing, making it live, and nourishing it with its breasts." Federico Zuccaro, *L'idea de'pittori, scultori ed architetti* (Rome: Marco Pagliarini, [1607] 1768), pp. 79, 93–94. Romano Alberti also uses the metaphor of suckling. See Leon Battista Alberti, *Trattato della nobiltà della pittura* (Rome: Francesco Zannetti, 1585), p. 2.

117. André Félibien, *Entretiens sur les vies et les ouvrages des plus excellens peintres anciens et modernes* (Paris: Denys Mariette, 1679), p. 243.

118. Lydie Bodiou, "Les singulières conversions du lait maternel à l'époque classique: Approche médicale et biologique," *Pallas* 85 (2011), pp. 141–51; Salvatore D'Onofrio, *Les fluide d'Aristote: Lait, sang et sperme dans l'Italie du Sud* (Paris: Les belles lettres, 2014); and Cousinié, *Esthétique des fluides.*

119. For more on this anecdote, see Denis Ribouillault, "Regurgitating Nature: On a Celebrated Anecdote by Karel van Mander about Pieter Bruegel the Elder," *Journal of Historians of Netherlandish Art* 8.1 (2016).

120. Karel van Mander, *The Lives of the Illustrious Netherlandish and German Painters*, ed. and trans. Hessel Miedema (Doornspijk: DAVACO, [1604] 1994), p. 190.

121. Consider this example, taken at random, from Pontormo: "Friday the thigh; ten oz of bread, an omelette and I finished the figure." Jacopo da Pontormo, *Pontormo's Diary*, ed. Rosemary Mayer (New York: Out of London Press, 1979), p. 113. See Jean-Claude Lebensztejn, *Dossier Pontormo: Le journal de Pontormo* (Paris: Macula, 1984), p. 47. For other anecdotes pertaining to the porosity between food and painting, see Wajeman, "Manger la peinture," pp. 120–22.

122. Paolo Pino, *Paolo Pino's "Dialogo di pittura": A Translation with Commentary*, trans. Mary Pardo (Ann Arbor, MI: University Microfilms International, 1985), pp. 376–78.

123. Cited in Giorgio Agamben, *Stanzas: Word and Phantasm in Western Culture*, trans. Ronald L. Martinez (Minneapolis: University of Minnesota Press, 1993), p. 25. For the original text, see Alberti, *Trattato della nobilità della pittura*, chap. 1, p. 17.

124. "By my art everyone's brain becomes wisdom." The engraving figures in Johann Theodore de Bry and Johann Israël, *Emblemata saecularia, mira et iucunda varietate saeculi huius mores ita exprimentia . . .* , Frankfurt, 1596, f. 44.

125. On the *phantasmata*, see Jackie Pigeaud, *Folie et cures de la folie chez les médecins de l'antiquité gréco-romaine* (Paris: Les Belles Lettres, 2010), p. 99, and Carl Havelange, *De l'oeil et du monde: Une histoire du regard au seuil de la modernité* (Paris: Fayard, 1998), pp. 164–65.

126. Poor digestion is digestion that does not cook the foodstuff. It thickens the blood and thus generates sediments. In his reading of Problem XXX in Aristotle, Jackie Pigeaud explains that "black bile is a residue, a sediment, of what is not cooked, since digestion is understood to be a cooking." In the words of Aristotle, "Even if (these symptoms) cease, quartan fevers occur in the survivors; for the sediment of what is

unconcocted is very fixed and becomes intense in the body, just like black bile." Aristotle, *Problems*, ed. and trans. Robert Mayhew, Loeb Classical Library, 71 (Cambridge, MA: Harvard University Press, 2011), p. 23.

127. For more on this print, see especially Ronald Paulson, *Hogarth*, Vol. 3, *Art and Politics, 1750–1764* (Cambridge, UK: Lutterworth Press, 1993), pp. 251–63; Bernd W. Krysmanski, *Hogarth's Enthusiasm Delineated: Nachahmung als Kritik am Kennertum: Eine Werkanalyse*, 2 vols. (Hildesheim: G. Olms, 1996); Bernd W. Krysmanski, "We See a Ghost: Hogarth's Satire on Methodists and Connoisseurs," *Art Bulletin* 80.2 (1998), pp. 292–310; and Oliver Seifert, ed., *Panis angelorum: Das brot der engel, Kulturgeschichte der Hostie* (Ulm: Jan Thorbecke Verlag, 2004), pp. 160–63.

128. Paulson, *Hogarth*, pp. 251–57. I leave aside here the strictly artistic dimension of the satire.

129. Another of Hogarth's engravings, *Credulity, Superstition, and Fanaticism* (1762), takes up, with a few variations, the basic outline of *Enthusiasm Delineated*, and places the ingestion of images within the general category of demonic behaviors. Ingesting and vomiting appear as the result of the worship of a little statue of the Virgin (like the *Schabmadonnen* we saw in part 1) with little devils and witches always standing close by.

130. Paulson, *Hogarth*, p. 260.

131. Cf. Krysmanski, "We See a Ghost," p. 300.

132. Paulson, *Hogarth*, pp. 257–58.

133. See part 1 of this book.

134. Rigaux, "Réflexions," pp. 157–58; Fabrizio Conti, *Witchcraft, Superstition, and Observant Francisca Preachers: Pastoral Approach and Intellectual Debate in Renaissance Milan* (Turnhout: Brepols, 2015), pp. 159–218; Ralph Dekoninck, "Les Silènes de Gumppenberg: L'*Atlas Marianus* et la matière des images miraculeuses de la Vierge au regard du culte marial dans les anciens Pays-Bas," in Olivier Christin, Fabrice Flückiger, and Naïma Ghermani, eds., *Marie mondialisée: L'*Atlas Marianus *de Wilhelm Gumppenberg et les topographies sacrées de l'époque modern* (Neuchâtel: Éditions Alphil-Presses universitaires suisses, 2014), p. 212. As Euan Cameron has emphasized, Gerson made a distinction between practices authorized by the Church and those that were not so authorized, but he allowed for a significant number of practices that were undetermined and considered by the ministers to be more or less suspect. Euan Cameron, *Enchanted Europe: Superstition, Reason, and Religion* (Oxford: Oxford University Press, 2010), pp. 50–51.

135. On the terms of this accusation, see François Lecercle, "'Des yeux pour ne point

voir': Avatars de l'idolâtrie chez les théologiens catholiques, au XVIe siècle," in *L'idolâtrie* (Rencontres de l'École du Louvre) (Paris: La Documentation Nationale, 1990), pp. 35–51.

136. Cf. Lecercle, "'Des yeux pour ne point voir,'" pp. 42–43.

137. Cf. Margarethe Ruff, *Zauberpraktiken als Lebenshilfe: Magie im Alltag vom Mittelalter bis heute* (Frankfurt: Campus, 2003), p. 154.

138. Rosa Mair, "Brixner Visitationsberichte 1663–1685," (PhD diss., Universität Innsbruck, 1978), p. 214; Ruff, *Zauberpraktiken als Lebenshilfe*, p. 154.

139. But as Joseph L. Koerner has pointed out, "idolatry is an accusation, not a belief." Koerner, *The Reformation of the Image* (London: Reaktion Books, 2004), p. 98.

140. François Lemée, *Traité des statues*, ed. Diane H. Bodart and Hendrik Ziegler, 2 vols. (Weimar: VDG, [1688] 2012), chap. 1, vol. 1, p. 11, and commentary vol. 2, p. 105.

141. Ibid., chap. 2, p. 59 and vol. 2, p. 108 for the commentary.

142. "[T]hen they climbed down; they came bringing the amaranth seed [image] which they had captured. They took it with them to their homes, for it was in truth their captive. They ate it. They offered it to each of their kin and to those of the neighborhood; they ate it all." Bernardino de Sahagún, *General History of the Things of New Spain: Florentine Codex*, trans. Arthur J. O. Anderson and Charles E. Dibble (Salt Lake City: University of Utah Press, 1950–82), p. 147. On the ingestion of these images, see Elizabeth H. Boone, "Incarnations of the Aztec Supernatural: The Image of Huizilopochtli in Mexico and Europe," *Transactions of the American Philosophical Society* 79.2 (1989), pp. 34–40; Carlos Jáuregui, "Saturnal cannibal: Fronteras, reflejos, y paradojas en la narrativa sobre el antropófago," *Revista de crítica literaria latinoamericana* 26.51 (2000), pp. 26–27; and Kristin Dutcher Mann, "Christmas in the Missions of Northern New Spain." *Americas* 66.3 (2010), p. 338.

143. Cf. Boone, "Incarnations of the Aztec Supernatural," p. 37.

144. Alain Manesson-Mallet, *La Description de l'univers, suite de l'Europe ancienne et moderne, des terres Australes et de l'Amérique* (Paris: Denis Thierry, 1683), vol. 5, p. 311, fig. 135. The Diocesan journals from the beginning of the twentieth century were to echo this judgement, condemning the ingestion of images as a "false devotion" that "appears . . . very much to approach paganism and fetishism." Cf. *La semaine religieuse de l'Archidiocèse d'Albi: Organe officiel hebdomadaire de l'archevêché*, March 28, 1903, p. 211.

145. Cited in Ralph Dekoninck, "Une idolâtrie iconoclaste? Usures et brisures pieuses des images saintes," in Agnès Lafont, Christian Belin, and Nicholas Myers, eds., *L'Image brisée aux XVIe et XVIIe siècles / Breaking the Image in the Renaissance* (Paris: Classiques Garnier, 2019), p. 163.

146. Chrestien, *Epigramme à François d'Amboise*, ms. Latin 8586, BnF, cited in Émile and Eugène Haag, *La France protestante* (Paris: Fischbacher, 1884), vol. 4, p. 374.

147. On this aspect, see part 3 below.

148. Frank Lestringant, *Une sainte horreur ou le voyage en eucharistie, XVI–XVIIe siècles* (Geneva: Droz, 2012); Aden Kumler, "The 'Genealogy of Jean le Blanc': Accounting for the Materiality of the Medieval Eucharist," in Christy Anderson, Anne Dunlop, and Pamela H. Smith, eds., *The Matter of Art: Material, Practices, Cultural Logics, c. 1250–1750* (Manchester: Manchester University Press, 2015), p. 121.

149. Lestringant, *Une sainte horreur*, pp. 48–49, 55; Leplatre, *"Un goût à la voir nonpareil,"* pp. 164–68. For a discussion of the debates generated by the assimilation of the Eucharist to cannibalism, see Vincent Vandenberg, *De chair et de sang: Images et pratiques du cannibalisme de l'Antiquité au Moyen Âge* (Rennes: PUR, 2014), pp. 68–79.

150. *La légende véritable de Jean le Blanc,* in Anatole de Montaiglon, *Recueil de poésies françoises des XVe et XVIe siècles, morales, facétieuses, historiques* (Paris, 1855–1878), vol. 8, pp. 105–23. Cf. Lestringant, *Une sainte horreur*, pp. 103–105; Kumler, "'The Genealogy of Jean le Blanc,'" pp. 119–21.

151. On this engraving, see Kumler, "The Genealogy of Jean le Blanc.'"

152. Cf. Seifert, *Panis angelorum*, p. 162.

153. Harald Rye-Clausen, *Die Hostienmühlenbilder im Lichte mittelalterlicher Frömmigkeit* (Stein am Rhein: Christiana, 1981); Rubin, *Corpus Christi*, pp. 312–13; Seifert, *Panis angelorum*, pp. 122–23; Kumler, "The Genealogy of Jean le Blanc,'" pp. 132–33.

154. Henry Stephen [Henri Estienne], *A World of Wonders, or An Introduction to a Treatise Touching on the Conformity of Ancient and Modern Wonders or A Preparative Treatise to the Apologie for Herodotus*, trans. Anonymous (Edinburgh: Andrew Hart and Richard Lawson, 1608), p. 312. Spelling slightly modified.

155. In his *Colloquies*, Erasmus describes a scene involving a dialogue between a man, Ogygius, who is criticized by another, Menedemus, for his superstition. Erasmus, "A Pilgrimage for Religion's Sake," in J. K. Sowards ed., *Collected Works of Erasmus*, trans. and annot. Craig R. Thompson (Toronto: University of Toronto Press, 1997) vol. 40, pp. 619–74. Cf. André Godin, "Du bon usage du sacré: Érasme de Rotterdam," *Les Cahiers du Centre de Recherches Historiques* 9 (2009), p. 5; Dekoninck, "Les Silènes de Gumppenberg," p. 211.

156. Krysmanski, *Hogarth's Enthusiasm Delineated*, p. 367. In a much less convincing analysis, Paulson suggests a connection between this figure and *The Ecstasy of St. Margaret of Cortona* by Giovanni Lanfranco at Palazzo Pitti. Paulson, *Hogarth*, pp. 258–59.

157. Ibid., p. 258. The unseemliness and "bad taste" contribute to the reply to Reynolds' taunt. On the scale of taste and madness, see Jean-Claude Lebensztejn, "Le goût du sang," in *Déplacements* (Brussels: Les presses du réel, 2013), pp. 114–17.

158. Krysmanski, *Hogarth's Enthusiasm Delineated*, p. 371.

159. John Ireland, *A Supplement, to Hogarth Illustrated*, 2 vols. (London: Boydell, 1798), vol. 2, p. 240. Cf. Paulson, *Hogarth*, p. 258; Krysmanski, "We See a Ghost," p. 298.

160. Brantôme, *Œuvres complètes de Pierre de Bourdeille seigneur de Brantôme*, ed. Louis Jean Nicolas Monmerqué (Paris: Louis Jean Nicolas Monmerqué, 1822–1823), vol. 7, p. 338. It is possible that Brantôme was inspired by François Rabelais who, in the first edition of Pantagruel, spoke of "*mangeresses d'Ymaiges* et de théologiennes," Rabelais, *Pantagruel: Les horribles et espouventables faictz et prouesses* . . . (Lyon, 1530), chap. 11, s.p. Cf. Lazare Sainéan, *La langue de Rabelais* (Paris: De Boccard, 1922–1923), p. 267.

161. Brantôme, "Discours sur les couronnels de l'infanterie de France," in Brantôme, *Œuvres complètes de Pierre de Bourdeille seigneur de Brantôme*, ed. Ludovic Lalanne (Paris, Jules Renouard, 1873), vol. 6, p. 86.

162. "On dit d'un bigot, d'un faux dévot, que c'est un mangeur de Crucifix, un mangeur d'images." *Dictionnaire de l'Académie françoise dédié au Roy (Le)* (Paris: Jean Baptiste Coignard, 1694), vol. 2, p. 20. This definition was to be included in all later editions of the dictionary.

163. Pierre Jurieu, a Protestant, also had recourse to this term when describing Catholics: "Today, those that we call *eaters of Images* are often rascals who, under cover of this false devotion, foist on the people a life that is full of crimes." Pierre Jurieu, *Histoire du calvinisme et celle du papisme mises en parallèle* . . . (Rotterdam: Reinier Leers, 1683), p. 544.

164. *Essais de poesie du sieur de La Vergne* (Paris: Pierre Le Petit, 1643). Cited in Emmanuel-Louis-Nicolas Viollet-le-Duc, *Catalogue des livres composant la bibliothèque poétique de M. Viollet le Duc* . . . (Paris: L. Hachette, 1843), p. 456.

165. There are also many examples of stamping with this image of the saint to be found in Spain and in many of the Hispanic colonies. Cf. Francisco de San Bernardo, *Vida del prodigioso Job de estos siglos, el venerable Padre fray Thomas de la Virgen* . . . (Madrid, 1747), pp. 372–73.

166. Jean Barrin, *The monk unvail'd* (London: Jonathan Edwin, 1678), pp. 28–30.

167. This rationalism undertook to finally dispense with the "*sphère du vraisemblable* (sphere of the plausible)" that had prevailed throughout the long Middle Ages. Cf. Schmitt, *Le Corps, les rites*, p. 88. On the disjunction of body and mind, that is, of the

physical and cognitive faculties, that took place progressively at the end of the sixteenth century, see Michel Foucault, *The Order of Things: An Archaeology of the Human Sciences*, trans. Alan Sheridan (New York: Vintage Books, 1994);

Philippe Descola, *Beyond Nature and Culture*, trans. Janet Lloyd (Chicago: University of Chicago Press, 2013), pp. 174–79; Viktoria von Hoffmann, *From Gluttony to Enlightenment: A World of Taste in Early Modern Europe* (Champaign, IL: University of Illinois Press, 2016), pp. 62–72; and Viktoria von Hoffmann, "Le sensible et le culinaire: Les prémices d'une artification au XVIIIe siècle," in Julia Csergo and Frédérique Desbuissons, ed., *Le cuisinier et l'art: Art du cuisinier et cuisine d'artiste (XVIe-XXIe siècle)* (Paris: INHA/Menu fretin, 2018), p. 18.

168. Hoffmann, *From Gluttony to Enlightenment*, chap. 3.

169. Paulson, *Hogarth*, p. 260.

170. Cf. David R. Blanks and Michael Frassetto, eds., *Western Views of Islam in Medieval and Early Modern Europe: Perception of Other* (London: Macmillan, 1999).

171. It is worth pointing out this change in perspective since it constitutes, like Montesquieu's *Lettres persanes*, evidence of the development of cultural relativism during the Enlightenment.

172. On superstitions in the seventeenth century faced with Cartesianism, see Koen Vermeir, "Tout dépend des circonstances: Superstition, lois de la nature et dissolution du préternaturel au XVIIIe siècle," in Olivier Christin, Fabrice Flückiger, and Naïma Ghermani, eds., *Marie mondialisée: L'*Atlas Marianus *de Wilhelm Gumppenberg et les topographies sacrées de l'époque moderne* (Neuchâtel: Éditions Alphil-Presses universitaires suisses, 2014), p. 47 et seq.

173. Michel Foucault, *History of Madness,* ed. Jean Khalfa, trans. Jonathan Murphy and Jean Khalfa (London: Routledge, 2006), p. 89.

174. Ibid., pp. 91–92.

175. On the religious themes in this episode, I refer the reader to Cyril Gerbron's extremely subtle analysis, "La question religieuse dans 'Trust No Bitch' (*Orange Is the New Black*, season 3, episode 13)," *Débordements*, January 27, 2018, http://debordements.fr/La-question-religieuse-dans-Trust-No-Bitch. The authors of the episode, Jim Danger Gray, Jenjii Kohan, and Phil Abraham, echo the popular story of a "miraculous" piece of toast that was owned by a woman called Diana Duyser. In 2000, Duyser sold the toast on Ebay to an online casino, claiming the toast "carried" on its surface an image of the Virgin Mary. The toast sold for $28,000.

176. *Acheiropoieta* or made without hands. Concerning this tradition, see especially Ernst Kitzinger, "The Cult of Images in the Age before Iconoclasm," *Dumbarton Oaks Papers*, 8 (1954), pp. 112–15; Hans Belting, *Likeness and Presence: A History of the Image before the Era of Art,* trans. Edmund Jephcott (Chicago: University of Chicago Press, 1996), pp. 49–57; Michele Bacci, *Il pennello dell'Evangelista: Storia delle immagini sacre attribuite a San Luca* (Pisa: GISEM, 1998); and Hans Belting, *La vraie image: Croire aux images?* (Paris: Gallimard, 2007).

177. Saint Thomas Aquinas, for example, likens madfolk to children in his *Summa Theologica.* Cf. Didier Lett, "L'enfance: *Aetas infirma, aetas infima,*" *Médiévales* 15 (1988), p. 90.

178. Foucault, *History of Madness.*

179. Hence also the role played by children in the carnivalesque inversions.

180. Bernard de Gordon, *De conservatione vitae humanae vitae humanae*, ed. D. Joachimi Baudisii (Leipzig, 1570), pp. 2–3.

181. Jacob and Wilhelm Grimm, *The Original Folk and Fairy Tales of the Brothers Grimm,* ed. and trans. Jack Zipes. Illustrations by Andrea Dezsö (Princeton, NJ: Princeton University Press, 2014), pp. 43–49 (see pp. 46–47 for the description of the house). But one might just as well take as an example the comic strip *Gingerbread*, published in *Little Jack Horner's Picture Book* (1880) in which disobedient children find themselves trapped by edible letters, or again the Christmas scene in Jean Renoir's film, *La grande illusion* (1937), where little Lotte, upon seeing for the first time the manger scene made for her by Lieutenant Maréchal (played by Jean Gabin) and Lieutenant Rosenthal (played by Marcel Dalio), is overcome by her emotions and exclaims to her mother that she wants to eat the baby Jesus—the desire to possess morphing immediately into the desire to incorporate—to which the mother (played by Dita Parlo) replies, "Aber das ist doch nichts zum essen! (But that is not to eat!)" and Lieutenant Maréchal then declares, "Streng verboten (Strictly forbidden)." The adults see Lotte's behavior as a sign of the naive and unreasoning nature of the child.

182. See the third part of this book for more on these figurative edibles. The engraving dates from second half of the sixteenth century.

183. Hans Sachs, *Das Schlaraffenland* [1530], in Edmund Goetze and Carl Drescher, eds., *Sämtliche Fabeln und Schwänke von Hans Sachs* (Halle: Niemeyer, 1893), vol. 1, pp. 8–11. Cf. Guy Borgnet, "Le pays de Cocagne dans la littérature allemande: Des origines à Hans Sachs," in Danielle Buschinger and Wolfgang Spiewok, eds., *Gesellschaftsutopien im Mittelalter: Discours et figures de l'utopie au Moyen Âge* (Greifswald: Reineke Verlag, 1994), pp. 15–27.

184. A pastry of little importance was said to be "only good for children." Cf. Rolande Bonnain, "D'une patisserie cérémonielle: Usage de l'oublie," *Ethnologie française* 23.4 (1993), pp. 553 and 556.

185. Alexis Desgagnés, "De Gillray à Cruickshank: Répétition historique, caricature et *praxis* de l'histoire," in Ségolène Le Men, ed., *L'art de la caricature* (Nanterre: Presses Universitaires de Paris Ouest, 2011), pp. 309–17.

186. Ibid., p. 313.

187. A caricature of these gingerbread stands, also in connection with Napoleon, can be seen in the engraving by Charles Williams and George Moutard, *A Political Fair* (1807; The British Museum, London).

188. Since Antiquity, the figure of the anthropophage has been a frequent personification of political violence. See Vandenberg, *De chair et de sang*, and for the Middle Ages, Angelica Montanari, *Il fiero pasto: Antropofagie medievali* (Bologna: Il Mulino, 2015), pp. 69–75.

189. See Pauline Piettre, "Catéchèse et instruction religieuse en France depuis le XIXe siècle," *Transversalités* 115.3 (2010), pp. 27–40.

190. The caricature was published in *Le Charivari*, April 9, 1833, Delteil, no. 157.

191. David S. Kerr, *Caricature and French Political Culture 1830–1848: Charles Philippon and the Illustrated Press* (Oxford: Clarendon Press, 2000), p. 154.

192. Loys Delteil, *Honoré Daumier: The Early Lithographs, Catalogue raisonné 1830–1837*, trans. Robin Orr Bodkin (San Francisco: Alan Wofsy Fine Arts, 2005), no. 2155. There is also a satirical medal (Musée Carnavalet, Paris) engraved the same year, designed after Daumier, with the same scene on the front, and on the back a scene showing Léon Faucher giving a speech before two people seated at table, with the inscription, "*Sic itur ad ministerium.*"

193. Michel Papaud, "La répression durant le ministère de Léon Faucher (January–May 1849)," in Philippe Vigier and Alain Faure, eds., *Maintien de l'ordre et polices en France et en Europe au XIXe siècle* (Paris: Créaphis, 1987), pp. 96–97.

194. From the period of the Dreyfuss Affair, we find in the April 2, 1899 edition of the illustrated weekly *La Silhouette,* an antisemitic caricature by Bobb showing a fair stand with a gallery of gingerbread politicians.

195. Argus, "Chronique," *La semaine des familles*, April 20, 1872, p. 47.

196. "La foire au pain d'épice (The Gingerbread Fair)," by André Gil in *L'Éclipse*, May 7, 1876.

197. There are numerous avatars of this image. As Jean-Marc Alexandre and Pierre Curie have informed me, we find still today lollipops in the form of Pope Francis and candies with the image of Queen Astrid. People eat these sweets as a sign of devotion, or, conversely, with irreverence.

198. Pliny the Elder, *Natural History, XXXV*, ed. Jeffrey Henderson, trans. H. Rackham, Loeb Classical Library, 394 (Cambridge, MA: Harvard University Press, 1952), pp. 309, 311.

199. See Korsmeyer, *Making Sense of Taste*, p. 19 and more generally chap. 1.

200. Cf. Leplatre, *"Un gout à la voir nonpareil,"* pp. 68–69.

201. Cf. Korsmeyer, *Making Sense of Taste*, pp. 14–15, on Plato and the mastering of animal appetites. See also Wajeman, "Manger la peinture," pp. 122–23, on how it is only children who are taken in by painting's illusions.

202. See Gérard Simon, "La théorie cartésienne, réponse à Kepler et rupture avec la problématique médiévale," in Joël Biard and Roshdi Rashed, ed., *Descartes et le Moyen Âge* (Paris: Vrin, 1997), p. 107.

203. On the evolution of the place accorded to taste in the thought of the modern era, see Hoffmann, *From Gluttony to Enlightenment*, pp. 87–96, and Hoffmann, "Le sensible et le culinaire."

204. See Jacqueline Lichtenstein, *The Blind Spot: An Essay on the Relations between Painting and Sculpture in the Modern Age*, trans. Chris Miller (Los Angeles: Getty Research Institute, 2008), and Leplatre, *"Un gout à la voir nonpareil,"* pp. 85 et seq. and 239 et seq. for the role of the still life in this debate.

205. Denis Diderot, "J.-B. S. Chardin (*Salon of 1763*)," *Neoclassicism and Romanticism 1750-1850: An Anthology of Sources and Documents*, ed. and trans. Lorenz Eitner (New York: Harper & Row, 1989), p. 58 and and Jean-Claude Lebensztejn, "Note sur Diderot et la magie de l'art," in *Déplacements* (Brussels: Les presses du réel, 2013), p. 41.

206. Ibid., p. 41. Diderot also brings up Rembrandt's painting as having to be seen from a distance. Cf. Érika Wicky, "La peinture à vue de nez, ou La juste distance du critique d'art, de Diderot à Zola," *RACAR* 39. 1 (2014), pp. 78–79.

207. Diderot, "J.-B. S. Chardin (*Salon of 1763*)," p. 59. Cf. Lichtenstein, *The Blind Spot*, pp. 55–56; and Lebensztejn, "Note sur Diderot," p. 41.

208. For Lebensztejn, although the operation of painting may seem magical, it must be concentrated "in the transmutation produced by the distancing of the painting." Ibid., p. 43.

209. Lichtenstein, *The Blind Spot*, p. 57. On this appreciation "at a distance," see also Wicky, "La peinture à vue de nez," pp. 76–89.

210. Hoffmann, *From Gluttony to Enlightenment*, p. 118.

211. On the transformation of the bodily sense (gustatory taste) into the faculty of judgement (artistic taste), see Robert Klein, "Judgement and Taste in Cinquecento Art Theory," in *Form and Meaning: Essays on the Renaissance and Modern Art*, trans. Madeline Jay and Leon Wieseltier (New York: Viking Press, 1979), pp. 161–69; Flandrin, "From Dietetics to Gastronomy," pp. 428–29; Martial Guédron, "Physiologie du bon goût: La hiérarchie des sens dans les discours sur l'art en France au XVIIIe siècle," in Ralph Dekoninck, Agnès Guiderdoni-Bruslé, and Nathalie Kremer, eds., *Aux limites de l'imitation: L'ut pictura poesis à l'épreuve de la matière (XVIe–XVIIIe siècles)* (Amsterdam: Rodopi, 2009), pp. 39–49; Lebensztejn, "Le goût du sang"; and Hoffmann, *From Gluttony to Enlightenment*, p. 114.

212. As Jean-Christophe Abramovici has noted, there was certainly a positive meaning in the culinary terms applied to painting in the eighteenth century, and in particular to the use of the term *ragoût* (stew), but it was short-lived and used only for recipes, for the actual doing. Jean-Christophe Abramovici, "Du ragoût en peinture," in Julia Csergo and Frédérique Desbuissons, eds., *Le cuisinier et l'art: Art du cuisinier et cuisine d'artiste (XVIe–XXIe siècle)* (Paris: INHA/Menu fretin, 2018), pp. 218–21.

213. Cf. Lichtenstein, *The Blind Spot*, pp. 55–56.

214. André Rouquet, *L'art nouveau de la peinture en fromage, ou en ramequin, inventée pour suivre le louable projet de trouver graduellement des façons de peindre inférieures à celles qui existent* (Marolles, 1755), pp. 6–7: "When I realized that cheese had the plastic and agglutinative qualities that rendered applicable to a new way of painting, . . . I resolved to eat my cheeses, and it was the happiest resolution that I could have taken, since it occasioned the discovery of painting in ramekin . . . . I made this great discovery the day that I put my cheese in an omelette." The "recipe" is given on p. 15 et seq. I am grateful to Pierre Von-Ow for having pointed out this text to me.

215. Ibid., pp. 16–17.

216. Ibid., p. 17.

217. Ibid., pp. 17–18.

218. Lichtenstein, *The Blind Spot*, pp. 171–73, and Frédérique Desbuissons, "The Studio and the Kitchen: Culinary Ugliness as Pictorial Stigmatisation in Nineteenth-Century France," in Andreï Pop and Mechtild Widrich, eds., *Ugliness: The Non-Beautiful in Art*

and Theory (London: I. B. Tauris, 2013), pp. 104–21. See also Wicky, "La peinture à vue de nez," p. 80 on Courbet's "cheeses."

219. Desbuissons, "The Studio and the Kitchen."

220. Émile Zola, *Mes haines: Causeries littéraires et artisques, Mon Salon, Édouard Manet, étude biographique et critique* (Paris: M. Charpentier, 1893), pp. 295–96.

CHAPTER THREE: SHARING IMAGES

1. On commensality as a rite of admission into a particular group or society, see Arnold Van Gennep, *The Rites of Passage*, trans. Monika B. Vizedom and Gabrielle L. Caffee (Chicago: University of Chicago Press, [1909] 1960), pp. 29, 164–65, and Milad Doueihi, *A Perverse History of the Human Heart* (Cambridge, MA: Harvard University Press, 1997), p. 5. For a semiotic approach to commensality, see Jean-Jacques Boutaud, *Le sens gourmand: De la commensalité, du goût, des aliments* (Paris: Jean-Paul Rocher, 2005), pp. 23–80.

2. In the context of meals, that will be our focus here, this function is generally attributed to verbal language. As Doueihi writes, "The concept of the meal around the table is, so to speak, an institutionalized gathering that functions to set apart a space and a time where eating and speaking converge and intersect. The meal around the table recognizes that eating and speaking are two forms of expression and communication akin to each other, two separate languages that can come together and can be substituted for each other." Doueihi, *A Perverse History of the Human Heart*, p. 5. My thesis is that images can play an equivalent role in this symbolic relationship by accompanying or substituting for the spoken word.

3. Hubert Damisch, "Titres," in *Fenêtre jaune cadmium, ou Les dessous de la peinture* (Paris: Seuil, 1984), p. 183.

4. Jean-Louis Schefer, *L'hostie profanée: Histoire d'une fiction théologique* (Paris: P. O. L., 2007), pp. 145 and 147.

5. René Girard tried to see in sacrifice, first in blood sacrifice and later symbolic sacrifice, a way of resolving the violence of humanity. René Girard, *Violence and the Sacred*, trans. Patrick Gregory (Baltimore, MD: Johns Hopkins University Press, 1977). For more on these readings, see Christoph Auffarth, "Le rite sacrificial antique: La longue durée et la fin du sacrifice," *Kermos* 25 (2012), p. 298.

6. See Marcel Detienne and Jean-Pierre Vernant, *The Cuisine of Sacrifice among the Greeks,* trans. Paula Wissing (Chicago: University of Chicago Press, 1989). The studies collected in this volume argue against a universal understanding of sacrifice such as is to

be found in the works of James George Frazer, Marcel Mauss, Robertson Smith, Émile Durkheim, Ernst Cassirer, and Sigmund Freud. On this point, see Marcel Detienne, "Culinary Practices," in *The Cuisine of Sacrifice among the Greeks*, pp. 1–20. For more on this refutation, see also Auffarth, "Le rite sacrificial antique."

7. Detienne is careful to warn us against the ethnocentric temptation to see the pagan "blood" sacrifice and the Christian "symbolic" sacrifice as two moments in the history of religion, signaling thus humanity's "trajectory" toward civilization. Detienne, "Culinary Practices," pp. 13–20. For a perspective on the topic that differs from that of Detienne and Vernant, see Cristiano Grottanelli, "La viande et ses rites," in Jean-Louis Flandrin and Massimo Montanari, eds., *Histoire de l'alimentation* (Paris: Fayard, 1996), pp. 117–32.

8. Jean-Claude Lacam, "La gourmandise des dieux: Les gâteaux sacrés des Tables de Gubbio (IIIe–IIe s. av. J.-C.)," *Mélanges de l'École française de Rome—Antiquité* 124.2 (2012), p. 561.

9. We might quite simply recall here that the images, such as frescoes, icons, sculptures, and engravings, that were diverted from their original goals show that the eye was not the only human organ involved in experiencing them.

10. Lacam, "La gourmandise des dieux," p. 566.

11. George Galavaris, *Bread and the Liturgy: The Symbolism of Early Christian and Byzantine Bread Stamps* (Madison: University of Wisconsin Press, 1970), pp. 22–25.

12. Cf. Margarete Bieber, *Skenika: Kuchenform mit Tragödienszene, Maske aus dem Kerameikos* (Berlin: G. Reimer, 1915), pp. 26–27 and plate IIIa.

13. Cf. Ibid., pp. 27–28, plate IIIb. See also Galavaris, *Bread and the Liturgy*, pp. 24–25.

14. Plutarch, *Moralia, V: Isis and Osiris, The E at Delphi, The Oracles at Delphi No Longer Given in Verse, The Obsolescence of Oracles*, trans. Frank Cole Babbitt, Loeb Classical Library, 306 (Cambridge, MA: Haravard University Press, 1936), p. 123. Cf. Galavaris, *Bread and the Liturgy*, p. 23.

15. Lacam, "La gourmandise de dieux," pp. 558–61.

16. Charles Victor Daremberg and Edmond Saglio, *Dictionnaire des antiquités grecques et romaines d'après les textes et les monuments* (Paris: Hachette, 1877–1919), III, 2, sv. "Libum," p. 1238: "*Libum, Liba*: sacred cakes offered to the gods. The *liba* were made, under the supervision of the pontiffs, by *fictores* specially charged with this task."

17. See Clifford Ando, quoted in Christopher A. Faraone and F. S. Naiden, eds., *Greek and Roman Animal Sacrifice: Ancient Victims, Modern Observers* (Cambridge, UK: Cambridge University Press, 2012), pp. 196–97.

18. "Et sciendum in sacris simulate pro veris accipi: unde cum de animalibus quae difficile inveniuntur est sacrificandum, de pane vel cera fiunt et pro veris accipiuntur." Maurus Servius Honoratus, *Commentary on the Aeneid of Vergil*, Georgius Thilo, ed., (Perseus Digital Library), book 2, chap. 116. See also Gérard Capdeville, "Substitution de victimes dans les sacrifices d'animaux à Rome," *Mélanges de l'Ecole Française de Rome Antiquité* 83.2 (1971), pp. 294–95.

19. John Scheid, *Quand faire, c'est croire: Les rites sacrificiels des Romains* (Paris: Aubier, 2011), pp. 29, 296–97. As Lacam writes, this configuration honored the divinity. Lacam, "La gourmandise des dieux," pp. 563.

20. Scheid, *Quand faire, c'est croire*, pp. 242, 241–43.

21. Ibid., p. 268. See also Lacam, "La gourmandise des dieux," p. 565.

22. John Scheid, "Sacrifice et banquet à Rome: Quelques problèmes," *Mélanges de l'École française de Rome — Antiquité* 97.1 (1985), p. 193.

23. Scheid, *Quand faire, c'est croire*, pp. 182–88, 274.

24. On the rite of initiation as a rite of passage, see Van Gennep, *The Rites of Passage*, chap. 6, esp. pp. 87–97.

25. Robert Kriech Ritner, *The Mechanics of Ancient Egyptian Magical Practice* (Chicago: Oriental Institute of the University of Chicago, 2008), pp.104–109.

26. Wine also had a fundamental role, but here my interest is limited to bread since naturally it alone could receive an image. Furthermore, we also find the persistence of animal sacrifice in the Church of the East in the Greek, Syriac, Arab, and Armenian cultures. Cf. Cristiano Grottanelli, "La viande et ses rites," in Jean-Louis Flandrin and Massimo Montanari, eds., *Histoire de l'alimentation* (Paris: Fayard, 1996), pp. 117–32.

27. Galavaris, *Bread and the Liturgy*; Schefer, *L'hostie profanée*, p. 152.

28. Galavaris, *Bread and the Liturgy*, pp. 30–39; Schefer, *L'hostie profanée*, pp. 142, 152.

29. Cf. Schefer, *L'hostie profanée*, p. 159.

30. Galavaris, *Bread and the Liturgy*, pp. 40–108.

31. Ibid., pp. 62–69.

32. Ibid., p. 65.

33. Ibid., pp. 84–87.

34. Ibid., p. 65.

35. *Zéon* ("hot water") was added immediately after the Eucharistic Canon in reference to the "fervor of faith, full of the Holy Spirit." See Michael J. Kuchera, "The Holy Eucharist in the Byzantine Rite: The Henosis and the Zeon," in Georges-Henri Ruyssen,

ed., *The Holy Eucharist in Eastern Canon Law: From the Wellspring of the Canons, Acts of the Bratislava Symposium, 14–17 April, 2009* (Rome: Pontificio Istituto Orientale, 2010), pp. 247–63.

36. Georgia Frank, "L'eucharistie et la mémoire sensorielle selon Jean Chrysostome," in Nicole Bériou, Béatrice Caseau, and Dominique Rigaux, eds., *Pratiques de l'eucharistie dans les églises d'Orient et d'Occident (Antiquité et Moyen Âge),* vol. 2: *Les réceptions* (Turnhout: Brepols, 2009), p. 769.

37. The sacrificial dimension was to be increasingly depicted in the Byzantine world, notably from the end of the twelfth century, through the iconography of the *melismos* or Lamb of God that appeared in the mosaics, frescoes, and liturgical fabrics in the form of a child placed on the paten or the chalice, ready to be dismembered. See Schefer, *L'hostie profanée*, pp. 212–15; Vasileios Marinis, "Piety, Barbarism, and the Senses in Byzantium," in Sally M. Promey, ed., *Sensational Religion: Sensory Cultures in Material Practice* (New Haven, CT: Yale University Press, 2014), pp. 321–40; Marie-Hélène Congourdeau, "L'enfant immolé: Hyper-réalisme et symbolique sacrificielle à Byzance," in Nicole Bériou, Béatrice Caseau, and Dominique Rigaux, eds., *Pratiques de l'Eucharistie dans les églises d'Orient et d'Occident (Antiquité et Moyen Âge)*, vol. 1: *Institution* (Turnhout: Brépols, 2009), pp. 292, 297.

38. For more on the history of the stamped host, see especially Jean Mabillon, *Dissertatio de pane eucharistico, azymo, ac fermentato: Suivie de la Revelation de saint Ildefonse*, in *Ouvrages posthumes de D. Jean Mabillon et de D. Thierri Ruinart, Bénédictins de la congrégation de Saint Maur* (Paris: Jean François Babutt and Jean-François Josse, 1724), pp. 101–97; Francesco Berlendi, *Delle Obblazioni all'altare antiche e moderne, o sia la storia intera dello Stipendio della Messa* (Venice: Apresso Angelo Pasinelli, 1736); Henri Leclercq, "Fer à hosties," in *Dictionnaire d'archéologie chrétienne et de liturgie* (Paris: Letouzé et Ané, 1922), pp. 1366–68; Claude Macherel and Jean Steinauer, *L'État de ciel: Portrait de ville avec rite, La Fête-Dieu de Fribourg (Suisse)* (Fribourg: Méandre Éditions, 1989); Miri Rubin, *Corpus Christi: The Eucharist in Late Medieval Culture* (Cambridge, UK: Cambridge University Press, 1991); Patricia Sela del Pozo Coll, "La devoción a la hostia consagrada en la Baja Edad Media castellana: Fuentes textuales, materiales e iconográficas para su studio," *Anales de Historia del Arte* 16 (2006), pp. 25–58; Patricia Sela del Pozo Coll, "Imágenes en las hostias eucarísticas: Origen y significación de motivos iconográficos presentes en un medio secundario," in Ines Monteira Arias, Belen Munoz Martinze, and Fernando Villasenor Sebatian, eds., *Relegados al margen: Marginalidad y espacios marginales en la*

cultura medieval (Madrid: CSIC Insituto de Historia, 2009), pp. 257–72; Schefer, *L'hostie profanée*, especially pp. 129–170; Aden Kumler, "The Multiplication of the Species: Eucharistic Morphology in the Middle Ages," *RES: Anthropology and Aesthetics* 59–60 (Spring–Autumn 2011), pp. 179–91; Aden Kumler, "The 'Genealogy of Jean le Blanc': Accounting for the Materiality of the Medieval Eucharist," in Christy Anderson, Anne Dunlop, and Pamela H. Smith, eds., *The Matter of Art: Material, Practices, Cultural Logics, c. 1250–1750* (Manchester: Manchester University Press, 2015), pp. 119–40; Kathryn M. Rudy, "Sewing the Body of Christ: Eucharist Wafer Souvenirs Stitched into Fifteenth-Century Manuscripts, Primarily in the Netherlands," *Journal of Historians of Netherlandish Art* 8.1 (Winter 2016).

39. "Quod sacerdotes debeant hostias facere per se Ipsos." Guillelmi Duranti, *Rationale Divinorum Officiorum*, eds. David Anselme and Timothy Thibodeau (Turnhout: Brepols, 1995), liber IV, 30, 6 (60). Cf. Marti Sunyol I Busquets, "Estudi d'un hostier medieval del 1339," *Acta historica et archaeologica mediaevalia* 9 (1988), pp. 478–79; Pozo Coll, "Imágenes en las hostias eucarísticas," p. 260; Kumler, "Multiplication of the Species," pp. 181–84; Kumler, "The 'Genealogy of Jean le Blanc,'" pp. 125–28. The wafers could sometimes be made by *oublieurs* (wafer makers). Cf. Rolande Bonnain, "D'une pâtisserie cérémonielle: Usage de l'oublie," *Ethnologie française* 23.4 (1993), pp. 544, 545–46: Article 19 of the statutes of the pastrycooks and wafer makers of Paris stipulated in 1586 "that the master pastrycooks and wafer makers of the town and surrounding areas of Paris be allowed to measure the wheat at the customary hour because the finest wheat is not too good to be used for pastries and also bread for singing mass and communion, where the body of Jesus Christ is celebrated." But, at the Council of Milan (1576), Charles Borromeo was to seek to put an end to this "mixing of genres." Bonnain, "D'une pâtisserie cérémonielle," p. 558n23.

40. Cf. Mabillon, *Dissertatio de pane eucharistico, azymo, ac fermentato*, pp. 135, 157, 189.

41. Ibid., p. 138; Berlendi, *Delle Obblazioni all'altare antiche e moderne*, p. 17; Schefer, *L'hostie profanée*, pp. 132, 137, 153–55. In 1136, Honorarius of Autun, was in turn to refer to "the image of the Lord stamped on the host that is in the form of a coin."

42. The Latin Church adopted the use of unleavened bread at the Council of Toledo (693). Busquets, "Estudi d'un hostier medieval del 1339," p. 476; Schefer, *L'hostie profanée*, pp. 132, 135–36, 151–63; Pozo Coll, "La devoción a la hostia consagrada," pp. 136–38. As Macherel and Steinauer have noted, the host was no longer a common bread, and making it required a certain technical skill. Now, this "change implied the pure and simple

suppression of the last surviving direct link between the people, their productions, and their oblations, and the supernatural operations carried out by the clerics, both in the name of the people and of Christ, on the altar table." Macherel and Steinauer, *L'État de ciel*, p. 85.

43. See Xavier Barbier de Montault, "L'hostie," in *Œuvres complètes* (Paris: Vivès, 1892), tome VI, vol. 1, pp. 178–80. On the care given to the preparation and cooking, see Rubin, *Corpus Christi*, pp. 42–43; Kumler, "Multiplication of the Species," pp. 186–87.

44. Pozo Coll, "La devoción a la hostia consagrada," p. 41; Kumler, "Multiplication of the Species," p. 185.

45. Kristen Van Ausdall, "Communicating with the Host: Imagery and Eucharistic Contact in Late Medieval and Early Renaissance Italy," in *Push Me Pull You: Imaginative and Emotional Interaction in Late Medieval and Renaissance Art* (Leiden: Brill, 2011), vol. 1, p. 449.

46. There were nonetheless a few interdictions promulgated such as the one pertaining to the use of the motif of the lamb. Cf. Galavaris, *Bread and the Liturgy*, p. 26; Pozo Coll, "Imágenes en las hostias eucarísticas," p. 271.

47. Mabillon, *Dissertatio de pane eucharistico, azymo, ac fermentato*, p. 128.

48. In the middle of the fourteenth century, William Russell, Bishop of Sodor (Isle of Man), also specified that the host should be "inscribed." Cf. Rubin, *Corpus Christi*, p. 39.

49. Honorarius of Autun, *De Gemma Animae*, book I, chap. 35, cited in Kumler, "Multiplication of the Species," p. 188. Cf. Schefer, *L'hostie profanée*, p. 54.

50. Berlendi, *Delle Obblazioni all'altare antiche e moderne*, p. 20

51. Kumler, "Multiplication of the Species," p. 186. As Schefer points out (*L'hostie profanée*, p. 151), the word *hostia* was not used before the thirteenth century. Before that time, one used the terms, *oblata* or *corpus*. From the beginning of the fifteenth century, the terms *Corpus Christi* or *Domini* were to be used more freely. Frédéric Tixier, *La monstrance eucharistique, XIIIe–XVIe siècle* (Rennes: PUR, 2014), pp. 15–21.

52. Pozo Coll, "Imágenes en las hostias eucarísticas," p. 262.

53. The dogma of transubstantiation was grafted onto Saint Ambrose's "theory of the miraculous transformation of the eucharistic bread and wine." It echoed also the contentious debates between the proponents of a symbolic reading of the Eucharist (Augustine, Ratramnus, Berengar of Tours) and the defenders of a realist understanding of it (Paschasius Radbertus). Cf. Macherel and Steinauer, *L'État de ciel*, pp. 83–87; Schefer, *L'hostie profanée*, pp. 109–10, 136–37, 185–86. According to Macherel and Steinauer, the image was

supposedly introduced with the purpose of revivifying a rite that had experienced an "extraordinary decline" between the ninth and twelfth centuries: "The greater part of the believers avoided a mass and communion table that, in terms of participation and symbolic exchange, offered them nothing more than insubstantial crumbs." Macherel and Steinauer, *L'État de ciel*, p. 86.

54. Cyril Gerbron has noted, "to make present Christ's sacrifice is to make present its redeeming powers, projecting thus the community towards the last days." Cyril Gerbron, *Fran Angelico: Liturgie et mémoire* (Turnhout: Brepols, 2016), p. 67.

55. Nicole Bériou, "L'eucharistie dans l'imaginaire des prédicateurs," in Nicole Bériou, Béatrice Caseau, Dominique Rigaux, eds., *Pratiques de l'eucharistie dans les Églises d'Orient et d'Occident (Antiquité et Moyen Âge),* vol. 2: *Les réceptions* (Turnhout: Brepols, 2009), pp. 881–83.

56. The *manducatio per visum* is discussed by William of Saint-Thierry in *De sacramento altaris liber*, PL, 180, cols. 341–66, and see especially 355. On this point, see also among others Macherel and Steinauer, *L'état de ciel*, p. 71 et seq.; Rubin, *Corpus Christi*, pp. 63–64; Charles Caspers, "The Western Church during the Late Middle Ages: *Augenkommunion* or Popular Mysticism?," in Charles Caspers, Gerard Lukken, and Gerard Rouwhorst, *Bread of Heaven: Customs and Practices surrounding Holy Communion, Essays in the History of Liturgy and Culture* (Kampen: Kok Pharos, 1995), pp. 83–97; Heike Schlie, *Bilder des Corpus Christi: Sakramentaler Realismus von Jan van Eyck bis Hieronymus Bosch* (Berlin: Mann Verlag, 2002), pp. 199–202; Achim Timmermann, *Real Presence: Sacrament Houses and the Body of Christ c. 1270–1600* (Turnhout: Brepols, 2009), pp. 3–7; Tixier, "La monstrance *eucharistique*," pp. 15–18, 25–98.

57. Schlie, *Bilder des Corpus Christi.*

58. Roger S. Wieck, "The Sacred Bleeding Host of Dijon in Books of Hours," in *Quand la peinture* était *dans les livres: Mélanges en l'honneur de François Avril* (Turnhout: Brepols, 2007), pp. 393–404.

59. On the elevation of the host and the decree concerning it, see Edouard Dumoutet, *Corpus Domini, aux sourves de la piété eucharistique médiévale* (Paris: G. Beauchesne, 1942), p. 44n1. See also Rubin, *Corpus Christi*, p. 49 et seq.; Macherel and Steinauer, *L'État de ciel*, pp. 88–90, 93; Pozo Coll, "Imágenes en las hostias eucarísticas," p. 257.

60. Schlie, *Bilder des Corpus Christi*, pp. 92–96; Uwe Albrecht, ed., *Corpus der Mittelalterlichen Holzskulptur und Tafelmalerei in Schleswig-Holstein*, Bd. 1 (Kiel: Ludwig, 2005), pp. 272–82.

61. See especially Jean-Claude Schmitt, "La culture de *l'imago*," *Annales Histoire, sciences sociales* 51.1 (1996), pp. 3–36; Jean Wirth, *L'image à l'époque romane* (Paris: Cerf, 1999), pp. 35–40; Schefer, *L'hostie profanée*, p. 149: "The bread and the wine, although they are mystically the body of Christ, represent or depict equally the participation of the faithful, united in the Church, with the mystical body of the Savior."

62. Georges Didi-Huberman, *La Ressemblance par contact: Archéologie, anachronisme et modernité de l'empreinte* (Paris: Éditions de Minuit, 2008), p. 72.

63. Didi-Huberman, *La Ressemblance par contact,* pp. 72–73.

64. Cf. Brigitte Miriam Bedos-Rezak, "Medieval Identity: A Sign and a Concept," *American Historical Review* 105.5 (2000), pp. 1489–1533; Brigitte Miriam Bedos-Rezak, "Une image ontologique: Sceau et ressemblance en France préscolastique (1000–1200)," in Alain Erlande-Bradenburg and Jean-Michel Leniaud, eds., *Études d'histoires de l'art offertes à Jacques Thirion: Des premiers temps chrétiens au XXe siècle* (Paris: École des chartes, 2001), pp. 39–50; Brigitte Miriam Bedos-Rezak, "In Search of a Semiotic Paradigm: The Matter of Sealing in Medieval Thougth and Praxis (1050–1400)," in Noël Adams, John Cherry, and James Robinson, eds., *Good Impressions: Image and Authority in Medieval Seals* (London: British Museum Research Publication, 2008), pp. 1–7; Brigitte Miriam Bedos-Rezak, "Ego, Ordo, Communitas: Seals and the Medieval Semiotics of Personality (1200–1350)," in Markus Späth, ed., *Die Bildlichkeit korporativer Siegel im Mittelalter Kunstgeschichte und Geschichte im Gespräch* (Cologne: Böhlau Verlag, 2009), pp. 47–64. This paradigm draws part of its legitimacy from the metaphor, widely used by theologians, of man as an imprint of the seal of God. Cf. Bedos-Rezak, "Medieval Identity," pp. 1504, 1522–26; Bedos-Rezak, "In Search of a Semiotic Paradigm," p. 2. On the seal as an analog for the host, see also Kumler, "Multiplication of the Species," pp. 187–91.

65. Bedos-Rezak, "In Search of a Semiotic Paradigm," p. 3.

66. Bedos-Rezak, "Medieval Identity," p. 1521: "I propose to interpret the extension of sealing as a manifestation of a new semiotics in which . . . immanence rather than transcendence governed the rapport between signifier and signified, thereby making possible new forms for the representation of reality." See also Bedos-Rezak, "Une image," p. 46.

67. Didi-Huberman, *La Ressemblance par contact*, pp. 53–54. For more on this other material, anthropological, and historical approach, see equally the conclusions of Bedos-Rezak, "Medieval Identity," especially pp. 1516–21.

68. The body of Christ is not divided up in the host. See among others Caroline

Walker Bynum, *Fragmentation and Redemption: Essays on Gender and the Human Body in Medieval Religion* (New York: Zone Books, 1992), p. 280; Olivier Leplatre, *"Un goût à la voir nonpareil." Manger les images: Essais d'iconophagie* (Paris: Kimé, 2018), p. 149 et seq.; Bériou, "L'eucharistie dans l'imaginaire des prédicateurs," pp. 888–89.

69. Didi-Huberman, *La Ressemblance par contact*, pp. 73–74.

70. Louis Petit de Juleville, "Un gaufrier du XIIIe siècle," *Annales Archéologiques* 13 (1853), pp. 43–44, and Pozo Coll, "Imágenes en las hostias eucarísticas," p. 271.

71. The principle of the many in the One is signified in this latter inscription. As Schefer notes, to distinguish their practice from the Jewish rite of Passover and from its use of shared unleavened bread, the Christians invoked the triune God in their celebration of the mystery. Schefer, *L'hostie profanée*, pp. 133–34.

72. We should not forget here, as Peter Brown has shown, that the rite establishes a relation of identity which is the precondition for the transformation of the community into a family. Peter Brown, *The Cult of the Saints: Its Rise and Function in Latin Christianity* (Chicago: University of Chicago Press, 2015), pp. 30–31.

73. For more on this mutual incorporation, see Schmitt, "La culture de *l'imago*," and Leplatre, *"Un goût à la voir nonpareil,"* pp. 149 and 189.

74. Saint Augustine, *The Confessions,* trans. Maria Boulding, OSB (New York: New City Press, 1997), p. 173.

75. Bernard of Clairvaux, *On the Song of Songs IV*, trans. Irene Edmonds (Kalamazoo, MI: Cistercian Publications, 1980), p. 53.

76. Guillaume Durand, *Guillelmi Duranti Rationale Divinorum Officiorum: I-IV*, A. Davril and Timothy M. Thibodeau, ed. (Turnhout: Brepols, 1995), pp. 443; William Durand, *Rationale IV: On The Mass and Each Action Pertaining to It,* trans. Timothy M. Thibodeau (Turnhout: Brepols, 2013), p. 334.

77. Honorarius Augustodunensis, *Eucharistion*, *Patrologia cursus completus: Series Latina*, ed. Jean-Paul Migne (Paris: 1844–1865), vol. 172, col. 555B. See also Kumler, "Multiplication of the Species," p. 187.

78. Luca Pinelli, *Brief Meditations of the Most Holy Sacrament and of Preparation, for Rescuing the Same, and of Some Other Things Apertaining to the Greatness and Devotion of So Worthy A Mystery*, ed., Henry Garnet (London: V. Simmes, ca. 1600), p. 5. Emphasis is mine and English spelling is modernized.

79. Giovanni Careri, *La torpeur des ancêtres: Juifs et chrétiens dans la chapelle Sixtine* (Paris: Éditions de l'École des Hautes Études en Sciences Sociales, 2013), chap. 1.

80. For more on this taking on of likeness, see Robert Javelet, et al., "Image et ressemblance," in *Dictionnaire de spiritualité ascétique et mystique, doctrine et histoire*, tome VII/16, vol. II/2. (Paris: Beauchesne, 1971), 1401–72.

81. The Discalced Carmelite, Theodoric of Saint-René, wrote in his *Remarques historiques données à l'occasion de la sainte hostie miraculeuse* (1725): "The goal of the institution of the eucharist is not to give health and long bodily life to those who take communion worthily, nor is it to strike with illness or bodily death those who take communion unworthily. Each time that a Christian worthily receives the Body of Jesus Christ, he is assured of receiving an increase of justifying grace and of being fortified in these duties, because Jesus Christ established the Sacrament of the Eucharist for this purpose." Theodoric of Saint-René, cited in Schefer, *L'hostie profanée*, p. 114. On the notion of *effectus* in the eucharistic sacrament, see Giorgio Agamben, *Opus Dei: An Archaeology of Duty*, trans. Adam Kotsko (Stanford: Stanford University Press, 2013), pp. 55–78.

82. This unity in Christ is accompanied by unity in the Church. See Jérôme Baschet, *La Civilisation féodale de l'an mil à la colonisation de l'Amérique* (Paris: Flammarion, 2006), p. 516: "By incorporating themselves into the Body of Christ (the host), the faithful *incorporate* themselves into the body of Christ (the Church)."

83. Charles Sanders Peirce, "[from] On the Algebra of Logic: A Contribution to the Philosophy of Notation," *The Essential Peirce: Selected Philosophical Writings*, eds. Nathan Houser and Christian Kloesel (Bloomington: Indiana University Press, 1992), vol. 1, pp. 225–28.

84. According to Schefer, "the sign is the summon of its referent, and by its consecration it is transformed into the thing itself." Schefer, *L'hostie profanée*, pp. 133 and 149.

85. As a degraded imprint of God, the communicant regains through ingestion a lost original likeness.

86. We can see this action as a trial, as we do in Numbers 5:11–34, or again a direct punishment, as in Jeremiah 8:14, "For the Lord God has doomed us to perish and given us poisoned water to drink, because we have sinned against him."

87. The Christian reading of this episode that we find in the Church Fathers is quite different. Martine Dulaey, "La geste de Moïse dans l'œuvre d'Augustin (2): La présence de Dieu au désert et la figure de Moïse," *Revue d'études augustiniennes et patristiques* 57 (2011), pp. 209–10. The drinking of the water was rather, for them, a sign of the conversion of the people as they incorporated God's truth. For Saint Augustine (*Contra Faustum* 22:93 and *Expositions of the Psalms* 73:16), the trial transforms the pagans into members

of the body of Christ. As Martine Dulaey writes, "The impious worship an idol that is like the head of the society of idolators, made of gold, because it is the object of a worship preached by the so-called wise of this world. But its apparent beauty disappears in the face of the fire that Christ has come to set alight on earth. Reduced to dust, that is, humiliating themselves and submitting to the word of God, the pagans pass into the body of Christ." Dulaey, "La geste de Moïse dans l'œuvre d'Augustin (2)," p. 209.

88. Cf. Gérard Haddad, *Eating the Book: Dietary Rites and Paternal Function,* trans. David Jacobson (New York: Agincourt Press, 2013), p. 45

89. "Cum in servis suspicio furti habetur, ducuntur ad sacerdotum, qui crustum panis, carmine infectum dat singulis. Quod cum haeserit, manifestum furti reum adserit." *Acronis et Porphirionis Comment., in Q. Horatium Flaccum*, cited in Federico Patetta, *Le Ordalie: Studio di storia del diritto e scienza del diritto comparator* (Turin: Fratelli Bocca, 1890), p. 140. Gustave Glotz thinks that this is more a Frankish custom. Gustav Glotz, *L'Ordalie dans la Grèce primitive: Étude de droit et de mythologie* (Paris: Fontemoing, 1904), pp. 110–11.

90. Warren Hastings, "On the Trial by Ordeal among the Hindus by Alí Ibráhím Káhn," in *Asiatick Researches or Transactions of the Society Instituted in Bengal* (Calcutta: Manuel Cantopher, 1788), p. 391. See also Glotz, *L'Ordalie dans la Grèce primitive*, pp. 115–16.

91. Derek A. Rivard, *Blessing the World: Ritual and Lay Piety in Medieval Religion* (Washington, DC: Catholic University of America Press, 2009), pp. 263–64. For more general information on the *iudicium panis*, see Patetta, *Le Ordalie*, pp. 215–16; Andrea Mareschi and Francesca Tasca, "Aux limites de l'hérésie et de la magie: L'ordalie du pain et du fromage," *Food and History* 16.1 (2018), pp. 49–67. The Fourth Lateran Council was to ban trials by ordeal, but people continued nonetheless to resort to them. Cf. Julie Jourdain, "Ordalie, image et sermon après le concile de Latran IV," *Cahiers de Recherches Médiévales et Humanistes* 25 (2013), pp. 389–404. The *iudicium panis et casei* is described in the *Ordines*, A, 26–28, B, XVII, 6; Eugène de Rozière, *Recueil général des formules usitées dans l'Empire des Francs du Ve au Xe siècle* (Paris: Auguste Durand, 1861), vol. 2, pp. 876, 878.

92. Cf. Jourdain, "Ordalie," p. 400.

93. Robert Jacob, *La grâce des juges: L'institution judiciaire et le sacré en Occident* (Paris: Presses universitaires de France, 2014), pp. 17–108.

94. Boccaccio, *The Decameron of Giovanni Boccaccio*, trans. J. M. Rigg (London, [1903] 1921), VIII, 6.

95. As Bonnain notes, the cake was "a privileged instrument for the establishment

of links through gifting or offering." Bonnain, "D'une pâtisserie cérémonielle," p. 547. For Henri Bresc, "Latin Christendom expressed its unity through the rhythms and rites imposed or suggested by the Church." Henri Bresc, "Europe: Town and Country (Thirteenth-Fifteenth Century)," in André Burguière, Christiane Klapisch-Zuber, Martine Segalen, and Francoise Zonabend, eds., *A History of the Family*, vol. 1: *Distant Worlds, Ancient Worlds*, trans. Sarah Hanbury Tenison, Rosemary Morris, and Andrew Wilson (Cambridge, MA: Belknap Press of Harvard University Press, 1996), p. 437.

96. Galavaris, *Bread and the Liturgy*, pp. 109–17.

97. Ibid., pp. 133–36.

98. Cf. Françoise Desportes, "Food Trades," in Jean-Louis Flandrin and Massimo Montanari, eds., *Food: A Culinary History from Antiquity to the Present*, trans. Clarissa Botsford, et al. (New York: Columbia University Press, 1999), p. 281; Bonnain, "D'une pâtisserie," pp. 542–43. It is relatively difficult to be sure about the ingredients used in these desserts because, as Bonnain writes, "in common and poetic language, white breads and cakes were often confused."

99. For more on these two molds, see Helga Giersiepen, *Die Inschriften der Stadt Aachen* (Düsseldorf: Reichert Verlag, 1993), p. 30, cat. 46 and 47; Marc Bussagli, ed., *Les ailes de Dieu: Messagers et guerriers ailés entre Orient et Occident* (Milan: Silvana, 2000), p. 222.

100. Alain Erlande-Brandenburg, Pierre-Yves Le Pogam, and Dany Sandron, *Musée national du Moyen Âge: Guide to the Collections*, trans. Pamela Hargreaves (Paris, RMN, 1993), pp. 62–63.

101. Cristina Mazzoni, *Cooking, Eating, and Spiritual Writing* (London: Continuum, 2005), p. 75.

102. The sale of these cakes provided a not insignificant source of income for the religious communities. Cf. Mazzoni, *Cooking*, p. 76.

103. Jacques Albin-Simon Colllin de Plancy, *Dictionnaire critique des reliques et des images miraculeuses* (Paris: Guien.), 1821–22, III, p. 228. On the life and functioning of the community of the *Génovéfains*, see Isabelle Brian, *Messieurs de Sainte-Geneviève. Religieux et curés de la Contre-Réforme à la Révolution* (Paris: Cerf, 2001).

104. Mazzoni, *Cooking*, p. 81. In the ancient world, we see evidence of other pastries in the form of a woman's breast, such as the kyribanas that were eaten in Laconia solely by woman at the time of their marriage. Atheneaus of Naucratis, *The Learned Banqueters*, ed. and trans. S. Douglas Olson, Loeb Classical Library, vol. VII (Cambridge, MA: Harvard University Press, 2011), p. 277. Cf. Galavaris, *Bread and the Liturgy*, p. 25. Pastries

in the form of breasts also appear in a recipe created by the Futurist artist Marisa Mori in the 1930s. See Jennifer Griffiths, "Marisa Mori's Futurist Breasts," *Gastronomica* 12.4 (2012), pp. 20–26.

105. Mazzoni, *Cooking*, p. 84.

106. Ibid., p. 78.

107. In Baden Baden, for example, the Cistercian nuns of Lichtenthal Abbey used such molds to make cakes at Christmas and Easter, giving them out to the benefactors of their convent. Once again, this came down to establishing, through the production of edible images, a connection between the institution and the wider community. Cf. Christiaan Schrickx, "Bethlehem in de Bangert: Een historische en archeologische studie naar de ontwikkeling van een vrouwenklooster onder de Orde van het Heilig Kruis in het buitengebied van Hoorn (1475–1572)," PhD diss. Universiteit Leiden, 2015, pp. 303–304.

108. Bonnain, "D'une pâtisserie cérémonielle," pp. 542 and 558n6.

109. On the Poor Clares of Monteluce, see Peter Höhler, "Il monastero delle clarisse di Monteluce in Perugia (1218–1400)." In Roberto Rusconi, ed. *Il movimento religioso femminile in Umbria nei secoli XIII–XIV. Atti del Convegno internazionale di studio nell'ambito delle celebraioni per l'VII centenario delle nascità di S. Francesco d'Assisi* (Florence: La Nuova Italia Editrice, 1984), pp. 161–82.

110. The monogram IHS, adored by Saint Bernardino of Siena, showed also the relationship between the Clarisse nuns and the Franciscans.

111. See the comments below pertaining to the secular *cialde*.

112. The sermon, originally in Latin, was published later in German by Johannes Adelphum in 1514. Cf. Johannes Geiler von Kaysersberg, *Passion Des Here[n] Jesu, Fürgeben vnd geprediget gar betrachtiglich (particuliert) vnd geteilt in stückes weiß eins süßen Lebkuochen vßzuogeben (per quadragesima[m]) als durch die gantze fasten allen tag wol ein Predig daruß zuonemen ist*. Straßburg, 1514, fol. 7r–13v. (although the pagination is slightly off). A digital copy made by the Bayerischen Staatsbibliothek is available online at: https://daten.digitale-sammlungen.de/~db/0002/bsb00020110/images/. For more on Geiler of Kaysersberg, see Rita Voltmer, *Wie der Wächter auf dem Turm: ein Prediger und seine Stadt: Johannes Geiler von Kaysersberg (1445–1510) und Straßburg* (Porta-Alba: Trèves, 2005); Rita Voltmer, "Political Preaching and a Design of Urban reform: Johannes Geiler of Kaysersberg and Strasbourg," *Franciscan Studies* 71 (2013), pp. 71–88.

113. Geiler, *Passion*, fol. 7v.

114. Ibid., fol. 8r. (step 1).

115. Ibid., fol. 8r. (steps 2 and 3).

116. Ibid., fol. 8r. (steps 4 and 5).

117. Ibid., fol. 8r.–v.

118. This is the point of Geiler's reference to John 6:27.

119. Behind this analogy, we can see the image of the seal, used by the theologians when they spoke of the resemblance of the Son to the Father. See above regarding the host, and see also Didi-Huberman, *La Ressemblance*, pp. 54–55.

120. Geiler, *Passion*, fol. 9r.

121. Ibid., fol. 9v.

122. Ibid.

123. Ibid., fol. 10v.

124. Ibid., fol. 13r.

125. Ibid., fol. 10r.

126. Ibid., fol. 13r.

127. The verb *schlagen*, used in this text, was also used to mean "to mint [beat] coins."

128. Geiler, *Passion*, fol. 12r.

129. Ibid., fol. 13r.

130. Ibid., fol. 12v.

131. Many molds depicting the Crucifixion have survived and are to be found today in collections. Cf. Hans Jürgen Hansen, ed., *Kunstgeschichte des Backwerks: Geschichte und Entwicklung der Gebäckarten und ihrer Formen* (Oldenbourg: Gerhard Stalling, 1968), p. 75.

132. "Also sag ich, wir hie zuo Straßburg seind alle ein leib, unnd wir seint glider." Cited in Voltmer, *Wie der Wächter*, p. 251.

133. See Voltmer, *Wie der Wächter*, pp. 251–69; Voltmer, "Political Preaching," pp. 79–80.

134. Voltmer, *Wie der Wächter*, p. 735 et seq.

135. Voltmer, "Political Preaching," pp. 71–75.

136. Ibid. pp. 82–83.

137. The notion of the family is changeable: its perimeter, structure, and legal reality vary across times and places. I am thinking here of the family as an entity constituted around a fire and comparable to a house (domus). It might contain, therefore, both cognate and agnate members of the same family, as well as persons assigned to the master's service. For more on these nuances, see Yan Thomas, "Fathers as Citizens of Rome, Rome as a City of Fathers (Second Century BC–Second Century AD)," in André

Burguière, Christiane Klapisch-Zuber, Martine Segalen, and Francoise Zonabend, eds., *A History of the Family*, vol. 1., trans. Sarah Hanbury Tenison, Rosemary Morris, and Andrew Wilson (Cambridge, MA: Belknap Press of Harvard University Press, 1996), vol. 1, pp. 318–78; Bresc, "Europe: Town and Country," pp. 430–66.

138. Cf. for a starting point, Van Gennep, *The Rites of Passage*; Charles de La Roncière, "Tuscan Notables on the Eve of the Renaissance," in Georges Duby and Philippe Ariès, eds., *A History of Private Life*, vol. 2: *Revelations of the Medieval World*, trans. Arthur Goldhammer (Cambridge, MA: Belknap Press of Harvard University Press, 1988), p. 247.

139. On the molds used in the domestic sphere, see notably Hansen, *Kunstgeschichte des Backwerks*, pp. 43–107; Frank Matthias Kammel and Ulrich G. Großmann, eds., *Spiegel der Seligkeit: Privates Bild und Frömmigkeit im Spätmittelalter* (Nuremberg: Germanisches Nationalmuseum, 2000), pp. 359–61; Gerald Volker Grimm, "Die Mitteleuropäischen backmodel des 15. Jahrhunderts: Werkgruppen, Chronologie, Verbreitung," in Lutz Grunwald, ed., *Den Töpfern auf der Spur: Orte der Keramikherstellung im Licht der neuesten Forschung* (Mainz: RGZM-Tagungen 21, 2015), pp. 349–58; Schrickx, *Bethlehem in de Bangert*, pp. 263–70; Christa Fischer, *Stolze Reiter, schöne Damen: Die Bilderwelt der Gebäckmodel* (Ostfildern: Jan Thorbecke Verlag, 2012). See also the collection of the Schweizerisches Landesmuseum of Zürich that has made many molds (*gebäckmodel*) available for viewing online.

140. Claus Stalburg and his wife Margarethe vom Rhein had fourteen children. For more on Stalburg's inventory see Friedrich Bothe, *Frankfurter Patriziervermögen im 16. Jahrhundert: Ein Beitrag zur Charakteristik der bürgerlichen Vermögen und der bürgerlichen Kultur* (Berlin: Alexander Duncker Verlag, 1908), pp. 113–15 (the Baptism is number 5); Hansen, *Kunstgeschichte des Backwerks*, p. 55; Kammel and Großmann, *Spiegel der Seligkeit*, p. 361.

141. Many other molds of this type can be found. We have, for example, those by Eberhard-Wüest (1634), Schweizerisches Landesmusem of Zürich (inv. LM-50718), and by Thurn-Seiler (1646), Schweizerisches Landesmusem of Zürich (inv. LM-71473).

142. Among these molds, we might mention the following subjects: Adam and Eve (1510), Samson and Delilah (1510), the story of Romulus and Remus (1512), the Baptism of Christ (1512), David and Bathsheba (1512), the Flight into Egypt (1514), the Rape of Lucretia (1515), Saint Sebastian (1517), a Moorish Dance, and so on. One of the molds that had belonged to Stalburg, showing four men around a fountain with four young women, is today in the collection of the Historisches Museum Frankfurt (inv. X10962).

143. Stalburg was also a close friend of the humanist Philip Melanchthon.

144. As Françoise Piponnier points out, waffle irons were relatively expensive: "Only professionals and the wealthiest private kitchens possessed waffle irons and griddles." Françoise Pipponier, "From Hearth to Table: Late Medieval Cooking Equipment," in Jean-Louis Flandrin and Massimo Montanari, eds., *Food: A Culinary History*, trans. Clarissa Botsford, et al. (New York: Columbia University Press, 1999), p. 341.

145. Walter Hildburgh, "Germanic Wafering-Irons of the Sixteenth Century," *Proceedings of the Society of Antiquaries of London*, ser. 2, 26 (1914), p. 146.

146. The bibliography on the *cialde* is not extensive, and the works often date from some time ago: Adamo Rossi, "Francesco di Valeriano detto il Roscetto ed i suoi figli Federico e Cesarino," *Giornale di erudizione artistica* 2, fasc. 4 (1873), pp. 89–136; Hildburgh, "Germanic Wafering-Irons"; Walter Hildburgh, "Italian Wafering-Irons of the Fifteenth and Sixteenth Century," *Proceedings of the Society of Antiquaries of London*, ser. 2, 27 (1905), pp. 161–201; Hanna Kronberger-Frentzen, *Die alte Kunst der süssen Sachen: Backformen und Waffeleisen vergangener Jahrhunderte* (Hambourg: Broschek Verlag, 1959); Giovanni Ranieri Fascetti, *I Ferri da cialda: Documenti del costume e del gusto fra Rinascimento dei miti ed eucaristia profana* (Pisa: ETS, 1997); Jacqueline Marie Musacchio, *Art, Marriage, and Family in the Florentine Renaissance Palace* (New Haven, CT: Yale University Press, 2008), pp. 32–33; Deborah L. Krohn, "Wafering Iron," in Andrea Bayer, ed., *Art and Love in Renaissance Italy* (New Haven, CT: Yale University Press, 2009), exhibition catalog, pp. 116–17, ; Oleg Zastrow, "Antiche inedite schiacce decorate artisticamente," *Rassegna di studi et di notizie* 34, anno 38 (2012), pp. 245–76.

147. Although rare, portraits can be found, such as for example with the wafering-irons belonging to Simone de Antonio da Parnaciano, 1532, in the collection of the Galleria Nazionale dell'Umbria in Perugia. On the front, we see the bull, symbol of Saint Luke the Evangelist, with the inscription, "Quiste ferra sonno de Semone de Antonio da Parnaciano fatte nel MDXXXII (These irons are of Semone of Antonio da Parnaciano; made in 1532)," and on the back, there is a portrait with the inscription, "Mangiate dele cialde epoi bevete che pigliarite l'orso sense rete (Eat of the wafers and then drink, that you may take the bear without a net)." Cf. Hildburgh, "Italian Wafering-Irons," p. 190 and figs. 24a–b.

148. Musacchio, Art, Marriage, and Family," p. 33 (weddings), pp. 41–42 (baptisms); Marta Ajmar and Flora Dennis, eds., *At Home in Renaissance Italy: Art and Life in the Italian House, 1400–1600* (New York: Abrams, 2006), p. 361n50. Hildburgh ("Italian Wafering-Irons") mentions also the occurrence of host presses in the account book of the Opera del Duomo. The consuls of the Woolmakers Guild were served cialde in 1417 for the feast

of San Giovanni. On the service and dishes involved in social representation, see Allen J. Grieco, "Food and Social Classes in Late Medieval and Renaissance Italy," in Jean-Louis Flandrin and Massimo Montanari, eds. *Food: A Culinary History*, trans. Clarissa Botsford, Arthur Goldhammer, et al. (New York: Columbia University Press, 1999), pp. 302–12; Charles de La Roncière, "Tuscan Notables on the Eve of the Renaissance."

149. Musacchio, *Art, Marriage, and Family*, p. 33.

150. Cristoforo da Messisbugo, *Banchetti, compositioni di vivande et apparacchio generale* (Ferrare: Giovanni de Buglhat et Antonio Hucher Compagni, 1549), s.p. The sumptuary laws placed no limits on the quantity of *cialde* that could be produced. Cf. Ronald E. Rainey, "Sumptuary Legislation in Renaissance Florence" (PhD diss., Columbia University, 1985), p. 785.

151. Cf. Rossi, "Francesco di Valeriano."

152. On the patrilineal line and alimentary obligation in the Latin world, the heritage of which was strong in Europe in the Middle Ages, see Thomas, "Fathers as Citizens of Rome."

153. Hans Belting, *An Anthropology of Images: Picture, Medium, Body*, trans. Thomas Dunlap (Princeton, NJ: Princeton University Press, 2011), p. 62.

154. Cf. Bedos-Rezak, "In Search of a Semiotic Paradigm," p. 2.

155. Genealogy is certainly present in the irons belonging to Simone de Antonio da Parnaciano in the form of the name (Simone son of Antonio da Parnaciano); however, the linking of the portrait with the *motto*, "Eat of the wafers and then drink, that you may take the bear without a net," suggests more the celebration of the strength and courage of one man.

156. As Charles de Miramon has noted, between the end of antiquity and up to the fourteenth century transmission via the flesh predominated over blood. It was in the fourteenth and fifteenth centuries that blood was to make its return with the concept of "bloodline," fusing the notions of blood and line of descent. Charles de Miramon, "Aux origines de la noblesse et des princes du sang: France et Angleterre au XIVe siècle," in Maaike van der Lugt and Charles de Miramon, eds., *L'hérédité entre Moyen Âge et Époque moderne, Perspectives historiques* (Florence: Sismel, 2008), pp. 200–201.

157. We should recall that Galen's ideas on medicine, widely shared in the Renaissance, included the view of digestion as the process by which a foodstuff was turned into blood. The philosopher and physician Marsilius Ficinus writes, "Blood is produced by the liver that uses, for carrying out this function, the elements derived from digestion." Marsile Ficin, *Sulla Vita*, ed. Alessandra Tarabochia Canavero (Milan: Rusconi,

1995), vol. 2, book 4, pp. 139–140. On the mind, digestion, and blood, see Robert Klein, "*Spirito peregrino*," in Robert Klein, *Form and Meaning: Essays on the Renaissance and Modern Art*, trans. Madeline Jay and Leon Wieseltier (New York: Viking Press, 1979), p. 45; Nella Bianchi Bensimon, "Alimentation et mélancolie dans le *De vita libri tres* de Marsile Ficin," in Adelin Charles Fiorato and Anna Fontes Baratto, eds., *La table et ses dessous: Culture, alimentation et convivialité en Italie, XIVe–XVIe siècle* (Paris: Presses de la Sorbonne Nouvelle, 1999), pp. 55–71.

158. The relationship established by ingesting the heraldic arms could function like the ancient Roman stemmata scrolls. In fact, for Christiane Klapisch-Zuber, those stemmata scrolls were a "metaphor of blood flows . . . and of the circulation of the vital humors transmitting life and identity." Christiane Klapisch-Zuber, *L'ombre des ancêtres: Essai sur l'imaginaire médiéval de la parenté* (Paris: Fayard, 2000), p. 26. See also ibid., pp. 20–21, and Scheid, *Quand faire, c'est croire*, p. 162.

159. See Klapisch-Zuber, *La maison et le nom: Stratégies et rituels dans l'Italie de la Renaissance* (Paris: Éditions de l'École des Hautes Études en Sciences Sociales, 1990), especially chap. 3. The idea of the family is not reducible to blood ties, even if these links are essential. On domestic society, lineage, and the structure of family relations in the Middle Ages and into the modern era, see Jack Goody, *The Development of the Family and Marriage in Europe* (Cambridge, UK: Cambridge University Press, 1983), pp. 222–39; Bresc, "Europe: Town and Country," pp. 430–66; Jean-Louis Flandrin, *Families in Former Times: Kinship, Household, and Sexuality,* trans. Richard Southern (Cambridge, UK: Cambridge University Press, 1979); Charles de La Roncière, "Tuscan Notables on the Eve of the Renaissance," especially pp. 157–65.

160. For example: "Gli si fa che non errei ricordate al patron portare i ferre" (irons dating from 1491 belonging to Ser Bernardino de la Via Nova, Perugia, Galleria Nazionale dell'Umbria.863) and "Ser Ieronimo de Bartolomeo a facts fare a chi non rende no li vol prestare" (irons dating from 1486–1500, Perugia, Galleria Nazionale dell'Umbria).

161. Charles de La Roncière, "Tuscan Notables on the Eve of the Renaissance," pp. 164–65.

162. Cf. Musacchio, "Art, Marriage, and Family," pp. 32–33.

163. Krohn, *Art and Love in Renaissance Italy*, p. 116.

164. A pair of irons in the collection of the Victoria and Albert Museum (inv. M.443-1924) belonging to the Pacca family and dating from 1481 also shows the coats of arms of two families. Furthermore, we find a variant of this linking of two families by means of

a double-sided dessert item in the sugar coins bearing the portraits of Costanzo Sforza and Camilla Marzano d'Aragona that were distributed by the figure of Fortune's Influence (*Influsso de Fortuna*) at their wedding banquet on May 29, 1475: "in spalla haveva una mastella de çuccharo dorata & dipinta piena dimoneta di çucchero doro & dargento cum la testa del Signore & de Madonna naturale & in meço di questi denari era una biscia pur di çucchero. . . ." *Ordine delle Noççe dello Illustrissimo Signore Meser Costantio Sfortia et della Illustrissima Madonna Cammilla de Aragonia sua consorte nellanno 1475*, Vatican, Biblioteca Apostolica, Ms. Urb. Lat. 899, fol. 78v. Cf. Jane Bridgeman's introduction and English translation in *A Renaissance Wedding: The Celebrations at Pesaro for the Marriage of Costanzo Sforza and Camilla Marzano d'Aragona (26–30 May 1475)*, ed. and trans. Jane Bridgeman and Alan Griffiths (London: Harvey Miller, 2013), pp. 92–93, 149.

165. See also the examples noted by Pozo Coll, "La devoción a la hostia consagrada," pp. 39–40, where the inscriptions are in the first person; Busquets, "Estudi d'un hostier medieval del 1339," p. 482.

166. Horst Bredekamp, *Image Acts: A Systematic Approach to Visual Agency*, ed. and trans. Elizabeth Clegg (Berlin: De Gruyter, 2021), p. 35. Seen from this perspective, the *cialda* forms part of a long tradition of "works of art that speak." Ibid., pp. 63–75.

167. Horst Bredekamp, *Image Acts*, p. 63. For Jean Wirth, it is the inscription that makes the image performative, rather than the specific qualities of the image. This is because an image cannot "formulate an utterance." Jean Wirth, *Qu'est-ce qu'une image?* (Geneva: Droz, 2013), p. 88.

168. The term *patrone* (or *padrone* in the *Vocabolario degli Accademici della Crusca* [Venice: Appresso Iacopo Sarzina, 1612], p. 584) designates the master and protector, that is, the one who has dominion (*dominus*) over the household. The term occurs often on the irons. For example, in the irons belonging to Giovanni Battista de S. Pietro de S. Lorenzo (1512, Perugia, Galleria Nazionale dell'Umbria): "Giovam Batiste de S Pietro de S Lorenzo e *patrone* de li ferra como penso MDXII." One of the essential duties of the *patrone* (or *paterfamilias*) was to feed the members of his household. Cf. Georges Duby, "Private Power, Public Power," in Georges Duby and Philippe Ariès, eds. *A History of Private Life*, vol. 2: *Revelations of the Medieval World*, trans. Arthur Goldhammer (Cambridge, MA: Belknap Press of Harvard University Press, 1988), pp. 17–19.

169. In this way, as Charles de Miramon writes, blood is a "social coat of arms." Miramon, "Aux origines de la noblesse et des princes du sang," p. 158. For more on blood nobility, see Claudio Donati, *L'idea di nobiltà in Italia: Secoli XIV–XVII* (Bari: Laterza, 1988).

170. In the fifteenth and sixteenth centuries, stamped wafers were often made especially for private masses, where they were substitutes for the usual host wafers. Pozo Coll mentions irons bearing the inscription "SON DEN BERNAT CUGOT" with a depiction of the Lamb of the Resurrection and the inscription, "AGNUS DEI QUI TOLLIS PECATA" on the other side. The custom was, however, condemned after the Council of Trent. Pozo Coll, "La devoción a la hostia consagrad," p. 39 See Bonnain, "D'une pâtisserie cérémonielle," p. 558n23.

171. Aulus Gellius, *Attic Nights*, trans. John C. Rolfe, Loeb Classical Library, 200 (Cambridge, MA: Harvard University Press, 1927), book 10, chap. 18, pp. 260–63. The story is also related by Valerius Maximus in his *Memorable Deeds and Sayings*, trans. D. R. Shackleton Bailey, Loeb Classical Library, 492 (Cambridge, MA: Harvard University Press, 2000), vol. 1, book 4, chap. 6, pp. 407–409.

172. Girolamo Tartarotti, *Del congresso notturno delle lammie, libri tre* (Rovereto: Gianbatista Pasquali, 1749), p. 177.

173. Tartarotti, *Del congresso notturno delle lammie*. The story of Artemisia brings together two modes of observing remembrance: on the one hand, Artemisia's building of the funeral monument in the form of the "mausoleum" to preserve the memory of her husband publicly and symbolically, and on the other hand, the eating of his ashes, representing her own personal and emotional remembrance. These are two distinct modalities, therefore, and they establish a separation between physical and symbolic remembrance. Cf. Piero Camporesi, *Les Baumes de l'amour* (Paris: Hachette, 1997), pp. 29–30.

174. On incorporation as a way of mourning a loved one by rendering the deceased person eternal, see Doueihi, *A Perverse History of the Human Heart*, pp. 4–13, and for the story of Artemisia, queen of Caria, ibid., 93–102.

175. Michel de Montaigne, *The Complete Essays of Montaigne*, trans. Donald M. Frame (Stanford, CA: Stanford University Press, 1998), p. 438. See Antoine Compagnon, *Nous, Michel de Montaigne* (Paris: Seuil, 1980), pp. 179–84.

176. According to Pierre Fédida, "one can hypothesize that, beyond the physical ingestion of a foodstuff, cannibalism is connected with *a way of conceiving human identification and descent*." Pierre Fédida, "Le cannibale mélancolique," in *L'absence* (Paris: Gallimard/Folio Essais, 1978), pp. 88-89.

177. Marie Paule Duminil suggests that this theory goes back to the followers of Pythagoras. The Pythagorean, Hippon of Rhegium, was supposedly the first to have formulated it. The theory also has echoes in Plato (*Timaeus*, 73b, 91a) before it appears

in Aristotle. Marie Paule Duminil, "Les theories biologiques sur la génération en Grèce antique," *Pallas: Revue d'études antiques* 31 (1984), pp. 103–104.

178. A similar specialty, known as *pan de muerto*, exists in Mexico. Cf. Juanita Garciagodoy, *Digging the Days of the Dead: A Reading of Mexico's Dias de Muertos* (Niwot: University Press of Colorado, 1998), pp. 15, 135–37.

179. For more on the anthropological stakes involved with these cakes, see Salvatore D'Onofrio, *Les fluides d'Aristote: Lait, sang et sperme dans l'Italie du Sud* (Paris: Les belles lettres, 2014), pp. 151–62. We find analogous rites in Northern Italy. See ibid., p. 157. And Giorgio Vasari speaks of similar cakes being served at the banquets of the Company of the Cazzuola (Compagnia della Cazzuola): "These first viands finished, which formed a sort of relish, dead men's bones were set all the way down the table in place of fruits and sweetmeats, as if the supper, which was scarcely begun, were finished; which reliquary fruits were of sugar." Giorgio Vasari, *Lives of the Painters, Sculptors and Architects*, trans. Gaston du C. de Vere (New York: Alfred A. Knopf, 1996), vol. 2, p. 528.

180. D'Onofrio, *Les fluides d'Aristote*, p. 152

181. Ibid., p. 158.

182. Ibid., p. 154.

183. D'Onofrio, referring to a study by Giuseppe Pitrè, *Medicina popolare siciliana* (Palermo: Clausen, 1896), p. 128 on popular medicine in the South of Italy, writes of "the belief according to which, in Sicily, the seminal fluid comes down from 'the marrow in the backbone,' i.e., from the extended marrow with which it maintains a physical analogy since it circulates from the head to the phallus, passing through the vertebral column." D'Onofrio, *Les fluides d'Aristote*, p. 158. This connection, deriving from the "theory of agnatic consanguinity," and going back "to Aristotle's *On the Generation of Animals*," with intermediaries such as Montaigne, "sees the sperm as the vehicle of the blood." Ibid., p. 158.

184. Ibid., p. 153.

185. Cf. Garciagodoy, *Digging the Days of the Dead*, pp. 15 et seq. and 233 et seq.; Kristin Congdon, "Making Merry with Death: Iconic Humor in Mexico's Day of the Dead," in Peter Narvaez, ed., *Of Corpse: Death and Humor in Folkore and Popular Culture* (Logan, UT: Utah State University Press, 2003), pp. 198–220; and Stanley Brandes, *Skulls to the Living, Bread to the Dead: Celebrations of Death in Mexico and Beyond* (Malden: Blakwell, 2006).

186. In addition to the film with its turbulent history, see Sergei Eisenstein, "The Day of the Dead," in Carole Naggar and Fred Ritchin, eds., *Mexico Through Foreign Eyes: Visto por ojos extranjeros, 1850–1990* (New York: W. W. Norton, 1993), pp. 154–55. For more

on the impact of Eisenstein in Mexico, see Antonio Somaini, "*Que Viva Mexico!* et le tournant archéologique dans l'œuvre d'Eisenstein," in Laurence Schifano and Antonio Somaini, eds., *Eisenstein leçons mexicaines: Cinéma, anthropologie, archéologie dans le mouvement des arts* (Paris: Presses universitaires de Paris-Ouest, 2016), pp. 49–62; Rose-Marie Godier, "*Calaveras* ou les écarts de la pensée: Une vision de Georges Bataille," in Laurence Schifano and Antonio Somaini, eds., *Eisenstein leçons mexicaines: Cinéma, anthropologie, archéologie dans le mouvement des arts* (Paris: Presses universitaires de Paris-Ouest, 2016), p. 311; Evgenia Giannouri, "Voyages dans les reflets et autres déplacements analogiques: Le Yucatan de S. M. Eisenstein, Robert Smithson et John Lloyd Stephens," in Laurence Schifano and Antonio Somaini, eds., *Eisenstein leçons mexicaines: Cinéma, anthropologie, archéologie dans le mouvement des arts* (Paris: Presses universitaires de Paris-Ouest, 2016), pp. 358–59; Marie Rebecchi and Elena Vogman, "The Anthropology of Rhythm," in Marie Rebecchi and Elena Vogman, *Sergei Eisenstein and the Anthropology of Rhythm* (Rome: Produzioni Nero, 2017), pp. 9–20. For an historical-anthropological approach to its continuing effect, see Garciagodoy, *Digging the Days of the Dead*, chap. 5.

187. Congdon, "Making Merry with Death," p. 200. Eisenstein himself writes, "This is Mexican defiance of death, an affirmation of the vitality of life." See Eisenstein, "The Day of the Dead," p. 154.

188. Congdon, "Making Merry with Death," p. 200.

189. Ibid., p. 207. See also Garciagodoy, *Digging the Days of the Dead*, p. 138.

190. Kristen Congdon quotes the remarks of María Antonieta Sánchez de Escamilla, a nursery school teacher from Puebla City, Mexico, who says to her schoolchildren, "our loved ones never really die while we remember them." Congdon, "Making Merry with Death," p. 200.

191. Stephanie Jones, "Q&A with Stephanie Jones," *Vhcle* 11 (2013), pp. 50–55.

192. Pliny the Elder, *Natural History, XXXV*, trans. H. Rackham, ed. Jeffrey Henderson, Loeb Classical Library, 394 (Cambridge, MA: Harvard University Press, 1952), pp. 370–73.

193. These "images to eat" might also be thought of as a sort of tribute to the sugar cameos, produced by the chef François-René Le Goullon during the last years of the eighteenth century, that Johann Wolfgang von Goethe liked to collect (Klassik Stiftung Weimar). For more on the "classical candy-boxes," see Andrea Linnebach, "Das Publikum der Antiken: Kunsthaus und Museum Fridericianum in Kassel als Ziel von Bildungs- und Forschungsreisen der europaïschen Aufklärung," in Alexis Joachimides,

Charlotte Schreiter, and Rüdiger Splitter, eds. *Auf dem Weg zum Museum: Sammlung und Präsentation antiker Kunst an deutschen Fürstenhöfen des 18. Jahrhunderts* (Kassel: Kassel University Press, 2016), pp. 191–94.

194. The stamps, produced from molds in bronze and iron, measured 20 x 10 cm for the largest ones, and 12.5 x 8 cm for the smallest. Cf. Angiolo Pasqui, "Notizie degli Scavi: Regione I (Latium et Campania), IV: Ostia," *Atti della Reale Accademia dei Lincei* 3, serie 5, anno 303 (1906), pp. 357–73; Waldemar Deonna, "Notes d'archéologie suisse, V: ΥΓΙΕΙΑ," *Anzeiger für schweizerische Altertumskunde* 21 (1919), pp. 88–89; and Bieber, *Skenika*, pp. 24–31.

195. Pasqui, "Notizie degli Scavi," especially pp. 372–73.

196. Ibid., p. 372. See also Bieber, *Skenika*, p. 26, and Hansen, *Kunstgeschichte des Backwerks*, p. 44.

197. Juvenal, *The Satires*, 10.77–81. This translation is from Maryl B. Gensheimer, *Decoration and Display in Rome's Imperial Thermae: Messages of Power and their Popular Reception at the Baths of Caracalla* (New York: Oxford University Press, 2018), p. 242. For a translation in context, see Juvenal, *The Satires*, pp. 88–89.

198. Paul Veyne, *Bread and Circuses: Historical Sociology and Political Pluralism*, trans. Brian Pearce (London: Allen Lane, 1990), pp. 10–13. As Veyne writes in the French original, one gives "to show the people that one feels a duty towards them and to pay them homage," and, at the same time, to show "that one owes them nothing, and that one possesses an essential superiority, in the way of a great lord distributing tips to the little people." Paul Veyne, *Le pain et le cirque: Sociologie historique d'un pluralisme politique* (Paris: Seuil, 1976), p. 489.

199. There could also be a free or low-cost distribution of wheat. Cf. Veyne, *Bread and Circuses*, pp. 236–37.

200. Ibid., pp. 214–16.

201. For more on these meals, see Waldemar Deonna and Marcel Renard, *Croyances et superstitions de table dans la Rome antique* (Brussels: Latomus, 1961), chap. 5, pp. 107–39.

202. Petronius, *Satyricon*, ed. and trans. Gareth Schmeling, Loeb Classical Library, 15 (Cambridge, MA: Harvard University Press, 1936), pp. 137–39, 211.

203. Deonna and Renard, *Croyances et superstitions*, p. 137. This change in appearance was often to be *de rigueur* during the Renaissance. Cf., Fanny Kieffer, "La confiserie des Offices: Art, sciences et magnificence à la cour des Médicis," *Predella* 33 (2013), p. 95.

204. Aristotle, *Mechanics*, trans. E. S. Forster, in Jonathan Barnes, ed., *The Complete Works of Aristotle,* (Princeton, NJ: Princeton University Press, 1984), vol. 2, 847a11–12,

p. 1299. As Patricia Falguières notes, "the wonder is not related to a theory of the fantastic, but to logic and *the temporality of knowledge*." Patricia Falguières, "Poétique de la machine," in Philippe Morel, ed., *L'art de la Renaissance entre science et magie* (Paris: Somogy, 2006), p. 429.

205. On wonderment and the mechanics of the *thaumaston*, see Patricia Falguières, "Moving Picture: Aristote et la machine cinema," *Les Cahiers du Musée National d'Art Moderne* 94 (2005–2006), pp. 96–115, and see also Falguièrers, "Poétique de la machine."

206. On edible sculptures and the art of the table, see Katherine J. Watson, "Sugar Sculpture for Grand Ducal Weddings from the Giambologna Workshop," *Connoisseur* 199 (1978), pp. 20–26, and Zeev Gourarier, *Arts et manières de table en Occident, des origines à nos jours* (Thionville: Gérard Klopp, 1994), and "Modèle de cour et usages de table: Les origines," in Jean-Pierre Babelon, ed., *Versailles et les tables royales en Europe: XVIIe–XIXe siècles* (Paris: RMN, 1993), pp. 15–32; Maria-Anna Fabbri dall'Oglio, *Il Trionfo dell'effimero: Lo sfarzo e il lusso dei banchetti nella cornice fastosa della Roma barocca, Viaggio nell'evoluzione del gusto e della tavola nell'Italia tra Sei e Settecento* (Rome: Ricciardi e Associati, 2002); Fanny Kieffer, "La confiserie des Offices"; Raffaella Morselli and Roberta Piccinelli, "Breve ragguaglio delle sculture in zucchero in epoca moderna: Ovvero *saccarum triumphans* alla corte di Carlo II Gonzaga Nevers," in Andrea Merlotti, ed., *Le tavole di corte tra Cinquecneto e Settecento* (Rome: Bulzoni, 2013), pp. 217–50; Roberta Piccinelli, "Sculture effimere per banchetti nuziali," in Paolo Venturelli, ed., *Vincoli d'amore: Spose in casa Gonzaga* (Milan: Skira, 2013), pp. 69–76; June Di Schino, "The Significance and Symbolism of Sugar Sculpture at Italian Court Banquets," in Marc McWilliams, ed., *Food and Material Culture: Proceedings of the Oxford Symposium on Food and Cookery* (Totnes: Prospect Books, 2014), pp. 111–22; Marcia Reed, "Court and Civic Festivals," in Marcia Reed, ed., *The Edible Monument: The Art of Food for Festivals* (Los Angeles: Getty Research Institute, 2015), pp. 27–71; Joseph Imorde, "Edible Prestige," in Marcia Reed, ed., *The Edible Monument: The Art of Food for Festivals* (Los Angeles: Getty Research Institute, 2015), pp. 101–23; Grégory Ems, "De sucre et de papier: Mises en scène et mises en bouche des mets aux XVIe et XVIIe siècles," *Dix-septième siècle* 271.2 (2016), pp. 195–218. The oldest mention of sugar sculpture goes back to the ninth century, during the reign of the Caliph Al Zahir. Fabbri dall'Oglio, *Il Trionfo dell'effimero*, p. 77; Morselli and Piccinelli, "Breve ragguaglio delle sculture in zucchero," p. 219.

207. Bridgeman, *A Renaissance Wedding*, p. 115. The booklet of the banquet was published in 1475 (British Library, I.A. 31753 *Sforzia, Constantio Signore di Pesaro*). An illuminated

manuscript version is held in the Biblioteca Vaticana (Urb. Lat. 899). See Fabbri dall'Oglio, *Il Trionfo dell'effimero*, pp. 86–87; Bridgeman, *A Renaissance Wedding*, pp. 90, 115, 122; Morselli and Piccinelli, "Breve ragguaglio delle sculture in zucchero," p. 220; Piccinelli, "Sculture effimere per banchetti nuziali," pp. 69–70. In the latter two articles, an error has been introduced into the texts with the names (it should be Costanzo Sforza and Camilla Marzano d'Aragona, and not, as written, Constanza Sforza and Camillo d'Aragona).

208. Messisbugo, *Banchetti*, s.p. For the sosamelli dough, a Neapolitan specialty, see Ken Albala, *Food in Early Modern Europe* (Westport/London: Greenwood Press, 2003), p. 125. For more on these meals, see Maurizio Bettini and Omar Calabrese, *BizzarraMente: Eccentrici e stravaganti dal mondo antico alla modernità* (Milan: Feltrinelli, 2002), pp. 223–26; and Diane Bodart and Valérie Boudier, "Le banquet de la Renaissance: Images et usages," *Predella* 33 (2013), pp. 9–20. For other meals preceding these, see Fabbri dall'Oglio, *Il Trionfo dell'effimero*, pp. 85–89; Morselli and Piccinelli, "Breve ragguaglio delle sculture in zucchero," p. 220 et seq.; and Piccinelli, "Sculture effimere per banchetti nuziali."

209. Watson, "Sugar Sculpture for Grand Ducal"; Kieffer, "La confiserie des Offices," pp. 92–93; Morselli and Piccinelli, "Breve ragguaglio delle sculture in zucchero," pp. 225–26; and Di Schino, "The Significance and Symbolism of Sugar Sculpture," p. 111.

210. Cf. Ivan Day, "Eating the Edifice" (lecture, Getty Research Institute, Los Angeles, CA, January 31, 2016).

211. Ems, "De sucre et de papier," p. 197.

212. Jean Polit, cited in ibid.

213. Ems, "De sucre et de papier," p. 198.

214. Ibid., p. 199; Kieffer, "La confiserie des Offices," p. 86; Reed, "Court and Civic Festivals," pp. 29–31.

215. The symbols, however, could sometimes be hard for people to decipher; so, inscriptions might be added, as was the case with the two hundred figures adorning the banquet given in Venice, in 1574, in honor of King Henri III of France. Cf. Piccinelli, "Sculture effimere per banchetti nuziali," p. 70.

216. Cf. Morselli and Piccinelli, "Breve ragguaglio delle sculture in zucchero," pp. 225–26; Reed, "Court and Civic Festivals," pp. 29–31; Ems, "De sucre et de papier," p. 202.

217. For the engraving, see Francesco Orilia, *Il Zodiaco, over, idea di perfettione di prencipi* (Naples: Ottavio Beltrano, 1630), p. 456. See Marcia Reed, "Feasting in the Streets: Carnivals and the Cuccagna," in Marcia Reed, ed., *The Edible Monument: The Art of Food for Festivals* (Los Angeles: Getty Research Institute, 2015), p. 91; John L. Varriano, *Tastes*

and Temptations: Food and Art in Renaissance Italy (Berkeley: University of California Press, 2009), p. 185.

218. "Con simil artificio, ma con roba di grascia, fù architettata la Porta dedicata alla Vigilanza, come la principal cura, che dee tener desto il Prencipe, sia la copia, & l'abbondanza delle cose da mangiare, perche la plèbe minuta è più ventre, che capo. Di queste materie, fù ornato il Trionfo, come può vedersi dal ritratto d'essa.... [I]n conformità di quest'arco, se l'accompagnò per tutta la strada un pergolato soltissimo della medesima roba... della Piazza larga (il che importò lunghissimo tratto di strada) si coverse di simil ornamento; e fu bel vedere, egualemente al popolo, godendo di quel, che più desidera, e del Prencipe, scorgendo gli effetti della sua Vigilanza, come era la massa di tanto viveri." Francesco Orilia, *Il Zodiaco*, pp. 455–57.

219. Ibid., p. 457. Feast days on which food is distributed to the people occur in European cities in the modern era, e.g., Bologna's Festa della Porchetta. Cf. Reed, "Feasting in the Streets," pp. 76–79.

220. For other examples of *Macchine di Cuccagna* in the seventeenth and eighteenth centuries, see the extremely interesting contribution in ibid., pp. 91–97.

221. Lisa Hsieh, "The Edible, Playable, and Wearable Architecture of Haus-Rucker-Co," *The Gradient*, October 23, 2015, https://walkerart.org/magazine/the-edible-playable-and-wearable-architecture-of-haus-rucker-co. For other examples of edible cities, see Alicia Rios, "Eat Art and Communities: From Oxford to Melbourne," *Food, Culture and Community* in the journal *Moving Worlds* 6.2 (2006), pp. 177–86.

222. Hsieh, "The Edible."

223. For more on the "partage du sensible," or "distribution of the sensible" as it is translated in the following English edition, as the real purpose of politics, see Jacques Rancière, *The Politics of Aesthetics: The Distribution of the Sensible*, trans. Gabriel Rockhill (London: Continuum, 2005). We should recall, however, along with Rancière that "politics" means here not "the exercise of, or struggle for power" but "the configuration of a specific space, the framing of a particular sphere of experience." Jacques Rancière, *Aesthetics and Its Discontents,* trans. Stephen Corcoran (Cambridge UK: Polity, 2009), p. 24.

224. On the Company, see especially Allen J. Grieco, "*Au pays de Cocagne:* Ulysse dans le chaudron," in Paul Noirot, ed., *L'Honnête volupté: Art culinaire, art majeur* (Paris: Études pour la valorisation de la recherche en sciences humaines, 1989), pp. 103–106; Bettini and Calabrese, *BizzarraMente*, pp. 227–30; Philippe Sénéchal, *Giovan Francesco Rustici (1475–1554)* (Paris: Arthéna, 2007), pp. 123–35; Tommaso Mozzati, *Giovanfrancesco Rustici:*

Le compagnie del paiuolo e della cazzuola, Arte, letteratura, festa nell'età della Maniera (Florence: Olschki, 2008), pp. 191–268; Varriano, *Tastes and Temptations*, pp. 171–201; Valérie Boudier, *La cuisine du peintre: Scène de genre et nourriture au Cinquecento* (Rennes: Presses universitaires de Rennes, 2010), pp. 232–33.

225. Vasari, *Lives of the Painters, Sculptors and Architects*, pp. 523–24.

226. Mozzati, *Giovanfrancesco Rustici*, p. 221, and Sénéchal, *Giovan Francesco Rustici*, p. 129. On the relation to the Christian model, see also Mozzati, *Giovanfrancesco Rustici*, pp. 194, 230.

227. Ibid., p. 250.

228. Ibid., pp. 230–31, 249–50.

229. On the Company of the Cauldron as a form of social organization, see Mozzati, *Giovanfrancesco Rustici*, pp. 191 et seq., 243–51.

230. Is it not their *originality* that guarantee them a place in Vasari's historiographical edifice?

231. *Disegni del convito fatto dall'illustrissimo signor senator Francesco Ratta all'illustrissimo public, eccelsi signori anziani & altra nobiltà terminando il suo confalonierato, li 28 febraro 1693* (Bologna: Per li Peri, 1693). Cf. Morselli and Piccinelli, "Breve ragguaglio delle sculture in zucchero," pp. 227–28, and Reed, "Court and Civic Festivals," pp. 61–64.

232. Imorde, "Edible Prestige," p. 105. On the gilding, see Kieffer, "La confiserie des Offices," p. 91.

233. Distant avatars of these trophies of the table, Daniel Spoerri's "snare-pictures," resulting from the "naturalization" of the leftovers of a meal and the arranging of the table vertically to transform it into a *painting*, might well appear as an end phase of this process of artification. See the catalogue of the exhibition organized by Françoise Bonnefoy, ed., *Restaurant Spoerri: Maison fondé en 1963, 1, place de la Concorde, Paris 75008* (Paris: Musée du Jeu de Paume, 2002), exhibition catalog.

234. Germano Celant, *Piero Manzoni* (New York: Sonnabend Press, 1972), p. 11; Freddy Battino and Luca Palazzoli, *Piero Manzoni: Catalogue raisonné* (Milan: Edizioni di Vanni Scheiwiller, 1991), pp. 104–105; Jean-Pierre Criqui, "Piero Manzoni and His Left-Overs," in Germano Celant, ed., *Piero Manzoni*, trans. Judith Aminoff, et al. (Milan: Arnoldo Mondadori Arte, 1991), exhibition catalog, p. 29; Auido Andrea Pautasso, *Piero Manzoni: Divorare l'arte* (Milan: Electa, 2015), especially pp. 63–86 for the performance.

235. Pautasso, *Piero Manzoni*, pp. 72, 88–89.

236. According to the account of Henk Peeters, who saw one of these performances,

"150 eggs marked with his thumbprint were swallowed down by the public, as they made direct contact with the work of art." Henk Peeters, cited in Pautasso, *Piero Manzoni*, p. 86. See also Henk Peeters, *Nul=0* 2 (1963), p. 18.

237. The artist Space Invader has also made use of the imprint, sharing his identifying image by producing and distributing in 2011 "Space Waffle," a limited edition set of 100 identical waffles.

238. The character's name is a pseudonym.

239. Cecilia Novero, *Antidiets of the Avant-Garde: From Futurist Cooking to Eat Art* (Minneapolis, MN: University of Minnesota Press, 2009), pp. 32–37; Chiara Di Stefano Frusi, "*Cucina futurista*: Entre renouveau des langages artistiques et mythe de la régénérescence," in Julia Csergo and Frédérique Desbuissons, eds., *Le cuisinier et l'art: Art du cuisinier et cuisine d'artiste (XVIe–XXIe siècle)* (Paris: INHA/Menu fretin, 2018), p. 227; Mélanie Boucher, "L'origine de l'usage des aliments en arts visuels au XXe siècle," in Julia Csergo et Frédérique Desbuissons, eds., *Le cuisinier et l'art: Art du cuisinier et cuisine d'artiste (XVIe–XXIe siècle)* (Paris: INHA/Menu fretin, 2018), p. 242.

240. Filippo Tommaso Marinetti, *The Futurist Cookbook*, trans. Suzanne Brill (San Francisco: Bedford Arts, 1989), pp. 26, 29.

241. Marinetti, *The Futurist Cookbook*, p. 29.

242. Ingesting the image and ingesting the other are frequently intermingled. It is not insignificant that the desire here passes through the ingestion of breasts, as with the Futurist artist Marisa Mori (see Griffiths, "Marisa Mori's Futurist Breasts") and in Michel Tournier's tale *Pierrot ou les secrets de la nuit*, illustrated by Danièle Bour. See, especially, the last plate of the tale in which Harlequin, Pierrot, and Colombine eat Colombine-Pierrette's "brioche breasts."

243. Novero, *Antidiets of the Avant-Garde*, pp. 194–97; Camille Paulhan, "Daniele Spoerri et la Eat Art Galerie," in Julia Csergo and Frédérique Desbuissons, eds., *Le cuisinier et l'art: Art du cuisinier et cuisine d'artiste (XVIe–XXIe siècle)* (Paris: INHA/Menu fretin, 2018), pp. 255, 259–60.

244. Wilhelm Freddie and Joergen Roos, *Spitze Horizonter* (1950), 35 mm film, Copenhagen, Statens Museum for Kunst.

245. There is a variant of these performances in the final scene of Peter Greenaway's film *The Cook, the Thief, His Wife, and Her Lover*, from 1989.

246. Ralf Beil, *Künstlerküche: Lebensmittel als Kunstmaterial von Schiele bis Jason Rhoades* (Cologne: DuMont, 2002), pp. 193–94.

247. Georgiana Colville, *Scandaleusement d'elles: Trente-quatre femmes surrealists* (Paris: Jean-Michel Place, 1999), p. 218; Novero, *Antidiets of the Avant-Garde*, p. 187.

248. As Johanne Lamoureux has suggested to me, we should include here, in parallel with the dissolution of the image, the transformation of the pictorial medium into the substance of performance. In a happening titled *The Smiling Workman* (1960), Jim Dine literally incorporated the contents of a pot of paint before writing on the surface of a canvas, "I love what I'm doing."

249. When the performance was staged at the Françoise Lambert Gallery in Milan, in 1971, it included the following technical setup: three microprojectors, color slides, Technicolor Super 8 film, floor to ceiling projection, and gingerbread cookies. For more on this performance, see Germano Celant, ed. *Dennis Oppenheim: Explorations* (Milan: Charta, 2001), pp. 16, 152–53; Nick Kaye, Dennis Oppenheim, and Amy van Winkle Oppenheim, *Dennis Oppenheim: Body to Performance, 1969–73* (Milan: Skira, 2016), pp. 199–201.

250. Microprojection-Feces, 6 ft diameter, 3000x enlargement. On the importance of *arte povera* for Oppenheim, see Celant, ed. *Dennis Oppenheim*, p. 10.

251. The accompanying statement reads: "A project dealing with activation of digestive processes. Situation created in which first a symbolically human form is slowly broken down and subjected to the linearity of the intestinal track . . . it is used to fill an internal space . . . and by emptying the stomach beforehand, this material is allowed full occupancy. It takes over the space, forcing itself into a linear housing, and is held captive to gastric processes, additional breakdown and depletion. Here the process of making (changes) is linked with that of a life sustaining interaction. The residue (waste products) become the finished work." Celant, *Dennis Oppenheim*, p. 152; Kaye, Oppenheim, and van Winkle Oppenheim, *Dennis Oppenheim*, p. 200.

252. Several series of sheets were made by the Rugg Road Paper Company in Somerville, Massachusetts, and by Snake Knob Paperworks in North Carolina. Cf. Anne de Fornel, *John Cage* (Paris: Fayard, 2019), pp. 172–73.

253. Fornel, *John Cage*, p. 173.

254. Ibid., pp. 173–74. The drawings have, for the most part, gone into museum collections, notably that of the Museum of Modern Art. In 1995, the chef Michael Silver did nonetheless create a soup recipe based on one of Cage's drawings. He had bought the drawing on the art market, and he served the soup to a few of his friends on the day following the closure of his restaurant at the Isabella Stewart Gardner Museum.

CONCLUSION: A SHORT SWEET

1. Aristotle, *On the Soul, Parva Naturalia, On Breath*, trans. W. S. Hett, Loeb Classical Library, 288 (Cambridge, MA: Harvard University Press, 1957), III, 7, p. 177; Emanuele Coccia correctly notes, "The being of images is necessary for this reason . . . because it constitutes but one element that permits nature to pass from the spiritual to the corporeal domain and vice versa." Emanuele Coccia, *Sensible Life: A Micro-ontology of the Image*, trans. Scott Alan Stuart (New York: Fordham University Press, 2016), p. 26.

2. W. J. T. Mitchell, *What do Pictures Want?: The Lives and Loves of Images* (Chicago: University of Chicago Press, 2005), pp. xv–xvi.

3. Jasper Johns, cited in Kirk Varnedoe, "Introduction: A Sense of Life," in Kirk Varnedoe, ed., *Jasper Johns: A Retrospective* (New York: MoMA Publications, 1996), p. 23.

4. This has been a common recipe since Giovan Francesco Caroto's *Portrait of a Child with a Drawing* (ca. 1523) at Museo di Castelvecchio in Verona.

5. For more on this painting, see Thierry Beherman, *Godfried Schalcken* (Paris: Maeght, 1988), p. 248, cat. 155; Peter Hecht, "Art Beats Nature and Painting Does so Best of All: The Paragone Competition in Duquesnoy, Dou and Schalcken," *Semiolus* 29 (2002), pp. 184–201, 196 et seq.; Anja K. Sevcik, "Junge mit Pfannkuchenmaske, 1670–1680," in *Schalcken: Gemalte Verführung* (Cologne: Wallraf-Richartz-Museums, 2015), exhibition catalog, pp. 158–60.

6. Maurice Blanchot, *Friendship*, trans. Elizabeth Rottenberg (Stanford: Stanford University Press, 1997), p. 40.

Bibliography

ABBREVIATIONS

PGM: Karl Preisendanz et Albert Henrichs. *Papyri Graecae Magicae. Die Griechischen Zauberpapyri.* 2 vols. Stuttgart: Teubner, second edition, 1974.

PG: *Patrologiae Cursus Completus. Series Graeca.* 161 vols. Ed. Jacques-Paul Migne. Paris, 1857–1866.

PL: *Patrologiae Cursus Completus. Series Latina.* 221 vols. Ed. Jacques-Paul Migne. Paris, 1844–1855.

PRIMARY SOURCES

Acta Sanctorum Aprilis Tomus III. Brussels: Société des Bollandistes, 1675.

Actes de Mar Mari (Les). Eds. C. and F. Jullien. In *Corpus scriptorum christianorum orientalium*, vol. 603, *Scriptores Syri*, t. 235. Louvain: Peeters, 2003.

Alberti, Leon Battista. *Trattato della nobiltà della pittura.* Rome: Francesco Zannetti, 1585.

An Anthology of Classical Myth: Primary Sources in Translation. Eds. Stephen Trzaskoma, R. Scott Smith, Stephen Brunet, and Thomas G. Palaima. Indianapolis: Hackett, 2004.

Aristotle. *L'homme de génie et la mélancolie.* Ed. Jackie Pigeaud. Paris: Payot & Rivages, 2006.

———. *Mechanics.* Trans. E. S. Forster. In *The Complete Works of Aristotle,* vol. 2. Ed. Jonathan Barnes. Princeton, NJ: Princeton University Press, 1984.

———. *On the Soul, Parva Naturalia, On Breath.* Trans. W. S. Hett. Loeb Classical Library, 288. Cambridge, MA: Harvard University Press, 1957.

———. *Problems.* Ed. and trans. Robert Mayhew. Loeb Classical Library, 71. Cambridge, MA: Harvard University Press, 2011.

Atheneaus of Naucratis. *The Learned Banqueters.* Ed. and trans. S. Douglas Olson. Loeb Classical Library, 204. Cambridge, MA: Harvard University Press, 2011.

Aulus Gellius. *Attic Nights.* Trans. John C. Rolfe. Loeb Classical Library, 200. Cambridge, MA: Harvard University Press, 1927.

Avicenna. *The Canon of Medicine*, vol. 1. Trans. O. Cameron Gruner and Mazar H. Shah. Chicago: Kazi Publications, Inc., 1999.

Barrin, Jean. *The Monk Unvail'd.* London: Jonathan Edwin, at the Three Roses in Ludgate Street, 1678.

Berlendi, Francesco. *Delle Obblazioni all'altare antiche e moderne, o sia la storia intera dello Stipendio della Messa.* Venice: Apresso Angelo Pasinelli, 1736.

Bernard of Clairvaux. *The Works of Saint Bernard of Clairvaux*, vol. 2. Trans. Killian Walsh. Kildale: Irish University Press, 1971.

Bernard of Clairvaux. *On the Song of Songs IV.* Trans. Irene Edmonds. Kalamazoo, MI: Cistercian Publications, 1980.

Bernardino de Sahagún. *General History of the Things of New Spain: Florentine Codex.* Trans. Arthur J. O. Anderson and Charles E. Dibble. Salt Lake City, UT: University of Utah Press, 1950–1982.

Bertondelli, Girolamo. *Miracoli operati dall'Onnipotenza divina per mezo degli Agnus Papali Benedetti dalla Santa Memoria d'Innocentio XI.* Venice: Dominico Louisa, 1691.

Boccaccio. *The Decameron of Giovanni Boccaccio.* Trans. J. M. Rigg. London, [1903] 1921, VIII, 6.

Böttiger, Karl August. "Die Römische Bonbonnière." *Journal des Luxus und der Moden* 7 (1792), p. 54 et seq.

Bouille, Pierre. *Brève histoire de l'invention et miracles de l'image de Nostre Dame de Foy, trouvée en un chesne à Foy les Dinant, l'an 1609.* Liège: Jean Ouwerx, 1620.

———. *Dame de la Foy: Histoire de la découverte et merveilles de l'image Nostre Dame de Foy trouvée en un chesne près la ville de Dinan pays de Liège l'an MDCIX.* Liège: Jean Ouwerx, 1627.

Brantôme, Pierre de Bourdeille. Œuvres *complètes de Pierre de Bourdeille seigneur de Brantôme.* Ed. Louis Jean Nicolas Monmerqué. Paris: Foucault Libraire, 1822–1823.

———. "Discours sur les couronnels de l'infanterie de France." In *Œuvres completes de Pierre de Bourdeille seigneur de Brantôme.* Ed. Ludovic Lalanne. Paris: Jules Renouard, 1873.

Bry, Johann Theodor, and Johann de Israël. *Emblemata saecularia, mira et iucunda varietate saeculi huius mores ita exprimentia . . . .* Frankfurt, 1596.

Calvin, John. *Commentaries on the First Twenty Chapters of the Book of the Prophet Ezekiel.* Trans. Thomas Myers. Grand Rapids: W. M. B. Eerdmans, 1948.

Caputo, Filocalo. *Il Monte Carmelo in cui si tratta della miracolosa imagine di N.S. del Carmine del Regio Convento di Napoli.* Naples: Lazaro Scoriggio, 1636.

Cennini, Cennino. *The Book of the Art of Cennino Cennini.* Trans. Christina J. Herringham. London: George Allen, 1899.

Chastain, Jean. *Le moine sécularisé.* Cologne: Chez Pierre du Marteau, 1678.

Collections grecques de miracles: Saint Thècle, Saints Côme et Damien, Saint Cyr et Jean (extraits), Saint Georges. Ed. André-Jean Festugière. Paris: Picard, 1971.

Collin de Plancy, Jacques Albin-Simon. *Dictionnaire critique des reliques et des images miraculeuses.* Paris: Guien, 1821–1822.

Coton, Pierre. *Institution catholique.* Paris: Claude Chappelet, 1610.

Damascus, Saint John of. *Three Treatises on the Divine Images.* Trans. Andrew Louth. New York: St. Vladimir's Seminary Press, 2003.

Decrees of the Ecumenical Councils, vol. 1. Ed. Norman P. Tanner. London/Washington, DC: Sheed & Ward and Georgetown University Press, 1990.

Dictionnaire de l'Académie françoise dédié au Roy (Le), 2 vols. Paris: Jean Baptiste Coignard, 1694.

Diderot, Denis. "J.-B. S. Chardin (*Salon of 1763*)." In *Neoclassicism and Romanticism 1750–1850: Sources and Documents*, vol. 1. Ed. and trans. Lorenz Eitner. New Jersey: Englewood Cliffs, 1970.

Dioscorides, Pedanius of Anazarbus. *De materia medica.* Trans. Lily Y. Beck. Hildesheim/Zürich/New York: G. Olms-Weidmann, 2005.

———. *The Greek Herbal of Dioscorides.* Ed. Robert T. Gunther. Royal Oak: Hafner Publishing, 1968.

Disegni del convito fatto dall'illustrissimo signor senatore Francesco Ratta all'illustrissimo publico, eccelsi signori anziani & altra nobiltà terminando il suo confalonierato, li 28 febraro 1693. Bologna: Per li Peri, 1693.

Du Bellay, Joachim. *The Regrets with The Antiquities of Rome, Three Latin Elegies, and The Defense and Enrichment of the French Language.* Ed. and trans. Richard Helgerson. Philadelphia: University of Pennsylvania Press, 2006.

Durand, Guillaume. *Guillelmi Duranti Rationale Divinorum Officiorum: I–IV.* Eds. A. Davril and Timothy M. Thibodeau. Turnhout: Brepols, 1995.

———. *Rationale IV: On The Mass and Each Action Pertaining to It.* Trans. Timothy M. Thibodeau. Turnhout: Brepols, 2013.

Erasmus. "A Declamation on the Subject of Early Liberal Education for Children." In *Collected Works of Erasmus*, vol. 26. Ed. J K. Sowards. Trans. and annot. Beert C. Verstraete. Toronto: University of Toronto Press, 1985.

———. "A Pilgrimage for Religion's Sake." In *Collected Works of Erasmus*, vol. 40. Ed. J. K. Sowards. Trans. and annot. Craig R. Thompson. Toronto: University of Toronto Press, 1997.

Estienne, Henri. *L'introduction au traité de la conformité des merveilles anciennes avec les modernes ou traité préparatif à l'apologie pour Hérodote*. Genève, 1566.

Eusebius's Ecclesiastical History. Trans. C. F. Cruse. Peabody, MA: Hendrickson, 1998.

Fabre, Pierre-Jean. *L'abrégé des secrets chymiques, ou L'on void la nature des animaux végétaux & minéraux entièrement découverte . . . .* Paris: Antoine de Sommaville, 1636.

Félibien, André. *Entretiens sur les vies et les ouvrages des plus excellens peintres anciens et modernes*. Paris: Denys Mariette, 1679.

Ficin, Marsile. *Sulla Vita*. Ed. Alessandra Tarabochia Canavero. Milan: Rusconi, 1995.

Galen. *Claudii Galeni opera omnia*, 20 vols. Ed. and trans. C. G. Kühn. Leipzig, 1821–1833. Reprinted Hildesheim: G. Olms, 1964–1965.

———. *On the Natural Faculties*. Trans. A. J. Brock. Loeb Classical Library, 71. Cambridge, MA: Harvard University Press, 1916.

Geiler von Kaysersberg, Johannes. *Passion Des Here[n] Jesu: Fürgeben vnd geprediget gar betrachtiglich (particuliert) vnd geteilt in stückes weiß eins süßen Lebkuochen vßzuogeben (per quadragesima[m]) als durch die gantze fasten allen tag wol ein Predig daruß zuonemen ist*. Straßburg, 1514.

Gordon, Bernard de. *De Conservatione vitae humanae*. Ed. D. Joachimi Baudisii. Leipzig, 1570.

Graminaeus, Theodor. *Beschreibung derer fürstlicher güligscher etc. Hochzeit* (Cologne, 1587)

———. *Furstliche Hochzeit so der durchluchtig hochgeborner Furst und Herr, Herr Wilhelm Hertzog zu Gulich Cleve und Berg . . . und der durchleuchtige(n) hochgebornen Furstinen Frewlin Jacobae gebornen Marggraffinen zu Baden etc*. Cologne, 1587.

Gregory of Tours. *The History of the Franks*. Trans. Lewis Thorpe. London: Penguin, 1974.

Grimm, Jacob and Wilhelm. *The Original Folk and Fairy Tales of the Brothers Grimm*. Ed. and trans. Jack Zipes. Illustrations by Andrea Dezsö. Princeton, NJ: Princeton University Press, 2014.

Guillelmi, Duranti. *Rationale Divinorum Officiorum*. Eds. David Anselme and Timothy Thibodeau. Turnhout: Brepols, 1995.

Guizzelmi, Giuliano di Francesco. *Historia della apparition et altri miracoli di Madonna Sancta del Carcere di Prato.* Prato: Biblioteca Roncioniana, 1505, codex 87.

Gumppenberg, Wilhelm. *Atlas Marianus sive De imaginibus Deiparae per orbem christianum miraculosis*, t. III. Ingolstadt, 1659.

Herodas. *Mimiambs.* Ed. and trans. Graham Zanker. Oxford: Oxbow Books, 2009.

Hill, John. *A History of the Materia Medica.* London: T. Longman, C. Hitch & L. Hawes, 1751, p. 186.

Horace, *Satires I.* Trans. P. Michael Brown. Warminster, UK: Aris & Phillips, 1993.

Incomplete Commentary on Matthew (Opus imperfectum), vol. 2. Ed. Thomas C. Oden. Trans. James A. Kellerman. Downers Grove, IL: Intervarsity Press, 2010.

Ireland, John. *A Supplement to Hogarth Illustrated*, 2 vols. London: Boydell, 1798.

Jacquet, Claude. *Histoire de l'origine, du progrès, et de l'état présent de la sainte chapelle située dans l'illustre Abaie des Ermites, ou D'Einsiedeln de l'Ordre de S. Benoit, en Suisse*, 2nd edition. Einsiedeln: J. E. Kälin, 1699.

———. and Abbé Nicolas. *Histoire de la S. chapelle de Notre-Dame-des-Ermites . . . revue, corrigée, &augmentée de deux cens soixante miracles.* Einsiedeln: Jean-Everhard Kälin, 1750.

John Chrysostom. Trans. Wendy Mayer and Pauline Allen. London: Routledge, 2000.

Journal de voyage de Michel de Montaigne en Italie, par la Suisse et l'Allemagne en 1580 et 1581. Ed. Alexandre d'Ancona. Città di Castello: S. Lapi, 1889

Julian the Emperor. Trans. C. W. King. London: George Bell & Sons, 1888.

Jurieu, Pierre. *Histoire du calvinisme et celle du papisme mises en parallèle: Ou apologie pour les Reformateurs, pour la Reformation, et pour les Reformez . . . .* Rotterdam: Reinier Leers, 1683.

Juvenal. *The Satires.* Trans. Niall Rudd. Oxford: Clarendon Press, 1991.

Kosmas und Damian: Texte und Einleitung. Ed. Ludwig Deubner. Leipzig: B. G. Teubner, 1907.

L'Ami du clergé paroissial: Supplément à l'Ami du clergé. Langres, 1899–1905, p. 561.

La petite guerre, March 25, 1903.

La semaine religieuse de l'Archidiocèse d'Albi: Organe officiel hebdomadaire de l'archevêché, March 28, 1903, p. 221.

L'Éclaireur de l'Ain, July 6, 1902, p. 2.

Lemée, François. *Traité des statues*, 2 vols. Eds. Diane H. Bodart and Hendrik Ziegler. Weimar: VDG, 2012.

Lennio, Levino. *Della complessione del corpo humano libri due, sommamente necessarij a tutti colori, che studiano alla sanita . . . .* Venezia: Appresso Dominico Nicolino, 1564.

Letters of Saint Catherine of Siena, vol. 4. Trans. Suzanne Noffke, OP. Tempe, AZ: Arizona Center for Medieval and Renaissance Studies, 2008.

Luther, Martin. *Von dem geweichten wasser, und des Bapsts Agnus Dei.* Augsbourg, 1539.

Mabillon, Jean. *Dissertatio de pane eucharistico, azymo, ac fermentato: Suivie de la Revelation de saint Ildefonse.* In *Ouvrages posthumes de D. Jean Mabillon et de D. Thierri Ruinart: Bénédictins de la congrégation de Saint Maur.* Paris: Jean François Babutt and Jean-François Josse, 1724, pp. 101–97.

Magick of Kirani, King of Persia, and of Harpocration containing the Magical and Medicinal Vertues of Stones, Herbs, Fishes, Beasts and Birds. . . . Early English Books Online. London, 1685.

Manesson-Mallet, Allain. *La Description de l'univers, suite de l'Europe ancienne et moderne, des terres Australes et de l'Amérique*, tome 5. Paris: Denis Thierry, 1683.

Mango, Cyril. *The Art of the Byzantine Empire: Sources and Documents.* Englewood Cliffs, NJ: Prentice-Hall, 1972.

Mansi, Jean-Dominique. *Sacrorum conciliorum nova et amplissima collectio*, 31 vols. Florence, 1759.

Marinetti, Filippo Tommaso. *The Futurist Cookbook.* Trans. Suzanne Brill. San Francisco: Bedford Arts, 1989.

Mély, Fernand de. *Les lapidaires de l'Antiquité et du Moyen Âge*, vol. 3: *Les lapidaires grecs.* Ed. and trans. Fernard de Mély. Paris: Ernest Leroux, 1902.

Messisbugo, Cristoforo da. *Banchetti, compositioni di vivande e apparecchio generale.* Ferrare: Giovanni de Buglhat et Antonio Hucher Compagni, 1549.

Miracles of Saint Artemios (The): A Collection of Miracle Stories by an Anonymous Author of Seventh-Century Byzantium. Eds. Virgil S. Crisafulli and John W. Nesbitt. Trans. Virgil S. Crisafulli. Leiden: Brill, 1997.

Montaiglon, Anatole de. *Recueil de poésies françoises des XVe et XVIe siècles, morales, facétieuses, historiques*, 8 vols. Paris, 1855–1878.

Montaigne, Michel de. *The Complete Essays of Montaigne.* Trans. Donald M. Frame. Stanford, CA: Stanford University Press, 1998.

Montaigne, Michel de. *Montaigne's Travel Journal.* Trans. Donald M. Frame. San Francisco: North Point Press, 1983.

Murrell, John. *A Delightfull Daily Exercise for Ladies and Gentlewomen: Whereby is Set Foorth the Secrete Misteries of the Purest Preseruings in Glasses and Other Confrictionaries . . . .* London, 1621.

Opus caroli regis contra synodum (Libri carolini). Ed. Ann Freeman. Hanover: Hahn, 1998, III, 16.

Orilia, Francesco. *Il Zodiaco, over, idea di perfettione di prencipi* . . . . Naples: Ottavio Beltrano, 1630.

Petrarch, Francesco. *Letters on Familiar Matters: Rerum familiarum libri IX-XVI*. Trans. Aldo S. Bernardo. Baltimore, MD: Johns Hopkins University Press, 1985.

Petronius. *Satyricon*. Ed. and trans. Gareth Schmeling. Loeb Classical Library, 15. Cambridge, MA: Harvard University Press, 1936.

Piergili, Battista. *Vita della B. Chiara detta della Croce da Montefalco dell'Ordine di S. Agostino*. Foligno: Appresso Agostino Alterij, 1640.

Pinelli, Luca. *Brief Meditations of the Most Holy Sacrament and of Preparation, for Rescuing the Same, and of Some Other Things Apertaining to the Greatness and Devotion of So Worthy A Mystery*. Ed. Henry Garnet. London: V. Simmes, ca. 1600.

Pino, Paolo. *Paolo Pino's "Dialogo di pittura": A Translation with Commentary*. Trans. Mary Pardo. Ann Arbor, MI: University Microfilms International, 1985.

Pio da Carpi, Alberto. *Praeter praefationem et operis conclusionem, tres et viginti libri in locos lucubrationum variarum D. Erasmi Roterodami, quos censet ab eo recognoscendos et retractandos*. Ed. Josse Bade. Paris, 1531.

Pliny the Elder. *Natural History, XXXV*. Ed. Jeffrey Henderson. Trans. H. Rackham. Loeb Classical Library, 394. Cambridge, MA: Harvard University Press, 1952.

Plutarch. *Moralia V: Isis and Osiris, The E at Delphi, The Oracles at Delphi No Longer Given in Verse. The Obsolescence of Oracles*. Trans. Frank Cole Babbitt. Loeb Classical Library, 306. Cambridge, MA: Haravard University Press, 1936.

Pontormo, Jacopo da. *Pontormo's Diary*. Trans. Rosemary Mayer. New York: Out of London Press, 1979.

Rabelais, François. *Pantagruel: Les horribles et espouventables faictz et prouesses* . . . . Lyon, 1530.

———. *The Complete Works of François Rabelais*. Trans. Donald M. Frame. Berkeley: University of California Press, 1991.

Raymond of Capua. *The Life of St. Catherine of Siena*. Trans. George Lamb. London: Harvill Press, 1960.

Richeome, Louis. *Les Trois Discours pour la religion catholique, des miracles, des saints, et des images*. Bordeaux: S. Millange, 1597.

Rouquet, André. *L'art nouveau de la peinture en fromage, ou en ramequin, inventée pour suivre le louable projet de trouver graduellement des façons de peindre inférieures à celles qui existent*. Marolles, 1755.

Sachs, Hans. *Das Schlaraffenland.* In Edmund Goetze and Carl Drescher, eds. *Sämtliche Fabeln und Schwänke von Hans Sachs*, vol. 1. Halle: Niemeyer, 1893, pp. 8–11.

Saint Ambrose. *The Fathers of the Church: Saint Ambrose, Letters* 1–91. Trans. Sister Mary Melchior Beyenka. Washington, DC: Catholic University of America Press, 1954.

Saint Augustine. *The Confessions.* Trans. Maria Boulding, OSB. New York: New City Press, 1997.

———. *The Works of Saint Augustine: Sermons.* Trans. Edmund Hill, OP. Brooklyn, New York: New City Press, 1990.

Saint Basil Letters and Select Works. Ed. Philip Schaff. Grand Rapids, MI: Christian Classics Ethereal Library (A Select library of the Nicene and Post-Nicene Fathers of the Christian Church. Ed. Philip Schaff. Vol. 8 Basil: Letters and Selected works). Originally published in Buffalo: Christian Literature Co., 1886.

Saint Basil the Great: On Christian Doctrine and Practice. Trans. Mark DelCogliano. Yonkers, NY: St. Vladimir's Seminary Press, 2012.

San Bernardo, Francisco de. *Vida del prodigioso Job de estos siglos, el venerable Padre fray Thomas de la Virgen . . . .* Madrid, 1747.

Schamp, Jacques, and Robert Halleux, eds. *Les lapidaires grecs: Lapidaire orphique, kérygmes lapidaires d'Orphée, Socrate et Denys, lapidaire nautique, Damigéron-Evax.* Paris: Les Belles Lettres, 1986.

Seneca. *The Epistles 66–92.* 2 vols. Trans. Richard M. Gummere. Loeb Classical Library, 76. Cambridge, MA: Harvard University Press, 1920.

Stephen, Henry [Estienne, Henri]. *A World of Wonders, or An Introduction to a Treatise Touching on the Conformity of Ancient and Modern Wonders or A Preparative Treatise to the Apologie for Herodotus.* Trans. Anonymous. Edinburgh: Andrew Hart and Richard Lawson, 1608.

Surgery of Master Henry de Mondeville: Written from 1306 to 1320, vol. 1. Trans. Leonard D. Rosenman, MD. Philadelphia: Xlibris Corporation, 2003.

Swift, Jonathan. *Gulliver's Travels.* London: Oxford University Press, 1919.

Tartarotti, Girolamo. *Del congresso notturno delle lammie, libri tre.* Rovereto: Gianbatista Pasquali, 1749.

Tauler, Jean. *Sermons.* Trans. E. Hugueny, G. Théry and M. A. L. Corin. Paris: Cerf, 1991.

Theodore the Studite: Writings on Iconoclasm. Trans. Thomas Cattoi. New York: Newman Press, 2015.

Theodoret of Cyrus, *Historia religiosa*, c. 21 BCE; p. 82, col. 1431 et seq.

Three Byzantine Saints. Trans. Elizabeth Dawes and Norman H. Baynes. New York: St. Vladimir's Seminary Press, 1996.

Trismegistus, Hermes. *Les Cyranides*, I, K, Ω, 20–34. In Fernand de Mély, ed. and trans., *Les lapidaires de l'antiquité et du Moyen Âge*, vol. 3: *Les lapidaires grecs*. Paris: Ernest Leroux, 1902, pp. 51–52, 69.

Valerius Maximus. *Memorable Deeds and Sayings*, vol. 1. Trans. D. R. Shackleton Bailey. Loeb Classical Library, 492. Cambridge, MA: Harvard University Press, 2014.

Varia graeca sacra. Ed. Athanasios Papadopoulos-Kerameus. Petropoli, 1900.

Van Mander, Karel. *The Lives of the Illustrious Netherlandish and German Painters*. Ed. and trans. Hessel Miedema. Doornspijk: DAVACO, 1994.

Vasari, Giorgio. *Le Vite de' più eccellenti pittori, scultori ed architettori*. In *Le Opere di Giorgio Vasari*, 9 vols. Ed. Gaetano Milanesi. Florence: Sansoni, 1906.

———. *Lives of the Painters, Sculptors and Architects*, vols. 1–2. Trans. Gaston du C. de Vere. New York: Alfred A. Knopf, 1996.

Vie de Daniel le Stylite. In Hippolyte Delehaye, *Les Saints stylites*. Brussels/Paris: Société des Bollandistes/A. Picard, 1923, pp. 91–92.

Vie d'Étienne le Jeune par Étienne le Diacre (La). Ed. Marie-France Auzépy. London/New York: Routledge, 1997.

Viollet-le-Duc, Emmanuel-Louis-Nicolas, *Catalogue des livres composant la bibliothèque poétique de M. Viollet le Duc . . . .* Paris: L. Hachette, 1843.

Vocabolario degli Accademici della Crusca . . . . Venise: Appresso Giouanni Alberti, 1612

Voragine, Jacobus de. *The Golden Legend of Jacobus de Voragine*. Trans. Granger Ryan and Helmut Ripperger. New York: Arno Press, 1969.

Wichmans, Augustin-François. *Brabantia Mariana tripartita*. Anvers: Joannem Cnobbaert, 1632.

Zola, Émile. *Mes haines: Causeries littéraires et artistiques; Mon salon, Édouard Manet, étude biographique et critique*. Paris: M. Charpentier, 1893.

Zuccaro, Federico. *L'idea de' pittori, scultori ed architetti*. Rome: Marco Pagliarini, 1768.

SECONDARY WORKS

Abramovici, Jean-Christophe. "Du ragoût en peinture." In Julia Csergo and Frédérique Desbuissons, eds., *Le cuisinier et l'art: Art du cuisinier et cuisine d'artiste (XVIe–XXIe siècle)*. Paris: INHA/Menu fretin, 2018, pp. 217–22.

Agamben, Giorgio. *Opus Dei: An Archaeology of Duty*. Trans. Adam Kotsko. Stanford: Stanford University Press, 2013.

———. *Stanzas: Word and Phantasm in Western Culture*. Trans. Ronald L. Martinez. Minneapolis: University of Minnesota Press, 1993.

Agut-Mabordère, Damien, and Michel Chauveau, eds. *Héros, magiciens et sages oubliés de l'Égypte ancienne: Une anthologie de la littérature en égyptien démotique*. Paris: Les Belles Lettres, 2011.

Ajmar, Marta, and Flora Dennis, eds. *At Home in Renaissance Italy: Art and Life in the Italian House, 1400–1600*. New York: Abrams, 2006.

Albala, Ken. *Food in Early Modern Europe*. Westport/London: Greenwood Press, 2003.

Albert Llorca, Marlène. "Les statues habillées dans le catholicisme: Entre histoire de l'art, histoire religieuse et anthropologie." *Archives de sciences sociales des religions* 164 (2013), pp. 11–23.

Albrecht, Uwe, ed. *Corpus der Mittelalterlichen Holzskulptur und Tafelmalerei in Schleswig-Holstein*. Bd. 1. Kiel: Ludwig, 2005.

Alexandre-Bidon, Danièle, ed. *Le pressoir mystique: Actes du colloque de Recloses*. Paris: Cerf, 1990.

Alloa, Emmanuel, ed. *Penser l'image*. Dijon: Les Presses du réel, 2010.

Arabeyre, Patrick. "La lactation de saint Bernard à Châtillon-sur-Seine: Données et problèmes." In Patrick Arabeyre, Jacques Berlioz, and Philippe Poirrier, eds., *Vies et légendes de saint Bernard de Clairvaux: Création, diffusion, réception (XIIe–XXe siècles)*. Cîteaux: Commentarii Cistercienses, 1993, pp. 173–97.

Areford, David S. "Multiplying the Sacred: The Fifteenth-Century Woodcut as Reproduction, Surrogate, Simulation." In Peter Parshall, ed., *The Woodcut in Fifteenth-Century Europe*. Washington, DC: National Gallery of Art, 2009, pp. 118–53.

———. "Print Trouble: Notes on a Medium In Between." In Colum Hourihane, ed., *From Minor to Major: The Minor Arts in Medieval Art History*. Princeton, NJ: Princeton University Press, 2012, pp. 229–54.

Armengaud, Christine. *Le diable sucré: Gâteaux, cannibalisme, mort et fécondité*. Paris: La Martinière, 2000.

Auerbach, Erich. "Figura." In Erich Auerbach, *Scenes from the Drama of European Literature*. Minneapolis: University of Minnesota Press, 1984.

Auffarth, Christoph. "Le rite sacrificial antique: La longue durée et la fin du sacrifice." *Kermos* 25 (2012), pp. 297–303.

Augé, Marc. *Génie du paganisme*. Paris: Gallimard, 2008.

Auségache, Mireille. "Le minéral au secours du corps dans la pharmacopée médiévale occidentale (XIIe–XVe siècle)." In Danielle Jacquart and Nicolas Weill-Parot, eds., *Substances minérales et corps animés / Mineral Substances and Animates Bodies (1100–1500)*. Montreuil: Omniscience, 2012, pp. 147–77.

Austin, John L. *How to do Things with Words*. 2nd ed. Eds. J. O. Urmson and Marina Sbisà. Oxford: Clarendon Press, 1975.

Bacci, Michele. *Il pennello dell'Evangelista: Storia delle immagini sacre attribuite a San Luca*. Pisa: GISEM, 1998.

Bachelard, Gaston. *The Formation of the Scientific Mind*. Trans. Mary McAllester Jones. Manchester: Clinamen Press, 2002.

Baciocchi, Stéphane and Christophe Duhamelle, eds. *Reliques romaines: Invention et circulation des corps saints des catacombes à l'époque moderne*. Rome: EFR, 2016.

Baert, Barbara. "Nourished by Inwardness: The Beato Chiarito Tabernable (c. 1340)." *Annali dell'Università di Ferrara, Sezione Storia* 4 (2007), pp. 28–50.

———. "'Who touched my clothes?': The Healing of the Woman with the Haemorrhage (Mark 5:24–34; Luke 8:42–48 and Matthew 9:19–22) in Early Medieval Visual Culture." *Konsthistorisk Tidskrift* 79.2 (2010), pp. 65–90.

Bakhtin, Mikhaïl. *Rabelais and His World*. Trans. Hélène Iswolsky. Bloomington, IN: Indiana University Press, 1984.

Barber, Charles. "From Transformation to Desire: Art and Worship after Byzantine Iconoclasm." *Art Bulletin* 75.1 (1993), pp. 7–16.

Barbier de Montault, Xavier. "L'hostie." In Œuvres *complètes*, tome VI, vol. 1. Paris: Vivès, 1892, pp. 178–87.

Barre, Aurélie, and Olivier Leplatre. "L'iconophagie byzantine: Aspects du rituel eucharistique dans le christianisme oriental." *Food & History* 6.2 (2008), pp. 73–89.

Barthélémy, Dominique. "Ordalie." In Claude Gauvard, Alain de Libera, and Michel Zink, eds., *Dictionnaire du Moyen Âge*. Paris: Presses universitaires de France, 2006, pp. 1020–22.

Bartholeyns, Gil, Pierre-Olivier Dittmar, and Vincent Jolivet. *Image et transgression au Moyen Âge*. Paris: Presses universitaires de France, 2008.

Baschet, Jérôme. *La civilisation féodale de l'an mil à la colonisation de l'Amérique*, revised 3rd edition. Paris: Flammarion, 2006.

———, Jérôme. *L'iconographie* médiévale. Paris: Gallimard, 2008.

———, and Jean-Claude Schmitt, eds. *L'image: Fonctions et usages des images dans l'Occident médiéval*. Paris: Le Léopard d'or, 1996.

Battino, Freddy, and Luca Palazzoli. *Piero Manzoni: Catalogue raisonné*. Milan: Edizioni di Vanni Scheiwiller, 1991.

Bedos-Rezak, Brigitte Miriam. "*Ego, Ordo, Communitas*: Seals and the Medieval Semiotics of Personality (1200–1350)." In Markus Späth, ed., *Die Bildlichkeit korporativer Siegel im Mittelalter Kunstgeschichte und Geschichte im Gespräch*. Cologne: Böhlau Verlag, 2009, pp. 47–64.

———. "In Search of a Semiotic Paradigm: The Matter of Sealing in Medieval Thought and Praxis (1050–1400)." In Noël Adams, John Cherry, James Robinson, eds., *Good Impressions: Image and Authority in Medieval Seals*. London: British Museum Research Publication, 2008, pp. 1–7.

———. "Medieval Identity: A Sign and a Concept." *The American Historical Review* 105.5 (2000), pp. 1489–1533.

———. "Une image ontologique: Sceau et ressemblance en France préscolastique (1000–1200)." In Alain Erlande-Bradenburg and Jean-Michel Leniaud, eds., *Études d'histoires de l'art offertes à Jacques Thirion: Des premiers temps chrétiens au XXe siècle*. Paris: École des chartes, 2001, pp. 39–50.

Beherman, Thierry. *Godfried Schalcken*. Paris: Maeght, 1988.

Behrend, Heike. "Photo Magic: Photographs in Practices of Healing and Harming in East Africa." *Journal of Religion in Africa* 33.2 (2003), pp. 129–45

Beil, Ralf. *Künstlerküche: Lebensmittel als Kunstmaterial von Schiele bis Jason Rhoades*. Cologne: DuMont, 2002.

Belting, Hans. *An Anthropology of Images: Picture, Medium, Body*. Trans. Thomas Dunlap. Princeton, NJ: Princeton University Press, 2011.

———. *La vraie image: Croire aux images?* Paris: Gallimard, 2007.

———. *Likeness and Presence: History of the Image before the Era of Art*. Trans. Edmund Jephcott. Chicago: University of Chicago Press, 1996.

Bénézet, Jean-Pierre. *Pharmacie et médicament en méditerranée occidentale (XIIIe–XVe siècles)*. Paris: Honoré Champion, 1999.

Benjamin, Walter, "The Work of Art in the Age of Mechanical Reproduction." In Walter Benjamin, *Illuminations: Essays and Reflections*. Trans. Harry Zohn. New York: Schocken Books, 1969, pp. 217–251.

Bériou, Nicole, "L'eucharistie dans l'imaginaire des prédicateurs." In Nicole Bériou, Béatrice Caseau, Dominique Rigaux, eds., *Pratiques de l'eucharistie dans les* Églises *d'Orient et d'Occident (Antiquité et Moyen Âge)*, vol. 2: *Les réceptions*. Turnhout: Brepols, 2009, pp. 879–925.

Bettini, Maurizio, and Omar Calabrese. *BizzarraMente: Eccentrici e stravaganti dal mondo antico alla modernità*. Milan: Feltrinelli, 2002.

Bianchi Bensimon, Nella. "Alimentation et mélancolie dans le *De vita libri tres* de Marsile Ficin." In Adelin Charles Fiorato and Anna Fontes Baratto, eds., *La table et ses dessous: Culture, alimentation et convivialité en Italie, XIVe–XVIe siècle*. Paris: Presses de la Sorbonne Nouvelle, 1999, pp. 55–71.

Bieber, Margarete. *Skenika: Kuchenform mit Tragödienszene, Maske aus dem Kerameikos*. Berlin: G. Reimer, 1915.

Blanchot, Maurice. *Friendship*. Trans. Elizabeth Rottenberg. Stanford: Stanford University Press, 1997.

Blanks, David R., and Michael Frassetto, eds. *Western Views of Islam in Medieval and Early Modern Europe: Perception of Other*. London: Macmillan, 1999.

Bloch, Marc. *Les rois thaumaturges: Étude sur le caractère surnaturel attribué à la puissance royale particulièrement en France et en Angleterre*. Paris et Strasbourg, Istra, 1924. Republished Paris: Gallimard, 1983.

Blumenberg, Hans. *Paradigms for a Metaphorology*. Trans. Robert Savage. Ithaca, NY: Cornell University Press, 2010.

Blümner, Hugo. *Technologie und Terminologie der Gewerbe und Künste bei Griechen und Römern*, vol. 1. Leipzig: B. G. Teubner, 1875.

Bodart, Diane, and Valérie Boudier. "Le banquet de la Renaissance: Images et usages." *Predella* 33 (2013), pp. 9–20.

Bodiou, Lydie. "Les singulières conversions du lait maternel à l'époque Classique: Approche médicale et biologique." *Pallas* 85 (2011), pp. 141–51.

Boehm, Gottfried. "Die Wiederkehr der Bilder." In *Was ist ein Bild?* Munich: Wilhelm Fink, 1994, pp. 11–38.

Boespflug, François, and Nicolas Lossky, eds. *Nicée II, 787–1987, Douze siècles d'images religieuses: Actes du colloque international "Nicée II."* Paris: Cerf, 1987.

Bonnain, Rolande. "D'une pâtisserie cérémonielle: Usage de l'oublie." *Ethnologie française* 23.4 (1993), pp. 542–61.

Bonne, Jean-Claude. "Entre l'image et la matière: La choséité du sacré en Occident." In Jean-Marie Sansterre and Jean-Claude Schmitt, eds., *Les Images dans les sociétés médiévales: Pour une histoire comparée*. Special issue of the *Bulletin de l'Institut historique belge de Rome* 69 (1999), pp. 77–111.

———. "Représentation médiévale et lieu sacré." In Sofia Boesch-Gajano and Lucetta

Scaraffia, eds., *Luoghi sacri e spazi della santità*. Turin: Rosenberg & Sellier, 1990, pp. 565–71.

Bonnefoy, Françoise, ed. *Restaurant Spoerri: Maison fondée en 1963, 1, place de la Concorde, Paris 75008*. Paris: Musée du Jeu de Paume, 2002. Exhibition catalog.

Bonner, Campbell. *Studies in Magical Amulets Chiefly Graeco-Egyptian*. Ann Arbor: University of Michigan Press, 1950.

Boone, Elizabeth H. "Incarnations of the Aztec Supernatural: The Image of Huizilopochtli in Mexico and Europe." *Transactions of the American Philosophical Society* 79.2 (1989), pp. 1–107.

Borgnet, Guy. "Le pays de Cocagne dans la littérature allemande: Des origines à Hans Sachs." In Danielle Buschinger and Wolfgang Spiewok, eds., *Gesellschaftsutopien im Mittelalter: Discours et figures de l'utopie au Moyen Âge*. Greifswald: Reineke Verlag, 1994, pp. 15–27.

Bothe, Friedrich. *Frankfurter Patriziervermögen im 16. Jahrhundert: Ein Beitrag zur Charakteristik der bürgerlichen Vermögen und der bürgerlichen Kultur*. Berlin: Alexander Duncker Verlag, 1908.

Boucher, Mélanie. "L'origine de l'usage des aliments en arts visuels au XXe siècle." In Julia Csergo and Frédérique Desbuissons, eds., *Le cuisinier et l'art: Art du cuisinier et cuisine d'artiste (XVIe–XXIe siècle)*. Paris: INHA/Menu fretin, 2018, pp. 239–53.

Boudier, Valérie. *La cuisine du peintre: Scène de genre et nourriture au Cinquecento*. Tours/Rennes: Presses Universitaires Rennes, 2010.

Boulnois, Olivier. *Au-delà de l'image: Une archéologie du visuel au Moyen Âge, Ve–XVIe siècle*. Paris: Seuil, 2008.

Bourdieu, Pierre. "Les rites comme actes d'institution." *Actes de la recherche en sciences sociales* 43 (June 1982), pp. 58–63.

Boutaud, Jean-Jacques, *Le sens gourmand: De la commensalité, du goût, des aliments*. Paris: Jean-Paul Rocher, 2005.

Brague, Rémi. *The Legend of the Middle Ages: Philisophical Explorations of Medieval Christianity, Judaism, and Islam*. Trans. Lydia G. Cochrane. Chicago: University of Chicago Press, 2009.

Brandes, Stanley. *Skulls to the Living, Bread to the Dead: Celebrations of Death in Mexico and Beyond*. Malden/Oxford/Victoria: Blakwell, 2006.

Brauneck, Manfred. *Religiöse Volkskunst: Votivgaben, Andachtsbilder, Hinterglas, Rosenkranz, Amulette*. Cologne: DuMont, 1978.

Bredekamp, Horst. *Image Acts: A Systematic Approach to Visual Agency.* Ed. and trans. Elizabeth Clegg. Berlin: De Gruyter, 2021.

———. *Stratégies visuelles de Thomas Hobbes: Le Léviathan, archétype de l'État moderne. Illustrations des* œuvres *et portraits*, 3 vols. Paris: Éditions de la Maison des Sciences de l'Homme, 2003.

Bresc, Henri. "Europe: Town and Country (Thirteenth–Fifteenth Century)." In André Burguière, Christiane Klapisch-Zuber, Martine Segalen, and Françoise Zonabend, eds., *A History of the Family*, vol. 1: *Distant Worlds, Ancient Worlds.* Trans. Sarah Hanbury Tenison, Rosemary Morris, and Andrew Wilson. Cambridge, MA: Belknap Press of Harvard University Press, 1996, pp. 430–66.

Brian, Isabelle. *Messieurs de Sainte-Geneviève: Religieux et curés de la Contre-Réforme à la Révolution.* Paris: Cerf, 2001.

Bridgeman, Jane. *A Renaissance Wedding: The Celebrations at Pesaro for the Marriage of Costanzo Sforza and Camilla Marzano d'Aragona (26–30 May 1475)*, ed. and trans. Jane Bridgeman and Alan Griffiths. London: Harvey Miller, 2013.

Brown, Peter, *The Cult of the Saints: Its Rise and Function in Latin Christianity.* 2nd edition. Chicago: University of Chicago Press, 2015.

Bruna, Denis. *Enseignes de plomb et autres menues chosettes du Moyen Âge.* Paris: Le Léopard d'or, 2006.

Bury, Michael. *The Print in Italy, 1550–1620.* London: British Museum, 2001. Exhibition catalog.

Bussagli, Marc, ed. *Les ailes de Dieu: Messagers et guerriers ailés entre Orient et Occident.* Milan: Silvana, 2000.

Bynum, Caroline Walker. *Christian Materiality: An Essay on Religion in Late Medieval Europe.* New York: Zone Books, 2015.

———. *Fragmentation and Redemption: Essays on Gender and the Human Body in Medieval Religion.* New York: Zone Books, 1992.

———. *Holy Feast and Holy Fast: The Religious Significance of Food to Medieval Women.* Berkeley: University of California Press, 1988.

———. *Jesus as a Mother: Studies in the Spirituality of the High Middle Ages.* Berkeley: University of California Press, 1982.

———. "Seeing and Seeing Beyond: The Mass of St. Gregory in the Fifteenth Century." In Anne-Marie Bouché and Jeffrey Hamburger, eds., *The Mind's Eye: Art and Theology in the Middle Ages.* Princeton, NJ: Princeton University Press, 2005, pp. 208–40.

———. "Why All the Fuss about the Body? A Medievalist's Perspective." *Critical Inquiry* 22.1 (1995), pp. 1–33.

Cameron, Euan. *Enchanted Europe: Superstition, Reason, and Religion*. Oxford: Oxford University Press, 2010.

Camille, Michael. "Mouth and Meanings: Towards an Anti-iconography of Medieval Art." In *Iconography at the Crossroads: Papers from the Colloquium Sponsored by the Index of Christian Art*. Princeton, NJ: Princeton University Press, 1993.

———. *The Gothic Idol: Ideology and Image-Making in Medieval Art*. Cambridge: Cambridge University Press, 1989.

Camporesi, Piero. *Les baumes de l'amour*. Paris: Hachette, 1997.

———. *The Incorruptible Flesh: Bodily Mutation and Mortification in Religion and Folklore*. Trans. Tania Croft-Murray and Helen Elsom. Cambridge, UK: Cambridge University Press, 1988.

Capdeville, Gérard. "Substitution de victimes dans les sacrifices d'animaux à Rome." *Mélanges de l'Ecole Française de Rome—Antiquité* 83.2 (1971), pp. 283–323.

Careri, Giovanni. *La torpeur des ancêtres: Juifs et chrétiens dans la chapelle Sixtine*. Paris: Éditions de l'École des Hautes Études en Sciences Sociales, 2013.

Caspers, Charles. "The Western Church during the Late Middle Ages: *Augenkommunion* or Popular Mysticism?" In Charles Caspers, Gerard Lukken, and Gerard Rouwhorst, eds., *Bread of Heaven: Customs and Practices surrounding Holy Communion: Essays in the History of Liturgy and Culture*. Nijmegen/Kampen: Kok Pharos, 1995, pp. 83–97.

Cassegrain, Guillaume. *La Coulure: Histoires de la peinture en mouvement (XIe–XXIe siècles)*. Paris: Hazan, 2015.

———. *Représenter la vision: Figuration des apparitions miaculeuses dans la peinture italienne de la Renaissance*. Arles: Actes Sud, 2017.

Celant, Germano. *Piero Manzoni*. New York: Sonnabend Press, 1972.

———. ed. *Dennis Oppenheim: Explorations*. Milan: Charta, 2001.

Charuty, Giordana. "Du catholicisme méridional à l'anthropologie des sociétés chrétiennes." In Dionigi Albera, Anton Blo, and Christian Bromberger, eds., *L'anthropologie de la Méditerranée*. Paris/Aix-en-Provence: Maisonneuve/Larose/MMSH, 2001, pp. 359–85.

———, Jérémie Koering, Pierre-Olivier Dittmar, and Jean-Claude Schmitt. "Des images faites pour être détruites." *Perspective—Actualité en histoire de l'art* 2, "Détruire," (2018), pp. 19–36.

Christin, Olivier, and Fabrice Flückiger. "Introduction: L'*Atlas Marianus* de Wilhelm Gumppenberg: Une topographie sacrée à l'âge de la science Classique." In Olivier Christin, Fabrice Flückiger, and Naïma Ghermani, eds., *Marie mondialisée: L'*Atlas Marianus *de Wilhelm Gumppenberg et les topographies sacrées de l'époque moderne.* Neuchâtel: Éditions Alphil-Presses universitaires suisses, 2014, pp. 9–23.

Clair, Muriel. "Notre-Dame de Foy en Nouvelle-France (1669–1675): Histoire des statuettes de Foy et des *wampum* des Hurons chrétiens." *Annales de la Société archéologique de Namur* 83 (2009), pp. 167–92.

Coccia, Emanuele. *Sensible Life: A Micro-ontology of the Image.* Trans. Scott Alan Stuart. New York: Fordham University Press, 2016.

Colville, Georgiana. *Scandaleusement d'elles: Trente-quatre femmes surrealists.* Paris: Jean-Michel Place, 1999.

Compagnon, Antoine. *Nous, Michel de Montaigne.* Paris: Seuil, 1980.

Compton, Michael T. "The Association of Hygieia with Asklepios in Graeco-Roman Asklepieion Medicine." *Journal of the History of Medicine and Allied Sciences* 57.3 (2002), pp. 312–29.

Congdon, Kristin. "Making Merry with Death: Iconic Humor in Mexico's Day of the Dead." In Peter Narvaez, ed., *Of Corpse: Death and Humor in Folkore and Popular Culture.* Logan, UT: Utah State University Press, 2003, pp. 198–220.

Congourdeau, Marie-Hélène. "L'enfant immolé: Hyper-réalisme et symbolique sacrificielle à Byzance." In Nicole Bériou, Béatrice Caseau, and Dominique Rigaux, eds., *Pratiques de l'Eucharistie dans les églises d'Orient et d'Occident (Antiquité et Moyen Âge),* vol. 1: *Institution.* Turnhout: Brepols, 2009, pp. 291–307.

Conti, Fabrizio. *Witchcraft, Superstition, and Observant Francisca Preachers: Pastoral Approach and Intellectual Debate in Renaissance Milan.* Turnhout: Brepols, 2015.

Cordini, Guido. "*Non est in Toto Sanctior Orbe Locus*: Collecting Relics in Early Medieval Rome." In Martina Bagnoli, Holger A. Klein, and C. Griffith Mann, eds., *Treasures of Heaven: Saints, Relics, and Devotion in Medieval Europe.* New Haven, CT: Yale University Press, 2010, pp. 69–78.

Cousinié, Frédéric. *Esthétique des fluides: Sang, sperme, merde dans la peinture française du XVIIe siècle.* Paris: Éditions du Félin, 2011.

———. *Images et méditation au XVIIe siècle.* Rennes: Presses universitaires Rennes, 2007.

———. *Trajectoire des images: Culte marial et intermédialité dans la France du XVIIe siècle.* Paris: Éditions 1:1, 2017.

Criqui, Jean-Pierre. "Piero Manzoni and His Left-Overs." In Germano Celant, ed., *Piero*

Manzoni. Trans. Judith Aminoff, Paul Blanchard, Alain Degange, Claude Gintz, and Maev de la Guardia. Milan: Arnoldo Mondadori Arte, 1991. Exhibition catalog.

Cupperi, Walter. "Introduction: Never Identical." In Walter Cupperi, ed., *Multiples in Pre-Modern Art*. Zurich: Diaphanes, 2014, pp. 7–28.

Dagron, Gilbert. *Décrire et peindre: Essai sur le portrait iconique*. Paris: Gallimard, 2007.

Damisch, Hubert. "La peinture est un vrai trois." In *Fenêtre jaune cadmium ou Les dessous de la peinture*. Paris: Seuil, 1984, pp. 275–305.

———. "Titres." In Hubert Damisch, *Fenêtre jaune cadmium, ou Les dessous de la peinture*. Paris: Seuil, 1984, pp. 181–87.

Daremberg, Charles Victor, and Edmond Saglio. *Dictionnaire des antiquités grecques et romaines d'après les textes et les monuments*. Paris: Hachette, 1877–1919.

Dasen, Véronique. "Le pouvoir des pierres: De la *sphragis* au médicament estampillé dans le monde gréco-romain." In Thomas Galoppin and Cécile Guillaume-Pey, eds., *Ce que peuvent les pierres: Vie et puissance des matériaux lithiques entre rites et savoirs*. Liège: Presses universitaires de Liège, 2021, pp. 135–62.

———. "Magic and Medicine: Gems and the Power of Seals." In Chris Entwistle and Noël Adams, eds., *"Gems of Heaven": Recent Research on Engraved Gemstones in Late Antiquity, c. AD 200–600*. London: British Museum, 2011, pp. 69–74.

———. "Magical Milk Stones?" In Juan Francisco Martos Montiel, Cristobal Macias Villalobos, and R. Caballero Sanchez, eds., *Plutarco, entre dioses y Astros: Homenaje al profesor Aurelio Pérez Jiménez de sus discípulos, colegas y amigos*, vol. 2. Zaragoza: Libros Pòrtico, 2019, pp. 1035–1048.

———. "Métamorphoses de l'utérus, d'Hippocrate à Ambroise Paré." *Gesnerus: Revue trimestrielle d'histoire de la médecine et des sciences naturelles* 59 (2002), pp. 167–86.

———. "*Probaskania*: Amulets and Magic in Antiquity." In Dietrich Boschung and Jan N. Bremmer, eds., *The Materiality of Magic*. Paderborn: Wilhelm Fink, 2015, pp. 177–203.

———, and Árpád M. Nagy. "Gems." In David Frankfurter, ed., *Guide to the Study of Ancient Magic*. Leiden: Brill, 2019, pp. 416–55.

———, and Árpád M Nagy. "Le serpent léontocéphale Chnoubis et la magie de l'époque romaine impériale." *Anthropozoologica* 47.1 (2012), pp. 291–314.

———, and Michel Spieser, eds. *Les Savoirs magiques et leur transmission de l'Antiquité à la Renaissance*. Florence: Sismel, 2014.

Davila, Thierry. "Esthétique et clinique: Brève introduction à l'art médecin." *Les Cahiers du MNAM* 67 (1999), pp. 92–111.

Day, Ivan, "Eating the Edifice." Lecture given at the Getty Research Institute, Los Angeles, CA, January 31, 2016.

Dekoninck, Ralph. "Les Silènes de Gumppenberg: L'*Atlas Marianus* et la matière des images miraculeuses de la Vierge au regard du culte marial dans les anciens Pays-Bas." In Olivier Christin, Fabrice Flückiger, and Naïma Ghermani, eds., *Marie mondialisée: L'*Atlas Marianus *de Wilhelm Gumppenberg et les topographies sacrées de l'époque moderne.* Neuchâtel: Éditions Alphil-Presses universitaires suisses, 2014, pp. 211–21.

———. "*Propagatio imaginum*: The Translated Images of Our Lady of Foy." In Christine Göttler and Mia Mochizuki, eds., *The Nomadic Object: The Challenge of World for Early Modern Religious Art.* Leiden: Brill, 2018, pp. 241–67.

———. "Une idolâtrie iconoclaste? Usures et brisures pieuses des images saintes." In Agnès Lafont, Christian Belin, and Nicholas Myers, eds., *L'image brisée aux XVIe et XVIIe siècles / Breaking the Image in the Renaissance.* Paris: Classiques Garnier, 2019, pp. 155–66.

———, Annick Delfosse, and Christian Pacco, eds. *Foy-Notre-Dame: Art, politique et religion*, special issue of the *Annales de la Société archéologique de Namur* 83 (2009), pp. 153–66.

Delatte, Armand. "Étude sur la magie grecque: V. Akephalos Theos." *Bulletin de correspondance hellénique* 38 (1914), pp. 189–249.

Delehaye, Hippolyte. *Les Origines du culte des martyrs.* Bruxelles: Bureaux de la Société des Bollandistes, 1912.

———. "Les recueils antiques de miracles des saints." *Analecta Bollandiana* 43 (1925), pp. 305–25.

Delteil, Loys. *Honoré Daumier: The Early Lithographs. Catalogue raisonné 1830–1837.* Trans. Robin Orr Bodkin. San Francisco: Alan Wofsy Fine Arts, 2005.

Deonna, Waldemar. "Notes d'archéologie suisse V: ΥΓΙΕΙΑ." *Anzeiger für schweizerische Altertumskunde* 21 (1919), pp. 87–95.

———, and Marcel Renard. *Croyances et superstitions de table dans la Rome antique.* Brussels: Latomus, 1961.

Derchain, Philippe. "À propos de performativité: Pensers anciens et articles récents." *Göttinger Miszellen. Beiträge zur* ägyptologischen *Diskussion* 110 (1989), pp. 13–18.

Desbuissons, Frédérique. "The Studio and the Kitchen: Culinary Ugliness as Pictorial Stigmatisation in Nineteenth-Century France." In Andreï Pop and Mechtild Widrich, eds., *Ugliness: The Non-Beautiful in Art and Theory.* London: I. B. Tauris, 2013, pp. 104–21.

Descola, Philippe. *Beyond Nature and Culture*. Trans. Janet Lloyd. Chicago: University of Chicago Press, 2013.

———. *La composition des mondes: Entretiens avec Pierre Charbonnier*. Paris: Flammarion, 2014.

———. "La fabrique des images." *Anthropologie et sociétés* 30.3 (2006), pp. 167–82.

———. "L'envers du visible: Ontologie et iconologie." In Thierry Dufrêne and Anne-Christine Taylor, eds., *Cannibalismes disciplinaires. Quand l'histoire de l'art et l'anthropologie se rencontrent*. Paris: INHA/Musée du quai Branly, 2009, pp. 25–36.

———. "Ontologie des images (suite) (1)." *Collège de France*, March 10, 2010. https://www.college-de-france.fr/fr/agenda/cours/ontologie-des-images-suite/ontologie-des-images-suite-1-0.

———, and Tim Ingold. *Être au monde: Quelle expérience commune?* Lyon: Presses universitaires de Lyon, 2014. Debate presented by Michel Lussault.

———, ed. *La fabrique des images: Visions du monde et formes de la représentation*. Paris: Somogy/Musée du quai Branly, 2010. Exhibition catalog.

Desgagnés, Alexis. "De Gillray à Cruikshank: Répétition historique, caricature et *praxis* de l'histoire." In Ségolène Le Men, ed., *L'art de la caricature*. Nanterre: Presses universitaires de Paris Ouest, 2011, pp. 309–17.

Desportes, Françoise. "Food Trades." In Jean-Louis Flandrin and Massimo Montanari, eds., *Food: A Culinary History from Antiquity to the Present*. Trans. Clarissa Botsford, Arthur Goldhammer, Charles Lambert, and Frances M. López-Morillas. New York: Columbia University Press, 1999 pp. 275–86.

Detienne, Marcel, and Jean-Pierre Vernant. "Culinary Practices and the Spirit of Sacrifice." In *The Cuisine of Sacrifice Among the Greeks*. Trans. Paula Wissing. Chicago: University of Chicago Press, 1989, pp. 1–20.

———. *The Cuisine of Sacrifice among the Greeks*. Trans. Paula Wissing. Chicago: University of Chicago Press, 1989

Didi-Huberman Georges. *La Ressemblance par contact: Archéologie, anachronisme et modernité de l'empreinte*. Paris: Éditions de Minuit, 2008.

———. *L'image ouverte: Motifs de l'incarnation dans les arts visuels*. Paris: Gallimard, 2007.

Dinzelbacher, Peter. "Religiöses Erleben von bildender Kunst in autobiographischen und biographischen Zeugnissen des Hoch- und Spätmittelalters." In Klaus Schreiner, ed., *Frömmigkeit im Mittelalter: Politisch-soziale Kontexte, visuelle Praxis, körperliche Ausdrucksformen*. Munich: Wilhelm Fink, 2002, pp. 299–330.

Di Schino, June. "The Significance and Symbolism of Sugar Sculpture at Italian Court Banquets." In Marc McWilliams, ed., *Food and Material Culture: Proceedings of the Oxford Symposium on Food and Cookery*. Totnes: Prospect Books, 2014, pp. 111–22.

Di Stefano Frusi, Chiara. "*Cucina futurista*: Entre renouveau des langages artistiques et mythe de la régénérescence." In Julia Csergo and Frédérique Desbuissons, eds., *Le cuisinier et l'art: Art du cuisinier et cuisine d'artiste (XVIe–XXIe siècle)*. Paris: INHA/ Menu fretin, 2018, pp. 223–38.

Dobschütz, Ernst von. *Christusbilder: Untersuchungen zur christlichen Legende*. Leipzig: J. C. Hinrichs, 1899.

Dölger, Franz Joseph. "Heidnische und christliche Brotstempel mit religiösen Zeichen." In Franz Joseph Dölger, *Antike und Christentum: Kultur-und-Religionsgeschichtliche Studien*, vol. 1. Munster: Aschendorff, 1929, pp. 1–46.

Donati, Claudio. *L'idea di nobiltà in Italia: Secoli XIV–XVII*. Bari: Laterza, 1988.

D'Onofrio, Salvatore. *Les fluides d'Aristote: Lait, sang et sperme dans l'Italie du Sud*. Paris: Les belles lettres, 2014.

Doueihi, Milad. *A Perverse History of the Human Heart*. Cambridge, MA: Harvard University Press, 1997.

Duby, Georges. "Private Power, Public Power." In Georges Duby and Philippe Ariès, eds., *A History of Private Life*, vol. 2: *Revelations of the Medieval World*. Trans. Arthur Goldhammer. Cambridge, MA: Belknap Press of Harvard University Press, 1988, pp. 17–19.

———, Dominique Barthélemy, and Charles de La Roncière. "Tuscan Notables on the Eve of the Renaissance." In Georges Duby and Philippe Ariès, eds., *A History of Private Life*, vol. 2: *Revelations of the Medieval World*. Trans. Arthur Goldhammer. Cambridge, MA/London: Belknap Press of Harvard University Press, 1988, pp. 157–310.

Dulaey, Martine. "La geste de Moïse dans l'œuvre d'Augustin (2): La présence de Dieu au désert et la figure de Moïse." *Revue d'études augustiniennes et patristiques* 57 (2011), pp. 189–237.

Duminil, Marie Paule. "Les théories biologiques sur la génération en Grèce antique." *Pallas. Revue d'études antiques* 31 (1984), pp. 97–112.

Dumoutet, Edouard. *Corpus Domini, aux sources de la piété eucharistique médiévale*. Paris: G. Beauchesne, 1942.

Dunand, Françoise. *Corps vivants des Dieux: Les statues animées dans le monde méditerranéen antique*. Paris: Picard, 2018.

Dupeux, Cécile. "La lactation de saint Bernard de Clairvaux: Genèse et évolution d'une image." In Françoise Dunand, Jean-Marie Spieser, and Jean Wirth, eds., *L'image et la production du sacré*. Paris: Méridiens Klincksieck, 1991, pp. 165–93.

Dupront, Alphonse. "Pèlerinages et lieux sacrés." In *Mélanges en l'honneur de Fernand Braudel: Méthodologie de l'histoire et des sciences humaines*, 2 vols. Toulouse: Privat, 1973, pp. 189–206.

Dutcher Mann, Kristin. "Christmas in the Missions of Northern New Spain." *Americas* 66.3 (2010), pp. 331–51.

Eisenstein, Sergei. "The Day of the Dead." In Carole Naggar and Fred Ritchin, eds., *México Through Foreign Eyes: Visto por ojos extranjeros, 1850–1990*. New York: W. W. Norton, 1993, pp. 154–55.

Ems, Grégory, "De sucre et de papier: Mises en scène et mises en bouche des mets aux XVIe et XVIIe siècles." *Dix-septième siècle* 271.2 (2016), pp. 195–218.

Erlande-Brandenburg, Alain, Pierre-Yves Le Pogam, and Dany Sandron. *Musée national du Moyen Âge: Guide to the Collections*. Trans. Pamela Hargreaves. Paris, RMN, 1993.

Étienne, Marc. *Héka: Magie et envoûtement dans l'Égypte ancienne*. Paris: RMN, 2000.

Fabbri dall'Oglio, Maria-Anna. *Il Trionfo dell'effimero: Lo sfarzo e il lusso dei banchetti nella cornice fastosa della Roma barocca, Viaggio nell'evoluzione del gusto e della tavola nell'Italia tra Sei e Settecento*. Rome: Ricciardi e Associati, 2002.

Fabre, Pierre-Antoine. *Décréter l'image? La XXVe Session du Concile de Trente*. Paris: Les Belles Lettres, 2013.

———. "L'image possible: La femme qui perdait son sang à Panéas, et que Jésus miraculeusement guérit, dans le discours de l'image chrétienne." In Barbara Baert, ed., *The Woman with the Blood Flow (Mark 5:24–34): Narrative, Iconic, and Anthropological Spaces*. Louvain/Walpole, MA: Peeters, 2014, pp. 311–31.

Falguières, Patricia. "Moving Picture: Aristote et la machine cinéma." *Les Cahiers du Musée National d'Art Moderne* 94 (2005–2006), pp. 96–115.

———. "Poétique de la machine." In Philippe Morel, ed., *L'art de la Renaissance entre science et magie*. Rome/Paris: Somogy, 2006, pp. 401–49.

Faraone, Christopher A. *Talismans and Trojan Horses: Guardian Satues in Ancient Greek Myth and Ritual*. Oxford: Oxford University Press, 1992.

———. "Text, Image and Medium: The Evolution of Graeco-Roman Magical Gemstones." In Chris Entwistle and Noël Adams, eds., *"Gems of Heaven": Recent Research on Engraved Gemstones in Late Antiquity, c. AD 200–600*. London: British Museum, 2011, pp. 50–61.

———, and F. S. Naiden, eds. *Greek and Roman Animal Sacrifice: Ancient Victims, Modern Observers*. Cambridge, UK: Cambridge University Press, 2012.

Fascetti, Giovanni Ranieri. *I Ferri da cialda: Documenti del costume e del gusto fra Rinascimento dei miti ed eucaristia profana*. Pise: ETS, 1997.

Fédida, Pierre. "Le cannibale mélancolique." In *L'absence*. Paris: Gallimard/Folio Essais, 1978.

Ferrand, Jean. *Disquisitio reliquiaria sive de suscipienda, et suspecta earundem numero Reliquiarum, quae in diversis Ecclesiis servantur, multitudine*. Lyon: Lavrentii Anisson, 1647.

Festugière, André-Jean. *Les Moines d'Orient*. Paris: Cerf, 1961.

Fischer, Christa. *Stolze Reiter, schöne Damen: Die Bilderwelt der Gebäckmodel*. Ostfildern: Jan Thorbecke Verlag, 2012.

Flanagan, Marie Therese. *The Transformation of the Irish Church in the Twelfth and Thirteenth Centuries*. Woodbridge: Boydell Press, 2010.

Flandrin, Jean-Louis. *Families in Former Times: Kinship, Household, and Sexuality*. Trans. Richard Southern. Cambridge, UK: Cambridge University Press, 1979.

———. "From Dietetics to Gastronomy: The Liberation of the Gourmet." In Jean-Louis Flandrin and Massimo Montanari, eds., *Food: A Culinary History from Antiquity to the Present*. Trans. Clarissa Botsford, Arthur Goldhammer, Charles Lambert, and Frances M. López-Morillas. New York: Columbia University Press, 1999 pp. 418–32.

———, and Massimo Montanari, eds. *Food: A Culinary History from Antiquity to the Present*. Trans. Clarissa Botsford, Arthur Goldhammer, Charles Lambert, Frances M. López-Morillas, and Sylvia Stevens. New York: Columbia University Press, 1999.

Flood, Finbarr Barry. "Mimesis, Mediation and the Ingestion of the Sacred in Christianity and Islam." In Sally M. Promey, ed., *Sensational Religion: Sensory Cultures in Material Practice*. New Haven, CT: Yale University Press, 2014, pp. 459–93.

———. *Technologies de dévotion dans les arts de l'Islam: Pèlerins, reliques et copies*. Paris: Musée du Louvre/Hazan, 2019.

Fornel, Anne de. *John Cage*. Paris: Fayard, 2019.

Foucault, Michel. *History of Madness*. Ed. Jean Khalfa. Trans. Jonathan Murphy and Jean Khalfa. London: Routledge, 2006.

———. *The Order of Things: An Archaeology of the Human Sciences*. Trans. Alan Sheridan. New York: Vintage Books, 1994.

France, James. *Medieval Images of Saint Bernard of Clairvaux*. Kalamazoo: Cistercian Publications, 2007.

Francis, James A. "Living Icons: Tracing a Motif in Verbal and Visual Representation from the Second to the Fourth Centuries C.E." *American Journal of Philology* 124.4 (2003), pp. 575–600.

Frank, Georgia. "L'eucharistie et la mémoire sensorielle selon Jean Chrysostome." In Nicole Bériou, Béatrice Caseau, and Dominique Rigaux, eds., *Pratiques de l'eucharistie dans les églises d'Orient et d'Occident (Antiquité et Moyen Âge)*, vol. 2: *Les réceptions*. Turnhout: Brepols, 2009, pp. 765–77.

———. "The Pilgrim's Gaze in the Age before Icons." In Robert Nelson, ed., *Visuality before and beyond the Renaissance: Seeing as Others Saw*. Cambridge, UK: Cambridge University Press, 2000, pp. 98–114.

Frankfurter, David. "The Laments of Horus in Coptic: Myth, Folklore, and Syncretism in Late Antique Egypt." In Ueli Dill and Christine Walde, eds., *Antike Mythen: Medien, Transformationen und Konstruktionen: Fritz Graf zum 65. Geburtstag*. Berlin: De Gruyter, 2009, pp. 229–47.

———. "Narrating Power: The Theory and Practice of the Magical *Historiola* in Ritual Spells." In Marvin Meyer and Paul Mirecki, eds., *Ancient Magic and Ritual Power*. Leiden: Brill, 1995, pp. 457–76.

Frazer, James George. *The Golden Bough: A Study in Magic and Religion*, 2 vols., abridged edition. New York: Macmillan, 1922.

Freddie, Wilhelm and Joergen Roos. *Spitze Horizonter*, 1950. 35 mm film. Copenhagen, Statens Museum for Kunst.

Freedberg, David. *The Power of Images: Studies in the History and Theory of Response*. Chicago: University of Chicago Press, 1989.

Freeman, Ann. "Carolingian Orthodoxy and the Fate of the Libri Carolini." *Viator* 16 (1985), pp. 65–108

Fricke, Beate. "A Liquid History: Blood and Animation in Late Medieval Art." *RES—Anthropology and Aesthetics* 63–64 (2013), pp. 53–69.

Frontisi-Ducroux, Françoise. *Dédale: Mythologie de l'artisan en Grèce ancienne*. Paris: La Découverte, 2000.

Frugoni, Chiara. "Le mistiche, le visioni e l'iconografia: Rapporti ed influssi." In *La mistica femminile del Trecento*. Todi: Accademia Tudertina, 1982, pp. 5–45.

Gaillard-Seux, Patricia. "Sympathie et antipathie dans l'*Histoire Naturelle* de Pline l'Ancien." In Nicoletta Palmieri, ed., *Rationnel et irrationnel dans la médecine antique et médiévale: Aspects historiques, scientifiques et culturels*. Saint-Étienne: Publications de l'université de Saint-Etienne, 2003, pp. 113–28.

Galavaris, George. *Bread and the Liturgy: The Symbolism of Early Christian and Byzantine Bread Stamps*. Madison, WI: University of Wisconsin Press, 1970.

Garciagodoy, Juanita. *Digging the Days of the Dead: A Reading of Mexico's Dias de Muertos*. Niwot: University Press of Colorado, 1998.

Gasse, Annie. *Les stèles d'Horus sur les crocodiles*. Paris: RMN, 2004.

Geary, Patrick J. *Le vol des reliques au Moyen Âge*. Paris: Aubier, 1993.

Gell, Alfred. *Art and Agency: An Anthropological Theory*. Oxford: Clarendon Press, 1998.

Gensheimer, Maryl B. *Decoration and Display in Rome's Imperial Thermae: Messages of Power and their Popular Reception at the Baths of Caracalla*. New York: Oxford University Press, 2018.

Genovese, Valeria E. *Statue vestite e snodate: Un percorso*. Pise: Edizioni della Normale, 2011.

Gerard, Martine, Catherine Gerard, Alain Person, and Jean-Pierre Sodini. "Argiles et eulogies en forme de jetons: Qal'at Sem'an en est-il une source possible?" In Henry Maguire, ed., *Materials Analysis of Byzantine Pottery*. Washington, DC: Dumbarton Oaks Research Library and Collection, 1998, pp. 9–24.

Gerbron, Cyril. *Fran Angelico: Liturgie et mémoire*. Turnhout: Brepols, 2016.

———. "La question religieuse dans 'Trust No Bitch' (*Orange Is the New Black*, season 3, episode 13)." *Débordements*, January 27, 2018. http://debordements.fr/La-question-religieuse-dans-Trust-No-Bitch.

Giannouri, Evgenia. "Voyages dans les reflets et autres déplacements analogiques: Le Yucatan de S. M. Eisenstein, Robert Smithson et John Lloyd Stephens." In Laurence Schifano and Antonio Somaini, eds., *Eisenstein—Leçons mexicaines: Cinéma, anthropologie, archéologie dans le mouvement des arts*. Paris: Presses universitaires de Paris-Ouest, 2016, pp. 353–72.

Giffin, Erin. "Détruire, reconstruire, redéfinir: La fragmentation volontaire de la Santa Casa de Loreto et ses altérations répliquées." *Perspective* 2 (2018), pp. 209–17.

Giersiepen, Helga. *Die Inschriften der Stadt Aachen*. Düsseldorf: Reichert Verlag, 1993.

Girard, René. *Violence and the Sacred*. Trans. Patrick Gregory. Baltimore, MD: Johns Hopkins University Press, 1977.

Glotz, Gustave. *L'Ordalie dans la Grèce primitive: Étude de droit et de mythologie*. Paris: Fontemoing, 1904.

Godier, Rose-Marie. "*Calaveras* ou les écarts de la pensée: Une vision de Georges Bataille." In Laurence Schifano and Antonio Somaini, eds., *Eisenstein—Leçons mexicaines: Cinéma, anthropologie, archéologie dans le mouvement des arts*. Paris: Presses universitaires de Paris-Ouest, 2016, pp. 305–15.

Godin, André. "Du bon usage du sacré: Érasme de Rotterdam." *Les Cahiers du Centre de Recherches Historiques* 9 (2009).

Goody, Jack. *The Development of the Family and Marriage in Europe*. Cambridge, UK: Cambridge University Press, 1983.

Gorrini, Maria Elena. "Healing Statues in the Greek and Roman World." In Ildikò Csepregi and Charles Burnett, eds., *Ritual Healing: Magic, Ritual and Medical Therapy from Antiquity until the Early Modern Period*. Florence: Sismel, 2012, pp. 107–30.

Gourarier, Zeev. *Arts et manières de table en Occident, des origines à nos jours*. Thionville: Gérard Klopp, 1994.

———. "Modèle de cour et usages de table: Les origines." In Jean-Pierre Babelon, ed., *Versailles et les tables royales en Europe: XVIIe–XIXe siècles*. Paris: RMN, 1993, pp. 15–32.

Grabar, André. *L'iconoclasme byzantin: Le dossier archéologique*. Paris: Flammarion, 1984.

———. *Martyrium: Recherches sur le culte des reliques et l'art chrétien antique*. Paris: Collège de France, 1946.

———. "Quelques reliquaires de saint Démétrios et le martyrium du saint à Salonique." *Dumbarton Oaks Papers* 5 (1950), pp. 1–28.

———. "Un nouveau reliquaire de saint Démétrius." *Dumbarton Oaks Papers* 8 (1954), pp. 305–14.

Gregory, Max Bonnet, Bruno Krusch, and Wilhelm Arndt, *In gloria martyrum*. In *Gregorii Turonensis Opera*. Hannover: Impensis Bibliopolii, 1969, 42.21–26.

Grieco, Allen J. "*Au pays de Cocagne*: Ulysse dans le chaudron." In Paul Noirot, ed., *L'Honnête volupté: Art culinaire, art majeur*. Paris: Études pour la valorisation de la recherche en sciences humaines, 1989, pp. 103–106.

———. "Food and Social Classes in Late Medieval and Renaissance Italy." In Jean-Louis Flandrin and Massimo Montanari, eds., *Food: A Culinary History from Antiquity to the Present*. Trans. Clarissa Botsford, Arthur Goldhammer, Charles Lambert, and Frances M. López-Morillas. New York: Columbia University Press, 1999, pp. 302–12.

Griffiths, Jennifer. "Marisa Mori's Edible Futurist Breasts." *Gastronomica* 12.4 (2012), pp. 20–26.

Grimm, Gerald Volker. "Die Mitteleuropäischen backmodel des 15. Jahrhunderts: Werkgruppen, Chronologie, Verbreitung." In Lutz Grunwald, ed., *Den Töpfern auf der Spur: Orte der Keramikherstellung im Licht der neuesten Forschung*. Mainz: RGZM-Tagungen 21, 2015, pp. 349–58.

Grottanelli, Cristiano. "La viande et ses rites." In Jean-Louis Flandrin and Massimo Montanari, eds., *Histoire de l'alimentation*. Paris: Fayard, 1996, pp. 117–32.

Grumel, Venance. "L'iconologie de saint Théodore Studite." *Échos d'Orient* 20.123 (1921), pp. 257–68.

Guédron, Martial. "Physiologie du bon goût: La hiérarchie des sens dans les discours sur l'art en France au XVIIIe siècle." In Ralph Dekoninck, Agnès Guiderdoni-Bruslé, and Nathalie Kremer, eds., *Aux limites de l'imitation: L'ut pictura poesis à l'épreuve de la matière (XVIe–XVIIIe siècles)*. Amsterdam: Rodopi, 2009, pp. 39–49.

Guichard, Pierre, and Jean-Pierre Cuvillier. "Barbarian Europe." In André Burguière, Christiane Klapisch-Zuber, Martine Segalen, and Françoise Zonabend, eds., *A History of the Family*, vol. 1: *Distant Worlds, Ancient Worlds*. Trans. Sarah Hanbury Tenison, Rosemary Morris, and Andrew Wilson. Cambridge, MA: Belknap Press of Harvard University Press, 1996, pp. 318–78.

Haag, Émile and Eugène. *La France protestante*. Paris: Fischbacher, 1884.

Haddad, Gérard. *Eating the Book: Dietary Rites and Paternal Function*. Trans. David Jacobson. New York: Agincourt Press, 2013.

Halbritter, Roland. "Südtiroler Breverln: Amulette zwischen Magie und Glaube?" *Der Schlern* 72.1 (1998), pp. 39–64.

Hamburger, Jeffrey. *The Visual and the Visionary: Art and Female Spirituality in Late Medieval Germany*. New York: Zone Books, 1998.

Hansen, Hans Jürgen, ed. *Kunstgeschichte des Backwerks: Geschichte und Entwicklung der Gebäckarten und ihrer Formen*. Oldenbourg: Gerhard Stalling, 1968.

Haquin, André. "La dévotion à Notre-Dame de Foy au Québec (XVIIe siècle) et à New York (XXe siècle)." *Annales de la Société archéologique de Namur* 83 (2009), pp. 193–204.

Harris, Thomas. *Red Dragon*. New York: Putnam, 1981.

Hastings, Warren. "On the Trial by Ordeal among the Hindus by Alí Ibráhím Káhn." In *Asiatick Researches or Transactions of the Society Instituted in Bengal*. Calcutta/London: Manuel Cantopher, 1788, pp. 389–401.

Havelange, Carl. *De l'oeil et du monde: Une histoire du regard au seuil de la modernité*. Paris: Fayard, 1998.

Hecht, Peter. "Art Beats Nature, and Painting Does so Best of All: The Paragone Competition in Duquesnoy, Dou and Schalcken." *Semiolus* 29 (2002), pp. 184–201.

Hemelryck, Tania van. "Mascher l'escripture: Livre, lecture et nourriture aux XIVe et XVe siècles." In Nelly Labère, ed., *Être à table au Moyen Âge*. Madrid: Casa de Velazquez, 2010.

Hildburgh, Walter. "Germanic Wafering-Irons of the Sixteenth Century." *Proceedings of the Society of Antiquaries of London*, ser. 2, 26 (1914), pp. 141–49.

———. "Italian Wafering-Irons of the Fifteenth and Sixteenth Century." *Proceedings of the Society of Antiquaries of London*, ser. 2, 27 (1915), pp. 161–201.

Hoffmann, Viktoria von. *From Gluttony to Enlightenment: A World of Taste in Early Modern Europe*. Champaign, IL: University of Illinois Press, 2016.

———. "Le sensible et le culinaire: Les prémices d'une artification au XVIIIe siècle." In Julia Csergo and Frédérique Desbuissons, eds., *Le cuisinier et l'art: Art du cuisinier et cuisine d'artiste (XVIIIe–XXIe siècles)*. Paris: INHA/Menu fretin, 2018, pp. 17–29.

Höhler, Peter. "Il monastero delle clarisse di Monteluce in Perugia (1218–1400)." In Roberto Rusconi, ed., *Il movimento religioso femminile in Umbria nei secoli XIII–XIV: Atti del Convegno internazionale di studio nell'ambito delle celebraioni per l'VII centenario delle nascità di S. Francesco d'Assisi*. Florence: La Nuova Italia Editrice, 1984, pp. 161–82.

Holmes, Megan. *The Miraculous Image in Renaissance Florence*. New Haven, CT: Yale University Press, 2013.

Hölscher, Tonio. *La vie des images grecques: Sociétés de statues,* Rôles *des artistes et notions esthétiques dans l'art grec ancien*. Paris: Hazan, 2015.

Hornung, Erik. *Conceptions of God in Ancient Egypt: The One and the Many*. Trans. John Baines. Ithaca, NY: Cornell University Press, 1982.

Houseman, Michael, and Carlo Severi. *Naven, or, The Other Self: A Relational Approach to Ritual Action*. Leiden: Brill, 1998.

Hsieh, Lisa. "The Edible, Playable, and Wearable Architecture of Haus-Rucker-Co." *The Gradient*, October 23, 2015. https://walkerart.org/magazine/the-edible-playable-and-wearable-architecture-of-haus-rucker-co.

Hübner, Wolfgang. "La mélothésie zodiacale à la Renaissance." In Véronique Dasen and Michel Spieser, eds., *Les savoirs magiques et leur transmission*, pp. 301–30.

Imbach, Josef. *Marienverehrung zwischen Glaube und Aberglaube*. Düsseldorf: Patmos, 2008.

Imorde, Joseph. "Edible Prestige." In Marcia Reed, ed., *The Edible Monument: The Art of Food for Festivals*. Los Angeles: Getty Research Institute, 2015, pp. 101–23.

Ingold, Tim. *Being Alive: Essays on Movement, Knowledge and Description*. London: Routledge, 2011.

———. *Faire: Anthropologie, archéologie, art et architecture*. Paris, Éditions Dehors, 2017.

———. *Lines: A Brief History*. London: Routledge, 2007.

———. *Marcher avec les dragons*. Le Kremlin-Bicêtre: Zones sensibles, 2013.

_____. "La nourriture et le corps au Moyen Âge." *Cahiers de recherches médiévales et humanistes* 13 (2006), pp. 259–66.

Jacob, Robert. *La grâce des juges: L'institution judiciaire et le sacré en Occident*. Paris: Presses universitaires de France, 2014.

Jacobs, Fredrika H. *Votive Panels and Popular Piety in Early Modern Italy*. Cambridge, UK: Cambridge University Press, 2013.

Jacquart, Danielle. *La médecine médiévale dans le cadre parisien (XIVe–XVe siècle)*. Paris: Fayard, 1998.

Jaksch, Peter Karl. *Gesetzlexikon im geistlichen, Religions- und Toleranzfache, wie auch in Güter- Stiftungs- Studien- und Zensurssachen* für das *Königreich Böhmen von 1601 bis Ende 1800*. Prague, 1828.

Jáuregui, Carlos, "Saturnal cannibal: Fronteras, reflejos, y paradojas en la narrativa sobre el antropófago." *Revista de crítica literaria latinoamericana* 26.51 (2000), pp. 9–39.

Javelet, Robert, Paul Lamarche, Leo Scheffczyk, and Aimé Solignac. "Image et ressemblance." In *Dictionnaire de spiritualité ascétique et mystique, doctrine et histoire*, tome VII/16, vol. II/2. Paris: Beauchesne, 1971, ca. 1401–1472.

Jeanneret, Michel. *A Feast of Words: Banquets and Table Talk in the Renaissance*. Chicago: University of Chicago Press, 1991.

Jelinkova-Reymond, Eva. *Les Inscriptions de la statue guérisseuse de Djed-Her-le-Sauveur*. Cairo: Institut français d'archéologie orientale, 1956.

Johnson, Trevor. *Magistrates, Madonnas and Miracles: the Counter-Reformation in the Upper Palatinate*. Farnham, UK: Ashgate, 2009.

Jones, Stephanie. "Q&A with Stephanie Jones." *Vhcle* 11 (2013), pp. 50—55.

Jouanna, Jacques. *Hippocrates*. Trans. M. B. DeBevoise. Baltimore, MD: Johns Hopkins University Press, 1999.

_____. "Médecine rationnelle et magie: Le statut des amulettes et des incantations chez Galien." *Revue des études grecques* 124.1 (2011), pp. 47–77.

Jourdain, Julie. "Ordalie, image et sermon après le concile de Latran IV." *Cahiers de Recherches Médiévales et Humanistes* 25 (2013), pp. 389–404.

Julia, Dominique. "L'Église post-tridentine et les reliques: Tradition, controverse et critique (XVIe–XVIIIe siècle)." In Pierre Boutry, Pierre Antoine Fabre, and Dominique Julia, eds., *Reliques modernes: Cultes et usages chrétiens des corps saints des Réformes aux revolutions*, vol. 1. Paris: École des Hautes Études en Sciences Sociales, 2009, pp. 69–120.

Kammel, Frank Matthias, and Ulrich G. Großmann, eds. *Spiegel der Seligkeit: Privates Bild und Frömmigkeit im Spätmittelalter.* Nuremberg: Germanisches Nationalmuseum, 2000.

Kaplan, Michel. "De la dépouille à la relique: Formation du culte des saints à Byzance du Ve au XIIe siècle." In Édina Bozóky and Anne-Marie Helvétius, eds., *Les reliques: Objets, cultes, symboles: Actes du colloque international de l'Université du Littoral-Côte d'Opale (Boulogne-sur-Mer), 4–6 septembre 1997.* Turnhout: Brepols, 1999, pp. 19–38.

Karr Schmidt, Suzanne, and Kimberly Nichols. *Altered and Adorned: Using Renaissance Prints in Daily Life.* New Haven, CT: Yale University Press, 2011.

Kaye, Nick, Dennis Oppenheim, and Amy van Winckel Oppenheim. *Dennis Oppenheim: Body to Performance, 1969–73.* Milan: Skira, 2016.

Kerr, David S. *Caricature and French Political Culture 1830–1848: Charles Philippon and the Illustrated Press.* Oxford: Clarendon Press, 2000.

Kessler, Herbert, and Johanna Zacharias. *Rome 1300: On the Path of the Pilgrim.* New Haven, CT: Yale University Press, 2000.

Kieffer, Fanny. "La confiserie des Offices: Art, sciences et magnificence à la cour des Médicis." *Predella* 33 (2013), pp. 85–102.

Kilgour, Maggie. *From Communion to Cannibalism: An Anatomy of Metaphors of Incorporation.* Princeton, NJ: Princeton University Press, 1990.

King, Helen. *Greek and Roman Medicine.* London: Bristol Classical Press, 2001.

Kitzinger, Ernst. "The Cult of Images in the Age before Iconoclasm." *Dumbarton Oaks Papers* 8 (1954), pp. 83–150.

Klapisch-Zuber, Christiane. *La maison et le nom: Stratégies et rituels dans l'Italie de la Renaissance.* Paris: Éditions de l'École des Hautes Études en Sciences Sociales, 1990.

———. *L'ombre des ancêtres: Essai sur l'imaginaire médiéval de la parenté.* Paris: Fayard, 2000.

Klein, Robert. *Form and Meaning: Essays on the Renaissance and Modern Art.* Trans. Madeline Jay and Leon Wieseltier. New York: Viking Press, 1979.

———. "Judgement and Taste in Cinquecento Art Theory." In Robert Klein, *Form and Meaning: Essays on the Renaissance and Modern Art.* Trans. Madeline Jay and Leon Wieseltier. New York: Viking Press, 1979, pp. 161–69.

———. "*Spirito peregrino.*" In Robert Klein, *Form and Meaning*, pp. 62–85.

Koenig, Yvan. "Conclusion." In Yvan Koenig, ed., *La magie en Égypte: À la recherche d'une définition.* Paris: La Documentation française/Musée du Louvre, 2002, pp. 399–413.

———. "Introduction." In Yvan Koenig, ed., *La magie en Égypte: À la recherche d'une définition*. Paris: La Documentation française/Musée du Louvre, 2002, pp. 9–13.

Koering, Jérémie. "Titien l'iconophage." *Venezia Cinquecento* 21.41 (2011), pp. 5–37.

———. "To Drink Pictures: Fluids, Imagination and Image-Making in the Renaissance." In Ulrich Pfisterer and Christine Tauber, eds., *Einfluss, Strömung, Quelle: Aquatische Metaphern der Kunstgeschichte*. Bielefeld: Transcript Verlag, 2018, pp. 23–47.

———. "Un artiste affamé: Privation, mélancolie et innutrition dans la *Vie* de Taddeo Zuccaro." In René Démoris, Florence Ferran, and Corinne Lucas-Fiorato, eds., *Art et violence: Vies d'artistes entre XVIe et XVIIIe siècles, Italie, France, Angleterre*. Paris: Desjonquères, 2012, pp. 146–59.

———, and Isolde Pludermacher. "Les graffitis d'artistes: Signes de dévotion artistique, Rome, Latium, XVe–XIXe siècles." *Revue de l'art* 184 (2014), pp. 25–34.

Koerner, Joseph L. *The Reformation of the Image*. London: Reaktion Books, 2004.

Kolta, Kamal Sabri, and Doris Schwarzmann-Schafhauser. *Die Heilkunde im Alten* Ägypten*: Magie und Ratio in der Krankheitsvorstellung und therapeutischen Praxis*. Stuttgart: Franz Steiner, 2000.

Korsmeyer, Carolyn. *Making Sense of Taste: Food and Philosophy*. Ithaca, NY: Cornell University Press, 2002.

Köster, Kurt. "Mittelalterliche Pilgerzeichen." In Lenz Kriss-Rettenbeck and Gerda Möhler, eds., *Wallfahrt kennt keine Grenzen: Themen zu einer Ausstellung des Bayerischen Nationalmuseums und des Adalbert Stifter Vereins, München*. Regensburg: Verlag Schnell & Steiner, 1984, pp. 203–23.

Kriss-Rettenbeck, Lenz. *Bilder und Zeichen religiösen Volksglaubens*. Munich: Georg D. W. Callwey, 1963.

Krohn, Deborah L. "Wafering Iron." In Andrea Bayer, ed., *Art and Love in Renaissance Italy*. The Metropolitan Museum of Art (New York, NY). New Haven, CT/London: Yale University Press, 2009, pp. 116–17. Exhibition catalog.

Kronberger-Frentzen, Hanna. *Die alte Kunst der süssen Sachen: Backformen und Waffeleisen vergangener Jahrhunderte*. Hambourg: Broschek Verlag, 1959.

Krysmanski, Bernd W. *Hogarth's Enthusiasm Delineated: Nachahmung als Kritik am Kennertum, eine Werkanalyse*, 2 vols. Hildesheim: G. Olms, 1996.

———. "We See a Ghost: Hogarth's Satire on Methodists and Connoisseurs." *Art Bulletin* 80.2 (1998), pp. 292–310.

Kuchera, Michael. "The Holy Eucharist in the Byzantine Rite: The Henosis and the

Zeon." In George-Henri Ruyssen, ed., *The Holy Eucharist in Eastern Canon Law: From the Wellspring of the Canons, Acts of the Bratislava Symposium, 14–17 April 2009*. Rome: Pontifico Istituto Orientale, 2010.

Kühne-Wespi, Carina. "Papyrus trinken und Hieroglyphen essen: Praktiken der Schriftverinnerlichung im pharaonischen Ägypten." In Carina Kühne-Wespi, Klaus Oschema, and Joachim F. Quack, eds., *Zerstörung von Geschriebenem: Historische und transkulturelle Perspektiven*. Berlin/Boston: De Gruyter, 2019, pp. 341–58.

Kumler, Aden. "The 'Genealogy of Jean le Blanc': Accounting for the Materiality of the Medieval Eucharist." In Christy Anderson, Anne Dunlop, and Pamela H. Smith, eds., *The Matter of Art: Material, Practices, Cultural Logics, c. 1250–1750*. Manchester: Manchester University Press, 2015, pp. 119–40.

———. "The Multiplication of the Species: Eucharistic Morphology in the Middle Ages." *RES: Anthropology and Aesthetics* 59–60 (Spring–Autumn 2011), pp. 179–91.

Kürzeder, Christoph. *Als die Dinge heilig waren: Gelebte Frömmigkeit im Zeitalter des Barock*. Regensburg: Schnell & Steiner, 2005.

Lacam, Jean-Claude. "La gourmandise des dieux: Les gâteaux sacrés des Tables de Gubbio (IIIe–IIe s. av. J.-C.)." *Mélanges de l'École française de Rome—Antiquité* 124.2 (2012), pp. 551–76.

Lacau, Pierre. "Les statues 'guérisseuses' dans l'ancienne Égypte." *Monuments et mémoires de la Fondation Eugène Piot* 25.1–2 (1921), pp. 189–210.

Lakey, Christophe. "The Curious Case of the *Chiarito Tabernacle*: A New Interpretation." *Getty Research Journal* 4 (2012), pp. 13–30.

La Roncière, Charles de. "Tuscan Notables on the Eve of the Renaissance." In Georges Duby and Philippe Ariès, eds., *A History of Private Life*, vol. 2: *Revelations of the Medieval World*. Trans. Arthur Goldhammer. Cambridge, MA: Belknap Press of Harvard University Press, 1988, pp. 157–310.

Lassus, Jean. "Une image de saint Syméon le Jeune sur un fragment de reliquaire syrien du musée du Louvre." *Monuments et mémoires de la Fondation Eugène Piot* 51 (1960), pp. 129–48.

Latour, Bruno, *We Have Never Been Modern*. Trans. Catharine Porter. Cambridge, MA: Harvard University Press, 1993.

———. *Sur le culte moderne des dieux faitiches*, suivi de *Iconoclash*. Paris: La Découverte, 2009.

Lebensztejn, Jean-Claude. *Dossier Pontormo: Le journal de Pontormo*. Paris: Macula, 1984.

———. "Le goût du sang." In *Déplacements*. Brussels: Les presses du réel, 2013, pp. 98–124.

———. "Note sur Diderot et la magie de l'art." In *Déplacements*. Brussels: Les presses du réel, 2013, pp. 34–65.

Lecercle, François. "'Des yeux pour ne point voir': Avatars de l'idolâtrie chez les théologiens catholiques au XVIe siècle." In *L'idolâtrie* (Rencontres de l'École du Louvre). Paris: La Documentation Nationale, 1990, pp. 35–51.

———. "L'infigurable." In Jean Céard, Marie-Madeleine Fontaine, and Jean-Claude Margolin, eds., *Le Corps à la Renaissance: Actes du XXXe Colloque de Tours, 2–11 juillet 1987*. Paris: Aux amateurs de livres, 1990, pp. 173–86.

Leclercq, Henri. "Fer à hosties." In *Dictionnaire d'archéologie chrétienne et de liturgie*. Paris: Letouzey et Ané, 1922, pp. 1366–68.

Le Goff, Jacques. "The Marvelous in the Medieval West." In *The Medieval Imagination*. Trans. Arthur Goldhammer. Chicago: University of Chicago Press, 1988, pp. 27–44.

Leitzmann, H., ed. *Das Leben des heiligen Symeon Stylites*, vol. 4, series 32. Texte und Untersuchungen zur Geschichte der altchristlichen Literatur. Leipzig, 1908.

Lembke, Katja, ed. *Madonna: Frau, Mutter, Kultfigur*. Dresden: Sandstein, 2015. Exhibition catalog.

Leone, Massimo. "Le Dieu mâché: Idéologies du sens religieux et mastication." *Lexia: Rivista di semiotica*. Special issue of *Cibo e identità culturale* 19–20 (2015), pp. 247–64.

Leplatre, Olivier. *"Un goût à la voir nonpareil": Manger les images, essais d'iconophagie*. Paris: Kimé, 2018.

Lepoittevin, Anne. "*Picciolini, picolini* et *piccioli*: La fabrique romaine des *Agnus Dei* (1563–1700)." *Archives de sciences sociales des religions* 183 (2018), pp. 87–117.

Lestringant, Frank. *Une sainte horreur ou le voyage en eucharistie, XVI–XVIIe siècles*. Geneva: Droz, 2012.

Lett, Didier. "L'enfance: *Aetas infirma, aetas infima*." *Médiévales* 15 (1988), pp. 85–95.

Lichtenstein, Jacqueline. *The Blind Spot: An Essay on the Relations between Painting and Sculpture in the Modern Age*. Trans. Chris Miller. Los Angeles: Getty Research Institute, 2008.

Linnebach, Andrea. "Das Publikum der Antiken: Kunsthaus und Museum Fridericianum in Kassel als Ziel von Bildungs- und Forschungsreisen der europaïschen Aufklärung." In Alexis Joachimides, Charlotte Schreiter, and Rüdiger Splitter, eds., *Auf dem Weg zum Museum: Sammlung und Präsentation antiker Kunst an deutschen Fürstenhöfen des 18. Jahrhunderts*. Kassel: Kassel University Press, 2016, pp. 191–210.

Lubac, Henri de. *Corpus mysticum: The Eucharist and the Church in the Middle Ages.* Trans. Gemma Simmonds, CJ, with Richard Price and Christopher Stephens. Notre Dame, IN: University of Notre Dame Press, 2007.

Macé, Marielle. *Styles: Critiques de nos formes de vie.* Paris: Gallimard, 2016.

MacGregor, Arthur. "Medicinal *Terra Sigillata*: A Historical, Geographical and Typological Review." In Christopher J. Duffin, Richard T. J. Moody, and Christopher Gardner-Thorpe, eds., *A History of Geology and Medicine.* London: Geological Society of London, 2013, pp. 113–36.

Macherel, Claude, and Jean Steinauer. *L'État de ciel: Portrait de ville avec rite, La Fête-Dieu de Fribourg (Suisse).* Fribourg: Méandre Éditions, 1989.

Maguire, Henry. "Magic and the Christian Image." In Henry Maguire, ed., *Byzantine Magic.* Washington, DC: Dumbarton Oaks Research Library and Collection, 1995, pp. 51–71.

Mair, Rosa. "Brixner Visitationsberichte 1663–1685." PhD Diss. Universität Innsbruck, 1978.

Mangenot, Eugène. "*Agnus Dei.*" In E. Amman, E. Mangenot, and A. Vacant, eds., *Dictionnaire de théologie catholique.* Paris: Letouzey et Ané, 1923, pp. 605–14.

Maniura, Robert. *Art and Miracle in Renaissance Tuscany.* Cambridge, UK: Cambridge University Press, 2018.

———. "The Images and Miracles of Santa Maria delle Carceri." In Erik Thunø and Gerhard Wolf, eds., *The Miraculous Image in the Late Middle Ages and Renaissance.* Rome: "L'Erma" di Bretschneider, 2004, pp. 86–95.

Mareschi, Andrea, and Francesca Tasca. "Aux limites de l'hérésie et de la magie: L'ordalie du pain et du fromage." *Food and History* 16.1 (2018), pp. 49–67.

Marganne, Marie-Hélène. "Les médicaments estampillés dans le corpus galénique." In Armelle Debru, ed., *Galen on Pharmacology: Philosophy, History, and Medicine.* Leiden: Brill, 1997, pp. 153–74.

Marin, Louis. *Food for Thought.* Trans. Mette Hjort. Baltimore, MD: Johns Hopkins University Press, 1989.

———. *Les pouvoirs de l'image: Gloses.* Paris: Seuil, 1993.

———. *Portrait of the King.* Trans. Martha M. Houle. Minneapolis: University of Minnesota Press, 1988.

Marinis, Vasileios. "Piety, Barbarism, and the Senses in Byzantium." In Sally M. Promey, ed., *Sensational Religion: Sensory Cultures in Material Practice.* New Haven, CT: Yale University Press, 2014, pp. 321–40.

Markus, Robert. *Au risque du christianisme: L'émergence du modèle chrétien (IVe–VIe siècle).* Lyon: Presses universitaires Lyon, 2012.

Martin, Michaël. *Magie et magiciens dans le monde gréco-romain.* Arles: Errance, 2005.

Maspéro, Gaston. *Études de mythologie et d'archéologie égyptiennes.* Paris: Ernest Leroux, 1893.

Mastrocinque, Attilio. "Le pouvoir de l'écriture dans la magie." *Cahiers "Mondes anciens": Histoire et anthropologie des mondes anciens* 1 (2010), pp. 1–10.

———. *Les intailles magiques du département des Monnaies, Médailles et Antiques.* Paris: Éditions BnF, 2014.

Maurus Servius Honoratus. *Commentary on the Aeneid of Vergil*, ed., Georgius Thilo. Perseus Digital Library, A. 2. 116.

Mauss, Marcel, "Techniques of the Body." In *Techniques, Technology and Civilization.* New York: Durkheim Press/Berghahn Books, 2006. *Journal de Psychologie* XXXII 3-4 (1936), pp. 271–93

Mayeur-Jaouen, Catherine. "La fonction sacrale de l'image dans l'Égypte contemporaine: De l'imagerie traditionnelle à la révolution photographique." In Bernard Heyberger and Silvia Naef, eds., *La Multiplication des images en pays d'Islam: De l'estampe à la télévision (17e–21e siècle).* Wurzbourg: Ergon, 2003, pp. 57–80.

Mazzini, Innocenzo. "Diet and Medicine in the Ancient World." In Jean-Louis Flandrin and Massimo Montanari, eds., *Food: A Culinary History from Antiquity to the Present.* Trans. Clarissa Botsford, Arthur Goldhammer, Charles Lambert, and Frances M. López-Morillas. New York: Columbia University Press, 1999, pp. 302–26.

Mazzoni, Cristina. *Cooking, Eating, and Spiritual Writing.* London: Continuum, 2005.

Metzger, Catherine. *Les Ampoules à eulogie du musée du Louvre.* Paris: RMN, 1981.

Michel, Simone, Peter Zazoff, and Hilde Zazoff, eds. *Die magischen Gemmen im Britischen Museum.* London: British Museum Press, 2001.

Mikuž, Jure. *Le sang et le lait dans l'imaginaire médiéval.* Ljubljana: Zalozba ZRC, 2013.

Miller, Patricia Cox. *The Corporeal Imagination.* Philadelphia: University of Pennsylvania Press, 2009.

Miramon, Charles de. "Aux origines de la noblesse et des princes du sang: France et Angleterre au XIVe siècle." In Maaike van der Lugt and Charles de Miramon, eds., *L'hérédité entre Moyen Âge et Époque moderne: Perspectives historiques.* Florence: Sismel, 2008, pp. 158–210.

Mitchell, W. J. T. *What do Pictures Want?: The Lives and Loves of Images.* Chicago: University of Chicago Press, 2005.

Mondzain, Marie-José. *Image, Icon, Economy: The Byzantine Origins of the Contemporary Imaginary.* Stanford, CA: Stanford University Press, 2005.

Montanari, Angelica A. *Il fiero pasto: Antropofagie medievali.* Bologna: Il Mulino, 2015.

Morel, Philippe. *Les grottes maniéristes en Italie au XVIe siècle: Théâtre et alchimie de la nature.* Paris: Macula, 1998.

Morselli, Raffaella, and Roberta Piccinelli. "Breve ragguaglio delle sculture in zucchero in epoca moderna: Ovvero *saccarum triumphans* alla corte di Carlo II Gonzaga Nevers." In Andrea Merlotti, ed., *Le tavole di corte tra Cinquecneto e Settecento.* Rome: Bulzoni, 2013, pp. 217–50.

Moulinier, Laurence. "Le sang au Moyen Age, entre savoir et questionnements, science et imaginaire." In *1453, Rencontres européennes.* Bordeaux: Éditions confluences, 2004, pp. 53–73.

Mozzati, Tommaso. *Giovanfrancesco Rustici: Le compagnie del paiuolo e della cazzuola, Arte, letteratura, festa nell'età della Maniera.* Florence: Olschki, 2008.

Muller, Aislinn. "The *agnus dei*, Catholic devotion, and Confessional Politics in Early Modern England." *British Catholic History* 34.1 (2018), pp. 1–28.

Musacchio, Jacqueline Marie. *Art, Marriage, and Family in the Florentine Renaissance Palace.* New Haven: Yale University Press, 2008.

Nagel, Alexander. *Medieval Modern: Art out of Time.* London: Thames & Hudson, 2012.

———. *The Controversy of Renaissance Art.* Chicago: University of Chicago Press, 2011.

———, and Christopher Wood. *Anachronic Renaissance.* New York: Zone Books, 2010.

Nagy, Árpád M. "*Daktylios Pharmakites*: Magical Healing Gems and Rings in the Graeco-Roman World." In Ildikò Csepregi and Charles Burnett, eds., *Ritual Healing: Magic, Ritual and Medical Therapy from Antiquity until the Early Modern Period.* Florence: Sismel, 2012, pp. 71–106.

———. "Engineering Ancient Amulets: Magical Gems of the Roman Imperial Period." In Dietrich Boschung and Jan N. Bremmer, eds., *The Materiality of Magic.* Paderborn: Wilhelm Fink, 2015, pp. 205–40.

———. "Étude sur la transmission du savoir magique: L'histoire post-antique du schéma anguipède (Ve–XVIIe siècles)." In Véronique Dasen and Michel Spieser, eds., *Les savoirs magiques et leur transmission*, pp. 131–55.

Neher, André. *Prophètes et prophéties: L'essence du prophétisme.* Paris: Payot & Rivages, 2004.

Nelson, Robert S. "To Say and to See: Ekphrasis and Vision in Byzantium." In Robert

S. Nelson, ed., *Visuality before and beyond the Renaissance: Seeing as Others Saw*. Cambridge, UK: Cambridge University Press, 2000, pp. 143–68.

Nicoud, Marilyn. "Savoirs et pratiques diététiques au Moyen Âge." *Cahiers de recherches médiévales et humanistes* 13 (2006), pp. 239–47.

Nissen, Cécile. *Entre Asclépios et Hippocrate: Étude des cultes guérisseurs et des médecins en Carie*. Liège: Presses universitaires de Liège, 2009.

Noble, Louis. *Medicinal Cannibalism in Early Modern English Literature and Culture*. New York: Palgrave Macmillan, 2011.

Novero, Cecilia. *Antidiets of the Avant-Garde: From Futurist Cooking to Eat Art*. Minneapolis: University of Minnesota Press, 2009.

Öffner, Richard. *A Critical and Historical Corpus of Florentine Painting*, section 3: *The Fourteenth Century*, vol. 5. New York: Institute of Fine Arts, New York University, 1956.

Ottosson, Per-Gunnar. *Scholastic medicine and philosophy: A study of Commentaries on Galen's* Tegni *(ca. 1300–1450)*. Naples: Bibliopolis, 1984.

Pacco, Christian. "La statuette miraculeuse de Foy Notre-Dame, état de la question." *Annales de la Société archéologique de Namur* 83 (2009), pp. 131–52.

Papaud, Michel. "La répression durant le ministère de Léon Faucher (janvier–mai 1849)." In Philippe Vigier and Alain Faure, eds., *Maintien de l'ordre et polices en France et en Europe au XIXe siècle*. Paris: Créaphis, 1987, pp. 87–102.

Pasqui, Angiolo. "Notizie degli Scavi. Regione I (Latium et Campania). IV. Ostia." *Atti della Reale Accademia dei Lincei 3*, serie 5, anno 303 (1906), pp. 357–73.

Patetta, Federico. *Le Ordalie: Studio di storia del diritto e scienza del diritto comparator*. Turin: Fratelli Bocca, 1890.

Paulhan, Camille. "Daniele Spoerri et la Eat Art Galerie." In Julia Csergo and Frédérique Desbuissons, eds., *Le cuisinier et l'art: Art du cuisinier et cuisine d'artiste (XVIe–XXIe siècle)*. Paris: INHA/Menu fretin, 2018, pp. 255–66.

Paulson, Ronald. *Hogarth*, vol. 3: *Art and Politics, 1750–1764*. Cambridge: Lutterworth Press, 1993.

Pautasso, Auido Andrea. *Piero Manzoni: Divorare l'arte*. Milan: Electa, 2015.

Peers, Glenn. "Object Relations: Theorizing the Late Antique Viewer." In Scott Fitzgerald Johnson, ed., *The Oxford Handbook of Late Antiquity*. Oxford: Oxford University Press, 2012, pp. 970–93.

Peeters, Henk. *Nul=0* 2 (1963).

Peirce, Charles S. "[from] On the Algebra of Logic: A Contribution to the Philosophy of

Notation." In *The Essential Peirce: Selected Philosophical Writings*, vol. 1. Eds. Nathan Houser and Christian Kloesel. Bloomington: Indiana University Press, 1992, pp. 225–28.

Pentcheva, Bissera V. "The Performative Icon." *Art Bulletin* 88.4 (2006), pp. 631–55.

———. *The Sensual Icon: Space, Ritual, and the Senses in Byzantium*. University Park, PA: Pennsylvania State University Press, 2010.

Pératé, André. "Note sur le groupe de Panéas." *Mélanges d'archéologie et d'histoire* 5 (1885), pp. 303–12.

Pereda, Felipe. *Images of Discord: Poetics and Politics of the Sacred image in Fifteenth-Century Spain*. Trans. Consuelo Lopez-Morillas. London/Turnhout: Harvey Miller, 2018.

Petit de Juleville, Louis. "Un gaufrier du XIIIe siècle." *Annales Archéologiques* 13 (1853), pp. 43–44.

Piccinelli, Roberta. "Sculture effimere per banchetti nuziali." In Paolo Venturelli, ed., *Vincoli d'amore: Spose in casa Gonzaga*. Milan: Skira, 2013, pp. 69–76.

Piette, Albert. *Contre le relationnisme: Lettre aux anthropologues*. Lormont: Le Bord de l'eau, 2014.

Piettre, Pauline. "Catéchèse et instruction religieuse en France depuis le XIXe siècle." *Transversalités* 115.3 (2010), pp. 27–40.

Pigeaud, Jackie. *Folie et cures de la folie chez les médecins de l'antiquité gréco-romaine*. Paris: Les Belles Lettres, 2010.

———. *La maladie de l'âme: Étude sur la relation de l'âme et du corps dans la tradition médico-philosophique antique*. Paris: Les Belles Lettres, 1981.

Pipponier, Françoise. "From Hearth to Table: Late Medieval Cooking Equipment." In Jean-Louis Flandrin and Massimo Montanari, eds., *Food: A Culinary History from Antiquity to the Present*. Trans. Clarissa Botsford, Arthur Goldhammer, Charles Lambert, and Frances M. López-Morillas. New York: Columbia University Press, 1999 pp. 339–46.

Pitarakis, Brigitte. "Magie, santé, piété privée: Les vertus du motif du lion sur les amulettes paléobyzantines." In Véronique Dasen and Michel Spieser, eds., *Les savoirs magiques et leur transmission*. Florence: Sismel, 2014, pp. 371–96.

Pitrè, Giuseppe. *Medicina popolare siciliana*. Palermo: Clausen, 1896.

Platelle, Henri. "Guibert de Nogent et le *De pignoribus sanctorum*." In Édina Bozóky and Anne-Marie Helvétius, eds., *Les reliques: Objets, cultes, symboles: Actes du colloque international de l'Université du Littoral-Côte d'Opale (Boulogne-sur-Mer), 4–6 septembre 1997*. Turnhout: Brepols, 1999, pp. 109–21.

Plesch, Véronique. "Destruction or Preservation? The Meaning of Graffiti on Paintings in Religious Sites." In Virginia Chieffo Raguin, ed., *Art, Piety and Destruction in the Christian West, 1500–1700*. Farnham, UK: Ashgate, 2010, pp. 137–72.

———. "Using or Abusing? On the Significance of Graffiti on Religious Mural Paintings." In Luis Urbano Afonso and Vitor Serrao, eds., *Out of the Stream: Studies in Medieval and Renaissance Mural Painting*. Newcastle: Cambridge Scholars, 2007, pp. 42–68.

Pozo Coll, Patricia Sela del. "Imágenes en las hostias eucarísticas: Origen y significación de motivos iconográficos presentes en un medio secundario." In Ines Monteira Arias, Belen Munoz Martinze, and Fernando Villasenor Sebatian, eds., *Relegados al margen: Marginalidad y espacios marginales en la cultura medieval*. Madrid: CSIC Instituto de Historia, 2009, pp. 257–72.

Pouchelle, Marie-Christine. "Le sang et ses pouvoirs au Moyen Age." In Arlette Farge, ed., *Affaires de sang*. Paris: Imago, 1988, pp. 17–41.

———. "Une parole médicale prise dans l'imaginaire: Alimentation et digestion chez un maître chirurgien du XIVe siècle." In Jean-Claude Margolin and Robert Sauzet, eds., *Pratiques et discours alimentaires à la Renaissance: Actes du colloque de Tours de mars 1979*. Paris: Maisonneuve et Larose, 1982, pp. 179–92.

Price, Campbell. "On the Function of 'Healing' Statues." In Campbell Price, Roger Forshaw, Andrew Chamberlain, and Paul T. Nicholson, eds., *Mummies, Magic and Medicine in Ancient Egypt: Multidisciplinary Essays for Rosalie David*. Manchester: Manchester University Press, 2016, pp. 169–82.

Pritchard, James B., ed. *Ancient Near Eastern Texts Relating to the Old Testament*. Princeton, NJ: Princeton University Press, 1969.

Rainey, Ronald E. "Sumptuary Legislation in Renaissance Florence." PhD Diss. Columbia University, 1985.

Rancière, Jacques. *Aesthetics and Its Discontents*. Trans. Steven Corcoran. Cambrige, UK/ Malden, MA: Polity, 2009.

———. *The Politics of Aesthetics: The Distribution of the Sensible*. Trans. Gabriel Rockhill. London: Continuum, 2005.

Rebecchi, Marie, and Elena Vogman. "The Anthropology of Rhythm." In Marie Rebecchi and Elena Vogman, *Sergei Eisenstein and the Anthropology of Rhythm*. Rome: Produzioni Nero, 2017, pp. 9–20.

Reed, Marcia. "Court and Civic Festivals." In Marcia Reed, ed., *The Edible Monument: The Art of Food for Festivals*. Los Angeles: Getty Research Institute, 2015, pp. 27–71.

———. "Feasting in the Streets: Carnivals and the Cuccagna." In Marcia Reed, ed., *The Edible Monument: The Art of Food for Festivals*. Los Angeles: Getty Research Institute, 2015, pp. 73–99.

Reesing, Ingmar, and Michael Hoyle. "Notre-Dame de Foy: The Reuse and Dissemination of a Late Medieval Figurine of the Virgin in the Low Countries." *Simiolus. Netherlands Quarterly for the History of Art* 33.3 (2007/2008), pp. 145–65.

Restif, Bruno. "Les statues touchées et malmenées dans le cadre de rites religieux en Bretagne (XVIIe–XXe siècle): Attestations, silences, enjeux internes au catholicisme." Conference presentation *La Statuaire entre hommages et outrages: Corps rossés, blâmés ou adorés de la sculpture moderne en Europe et Nouvelle Espagne (XVIe–XVIIIe siècle)*, Toulouse, November 14–16, 2012.

Ribouillault, Denis. "Regurgitating Nature: On a Celebrated Anecdote by Karel van Mander about Pieter Bruegel the Elder." *Journal of Historians of Netherlandish Art* 8.1 (2016).

Richter, Erwin. "Esszettel." In *Reallexikon zur Deutschen Kunstgeschichte*, vol. 6. Munich, 1973, col. 42–48.

Rigaux, Dominique. "Autour de la messe de saint Grégoire: Visée pastorale et réalisme rural." In Nicole Bériou, Béatrice Caseau, Dominique Rigaux, eds., *Pratiques de l'eucharistie dans les* Églises *d'Orient et d'Occident (Antiquité et Moyen Âge)*, vol. 2: *Les receptions*. Paris: Institut d'Études Augustiniennes, 2009, pp. 951–83.

———. "Réflexions sur les usages apotropaïques de l'image peinte: Autour de quelques peintures murales novaraises du Quattrocento." In Jérôme Baschet and Jean-Claude Schmitt, eds., *L'image: Fonctions et usages des images dans l'Occident médiéval*. Paris: Le Léopard d'or, 1996, pp. 155–77.

———. "Usages apotropaïques de la fresque dans l'Italie du Nord au XVe siècle." In François Boespflug and Nicolas Lossky, eds., *Nicée II, 787–1987: Douze siècles d'images religieuses: Actes du colloque international "Nicée II."* Paris: Cerf, 1987, pp. 317–31.

Riley, Gillian. "'Eat Your Words!': Seventeenth-Century Edible Letterforms." *Gastronomica* 1.1 (2001), pp. 45–59.

Rintelen, Michael. "Schluckbilder und Esszettel: Fragmente zum Thema Schauen und Essen." In Daniel Hees and Gundolf Winter, eds., *Kreativität und Werkerfahrung: Festschrift für Ilse Krahl zum 65. Geburtstag*. Duisburg: Gilles und Francke, 1988, pp. 112–16.

Rios, Alicia. "Eat Art and Communities: From Oxford to Melbourne." *Food, Culture and Community* in the journal *Moving Worlds* 6.2 (2006), pp. 177–86.

Ritner, Robert Kriech. *The Mechanics of Ancient Egyptian Magical Practice.* Chicago: Oriental Institute of the University of Chicago, 2008.

Rivard, Derek A. *Blessing the World: Ritual and Lay Piety in Medieval Religion.* Washington, DC: Catholic University of America Press, 2009.

Robert, Aurélien. "Le corps d'après: La Chute entre théologie et médecine (XIIe–XIVe siècle)." In Gianluca Briguglia and Irène Rosier-Catach, eds., *Adam, la nature humaine avant et après: Épistémologie de la Chute.* Paris: Publications de la Sorbonne, 2016, pp. 173–204.

Robinson, James, and Lloyd De Beer, eds. *Matter of Faith: An Interdisciplinary Study of Relics and Relic Veneration in the Medieval Period.* London: British Museum, 2014.

Roccati, Alessandro. "Qu'est-ce que le texte magique?" In Yvan Koenig, *La magie en Égypte: À la recherche d'une definition.* Paris: La Documentation française/Musée du Louvre, 2002, pp. 71–79.

Rossi, Adamo. "Francesco di Valeriano detto il Roscetto ed i suoi figli Federico e Cesarino." *Giornale di erudizione artistica* 2, fasc. IV, 1873, pp. 89–136.

Rothkegel, Rüdiger. "Mittelalterliche und neuzeitliche Tonstatuetten aus dem Kanton Zug." *Zeitschrift* für *Schweizerische Archäologie und Kunstgeschichte* 63.1 (2006), pp. 141–98.

Rozière, Eugène de. *Recueil général des formules usitées dans l'Empire des Francs du Ve au Xe siècle.* Paris: Auguste Durand, 1861.

Rubin, Miri. *Corpus Christi: The Eucharist in Late Medieval Culture.* Cambridge, UK: Cambridge University Press, 1991.

Rudy, Kathryn M. "Sewing the Body of Christ: Eucharist Wafer Souvenirs Stitched into Fifteenth-Century Manuscripts, Primarily in the Netherlands." In *Journal of Historians of Netherlandish Art* 8.1 (Winter 2016).

Ruff, Margarethe. *Zauberpraktiken als Lebenshilfe: Magie im Alltag vom Mittelalter bis heute.* Frankfurt: Campus, 2003.

Rye-Clausen, Harald. *Die Hostienmühlenbilder im Lichte mittelalterlicher Frömmigkeit.* Stein am Rhein: Christiana, 1981.

Sabatini, Francesco, Sergio Raffaelli, and Paolo D'Achille. *Il volgare nelle chiese di Roma: messaggi graffiti, dipinti e incisi dal IX al XVI secolo.* Rome: Bonacci, 1987.

Sainéan, Lazare. *La langue de Rabelais*, 2 vols. Paris: De Boccard, 1922–1923.

Sansterre, Jean-Marie. "Les justifications du culte des reliques dans le haut Moyen Âge." In Édina Bozóky and Anne-Marie Helvétius, eds., *Les reliques: Objets, cultes, symboles:*

Actes du colloque international de l'Université du Littoral-Côte d'Opale (Boulogne-sur-Mer), 4–6 septembre 1997. Turnhout: Brepols, 1999, pp. 81–93.

_____. "Sacralité et pouvoir thaumaturgique des statues mariales (Xe siècle–première moitié du XIIIe siècle)." *Revue Mabillon* 22 (2011), pp. 53–77.

_____. "Vivantes ou comme vivantes: L'animation miraculeuse d'images de la Vierge entre Moyen Âge et époque moderne." *Revue de l'histoire des religions* 232.2 (2015), pp. 155–82.

Scavizzi, Giuseppe. *The Controvery on Images from Calvin to Baronius*. New York: Peter Lang, 1992.

Schefer, Jean-Louis. *L'hostie profane: Histoire d'une fiction théologique*. Paris: P. O. L., 2007.

Scheid, John. *Quand faire, c'est croire: Les rites sacrificiels des Romains*. Paris: Aubier, 2011.

_____. "Sacrifice et banquet à Rome: Quelques problèmes." *Mélanges de l'École française de Rome—Antiquité* 97.1 (1985), pp. 193–206.

Schlie, Heike. *Bilder des Corpus Christi: Sakramentaler Realismus von Jan van Eyck bis Hieronymus Bosch*. Berlin: Mann Verlag, 2002.

Schmidt, Peter. "Die Kupferstiche des Meisters E. S. zur Wallfahrt nach Einsiedeln: Einige Überlegungen zum Publikum, Programm und Kontext." In *Artibus: Kulturwissenschaft und deutsche Philologie (Festschrift für Dieter Wuttke)*. Wiesbaden: Stephan Füssel, 1994, pp. 293–318.

Schmitt, Jean-Claude. "Introduction." In Jérôme Baschet and Pierre-Olivier Dittmar, eds., *Les images dans l'Occident médiéval*. Turnhout: Brepols, 2015, pp. 7–18.

_____. "La culture de l'*imago*." *Annales, Histoire, sciences sociales* 51.1, (1996), pp. 3–36.

_____. *Le Corps des images: Essais sur la culture visuelle au Moyen Âge*. Paris: Gallimard, 2002.

_____. *Le Corps, les rites, les rêves, le temps: Essais d'anthropologie médiévale*. Paris: Gallimard, 2001.

_____. "L'Occident, Nicée II et les images du VIIIe au XIIIe siècle." In François Boespflug and Nicolas Lossky, eds., *Nicée II, 787–1987: Douze siècles d'images religieuses: Actes du colloque international "Nicée II."* Paris: Cerf, 1987, pp. 271–301.

Schneegasse, C. "Schluckbildchen: Ein Beispiel der 'Populärgraphik' zur aktiven Aneignung." *Volkskunst: Zeitschrift für volkstümliche Sachkultur* 6 (1983), pp. 27–32.

Schönborn, Christoph. *L'icône du Christ: Fondements théologiques*. Paris: Cerf, 1986.

Schrickx, Christiaan. "Bethlehem in de Bangert: Een historische en archeologische studie naar de ontwikkeling van een vrouwenklooster onder de Orde van het Heilig Kruis in het buitengebied van Hoorn (1475–1572)." PhD Diss. Universiteit Leiden, 2015.

Scott, Nora E. "The Metternich Stela." *Metropolitan Museum of Art Bulletin* 9.8 (April 1951), pp. 201–17.

Seifert, Oliver, ed. *Panis angelorum: Das brot der engel: Kulturgeschichte der Hostie*. Ulm: Jan Thorbecke Verlag, 2004.

———. "La devoción a la hostia consagrada en la Baja Edad Media castellana: Fuentes textuales, materiales e iconográficas para su studio." *Anales de Historia del Arte* 16 (2006), pp. 25–58.

Sénéchal. Philippe. *Giovan Francesco Rustici (1475–1554)*. Paris: Arthéna, 2007.

Sensi, Mario. "Santuari, culti e riti 'ad repellendam pestem' tra medioevo ed età moderna." In Sofia Boesch Gajano and Lucetta Scaraffia, eds., *Luoghi sacri e spazi della santità*. Turin: Rosenberg e Sellier, 1990, pp. 135–49.

Serragli, Silvio. *La Santa Casa Abbellita*. Loreto: Paolo and Giovanni Battista Serafini Fratelli, 1634.

Sevcik, Anja K. "Junge mit Pfannkuchenmaske, 1670–1680." In *Schalcken: Gemalte Verführung*. Cologne: Wallraf-Richartz-Museums, 2015, pp. 158–60. Exhibition catalog.

Shepard, Dorothy M. *Introducing the Lambeth Bible: A Study of Texts and Imagery*. Turnhout: Brepols, 2007.

Sherman, E. J. "Djedhor the Saviour: Statue Base OI 10589." *Journal of Egyptian Archaeology* 67 (1981), pp. 82–102.

Shiff, Richard. "Johns Metanoid, Metanoid Johns." In James Rondeau and Douglas Druick, eds., *Jasper Johns: Gray*. Chicago: Art Institute of Chicago, 2007, pp. 120–41. Exhibition catalog.

Signori, Gabriela. *Wunder: Eine historische Einführung*. Frankfurt: Campus, 2007.

Silva Veiga, Paula Alexandra da. *Health and Medicine in Ancient Egypt: Magic and Science*. Oxford: BAR International Series, 2009.

Silver, Larry. "Full of Grace: 'Mariolatry' in Post-Reformation Germany." In Michael W. Cole and Rebecca Zorach, eds., *The Idol in the Age of Art: Objects, Devotions and the Early Modern World*. London: Routledge, 2016, pp. 289–316.

Simon, Gérard. "La théorie cartésienne de la vision: Réponse à Kepler et rupture avec la problématique médiévale." In Joël Biard and Roshdi Rashed, eds., *Descartes et le Moyen Âge*. Paris: Vrin, 1997, pp. 107–17.

Simondon, Gilbert. *Imagination et invention (1965–1966)*. Paris: Presses universitaires de France, 2014.

———. *De l'individuation psychique et collective*. Paris: Aubier, 2007.

Sladeczek, Franz-Josef. "Les copies de la statue miraculeuse d'Einsiedeln." In Cécile Dupeux, Pieter Jezler, and Jean Wirth, eds., *Iconoclasme: Vie et mort de l'image médiévale*. Paris: Somogy, 2001, cat. 102, pp. 250–51. Exhibition catalog.

Sodini, Jean-Pierre. "La terre des semelles: Images pieuses ramenées par les pèlerins des Lieux saints (Terre sainte, Martyria d'Orient)." *Journal des savants* (2011), pp. 77–140.

Somaini, Antonio. "*Que Viva Mexico!* et le tournant archéologique dans l'œuvre d'Eisenstein." In Laurence Schifano and Antonio Somaini, eds., *Eisenstein—Leçons mexicaines: Cinéma, anthropologie, archéologie dans le mouvement des arts*. Paris: Presses universitaires de Paris-Ouest, 2016, pp. 39–74.

Spencer, Brian. *Pilgrim Souvenirs and Secular Badges*. London: Boydell & Brewer, 2010.

Sperling, Jutta. "Squeezing, Squirting, Spilling Milk: The Lactation of Saint Bernard and the Flemish *Madonna Lactans* (ca. 1430–1530)." *Renaissance Quarterly* 71 (2018), pp. 868–918.

Spier, Jeffrey. "An Antique Magical Book Used for Making Sixth-Century Byzantine Amulets?" In Véronique Dasen and Michel Spieser, eds., *Les Savoirs magiques et leur transmission*, pp. 43–66.

———. *Late Antique and Christian Gems*. Wiesbaden: L. Reichert, 2007.

Spieser, Michel. "Christianisme et magie du IIIe au VIIe siècle." In Véronique Dasen and Michel Spieser, eds., *Les savoirs magiques et leur transmission*. Florence: Sismel, 2014, pp. 333–51.

Sternberg-el Hotabi, Heike. *Untersuchungen zur Überlieferungsgeschichte der Horusstelen: Ein Beitrag zur Religionsgeschichte Ägyptens im 1. Jahrtausend v. Chr.*, vol. 1. Wiesbaden: Harrassowitz, 1999.

Stoichita, Victor I. *Visionary Experience in the Golden Age of Spanish Art*. London: Reaktion Books, 1995.

Sugg, Richard. *Mummies, Cannibals and Vampires: The History of Corpse Medicine from the Renaissance to the Victorians*. London: Routledge, 2011.

Sunyol I Busquets, Marti. "Estudi d'un hostier medieval del 1339." *Acta historica et archaeologica mediaevalia* 9 (1988), pp. 475–93.

Tallet, Pierre, Frédéric Payraudeau, Chloé Ragazzoli, and Claire Somaglino. *L'Égypte pharaonique: Histoire, société et culture*. Paris: Armand Colin, 2019.

Taylor, Charles. *Sources of the Self: The Making of Modern Identity*. Cambridge, MA: Harvard University Press, 1989.

Thomas, Yan. "Fathers as Citizens of Rome, Rome as a City of Fathers (Second Century BC–

Second Century AD)." In André Burguière, Christiane Klapisch-Zuber, Martine Segalen, and Françoise Zonabend, eds., *A History of the Family*, vol. 1: *Distant Worlds, Ancient Worlds*. Trans. Sarah Hanbury Tenison, Rosemary Morris, and Andrew Wilson. Cambridge, MA: Belknap Press of Harvard University Press, 1996.

Thunø, Erik and Gerhard Wolf, eds. *The Miraculous Image in the Late Middle Ages and Renaissance*. Rome: "L'Erma" di Bretschneider, 2004.

Timmermann, Achim. *Real Presence: Sacrament Houses and the Body of Christ c. 1270–1600*. Turnhout: Brepols, 2009.

Tixier, Frédéric. *La monstrance eucharistique, XIIIe–XVIe siècle*. Rennes: Presses universitaires Rennes, 2014.

Tobler, Mathilde. "'Wahre Abbildung': Marianische Gnadenbildkopien in der schweizerischen Quart des Bistums Konstanz." *Der Geschichtsfreund: Mitteilungen des Historischen Vereins Zentralschweiz* 144 (1991), pp. 5–426.

Tomasi, Michele, ed. *L'art multiplié: Production de masse, en série, pour le marché dans les arts entre Moyen Âge et Renaissance*. Rome: Viella, 2011.

Tuerk, J. "An Early Byzantine Inscribed Amulet and its Narratives." *Byzantine and Modern Greek Studies* 23 (1999), pp. 25–42.

Van Ausdall, Kristen. "Communicating with the Host: Imagery and Eucharistic Contact in Late Medieval and Early Renaissance Italy." In *Push Me Pull You: Imaginative and Emotional Interaction in Late Medieval and Renaissance Art*, vol. 1. Leiden: Brill, 2011, pp. 447–86.

Van den Ven, Paul. *La vie ancienne de S. Syméon Stylite le Jeune (521–592)*, 2 vols. Brussels: Société des Bollandistes, 1962–1970.

Vandenberg, Vincent. *De chair et de sang: Images et pratiques du cannibalisme de l'Antiquité au Moyen Âge*. Rennes: Presses universitaires Rennes, 2014.

Van Eck, Caroline. *François Lemée et la statue de Louis XIV sur la place des Victoires: Les origines des théories ethnologiques du fétichisme*. Paris: Éd. De la Maison des sciences de l'homme, 2013.

Van Gennep, Arnold, *The Rites of Passage*. Trans. Monika B. Vizedom and Gabrielle L. Caffee. Chicago: University of Chicago Press, [1909] 1960.

Vanhoye, Albert. "L'utilisation du livre d'Ézéchiel dans l'Apocalypse." *Biblica* 43.3 (1962), pp. 436–76.

Varnedoe, Kirk. "Introduction: A Sense of Life." In Kirk Varnedoe, ed., *Jasper Johns: A Retrospective*. New York: MoMA Publications, 1996.

Varriano, John L. *Tastes and Temptations: Food and art in Renaissance Italy*. Berkeley: University of California Press, 2009.

Vauchez, André. *Sainthood in the Later Middle Ages*. Trans. Jean Birrell. Cambridge, UK: Cambridge University Press, 1997.

———. *Saints, prophètes et visionnaires: Le pouvoir surnaturel au Moyen Âge*. Paris: Albin Michel, 1999.

Vermeir, Koen. "Tout dépend des circonstances: Superstition, lois de la nature et dissolution du préternaturel au XVIIIe siècle." In Olivier Christin, Fabrice Flückiger, and Naïma Ghermani, eds., *Marie mondialisée: L'*Atlas Marianus *de Wilhelm Gumppenberg et les topographies sacrées de l'époque moderne*. Neuchâtel: Éditions Alphil-Presses universitaires suisses, 2014, pp. 47–61.

Vetta, Massimo. "The Culture of the Symposium." In Jean-Louis Flandrin and Massimo Montanari, eds., *Food: A Culinary History from Antiquity to the Present*. Trans. Clarissa Botsford, Arthur Goldhammer, Charles Lambert, and Frances M. López-Morillas. New York: Columbia University Press, 1999, pp. 96–105

Veyne, Paul. *Bread and Circuses: Historical Sociology and Political Pluralism*. Trans. Brian Pearce. London: Allen Lane, 1990.

———. *Le pain et le cirque: Sociologie historique d'un pluralisme politique*. Paris: Seuil, 1976.

Vikan, Gary. "Art, Medicine, and Magic in Early Byzantium." *Dumbarton Oaks Papers* 38 (1984), pp. 65–86.

———. *Byzantine Pilgrimage Art*. Washington, DC: Dumbarton Oaks, 1982.

———. "Ruminations on Edible Icons: Originals and Copies in the Art of Byzantium." In *Studies in the History of Art*, 20, Symposium Papers VII: Retaining the Original: Multiple Originals, Copies, and Reproductions. Washington, DC: National Gallery of Art, 1989, pp. 47–59.

Voltmer, Rita. "Political Preaching and a Design of Urban reform: Johannes Geiler of Kaysersberg and Strasbourg." *Franciscan Studies* 71 (2013), pp. 71–88.

———. *Wie der Wächter auf dem Turm: Ein Prediger und seine Stadt: Johannes Geiler von Kaysersberg (1445–1510) und Straßburg*. Porta-Alba: Trèves, 2005.

Wajeman, Lise. "Manger la peinture." In François Lecercle, Emmanuelle Hénin, and Lise Wajeman, eds., *La Théorie subreptice: Anecdotes picturales de la Renaissance aux Lumières*. Turnhout: Brepols, 2012, pp. 109–27.

Wall, Wendy. *Recipes for Thought: Knowledge and Taste in the Early Modern English Kitchen*. Philadelphia: University of Pennsylvania Press, 2016.

Watson, Katherine J. "Sugar Sculpture for Grand Ducal Weddings from the Giambologna Workshop." *Connoisseur* 199 (1978), pp. 20–26.

Weill-Parot, Nicolas. *Les "Images astrologiques" au Moyen Âge et à la Renaissance: Spéculations intellectuelles et pratiques magiques (XIIe–XVe siècle).* Paris: Champion, 2002.

Weiss, Jeffrey. "Painting Bitten by a Man." In Jeffrey Weiss, ed., *Jasper Johns: An Allegory of Painting, 1955–1965.* National Gallery of Art, Washington, DC. New Haven, CT: Yale University Press, 2007, pp. 2–28. Exhibition catalog.

Wicky, Érika. "La peinture à vue de nez ou la juste distance du critique d'art, de Diderot à Zola." *RACAR* 39.1 (2014), pp. 76–89.

Wieck, Roger S. "The Sacred Bleeding Host of Dijon in Books of Hours." In *Quand la peinture* était *dans les livres: Mélanges en l'honneur de François Avril.* Turnhout: Brepols, 2007, pp. 393–404.

Willems, Harco. *The Coffin of Heqata (Cairo JdE 36418): A Case Study of Egyptian Funerary Culture of the Early Middle Kingdom.* Louvain: Peeters/Departement Oriëntalistiek, 1996.

Wirth, Jean. *L'image à l'époque gothique (1140–1280).* Paris: Cerf, 2008.

———. *L'image à l'époque romane.* Paris: Cerf, 1999.

———. *Qu'est-ce qu'une image?* Geneva: Droz, 2013.

———. "Structure et fonctions de l'image chez saint Thomas d'Aquin." In Jérôme Baschet and Jean-Claude Schmitt, eds., *L'image: Fonctions et usages des images dans l'Occident medieval.* Paris: Le Léopard d'or, 1996, pp. 39–58.

Wood, Christopher. *Forgery, Replica, Fiction: Temporalities of German Renaissance Art.* Chicago: Chicago University Press, 2008.

Wunderlin, Dominik. "Guérir par ingestion: La consommation d'images de dévotion bénites est censée apporter la guérison." In Cécile Dupeux, Pieter Jezler, and Jean Wirth, eds., *Iconoclasme: Vie et mort de l'image médiévale.* Paris: Somogy, 2001, pp. 256–57. Exhibition catalog.

Zastrow, Oleg. "Antiche inedite schiacce decorate artisticamente." *Rassegna di studi et di notizie* 34, anno 38 (2012), pp. 245–76.

Zivie-Coche, Christiane. "Noms divins et pratiques magiques en Égypte ancienne." In Olivier Boulnois and Brigitte Tambrun, eds., *Les noms divins.* Paris: Cerf, 2016, pp. 69–84.

Zwierlein-Diehl, Erika. "Antike Gemmen im Mittelalter: Wiederverwendung, Umdeutung, Nachahmung." In Dietrich Boschung and Susanne Wittekind, eds., *Persistenz und Rezeption: Weiterverwendung, Wiederverwendung und Neuinterpretation antiker Werke im Mittelalter.* Wiesbaden: Reichert, 2008, pp. 237–84.

———. "Magical Gems in the Medieval and Early-Modern Periods: Tradition, Transformation, Innovation." In Véronique Dasen and Michel Spieser, eds., *Les savoirs magiques et leur transmission.* Florence: Sismel, 2014, pp. 87–130.

———. *Magische Amulette und andere Gemmen des Instituts* für *Altertumskunde der Universität zu* Köln. Opladen: Westdeutscher Verlag, 1992.

Index

Zone Books series design by Bruce Mau
Image placement and production by Julie Fry
Typesetting by Meighan Gale
Printed and bound by Maple Press